MATTHEW

A Commentary in the Wesleyan Tradition

Robert S. Snow
and Arseny Ermakov

Beacon Hill Press of Kansas City
PO Box 419527
Kansas City, MO 64141
www.BeaconHillBooks.com

ISBN 978-0-8341-3831-5

Printed in the United States of America

Cover Design: J.R. Caines
Interior Design: Sharon Page

Library of Congress Cataloging-in-Publication Data
Names: Snow, Robert S., author. | Ermakov, Arseny, 1980- author.
Title: Matthew : a commentary in the Wesleyan tradition / Robert Snow, Arseny Ermakov.
Description: Kansas City : Beacon Hill Press of Kansas City, [2019] | Series: New Beacon Bible commentary | Includes bibliographical references. | Summary: "This is a Bible commentary, in the Wesleyan tradition, of the book of Matthew"—Provided by publisher.
Identifiers: LCCN 2019037199 (print) | LCCN 2019037200 (ebook) | ISBN 9780834138315 (paperback) | ISBN 9780834138322 (ebook)
Subjects: LCSH: Bible. Matthew—Commentaries.
Classification: LCC BS2575.53 .S64 2019 (print) | LCC BS2575.53 (ebook) | DDC 226.2/077—dc23
LC record available at https://lccn.loc.gov/2019037199
LC ebook record available at https://lccn.loc.gov/2019037200

10 9 8 7 6 5 4 3 2 1

DEDICATION

To
Kent E. Brower
Mentor, Colleague, Friend

COMMENTARY EDITORS

CONTENTS

GENERAL EDITORS' PREFACE

The purpose of the New Beacon Bible Commentary is to make available to pastors and students in the twenty-first century a biblical commentary that reflects the best scholarship in the Wesleyan theological tradition. The commentary project aims to make this scholarship accessible to a wider audience to assist them in their understanding and proclamation of Scripture as God's Word.

Writers of the volumes in this series not only are scholars within the Wesleyan theological tradition and experts in their field but also have special interest in the books assigned to them. Their task is to communicate clearly the critical consensus and the full range of other credible voices who have commented on the Scriptures. Though scholarship and scholarly contribution to the understanding of the Scriptures are key concerns of this series, it is not intended as an academic dialogue within the scholarly community. Commentators of this series constantly aim to demonstrate in their work the significance of the Bible as the church's book and the contemporary relevance and application of the biblical message. The project's overall goal is to make available to the church and for her service the fruits of the labors of scholars who are committed to their Christian faith.

The *New International Version* (NIV) is the reference version of the Bible used in this series; however, the focus of exegetical study and comments is the biblical text in its original language. When the commentary uses the NIV, it is printed in bold. The text printed in bold italics is the translation of the author. Commentators also refer to other translations where the text may be difficult or ambiguous.

The structure and organization of the commentaries in this series seeks to facilitate the study of the biblical text in a systematic and methodical way. Study of each biblical book begins with an ***Introduction*** section that gives an overview of authorship, date, provenance, audience, occasion, purpose, sociological/cultural issues, textual history, literary features, hermeneutical issues, and theological themes necessary to understand the book. This section also includes a brief outline of the book and a list of general works and standard commentaries.

The commentary section for each biblical book follows the outline of the book presented in the introduction. In some volumes, readers will find section ***overviews*** of large portions of scripture with general comments on their overall literary structure and other literary features. A consistent feature of the commentary is the paragraph-by-paragraph study of biblical texts. This section has three parts: ***Behind the Text***, ***In the Text***, and ***From the Text***.

The goal of the ***Behind the Text*** section is to provide the reader with all the relevant information necessary to understand the text. This includes specific historical situations reflected in the text, the literary context of the text, sociological and cultural issues, and literary features of the text.

In the Text explores what the text says, following its verse-by-verse structure. This section includes a discussion of grammatical details, word studies, and the connectedness of the text to other biblical books/passages or other parts of the book being studied (the canonical relationship). This section provides transliterations of key words in Hebrew and Greek and their literal meanings. The goal here is to explain what the author would have meant and/or what the audience would have understood as the meaning of the text. This is the largest section of the commentary.

The ***From the Text*** section examines the text in relation to the following areas: theological significance, intertextuality, the history of interpretation, use of the Old Testament scriptures in the New Testament, interpretation in later church history, actualization, and application.

The commentary provides ***sidebars*** on topics of interest that are important but not necessarily part of an explanation of the biblical text. These topics are informational items and may cover archaeological, historical, literary, cultural, and theological matters that have relevance to the biblical text. Occasionally, longer detailed discussions of special topics are included as ***excursuses.***

We offer this series with our hope and prayer that readers will find it a valuable resource for their understanding of God's Word and an indispensable tool for their critical engagement with the biblical texts.

Roger Hahn, Centennial Initiative General Editor
Alex Varughese, General Editor (Old Testament)
George Lyons, General Editor (New Testament)

AUTHORS' PREFACE

In the writing of this commentary, we have quickly discovered the enormity of the task at hand. Countless hours of thinking, conversing, reading, writing, editing, and proofreading went into this book. The journey of interpretation was filled with moments of desperation and great discoveries, with deep thinking about practical applications and challenges posed by this Gospel for the modern church, along with the painstaking process of formulating thoughts and wordsmithing.

Readers will see quickly that we have engaged a number of conversation partners along the way: Davies and Allison, Guelich, Gundry, Hagner, Keener, Luz, Nolland, France, and many others. There are likely places where their ideas have come through even unbeknownst to us. We hope that all this effort and all of these voices will help readers grasp Matthew's message better and that the book will serve the modern holy people of God in their mission.

We also hope that this commentary provides fresh insight into holiness themes in Matthew's Gospel. One important contribution that this Gospel makes for those in Wesleyan-holiness traditions is that purity of heart is inextricably linked to purity of action, both of which are enabled by the indwelling presence of Immanuel: God with us. It is our hope that you will see the various ways in which the holy God desires to form a holy people so that they might be light and agents of salvation to the sick, tormented, and marginalized.

We have also attempted to demonstrate how Matthew's presentation of Jesus is thoroughly shaped by the Scriptures of Israel and its traditions. Of all the Gospels, Matthew draws explicit attention to the influence of the OT. One can only understand Jesus as Messiah, Christ, Lord, and Son of Man in light of the OT, "so that the scriptures . . . may be fulfilled" (Matt 26:56 NRSV).

The issue of holiness and the influence of the OT on the NT has been a lifelong area of study for the editor of his commentary, Dr. Kent E. Brower, whose early research considered the influence of the OT on Mark's Passion Narrative, and his recent publications are dedicated to exploration of holiness and community in the NT. Dr. Brower was our PhD adviser. In our own doctoral research, we have examined the influence of various OT voices on the Gospel of Mark, its Christology, and ecclesiology.

As the authors of this commentary, we are delighted to dedicate this volume to our mentor and colleague, Dr. Brower. Much of our own thinking on holiness and intertextuality has been shaped by him, and it is our hope that this commentary reflects that profound scholarly influence. Any shortcomings in this area, or elsewhere, are, of course, the fault of the authors!

We also would like to thank our families, academic institutions, faith communities, friends, and colleagues for their continual support, encouragement, and insightful conversations.

Robert S. Snow and Arseny Ermakov
Calgary and Melbourne
Easter 2019

ABOUT THE AUTHORS

Robert S. Snow has written chs 1—16. He is Associate Professor of New Testament at Ambrose University in Calgary, Alberta, Canada where he has been a member of the faculty since 2006. His current research interests include the relationship between the spiritual gifts in 1 Cor 12—14 and holiness as well as thematic connections between various depictions of heavenly temples in biblical and extrabiblical texts. He is an ordained elder in the Church of the Nazarene and serves regularly in his local church.

Arseny Ermakov has written chs 17—28. He is Senior Lecturer in Biblical Studies at Eva Burrows College, University of Divinity, Melbourne, Australia. His primary research interests lay in the area of holiness and purity in the Bible and the ancient world. He also is an ordained elder in the Church of the Nazarene.

ABBREVIATIONS

With a few exceptions, these abbreviations follow those in *The SBL Handbook of Style* (Alexander 1999).

General

→	see the commentary at
↔	intertextual relationship between two—usually—OT and NT texts
//	Synoptic parallel to
2T	Second Temple
2TJ	Second Temple Judaism
2TP	Second Temple period
Aram.	Aramaic
BCE	before the Common Era
bk.	book
ca.	circa, approximate time
CE	Common Era
ch	chapter
chs	chapters
DSS	Dead Sea Scrolls
e.g.	*exempli gratia*, for example
esp.	especially
ET	English translation
etc.	*et cetera*, and the rest
Gk.	Greek
HB	Hebrew Bible
Heb.	Hebrew
idem	the same
i.e.	*id est*, that is
Lat.	Latin
lit.	literal; literally
LXX	Septuagint (Greek translation of the OT)
MS	manuscript
MSS	manuscripts
MT	Masoretic Text (of the OT)
n.	note
n.d.	no date
n.p.	no place; no publisher; no page
NT	New Testament
OT	Old Testament
s.v.	*sub verbo*, under the word
v	verse
vs.	versus
vv	verses

Modern English Versions

KJV	King James Version
NEB	New English Bible
NETS	New English Translation of the Septuagint
NIV	New International Version
NKJV	New King James Version
NRSV	New Revised Standard Version

Print Conventions for Translations

Bold font	NIV (bold without quotation marks in the text under study; elsewhere in the regular font, with quotation marks and no further identification)
Bold italic font	Author's translation (without quotation marks)

Behind the Text:	Literary or historical background information average readers might not know from reading the biblical text alone
In the Text:	Comments on the biblical text, words, phrases, grammar, and so forth
From the Text:	The use of the text by later interpreters, contemporary relevance, theological and ethical implications of the text, with particular emphasis on Wesleyan concerns

Ancient Sources

Old Testament

Gen	Genesis
Exod	Exodus
Lev	Leviticus
Num	Numbers
Deut	Deuteronomy
Josh	Joshua
Judg	Judges
Ruth	Ruth
1—2 Sam	1—2 Samuel
1—2 Kgs	1—2 Kings
1—2 Chr	1—2 Chronicles
Ezra	Ezra
Neh	Nehemiah
Esth	Esther
Job	Job
Ps/Pss	Psalm/Psalms
Prov	Proverbs
Eccl	Ecclesiastes
Song	Song of Songs/ Song of Solomon
Isa	Isaiah
Jer	Jeremiah
Lam	Lamentations
Ezek	Ezekiel
Dan	Daniel
Hos	Hosea
Joel	Joel
Amos	Amos
Obad	Obadiah
Jonah	Jonah
Mic	Micah
Nah	Nahum
Hab	Habakkuk
Zeph	Zephaniah
Hag	Haggai
Zech	Zechariah
Mal	Malachi

(Note: Chapter and verse numbering in the MT and LXX often differ compared to those in English Bibles. To avoid confusion, all biblical references follow the chapter and verse numbering in English translations, even when the text in the MT and LXX is under discussion.)

New Testament

Matt	Matthew
Mark	Mark
Luke	Luke
John	John
Acts	Acts
Rom	Romans
1—2 Cor	1—2 Corinthians
Gal	Galatians
Eph	Ephesians
Phil	Philippians
Col	Colossians
1—2 Thess	1—2 Thessalonians
1—2 Tim	1—2 Timothy
Titus	Titus
Phlm	Philemon
Heb	Hebrews
Jas	James
1—2 Pet	1—2 Peter
1—2—3 John	1—2—3 John
Jude	Jude
Rev	Revelation

Apocrypha

Bar	Baruch
Jdt	Judith
1—2 Macc	1—2 Maccabees
3—4 Macc	3—4 Maccabees
Sir	Sirach/Ecclesiasticus
Tob	Tobit
Wis	Wisdom of Solomon

OT Pseudepigrapha and NT Apocrypha

Apoc. Ab.	*Apocalypse of Abraham*
(Arab.) Gos. Inf.	*Arabic Gospel of the Infancy*
2 Bar.	*2 Baruch*
3 Bar.	*3 Baruch*
4 Bar.	*4 Baruch*
1 En.	*1 Enoch (Ethiopic Apocalypse)*
2 En.	*2 Enoch (Slavonic Apocalypse)*
4 Ezra	*4 Ezra*
Jub.	*Jubilees*
Pss. Sol.	*Psalms of Solomon*
Sib. Or.	*Sibylline Oracles*
T. Adam	*Testament of Adam*
T. Dan	*Testament of Dan*
T. Iss.	*Testament of Issachar*
T. Job	*Testament of Job*
T. Levi	*Testament of Levi*
T. Sol.	*Testament of Solomon*

Dead Sea Scrolls and Related Texts

CD	Cairo Genizah copy of the *Damascus Document*
DSS	Dead Sea Scrolls
1QH	*Thanksgiving Hymns*
1QM	*War Scroll*
1QpHab	*Pesher Habakkuk*
1QS	*Rule of the Community*
1QSa	*Rule of the Congregation* (appendix a to 1QS)
1QSb	*Rule of the Blessings* (appendix b to 1QS)
4Q159	Ordinances
4Q164	Isaiah Pesher
4Q174	*Florilegium*
4Q242	*Prayer of Nabonidus*
4Q268	*Damascus Document*
4Q521	*Messianic Apocalypse*
11Q20	*Temple Scroll*
4QMMT B	*Miqṣat Ma'aśê ha-Torah* (Some Observances of the Law)

Eusebius

HE	*Historia Ecclesiastica*

John Chrysostom

Hom. Matt.	*Homiliae in Matthaeum*

Josephus

Ant.	*Jewish Antiquities*
J.W.	*Jewish War*

Pliny the Elder

Nat. Hist.	*Natural History*

Rabbinic Texts

m. 'Abot	*Mishnah Avot*
b. B. Meṣ.	*Babylonian Bava Metzi'a*
b. Bek.	*Babylonian Bekorot*
b. Ber.	*Babylonian Berakot*
m. Ber.	*Mishnah Berakot*
m. Git.	*Mishnah Gittin*
m. Ned.	*Mishnah Nedarim*
b. Šabb.	*Babylonian Šabbat*
m. Šabb.	*Mishnah Šabbat*
m. Sanh.	*Mishnah Sanhedrin*
m. Šeqal.	*Mishnah Sheqalim*
Midr. Qoh.	*Midrash Qohelet Rabbah*
Sop.	*Masekhet Soperim*
y. Ta'an.	*Jerusalem Ta'anit*
b. Yebam.	*Babylonian Yebamot*
b. Yoma	*Babylonian Yoma*

Tacitus

Ann.	*Annals*

Contemporary Sources

AB	Anchor Bible
ABD	*Anchor Bible Dictionary*
ACCS	Ancient Christian Commentary on Scripture
AGJU	Arbeiten zur Geschichte des antiken Judentums und des Urchristentums
BDAG	Bauer, Walter, Frederick W. Danker, William F. Arndt, and F. Wilbur Gingrich. *Greek-English Lexicon of the New Testament and Other Early Christian Literature.*
BDB	Brown, Francis, S. R. Driver, and Charles A. Briggs. *A Hebrew and English Lexicon of the Old Testament.*
BECNT	Baker Exegetical Commentary on the New Testament
BibInt	*Biblical Interpretation*
BTB	*Biblical Theology Bulletin*

BZNW	Beihefte zur Zeitschrift für die neutestamentliche Wissenschaft und die Kunde der älteren Kirche
CBQ	*Catholic Biblical Quarterly*
CCT	Chalice Commentaries for Today
DJG	*Dictionary of Jesus and the Gospels*
DNTB	*Dictionary of New Testament Background*
DOTP	*Dictionary of the Old Testament Prophets*
EBC	Expositor's Bible Commentary
EDEJ	*Eerdmans Dictionary of Early Judaism*
ETL	*Ephemerides Theologicae Lovanienses*
EvQ	*Evangelical Quarterly*
ExpTim	*Expository Times*
HBT	*Horizons in Biblical Theology*
HTR	*Harvard Theological Review*
HvTSt	*Hervormde teologiese studies*
ICC	International Critical Commentary
JATS	*Journal of the Adventist Theological Society*
JBL	*Journal of Biblical Literature*
JCP	*Jewish and Christian Perspectives*
JETS	*Journal of the Evangelical Theological Society*
JRS	*Journal of Roman Studies*
JSNT	*Journal for the Study of the New Testament*
JSNTSup	Journal for the Study of the New Testament Supplement Series
JSOT	*Journal for the Study of the Old Testament*
JSOTSup	Journal for the Study of the Old Testament Supplement Series
JTS	*Journal of Theological Studies*
LNTS	Library of New Testament Studies
MAJT	*Mid-America Journal of Theology*
NCBC	New Cambridge Bible Commentary
NIB	*The New Interpreter's Bible*
NIBC	New International Bible Commentary
NICNT	The New International Commentary on the New Testament
NIDB	*New Interpreter's Dictionary of the Bible*
NIGTC	New International Greek Testament Commentary
NovT	*Novum Testamentum*
NSBT	New Studies in Biblical Theology
NTS	*New Testament Studies*
PG	Patrologia graeca
SBL	Society of Biblical Literature
SBLDS	Society of Biblical Literature Dissertation Series
SBLMS	Society of Biblical Literature Monograph Series
SBLRBS	Society of Biblical Literature Resources for Biblical Study
SBT	Studies in Biblical Theology
SCM	Student Christian Movement
SJSJ	Supplements to the Journal for the Study of Judaism
SJT	*Scottish Journal of Theology*
SNTSMS	Society for New Testament Studies Monograph Series
SPCK	Society for the Promotion of Christian Knowledge
TDNT	*Theological Dictionary of the New Testament*
TS	*Theological Studies*
TynBul	*Tyndale Bulletin*
TZ	*Theologische Zeitschrift*
VT	*Vetus Testamentum*
WBC	Word Biblical Commentary
WUNT	Wissenschaftliche Untersuchungen zum Neuen Testament
ZNW	*Zeitschrift* für die neutestamentliche Wissenschaft

Greek Transliteration

Greek	Letter	English
α	*alpha*	*a*
β	*bēta*	*b*
γ	*gamma*	*g*
γ	*gamma nasal*	*n* (before γ, κ, ξ, χ)
δ	*delta*	*d*
ε	*epsilon*	*e*
ζ	*zēta*	*z*
η	*ēta*	*ē*
θ	*thēta*	*th*
ι	*iōta*	*i*
κ	*kappa*	*k*
λ	*lambda*	*l*
μ	*mu*	*m*
ν	*nu*	*n*
ξ	*xi*	*x*
ο	*omicron*	*o*
π	*pi*	*p*
ρ	*rhō*	*r*
ῥ	initial *rhō*	*rh*
σ/ς	*sigma*	*s*
τ	*tau*	*t*
υ	*upsilon*	*y*
υ	*upsilon*	*u* (in diphthongs: *au, eu, ēu, ou, ui*)
φ	*phi*	*ph*
χ	*chi*	*ch*
ψ	*psi*	*ps*
ω	*ōmega*	*ō*
ʽ	rough breathing	*h* (before initial vowels or diphthongs)

Hebrew Consonant Transliteration

Hebrew/ Aramaic	Letter	English
א	*alef*	ʾ
ב	*bet*	*b*
ג	*gimel*	*g*
ד	*dalet*	*d*
ה	*he*	*h*
ו	*vav*	*v* or *w*
ז	*zayin*	*z*
ח	*khet*	*ḥ*
ט	*tet*	*ṭ*
י	*yod*	*y*
כ/ך	*kaf*	*k*
ל	*lamed*	*l*
מ/ם	*mem*	*m*
נ/ן	*nun*	*n*
ס	*samek*	*s*
ע	*ayin*	ʿ
פ/ף	*pe*	*p; f* (spirant)
צ/ץ	*tsade*	*ṣ*
ק	*qof*	*q*
ר	*resh*	*r*
שׂ	*sin*	*ś*
שׁ	*shin*	*š*
ת	*tav*	*t; th* (spirant)

BIBLIOGRAPHY

Alexander, P. 1999. "The Parting of the Ways" from the Perspective of Rabbinic Judaism. Pages 1-25 in *Jews and Christians: The Parting of the Ways A.D. 70 to 135*. Edited by J. D. G. Dunn. Grand Rapids: Eerdmans.

Allison, D. C. 1984. Elijah must come first. *JBL* 103/2:256-58.

———. 1993. *The New Moses: A Matthean Typology*. Edinburgh: T&T Clark.

Ambraseys, N. 2009. *Earthquakes in the Mediterranean and Middle East: A Multidisciplinary Study of Seismicity up to 1900*. Cambridge: Cambridge University Press.

Anderson, B. W. 2000. *Out of the Depths: The Psalms Speak for Us Today*. 3rd ed. Louisville, KY: Westminster John Knox Press.

Aune, D. E. 1983. *Prophecy in Early Christianity and the Ancient Mediterranean World*. Grand Rapids: Eerdmans.

———. 1988. *Greco-Roman Literature and the New Testament: Selected Forms and Genres*. Atlanta: Scholars.

Bailey, K. E. 1980. *Through Peasant Eyes: More Lucan Parables, Their Culture and Style*. Grand Rapids: Eerdmans.

———. 1995. Middle Eastern Oral Tradition and the Synoptic Gospels. *ExpTim* 106:363-67.

Balch, D. L. 1988. Household Codes. Pages 25-50 in *Greco-Roman Literature and the New Testament: Selected Forms and Genres*. Edited by David E. Aune. Atlanta: Scholars.

Barth, K. 2004. *Church Dogmatics, Volume 2: The Doctrine of God, Part 2*. Edited by T. F. Torrance and G. Bromiley. Edinburgh: T&T Clark International.

Barton, S. C. 1994. *Discipleship and Family Ties in Mark and Matthew*. SNTSMS 80. Cambridge: Cambridge University Press.

Bauckham, R. 1986. The Coin in the Fish's Mouth. Pages 219-52 in *Gospel Perspectives 6: The Miracles of Jesus*. Edited by D. Wenham and C. Blomberg. Sheffield: JSOT Press.

———. 1988. Jesus' Demonstration in the Temple. Pages 72-89 in *Law and Religion: Essays on the Place of the Law in Israel and Early Christianity*. Edited by Barnabas Lindars. Cambridge: James Clarke & Co.

———. 1998a. *God Crucified: Monotheism and Christology in the New Testament*. Carlisle: Paternoster.

———. 1998b. *The Gospels for All Christians: Rethinking Gospel Audiences*. Edinburgh: T&T Clark.

______. 2006. *Jesus and the Eyewitnesses: The Gospels as Eyewitness Testimony*. Grand Rapids: Eerdmans.

———. 2008. *Jesus and the God of Israel: God Crucified and Other Studies on the New Testament's Christology of Divine Identity*. Grand Rapids: Eerdmans.

Bauer, D. R. 1992. Son of David. Pages 766-69 in *Dictionary of Jesus and the Gospels*. Edited by J. B. Green and S. McKnight. Downers Grove, IL: InterVarsity Press.

Bauer, W., W. Arndt, and F. Danker. 2000. *A Greek-English Lexicon of the New Testament and Other Early Christian Literature*. 3rd ed. Chicago: University of Chicago.

Beale, G. K., and D. A. Carson. 2007. *Commentary on the New Testament Use of the Old Testament*. Grand Rapids: Baker / Nottingham: Apollos.

Berg, I. C. 2014. *Irony in the Matthean Passion Narrative*. Minneapolis: Fortress Press.

Black, M. 1967. *An Aramaic Approach to the Gospels and Acts*. Oxford: Clarendon.

Blomberg, C. L. 2007. *The Historical Reliability of the Gospels*. Downers Grove, IL: IVP Academic / Nottingham: Apollos.

———. 2012. *Interpreting the Parables*. 2nd ed. Downers Grove, IL: IVP Academic.

Boda, Mark J., and J. Gordon McConville. 2012. *Dictionary of the Old Testament Prophets*. Downers Grove, IL: InterVarsity Press.

Bonhoeffer, D. 1959. *The Cost of Discipleship*. London: SCM Press.

Booth, R. P. 1986. *Jesus and the Laws of Purity: Tradition History and Legal History in Mark 7*. Sheffield: JSOT.

Borg, M. J. 1984. *Conflict, Holiness, and Politics in the Teachings of Jesus*. New York: E. Mellen.

Botha, P. J. J. 2012. *Orality and Literacy in Early Christianity*. Biblical Performance Criticism 5. Eugene, OR: Cascade Books.

Bourgel, J. 2010. The Jewish Christians' Move from Jerusalem as a Pragmatic Choice. Pages 107-38 in *Studies in Rabbinic Judaism and Early Christianity*. Edited by D. Jaffé. Leiden: Brill.

Boyer, M. G. 2017. *Divine Presence: Elements of Biblical Theophanies*. Eugene, OR: Wipf & Stock.

Brandon, S. G. F. 1957. *The Fall of Jerusalem and the Christian Church*. London: SPCK.
Brower, K. E. 1978. "The Old Testament in the Markan Passion Narrative." PhD thesis. University of Manchester.
———. 2004. Jesus and the Lustful Eye: Glancing at Matthew 5:28. *EvQ* 76:291-309.
———. 2005. *Holiness in the Gospels*. Kansas City: Beacon Hill Press of Kansas City.
______. 2007. The Holy One and His Disciples: Holiness and Ecclesiology in Mark. Pages 57-75 in *Holiness and Ecclesiology in the New Testament*. Edited by K. E. Brower and A. Johnson. Grand Rapids: Eerdmans.
———. 2012. *Mark: A Commentary in the Wesleyan Tradition*. Kansas City: Beacon Hill Press of Kansas City.
Brower, K. E., and M. W. Elliott, eds. 2013. *The Reader Must Understand: Eschatology in Bible and Theology*. Eugene: Wipf & Stock.
Brown, R. E. 1968. *New Testament Essays*. Garden City, NY: Doubleday.
———. 1977. *The Birth of the Messiah: A Commentary on the Infancy Narratives in Matthew and Luke*. Garden City, NY: Doubleday.
______. 1994. *The Death of the Messiah: from Gethsemane to the Grave: A Commentary on the Passion Narrative in the Four Gospels.* New Haven, CT: Yale University Press.
———. 1997. *An Introduction to the New Testament*. New York: Doubleday.
Byrskog, S. 2000. *Story as History—History as Story: The Gospel Tradition in the Context of Ancient Oral History*. WUNT 123. Tübingen: Mohr Siebeck.
Cane, A. 2017. *The Place of Judas Iscariot in Christology*. London: Routledge.
Card, M. 2013. *Matthew: The Gospel of Identity.* Downers Grove, IL: IVP Books.
Cargal, T. 1991. "His Blood Be Upon Us and Upon Our Children": A Matthean Double Entendre? *New Testament Studies* 37/1: 101-12.
Carson, D. A. 1984. *Matthew.* Vol. 8 of Expositor's Bible Commentary. Grand Rapids: Zondervan.
Carter, W. 2000. Evoking Isaiah: Matthean Soteriology and an Intertextual Reading of Isaiah 7-9 and Matthew 1:23 and 4:15-16. *JBL* 19:503-20.
Casey, M. 1976. The Son of Man Problem. *ZNW* 67:147-54.
Chilton, B. D., and C. A. Evans. 1997. *Jesus in Context: Temple, Purity and Restoration*. AGJU 39. Leiden: Brill.
Chilton, B. D., and J. Neusner. 1995. *Judaism in the New Testament: Practices and Beliefs*. London: Routledge.
Chilton, B. D., P. W. Comfort, and M. O. Wise. 2000. Temple, Jewish. Pages 1167-83 in *Dictionary of New Testament Background*. Edited by C. A. Evans and S. E. Porter. Downers Grove, IL: InterVarsity Press.
Chrysostom, J. 1859. "Homily on the betrayal of Judas (*Eis Ten Prodosian Tou Iouda*)." Pages 373-92 in Patrologia Graeca. Vol. 49. Edited by J.-P. Migne. Paris: Imprimerie Catholique.
Collins, A. Y. 2007. Mark: A Commentary. Hermeneia: A Critical and Historical Commentary on the Bible. Minneapolis: Fortress Press.
Collins, J. J. 1997. *Seers, Sibyls, and Sages in Hellenistic-Roman Judaism*. SJSJ 54. Leiden: Brill.
Collins, K. J. 2003. *John Wesley: A Theological Journey*. Nashville: Abingdon.
Cousland, J. R. C. 1999. The Feeding of the Four Thousand Gentiles in Matthew? Matthew 15:29-39 as a Test Case. *NovT* 41:1-23.
Daube, D. 1972-73. Responsibilities of Master and Disciples in the Gospels. *NTS* 19:1-15.
Davidson, R. M. 2006. Did King David Rape Bathsheba?: A Case Study in Narrative Theology. *JATS* 17:81-95.
Davies, E. W. 2003. *The Dissenting Reader: Feminist Approaches to the Hebrew Bible*. Aldershot, UK / Burlington, VT: Ashgate.
Davies, R. E., ed. 1989. *The Works of John Wesley*. Vol. 9: *The Methodist Societies: History, Nature, and Design*. Nashville: Abingdon Press.
Davies, W. D. 1994. *The Gospel and the Land: Early Christianity and Jewish Territorial Doctrine*. Sheffield: JSOT.
Davies, W. D., and D. C. Allison. 1988. *The Gospel According to Saint Matthew*. ICC. Vol. 1: Matthew 1-7. Edinburgh: T&T Clark.
———. 1991. *The Gospel According to Saint Matthew*. ICC. Vol. 2: Matthew 8-18. Edinburgh: T&T Clark.
———. 2004. *The Gospel According to Saint Matthew*. ICC. Vol. 3: Matthew 19-28. Edinburgh: T&T Clark.

Deasley, A. R. G. 2000. *Marriage and Divorce in the Bible and the Church*. Kansas City: Beacon Hill Press of Kansas City.

Deines, R. 2008. Not the Law but the Messiah: Law and Righteousness in the Gospel of Matthew: An Ongoing Debate. Pages 53-83 in *Built Upon the Rock: Studies in the Gospel of Matthew*. Edited by D. M. Gurtner and J. Nolland. Grand Rapids: Eerdmans.

Derrett, J. D. M. 1970. *Law in the New Testament*. London: Darton, Longman and Todd.

deSilva, D. A. 2004. *An Introduction to the New Testament: Contexts, Methods and Ministry Formation*. Downers Grove, IL: IVP Academic.

Dodd, C. H. 1961. *Parables of the Kingdom*. Rev. ed. London: Collins.

Donaldson, T. L. 1985. *Jesus on the Mountain: A Study in Matthean Theology*. Sheffield: JSOT.

———. 1996. Guiding Readers—Making Disciples: Discipleship in Matthew's Narrative Strategy. Pages 30-49 in *Patterns of Discipleship in the New Testament*. Edited by R. N. Longenecker. Grand Rapids: Eerdmans.

Douglas, S. 2016. *Early Church Understandings of Jesus as the Female Divine: The Scandal of the Scandal of Particularity*. LNTS 557. London and New York: Bloomsbury T&T Clark.

Downing, F. G. 1992. *Cynics and Christian Origins*. Edinburgh: T&T Clark.

Droge, A. J., and J. D. Tabor. 1992. *A Noble Death: Suicide and Martyrdom Among Christians and Jews in Antiquity*. San Francisco: HarperCollins.

Dunn, J. D. G. 1996. *Christology in the Making: A New Testament Inquiry into the Origins of the Doctrine of the Incarnation*. 2nd ed. Grand Rapids: Eerdmans.

———. 2003. *Christianity in the Making*. Vol. 1: *Jesus Remembered*. Grand Rapids: Eerdmans.

———. 2004. Jesus and Purity: An Ongoing Debate. *NTS* 48/4:449-67.

———. 2006a. Did Jesus Attend the Synagogue? Pages 206-22 in *Jesus and Archaeology*. Edited by J. H. Charlesworth. Grand Rapids: Eerdmans.

———. 2006b. *The Parting of the Ways: Between Christianity and Judaism and Their Significance for the Character of Christianity*. 2nd ed. London: SCM Press.

Edwards, D. L., and J. R. W. Stott. 1989. *Evangelical Essentials: A Liberal-Evangelical Dialogue*. Downers Grove, IL: InterVarsity.

Ehrman, B. D. 2004. *The New Testament: A Historical Introduction to the Early Christian Writings*. 3rd ed. New York/Oxford: Oxford University Press.

Ellis, E. E. 1997. New Testament Teaching on Hell. Pages 199-219 in *Eschatology in Bible & Theology: Evangelical Essays at the Dawn of a New Millennium*. Downers Grove, IL: InterVarsity.

Eppstein, V. 1964. The Historicity of the Gospel Account of the Cleansing of the Temple. *ZNW* 55:42-58.

Ermakov, A. 2014a. The Holy One of God in Markan Narrative. *HBT* 36/2:159-84.

———. 2014b. Purity in the Synoptic Gospels. Pages 89-113 in *Purity: Essays in Bible and Theology*. Edited by A. Brower Latz and A. Ermakov. Eugene, OR: Pickwick.

Esler, P. F. 2006. *Ancient Israel: The Old Testament in Its Social Context*. Minneapolis: Fortress Press.

Evans, C. A. 1997. Jesus' Action in the Temple: Cleansing or Portent of Destruction? Evidences. Pages 419-28 in *Jesus in Context: Temple, Purity, and Restoration*. Edited by C. Evans and B. Chilton. Leiden: Brill.

———. 2012. *Matthew*. NCBC. New York: Cambridge University.

Evans-Grubbs, J. 2013. Infant Exposure and Infanticide. Pages 222-333 in *The Oxford Handbook of Childhood and Education in the Classical World*. Edited by Judith Evans Grubbs, Tim Parkin, and Roslynne Bell. Oxford: Oxford University Press.

Eve, E. 2013. *Behind the Gospels: Understanding the Oral Tradition*. London: SPCK.

Ferguson, E. 2009. *Baptism in the Early Church: History, Theology, and Liturgy in the First Five Centuries*. Grand Rapids: Eerdmans.

Fiore, Benjamin. 2000. Cynicism and Skepticism. Pages 242-45 in *Dictionary of New Testament Background*. Edited by C. A. Evans and S. E. Porter. Downers Grove, IL: InterVarsity Press.

Fletcher-Louis, C. H. T. 2002. Jesus, the Temple and the Dissolution of Heaven and Earth. Pages 117-41 in *Apocalyptic in History and Tradition*. Edited by J. Barton and C. C. Rowland. Sheffield: Sheffield Academic Press.

______. 2013. The Destruction of the Temple and the Relativization of the Old Covenant: Mark 13:31 and Matthew 5:18. Pages 145-69 in *The Reader Must Understand: Eschatology in Bible and Theology*. Edited by K. E. Brower and M. W. Elliot. Eugene, OR: Wipf and Stock Publishers.

France, R. T. 1989. *Matthew: Evangelist and Teacher*. London: Paternoster.

———. 2007. *The Gospel of Matthew*. NICNT. Grand Rapids: Eerdmans.

Fuller, R. H. 1954. *The Mission and Achievement of Jesus: An Examination of the Presuppositions of New Testament Theology*. London: SCM Press.
Gaebelein, F. E., J. D. Douglas, and D. Polcyn. 1985. *Matthew, Mark, Luke*. EBC 8. Grand Rapids: Zondervan.
Garland, D. E. 2001. *Reading Matthew: A Literary and Theological Commentary on the First Gospel.* Macon, GA: Smyth & Helwys Publishing.
Gerhardsson, B. 1998. *Memory and Manuscript: Oral Tradition and Written Transmission in Rabbinic Judaism and Early Christianity with Tradition and Transmission in Early Christianity.* Biblical Resources Series. Grand Rapids: Eerdmans.
Glatt-Gilad, D. A., and J. H. Tigay. 1996. Phylacteries. Page 854 in *The HarperCollins Bible Dictionary*. Edited by P. J. Achtemeier et al. San Francisco: HarperSanFrancisco.
Goldingay, J. 2005. *The Message of Isaiah 40-55: A Literary-Theological Commentary*. London / New York: T&T Clark.
Goodacre, M. 2001. The Synoptic Problem: A Way Through the Maze. Sheffield: Sheffield Academic Press.
———. 2002. The Case Against Q: Studies in Marcan Priority and the Synoptic Problem. Harrisburg, PA: Trinity Press International.
Goulder, M. D. 1974. *Midrash and Lection in Matthew: The Speaker's Lectures in Biblical Studies, 1969-71*. London: SPCK.
Gray, T. C. 2008. *The Temple in the Gospel of Mark.* WUNT 242. Tübingen: Mohr Siebeck.
Greathouse, W. M. 1979. *From the Apostles to Wesley: Christian Perfection in Historical Perspective.* Kansas City: Beacon Hill Press of Kansas City.
Green, J. B., S. McKnight, and I. H. Marshall. 1992. *Dictionary of Jesus and the Gospels*. Downers Grove, IL: InterVarsity.
Guelich, R. A. 1982. *The Sermon on the Mount: A Foundation for Understanding*. Waco, TX: Word Books.
Gundry, R. H. 1976. *Sōma in Biblical Theology: With Emphasis on Pauline Anthropology*. Cambridge / New York: Cambridge University.
———. 1982. *Matthew: A Commentary on His Literary and Theological Art*. Grand Rapids: Eerdmans.
Gunther, J. J. 1973. The Fate of the Jerusalem Church. The Flight to Pella. *TZ* 29:81-94.
Hagner, D. A. 1993. *Matthew 1-13*. WBC 33A. Dallas: Word Books.
———. 1995. *Matthew 14-28*. WBC 33B. Dallas: Word Books.
———. 2007. Holiness and Ecclesiology: The Church in Matthew. Pages 40-56 in *Holiness and Ecclesiology in the New Testament*. Edited by K. E. Brower and Andy Johnson. Grand Rapids: Eerdmans.
———. 2012. *The New Testament: A Historical and Theological Introduction*. Grand Rapids: Baker Academic.
Hahn, R. L. 2007. *Matthew: A Commentary for Bible Students*. Indianapolis: Wesleyan Publishing House.
Harrington D. J. 1991. The Gospel of Matthew. Sacra Pagina 1. Collegeville, MN: Liturgical Press.
Harrington, H. K. 2012. Leviticus. Pages 70-78 in *Women's Bible Commentary.* Revised and updated. Edited by Carol A. Newsom, et al. Louisville, KY: Westminster John Knox Press.
Harris, W. V. 1994. Child-Exposure in the Roman Empire. *JRS* 84:1-22.
Hartman, L. 1997. *"Into the Name of the Lord Jesus": Baptism in the Early Church*. Edinburgh: T&T Clark.
Harvey, R. J. 2016. "Judas Iscariot, Betrayal and Idolatry." PhD thesis. Newcastle, NSW: University of Newcastle.
Hays, R. B. 1989. *Echoes of Scripture in the Letters of Paul*. New Haven, CT: Yale University.
———. 2008. *Seeking the Identity of Jesus: A Pilgrimage*. Grand Rapids: Eerdmans.
———. 2014. *Reading Backwards: Figural Christology and the Fourfold Gospel Witness*. Waco, TX: Baylor University.
Hengel, M. 1977. *Crucifixion in the Ancient World and the Folly of the Message of the Cross*. Philadelphia: Fortress Press.
———. 1985. *Studies in the Gospel of Mark*. Philadelphia: Fortress Press.
Hill, D. 1972. *The Gospel of Matthew.* The New Century Bible Commentary. London: Marshall, Morgan & Scott.
Hoehner, H. W. 1980. *Herod Antipas*. Grand Rapids: Zondervan.
______. Herodian Dynasty. Pages 317-26 in *Dictionary of Jesus and the Gospels.* Edited by J. B. Green and S. McKnight. Downers Grove, IL: InterVarsity Press.

Hooker, M. D. 1967. *The Son of Man in Mark: A Study of the Background of the Term "Son of Man" and Its Use in St. Mark's Gospel*. London: SPCK.
———. 1994. *Not Ashamed of the Gospel: New Testament Interpretations of the Death of Christ*. Carlisle: Paternoster Press.
______. 1997. *Beginnings: Keys that Open the Gospels.* Harrisburg, PA: Trinity Press International.
Huffman, D. S. 1992. Genealogy. Pages 253-59 in *Dictionary of Jesus and the Gospels.* Edited by J. B. Green and S. McKnight. Downers Grove, IL: InterVarsity Press.
Hultgren, A. J. 2000. *The Parables of Jesus: A Commentary*. Grand Rapids: Eerdmans.
Hurtado, L. W. 1983. *Mark: A Good News Commentary.* San Francisco: Harper & Row.
———. 2003. *Lord Jesus Christ: Devotion to Jesus in Earliest Christianity*. Grand Rapids: Eerdmans.
———. 2014. Oral Fixation and New Testament Studies? "Orality," "Performance" and Reading Texts in Early Christianity. *NTS* 60:321-40.
Instone-Brewer, D. 2002. *Divorce and Remarriage in the Bible: The Social and Literary Context*. Grand Rapids: Eerdmans.
———. 2003. *Divorce and Remarriage in the Church: Biblical Solutions for Pastoral Realities*. Downers Grove, IL: IVP Books.
Jackson, B. 2008. *Essays on Halakhah in the New Testament.* JCP 16. Leiden: Brill.
Jeremias, J. 1966. *Rediscovering the Parables*. New York: Scribner's Sons.
______. 1971. *New Testament Theology: Part One, The Proclamation of Jesus.* London: SCM Press.
———. 1977. *The Eucharistic Words of Jesus*. Philadelphia: Fortress Press.
Jeremias, J., and S. H. Hooke. 1972. *The Parables of Jesus*. Translated by S. H. Hooke. 3rd rev. ed. London: SCM Press.
Johnson, L. T. 2010. *The Writings of the New Testament: An Interpretation.* Philadelphia: Fortress Press.
———. 2011. *Prophetic Jesus, Prophetic Church: The Challenge of Luke-Acts to Contemporary Christians*. Grand Rapids: Eerdmans.
Josephus. 1927-28. *The Jewish War*. Volumes I-III. Loeb Classical Library. Translated by H. St. J. Thackeray. Cambridge, MA: Harvard University Press.
———. 1930-65. *Jewish Antiquities*. Volumes I-IX. Loeb Classical Library. Translated by Ralph Marcus. Cambridge, MA: Harvard University Press.
Justin (Martyr). 2003. *Dialogue with Trypho*. Vol. 3: Selections from the Fathers of the Church. Translated by T. B. Falls. Washington: The Catholic University of America Press.
Keck, L. E., ed. 1995. *The New Interpreter's Bible*, Vol. 8. Nashville: Abingdon Press.
Keener, C. S. 1999. *A Commentary on the Gospel of Matthew*. Grand Rapids: Eerdmans.
———. 2009. *The Gospel of Matthew: A Socio-Rhetorical Commentary*. Grand Rapids: Eerdmans.
———. 2011. *Miracles: The Credibility of the New Testament Accounts*. Grand Rapids: Baker Academic.
Kelber, W. H. 1997. *The Oral and the Written Gospel: The Hermeneutics of Speaking and Writing in the Synoptic Tradition, Mark, Paul and Q*. Bloomington and Indianapolis: Indiana University Press.
Kerr, A. J. 1997. Matthew 13:25: Sowing Zizania among Another's Wheat: Realistic or Artificial? *JTS* 48:108-9.
Kingsbury, J. D. 1969. *The Parables of Jesus in Matthew 13: A Study in Redaction-Criticism*. Richmond, VA: John Knox.
———. 1988. *Matthew as Story*. 2nd ed. Philadelphia: Fortress.
Kistemaker, S. J. 1980. *The Parables of Jesus*. Grand Rapids: Baker Book House.
Kister, M. 2010. Divorce, Reproof, and Other Sayings in the Synoptic Gospels: Jesus Traditions in the Context of "Qumranic" and Other Texts. Pages 195-239 in *Text, Thought, and Practice in Qumran and Early Christianity: Proceedings of the Ninth International Symposium of the Orion Center for the Study of the Dead Sea Scrolls and Associated Literature, Jointly Sponsored by the Hebrew University Center for the Study of Christianity, 11-13 January, 2004*. Edited by R. Clements and D. R. Schwartz. Leiden: Brill.
Kittel, G., G. W. Bromiley, and G. Friedrich, eds. 1964-76. *Theological Dictionary of the New Testament*. Grand Rapids: Eerdmans.
Klassen, W. 1996. *Judas: Betrayer or Friend of Jesus?* Minneapolis: Fortress Press.
Klauck, H.-J. 1997. *Judas, ein Jünger des Herrn*. Freiburg-in-Brisgau: Herder.
Koester, C. 1989. The Origin and Significance of the Flight to Pella Tradition. *Catholic Biblical Quarterly* 51:90-106.
Kreitzer, L. J. 1997. Parousia. Pages 856-75 in *The Dictionary of the Later New Testament and Its Developments: A Compendium of Contemporary Biblical Scholarship*. Edited by Peter Davids and R. P. Martin. Downers Grove, IL: IVP.
Lachs, S. T. 1975. On Matthew 23:27-28. *HTR* 68:385-88.

Ladd, G. E. 1974. *The Presence of the Future: The Eschatology of Biblical Realism*. London: SPCK.
Laeuchli, S. 1953. Origen's Interpretation of Judas Iscariot. *Church History* 22/4:253-68.
Lammé, N. 2012. The Blasphemy against the Holy Spirit: The Unpardonable Sin in Matthew 12:22-32. *MAJT* 23:19-51.
Lee, P. 2001. *New Jerusalem in the Book of Revelation: A Study of Revelation 21-22 in the Light of Its Background in Jewish Tradition*. WUNT II, Bk. 129. Tübingen: Mohr Siebeck.
Lindars, B. 1983. *Jesus, Son of Man: A Fresh Examination of the Son of Man Sayings in the Gospels in the Light of Recent Research*. Grand Rapids: Eerdmans.
Lohmeyer, E. 1961. *Lord of the Temple: A Study of the Relation between Cult and Gospel*. Edinburgh, London: Oliver & Boyd.
Longman, T. 2013. *The Baker Illustrated Bible Dictionary*. Grand Rapids: Baker Books.
Lunde, J. M. 1992. Heaven and Hell. Pages 307-12 in *Dictionary of Jesus and the Gospels*. Edited by J. B. Green and S. McKnight. Downers Grove, IL: InterVarsity Press.
Luz, U. 1995. *The Theology of the Gospel of Matthew*. Translated by J. Bradford Robinson. New Testament Theology. Cambridge: Cambridge University Press.
———. 2001. *Matthew 8-20*. Hermeneia. Minneapolis: Fortress.
———. 2005. *Matthew 21-28*. Rev. ed. Hermeneia. Minneapolis: Fortress.
———. 2007. *Matthew 1-7*. Rev. ed. Hermeneia. Minneapolis: Fortress.
Maccoby, H. 1999. *Ritual and Morality: The Ritual Purity System and Its Place in Judaism*. Cambridge: Cambridge University Press.
Malina, B. J. 2001. *The New Testament World: Insights from Cultural Anthropology*. 3rd ed. Revised and Expanded. Louisville, KY: Westminster John Knox.
Malina, B. J., and R. L. Rohrbaugh. 2003. *Social-Science Commentary on the Synoptic Gospels*. 2nd ed. Minneapolis: Fortress.
Manson, T. W. 1957. *The Sayings of Jesus: As Recorded in the Gospels According to St. Matthew and St. Luke*. Grand Rapids: Eerdmans.
Marcus, J. 1988. The Gates of Hades and the Keys of the Kingdom (Matt 16:18-19). *CBQ* 50:443-55.
———. 2009a. Birkat Ha-Minim Revisited. *NTS* 55/4:523-51.
———. 2009b. *Mark 8-16*. New Haven, CT: Yale University Press.
Marshall, I. H. 1980. *Last Supper and Lord's Supper*. Exeter: Paternoster.
McComiskey, D. S. 2010. Exile and Restoration from Exile in the Scriptural Quotations and Allusions of Jesus. *JETS* 53:673-96.
McEleney, N. J. 1994. The Unity and Theme of Matthew 7:1-12. *CBQ* 56:490-500.
McGowan, A. B. 2014. *Ancient Christian Worship: Early Church Practices in Social, Historical, and Theological Perspective*. Grand Rapids: Baker Academic.
McIver, R. K. 2011. *Memory, Jesus, and the Synoptic Gospels*. SBLRBS 59. Atlanta: Society of Biblical Literature.
McVann, M. 1998. Family Centeredness. Pages 75-79 in *Handbook of Biblical Social Values*. Edited by J. J. Pilch and B. J. Malina. Peabody, MA: Hendrickson Publishers.
Meier, J. P. 1996. The Miracles of Jesus: Three Basic Questions. *Dialogue* 29:1-15.
Menken, M. J. J. 1984. The References to Jeremiah in the Gospel according to Matthew (Matt 2:17, 16:14, 27:9). *ETL* 60:5-24.
Metzger, B. M. 1975. *A Textual Commentary on the New Testament*. London: United Bible Societies.
Milgrom, J. 2001. *Leviticus 23-27: A New Translation with Introduction and Commentary*. 1st ed. New Haven, CT: Yale University.
Morris, L. 1992. *The Gospel According to Matthew*. Grand Rapids: Eerdmans.
Mounce, R. H. 1991. *Matthew*. NIBC. Peabody, MA: Hendrickson.
Mullins, M. 2007. *The Gospel of Matthew: A Commentary*. Dublin: The Columba Press.
Neusner, J. 1973. *The Idea of Purity in Ancient Judaism*. Leiden: Brill.
———. 1991. The Mishnah: A New Translation. New Haven, CT: Yale University Press.
Newsom, C. A., S. H. Ringe, and J. E. Lapsley, eds. 2012. *Women's Bible Commentary*. 3rd ed. Revised and Updated. Louisville, KY: Westminster John Knox.
Neyrey, J. H. 1982. The Thematic Use of Isaiah 42:1-4 in Matthew 12. *Biblica* 63:457-73.
______. 1998. *Honor and Shame in the Gospel of Matthew*. Louisville, KY: Westminster John Knox Press.
Nicholson, E. W. 1982. The Covenant Ritual in Exodus xxiv 3-8. *VT* 32/1:74-86.
Nolland, J. 2005. *The Gospel of Matthew: A Commentary on the Greek Text*. NIGTC. Grand Rapids: Eerdmans / Bletchley: Paternoster.

Novakovic, L. 2003. *Messiah, the Healer of the Sick: A Study of Jesus as the Son of David in the Gospel of Matthew*. WUNT II/170. Tübingen: Mohr Siebeck.

______. 2007. 4Q521: The Works of the Messiah or the Signs of the Messianic Time? Pages 208-31 in *Qumran Studies: New Approaches, New Questions*. Edited by M. T. Davis and B. A. Strawn. Grand Rapids: Eerdmans.

Oden, T. C. 2012. *John Wesley's Teachings: Christ and Salvation*. Vol. 2. Grand Rapids: Zondervan.

Oropeza, B. J. 2011. *In the Footsteps of Judas and Other Defectors: The Gospels, Acts, and Johannine Letters*. Vol. 1: *Apostasy in the New Testament Communities*. Eugene, OR: Cascade Books.

Park, E. C. 1995. *The Mission Discourse in Matthew's Interpretation*. WUNT 2/81. Tübingen: J. C. B. Mohr (Paul Siebeck).

Patte, D. 1986. *The Gospel According to Matthew: A Structural Commentary on Matthew's Faith*. Philadelphia: Fortress Press.

Pennington, J. T. 2007. *Heaven and Earth in the Gospel of Matthew*. Leiden: Brill.

Pilch, J. J., and B. J. Malina. 1998. *Handbook of Biblical Social Values*. Peabody, MA: Hendrickson.

Pregeant, R. 2004. *Matthew*. CCT. St. Louis: Chalice Press.

Pritz, R. A. 1981. On Brandon's Rejection of the Pella Tradition. *Immanuel* 13:39-43.

Regev, E. 2004. Moral Impurity and the Temple in Early Christianity in Light of Ancient Greek Practice and Qumran Ideology. *HTR* 97/4:383-411.

Rhoads, D. M., J. Dewey, and D. Michie. 1999. *Mark as Story: An Introduction to the Narrative of a Gospel*. 2nd ed. Minneapolis: Fortress.

Robinson, T. H. 1927. *The Gospel of Matthew*. Moffatt's Commentary on the New Testament. New York and London: Harper and Brothers Publishers.

Rodriguez, R. 2010. *Structuring Early Christian Memory: Jesus in Tradition, Performance and Text*. LNTS 407. London: T&T Clark.

Saldarini, A. J. 1994. *Matthew's Christian-Jewish Community*. Chicago: University of Chicago Press.

———. 1996. Fringes. Page 854 in *The HarperCollins Bible Dictionary*. Edited by P. J. Achtemeier et al. San Francisco: HarperSanFrancisco.

Sanders, E. P. 1985. *Jesus and Judaism*. London: SCM Press.

———. 1992. *Judaism: Practice and Belief, 63 BCE-66 CE*. London: SCM.

———. 1995. *The Historical Figure of Jesus*. London: Penguin Books.

Schnackenburg, R. 2002. *The Gospel of Matthew*. Translated by R. R. Barr. Grand Rapids: Eerdmans.

Schrage, W. 1979. *synagōgē*. Pages 798-841 in vol. 7 of *TDNT*. Edited by G. Friedrich. Grand Rapids: Eerdmans.

Scott, B. B. 1989. *Hear then the Parable: A Commentary on the Parables of Jesus*. Minneapolis: Fortress Press.

Shirbroun, G. F. 1992. "Light." Pages 472-73 in *Dictionary of Jesus and the Gospels*. Edited by J. B. Green and S. McKnight. Downers Grove, IL: InterVarsity Press.

Sim, D. C. 1998. *The Gospel of Matthew and Christian Judaism*. Edinburgh: T&T Clark.

———. 1999. Angels of Eschatological Punishment in the Jewish and Christian Apocalyptic Traditions and in the Gospel of Matthew. *HvTSt* 55:693-718.

Smith, M. J. 2010. Political Context. Pages 79-104 in *The Content and the Setting of the Gospel Tradition*. Edited by Mark Harding and Alanna Nobbs. Grand Rapids: Eerdmans.

Snodgrass, K. R. 1992. Parable. Pages 591-601 in *Dictionary of Jesus and the Gospels*. Edited by J. B. Green and S. McKnight. Downers Grove, IL: InterVarsity Press.

———. 2008. *Stories with Intent: A Comprehensive Guide to the Parables of Jesus*. Grand Rapids: Eerdmans.

Snow, R. S. 2016. *Daniel's Son of Man in Mark: A Redefinition of the Jerusalem Temple and the Formation of a New Covenant Community*. Eugene, OR: Pickwick.

Soares Prabhu, G. M. 1976. *The Formula Quotations in the Infancy Narrative of Matthew: An Enquiry into the Tradition History of Mt 1-2*. Rome: Biblical Institute.

Soulen, R. N., and R. K. Soulen. 2011. *Handbook of Biblical Criticism*. 4th ed. Louisville, KY: Westminster John Knox Press.

Stanton, G. N. 1982. Matthew 11:28-30: Comfortable Words? *ExpTim* 94:3-9.

———. 1992. *A Gospel for a New People: Studies in Matthew*. Louisville, KY: Westminster/John Knox Press.

Stoops, R. F. 2000. Coinage: Jewish. Pages 222-25 in *Dictionary of New Testament Background*. Edited by C. A. Evans and S. E. Porter. Downers Grove, IL: InterVarsity Press.

Stott, J. R. W. 1989. *Essentials: A Liberal-Evangelical Dialogue*. Downers Grove, IL: InterVarsity Press.

Suggs, M. J. 1970. *Wisdom, Christology, and Law in Matthew's Gospel*. Cambridge: Harvard University.

Sullivan, D. 1992. New Insights in Matthew 27:24-25. *New Blackfriars* 73:453-57.
Talbert, C. H. 2010. *Matthew.* Paideia: Commentaries on the New Testament. Grand Rapids: Baker Academic.
Tasker, R. G. V. 1961. *Matthew: An Introduction and Commentary.* Tyndale New Testament Commentaries. London: Tyndale Press.
Taylor, M., ed. 2003. *Christianity, Poverty and Wealth: The Findings of Project 21.* London: SPCK.
Telford, W. R. 1980. *The Barren Temple and the Withered Tree.* Sheffield: JSOT Press.
Treggiari, S. 2003. Marriage and Family in Roman Society. Pages 132-82 in *Marriage and Family in the Biblical World.* Edited by Ken M. Campbell. Downers Grove, IL: IVP.
Turner, D. L. 2008. *Matthew.* BECNT. Grand Rapids: Baker Academic.
Twelftree, G. H. 1992. Demon, Devil, Satan. Pages 163-72 in *Dictionary of Jesus and the Gospels.* Edited by J. B. Green and S. McKnight. Downers Grove, IL: InterVarsity Press.
van de Sandt, H. 2005. Two Windows on a Developing Jewish-Christian Reproof Practice: Matt 18:15-17 and Did. 15:3. Pages 171-92 in *Matthew and the Didache: Two Documents from the Same Jewish-Christian Milieu?* Edited by H. van de Sandt. Minneapolis: Fortress Press.
Van De Walle, B. A. 2009. *The Heart of the Gospel: A. B. Simpson, the Fourfold Gospel, and Late Nineteenth-Century Evangelical Theology.* Eugene, OR: Pickwick.
Vermes, G. 1973. *Jesus the Jew: A Historian's Reading of the Gospels.* London: Collins.
Vine, C. E. W. 2014. *The Audience of Matthew: An Appraisal of the Local Audience Thesis.* LNTS 496. London: Bloomsbury.
Watts, R. E. 2015. Messianic Servant or the End of Israel's Exilic Curses?: Isaiah 53.4 in Matthew 8.17. *JSNT* 38:81-95.
Watts Henderson, S. 2006. *Christology and Discipleship in the Gospel of Mark.* SNTSMS 135. Cambridge: Cambridge University Press.
Wenham, D., and W. Walton. 2011. *Exploring the New Testament.* 2nd ed. Downers Grove, IL: IVP Academic.
Wenham, G. J. 1979. *The Book of Leviticus.* Grand Rapids: Eerdmans.
Wesley, J. 1978. *The Works of John Wesley.* 3rd ed. Kansas City: Nazarene Publishing House.
———. 1984. *The Works of John Wesley, Bicentennial Edition.* Vol. 1: Sermons I (1-33). Edited by Albert Outler. Nashville: Abingdon Press.
———. 1987a. *The Works of John Wesley.* Vol. 11: *The Appeals to Men of Reason and Religion and Certain Related Open Letters.* Edited by Gerald Cragg. Nashville: Abingdon Press.
———. 1987b. *The Works of John Wesley, Bicentennial Edition.* Vol. 4: Sermons IV (115-151). Edited by Albert Outler. Nashville: Abingdon Press.
Whybray, R. N. 1983. *The Second Isaiah.* Sheffield: Sheffield University Press.
Wright, N. T. 1992. *The New Testament and the People of God.* Vol. 1 of *Christian Origins and the Question of God.* Minneapolis: Fortress.
———. 1996. *Jesus and the Victory of God.* Vol. 2 of *Christian Origins and the Question of God.* Minneapolis: Fortress.
______. 2002. *Matthew for Everyone. Part 2: Chapters 16-28.* London: SPCK.
———. 2004. *Matthew for Everyone. Part 2: Chapters 16-28.* Louisville, KY: Westminster John Knox Press.
———. 2013. *Paul and the Faithfulness of God.* Vol. 4 of Christian Origins and the Question of God. Minneapolis: Fortress.
———. 2016. *The Day the Revolution Began: Reconsidering the Meaning of Jesus's Crucifixion.* San Francisco: HarperOne.
Yang, Y.-E. 1997. *Jesus and the Sabbath in Matthew's Gospel.* LNTS 139. Sheffield: Sheffield Academic.

TABLE OF SIDEBARS

INTRODUCTION

Matthew's place in the biblical canon as the first Gospel signals its importance for the early church. Its authoritative status was supported by the traditional belief that Matthew, an apostle of Jesus, composed his story first among other Gospels. Early church fathers paid particular attention to Matthew: the first Gospel was "most widely read, commented upon and used in patristic writings" (ACCS 1a:xxxvii). The first few generations of Christians learned the stories of Jesus' life from Matthew (ACCS 1a:xxxvii). Unique discourses in Matthew—such as the Sermon on the Mount, the Lord's Prayer, the Birth Narratives, the Beatitudes, and so forth—are deeply engrained in Christian discourse and thinking.

The church noticed the distinctive character of Matthew's Gospel early on. Each of the four Evangelists was given an allegorical symbol to capture his unique perspective. They corresponded to four mythical creatures from Ezek 1:10 (also Rev 4:6-8). Matthew was represented by "the winged creature with a face of a man." Irenaeus of Lyon (ca. 130-202 CE) explains this choice by Matthew's representation of Jesus. For him, the symbol of the divine man represents the emphasis on Christ's humanness: "This, then, is the Gospel of His humanity; for which reason it is, too, that [the character of] a humble and meek man is kept up through the whole Gospel" (*Against Heresies,* 3.11.8). Modern scholars might disagree with this assessment but unanimously agree on the distinctiveness of Matthew's voice. This commentary attempts to capture the first Gospel's special character and communicate it to a contemporary Wesleyan reader.

With the arrival of modern biblical criticism—with its drive to reconstruct "early Jesus tradition"—the Gospel of Matthew lost its preeminent place in theological scholarship because scholars believed that it reflects later Christian traditions. Despite this shift in scholarly interests, the Gospel of Matthew continues to play an important role in the life of the church and brings its distinctive voice into the conversation about Jesus, the kingdom of heaven, and the holy people of God. Its emphasis on communal living, cruciform mission, and formation of Christian identity enriches the dialogue that is taking place within a new generation of holiness people. This commentary invites us to hear what Matthew has to offer.

A. Title

The earliest manuscripts bearing the name Matthew come to us from the fourth century CE (though portions of the Matthean text appear in papyri $\mathfrak{P}^{64/67}$ and $\mathfrak{P}^{45}$ dated by early second and third century CE). Codex Sinaiticus, for example, simply refers to the Gospel as *kata matthaion* or "according to Matthew." Fifth-century manuscripts add *euangelion* or "gospel" to the title. Thus, the name of the book—as we have it now—was not given by the author himself but derives later from the period of formation of "the fourfold Gospel canon" (*NIB* 8:106) and is modeled on the introductory line from Mark 1:1. But other scholars disagree (Hengel 1985, 64-84; Turner 2008, 11-13), arguing that the inscription emerges as soon as other "gospels" appeared (Bauckham 2006, 304).

The word "gospel" or "good news" (Gk. *euangelion*) was originally used to refer to proclamation of royal news: birth in the family, ascension to the throne, victory in the battle, and so forth. In the OT, *euangelion* refers to the good news of YHWH's return, victory over his enemies, and liberation of his people (Isa 52:7). In early Christian literature, the word refers to the announcement of the inbreaking kingdom of God and salvific work of Christ, his death and resurrection. "Gospel" is also used to identify a genre of early Christian writing—akin to ancient biography—that recounts and interprets the events of Jesus' life and his teachings.

B. Author

As with the title, identification of the author comes from later Christian tradition and its attempt to connect the text with an eyewitness and the apostolic tradition. Eusebius mentions that out of the twelve apostles only Matthew and John have left "written memorials" and have done so "under the pressure of necessity" (*HE* 3.24.5). He also notes that Matthew preached among Jewish people and has composed his Gospel in Hebrew (*HE* 3.24.6).

This assertion is based on the witness of Papias, the bishop of Heirapolis (second century CE), whom Eusebius quotes later: "So then Matthew wrote the oracles in the Hebrew language, and everyone interpreted them as he was able" (*HE* 3.39.16). What are these oracles (*logia*)? Do they represent the Gospel as we have it now? Or are they detached recollections of Jesus' teaching? What does the phrase *Hebraidi dialektō* mean? Hebrew/Aramaic language or Jewish style of writing? Does *hērmēneusen* mean "translate" or "explain/interpret"? Donald Hagner suggests Papias' statement could be interpreted as a reference to a collection of sayings of Jesus in Aramaic that were later translated and used by other Gospel writers (2012, 196). However, a possibility remains that Papias' testimony is inaccurate altogether (France 1989, 66).

Modern scholarship raises questions about the provenance and authorship of the Gospel. Several factors are at play: ambiguity of ancient witness, the lack of concrete historical data, and even modern bias against church tradition. Moreover, some studies of the Matthean text do not support early assumptions. For example, there is no strong evidence that the existing Matthean text is a direct translation from the Hebrew/Aramaic original.

The almost universal assumption by scholarship of Markan priority (Mark written before Matthew) makes it easier to imagine Matthew using and correcting Mark rather than Mark's omission of 50 percent of Matthew's text and awkward correction of Matthew's Greek. In comparison with Mark, Matthew demonstrates "a consistently clearer, more concise and correct, use of Greek" (Johnson 2010, 166).

Scholarship is also divided on whether the Apostle Matthew is behind the Gospel. There are arguments to support Matthew's authorship as well as to question it. However, we don't have clear historical evidence to support either claim.

Whatever is the answer to the question of the historical identity of the author, one might agree with J. K. Brown that it "is not essential to the interpretation of the First Gospel" (*DJG*, 575). Taken on its own terms, the Gospel of Matthew appears to be anonymous; nowhere does the text *explicitly* reveal the identity of its author.

Richard Bauckham recognizes the complexity in attribution of the Gospel. Although references to "Matthew" as "the tax collector" in 9:9 and 10:3 do not provide a strong case, he suggests that they "could either be a pseudepigraphal claim to Matthean authorship or could reflect a role that the apostle Matthew actually played in the genesis of the Gospel" (2006, 302). In any case, the writer of the Gospel leaves his fingerprints everywhere in the text. This makes it possible to reconstruct a portrait of the implied author emerging from the narrative. According to Eugene Boring, the person who looks at his readers from the text is a teacher of the church that has Jewish background and uses Greek as his first language; perhaps a Jew who grew up in a Hellenistic city. The writer knows enough Hebrew for biblical interpretation and

Aramaic for everyday communication. He is familiar with rabbinic traditions and methods of interpretation. He knows the Jewish Scriptures well and appeals to them constantly; the Septuagint (Greek translation of the OT) is his text of choice (*NIB* 8:106-7).

C. Date and Location of Composition

Dating the Gospel of Matthew is complicated and often speculative. Historical evidence is limited. Three issues need to be considered: the literary relationships among the Synoptic Gospels, the fall of Jerusalem, and the usage of Matthew in early Christian writings (*DJG*, 576). In the past, scholars tended to date the appearance of the text in the first half of the second century mainly on the basis of the appearance of Trinitarian language (28:19) and the usage of *ekklesia* translated as "church" (16:18; 18:17).

However, this position has been abandoned since early Christian writings already demonstrate familiarity with the Matthean text (such as the *Didache*, the Letters of Ignatius, and the Gospel of Peter). Currently, scholars date Matthew in the second part of the first century CE; the dates range from 58 to 95 CE (*DJG*, 576). However, the "majority consensus" places Matthew between the mid-70s to 90 CE because, first, Matthew uses the Gospel of Mark as his source, thought to be composed in the late 60s CE (see Brower 2012, 27-28). Second, confrontation with the Pharisees (23:1-36) and the conflict between synagogue and *ecclesia* (10:16-23) is reflective of the situation within formative Judaism after the destruction of the temple (Brown 1997, 217).

Location of composition is also hard to ascertain. The traditional view places Matthew somewhere in Palestine since it was believed that the Gospel (or parts of it) was first written in Hebrew and among the Jews. That could fit well with some of Jewish features of the Gospel, such as the usage of Aramaic and attention to Jewish traditions and the Hebrew Scriptures (France 1989, 91-92).

However, Palestinian origins of the Gospel have been abandoned in favor of the idea that Matthew has composed his story of Jesus in Syria, specifically, Antioch. Some arguments for this location had been suggested. First, a sizable Jewish diaspora in this Hellenistic city could serve as a backdrop for engagement with Jewish traditions and conflicts in the Gospel. Second, Antioch is also known as one of leading Christian centers and some early documents that refer to Matthew are related to that church (Ignatius and possibly the *Didache*). Third, the usage of good Greek as well as Hebrew/Aramaic could fit in the multilingual context of this metropolis. Finally, Matthew adds "Syria" to the Markan description of the extent of Jesus' ministry (Mark 1:39 / Matt 4:24); this also could be interpreted as reference to the location (Brown 1997, 212). However, other places—such as Alexandria, Transjordan, Jerusalem, Tiberius, and even Sepphoris—have also been suggested (*DJG*, 576; France 1989, 93).

D. Sources

The answer to the question about written sources is predicated upon one's view of the relationship among the Synoptic Gospels (Matthew, Mark, and Luke). The Two Source Hypothesis is most popular, postulating that Matthew and Luke used Mark and an unknown source (Q) to compose their Gospels. According to this theory, Matthew draws upon several written sources.

First, Matthew uses the Gospel of Mark that was written earlier (in the 60s of the first century CE) and had been in circulation among early Christian communities. Overall, Matthew closely follows Mark's text in chronology and language. However, he makes a few editorial changes: improves Greek expressions, omits or changes certain passages (for example, Matt 12:22-37 / Mark 3:20-30), demonstrates a reverent attitude toward Jesus (for example, Matt 8:23-27 / Mark 4:35-41), and highlights the magnitude of miraculous events (Brown 1997, 204-5).

Second, Matthew also shares material with Luke that is not found in Mark. Scholars identify this document as a collection of Jesus' sayings and call it Q from the German word "quelle," which simply means "source." Both Matthew and Luke incorporate and adapt Q material in the light of their narratives and theological perspectives (*NIB* 8:95). Vivid examples of that are found in comparing two versions of "the Sermon on the Mount" (Matt 5:1—7:27 / Luke 6:17-48; 11:1-13).

The existence of this hypothetical source has been questioned. Mark Goodacre, for example, explains the presence of common material by Lukan dependence on and redaction of Matthew as well as having access to independent traditions (2002). He offers a revamped version of Farrer-Goulder hypothesis that finds no need for Q in a solution for the Synoptic problem: Matthew used Mark and Luke used both for composing his Gospel (Goodacre 2001).

Third, the Gospel also contains material that is found nowhere else. The most evident examples are Matthew's birth narrative (chs 1—2), stories about Peter (14:28-31; 16:17-19; 17:24-27), and insertions into the passion stories: Judas's death (27:1-10), the dream of Pilate's wife (27:19), washing hands and the crowd's response (27:24-25), events following Jesus' death (27:51-53), and the guards at the tomb (27:62-66; 28:11-15).

Fourth, Matthew uses OT scriptures as a source in a variety of ways (→ G. Matthew's Use of the Old Testament for more detailed explanation).

Older hypothesis of textual dependence attempted to explain the existence of the final form of the Matthean text on the basis of *written* sources. This approach often underestimates the place and interconnectedness of memory, orality, and literacy in the formation and preservation of the Gospel traditions. These days, *oral tradition* and *oral history* increasingly receive attention in NT studies. Scholars, reacting to the results of form-critical inquiry, have explored different avenues: the relationship between orality and writing

(Kelber 1997; Botha 2012); the place of individual and social memory in the formation of the Gospels (Dunn 2003; Rodriguez 2010; McIver 2011); and the role of eyewitness testimony (Byrskog 2000; Bauckham 2006). The issues of transmission and the spread of oral traditions have also not escaped scholarly attention (Gerhardsson 1998; Bailey 1995).

Scholars have reassessed the process of the formation of the Gospels in light of the practices of memorization, eyewitnessing, oral performances, and passing on of knowledge that were widespread in the ancient—predominantly oral—culture (as an opposite to our modern, text-based or even screen-based culture). Studies have highlighted the reliability of memory and oral traditions in preserving and transmitting knowledge. At the same time, they have uncovered the interplay between stability and fluidity, the relationship between individual and social memory, and the complexities related to remembering, eyewitness interpretation of events, construction of a testimony, oral performances, accommodation of change, and deliberate alterations. Moreover, the fact that formation, transmission, and then recording of oral tradition was influenced by many factors and belong to a variety of interconnected contexts, adds to the complexity of the issue at hand.

In that light, the Synoptic Gospels are envisaged to be based on memories of Jesus, his teaching and actions that were passed down by word of mouth from eyewitnesses to the next generation of his disciples (Dunn 2003, 125-32). Bauckham also claims that traditions about Jesus have originated with particular eyewitnesses whose names were preserved and who played the role of moderators and guarantors in the process of its transmission. The twelve apostles—from the center in Jerusalem and through the network of communities around the empire—played a major role in spreading and controlling oral tradition (2006, 290-357).

Scholarly discussion around oral tradition helps to understand that the Gospels did not appear in a vacuum but in the wider context of communal life of early Christianity and arose out of its oral practices. The Gospels not only contain oral tradition but are actually embedded in it and its performance in the early church. This is how evangelists knew stories about Jesus in the first place (Rodriguez 2010, 27-31). Perhaps similarities and differences among the Gospels could be explained by sharing and performing oral tradition.

As with other models of explanation of the genesis of gospel texts, the models of oral tradition have their limits. We don't have access to oral performances. This forces scholars to reconstruct orality on the basis of clues we get from the written text, which in turn creates a circular argument. Moreover, we can only speculate about particular circumstances, social contexts of transmission, and the length of transmission chains (in comparison to rabbinic ones). We do not know to what extent the evangelists used oral tradition, their memory, and written sources in the composition of the Gospels. Appearance of the written Gospels in their final forms at the early stages of Christian history also raises questions about the place, importance, and limitations of oral tradition (Eve 2013, 177; see also Hurtado 2014, 321-40).

E. First Readers

The issue of the first audience for Matthew is a complicated one; scholars had not often been able to provide a compelling argument (Vine 2014, 202-7). Although the Gospel could have been written to the wider church in *oikoumene* (Bauckham 1998*b*), it does not alleviate particular concerns Matthew raises by his editorial work. And one of these is the relationship between the Matthean audience and synagogue.

The text presupposes that some of Jesus' disciples still follow Jewish traditions and participate in synagogue life (10:17; 23:2-3; 24:20). Moreover, the early Christian community finds itself caught in a dramatic change within formative Judaism as it emerges in the wake of devastation of Jewish war and the destruction of the temple in 70 CE.

While other groups disappeared or dramatically weakened, the Pharisees and their scribes took leadership in shaping and reconstructing the religious life of faithful Jews. Establishment of the center of rabbinic teaching in Yavneh/Jamnia (Palestine) played an important role in projecting the Pharisaic vision for post-temple Judaism (but see discussion on historicity of Yavneh movement in Collins 1997, 3-5; Lee 2001, 206-15). The rabbinate have gradually consolidated power over synagogues and started drawing lines between "normative" Judaism as they understood it and the rest, "Their treatment of the Jewish Christians was in line with this general policy: they tried to exclude them from the synagogues and to persuade other Jews to ostracize them in social and even in commercial life" (Alexander 1999, 6).

Jewish followers of Jesus the Messiah found it hard to fit into that program and adjust to the rising domination of the Pharisees. In response, they provided an alternative vision and fostered their own sense of identity, structures, rules of communal life, and teaching based on Jesus' tradition (see Matt 18; *NIB* 8:100-101).

The signs of alienation and conflict with forming rabbinic Judaism are scattered across the text of Matthew. Drawing lines between "my church" (16:18) and "their synagogues" (4:23; 9:35; 12:9; 13:54; 23:34; see 10:17) culminates in identifying "the Jews" (28:15) as a separate group. The leaders of the disciples are called to behave in ways opposite of the rabbis of the time (23:4-12). Matthew's unique material emphasizes the divide even further: the scathing critique against the Pharisees and scribes (23:1-36) and the rejection of the Messiah by the religious leadership and the crowd (27:15-26).

On the rabbinic side of the conflict, the composition of *Birkat-ha-minim* (a curse on heretics) and its inclusion among the Eighteen Benedictions (Jewish public prayer) in the first century CE illustrates the struggle further. A later Palestinian recension of the prayer also included *notzerim* (Nazarenes or Christians) as an explanatory gloss on *minim* (Alexander 1999, 8-9). The church fathers took this prayer as an attack against Christians (*NIB* 8:100; also see Stanton 1992, 142-45, for a cautious treatment of the prayer in Matthean studies).

In this context of rising tensions, Matthew's first readers represent the Jewish *ecclesia* under persecution from the wider Jewish community. Though far from the complete "parting of the ways," the Christian community is in the time of transition—gradually departing from forming rabbinic Judaism and reorienting itself to the Gentile mission (see Saldarini 1994; Sim 1998).

However, these emerging differences and separation do not imply complete severing of ties or do not suggest anti-Semitism. For Matthew, the identity of the *ecclesia* is deeply rooted in Jewish faith. It is the God of Israel who is behind the Gospel story and assures his continued presence with the believers: "God with us" (1:23). Jesus the Messiah is "the son of David, the son of Abraham" (1:1), and the "king of the Jews" (2:2).

The twelve apostles—the new leaders of God's people—will judge "the twelve tribes of Israel" (19:28) and part of their mission is to proclaim the good news of God's reign to all "towns of Israel" (10:23), thus claiming authority over all of Israel (Schnackenburg 2002, 7). Their mission and self-understanding are rooted in the overall narrative and intentions of Hebrew Scriptures. The message is clear: Matthew's church—embracing both Jews and Gentiles—is the new holy people of God gathered around Jesus the Messiah on the mission of God in fulfillment of the Scriptures.

F. Matthew's Narrative

There have been some major shifts in understanding over the past sixty years on what constitutes a Gospel beginning with an approach known as form criticism in the mid-twentieth century. In this approach, the sayings and deeds of Jesus have been randomly placed by the Gospel authors because there is little evidence of creativity and intentionality in the ordering and presentation of their written form. This approach is clearly not with the final form of the text, but rather with the oral or written traditions from which it was composed. Therefore, Matthew's organization of the individual stories is likened to the process of stringing together pearls on a string.

For advocates of this method, much of the Gospel material does not tell us about the historical Jesus. Rather, on the basis of several criteria, one must distinguish between texts that reflect the beliefs and experiences of the early church and those that provide us with firm historical insight into the ministry of Jesus.

Recent scholars argue that the alleged tension between *the Christ of faith*, as that which in the Gospels is a product of the early church, and *the Jesus of history*, as that which actually can be traced to Jesus himself, is overdrawn. Scholarly consensus has shifted and now scholars place more emphasis on the final form of the biblical text. Even a prima facie reading of Matthew, Mark, or Luke indicates that these are carefully structured pieces of writing and are not just a series of randomly placed stories. This is evident in the assessment of Jack Kingsbury:

> The Gospel of Matthew is a unified narrative, or "artistic whole." The story it relates is governed, as will be seen, by a single, overarching "evaluative point of view." Moreover, the action, thought, and interactions are all organized by means of a coherent plot. This plot has a beginning, middle, and artful ending. (1988, 1-2)

This method of interpreting the Gospels is known as narrative criticism.

A narrative approach distinguishes between the grammar of a story and its discourse. Story grammar refers to the constituent parts of a story, such as settings, characters, plot, and resolution. In Matthew's Gospel, there is an overarching narrative that describes the birth of Jesus, his Galilean ministry, and then the plot dramatically slows when recounting his final days in Jerusalem culminating in the Messiah's crucifixion followed by his resurrection. This overarching narrative is made up of a variety of individual stories each of which have their own unique settings, characters, plot, and resolution, all of which develop Matthew's theological themes.

The discourse of a narrative is concerned with how the author tells the story. In Matthew, this is evident, for example, in the way he describes the characters, his ordering of the oral discourses and mighty deeds of Jesus, his use of unique terminology, and his use of the OT. Since Matthew's implied audience is composed of Christian communities with a predominately Jewish constituency and emerging Gentile presence, he will tell the story of Jesus in a way that makes Jesus' ministry relevant to this mixed audience and their experiences.

Many scholars agree that Matthew's audience not only is made up of Jew and Gentile alike but also is the object of non-Christian Jewish hostility. These Jewish detractors are likely those who refuse to accept that Jesus is the Jewish Messiah, such as the Pharisees who came to prominence after the temple's destruction in 70 CE. The vitriolic language of Jesus in Matt 23, which he directs toward the scribes and Pharisees for moral and religious corruption, is in some way connected with this hostility. It also bolsters the faith of Matthew's community to persevere as they know that Jesus himself dealt with such things from the same group of people. This is just one example in which we see the influence of Matthew in the way that he recounts the story for the sake of his audience.

We also see Matthew's influence in his emphasis on the Jewish and royal lineage of Jesus. This is abundantly evident in the introduction to the genealogy that highlights his royal and ethnic heritage: "This is the genealogy of Jesus the Messiah the son of David, the son of Abraham" (Matt 1:1). As we will see throughout the commentary, Matthew describes the identity of Jesus and his ministry in such a way to draw out his royal and Jewish status.

Some narrative-critical studies devalue the role of the historical world of the biblical text in favor of a strict emphasis on its literary and narrative features. But there is no reason to draw a hard line between history and literature. To study Matthew as a narrative does not obviate insights that come from the text's historical world either from the time that Jesus ministered or the time during which Matthew's text was composed. So, where appropriate, this commentary considers relevant layers of history whether it be the Second Temple or rabbinic periods. Matthew is still an ancient text, written to an ancient audience, during an ancient time, in an ancient place.

G. Matthew's Use of the Old Testament

One only has to read the first two chapters of Matthew to see why those responsible for the arrangement of the books of the NT in the third and fourth centuries of the church placed Matthew at the beginning. No less than five times in these chapters do we encounter the formula quotation, "All this took place to fulfill what the Lord had said through the prophet" (see 1:22), which expresses that Jesus and the events surrounding his birth fulfill OT prophecy. Jesus is the Jewish Messiah who comes in fulfillment of the Jewish Scriptures. Matthew quotes larger sections of the OT compared with Mark and Luke; see, for example, the longer quotations from Deuteronomy in Matthew's account of Jesus' temptation (4:1-11) compared with Luke's (Luke 4:1-13). There are many echoes and allusions to the OT in Matthew that underscore the formative role of the OT in his Gospel.

The scholarly term often used to refer to such analysis is known as intertextuality, which is defined as "any given use of language [in our case, Matthew's text] is intelligible only because and in terms of its *interconnection* with prior uses and understandings of its constituent metaphors, concepts, images, symbolic worlds, and terminology" (emphasis added; Soulen and Soulen 2011, 87). The prior uses for us are contained in the OT texts to which Matthew refers.

That Matthew uses the OT in his story of Jesus is obvious, but the ways in which the OT functions in his Gospel is much less clear because he doesn't always appear to evoke it in a consistent manner. For example, the first OT quotation is from Isa 7:14, found in Matt 1:23. The sign of Immanuel in Isa 7 is a symbol of judgment that will come upon Judah for Ahaz's refusal to ask Yahweh, the Lord, for a sign (see vv 16-17). However, Matthew presents the proclamation of the angel to Mary, that she will name him Jesus because "because he will save his people from their sins" (Matt 1:21), as the fulfillment of Isa 7:14. For Matthew, the sign of Immanuel, or God being with his people, is now fulfilled in Jesus who brings salvation for Israel whereas for Isaiah, several centuries before, the sign represented judgment that is to come upon Judah for Ahaz's disobedience in not requesting a sign. How are we as interpreters to make sense of Matthew's new understanding of Immanuel?

Another example that scholars have pondered is Matthew's statement that when Jesus and his family settle in Nazareth this "fulfilled what was said through the prophets, that he would be called a Nazarene" (Matt 2:23*b*). The problem here is that the OT does not associate the Messiah with Nazareth, let alone state that he would be called a Nazarene. How are we to understand Matthew's comment?

Our last example is found in Matt 8:17. Here Matthew links the fulfillment of Isa 53:4 ("He took up our infirmities and bore our diseases") with the healing ministry of Jesus who exorcised many demons "with a word and healed all the sick" (Matt 8:16*b*). Although this is the fullest quotation of Isa 53 in the Synoptic Gospels, there are other echoes of this text elsewhere in Matthew but only in relation to the passion of Jesus. But here there is no hint of his suffering. Rather, this section of the Gospel, Matt 8—9, recounts his mighty deeds and acts of power as Yahweh's anointed. What are we to make of the difference between the context of this OT quotation in Matt 8:17 with the content of the quotation itself?

Many of Matthew's quotations and allusions to the OT are much clearer in the contribution they make to Matthew's presentation of Jesus. However, in order to get the most from his use of the OT, it is crucial to adopt a clear method and to define clearly the terms that we use in this commentary.

1. *Quotation*: an explicit reference to an OT text that begins with "it is written" or "this was to fulfill." The examples discussed above, Matt 1:23 and 8:17, are such quotations. When analyzing quotations in Matthew, we will consider two items: (*a*) the differences in terminology between the version Matthew quotes and that of his source text, that is, the LXX, which is a Greek translation of the Hebrew OT, or the Masoretic Text, which is the Hebrew text of the OT; and (*b*) the significance of the literary context of the OT passage that Matthew quotes to determine any unstated thematic correspondences between the literary context of Matthew's citation and the literary context of the OT citation itself (Hays 1989, 20).

2. *Allusion*: a reference to an OT text by means of two or more terms embedded in Matthew's text. Once it is clear that Matthew is referring to a specific OT text in a passage, the interpreter must determine how much of the context of the OT text contributes to our understanding of its use in Matthew. Hays accurately notes that "as we move farther away from overt citation [into allusions], the source recedes into the discursive distance, the intertextual relations become less determinate, and the demand placed on the reader's listening powers grows greater" (1989, 23). This serves as a helpful reminder that more than one terminological correspondence is necessary between Matthew's text and the one he evokes so interpreters can establish an allusion with a higher degree of probability.

3. *Echo*: a much broader category that refers to more than one passage that may be at work behind a Matthean one not because the author intentionally refers to them but rather because his mind is so furnished with the scriptural imagery of the OT that he unconsciously uses it. Some scholars refer to this as "influence" in which one or more OT passages have influenced the author's mind but there are no explicit terminological connections.

Since allusions and echoes are more difficult to identify and to determine what meaning they provide for the narrative context in which they appear, an example of an allusion and then an echo might help clarify our approach. First, an allusion to Elijah the prophet is evident in Matthew's description of John the Baptist in 3:4: "John's clothes were made of camel's hair, and he had a leather belt around his waist. His food was locusts and wild honey." Since Matthew and his audience know the OT Scriptures so well, he evokes Elijah as the framework through which to view John by means of terminological correspondences with 2 Kgs 1:8 [LXX], in which the same terms are used to describe part of Elijah's clothing, specifically, "leather belt" and "his waist." Jesus confirms this allusion later in Matthew when he speaks of John as Elijah: "But I tell you, Elijah has already come, and they did not recognize him, but have done to him everything they wished. In the same way the Son of Man is going to suffer at their hands" (Matt 17:12). In light of these things, Elijah the prophet has returned in the person of John the Baptist.

An echo of the OT Scriptures is evident in the phrase "forty days and forty nights" that denotes the period of Jesus' fast in the Judean wilderness (4:2). In Exod 34:28, Moses is with the Lord on Sinai "for forty days and forty nights" and he did not eat or drink (see Deut 9:9). The prophet Elijah was also without food and drink for the same period of time several centuries later (1 Kgs 19:8). Beyond fasting, the connection between Jesus and Moses or Jesus and Elijah is not strong, although both Moses and Elijah fast in a wilderness setting.

Perhaps the strongest echo is Israel's wilderness wandering in which they spent not forty days but forty years in the wilderness (Num 14:33). Since Israel was in the wilderness so that the Lord could test them (Deut 8:2-3), and that Satan now comes to Jesus likewise in the wilderness to test him (Matt 4:1), this echo seems to be the strongest. Since there are a number of instances where the time frame of forty is used in the OT and that more than one background is informative, Matthew's use of it here functions as an echo.

H. Matthew's Key Theological Themes

1. Matthew's Christology

Jesus and his identity are at the center of the Matthean story. A multitude of voices offer their answer to the question: "What kind of man is this?" (8:27). While God the Father affirms Jesus as the beloved Son (3:17; 17:5), his opponents claim that he is possessed by Beelzebul (12:22-27). While John the Baptist confesses that he is "not worthy to carry" Jesus' sandals (3:11), the Pharisees (9:3) and the high priest call him a blasphemer (26:65). While the disciples recognize his messianic identity (16:16), the religious leaders slander him for being a friend of "tax collectors and sinners" (9:11). While pilgrim crowds announce him to be "the Son of David" (21:9), Jerusalem crowds perceive him as a prophet from Galilee (21:11). Jesus' own confessions (16:13; 24:36-37; 26:64) and secrecy around revealing his identity (8:4; 12:16; 16:20) add to the enigma of this divisive figure.

Matthew offers his vision right from the beginning: Jesus is the Messiah (Son of David), Son of Abraham, and the Son of God (see Matt 1). The evangelist connects these titles with Jesus' mission, his relationship with the people of God, and his divine identity; these play an important role in the developing drama of Matthean Christology. By means of narrative Christology—through titles, words, and deeds—Matthew leads the readers in unraveling the mystery. Like the Twelve, they are taken on a journey of discovery of who Jesus truly is.

a. The Messiah (the Son of David, the King of the Jews)

At the outset of the story, Matthew announces that Jesus is the Messiah (Gk. *Christos*—"Anointed one") who belongs to the royal house of David through Joseph's line (1:6, 16). He is a descendant of the legendary king David to whom God has promised an everlasting kingdom (2 Sam 7:1-17). The birth narratives utilize the titles "Messiah" and "Son of David" extensively (Matt 1:1, 16-18; 2:4) and even include the title "king of the Jews" (2:2) to highlight this.

Matthew illustrates what kind of Messiah Jesus is through the rest of the Gospel. Jesus exercises his messianic authority in healings (9:27-31; 20:29-34) and exorcisms (12:22-23; 15:21-28). The summary of the Messiah's deeds includes purification, resurrection, and proclamation of the good news (11:2-6). Jesus the Messiah brings salvation (1:21) and restoration to the people of God (15:29-31). But there is more.

The scene of Christ's entry to Jerusalem is filled with messianic sentiments and expectations (21:1-11). Jesus, the Son of David, enters the royal capital and exercises extraordinary authority over the temple by driving away traders, performing healings, and teaching in the holy place (21:12-17, 23-27). Here in Jerusalem, Jesus redefines the messianic notion even further—the Son of David also has a divine identity (22:41-45).

Peter's confession is a turning point in the narrative where recognition of Jesus as the Messiah by the disciples (16:13-20) is coupled with Jesus' prediction of his own suffering and death (16:21-23). From now on, the Twelve have to come to terms with the idea that suffering is the key aspect of the Messiah's mission. The title "Messiah" consistently appears throughout the Passion Narrative and is referenced by the high priest (26:63), the members of Sanhedrin (26:68), and Pilate himself (27:17, 22).

The Passion Narrative draws heavily on Isa 53 and the Psalms of the righteous sufferer to demonstrate that the suffering and death of the Messiah are divinely sanctioned. The title "the king of Jews" reappears again in the final scenes: where Herod failed (Matt 2:2), the Romans succeeded (27:11, 29, 37, 42). The King of the Jews takes up his throne—the cross; this is how redemption, restoration, and liberation of the people of God come to fulfillment.

b. Son of Abraham and Son of Man

The relationship between the Messiah and the people of Israel is a key aspect of Matthean Christology. He embodies faithful Israel and represents the people of God. Through direct citations and allusions, Matthew evokes scriptural traditions of corporate personality to describe Jesus' identity. From the beginning, Jesus is called "the son of Abraham" (1:1), which connects Jesus with the people of God. But for Matthew, Jesus is more than just a Jew; as the Messiah he represents the people of God. Matthew's unique story of the escape and return from Egypt perfectly illustrates the point (2:13-23). Jesus has repeated the path of the people of God and fulfilled the prophecy of Hos 11:1 about Israel: "Out of Egypt I called my son." Jesus reenacts the story of Israel. At the baptism (Matt 3:13-17), Jesus aligns himself with "the people of Jerusalem and all of Judea" and later acts on their behalf (*DJG*, 581).

In the temptation episode, Jesus also reenacts Israel's Exodus experience (4:1-11). After forty days in the desert—unlike the historical people of God—Jesus emerges as the faithful one. The theme of faithfulness and corporate representation continues in the Passion Narrative. Matthew employs the imagery of Isaiah's Suffering Servant (Isa 53) in picturing Christ to drive the point home—Jesus fully commits himself to the divine will and dies for and on behalf of the people of God (Matt 1:21; 20:28).

The representation of faithful Israel is also highlighted by the usage of "the Son of Man" language (10:23; 16:27-28; 24:30-31; 26:64) with its allusions to Dan 7 where a human-like figure represents Israel (*DJG*, 581). Thus, for Matthew, in suffering and vindication of the Son of Man, new Israel gathered around the Messiah has been vindicated (Wright 1992, 291-97).

c. Son of God (Immanuel, Lord, Wisdom)

From the beginning, Matthew identifies Jesus as "Immanuel"—"God with us" (Matt 1:23). But the coming of Jesus is not just a sign of the God's kingdom breaking in. The birth narrative is clear—Jesus himself is the embodiment of YHWH's presence. The conception and birth of Jesus from the Holy Spirit (1:18-25) presents the mystery of incarnation; Jesus' divine sonship is rooted in this act of divine intervention. The Son of God is not just manifesting the divine presence and actions through his ministry of proclamation and deeds of power (doing what the God of Israel promised to do) but he himself is God incarnate.

That disclosure of divine identity takes place throughout the whole Gospel narrative: the divine voice at the baptism (3:13-17), stilling the storm (8:23-27), confronting evil cosmic powers (8:28—9:1), offering forgiveness of sins (9:2-8), raising the dead (9:18-26), walking on water (14:22-32), Jesus' transfiguration (17:1-8), and the apocalyptic scenes of enthronement and universal authority (25:31-32; 26:64). Moreover, the motif of the continual divine presence in Christ bookends the whole story: In Christ, God is with his people (1:23) and will continue "to the very end of the age" (28:20).

Apart from the narrative disclosure and using the Son of God title, Matthew consistently refers to Jesus as "Lord." In Jewish tradition, the Hebrew word *adonai* and the Aramaic *maryah*—both meaning "Lord"—served as a deferential substitution for the divine name YHWH. These helped to avoid pronouncing the name of God during the reading of scripture (Hurtado 2003, 109). In Matt 3:3 "the way for the Lord" (or YHWH; see Isa 40:3) has been interpreted as a reference to Jesus (see Matt 1:22). Here and in other instances, Matthew appropriates and redefines the title "Lord" (Gk. *kyrios*) to highlight Jesus' divine identity. To drive the point even further, the evangelist also places the title in the explicit scenes of worship where people prostrate (*proskynein*) themselves before Christ in recognition of his divinity (4:9-10; 8:2; 9:18; 15:25; 14:32-33; 18:26; Hurtado 2003, 338).

Matthew also appropriates wisdom traditions to illustrate the divine identity. In 2TJ, personified Wisdom was portrayed as a heavenly being who existed before the creation of the world and could dwell on earth among human beings (1 En 42; Wis 6:12—11:1; Sir 24:8-12; Bar 3:37). Matthew evokes this tradition in relation to Jesus in ch 11 (see also 23:34-39). The statement from 11:19, "But wisdom is proved right by her deeds," equates the deeds of Messiah (11:2-6) with that of Wisdom; Jesus is divine Wisdom herself (France 1989, 303-5; see also Douglas 2016).

In Jesus, the divine Wisdom dwells among the people of God. The chapter also continues to evoke wisdom tradition in different ways (*DJG*, 580): the motif of hiddenness and revelation (Job 28; Wis 9↔Matt 11:25-27); the call to come (Sir 24:19↔Matt 11:28); to rest (Sir 6:287↔Matt 11:28); not to be weary (Wis 6:14↔Matt 11:28) and to accept the yoke (Sir 51:26↔Matt 11:30): "Put your neck under her [Wisdom's] yoke, and let your souls receive instruction" (NRSV).

Matthew's narrative Christology employs a variety of titles, scriptural motifs (Suffering Servant, righteous sufferer, wisdom, etc.), and stories to paint a comprehensive picture of Jesus' identity. Matthew goes far beyond "the gospel of Jesus' humanity"; even the language of Son of Man is no mere reference to his humanness but also to an elevated status in the heavenly realm (see 24:30-31; 25:31-46; 26:64). The references to his divine identity are hard to miss. At the end of the Gospel, the main question "what kind of man is this?" receives its answer. Jesus, the exalted and victorious Messiah, the Son of God, is the Lord over all nations and the entire universe (28:17-20).

2. Matthew's Community

a. Defining Identity

Matthew is often called "the gospel of the church." This highlights one of its key concerns—identity, mission, and the communal life of believers. For Matthew, the question "who is Jesus?" is followed by "what does it mean to be his followers?" These are inseparably connected. The notion of being a disciple is rooted in Jesus' identity, mission, and teaching; it is unashamedly Christ-centric and cross-shaped. Disciples—personally and communally—are those who are totally committed to Jesus, follow him, imitate his serving attitude, participate in the mission of God, and exhibit loyalty and obedience to God to the point of sacrificial self-giving (France 1989, 260-68).

Apart from discipleship language, Jesus also defines the community of followers in terms of household. They all are brothers and sisters who obey their heavenly Father—God (12:46-50). This is the new family as their real family ties might have been severed because of their commitment to Christ (8:21-22; 19:27-30). Matthew also abundantly uses imagery and language of the people of Israel to describe his community (10:1-15; 19:29). This highlights their identity as the reconstituted holy people of God who gathered around Jesus the Messiah and are bound to him by covenant relationship (26:26-29).

At the end of the Gospel, "The Great Commission" (28:17-20) recapitulates Matthew's vision of the church. It is a worshiping community gathered by and under the authority of the exalted Lord Jesus. He has sent and empowered it to participate in the mission of the Triune God—bringing people from all nations under the divine rule. The new people of God are also marked by living out Jesus' teaching, trust and faithfulness, and experience of his continual presence.

b. Patterns of Discipleship

By telling the story of Jesus' disciples, Matthew not only pursues historical interests but also demonstrates what it means to be a follower. A few interrelated patterns of discipleship emerge in Matthew's story. The first is the calling and empowerment of the Twelve for the mission of God. Jesus' call to follow him is inseparably connected with his ministry. Jesus' first proclamation of the good news (4:17) is followed by the calling of the first disciples (4:18-22): "Follow me, and I will send you out to fish for people." The mission does not proceed without them; it is a communal affair. The call is then followed by commissioning and sending out (10:1-15). The Twelve are not just followers or helpers; they are given authority to confront the evil cosmic powers and to participate in the holistic restoration of the people of God. They have become the empowered agents of the kingdom and Jesus' co-workers. A pattern emerges: from fishermen to followers to apostles (Watts Henderson 2006, 31-94). Other disciples in the Gospel demonstrate a similar response to the salvific grace of God: healing is often followed by a desire to follow Jesus and proclaim the good news (9:27-31; 20:29-34).

Second, the response to follow Jesus is a costly one. It requires complete self-denial—leaving everything behind for the sake of Jesus' mission and the kingdom of heaven. This often involves severing family ties, abandonment of pursuit for material gains, and social status (19:27-30). However, this renunciation does not come unnoticed; Jesus, the exalted Lord, will reward those who have been faithful to him: they "will receive a hundred times as much and will inherit eternal life" (19:29). This reveals another pattern of discipleship: self-denial is followed by a reward.

Third, one has to be prepared to suffer and even die for the sake of Jesus and the good news: "Whoever wants to be my disciple must deny themselves and take up their cross and follow me" (16:24). The mission of God is cruciform. Jesus shows the path for his disciples—suffer and die for others. Jesus' sacrifice was followed by resurrection and vindication. Here is the hope for the believers: the God of the living will bring his faithful to life and reward them at the time of great reversal in which "the last will be first" (19:30). Suffering and vindication are part of the pattern of Christian living.

Fourth, the disciples' misunderstanding is another motif that runs through Matthew. They constantly fail to grasp Jesus' identity and implications of his mission (13:51; 14:31; 16:12; 17:13). The revelation of divine mysteries is not always met with comprehension. At the same time, secondary characters in the story demonstrate perceptiveness of faith (20:29-34; 26:6-13). However, participation in the mission of God is not predicated on complete understanding of these truths; it is a journey of discovery, listening to God and learning on the way (13:11; 16:17; 17:5).

Fifth, the disciples' drive for positions of power and authority is met by Jesus' example and teaching on servanthood (18:10-14; 20:20-28; 23:1-12). Humble service and care for others is at the heart of this discipleship pattern: "Whoever wants to become great among you must be your servant" (20:26).

Sixth, Matthew also shows that the disciples' faith is often mixed with doubt: uncertainty about Jesus' identity (8:26), the provision of God (6:30), and Jesus' bodily resurrection (28:17). The acts of worship, adoration, and realities of ministry are faced by people of "little faith"; it's a part of the discipleship story. An unwavering faith is not a prerequisite for following Jesus but is something to be nourished and cultivated, something to strive for (Donaldson 1985, 45).

Seventh, the theme of betrayal runs through the Passion Narrative: Judas' plot (26:14-16), Jesus' warning (26:21-25, 31-35), abandonment at Gethsemane (26:56), and Peter's threefold denial (26:69-75). All of the apostles, the closest disciples, abandon their Lord. But this grim scene of disloyalty, betrayal, and denouncement is balanced by the faithfulness of female disciples who follow Jesus to the end and witness his crucifixion (27:55-56). Faithfulness and betrayal mark another pattern of discipleship.

Eighth, the disciples' failure to remain loyal highlights the final motif. Even though the mighty pillars of the church might stumble and fall, and even denounce their Master, Jesus does not hesitate to offer forgiveness and reconciliation (26:32) and reinstate them for the mission of God despite lingering doubt (28:16-20). Thus, for Matthew, on the path of Christian discipleship, human failure is met with divine grace and restoration that is freely offered.

c. Communal Living

For Matthew, the life of the community is based on Jesus' example, teaching, and interpretation of Scripture. There are a few key elements in his vision of communal life. First, it is a community of *love*. Love toward God and neighbor are the central commandments for Jesus' followers (22:24-40; 19:19). The Sermon on the Mount takes it even further—the disciples are called to imitate God's perfect love by embracing and forgiving enemies (5:43-48). Second, it is a community that includes and empowers the marginalized—women, children, disabled, Gentiles, poor, and "sinners" (4:18-25; 8:1-17; 9:1-13, 18-34; 15:21-31; 18:1-5; 20:29-34; 26:6-14; 27:55-56; 28:1-10).

Third, it is a community of boundless mercy. Followers are called to practice limitless forgiveness toward each other since they have experienced the same from God the Father (5:38-31; 6:14-15; 18:21-35). Fourth, it is a community of servanthood. The leaders are warned against employing culturally driven tyrannical (20:25) or hierarchical (23:8-10) patterns of leadership (Donaldson 1996, 46). Instead, they should emulate Christ by serving "the little ones," taking care of the vulnerable and embracing the position of powerlessness (18:1-10; 20:20-28).

However, Matthew calls the community members to sobriety and watchfulness (18:8-9; 24:36—25:30). Love and mercy go hand to hand with justice that reflects God's character (*DJG*, 582). This sometimes plays out in shocking and unexpected ways (20:1-16; 25:14-46). Being a member of the new people of God does not release one from accountability and responsibility. Unlimited forgiveness cannot be used to justify abuse and cover up sins. The Matthean Jesus warns the disciples about the perils of failure to extend forgiveness, to remain faithful, to serve others, and to keep others from stumbling and to do the will of God (7:21-29; 16:24-27; 18:6-9, 21-35): "Not everyone who says to me, 'Lord, Lord,' will enter the kingdom of heaven" (7:21). Believers have to keep in mind that Jesus is both the merciful Savior (1:21) and Judge (25:31-46). Matthew reminds his readers about the dialectic relationship between divine grace and judgment (Luz 1995, 132).

3. The Kingdom of Heaven

The kingdom of heaven is Matthew's language to talk about the reign of God. It is synonymous with "the kingdom of God" used by other gospel traditions. But unlike others, Matthew utilizes the Jewish circumlocution "heaven" (Heb. *shamayim*; Gk. *ouranos*) in reference to God. For the evangelist, this is not just a reflection of Jewish piety; he is making a theological point. This kingdom is radically different from earthly kingdoms and comes from the heavenly domain of God (see 6:4). This also underlines the fact that in the inbreaking of the kingdom in Jesus' ministry, heaven and earth are meeting together and divine rule is established in the human realm (Pennington 2007, 279-330).

As N. T. Wright and others have demonstrated, the notion of the kingdom of God is rooted in OT scriptures and 2TJ traditions (*DJG*, 471-72). Jews believed that the God of Israel will return to Zion (i.e., Jerusalem) to liberate and restore his people and rule as a king (e.g., Isa 40:1-10; Mic 4:1-8).

Jesus the Messiah enacted the traditions of YHWH's coming in his actions: restoring the people of Israel, overcoming cosmic powers of evil, journeying to and arriving at Jerusalem, establishing the new covenant at the Last Supper, and liberating the people of God through his suffering and death on the cross. Thus, Jesus has embodied YHWH's return and believed that the kingdom of heaven "was coming in and through his work" (Wright 1996, 651-52). Inauguration of the divine rule is taking place through Jesus the Messiah, the Son of God, and his mission: "But if it is by the Spirit of God that I drive out demons, then the kingdom of God has come upon you" (Matt 12:28).

The theme of the kingdom being established runs throughout the Gospel. In the beginning, John the Baptist and Jesus announce the arrival of the kingdom: "the kingdom of heaven has come near" (3:2; 4:17). The first part of the Gospel reveals the nature of God's reign: healings and forgiveness of sins point to holistic salvation (9:2-8; 15:30-31); befriending sinners and tax collectors—to hospitality (9:10-13); taking care of slaves, children, and women—to the transgressing of social and gender boundaries and reversing the pyramids of social power (8:5-13, 14-15; 9:18-25; 18:1-5; 19:13-15); confronting unclean spirits and religious authorities—to challenging power structures (8:21—9:1; 26:57—27:26); helping Gentiles—to demonstrating radical inclusion and challenging racial prejudices (8:5-13; 15:21-28).

The parables of the kingdom of heaven in Matt 13 reveal some of its mysteries. The notion of the kingdom is dynamic and often hard to grasp. Jesus explains that it has arrived but at the same time it is growing and spreading until it comes in its fullness (vv 31-33). As it is breaking into this world, different people react differently, and there are implications for accepting or resisting it (vv 1-8, 18-30, 36-43). And it is worthy of giving everything for its sake (vv 44-53).

In the second part of the Matthean narrative, Jesus vividly reenacts the Lord's appearance in the holy city and the temple and clashes with earthly powers that resist its arrival. In that conflict, Jesus, the King of the Jews, gives his life. This is a culminating point in ushering in the kingdom: death on the cross liberates the people of God from sins so that it can come in its fullness (Wright

2016, 219). Now people have been set free to live under God's rule. They are given power and authority—"the keys of the kingdom of heaven" (16:18-19)—to invite others into his domain (28:16-20), and to act in such a way as to disclose "in word and deed the character of the kingdom" (*DJG*, 475).

In this light, the Sermon on the Mount (5:1—7:29) is not a utopian picture of the future or simply an ethos for a new community. It is about a cruciform and missional way of being in this world (Wright 2016, 362-81). This is how the kingdom operates: through the new holy people of God who act as peacemakers, justice-hungry men and women, pure-in-heart followers, poor-in-spirit disciples, the merciful, the meek, and the martyrs. People who learn how to love, to embrace enemies, to selflessly give, to pray, to rely on God, and to suffer thus to embody a new righteousness and holiness (Wright 2016, 218). These are the new holy people of God—both Jews and Gentiles—who live under Christ's authority and through whose mission, life, and suffering "the saving rule of god will be brought to bear upon the world" (Wright 2016, 219).

I. The Commentary's Perspective

All studies of the Bible are guided by certain ways of reading the biblical text whether the interpreter/reader is aware of them or not. While there are a variety of ways the Bible is currently interpreted in the world of NT scholarship, two methods of biblical study will chart our course in this commentary on Matthew: narrative criticism and intertextuality.

The former considers Matthew as a story organized by means of an intentional structure and recounted through a variety of literary features. To refer to the text as a story does not mean that we are diminishing the historical and theological truthfulness of the events it contains, but, rather, we are advocating that Matthew communicates these things in the form of a narrative or story.

The latter, intertextuality, considers the correspondences between the text of Matthew and that of the OT whether they be quite overt, as in a quotation, or subtle, as in an allusion or echo. This is a crucial aspect of Matthean studies because the Scriptures for Matthew are not the NT writings but rather the OT, the source of his theological reflection on Jesus and the kingdom he inaugurates.

COMMENTARY

PART ONE: MATTHEW 1:1—16:28

Robert S. Snow

I. THE BIRTH OF THE MESSIAH: MATTHEW 1—2

A. The Genealogy of the Messiah (1:1-17)

BEHIND THE TEXT

Matthew begins with the genealogy of Jesus. This genealogy is selective, like genealogies in the OT (Davies and Allison 1988, 176-77). For example, Matthew has omitted three kings, Ahaziah, Joash, and Amaziah between Jehoram (Joram) and Uzziah (v 8*b*; see 1 Chr 3:11-12). He also leaves out Jehoahaz and Jehoiakim between Josiah and Jeconiah (Jehoiachin). The omissions enable him to achieve an even fourteen generations between Abraham and David (Matt 1:17).

Biblical genealogies are not always concerned with the actual genealogical descent of a figure. Rather, they reveal the significance and identity of an individual (Huffman 1992, 255). For example, the number fourteen by which Matthew structures his genealogy is the numerical value of David's name in Hebrew: "Thus there were fourteen generations in all from Abraham to David, fourteen from David to the exile to Babylon, and fourteen from the exile to the Messiah" (v 17). Another anomaly, in contrast with ancient genealogies, is Matthew's bold inclusion of four named women. This irregularity has theological significance for our understanding of God's saving purposes now revealed in Jesus Messiah.

IN THE TEXT

■ **1-17** Although not evident in the NIV, the first two words of Matthew's Gospel in Greek read "book of origin" or "book of beginning" (*biblos geneseōs*). In Gen 5:1 of the LXX, the same phrase introduces the genealogy of Adam, which is a subtle connecting point between Matthew's Gospel and the OT. His genealogy not only refers to a list of Jesus' ancestors but also, in light of the meaning of "genesis" ("origin" or "beginning"), it points to the origin of Jesus himself, perhaps implicitly like John 1:1.

Since Gen 5:1-32 recounts primeval material about the creation or beginning of Adam and Eve, among other things, "Matthew might have opened his gospel as he did in order to draw a parallel between one beginning and another beginning" (Davies and Allison 1988, 150). Through this evocation, Matthew elevates the birth of the Messiah to a cosmic level: just as the author of Genesis recorded the origins of the heavens and the earth and all that they contain, Matthew now speaks of another creation, a new creation, which is the Messiah himself!

Messiah

Matthew immediately identifies Jesus as "the Messiah" (1:1). The Greek word for Messiah is *christos*, from which we get the English word "Christ." Christ is not a surname for Jesus but functions as a title denoting a specific function. The root of the corresponding Hebrew word for *christ* means "anointed," and, in the OT, kings and priests were anointed for their respective vocations. Christ/Messiah as a title refers to Jesus' royal vocation to inaugurate God's reign on earth. This is similar to the functions of Israel's kings who would represent God's rule on earth by, for example, advocating obedience to the Mosaic law in order to maintain the status of Israel as a holy people. However, few of Israel's kings fulfilled this, and exile was the result (Deut 4:25-31).

During the time of exile and continuing into the 2TP, some segments of Judaism, such as the Pharisees and Essenes, expected God to anoint another human king to restore the nation. He does so in the person of Jesus, and Matthew's Gospel reveals what this restoration entails and how it will be accomplished. It is very different from what some groups were expecting, as we shall see.

In the second half of v 1, Matthew isolates two key figures in the history of Israel, **Abraham** and **David**. For Matthew, any consideration of the origins of Jesus must include Abraham, the father of Israel, and King David, Israel's greatest king. Here we see that Matthew has structured the first part of his genealogy around these two figures, as his concluding summary makes clear: **Thus there were fourteen generations in all from Abraham to David, fourteen from David to the exile to Babylon, and fourteen from the exile to the Messiah** (v 17).

Exile and Messiah are the organizing principles. By beginning his Gospel in this way, Matthew introduces his readers to King Jesus, who will deliver Israel from exile, as opposed to lead them into it like his predecessors. As a true son of Abraham, Jesus will create a new Israel in the midst of whom the holy presence of the exalted Christ will remain forever (28:20*b*).

Matthew has structured his genealogy in three parts, each with fourteen generations, although there are only thirteen in the third part. Scholars have offered a number of proposals for the numerical symbolism (see Davies and Allison 1988, 161-65). The most popular is that fourteen is the numerical value of the Hebrew letters that make up David's name, $d+w+d = 4+6+4 = 14$. Assigning numerical significance to words was common in ancient times, known as *gematria* (see Rev 13:18).

Through the use of **fourteen**, Matthew has structured an orderly genealogical account demonstrating that the birth of Messiah Jesus is in strict accordance with God's sovereign plan to bring salvation to his people, delivering them from the pain of that past. Second, since fourteen is the numerical value of David—Israel's greatest king—King Jesus, who originates from David, will bring salvation as God's anointed. He will defeat his adversaries, albeit in a very different manner from the military might of old.

Comparing Matthew's genealogy with Luke's, one noticeable difference is the former's inclusion of women. Genealogies do not typically reference women, although there are exceptions (e.g., Gen 11:29; 22:20-24; 35:22-26; Davies and Allison 1988, 170). Matthew mentions four women, in addition to Mary: **Tamar** (1:3*a*), **Rahab** (v 5*a*), **Ruth** (v 5*b*), and Bathsheba (**Uriah's wife** [v 6]). Studying Matthew from a narrative-critical perspective requires readers to determine why he includes them.

Scholars have offered at least a couple of reasons: (1) All of these women are Gentiles: **Tamar** and **Rahab** are likely Canaanites, **Ruth** is a Moabite and Bathsheba is a Hittite. In Matthew's genealogy, all of these Gentile women are mothers who contributed to the genealogy of Jesus by bearing sons. If Gentiles can play a role in the origins of Jesus, maybe Matthew has included them as a foreshadow of those places in the Gospel where Gentiles become the recipients of the gospel and full-fledged subjects of God's reign inaugurated through his Messiah. (2) The moral behavior and/or stature of these women fall short of expected Jewish moral standards: **Tamar** seduces her father-in-law **Judah** (Gen 38); **Rahab** is a prostitute (Josh 2:1); Naomi commands **Ruth** to lie at the feet of **Boaz**, in which "feet" likely refers to his genitals (Ruth 3:4-8); and **David** commits adultery with Bathsheba (2 Sam 11). Some argue, however, that David raped her (e.g., Davidson 2006, 89).

If God can use scandalous situations in the history of ancient Israel, which culminate in the coming of the Messiah, he can certainly work through this very present issue of a virgin who has conceived outside of her betrothed husband. The scandal is so serious that Joseph is contemplating divorcing her in secret because she has conceived outside of their sexual union.

FROM THE TEXT

During the ministry of Jesus, the most influential group of Jews are the Pharisees who fiercely maintain ritual purity and faithfulness to their oral law. This law is a series of additional laws to ensure obedience to the written Mosaic law. Their emphasis on purity ensures that they be holy as God is holy (Lev 20:26). The need to be set apart, which is what holiness meant to the Pharisees and most 2TP Jews, makes perfect sense given the ever-present profaning and paganizing influence of the Romans.

In Matthew's description of the origins of Jesus, we learn that God does not separate himself from human situations that are less than morally acceptable and ritually pure. In fact, these things culminate in the coming of Messiah Jesus. This trend continues when unclean Gentiles are the first ones to worship King Jesus (Matt 2:2); when God sends Mary, Joseph, and their child to an unclean land, Egypt (v 13); and when Jesus begins his ministry in the darkest place in the land of Israel, in the lands of Zebulun and Naphtali (4:13-16).

Holiness denominations have not always viewed the dark and sinful places of this world as opportunities for the reign of God to be made known, but rather have been busy adhering to certain moral codes that would separate them from such defiling places. Even at this early stage of Matthew's Gospel, it is clear that God uses scandalous situations for his saving purposes and does not shy away from entering into them so that redemption and salvation might come.

B. The Messiah as Immanuel (1:18-25)

BEHIND THE TEXT

Matthew begins this section with an introductory comment: "This is how the birth of Jesus the Messiah came about" (1:18*a*). The Greek word for "birth" is the same for genealogy in v 1: *genesis*. A more accurate translation might be "this is how the origin of Jesus the Messiah came about." In vv 1-16, Matthew provides his readers with a macroscopic view of the origin of Jesus beginning with the well-known father of the Jews, Abraham. Now he dramatically narrows the focus of his lens on the origin of Jesus beginning with Joseph. In both cases, it is clear that God's hand is at work whether through his use of women of questionable moral character and ethnicity or the angelic visitations of Joseph providing him with the knowledge he needs for his next move.

God makes his plans known to Joseph through dreams (1:20; 2:12, 13, 19). Nolland thinks Joseph's dreams are related to the patriarchal ones in Genesis (20:3; 31:11, 24; 46:2; 2005, 96-97). This forms another connection with the first book of the OT. As Davies and Allison point out, "Dreams are frequently vehicles of divine revelation in the OT . . . and they remain so in the intertestamental period literature" (1988, 207). The NT, and especially Matthew, is no exception (see also 27:19). As a result of his first dream, Joseph "took Mary home as his wife" (v 24) and "gave him the name Jesus" (v 25*b*).

IN THE TEXT

■ **18-19** Matthew begins his microscopic account with conflict and tension, which actually characterizes the rest of his story: Mary is already with child before any sexual encounter with Joseph. Since he is a law-abiding Jew, he will divorce her. There are provisions in OT law for determining if a virgin who is pledged to be married has either intentionally committed sexual sin or has been raped in a place where no one could hear her screams (Deut 22:23-27).

Joseph wants to avoid the public trial where these things are determined, which would invariably **expose her to public disgrace** (Matt 1:19; Davies and Allison 1988, 204-5). Rather, he wants simply **to divorce her quietly**. He likely would have drawn up a certificate of divorce. Moses refers to this provision in Deut 24:1, which would preserve his status as a law-abiding Jew. However, Joseph is making these plans ignorant of God's will, which will soon be made known to him: Mary is pregnant by **the Holy Spirit** (Matt 1:18*b*).

■ **20-21** Matthew records the first of four divine visitations that Joseph receives, all of which ensure the protection of the defenseless child Messiah. **After** Joseph **had considered** his plan to divorce Mary, an **angel of the Lord** appears **to him in a dream** (v 20). The Greek word for the verb **considered** connotes thinking very carefully about an issue. This verb only appears three times in the NT, and its second instance is in 9:4, where Jesus castigates the scribes for "thinking evil in [their] hearts" (NASB). In both cases, intellectual musings occur outside of divine knowledge, and in both cases something suprarational occurs in response (→ 9:6).

For Joseph, an **angel of the Lord** appears revealing the divine plan that includes an explanation of Mary's pregnancy. He is not to divorce his wife **because what is conceived in her is from the Holy Spirit. She will give birth to a son, and you are to give him the name Jesus, because he will save his people from their sins** (1:20*b*-21).

Angel of the Lord

References to "the angel of the Lord" occur early in the OT, most notably in Genesis. The angel also appears to Moses in Exod 3. He is not distinct from God himself but is rather a manifestation of him (Exod 3:2 ff.; see also Judg 6:12-18). In later Jewish texts, angels become distinct (e.g., Zech 1:8-17) and are named by the time of the NT (e.g., Luke 1:26).

Not unlike the angel that appears to Joseph in Matthew, an angel of the Lord appears to Hagar, after she becomes pregnant, announcing to her that she will give birth to a son, she will name him Ishmael, and why she will give him this name. Although Matthew is obviously not quoting Gen 16:11 in Matt 1:21, the angel's words to Joseph reflect the same literary pattern. One of the major functions of the "angel of the Lord," whether the figure is the Lord's manifest presence or a separate divine figure, is to herald words of promise and blessing for the sake of the Lord's people.

Although Jesus is still not the biological son of Joseph, he is essentially legally adopted as Joseph's child and legitimately becomes "the son of David, the son of Abraham" (1:1) (Hooker 1997, 27). Through his obedience, "Joseph, the Davidid, proves that he has made Jesus his own" (Davies and Allison 1988, 208). In the angel's proclamation, there is a connection between naming the child **Jesus** and his mandate of saving Israel from their sins (v 21).

The name *Jesus* is the Greek counterpart of the Hebrew name Joshua, which means "Yahweh is salvation." Jesus not only heralds salvation but also is the means of salvation. This is evident at numerous points in Matthew (e.g., 8:25; 9:2; 26:28). His mandate is to rescue Israel **from their sins**, which may come as a surprise in light of Jesus' parting words to his disciples that they are to "make disciples of all nations" (28:19). A closer look at the Abrahamic covenant demonstrates that a movement from Israel to the nations is natural.

Israel's founding father, Abraham, receives a promise that "I will make you into a great nation, and I will bless you; I will make your name great, and you will be a blessing" (Gen 12:2). Israel is God's nation that not only receives blessing from him but also is to be a blessing to "all peoples on earth" (v 3*b*).

This is captured clearly in Isa 49:6*b* in God's words to the servant, who represents Israel: "I will also make you a light for the Gentiles that my salvation may reach to the ends of the earth." However, the effects of the fall were too much for the nation as she almost continually rebelled against God, eventually leading to her exile in a foreign land.

A number of scholars argue that despite Israel returning to the land after this period, she still languishes due to the presence of sin within the nation (Wright 2013, 139-63). Jesus' ministry, then, begins with his baptism demonstrating that he is a new Israel, without sin, and subsequently calls others to live under a new reign of God. His reign is inaugurated by his authoritative words and mighty deeds leading to the rescue of ethnic Israel from her sins. She will then become light and blessing to the nations (e.g., Matt 5:14).

■ **22-25** In the first of five fulfillment formulas, Matthew expresses that **all this** [the birth of Jesus] **took place to fulfill what the Lord had said through the prophet: "The virgin will conceive and give birth to a son, and they will call him Immanuel" (which means "God with us")** (1:22-23). In many discussions of this quotation, scholars focus on the discrepancy between Matthew's text, which reads **virgin**, and the Hebrew OT, which uses the term "young woman" instead (Isa 7:14 NIV n.). For a helpful discussion of the many issues surrounding this, consult Brown 1977, 144-50.

According to Brown,

> For both the MT [the OT] and the LXX [the Septuagint], . . . the sign offered by Isaiah was not centered on the manner in which the child would be conceived [i.e., from a virgin], but in the providential timing whereby a child who would be born precisely when that people's fortunes had reached their nadir. (1977, 149)

In other words, Matthew's major point in citing Isa 7:14 is that the birth of Jesus means that Yahweh is now with his people and not that his mother is a virgin.

The vocation of Jesus to save Israel from **their sins** is "a sign" (Isa 7:14*a*), to use Isaiah's language, of **Immanuel**. The figure in King Ahaz's day is a sign of judgment that will take the form of an Assyrian invasion because of his failure to rely upon God for deliverance from aggressive neighbors (vv 15-25). However, the sign appears to be transposed into one of hope in 8:10 forming a taunt to the Assyrians: "Devise your strategy, but it will be thwarted; propose your plan, but it will not stand, for God is with us." While the sign initially signifies judgment, in the next chapter, it is associated with salvation.

Matthew clearly interprets it as the latter, namely, through the birth and ministry of Jesus, Yahweh will save his people from their sins. Matthew appears to overlook the immediate literary context of his OT quotation in Isa 7. However, there is an unstated correspondence between Matthew's understanding of Immanuel and its transposition into a sign of salvation in Isa 8. Israel's Davidic hopes are now being fulfilled. Jesus Messiah inaugurates a reign that leads with salvation bringing light and hope to his wayward people (France 2007, 57). This is **God with us**!

FROM THE TEXT

This passage reveals what is of ultimate importance in Matthew's understanding of Jesus: he is salvation! Since, as Paul says, "God was pleased to have all his fullness dwell in him" (Col 1:19), we see the heart of God revealed in Matthew's Gospel. As followers of Jesus who are indeed sent into "all nations" (Matt 28:19), our message and deeds should reflect the mandate of Jesus himself to bring rescue and deliverance.

The Israel of Jesus' day is really not that much different from the plight of many people in our global society. Every day, people suffer the effects of economic, social, and spiritual oppression to which the gospel of Jesus Christ and its message of salvation bring hope and healing. In one of his homilies on Matt 1:23, John Chrysostom, a fourth-century church father, comments that the naming of Immanuel comes as a result of the multitudes witnessing the presence of God among his people in tangible ways (*Hom. Matt.* 5.2-3). While Chrysostom recognizes that God has been among his people in the past, it has never been so openly until now.

C. Gentile Astrologers Worship Messiah Jesus (2:1-12)

BEHIND THE TEXT

Unlike Luke's birth narrative that portrays the birth of Jesus as triumphant and joyous (see Luke 2:10), Matthew's account is characterized by hostility and aggression. Yes, magi from the east wish to worship this king (Matt 2:2), but Herod, the client king of Israel, is threatened at the news of the "one who has been born king of the Jews" (v 2*a*). The aggression that results from Herod's fear of this child-King drives the plot of Matthew's birth narrative until the family reaches Nazareth, Jesus' home, until his baptism as an adult (3:13).

Matthew continues to tell the story of the origin of Jesus in a microscopic way, compared with the macroscopic view offered in the genealogy. However, through a series of five OT quotations in chs 1—2, the first one of which was introduced in 1:23, Matthew evokes key moments in Israel's history as well. The birth of Immanuel signals the long-awaited deliverance of Israel, and the next four quotations in this chapter provide further clarity on the significance of the coming of Jesus Messiah.

In 2:1, Matthew introduces the magi (*magoi*) who only appear in his birth account. They are astrologers from the east, possibly Persia, who specialize in reading stars to find guidance and wisdom. Luke uses the singular *magos* as a title to describe Elymas "the sorcerer" in Acts 13:8, which, in light of Paul's rebuke of this man in v 10, is associated with the demonic realm.

Matthew's *magoi* are clearly not in league with demons but rather are like the *magoi* described in other ancient sources: "those who possessed superior knowledge and ability, including astrologers, [and] oriental sages" (Davies and Allison 1988, 228). The *magoi* often predict the rise and reign of kings and emperors, according to a number of ancient sources (Davies and Allison 1988, 230), and these ones are no different.

IN THE TEXT

■ **1-2** The magi come to Jerusalem because of a **star** that represents **the one who has been born king of the Jews** (v 2). Pagan and Jewish sources alike associate the appearance of stars with the accession of kings. For example, in the story of Balaam a Gentile prophet "from the east" (Num 23:7 LXX) prophesies that "a star will come out of Jacob; a scepter will rise out of Israel" (Num 24:17), referring to an Israelite king who will be victorious over his adversaries (Davies and Allison 1988, 234; Luz 2007, 104-5). Balaam's star is interpreted as a priestly messiah at Qumran (CD 7:18-26; *T. Levi* 18:3). In light of Matthew's genealogy, the rising of this star signals the arrival of the Messiah, the Son of David and the King of the Jews. The ones who recognize this first are the intelligentsia of the Gentile world. A minority of scholars suggest that the magi are in fact Jewish, but they are **from the east**, which suggests a Babylonian or even Persian locale (France 2007, 66; Evans 2012, 51).

■ **3-4** When they hear that the star signals the arrival of a new king, **King Herod** and **all Jerusalem with him** are **disturbed**. They are united in their "inward turmoil" (BDAG 2000, 990), elicited by the arrival of this king. Herod will do everything within his power to eliminate the threat. He immediately enlists the help of the Jewish scholars, "the chief priests and scribes of the people" (NRSV), to determine exactly where the Messiah was to be born. The Gentile magi call Jesus "king of the Jews" (v 2), the usual Gentile appellation. Herod refers to him as **the Messiah**, a distinctly Jewish term (v 4). Matthew contrasts the Jewish insiders who fear the Messiah and wish to kill him, with the Gentile outsiders who come to worship him.

Herod the Great

Herod reigned as king over the Roman province of Judea from 37 to 4 BCE. Herod's father was Idumean, and this did not endear him to the Jewish populace. Israel's king must be completely Jewish and from the line of David. Further, he curried the favor of Rome to gain territory greater than his father, Antipater: Judea, Samaria, and Galilee. In an attempt to placate the Jews, Herod undertook an extreme makeover of the Jerusalem temple that began around 20 BCE and did not conclude until 60 CE. However, he also constructed a number of pagan temples, as well as an opulent home at Masada not far from Jerusalem.

Matthew's portrayal of Herod as paranoid and murderous finds support in other ancient sources. Josephus recounts disturbing moments from Herod's regency. He executed some of his sons and his wife because he suspected they were plotting a coup d'etat (*Ant.* 15.232-36; 16.392-94), and, at his death, he ordered the slaughter of hundreds of Jewish men to ensure lamentation (*Ant.* 17.180-81), which fortunately never happened (*Ant.* 17.193). Clearly the pithy statement attributed to the Roman emperor Augustus about Herod is quite accurate, which contains a play on words in Greek: "I would rather be Herod's pig (*hus*) than this son (*huios*)" (Macrobius, *Saturnalia* 2:4:11).

No widespread expectation of a royal Messiah cuts across the sectarian lines of 2TJ (Wright 1992, 307). At Qumran, two messiahs, one royal and the other priestly, were expected. However, in the *Psalms of Solomon*, a first-century BCE Pharisaic text, a royal messiah is expected to cleanse Jerusalem of all iniquity and restore her fortunes (*Pss. Sol.* 17). Later in Matthew, Peter confesses that Jesus is "the Messiah, the Son of the living God" (16:16), which comes to Peter as revelation. Herod associates the star with the Messiah (2:2-3).

■ **5-6** This Messiah is to be born **in Bethlehem in Judea . . . for this is what the prophet has written** (see Mic 5:2). Matthew's citation states that Bethlehem is **by no means least among the rulers of Judah**; the LXX states the opposite: "Bethlehem is very few in number to be among the thousands of [Judeans]." The phrase **who will shepherd my people Israel**, which is not found in either the LXX or MT of Micah, alludes to 2 Sam 5:2*b*: "You will shepherd my people Israel," in which the Lord commissions David as Israel's shepherd (France 2007, 72).

By means of his alterations to and expansion of Mic 5:2, Matthew elevates the significance of the place of Jesus' birth and highlights the pastoral role of the Messiah, in keeping with the role of David, Israel's shepherd (Ps 78:72). Jesus desires to shepherd his people (see Matt 9:36). The Messiah's birth and his subsequent ministry changes the status of this small town into something great.

■ **7-12** Herod **secretly** wishes to know two things from the magi: **the exact time the star had appeared** (v 7), and where Jesus is so that Herod **may go and worship him** (v 8*b*). The answer to the first question will confirm the child's age, which is around two years old (v 16*b*). This is ominous in light of Herod's initial fear at hearing about the Messiah's birth. Tension builds as the magi are **warned in a dream not to go back to Herod**, but **they returned to their country by another route** (v 12). Immediately after this, a dream provides Joseph with supernatural direction that ensures the safety of the defenseless child-King from the murderous jealousy of King Herod (v 13).

Even before this, however, divine guidance is evident: **the star they** [the magi] **had seen when it rose went ahead of them until it stopped over the place where the child was** (v 9). Although it is unclear in the Greek text of v 10: **when they saw the star, they were overjoyed**, the jubilation may come as a result of not merely seeing the star, but rather when it stops over the house of the child (see v 11). Upon entering the house and seeing **the child with his mother Mary, . . . they bowed down and worshiped him** (v 11*a*). The combination of joy and worship confirms for Matthew's audience that this is indeed the true King of the Jews through whom God is with his people (1:23).

As was customary when visiting royalty, the magi offer him their **gifts of gold, frankincense and myrrh** (2:11*b*). Davies and Allison note that "the magi seem to know, earthly treasure is to be given up to God (2.11; 6.19). Only heavenly treasure matters (6.20-1; 19.21)" (1988, 248). These gifts, namely gold and frankincense, evoke the eschatological gathering of the Gentiles to the Lord (Isa 60:1-7; *Pss. Sol. 17:31*). In Ps 72, Sheba brings gold to the Lord's Messiah (vv 8-15). The presence of the Gentile astrologers in Matthew represents the gathering of the Gentiles to Jesus Messiah.

By the end of the Gospel, a reversal occurs: the resurrected Messiah commands his followers to go to the Gentiles (see Matt 28:19-20). In the meantime, Matthew does not let us dwell long in this heavenly moment of adoration of Jesus, but quickly reminds us that someone else is also pursuing this child when he comments that the magi have been warned not to return to King Herod (2:12).

FROM THE TEXT

These twelve verses describe the Messiah's birth. It is no coincidence that a dominant theme is worship. The surprise is that Gentile intellectuals are the first to come, from a distance, to worship the child-King when the angel had announced that "he will save *his* people from their sins" (1:21). It becomes clear that not all of the Messiah's people will welcome his deliverance. The Jewish intelligentsia, along with their king, are frightened at his coming. In fact, King Herod seeks Jesus not to worship him, but to destroy him.

These two responses create a stark contrast, but also reveal two aspects of Christian worship. First, worship is christologically centered. From Matthew's perspective, the worship of the Lord is now redefined around Jesus. The magi, upon seeing him, prostrate themselves, which in Jewish tradition is reserved for the worship of the Lord (Num 20:6; 1 Chr 29:20; Acts 10:25-26; Rev 19:10) (Davies and Allison 1988, 248). This posture is commensurate for the worship of the one in whom the Lord is now revealed (Matt 1:23).

The first ones to worship the Messiah are Gentiles, which is unexpected in such a Jewish Gospel. The celestial realm, which is the source of revelation for these astrologers, only guides them so far. They do eventually have to ask Herod who then consults the leaders of Israel who in turn examine the scriptures (Keener 1999, 99). The light shown to those of other faiths, not unlike the pagan astrologer, is not complete without submission to the God revealed in Scripture.

Second, authentic worship, as the OT affirms, requires contrite and humble hearts. Herod's fear and insecurity prohibits him from worshiping God but actually emboldens his rejection of the Lord's Messiah. Later, the disciples only recognize Jesus as the Son of God and worship him when the winds of the stormy sea cease (14:32-33). Initially, their fcar clouded their perception of his presence on the water, prompting them to think he was a ghost (v 26). However, when the wind ceased, they worshiped him (vv 32-33). Through the presence of the Spirit of Christ in our hearts, joy and humility should be the hallmarks of our worship of the now exalted Messiah.

D. King Herod Seeks to Destroy Messiah Jesus (2:13-23)

BEHIND THE TEXT

Matthew now returns to Joseph who, because of continued divine guidance through dreams, stays one step ahead of the murderous Herod. Before Herod realizes that he has been duped by the magi (2:16), which comes from a divine prompting to return a different way (v 12), Joseph and his family are already in Egypt (vv 14-15).

After Herod's death, an angel appears once again to Joseph in a dream telling him that it is safe to return home (vv 19-20). However, he relocates to Nazareth in Galilee because he is warned, yet again, through a dream that Herod's son is reigning in Judea (v 22).

God's direct intervention in Joseph's life to ensure the Messiah's safety is a major theme in Matthew's birth narrative. Matthew validates this divine guidance by associating these locations with the fulfillment of OT prophecy and, moreover, retraces the journey of the ancient Israelites who, like the Messiah, came up from Egypt and, eventually, went to the promised land (Matt 2:21; Exod 4:19-20).

IN THE TEXT

■ **13-15** In v 13*a*, Matthew indicates that **an angel of the Lord** visits Joseph **in a dream, when they** [the magi] **had gone**. Because of a dream, the magi return a different way to the east to avoid Herod (v 12). God once again provides guidance (see 1:20) to protect his people. The angel instructs Joseph: **"Get up," he said, "take the child and his mother and escape to Egypt. Stay there until I tell you, for Herod is going to search for the child to kill him"** (2:13*b*). This divine insight confirms the disingenuous desire of Herod in v 8 who wishes to "worship" the Messiah when in reality he desires **to kill him**. Later the chief priests and elders successfully seek Jesus' execution (27:20; Hagner 1993, 35; Davies and Allison 1988, 260).

In good Hebraic literary form—in which the details of the command are repeated when it is carried out (see Exod 7:9-10)—Joseph got up and departed for Egypt, taking **the child and his mother during the night** (Matt 2:14). The nocturnal departure maintains the tension and uncertainty that Matthew introduced earlier in the chapter. Jesus remains there **until the death of Herod** and, for Matthew, his departure from Egypt fulfills **what the Lord had said through the prophet: "Out of Egypt I called my son"** (v 15). By placing the Hosea quotation at this point, which is before Matthew cites Jer 31:15 in Matt 2:18, he reflects the historical order of exodus and then exile (Hagner 1993, 36).

Matthew recapitulates major moments in the history of Israel, just as he did in the genealogy, to highlight that Israel's hope of full deliverance is finally met in Messiah Jesus. With this quotation from Hosea, the child-King "retraces in his own life the foundational experiences of Israel in being called by God out of Egypt" (Nolland 2005, 123). Further, like ancient Israel, Jesus is delivered from a pagan tyrant and now as God's faithful Son will himself deliver the nation (see 1:21*b*).

Matthew uses a different word for **son** (*ton huion mou*) in the quotation from the one he uses up to this point in Matt 2. When referring to Jesus as a child, he uses the word *teknon* and now, in this quotation, he shifts to *huios*, which he uses several times in ch 1. He does this to forge a connection between the nation of Israel and Jesus.

Luz suggests that **son** for Matthew also might refer to the son of God who reigns on David's throne (2007, 121), but the immediate context of Matt 2 recalls the plight of the nation as opposed to its past leaders. The word *huion* emphasizes the Jewish background of Jesus who, according to 1:1, is "the son [*huiou*] of David, the son [*huiou*] of Abraham." Joseph learns that Mary's son [*huion*] will be called "Jesus, because he will save his people from their sins" (v 21*b*). In his quotation of Hos 11:1, Matthew expresses a connection between the Lord's son, Israel, who came up from Egypt, and Jesus who likewise travels from Egypt to "the land of Israel" (2:20).

Scholars have noted that this citation is not a prophetic utterance but is in fact part of Hosea's recollection of the rebellious nature of Israel even after the Lord had delivered them from slavery in Egypt (Hos 11:2-4). Fulfillment here refers to the ultimate fulfillment of that foundational saving act of the Lord in which he delivers his people from Egypt. Evans comments that "the exodus of God's son, Israel, foreshadowed the deliverance of God's son Jesus, whose ministry will save God's people in an even greater way than they were saved long ago" (2012, 58). As we will see, this new son of the Lord does not repeat the past sins of the nation but becomes a model of obedience that characterizes life under the Lord's reign. According to Hagner, "In Egypt, in the exodus, and in the wilderness (see 4:1-11), Jesus is the embodiment of Israel, not only anticipating her victories but also participating in her sufferings (cf. Isa 63:8-9)" (1993, 36).

■ **16-18** After some time passed and the magi had not returned, Herod real- 2:16-18
ized that he was **outwitted by the Magi**. In response, **he was furious, and he gave orders to kill all the boys in Bethlehem and its vicinity who were two years old and under** (Matt 2:16). Herod's infanticide fulfills **what was said through the prophet Jeremiah** (v 17). Matthew quotes Jer 31:15 in Matt 2:18: **A voice is heard in Ramah, weeping and great mourning, Rachel weeping for her children and refusing to be comforted, because they are no more.**

It seems odd that Matthew highlights the fulfillment of OT prophecy concerning the slaughter of innocent children. However, the context of Jer 31:15 has a number of unstated correspondences with Matthew's birth narrative that center on hope, namely, the end of exile. The returnees from exile mentioned in Jer 31 include "the woman with child" (v 8*b* KJV). Just before this in the LXX version, the prophet declares, "The Lord saved his people" (v 7*b*), which coheres with the mandate of Jesus Messiah: "He will save his people" (Matt 1:21*b*; for additional correspondences, see Davies and Allison 1988, 267).

While it appears that Herod's ruthless military power marks anything but the end of exile, Matthew uses Jer 31 to communicate that this atrocity is not the end of the story. Just as Rachel once wept for those taken into exile and now mothers in Bethlehem mourn the loss of their sons, deliverance will come (Hagner 1993, 38). As we have already seen, a new nation, in the person of

Jesus Messiah, will come up from Egypt to bring an end to Israel's oppression. From what this Messiah ultimately delivers Israel will become apparent after his baptism (Matt 3:16-17).

■ **19-23** **An angel of the Lord** appears to Joseph **in a dream** (2:19) for a third time with detailed instructions: **Get up, take the child and his mother and go to the land of Israel, for those who were trying to take the child's life are dead** (v 20). As before, Matthew recounts Joseph's obedient fulfillment of a divine command (v 21).

Now that King Herod is dead, the holy family can return to the land of Israel. The angel does not command them to return to Bethlehem but, more broadly, to the land of Israel. This anticipates not only the final revelation Joseph receives in v 22*b* in which he is **warned in a dream** to avoid Jerusalem but also preserves Matthew's Exodus framework evident in the chapter (Hagner 1993, 39).

Unlike the other divine encounters Joseph has, this one comes in response to his personal fear about returning to Judea that is now under the control of Archelaus (v 22*b*), the son of King Herod. While Herod's other sons, Herod Antipas and Herod Philip, remained in control of their areas well after their father's death, the Romans dethroned Archelaus in 6 CE for his incompetence and ruthless behavior. According to Josephus, Archelaus inaugurated his rule by slaughtering three thousand Jewish citizens (*J.W.* 2:89). Joseph's fear is not unfounded.

Joseph chooses Nazareth in the region of Galilee as the new home for his family and **so was fulfilled what was said through the prophets, that he would be called a Nazarene** (v 23). The problem with this quotation is that it does not appear in the OT. Matthew refers to **the prophets** suggesting an evocation of a prophetic theme rather than a specific OT citation (Hagner 1993, 40; Nolland 2005, 128).

A number of scholars suggest the background of v 23 is the "Nazirite vow" in Num 6:1-21, or that it echoes the Hebrew word *nazir*, translated "holy" (e.g., Davies and Allison 1988, 226-27). The vow is characterized by austerity: no strong drink, uncut hair, and separation from the dead. This is unlikely. Jesus is accused in Matthew of being "a glutton and a drunkard, a friend of tax collectors and sinners" (11:19*b*) and resuscitated the dead by touch (9:23-26) (Hagner 1993, 41). It is more likely an allusion to Isa 11:1 that speaks of the restoration of the Davidic line inaugurating a messianic age (Isa 11—12), which is a prophetic theme (Jer 23:5-6; 33:15-16; Ezek 37:24-27; Mic 5:2-15 [1-14 HB]).

There is a faint terminological correspondence between Matt 2:23 and Isa 11:1 in which *Nazōraios* in Matt 2:23 alludes to the Hebrew term for "branch" in Isa 11:1: "A shoot will come up from the stump of Jesse; from his roots a Branch will bear fruit." Many 2TP Jews interpreted the "branch" of Isa 11:1 messianically as evident in the DSS (1QSb 5:20-29) and *Pss. Sol.*

17:29, 36, 37 (Evans 2012, 62-63). If Matthew is referring to this passage, he is finishing off his birth account where he began, with an implicit affirmation through Scripture that Jesus is indeed the Messiah, the Son of David, and that this is a fundamental category for interpreting the ministry of Jesus in the rest of the Gospel.

FROM THE TEXT

In the darkness and hostility in Matthew's birth narrative, especially evident in Matt 2, the Lord does not remain silent. Through dreams, which contain an angelic visitation, the Lord provides divine guidance for Joseph's next move and direction for the magi as well. We need to consider seriously divine encounters that come through dreams not only because they occur at a number of points in Scripture but also because they advance the saving purposes of God. The Spirit has come to indwell all of God's people, and Peter declares what this means at Pentecost: "In the last days it will be, God declares, that I will pour out my Spirit upon all flesh, and your sons and your daughters shall prophesy, and your young men shall see visions, and your old men shall dream dreams" (Acts 2:17 NRSV). Matthew gives us a picture of the ways in which God interacts with his people, in this case through dreams and divine encounters, and Luke invites us to experience these things so that God's saving purposes are made known.

II. THE MESSIAH PREPARES FOR MINISTRY: MATTHEW 3:1—4:11

A. John the Baptist (3:1-17)

1. A Call to Repentance (3:1-12)

BEHIND THE TEXT

From a young age, Jesus makes his home in Nazareth, a small village about twenty-four kilometers west of the southern part of the Sea of Galilee. Nazareth was an agricultural village with a population of about five hundred (Longman 2013, 1199). According to Matt 2, this reveals that he is the messianic Branch who comes to reign on David's throne. This does not guarantee a warm welcome, however. The familiarity with Jesus, who is known only as Joseph's son, leads to disbelief that hinders him from performing many miracles (Matt 13:54-57; see Mark 6:1-6).

In Matt 3:1, Matthew shifts from Nazareth to the wilderness areas of the Jordan River, east of Jerusalem, to introduce John the Baptist. John calls the inhabitants of Jerusalem and its environs to repent and confess their sins in preparation for the coming of the Lord. Immanuel, God with us, is soon to visit his people, but their hearts must be prepared for his coming.

For Jews living in the 2TP, life is not as it should be. The promises that Israel would be a great nation—possessing her own land as well as the gate of her enemies—have not come to fruition (Gen 12:1-3; 17:8; 22:16-18). She has not been gathered from the nations to become the purified, Spirit-filled people of God as promised in the Prophets (e.g., Ezek 36:24-32). Even though Israel has paid the penalty for her sin by spending seventy years in exile (Isa 40:1-2; Dan 9:1-24), many Jews longed for the exclusive reign of the Lord, not that of the Romans. They also hoped that the land would be cleansed from all iniquity, including the paganizing influence of Greco-Roman culture.

Some scholars conclude that exile never really ended (McComiskey 2010, 673-96; Wright 2013, 139-63). There is an experiential disconnection between promise and reality, between the promise made to Abraham and the reality of being ruled by the Romans coupled with the vast majority of Jews living outside of the land. Israel's exile has not ended because sin persists; the nation is not holy as the Lord is holy (Lev 20:26), a state to which the Pharisees and Essenes aspired in the 2T period (Brower 2005, 24-37). It is not difficult to see why John comes preaching about repentance, preparing hearts for the Lord's visitation through his anointed Son.

In the OT, the wilderness is associated with both preparation and deliverance. In Sinai, after having been rescued from the Egyptians, Israel receives the Mosaic covenant through which she becomes a "treasured possession," "a kingdom of priests," and "a holy nation" (Exod 19:5-6). In the wilderness, Moses prepares a new generation of Israelites for life in the promised land so that they will be obedient, live holy lives, and not be exiled from the land.

Later, Isaiah promises captive Israel that the Lord would manifest his saving presence in the wilderness when he delivered them from Babylon (Isa 40:3-5; 41:19-20; 43:14—44:5) and lead them to a glorified Jerusalem (ch 66). John's message of repentance followed by confession of sins, all of which occurs in the wilderness, coheres with the wilderness as a place of the Lord's saving activity, of the deliverance of his people as in Isaiah, which, for Matthew, is where the ministry of Jesus begins.

IN THE TEXT

■ **1-3** The setting for **John the Baptist**'s ministry is **the wilderness of Judea** (v 1). The term **baptist** (*baptistēs*) means "the one who baptizes," denoting John's role. Matthew uses the phrase "John the Baptist" five times, which highlights his importance in the Gospel.

John preaches, **Repent, for the kingdom of heaven has come near** (v 2). This call parallels the preaching of Jesus (4:17), showing the close link between the two (3:11). For additional parallels, see Davies and Allison (1988, 289). **Repent** in Greek means "change of mind" and in Hebrew means to "turn back" or "return." If Israel's exile has not ended, and it is sin that brings about exile, it is fitting that John calls Israel to repent (see Deut 30:2-3; 1 Kgs 8:46-51).

Repentance involves the whole person: heart, head, and hands. Turning to God results not only in trusting the Lord and his faithfulness but also in living lives of holiness and purity that reflect such a trusting relationship. However, judgment awaits those who refuse this call (Matt 3:7-10) and that of Jesus as well (11:20-21).

John calls Israel to repent because the rule of God, the meaning of the phrase **the kingdom of heaven**, is dawning in both salvation and judgment (Hagner 1993, 47; Nolland 2005, 138). Matthew prefers the phrase **kingdom of heaven** to kingdom of God. Heaven may be a circumlocution to avoid uttering the divine name. But Matthew does use kingdom of God as well, so its use may be purely stylistic (France 2007, 101).

Scholars differ on what it means that **the kingdom of God has come near**. Some argue that **has come near** means that in Jesus' ministry the reign of God has arrived, which is known as "realized eschatology" (Dodd 1961, 35). Others argue that the kingdom of God will not be manifested until the return of Christ; this is known as "futurist eschatology" (Fuller 1954, 25-32; Sanders 1985, 228-41).

A mediating view, known as "inaugurated eschatology," claims that already in the ministry of Jesus the reign of God is realized over sickness, death, and demons, but, at the same time, it has a dimension that is not yet fully realized until Jesus returns (Ladd 1974, 206; Wenham and Walton 2011, 175). The ambiguity inherent in the aspect of the perfect tense of the verb in Greek **has come near** implies "having drawn near and remaining near" (Hagner 1993, 47) or "that which has completed the process of 'coming near' is already present, not simply still on the way" (France 2007, 103). The reign of God draws near in the ministry of Jesus through his words and deeds and remains so through his followers (Matt 10:1), but it will not be manifested in its fullness until the Parousia (e.g., 25:31-46).

In 3:3, Matthew quotes Isa 40:3 to support his statement that John **is he who was spoken of through the prophet Isaiah**. Matthew explains John's "significance in terms of a scriptural model" (France 2007, 104) as he does with Jesus. Isaiah 40 assures Israel that the Lord will deliver the nation from captivity. The **voice** is that of John, who is now **calling in the wilderness, "Prepare the way for the Lord, make straight paths for him"** (Matt 3:3). In Isaiah, God is the Lord; here, Messiah Jesus comes as **the Lord** (see 8:26-27; 12:6; 22:43-45). Through Jesus, the Lord is present with his people (→ 1:23). John's ministry is preparing the Lord's way so that the people can receive his salvation. When the Lord returns to his people, exile is over (Deut 30:1-10; Isa 40:9-11).

■ **4-6** Matthew's description of John's clothing of **camel's hair** and **a leather belt around his waist** (Matt 3:4*a*) recalls Elijah the prophet (see 2 Kgs 1:8). John's diet of **locusts and wild honey** (Matt 3:4*b*) implies that he "abstained from flesh from which blood has been drained and took no strong drink" (Davies and Allison 1988, 297; see Jesus' comment on John in 11:18). The austere depiction of John (2 Kgs 1:8) aligns him with the simplicity to which Jesus calls his own disciples (Matt 6:25-34; 8:18-22; 10:10; 24:45).

The links with Elijah present John as a prophet, one who fulfills the call in Isaiah to prepare the way of the Lord, preparing the hearts of Israel for his coming reign through his messiah. Jesus even refers to John as Elijah (11:14; 17:11-13). John's bold rebuke of the Pharisees and Sadducees in Matt 3:7-10, as well as his call to repent (e.g., Isa 31:6; Jer 4:1), is characteristic of OT prophets (1 Kgs 17:1; Evans 2012, 69).

Many people from Judea respond to John's call to repentance. It is not likely that **all Judea and the whole region of the Jordan** confessed their sins and were baptized by him (Matt 3:5). The point is that this was the preparation of the people for the Lord. Large numbers from these areas responded to John's message, which demonstrates his far-reaching impact (see Josephus, *Ant.* 18.118). Later, Jesus addresses a crowd with the assumption that they have heard John preach (11:7-9).

Baptism

Despite the many references to baptism in the NT (e.g., Acts 2:38, 41; Rom 6:3-4; 1 Cor 1:13-17; Gal 3:27; 1 Pet 3:21), there is no reference to it as a rite of initiation in the OT. Also, baptism is not a rite for Gentiles who convert to Judaism in the 2TP, except for one reference in the Mishnah that likely reflects traditions after the destruction of the temple in 70 CE (Nolland 2005, 141; France 2007, 108 n. 47).

There are references to washing with water for purification (Ps 51:6-9 [8-11 HB]; Isa 4:4; Jer 4:14; Ezek 36:25-27) but nothing like baptism in the NT, which derived from John (Nolland 2005, 141). The inhabitants of Qumran used water for purification but as ceremonial washing, not initiation (France 2007, 108 n. 46). Jews also ceremonially washed when they attended synagogue (Evans 2012, 94-95). John's baptism, not unlike the promise in Ezek 36:25*a*, "I will sprinkle clean water on you, and you will be clean," is a symbolic event marking those who confess their sins as now purified and prepared for the coming of the Lord, Messiah Jesus.

Josephus recognizes the purifying significance of John's baptism. Jews came "for the purification of the body; supposing still that the soul was thoroughly purified beforehand by righteousness" (*Ant.* 18.117). In Matthew, a holy remnant is forming, a new manner of being Israel, which will come into its own when the Lord comes, the one for whom John prepares a way.

The purification symbolized by baptism is accompanied by confession of sin. Those who respond do so with their whole person, confessing sins with their mouths and being baptized with their bodies, just as the Lord calls Israel to repent with their whole being, marking the end of exile (Deut 30:1-3).

Unlike Mark and Luke, Matthew does not associate John's baptism with "the forgiveness of sins" (Mark 1:4; Luke 3:3), because "in Matthew's eyes, John only brought people to repentance in order to make them ready for the

Messiah. It is the Messiah's task to bring the world forgiveness" (Davies and Allison 1988, 301). Of the Synoptic Gospels, only Matthew explicitly describes the crucifixion as resulting in "the forgiveness of sins" (26:28). The culminating, redemptive work of Jesus on the cross, which began with John's ministry of preparation, effects the complete purification of those who repent (3:2; 4:17), bringing an end to exile (Ezek 36:24-25).

■ **7-10** This passage is unique to Matthew and is important for his characterization of what will become two major opponents of Jesus, **the Pharisees and Sadducees**.

Pharisees and Sadducees

The Pharisees are the major opponents of Jesus in Matthew. The term itself occurs twenty-nine times compared with twelve in Mark. Josephus recounts that they were highly influential among the Jewish populace in first-century Palestine (*Ant.* 18.12-15). Many Jews respected them because of their strict obedience to ancestral traditions that centered on ritual purity laws. These laws were based on Levitical regulations that preserved the holiness of the temple priests. The Pharisees, however, extended these laws to themselves in order to embody temple holiness in everyday life (Borg 1984, 73; see Mark 7:3-4 for these traditions). Later in Matthew, the Pharisees challenge Jesus on his alleged disregard for ritual purity as well as other ancestral laws that they follow to ensure a strict obedience to the Mosaic law (Matt 12:1-2; 15:1-2) and thereby live as holy people.

The Sadducees were an aristocratic group of Jews from the same priestly family. Although Matthew does not refer to them as much as the Pharisees, he does mention them seven times compared with Mark and Luke, who only refer to them once. They exercise their governing powers over the temple maintaining order in both the temple and Jerusalem lest the Romans intervene. It is the Sanhedrin, the judicial body of Palestinian Judaism, composed entirely of Sadducees, that pronounces the death penalty on Jesus (Matt 26:59-66). Finally, the Sadducees' desire to maintain the status quo gives rise to their disbelief in the resurrection (22:23), which would entail a complete reversal of the power structures of this age and from which this group currently acquires its power and money (Wright 1992, 211).

At seeing **the Pharisees and Sadducees coming to where he was baptizing**, John calls them a **brood of vipers** (3:7*a*). Matthew uses the term "vipers" two more times (12:24-37; 23:29-36) to portray the Pharisees as those who have the appearance of devotion but only speak and practice evil. In Ps 140:3 [4 HB], snakes and vipers describe the wicked whose words are poison (see also Prov 23:32; Evans 2012, 70). John reveals this pretention with his question, **Who warned you to flee from the coming wrath?** (Matt 3:7*b*).

Some feel it is unlikely they are coming to be baptized by John (Hagner 1993, 49; France 2007, 110). But this undermines his question about fleeing wrath if they did not intend to be baptized (Nolland 2005, 142). Possibly John perceives them as coming for repentance, and Matthew, the narrator, portrays them as having no intention to do so, which fits with the hostility of John toward them.

According to the OT, the Lord will intervene in judgment and wrath on the "day of the Lord" to deal with injustice and wickedness (Joel 2:1-11; Amos 2:6-16; Zeph 1:1-18; Zech 14:1-15). John appears surprised that they are giving heed to this day and his baptism of preparation for the Lord's coming. Some argue that the coming wrath will be the second coming of Jesus (Matt 16:27; 25:34-46). However, Jesus' interactions with the religious leaders result in their judgment much sooner (21:18-22). The Messiah's ministry inaugurates not only salvation in the present but judgment as well.

John calls the religious leaders to **produce fruit in keeping with repentance** (v 8). Repentance needs to be demonstrated and believers will be judged on the basis not only of belief but also of actions, because the Son of Man "will reward each person according to what they have done" (16:27). Jesus concludes the Sermon on the Mount with a call to action: "Therefore everyone who hears these words of mine and *puts them into practice* is like a wise man who built his house on the rock" (7:24; see also 5:16). Josephus records that John "commanded the Jews to exercise virtue, both as to righteousness towards one another, and piety towards God, and so to come to baptism" (*Ant.* 18.117 [Whiston]). Judaism was a religion not just of creeds but of deeds and expects the latter of the religious leaders.

3:7-10 Although the Jews are the Lord's chosen people, that is, they **have Abraham as** their **father** (v 9*a*), ethnicity and election does not guarantee salvation if fruit, or right behavior, is not manifested. John warns them **that out of these stones God can raise up children for Abraham** (v 9*b*). In other words, if the Pharisees and Sadducees do not repent and live lives pleasing to the Lord, he will find others.

The connection between **stones** and **children** is found in their similar spelling in Hebrew and Aramaic. This harsh response is a foreshadow of the Gentile mission, which Matthew develops later in the Gospel (Hagner 1993, 50), and "brutally wounds the pride of unrepentant Jews—even stones have more chance of being God's true people than they have" (France 2007, 112). Although Nolland argues that "there is not the slightest hint here of Gentiles replacing Jews, the opening to the Gentiles . . . is not out of keeping with the freedom of God . . . [who raises up children for Abraham from stones]" (Nolland 2005, 145). The usefulness, however, of Jew or Gentile for God's saving purposes is not contingent upon ethnic identity but by fruitful labor in the kingdom.

John then announces that their unequivocal judgment is very near, for **the ax is already at the root of the trees, and every tree that does not produce good fruit will be cut down and thrown into the fire** (v 10). Jesus himself reuses this imagery in 7:18-19, which refers to a faith characterized by inactivity (Hagner

1993, 51). Without acts of righteousness, the fire of judgment awaits (Mal 3:2; 4:1 [3:19 HB]; Jer 22:7; Evans 2012, 72). Like John, Jesus directs this imagery specifically at the Pharisees (→ Matt 12:33-34; these verses are a warning to those who have just accused Jesus of operating in league with Satan in 12:24).

Matthew is concerned with the faithfulness of the whole person. The Pharisees and Sadducees have refused to heed John's call to repentance. Their joint approach to John, despite their differences, represents a shared "hostile stance towards the early Christian movement" (Nolland 2005, 142).

■ **11-12** John highlights his preparatory ministry, the one who prepares the Lord's way (3:3). While he baptizes with **water for repentance**, Jesus **who is more powerful than I** [John]**, whose sandals I am not worthy to carry, . . . will baptize you with the Holy Spirit and fire** (v 11). This Holy Spirit-fire baptism is a prediction of what occurs on the day of Pentecost when 120 believers were waiting in the Upper Room to be "clothed with power from on high" (Luke 24:49*b*; Acts 1:5). The Spirit poured out at Pentecost comes from the exalted Jesus (2:32-33), which was accompanied by "tongues of fire" (2:3). Matthew's audience reads his gospel in light of Pentecost and their own baptism in the Holy Spirit. Matthew wrote some fifty years after Pentecost.

John's reference to the **Holy Spirit** and **fire** continues the purification theme associated with John's baptism (Matt 3:11). In the OT, fire purifies Israel for God's holy purposes and staves off his judgment (Isa 1:25; Ezek 22:18-22; Zech 13:9; Mal 3:2-4). However, in Matt 3:12, some will be judged (described as **burning up the chaff with unquenchable fire**) and others receive the reward of salvation (**gathering his wheat into the barn**). Jesus develops this eschatological theme of separation in ch 13 (e.g., vv 41-43, 49). John's ministry begins the process of winnowing that will continue in the Messiah's ministry and be completed when he returns as the heavenly judge (25:31-33).

FROM THE TEXT

For many Christians in the modern, Western world, the vitriolic language of John labeling the religious leaders as a "brood of vipers" and his divisive message of judgment for the unfaithful and salvation for the faithful may be difficult to accept. However, when it comes to moral purity and living lives where repentance is demonstrated in all aspects of our being, Scripture is uncompromising in the face of widespread lack of concern for holiness, not least in Israel herself.

In prophetic fashion echoing Ezek 34, John is addressing the religious leaders who live compromised lives. John Wesley was similarly unwavering when confronting the religious folks of his day. Kenneth Collins writes that

> Wesley rejects the notion that the Methodists were "gathering churches out of churches," because he now calls into question the earlier sanctity, even the soteriological status, of many within the Anglican communion who had subsequently joined the Methodists. (2003, 153)

Because of the depraved language and behavior that Wesley saw in these folks, Wesley labeled them as "barefaced heathens" (Davies 1989, 9:258). In the Wesleyan-holiness tradition, we, too, must reflect in our own lives the purity and holiness of God himself, which will invariably require us to stand up, albeit in a gracious way, against those who do not bear fruit worthy of repentance, but, rather, as Paul says in a similar context, may we speak "the truth in love" (Eph 4:15). Given that John addresses the religious leaders, those who lead the people of God must lead the way modeling holiness in their congregations and other ministry contexts.

2. The Baptism of Jesus (3:13-17)

BEHIND THE TEXT

All three Synoptic Gospels record the baptism of Jesus. It reveals Jesus' royal identity as God's Son and as a faithful Israelite fulfilling "all righteousness" (Matt 3:15). Matthew associates the arrest of John (see 4:12) with the beginning of Jesus' ministry. John likely continues his baptism of repentance until his arrest, but Matthew makes no further reference to it after John baptizes Jesus. When the one for whom John has prepared the way comes, Jesus begins his proclamation of the kingdom (see 4:12-17). This is the last time John appears as a character in the Gospel, other than when he sends his disciples to inquire about Jesus (11:2-6) and Matthew's record of his execution (14:3-12). The influence of his ministry, however, continues after his death (17:9-13; 21:23-27).

IN THE TEXT

■ **13-15** The adult Jesus now reenters the narrative. Having been raised in Nazareth, **Jesus came from Galilee to the Jordan to be baptized by John** (v 13). Given John's appraisal of Jesus as superior to him in v 11, he is not comfortable baptizing Jesus. He questions him: **I need to be baptized by you, and do you come to me?** (v 14). The question is only in Matthew. Jesus' response introduces an important theme: **"Let it be so now; it is proper for us to do this to fulfill all righteousness." Then John consented** (v 15).

Righteousness

Righteousness is widely discussed in biblical studies. Is it a status given to us by God through faith, as Luther argued? In the OT, righteousness describes God's own covenant faithfulness, or his own moral integrity, in which he acts savingly to restore his people (Ps 98:2-3; Isa 51:4-5; 52:10). In turn, covenant faithfulness/righteousness is required of God's people in the form of obedience to Torah. In a variety of texts (Gen 15:6; Pss 1:4-6; 11:7; 72:1; Isa 1:16-17; *Pss. Sol.* 3:3-12; Josephus, *Ant.* 6.88-94; 1QS 1:13) righteousness is a characteristic of those who adhere to God's commands (see Green, McKnight, and Marshall 1992, 411-16).

Righteousness is the language of relationship, of being rightly related to God and God to his people.

Many scholars locate righteousness in this passage as the human obedience of John and Jesus (France 2007, 120; Keener 1999, 131-32; Davies and Allison 1988, 325). However, the emphatic phrase **all righteousness** may also imply the faithfulness of the Lord. His righteousness, defined as faithfulness toward his people, is evident in two ways: (1) He has been divinely protecting the child Messiah in the birth narrative; and (2) He declares his familial affirmation of Jesus as his beloved Son following his baptism. That is, John and Jesus have been obedient in baptism, and the Lord responds with a declaration highlighting the love he has for his servant-Son. At the same time, Jesus' baptism begins a journey of obedience to the will of his father. Because righteousness is relational, it is only natural that **all righteousness** refers to both John/Jesus and the Lord.

■ **16-17** Immediately after Jesus is baptized, **heaven was opened, and he saw the Spirit of God descending like a dove and alighting on him** (v 16). Matthew may be alluding to Isa 64:1 [63:19*b* HB]: "If you should open heaven, trembling from you would seize the mountains, and they would melt" (NETS). However, the significance of this allusion for Matthew isn't based merely on the terminological correspondence of the phrase **heaven was opened**.

Thematic connections extend beyond Isa 64:1 [63:19*b* HB]. Beginning in 63:7, the prophet recalls the Exodus (vv 7-9). But Israel rebelled and grieved the Holy Spirit, resulting in her exile (v 10). However, vv 11-19 highlight the faithfulness of the Lord who delivered his people and the plea for him to deliver his people once again. The plea culminates in 64:1 [63:19*b* HB]: "O that you would tear open the heavens and come down" (NRSV).

This Isaianic background lies behind Matthew's presentation of John and Jesus. In Matthew, the exilic call to rend the heavens is answered through Jesus, the Lord's king, who receives the Spirit from the open heaven. The phrase **alighting on him** in the NIV is actually "coming upon him" in Greek. In Gen 1:2, a spirit of/from God was "upon/above the water" (LXX). A Qumran text alludes to Gen 1:2, stating that "over the humble his [the Lord's] Spirit hovers" (*Messianic Apocalypse* [4Q521 f2ii+4:6]). Perhaps Matthew is echoing Gen 1:2 in which the Spirit is now "upon/over" Jesus for his work as the beloved Son just as the Spirit of God in Gen 1 brought order out of chaos. A new creation occurs now.

It's more likely, however, that Matthew has in mind Isa 42:1 in which the Lord will put "my spirit upon him" (Davies and Allison 1988, 334-35; Keener 1999, 132). Later, Matthew applies Isa 42:1 to Jesus in Matt 12:18. This marks "a turning point in salvation-history, for only after the Spirit comes does the Messiah's ministry begin . . . So at the Jordan the messianic office is taken up" (Davies and Allison 1988, 335).

Several key points are made by this declaration. First, his sonship is inextricably linked to the notion of messiah and kingship in Scripture. The kings of Israel are considered sons of God. Jesus as God's Son fits with Matthew's portrayal of Jesus as a royal Messiah (Pss 2:7; 89:20-27 [21-28 HB]) and David's long-awaited son (see Matt 1:17-18; 2:2-6). All this is affirmed by the voice from heaven in 3:17: **This is my Son, whom I love; with him I am well pleased**.

Second, the baptismal scene and the forty days of wilderness testing that follow (3:13—4:11) evoke the exodus of Israel and her forty-year journey. Jesus as God's Son recalls the nation of Israel, who is also God's son. Israel as God's son is a designation associated with the Exodus (Exod 4:22; Hos 11:1). After the exodus, Israel journeys for forty years in the wilderness but disbelieves that the Lord will remain faithful (e.g., Exod 16:1-3). This exodus-wilderness pattern reappears in the Synoptic Gospels: Jesus, as true Israel, is affirmed as God's Son at his baptism. In the wilderness, he remains faithful to the Lord whereas Israel did the opposite (→ Matt 4:1-11).

Third, the second phrase, **whom I love**, expresses the familial love between God, who commissions his Son, and Jesus. In Gen 22:2, the phrase describes Abraham who is to "take your son, your only son, whom you love . . . and offer him there [land of Moriah] as a burnt offering" (NRSV; see vv 12, 16). If this is an allusion of Gen 22, Matthew may be foreshadowing the sacrifice of Abraham's true son, Jesus Messiah (Keener 1999, 134).

Fourth, a hint of suffering becomes stronger when we consider Isa 42, which introduces the Servant of Yahweh. We see similar terminology between Matt 3:17 (**with him I am well pleased**) and 12:18 ("in whom I delight"), in which Matthew quotes Isa 42:1. In other contexts, "well pleased" echoes passages describing God's delight in his people (Pss 44:3 [4 HB]; 149:4; Isa 62:4). In light of Matt 12:18 and the allusion to Isa 42:1 in this passage, Jesus is the servant Messiah and as such has a unique relationship with and mandate from his heavenly Father, which culminates with his death on the cross.

The baptism of Jesus identifies him not only as God's Son, Israel's king and the Lord's servant, but also as one who represents a restored nation centered around himself as one who is loved by the Lord and with whom he is well pleased. However, just as ancient Israel was tested in the wilderness after passing through the Red Sea, so will her long-awaited King.

FROM THE TEXT

In Matthew, Jesus as a new Israel demonstrates faithfulness to his heavenly Father through the guiding presence of the Holy Spirit (e.g., 4:1). This Trinitarian moment is the beginning of God's mission through his Son and, by implication, his people. Jesus will eventually call twelve disciples to participate with him in his work of preaching the gospel to the sick and marginalized (10:1-8).

Since Jesus represents the nation, this relationship is available to all of his followers. Like Jesus, we as God's people, through the indwelling Spirit, can unwaveringly trust in our heavenly Father (4:1-11). This relationship enables us, for example, to bring the light of the gospel into dark places (vv 15-17). The mission of God, to save and redeem not only souls but also the marginalized, is at work through his people. The baptism of Jesus marks the beginning of this mission.

B. Jesus Tested in the Wilderness (4:1-11)

BEHIND THE TEXT

After his baptism, the Spirit leads Jesus into the wilderness, the same setting for John's ministry. The wilderness is where true allegiances are made known (see Exod 16:1-3). Yahweh led Israel into the wilderness to prepare them for the promised land, but the Exodus generation refused to listen (Num 14:20-25). Now, where ancient Israel rebelled, Jesus, as both new Israel and messianic King, is obedient.

IN THE TEXT

■ **1-2** Why would Jesus be **led by the Spirit . . . to be tempted by the devil** (v 1), especially since the voice has just declared his love and pleasure for his Son? The answer may lie in the length of Jesus' fast: **forty days and forty nights** (v 2). This period—which, according to France, is an idiom "for a significant but limited period" (2007, 129)—has echoes from Scripture. Moses ascended Mount Sinai for forty days and forty nights and, like Jesus, ate or drank nothing during this time (Exod 24:18; 34:28). Likewise, Elijah is in the wilderness for this period but receives food from an angel before his forty-day journey to Horeb (1 Kgs 19:8). It also recalls Moses who remained faithful to Yahweh, like Jesus, while the rest of the nation fell into disobedience (Exod 32:1).

Unlike Moses and Elijah, however, Jesus does not experience any divine encounters until his time of testing is complete (Matt 4:11). Rather, he is tested by the devil during this time, much like Israel was tested in the wilderness for **forty** years. The Spirit of God was present during the wilderness wanderings of Israel (Num 11:17, 25, 29; Neh 9:20; Ps 106:33; Isa 63:10-14; see Davies and Allison 1988, 355). Now Jesus is tested just as God's son "Israel" was tested.

It is unlikely that the Spirit led Jesus into the desert for the sake of being tempted by the devil. The desert was sometimes understood as a dangerous place of demons (Davies and Allison 1988, 354). Rather, this is the testing of God's Son, the representative Israelite. In Deut 8, Moses reminds a new Israelite generation of the purpose of the wilderness wandering: "Remember how the Lord your God led you all the way in the wilderness these forty years, to humble and *test* you in order to know what was in your heart, whether or not you would keep his commands" (8:2). Of course, Jesus' temptation is days, not years, but the echoes of Israel's wilderness period are unmistakable.

The Greek word for "tempt" can mean "testing" (see Deuteronomy) or "seducing or enticing" (see Gal 6:1; Jas 1:13). In Matthew, it's a combination: God's testing of his Son occurs through the three seducing proposals of Satan. While France (2007, 127) and Nolland (2005, 162-63) favor "testing," either aspect demonstrates the unwavering faithfulness of Jesus.

The Devil

The Gospels employ several terms to refer to the devil. In this text alone, there are three: **devil** (vv 1, 5, 8), "tempter" (v 3), and "Satan" (v 10). Matthew uses the terms interchangeably. What is more significant is the narrative role that the devil/Satan plays. The term "tempter" denotes one who seduces. The meaning of "Satan" in Hebrew means "the accuser" (Job 1:6), which is close to the meaning for "devil" ("slanderer" [Zech 3:1 LXX]). The tempter wants to entice Jesus not to be faithful by miraculously providing sustenance for himself (Matt 4:3-4) or putting God to the test (vv 5-7).

■ **3-10** In the first temptation (vv 3-4), Satan takes advantage of Jesus' hunger. He tempts Jesus to demonstrate his sonship by performing a miracle: **tell these stones to become bread**. Jesus responds with a quotation from Deut 8:3 [LXX]: **Man shall not live on bread alone, but on every word that comes from the mouth of God**. (Luke's quotation is limited to the first half of the verse; see Luke 4:4.)

4:3-10 Jesus' responses to Satan all come from Deuteronomy (8:3, 6:16, and 6:13 respectively). The context of these passages highlights Israel's refusal to trust Yahweh to fulfill his promises. In Deut 6—8, Yahweh warns his son, ancient Israel, to remain faithful to him, and not repeat sins of the preceding generation. However, they failed (Deut 29:22-29 [21-28 HB]).

Distrust in the Lord and his promises finds its basis in the failure of Adam and Eve; Israel was guilty of the same thing. Now, in Matthew, God sends his faithful Son as a representative Israelite demonstrating faithfulness to God and as a king is commissioned to lead Israel out of exile.

Jesus' quotation of Deut 8:3 refers to Yahweh's testing of Israel who permitted them to hunger to see if they would trust him to provide. The Israelites wanted to kill Moses for bringing them into the wilderness only to die of hunger, but the Lord wants to know what is in their hearts (Exod 16:4). The Lord promises to provide manna, but they fail to follow his instruction (vv 5, 19-20, 24-28). Jesus, on the other hand, does not end his hunger through his own miraculous ability (see Matt 14:15-21 and 15:32-39). Rather, he trusts **every word that comes from the mouth of God** (4:4), something his ancestors should have done as well.

The setting for the next temptation shifts from the wilderness to the temple. Davies and Allison suggest that "the devil is asking Jesus to perform a spectacular miracle, to give the people a sign, and thus reveal his identity to

Israel": that he is the Messiah (1988, 366-67). While some dismiss the idea that this temptation has a messianic significance mainly because 2T Jews do not interpret Ps 91 in this way (Davies and Allison 1988, 367; Hagner 1993, 67), Jewish literature does associate the Messiah's reign with the temple (e.g., *Pss. Sol.* 17) and Satan tempts Jesus as "the Son of God," which is another way of denoting the Messiah.

Satan tempts Jesus to make a spectacular leap from the temple. Satan quotes an abbreviated form of Ps 91:11-12 to provide a scriptural warrant: **For it is written: "He will command his angels concerning you, and they will lift you up in their hands, so that you will not strike your foot against a stone"** (Matt 4:4). But again, the one who will be under the protection of Yahweh's angels is the one who trusts God (Ps 91:2) and makes him his refuge and dwelling (v 9). Satan is using this passage to put Yahweh to the test and deliberately ignores the literary context of a trusting relationship between the Psalmist and God.

This temptation encourages Jesus "to test the literal truth of God's promise of protection by deliberately creating a situation in which he will be obliged to act to save his Son's life" (France 2007, 133). Jesus' response from Deut 6:16 turns the table. This is not a test of Jesus but of Yahweh. **It is also written: "Do not put the Lord your God to the test"** (Matt 4:7). Jesus rejects Satan's interpretation of the psalm and reveals what Satan is attempting to do—to incite distrust in the faithfulness of God. Jesus will not put God to the test as his ancestors did at Massah and Meribah (Exod 17:1-7).

In the final temptation, **the devil took him to a very high mountain and showed him all the kingdoms of the world and their splendor** and promises all of what he sees to Jesus if only he would **bow down and worship me** (Matt 4:8-9). Unlike his disobedient ancestors who failed to be completely loyal to Yahweh (Deut 5:7-10; 6:4), Jesus' response expresses the distinctiveness of Judaism in contrast with the pagan religions of his day and that of ancient Israel: **Worship the Lord your God, and serve him only** (Matt 4:10*b*).

Satan's offer is a blatant disregard for the foundational belief of the Jews. Hence Jesus prefaces his response with the harsh rebuke, **Away from me, Satan!** (v 10*a*; → 16:23). Jesus cites Deut 6:13, replacing "fear" with **worship** and inserts the word **only**. Satan wants worship, and Jesus refuses. The adverb **only** is connected to the literary context of Deut 6:13 as well as Satan's offer (France 2007, 135).

Preceding Deut 6:13, Moses warns the Israelites not to forget that God delivered them from Egypt and gave them cities and houses (vv 10-12), material things. Then, in vv 13-14, Moses calls Israel to fear and serve God who has given them these things and not the gods of the nations. Matthew applies this to Satan and his alleged provisions. Jesus refuses to worship Satan in exchange for power, wealth, and security and thereby show distrust toward his Father.

He trusts **only** God. The Israelites, however, turned to pagan gods instead for peace and security.

Like Jesus' first temptation, this test appeals to royal authority befitting Matthew's anointed, Messiah, Son of God (France 2007, 134; Pss 2:8; 72:8-11). Jesus refuses to acquire such power outside of a trusting relationship with his heavenly Father. Power and authority will be his, but only through suffering and death, as Jesus will reveal on another mountain at the end of the Gospel (28:16-20) (France 2007, 135). As Terrence Donaldson rightly observes: "The first and last Matthean mountains stand as literary brackets within which the drama of the obedient, suffering, yet finally vindicated Son is played out" (1985, 194).

■ **11** Saying nothing further, **the devil left him, and angels came and attended him**. Luke 4:13 foreshadows a future encounter with the devil. Matthew doesn't but Jesus will soon encounter demons to which Matthew refers in summary form (Matt 4:24). After having fasted for so long, the **angels came and attended him**, much like an angel provided for Elijah in 1 Kgs 19:4-8 (Nolland 2005, 169 n. 62). Davies and Allison suggest the provision of manna as a background: "As God once miraculously gave Israel manna in the desert, so now he feeds his Son, his Son who, unlike Adam, did not succumb to temptation and so received the food which the first man ate in paradise before the fall" (1988, 374).

FROM THE TEXT

The baptism of Jesus reveals that he is both Israel's king and God's servant. In the temptation narrative, this is put to the test. Satan tempts Jesus to distrust God, just as Israel did in the wilderness, by circumventing his identity as God's servant. He tempts Jesus to exercise power outside of relationship with God. For example, Satan asks him to rule the world, which is a rule that has no place for the cross and suffering at the hands of adversaries (see Matt 16:21). It is the will of God that Jesus suffer and die and so Jesus remains completely obedient to his will (see 26:39).

The lure of power is no less real today than it was for Jesus two thousand years ago. The power and control evident in the world today is not the way of Christ, which is characterized by sacrifice and service for the good of others. The key to remaining faithful is purity of heart and mind, empowered by the indwelling Spirit. This purity is characterized by single-minded devotion to God and his word. Israel failed this test because she doubted that God would be faithful. We, like Jesus, can overcome temptations that would have us place our trust in any worldly power other than our heavenly Father.

III. THE KINGDOM OF GOD IN GALILEE: MATTHEW 4:12—16:20

A. A Great Light Has Dawned (4:12-25)

BEHIND THE TEXT

When John is arrested, Jesus relocates to Galilee (4:12). He settles in Capernaum where he begins his ministry to fulfill a prophecy from Isaiah (4:13-14). Capernaum is an administrative center having both a centurion (8:5) and a customs post (9:9) (France 2007, 141). It is located on a trade route and, hence, is a commercial center as well (Longman 2013, 274). Jesus will return to it during his Galilean ministry (9:1). But he will eventually pronounce judgment on it for refusing to repent (11:23-24). Jesus likely calls his first disciples in this city (4:18-22).

IN THE TEXT

■ **12-17** One possible reason that Jesus **withdrew to Galilee** could be the threat from Herod and John's arrest (v 12). Both John and Jesus are in the territory of Herod Antipas (14:3). However, Capernaum puts him even closer to Herod's new capital, Tiberias. Carter suggests that "his move, rather, challenges the Roman vassal's power by asserting there a different reign, God's empire (see 4:17)" (2000, 514).

Jesus settling **in Capernaum, which was by the lake in the area of Zebulun and Naphtali** (4:13), fulfills Isa 9:1-2 [8:23—9:1 HB], a text about the restoration of the northern kingdom of Israel after 722 BCE. Matthew's reference to the tribal allotments of Zebulun and Naphtali has long lost its geographical significance. Rather, the reference makes a theological connection between the place of the beginning of Jesus' ministry, Galilee, and the fulfillment of Isa 9 (France 2007, 141).

The quotation of Isa 9:1-2 (8:23—9:1 HB) does not exactly reflect the Hebrew or Greek texts. This quotation is either an earlier version of the Hebrew influenced by the LXX (Prabhu 1976, 104, cited in France 2007, 141 n. 12; Davies and Allison 1988, 380) or is largely Matthew's own editorial work (Nolland 2005, 172; Hagner 1993, 73-74). The string of five geographical references in Matthew's version, **Land of Zebulun and land of Naphtali, the Way of the Sea, beyond the Jordan, Galilee of the Gentiles** (Matt 4:15), demonstrates his concern for the theological significance of place, as in ch 2.

In the eighth century BCE, the Assyrians not only exiled Jews from here but also replaced them with pagans (2 Kgs 15:29; 17:24-41). Three centuries later, the banished non-Jewish women and children from Ezra's reforms (Ezra 10:1-5) contributed even further to the mixed population of this area. In the mid-second century BCE, Simon the Maccabee rescued Jews in Galilee from Seleucid reign and brought them to Judea (1 Macc 5:14-23). However, fifty years later, it came under Jewish reign accompanied by forced conversions to Judaism. But Gentile influence continued.

In the time of Jesus, the Romans constructed Sepphoris, the capital of Galilee, and Perea. Both would have been populated by Gentiles. The city of Tiberias also had a largely Gentile populace (Longman 2013, 1631). Isaiah's designation "Galilee of the Gentiles" is an apt description.

Carter argues that the references to the Gentiles in Matthew's quotation stress that these are occupied lands, Assyria in Isaiah's time and now Rome in Jesus', hence the need for God's people to be delivered (2000, 517). However, he reads into Matthew too much of an imperial agenda when he claims that "darkness does not denote some spiritual condition but . . . structures (such as imperialism) contrary to God's purposes" (2000, 517). Jesus first calls his hearers in Capernaum and Galilee to "repent" (Matt 4:17).

In this light, Jesus preaches the gospel in a part of Galilee predominately inhabited by Gentiles. However, for much of Matthew, Jesus is concerned with his own people and so he begins his ministry in the Jewish city of Capernaum, much smaller than the neighboring Sepphoris and Tiberias. There is no evidence of Jesus ever visiting these major cities.

For Isaiah, those who experience exile and dislocation are **the people living in darkness . . . those living in the land of the shadow of death** (Matt 4:16). In Isa 8:19-22, the prophet describes the fate of Israel for its disobedience, "consult[ing] mediums and spiritists" (v 19) as opposed to "God's instruction and the testimony of warning" (v 20*a*). Consequently, Isaiah describes rebellious Israel as having "no light of dawn" (v 20*b*) and seeing "only distress and darkness and fearful gloom" (v 22).

In Matthew's view, the promised deliverance has dawned with the coming of Jesus in which those in Galilee **have seen a great light** and for those in **the shadow of death a light has dawned** (Matt 4:16). Light represents God's presence with his people as well as their deliverance (Exod 31:21; Ps 27:1; Isa 60:19; Shirbroun 1992, 472-73). In Isa 42:6-7 and 49:6 the servant, as one who effects salvation on behalf of Yahweh, is "a light for the Gentiles, to open eyes that are blind, to free captives from prison" (42:6*b*-7*a*). Darkness, in contrast, is "a symbol of moral and spiritual bankruptcy" (Ps 107:10; Isa 42:6-7; Bar 59:2; Davies and Allison 1988, 385).

Linking the fulfillment of this prophecy with the ministry of Jesus, Matthew states in 4:17 **from that time on Jesus began to preach, "Repent, for the kingdom of heaven has come near."** Jesus as Immanuel, God with us, manifests the reign of God, the presence of God, who begins his ministry in a region known for darkness and despair. But the light of God's reign and deliverance is soon to be realized as Jesus proclaims the kingdom and heals sickness and disease (v 23). As was the case with John's preaching, the prerequisite for living under God's reign is repentance, defined as turning to God with the whole self, living lives characterized by holiness and purity. This repentance is key to deliverance from exile or the threat of exile (→ 3:2).

■ **18-22** Before healing the sick or exorcising any demons, Jesus calls four disciples in 4:18-22. Like Mark, Matthew wants to highlight the corporate dimension of Jesus' ministry—the reign of God will not be inaugurated through the Messiah alone but also through his followers, a new Israel.

Jesus' call to Peter, Andrew, James, and John to abandon their livelihoods would not just mean a change of vocation but also a change in identity since they are leaving their families as well: **James son of Zebedee and his brother John . . . were in a boat with their father Zebedee, preparing their nets** (v 21). According to Keener, "Family businesses . . . would have been common . . . ; keeping money in the family was economically as well as socially profitable" (1999, 152). Jesus himself explains the high cost of discipleship when he commands a would-be follower not to bury his father but rather "let the dead bury their own dead" (8:22*b*).

In both instances (4:18-20 and 21-22), the two groups immediately cease their activities and **follow** Jesus who **will send** them **out to fish for people** (v 19). France insightfully notes that despite their sudden departure, they will return home, for example, when Jesus and his disciples visit Peter's house in 8:14-15 (2007, 146). This is still a radical commitment. The call of Jesus makes uncompromising demands (see 8:18-22; 10:21-22, 34-37). Unlike the rabbi-disciple relationships of his day in which the would-be follower requests to follow a rabbi, Jesus does the opposite. Jesus calls them, and they in turn **fish for people** (see 10:6-7).

■ **23-25** These verses provide the narrative and theological context for interpreting the Sermon on the Mount in chs 5—7. Then, in chs 8—9, Matthew recounts the deeds of the Messiah in the successful proclamation of the kingdom in Galilee.

Not only is Jesus **teaching in their synagogues, proclaiming the good news of the kingdom** (4:23), but he also demonstrates that God's reign has drawn near by **healing every disease and sickness among the people**. France makes the point that Matthew's description of Jesus **healing every disease and sickness among the people** and that **news about him spread all over Syria** (v 24) depicts "a phenomenally successful and popular program of healing" (2007, 151).

This is the "inaugurated eschatology" of Jesus in which God's reign is realized now over sickness, disease, and demonic influence. Not surprisingly, **large crowds from Galilee, the Decapolis** [an area of Gentile territory east of Sea of Galilee], **Jerusalem, Judea and the region across the Jordan followed him** (v 25). There is a significant Jewish population in the region across the Jordan, but it is also part of the land (Nolland 2005, 185). Jesus' ministry of physical and spiritual healing of the large crowds are a sign that the sickness and oppression associated with exile is coming to an end. Wright asserts that Jesus "saw [his mighty works] as part of the inauguration of the sovereign and healing rule of Israel's covenant god" (1996, 191).

FROM THE TEXT

In this text, Matthew introduces the nature of the reign of God proclaimed by Jesus. Through his Messiah, God's reign changes the hopeless plight of those in darkness and under the shadow of death. When Jesus begins to proclaim God's reign, the sick and oppressed are healed, bringing them into the light. This proclamation spreads very quickly so that others from far distances bring folks to Jesus for deliverance.

There is a lesson for the church in this. The proclamation of the gospel—that God now reigns—is not mere teaching but is actually manifested in life-changing ways for those who respond. As Paul puts it, just over twenty years after the ministry of Jesus, "For the kingdom of God is not a matter of talk but of power" (1 Cor 4:20). As the church, our articulation of the gospel must not only be biblically and theologically informed but also demonstrated with results that point to the reality that God indeed reigns while sickness and oppression do not.

There are some, however, who claim that when the sick are not healed or the economically oppressed do not become rich, it is not the fault of God but is a lack of faith. While not to diminish the role of faith in divine healing, for example, we live in a fallen world because the reign of God has not yet come in its fullness. In the meantime, we continue to pray for the sick and care for the marginalized, which is all a reflection of the holy love of God for his people.

B. The Sermon on the Mount (5:1—7:29)

The next five chapters contain Jesus teaching (chs 5—7) and performing miraculous deeds (chs 8—9). Before the Sermon on the Mount, Matthew summarizes this ministry: "Jesus went throughout Galilee, teaching in their synagogues, proclaiming the good news of the kingdom, and healing every disease and sickness among the people" (4:23). Matthew repeats the language of 4:23 almost verbatim at the end of ch 9 that Jesus both proclaimed the kingdom and healed the sick (v 35). The identity of Jesus as God's Messiah, who proclaims the kingdom in both word and deed, unifies these five chapters of Matthew. It builds on the identity already established in chs 1 to 4. According to Guelich, Jesus is "the 'Messiah of Word' (5-7) and the 'Messiah of Deed' (8-9)" (1982, 56).

Some scholars argue that Jesus is teaching a new Torah due to typological parallels between Matt 2—5 and the Exodus story (see Allison 1993; Ehrman 2004, 96). However, Matthew's main concern is Jesus as Messiah (e.g., 1:1), not Jesus as Moses, in whom God's saving purposes are fully revealed for Israel. Jesus is Immanuel, God with us. Thus, one should not interpret the Sermon on the Mount from a Mosaic framework but, rather, a christological one that reveals God's ecclesiological and eschatological salvation for his people (Guelich 1982, 56, 142).

1. Beatitudes (5:1-16)

BEHIND THE TEXT

Makarisms or beatitudes occur in both pagan and Jewish literature (see Davies and Allison 1988, 431-34). Matthew's beatitudes reflect those used in eschatological contexts, which are "usually addressed to people in dire straits, and the promise to them is of future consolation" (Davies and Allison 1988, 432; Ps 72:17; Dan 12:12; Tob 13:14; *1 En.* 58:2-3). They either promise consolation for those in need or reward for those who have been faithful.

While the promised consolation lies in the eschatological future, Jesus does say that the "poor in spirit" receive the kingdom now (Matt 5:3, 10). This is the starting point for the disciples of Jesus. Those who repent and believe receive God's reign in the present. This prior reality must inform our reading of the ethical demands of ch 5 since these things "depend on this present reality brought about by Jesus" (Hagner 2007, 51). Jesus as "God with us" both in the flesh with his original disciples and now through his Spirit as exalted Lord, enables his people to live holy lives that reflect God's holy character.

IN THE TEXT

■ **1-2** The **crowds** recalls the "large crowds" that have come to Jesus for healing from a variety of geographical areas in v 25. The crowds who have come to the Messiah for healing now come to him to hear his teaching. For ease of communication, Jesus **went up on a mountainside and sat down** (v 1). The phrase **went up on a mountainside** may recall the same one used to describe Moses who likewise ascends a mountain, Mount Sinai (Exod 19:3; 24:15). This does not support the argument that Jesus teaches as a new Moses, but rather points to his authority to teach in the way Moses did. The disciples, which presumably includes the Twelve, although Matthew only recounts the calling of four, also **came to him** (v 1), and **he began to teach them** (v 2). This teaching is primarily directed at the disciples while the crowds listen in (France 2007, 156).

■ **3-12** To begin this discourse, Jesus consoles his followers with a series of Beatitudes. The Greek word for **blessed**, *makarios*, denotes one who is "fortunate or happy because of circumstances" (BDAG 2000, 610). Blessedness is a reality now because of consolation and reward that await in the future. While this is true for Jewish beatitudes generally, for Jesus, the consolation and blessedness of the future reaches into the present. Already, his disciples have received the kingdom.

While the first, second, and eighth beatitudes refer to circumstances (e.g., **the poor in spirit** [v 3]), the rest refer to dispositions, **hunger and thirst for righteousness** (v 6), and virtues, such as meekness (v 5). Both the dispositions and the virtues that Jesus lists constitute the core values of the reign of God, for which there is reward (France 2007, 159; Keener 1999, 166-67). The circumstances and dispositions are also virtues since they translate into a life of humility and obedience to God, which are necessary to participate in God's reign.

The first and last beatitudes have **the kingdom of heaven** as the reward, the dynamic reign of God (vv 3, 10), which one realizes in the present. This inclusio underscores that this section includes life under God's reign now. Further, there is irony and paradox: what is prized and valued in the kingdom of this world is very different in the kingdom of heaven. In the kingdom, it is blessed to mourn because comfort will come (v 4) and to lose life is to find it (16:25*b*).

Unlike Luke's "Blessed are you who are poor," Matthew refers to **the poor in spirit** (v 3*a*). This connotes a spiritual poverty, a desirable disposition for those wishing to live under God's reign. For these ones **theirs is the kingdom of heaven** (v 3*b*). In Isa 66:2, the Lord favors "those who are humble [or poor] and contrite in spirit." The Hebrew word for "humble" is also the word that's translated as "poor." The virtue of spiritual poverty is mentioned several times in the first-century BCE Jewish text *Psalms of Solomon* as well as at Qumran.

While **those who mourn** are obviously not "happy," they are in a blessed or favorable state because **they will be comforted**. When the reign of God does come and the Lord's favor is upon his people, according to Isa 61:2-3, those who mourn will be comforted, and they will receive "the oil of joy instead of mourning." Mourning is a hallmark of exilic life, but it will give way to comfort and joy, marking the end of exile (see Isa 57:18; Jer 31:15; Zech 8:19). This beatitude also echoes Isa 40. The prophet's announcement that captivity is now over begins with a consolation of "comfort" (v 1) for the "weary" and "weak" (v 29). With Jesus and his proclamation of God's reign, this comfort begins now. He heals and restores the sick and marginalized (Matt 4:23; 9:35); he calls the "weary and burdened" to himself (11:28).

Next, Jesus says, **Blessed are the meek** (5:5). The poor/meek will have their fortunes reversed when the Lord stretches out his hand against those who practice evil and oppression (Ps 37:11-13; Isa 61:1-2). Like Matt 5:5 (**they will inherit the earth**), Ps 37:11 refers not only to the meek but also to their reward (see v 11*a*).

This allusion could be intentional as the whole psalm focuses on the reversal of fortunes, the theme that defines vv 3-12 (France 2007, 166). While the psalm promises the land, Matthew envisages something much greater: a renewed earth characterized by the complete reign of God where the hostile, arrogant, and powerful have no place.

In the meantime, Matthew's audience is to be "the salt of the *earth*" (Matt 5:13) living under the authority of the ascended and exalted Jesus for whom "all authority in heaven and on *earth* has been given" (28:18). Some feel that Ps 37, with its emphasis on the restoration of the land, should be "divorced" from Matt 5:5 (e.g., Davies 1994, 362). However, the context of Ps 37:11 underscores Matthew's theme of reversal.

In Matt 5:6, Jesus declares, **Blessed are those who hunger and thirst for righteousness, for they will be filled**. While **righteousness** refers to moral integrity (France 2007, 167; Davies and Allison 1988, 453), it could also be a shorthand way of referring to God's own faithfulness to his people (Gundry 1982, 70; Hagner 1993, 93).

In some OT texts, **righteousness** refers to both: God's faithfulness to restore the fortunes of Israel (Ps 98:2-3; Isa 51:4-5; 52:10) and the type of behavior that he expects of them (Gen 6:9; 7:1; Deut 6:25; Pss 1:6; 15:2; → Matt 3:13-15 sidebar, "Righteousness"). The former option fits the preceding literary context because the vindication of **the poor in spirit, those who mourn**, and **the meek** will only occur when God acts in faithfulness to restore his people. For Matthew, this restoration and salvation has now begun through his anointed Son, Jesus Messiah.

The Greek word translated **filled** refers to a satiated state (BDAG 2000, 1087), which coheres with the reversals soon to come for the disadvantaged. Hagner suggests that Ps 107 (106 LXX) reflects the movement of this beatitude: in vv 5-6 the Psalmist refers to those who thirst and hunger, whom the Lord delivers, and then in v 9 he declares that "he satisfies the thirsty and fills the hungry with good things" (1993, 93). God is a righteous God who will act to "fill" his people.

The spiritual disposition of hungering and thirsting for righteousness understood as ethical faithfulness toward God and others relates to the next three beatitudes. God expects his people to be **merciful** (Matt 5:7), **pure in heart** (v 8), and **peacemakers** (v 9). In v 20, Jesus calls his disciples to a level of righteousness that surpasses that of the scribes and Pharisees.

In light of vv 7-9, this is not a call to greater ritual purity (→ v 20) but to hearts and actions that reflect God's righteousness of mercy, purity, and peace to the lost, the harassed, and the helpless. The new covenant that Messiah Jesus establishes with his people enables this righteousness. Under God's present reign, God's people are filled with that righteousness now (→ 6:33). Righteousness in this sense is both gift and demand (Brower 2005, 113).

Under God's reign, the **merciful** are happy **for they will be shown mercy** (5:7). France notes that, although mercy and forgiveness are closely related, mercy "is a generous attitude which is willing to see things from the other's point of view and is not quick to take offense or to gloat over others' shortcomings" (France 2007, 168). Here we get a clear picture of the nature of God's reign. It is characterized by mercy, which is embodied in the ministry of Jesus himself (9:12-13).

In 5:8, **Blessed are the pure in heart, for they will see God**, Matthew alludes to Ps 24. In the psalm, the one who is fit to "ascend the mountain of the Lord" and "stand in his holy place" (v 3) is "the one who has clean hands and a pure heart" (v 4*a*). Matthew's theme of reversal and vindication is also reflected in the psalm. Those who remain in a faithful trusting relationship with the Lord "will receive blessing . . . and vindication from God their Savior" (Ps 24:5).

The purity of heart to which Jesus and the Psalmist refer is not ritual purity but rather moral purity. That is, pure intention of the heart focused on obedience to God and not trusting "in an idol or swear[ing] by a false god" (v 4*b*). The holiness to which Jesus calls his followers is likewise centered on the heart from which evil springs and over which ritual purity has no control (→ Matt 15:1-20 and below on 5:21-48). Much of Jesus' teaching in the sermon is concerned with inward purity that animates outward acts of righteousness (6:1-18, 21; 7:16-20).

The reward for internal purity is to **see God** (5:8). This is usually the privilege of angels and very few humans (Exod 24:10; Isa 6:1). According to Davies and Allison, "There are two biblical traditions about seeing God. One seems to put this out of the realm of possibility (Exod 3.6; 19.21, . . .), the other to make it a blessed goal (Ps 11.7; 17.15; Job 19.26)" (1988, 457).

The salient feature in both traditions is the reality or prospect of being in the presence of God himself. This is the desire and goal of God's people, to be present with him for eternity, holy people with their holy God (Exod 33:15-16; Ezek 36:24-28; Rev 21:1-4). As Immanuel, the purity of God is manifested on earth, when Jesus touches the unclean leper (Matt 8:3) and ministers to a Gentile woman in her Gentile lands (15:21-28).

The holiness of God is manifested "by the integrity of being . . . identified wholly and unreservedly with the purposes of God in compassion and redemption for His lost and dying world" (Brower 2005, 115). Such identification with God's saving purposes enables his people to discern God at work in the most unpromising and unlikely places. This is something that the Pharisees miss when they question Jesus sharing table fellowship with sinners and tax collectors (9:10-13).

Similar to mercy and purity, peace is another highly prized feature of God's reign: **Blessed are the peacemakers, for they will be called children of God** (5:9). For Paul, the kingdom of God is characterized by "righteousness, peace and joy in the Holy Spirit" (Rom 14:17; see also Isa 9:6; 55:12). Those who seek peace when there is division and strife embody what it means to be his **children**. In Matt 5:44-45 those who love enemies and pray for persecutors likewise receive a unique familial status with God: "that you may be children of your Father in heaven" (v 45). Jesus himself provides practical instruction on reconciliation and peacemaking within the community in 18:15-17. In several Jewish texts, sonship becomes a reality in the eschaton (*Pss. Sol.* 17:27; *Sib. Or.* 3:702; Rom 8:23; Rev 21:7), but in Matthew, that familial relationship begins now. For example, Jesus teaches his disciples to address God as "our Father" (6:9).

The last two beatitudes focus on persecution, a likely fate for the peacemakers who intervene in hostile situations. The first is **those who are persecuted because of righteousness** (v 10*a*). Righteousness here refers to the moral responsibility placed on believers by the gospel in which we reflect the reign of God in mercy, purity, and peacemaking. The world, however, has little place for such things, and those who suggest otherwise are easily rebuffed or, worse yet, persecuted. Nonetheless, those who persevere have as their possession **the kingdom of heaven**—the present and future reign of God (v 10*b*).

In the last beatitude (v 11), Jesus expands on what persecution entails from living a righteous life: **Blessed are you when people insult you, persecute**

you, and falsely say all kinds of evil against you because of me. For Jesus, the prospect of such treatment becomes reality at the Jewish and Roman trials (26:67-68; 27:27-31). His disciples should not be surprised if they face the same things on account of him (10:17-19).

Counterintuitively from the world's perspective, Jesus exhorts his hearers to **rejoice and be glad, because great is your reward in heaven, for in the same way they persecuted the prophets who were before you** (v 12). In Jewish tradition, the prophets who spoke the truth were known for having suffered much as a result (2 Kgs 17:13-14; 2 Chr 36:16; Jer 26:7-9). Suffering for the gospel is a key aspect of what it means to follow Jesus (e.g., Matt 10:16-23; 16:24-27; 20:20-23).

Matthew does not define the rewards for this other than that there is a great reward in heaven. Some suggest relationship with God (France 2007, 173), comfort from God (Keener 1999, 166), or "divine approval" (Davies and Allison 1988, 464). As in reading other passages that promise heavenly rewards and other unknown treasures, interpreters should be cautious about identifying it with any precision (see also 1 Pet 1:4*b*-5; 1 Tim 6:19).

■ **13-16** The Beatitudes express truth about God and his reign, whether it is reversal of plight for the meek and poor or reward for the merciful in the future. At the same time, the Beatitudes manifest kingdom ethics in the present. Life under God's reign results in transformed lives characterized by humility, purity, and peace as well as welcome for the oppressed and marginalized. In light of this, Jesus declares that his disciples are **salt of the earth** (v 13) and **light of the world** (v 14).

In the ancient world, salt functioned both as a source of flavor and as a preservative. France suggests that it could be taken both ways (2007, 174). Davies and Allison list a variety of functions of salt and cautiously conclude that "given the various uses for salt . . . and its several symbolic associations, it is quite impossible to decide what one characteristic is to the fore in Mt 5.13" (1988, 473).

Since Jesus' declaration that his followers **are the salt of the earth** (v 13*a*) parallels the statement that they **are the light of the world** (v 14*a*), it could be that "the disciples, like salt, have several characteristic qualities . . . without which they would cease to be what they are and instead become useless" (Davies and Allison 1988, 473; see also Hagner 1993, 99).

There is also a warning here for Jesus' followers that their testimony not be taken for granted because it can lose its effectiveness and distinctiveness if not tended, just as salt can lose its ability to preserve (v 13) (France 2007, 175; Davies and Allison 1988, 474). Ancient salt is not the purified sodium chloride used today. It contained other minerals, and if the salt content gradually dissipates, then **the salt loses its saltiness** (France 2007, 175). In the same way, the witness of Jesus' followers begins to fade if they downplay the costly call of the gospel, which includes the acceptance of persecution (e.g., 10:17-19), the relinquishment of selfish desires (13:22; 16:24-25), and love for enemies (5:44).

Whatever Jesus intends by the metaphor of salt, it is clear that the disciples influence the world around them, which is made clearer by the following metaphor of **light**. Davies and Allison note that "it is not the Torah or the temple or Jerusalem or Israel or some group within Israel (such as the Pharisees) that is the salt or light of the world . . . but Jesus' followers (the 'you' is emphatic)" (1988, 472).

Thinking of the metaphor in this way, **light** relates to Jesus' baptism, in which he and his disciples embody a new Israel. The light of this redefined nation will shine not just for ethnic Israel but for the **world**. This foreshadows Matthew's Gentile mission, which will progressively unfold throughout the Gospel culminating in 28:19-20, hence fulfilling Isa 49:6: "I will also make you a light for the Gentiles, that my salvation may reach to the ends of the earth."

The reference to **a town built on a hill cannot be hidden** in Matt 5:14*b*, could refer to Nazareth, built on the side of a mount whose lights would be visible to others at night. Jesus also speaks about a light that is not meant to be **put . . . under a bowl** but, rather, the people of the house **put it on its stand, and it gives light to everyone in the house** (v 15). He then explains this metaphor in v 16 as **good deeds** that others may then see and **glorify your Father in heaven** as a result.

Kingdom ethics of showing mercy and making peace, for example, are tangible deeds, good works, which will draw people, Jew and Gentile alike, to the one whose character is mercy and peace, **your Father in heaven** (v 16*b*). The personal ethics that Jesus describes at various points in vv 21-48, which fulfill God's intention for the Law at Sinai, reveals the holy character of God himself and, moreover, that his people can reflect his character. For this reason, the faith community in whom Immanuel dwells are **salt** and **light**. Messiah Jesus who is with his people "always" (28:20) forms them into a holy people who reflect God's merciful and just ways to the **world**. This witness is not effected by one individual, but rather the community of believers whom Matthew addresses using the second-person plural "you" in both 5:13 and 14.

FROM THE TEXT

The Beatitudes both console the disenfranchised and encourage the faithful. In some Christian circles, folks seldom feel comfortable sharing their spiritual deprivation or emotional pain. Some may feel inadequate because of their own moral shortcomings in the face of a completely holy God. Holiness people, at times, have a tendency to portray God as an unmerciful judge and harsh critic who has little margin for mercy and grace. After all, he has a holy character to defend!

However, the ability of God to relate to his people with compassion and mercy is a crucial aspect of his holy character, which comes to fullest expression in the words and deeds of his Messiah. For the meek and humble, Jesus claims that they are "blessed" not only because they realize the truth about themselves but also because they are in a position to receive God's reign just as are the "poor in Spirit." The reign of God in Messiah Jesus is also for the spiritually deprived, the emotionally distressed, and the social outcast. Jesus begins his ministry in the place of "darkness" and in "the shadow of death" (Matt 4:16). The God revealed in Matthew is the same God of Exodus who hears the cries of his people and sees their misery (see Exod 2:23-25). God is a righteous and faithful God who knows the pain and the difficulty of his people (e.g., Exod 2:23) and his Messiah is no different. This is how our holy God relates to his people.

2. Fulfillment of the Law and Prophets (5:17-48)

BEHIND THE TEXT

In the Beatitudes, Jesus teaches that the kingdom is for those who recognize their need and also that the hallmarks of this kingdom are mercy, purity, and peace. Those who live in these ways reflect the holy character of God himself and participate with him in his mission to redeem the world. Consequently, Jesus declares that his followers are "the light of the world" (v 14).

Although it may appear that the content of the sermon changes in vv 17-48, it does not. In this section, Jesus builds upon the ethics he introduces in the Beatitudes. For example, the "pure in heart" (v 8*a*) do not look "at a woman lustfully" (v 28) and the "merciful" (v 7) are those who "love [their] enemies" (v 44). The major difference between the Beatitudes and this section is that the Mosaic law is now the framework.

When Jesus teaches that he has come to "fulfill" the Law, he means that his teaching intensifies it "precisely in its own direction" (Brower 2004, 302). That is, he emphasizes the transformation of heart and mind that then leads to outward acts of righteousness, something God always intended for his people, and thereby fulfills the intention of the Law. The transformation Jesus expects will result in a righteousness that exceeds that of the Pharisees (vv 18-20)!

Beginning in v 21, Jesus presents a collection of so-called antitheses. He quotes a series of traditional, taught laws and then develops them with an intensified precept, to which some refer as an antithesis. However, the precept centers not on an opposing idea but rather an intensified one related to the transformation of the heart.

Davies and Allison argue that "the contrast involves not contradiction but transcendence" (1988, 507; see also Keener 1999, 181-82). The term "transcendence" downplays the foundational role of the Law in Jesus' teaching, and his identity as God's Messiah who now speaks "the very word of God to his people" (Brower 2004, 295). The teaching Jesus gives is rooted in God's intention for the Mosaic law to form a holy people.

IN THE TEXT

■ **17-20** Verse 17 confirms the Jewish portrayal of Jesus that Matthew has depicted so far in his Gospel. No less than six times Matthew highlights that the birth of the Messiah as well as the beginning of his ministry fulfills OT prophecy. Further, Jesus' journey to and return from Egypt, flight from Herod, baptism by John, temptation in the wilderness, and now his Sermon on the Mount all point to the restoration of the nation of Israel. Jesus is the leader of this restoration as God's messianic King who now speaks God's word to Israel.

In light of this OT continuity, Jesus has not **come to abolish the Law or the Prophets** (v 17*a*). He has **not come to abolish them but to fulfill them** (v 17*b*). For Jesus, **the Law and the Prophets** are likely "a canon- or integrity-formula that summarizes God's revelation" of salvation thus far in the Scriptures of Israel (Deines 2008, 75). This coheres with twelve uses of Matthew's verb **to fulfill**, which focus on the fulfillment of Scripture, all of which highlight a "christology that perceives Jesus to be the Messiah Son of God who comes as the fulfillment of God's promise to his people" (Guelich 1982, 142; Deines 2008, 74). What Jesus says about the Law with "authority" (7:28) inaugurates a way of being the holy people of God through which God's intention for the Law is fulfilled in the lives of his people. Davies and Allison put it like this: "The *telos* [goal or purpose] which the Torah anticipated, namely, the Messiah, has come and revealed the law's definitive meaning" (1988, 486).

According to 5:18, the Law remains in effect **until heaven and earth disappear**, which, from a Jewish perspective, would be never (Nolland 2005, 220). Fletcher-Louis attempts to argue that this language is a metaphor for the destruction of the temple, which does coincide with the passing away of "this generation" at the temple's destruction (2013, 163; → Matt 24:34-35), but this has not persuaded most scholars.

The phrase appears to be in tension with the next temporal clause, which concludes the verse: the Law remains in effect **until everything is accomplished**. However, Jesus applies the phrase "until all these things have happened" (*heōs an panta tauta genētai* [24:34*b*]) to the destruction of the temple. Further, the same language reappears to describe the report of the guards about Jesus' crucifixion and resurrection: "everything that had happened" (*hapanta ta genomena* [28:11*b*]). Matthew juxtaposes this report with the women who are on their way to Galilee to be reunited with the resurrected Christ! The temple's destruction, the death and resurrection of Jesus as well as the sending of the women to the resurrected Jesus mark the accomplishment of "all things." A new eschatological age has dawned! As the Messiah who dies sacrificially for his people, "Jesus came bringing not a new law but a new covenant . . . God offers to his own a new starting point in relationship with himself and with others" (Guelich 1982, 29; see also Brower 2004, 296).

Associating the phrases **until heaven and earth disappear** and **until everything is accomplished** with events later in the Gospel provides a theological framework for interpreting the emphatic instruction of Jesus about the Law in v 18: **not the smallest letter** or **not the least stroke of a pen** of the Law **will by any means disappear** (v 18*b*).

The **smallest letter** likely refers to the smallest Hebrew letter, *yodh*, and the **least stroke of a pen** refers to the smallest lines that form Hebrew letters. Strict Pharisaic obedience to the Law, which in Matthew is a religion of outward performance (see Matt 23), disappears with the judgment of the most central symbol of Judaism, the temple, the redemptive death of Jesus on the cross, and his subsequent resurrection leading to the formation of new holy people of God. Their holiness is not founded upon obedience to scribal law, assuming that it's even possible, but rather upon the shed blood of Jesus that gives rise to a new covenant where sin is forgiven.

The question of the Law to which Jesus refers when he speaks of **these commands** (5:19) is not immediately clear. Is he speaking about the minute detail of the Mosaic law in v 18 or is it his description of a fulfilled Mosaic law in vv 21-48? France argues that scholars who identify **these commands** with those of Jesus is a "convenient suggestion" and ignore the fact that they are "the same as the jot and tittle of v. 18" (2007, 187).

Matthew's **therefore** at the beginning of v 19 continues to highlight the centrality of the Mosaic law and its continuing importance, but only those aspects of the Law as redefined or even "radicalized" (Brower 2005, 122) in the teaching of Jesus beginning in v 21. Further, in v 17, the minutiae of the Law will end at the death and resurrection of Jesus. This is anticipated in the ministry of Jesus himself where he clearly breaches the laws of ritual purity when he touches an unclean leper (8:3), for example.

Disciples of Jesus follow Torah but "only to the extent that it expressed conduct in keeping with the Father's will as revealed through Jesus Messiah" (Guelich 1982, 29). Therefore, **these commands** must refer to the Messiah who now teaches in the place of Moses and so **anyone who sets aside one of the least of these commands and teaches others accordingly will be called least in the kingdom of heaven, but whoever practices and teaches these commands will be called great in the kingdom of heaven** (5:19).

In v 20, Jesus now radicalizes the idea of **righteousness** in which the righteousness of the disciples must surpass **that of the Pharisees and the teachers of the law**; otherwise, they **will certainly not enter the kingdom of heaven**. It is unlikely that Jesus advocates a more rigorous obedience to the legal demands of the Mosaic law than the Pharisees practiced. Jesus envisages a **righteousness** that transforms the heart and mind, a radical righteousness that gives rise to righteous behaviors, which he describes in vv 21-47. This way of living comes from the law written on the heart "in which the Law becomes part of the interiority of the covenant people, not an external code . . . [and]

is based on the new relationship . . . brought to fruition by the death of Jesus Messiah" (Brower 2005, 122).

Members of this new covenant exercise a righteousness that welcomes tax collectors and sinners because it is singularly concerned for the restoration of the other, mirroring the righteousness of God himself (see 5:3-10). Jesus and his followers feed the hungry, welcome the sinner, heal the sick, not to earn righteousness but because they are righteous.

■ **21-26** Jesus begins each antithesis with the line **You have heard that it was said to the people long ago** (v 21*a*). This highlights the antiquity of the command originally given from God, through Moses, to the Israelites (Exod 24:3; Nolland 2005, 229). Restating what was once taught to the Israelites, Jesus says, **You shall not murder, and anyone who murders will be subject to judgment** (Matt 5:21*b*). Prohibition of murder is the sixth commandment (Exod 20:13 and Deut 5:17). This is given a rationale in Gen 9:6: one should not murder because humans are made in the divine image. This passage also warns that those who murder will themselves be judged (see also Deut 21:1-9).

In Matt 5:22, Jesus reveals what motivates murder and anger and prohibits this attitude. Just as one who murders is liable to judgment (v 21), **anyone who is angry with a brother or sister will be subject to judgment** (v 22*a*). Anger is tantamount to murder. Jesus then provides examples of other ways in which anger may manifest: **Anyone who says to a brother or sister, "Raca," is answerable to the court. And anyone who says, "You fool!" will be in danger of the fire of hell** (v 22*b*).

Raca is an Aramaism meaning "one who lacks intelligence," a "numbskull, fool" (BDAG 2000, 903). Likewise, **fool** is a term of derision likely having the same connotation as **raca**, or is merely the Greek translation of the Aramaic term for **raca** (BDAG 2000, 663). Davies and Allison suggest that the two terms are synonymous (1988, 514).

The penalty of labeling someone **raca** is trial before the Jewish court, and calling someone a **fool** carries a harsh sentence, **danger of the fire of hell**. These are warnings not to let anger gain a foothold lest Jesus' followers insult others, or it develops into murder. This first "antithesis" is a clear example of Jesus' radicalization of the Mosaic law that reveals God's holy purposes. Not only is it insufficient not to murder, but also, one must not let the heart be overcome with anger that would lead to harmful actions in word or deed.

Hell

The word *gehenna*, translated as "hell," is the Greek version of a Hebrew word referring to a desecrated valley where children were sacrificed to the Ammonite god Molek (2 Kgs 23:10). God pronounced judgment on this valley, located southwest of Jerusalem, in Jeremiah (7:30-32; 19:5-7) and, in Matt 23:15, Jesus refers to an ungodly person as "a child of hell [*gehenna*]." In the time of Jesus, it was a burning garbage dump, and sometimes the dead bodies of criminals were discarded there (Davies and Allison 1988, 514-15). Jesus' audience likely thought of this valley when he spoke about hell in Matthew (5:22, 29-30; 10:28; 18:9; 23:15, 33). *Gehenna* is a metaphor for hell and some believe that this valley is the eternal place of judgment (*1 En.* 27:1-2; 54:1-6; 56:3-4; 90:26-28; *4 Ezra* 7:36). Jesus' use of the term suggests that hell, like heaven, is a place prepared elsewhere (Matt 25:41).

Now that Jesus has considered offending parties, those who are given to anger, he turns to those that have been offended (5:23). In a hypothetical but very probable scenario, Jesus teaches, **If you are offering your gift at the altar and there remember that your brother or sister has something against you, leave your gift there in front of the altar** (vv 23-24*a*).

Jesus calls his followers not only to avoid anger (v 22), but if they have manifested a hostile attitude toward another person, it must be made right. To leave a sacrificial **gift at the altar** to **go and be reconciled** to the offended party echoes a number of prophetic texts in the OT that highlight care and concern for others over sacrificial ritual (Hos 6:6; Mic 6:8). Once reconciled, **then come and offer your gift** (Matt 5:24*b*). Reconciliation is the antidote to the fractures in relationship caused by anger and, moreover, is rooted in the character of God himself who comes to save his people from their rebellious state (see Rom 5:10).

Jesus exhorts his hearers to be reconciled with one another hastily: **Settle matters quickly with your adversary who is taking you to court** (Matt 5:25*a*). This picks up on the warning that one who labels another **"raca" is answerable to the court** (v 22). Restitution must be made **on the way, or your adversary may hand you over to the judge** resulting in imprisonment (v 25*b*). Those sent to jail for unresolved offenses will be there **until [they] have paid the last penny** (v 26).

Jesus is referring to the Roman system of punishment. There is no reference in Jewish literature for incarceration when one could not meet a court-imposed financial obligation (Nolland 2005, 234). **The last penny** refers to the *quadrans*, which is the smallest Roman coin. Verses 25-26 imply that just as the pagan judiciary is concerned with justice, so is God! This warning demonstrates the nature of God's reign and that injustice is to be put to right, even in the present. Restitution, reconciliation, and forgiveness must, however, be rooted in the heart (18:35), which Jesus drives home in 5:44-47.

■ **27-30** Next, Jesus quotes the commandment **You shall not commit adultery** (v 27). The following antithesis homes in on a misguided affection of the heart that, if left unchecked, can lead to adultery: **But I tell you that anyone who looks at a woman lustfully has already committed adultery with her in his heart** (v 28). The **look** does not refer to a passing glance at another's beauty but to conspiring and planning to possess a married woman for one's own ends (Keener 1999, 189). The Greek word translated **lustfully** is the same one used in the LXX for the word "covet" in the tenth commandment. Moses prohibits an Israelite from coveting a neighbor's property, which includes his wife (Exod 20:17). Brower notes that this commandment focuses on "the inner disposition of the person in the covenant community. For Jesus, then, the law is being intensified precisely in its own direction" (2004, 302).

Jesus calls for a transformed heart that loves the other perfectly and is not enslaved to a sexual desire that uses the opposite sex to gratify itself, such as in acts of adultery. "For Jesus, then, adultery defined as covetousness is the opposite of 'loving your neighbor as yourself'" (Brower 2004, 303). As with tolerating anger and engaging in the abusive language that stems from it, there will be judgment for those who persist in lust leading to sexual immorality; God has something to say about attitudes and behaviors that dehumanize the other.

Jesus calls his hearers not to tolerate anything in their lives that would make room for impurity and, ultimately, the absence of love. Speaking with hyperbole he says, **If your right eye causes you to stumble, gouge it out and throw it away. It is better for you to lose one part of your body than for your whole body to be thrown into hell. And if your right hand causes you to stumble, cut it off and throw it away. It is better for you to lose one part of your body than for your whole body to go into hell** (Matt 5:29-30). Reference to the **eye** in v 29 first expresses the lustful look and then to the **hand** in v 30, the means by which one engages in adultery (Nolland 2005, 238).

To **stumble** in Matthew is to veer off the path of salvation, either through
one's own attitudes and actions, as is the case here (see also 13:21; 18:8-9; 5:31-32
24:10), or through the actions of others that would cause believers to go astray (13:21; 18:6-7). By using this imagery, Jesus is not calling his disciples to literally injure themselves. This would not foster the love and holiness that God desires any more than obedience to external, Pharisaic legislation. Those who preach and teach these texts must communicate clearly that Jesus is not giving literal commands! Rather, he is saying that believers should not tolerate anything that would cause them to fall off the way. As Nolland indicates, "The goal is what is important, not the means" (2005, 239).

■ 31-32 Jesus quotes not a commandment but a provision found only in Deut 24:1-4 in which a husband could divorce his wife for a number of reasons subsumed under the following: "because he finds something indecent about her" (v 1*a*). Although the meaning of the Hebrew word translated "indecent" is unclear, it may refer to a disgraceful or shameful act in which a married woman exposes her pudenda (BDB 1979, 6172).

It is quite likely that Jewish males exploited an open-ended interpretation of "indecency" such that they were divorcing their wives for selfish reasons and not anything really indecent. Davies and Allison indicate that "divorce was relatively easy and was not considered a grave misdeed" during the time of Jesus (1988, 528). This is likely what prompts the Pharisees' question to Jesus: "Is it lawful for a man to divorce his wife for any and every reason?" (19:3).

Jesus warns that those who divorce their wives for any reason other than unfaithfulness **makes her the victim of adultery, and anyone who marries a divorced woman commits adultery** (5:32*b*). The divorced woman would automatically be guilty of adultery as she would be forced to remarry so that her husband could provide for her. Women, for the most part, did not work and have their choice of employment opportunities in the male-dominated, socioeconomic culture of the Greco-Roman world. According to v 32*b*, the next husband becomes an adulterer because he is having sexual relations with a woman who is still married to her original spouse who has divorced her for reasons other than marital unfaithfulness. Jesus teaches that marriage is not a bond based on convenience but, rather, unwavering commitment.

This passage is an important reminder that Christian marriage is a commitment for life and not one of convenience; divorce is an absolute last resort. The provision of Deut 24 does not reflect the ideal of Gen 2:23-24 in which the first man sings a hymn about the woman and the author concludes that man and woman "become one flesh" as Jesus himself affirms in Matt 19:4-6. Jesus says, "Therefore what God has joined together, let no one separate" (v 6*b*). Moses gave the legislation in Deuteronomy because Israel's "hearts were hard" (v 8). This is legislation to deal with human sin, providing a moral guideline for divorce or as France puts it, "a law which aims to control human failure" (2007, 213).

Christians who have ended up divorced have been outrightly ostracized or, less obviously, subtly censured by some faith communities. The same can be said for those guilty of adultery. Faith communities defined by the redemptive, covenant forming work of Jesus must show grace and mercy not only to the outsiders but to the insiders as well who have lost their way. If the church cannot even accept their own, at times, how will it ever accept the sinner and tax collector from the outside?

■ **33-37** The two injunctions, **Do not break your oath, but fulfill to the Lord the vows you have made** (v 33*b*), are not found in a specific OT text. Rather, "They represent the gist of a number of passages in the Law and elsewhere in the OT which require oaths and/or vows be taken seriously" (France 2007, 214). France suggests that they allude to false swearing against one's neighbor prohibited in the ninth commandment, or the third one in which one would misuse the Lord's name by providing a "false oath" (2007, 214). However, the legislation Jesus quotes ensures that God's people follow through on their commitments, and that it is not about making a deceptive oath to advance personal gain, per se, as in the ninth commandment.

In v 33*b*, the Greek word translated **do not break your oath** means a failure "to do what one has promised under oath" (BDAG 2000, 376). Unlike vows that where voluntary, oaths were, at times, required (Exod 22:11). As the second half of this legislation expresses, vows can be made to the Lord: **but fulfill to the Lord the vows you have made** (Matt 5:33*b*). Further, in the OT and elsewhere in Matthew, vows can be made to one another (Lev 5:4; Num

30:11 [12 HB]; Matt 14:7; 26:72). In contrast, Jesus does not want his believers to **swear an oath at all** (5:34*a*). This finds some basis in Deut 23:22 [23 HB]: "But if you refrain from making a vow, you will not be guilty," implying that since you did not make a vow, there is no promise to break.

Following Jesus' sweeping prohibition of making oaths is a series of scenarios by which one might swear **either by heaven, for it is God's throne; or by the earth, for it is his footstool; or by Jerusalem, for it is the city of the Great King. And do not swear by your head, for you cannot make even one hair white or black** (Matt 5:34*b*-36). Jesus does not want his followers swearing by heaven, earth, or Jerusalem because they are each connected to God.

If his followers swear by any of these and fail to make good on their promises, they profane God's holiness and faithfulness because he is a God of his word. According to France, "Oaths normally invoked God as the guarantor of the person's word, and it was this which made it so serious a matter to break them" (2007, 215; see also Keener 1999, 194-95). To swear by one's head is completely futile as humans, who **cannot make even one hair white or black**, do not compare with the almighty power of God for whom heaven is his throne and the earth is his footstool.

Rather, Jesus calls his disciples to a simple righteousness where they need to commit and stick with it. To rely on oaths and vows calls into question the legitimacy of one's commitment since **anything beyond this** [a simple yes or no] **comes from the evil one** (v 37). While the NIV has **evil one**, the Greek could also be rendered "evil." In either case, "evil" and **evil one** are associated with a realm that is hostile toward Jesus and his ministry.

■ **38-42** Jesus cites legislation repeated a few times in the Pentateuch: **You have heard that it was said, "Eye for eye, and tooth for tooth"** (Exod 21:24; Lev 24:20; Deut 19:21). In its original application, the OT laws of *lex talionis* required a physical punishment that met the crime: "eye for eye, tooth for tooth, hand for hand, foot for foot, burn for burn, wound for wound, bruise for bruise" (Exod 21:24-25). This reflects a strong concern for justice to highlight "the full seriousness of the crime committed (Dt. 19:21: 'show no pity') and making sure that the guilty party 'bear[s] the sin' and the whole community not be contaminated" (Nolland 2005, 256). Likely by the time of Jesus, these physical penalties became monetary (France 2007, 219; Nolland 2005, 256).

In contrast to *lex talionis*, Jesus calls his disciples to **not resist an evil person** (Matt 5:39*a*). Through four scenarios (vv 39*b*-42), we see that the disciples are not to resist those who perpetrate evil and even to give them more than they are demanding!

In the first one, if one is struck **on the right cheek, turn to them the other cheek also** (v 39*b*). Slapping someone on the right cheek would require a backhanded slap with the right hand, assuming the perpetrator was right-handed. A left-handed slap is considered especially offensive, which only heightens the intensity of this teaching (France 2007, 220; Nolland 2005, 197). As for the followers of Jesus, they will see no justice but, rather, are to turn the other cheek and so face the prospect of being struck again and hence submit to aggression. However, turning the other cheek represents a "preference for suffering wrong over feeding the spiral of violence" (France 2007, 258).

In the second, **if anyone wants to sue you and take your shirt, hand over your coat as well** (v 40). Old Testament legislation protects Israelites from having to relinquish their coats or outer garments, which function as a blanket for warmth (Exod 22:26-27 [25-26 HB]; Deut 24:12-13). Not unlike the first scenario, the disciples go above and beyond what the other party expects would happen. Jesus wants his disciples to value sacrificial service to others, even beyond what they need, over the possessions of this world (Keener 1999, 198). It is this type of love that fulfills the commandment to love your neighbor as yourself, which is itself a reflection of God's love. Behaving in these ways reflects the holiness that God always intended for Israel, and so that is why this love is the fulfillment of "the Law and the Prophets" (Matt 22:40).

Some suggest that turning the other cheek or offering one's outer garment is a form of resistance. The former "demonstrates that one does not value human honor [and so] . . . could constitute a form of resistance by showing contempt for the value of the insulter's . . . opinions" (Keener 1999, 198). The latter draws attention to the aggressiveness of "the plaintiff's demands [that] are not resisted, indeed they are exceeded, but they are in the process unmasked for what they are" (Nolland 2005, 259).

5:43-47 In 5:41, the third scenario draws upon Roman impressment laws, in which regular citizens and their possessions could be requisitioned for the state. The Greek word for "force" is often used to describe such moments of involuntary help. For example, Simon is compelled by the Romans to carry Jesus' cross (27:32). If this should happen to the disciples, they should double what is required: **If anyone forces you to go one mile, go with them two miles** (5:41). Since this practice is particularly associated with the Romans, it would be very difficult for a Jew in occupied Palestine to accept (France 2007, 222).

Finally, in the fourth scenario (v 42), Jesus calls his followers to **give to the one who asks you, and do not turn away from the one who wants to borrow from you**. Again, Jesus requires an unconditional response to one who has need, as in vv 40-41. The **one who asks** calls to mind a beggar on the street. The **one who wants to borrow** could require a higher sum of money as it is the borrower who sets the amount, which the lender, the disciples, must willingly give. For Jesus' followers, a life of selfless giving is a requirement. One must exercise discernment when lending money or giving to those in need. Sometimes these actions are genuinely helpful, but other times they are regressive, because they leave the person no further ahead when the gift is gone.

■ **43-47** Jesus quotes a portion of Lev 19:18, **love your neighbor**, and adds **hate your enemy** (Matt 5:43). While this addition is not explicitly stated in the OT law, it is likely rooted in invective OT passages where Gentiles who seek Israel's demise are worthy of hate and rejection (Pss 137:7-9; 139:21-22; France 2007, 224-25). This also coheres with "neighbor" in Lev 19:18 as referring exclusively to fellow Israelites where, earlier in this verse Israel is not to "seek revenge or bear a grudge against anyone *among your people*, but love your neighbor as yourself." The closest parallel to hating enemies is found in the DSS. In 1QS 1:9-10 there is to be love for "the sons of light" and hate for "the sons of darkness."

Jesus rejects this nationalistic sentiment of exclusivity and calls his followers to something extremely provocative: **But I tell you, love your enemies and pray for those who persecute you** (Matt 5:44). Jesus' followers, those who constitute a new Israel, must behave very different from their Jewish counterparts. They are to love enemies, including Rome, and pray for those who persecute them. This type of love is a prerequisite for those who wish to be **children of your Father in heaven** (v 45*a*). This call takes the preceding injunction to turn the other cheek to another level, wherein the disciples now seek the good of those who harass and trouble them (France 2007, 225).

In the second half of v 45, Jesus speaks to the character of God who **causes his sun to rise on the evil and the good, and sends rain on the righteous and the unrighteous**. His followers are to embody God's love both to **the evil** and **the unrighteous** because this is what God himself does. In loving their enemies, the disciples reflect the very nature of Israel's holy God, who loves them and remains faithful because of his love (Deut 7:8). With the coming of Jesus, we see God's love most fully revealed. His Son comes specifically for the enemies of God, the sinners (Matt 9:13*b*; Rom 5:8), and with whom he forms a new covenant relationship in order to save and redeem.

Jesus concludes his teaching with two sets of rhetorical questions that basically emphasize the cultural norm of only loving **those who love you** (v 46*a*). There is no **reward** for behaving like **tax collectors**, a highly despised group, who also love those who love them in return (v 46*b*). Similarly, there is nothing unique about greeting fellow Israelites, **your own people**, since **even pagans do that** (v 47).

■ **48** The idea that Jesus is calling his disciples to be like their heavenly Father is made explicit here. The call to love unconditionally and in extraordinary ways, for which there are no parallels in the rest of society, leads to this radical concluding statement: **Be perfect, . . . as your heavenly Father is perfect**.

The radical love Jesus described in vv 43-47 reflects the holy love of God. This verse strongly echoes the one in Lev 19:2: "Speak to the entire assembly of Israel and say to them: 'Be holy because I, the LORD your God, am holy.'" For Matthew, there is correspondence in meaning between "holy" and the word translated as **perfect**, which is not perfection of actions but rather of being wholly transformed into one who loves unconditionally as God himself does.

In Matt 19, a man asks Jesus what he must to do have eternal life (v 16). Jesus responds that obedience to the commandments *and* selling one's possession leads to "perfection." To give all unreservedly to the call of the gospel is to be a complete or a **perfect** disciple of Jesus. In 5:48, then, Jesus is not advocating another level of moral rigor or sacrifice, but rather a complete willingness to obey him and the call of the gospel, which is to love God and neighbor completely (see Matt 22:36-40; Hagner 2007, 49).

No disciple of Jesus is exempt from the demands of the greater righteousness, which, like perfection, is a call to wholehearted devotion to Jesus (5:20; Brower 2005, 124-25). The disciples will "prove themselves worthy of the kingdom of God by overcoming enmity, crossing religiously defined . . . and ethnic boundaries with the aim of loving everyone into the presence of God" (Deines 2008, 81). This is only possible by the new covenant Jesus establishes with his people in which we embody the presence of Jesus Immanuel, who is God with us.

This exhortation rounds off the entire section of teaching, beginning in v 21, which explains the ways in which Jesus radicalizes the Law. The motivation for each of the teachings that Jesus expounds, whether it is seeking reconciliation with an offended party or turning the other cheek, is love for the other and in this way the Law and the Prophets are now fulfilled.

FROM THE TEXT

The Sermon on the Mount contains some of the most difficult teaching of Jesus, specifically in 5:21-48. For some, these expectations of Jesus are impossible to obey and, as such, depict legislation that only applies to Jesus, for example. However, this is to view the moral exhortations of Jesus from a Pharisaic framework of performance, another set of behavioral guidelines to be followed. Many holiness denominations are guilty of performance-based religion. But this is not the way of Christ!

Jesus Messiah has come to fulfill the Law and the Prophets for the sake of God's saving purposes on earth. In Matthew, Jesus makes this fulfillment possible by establishing a new covenant in his blood that is vindicated at his resurrection whereby a holy community is formed and shaped around him and his saving presence. This means that everyone who desires to follow him is enabled, through the Spirit, to live a complete and whole life characterized by love for God and others both inside and out.

We can love as God loves, which will then lead to the behaviors and transformed attitudes that Jesus describes beginning in v 21. In the present, we can live lives that are animated by "a totally God-centered and neighbor-centered mind-set" (Brower 2005, 125). To love our neighbor, regardless of their color of skin, socioeconomic class, or sexual orientation, is to participate with God in his holy mission to redeem the lost. When we, or others in our faith communities, stray from such a mind-set, forgiveness is still available to us and them as well.

3. True Righteousness (6:1-18)

BEHIND THE TEXT

Matthew 5 ends with the exhortation "be perfect, therefore, as your heavenly Father is perfect" (v 48). This is a call to a life of inward purity and holiness of heart in which disciples of Jesus demonstrate God's character in ways that are countercultural and truly "other," reflecting the "otherness" of God's holy love, which issues in acts of mercy. If Christian holiness is merely an inward disposition and does not lead to acts of mercy, it becomes reduced to a private pietism. In this teaching, which begins in 5:21, Jesus is not legislating a new set of laws but, rather, provides a series of depictions of what lives that fulfill the Law and Prophets look like.

In Matt 6, Jesus expects his followers to engage in customary acts of righteousness or faithfulness toward God and others, but, as with ch 5, these acts need to come from a heart of pure motives. This reflects a theme throughout Scripture that God looks on the heart (Davies and Allison 1988, 576). Those who pride themselves on their acts of outward piety are hypocrites, a term Jesus repeats three times (6:2, 5, 16).

At the same time, a faith not lived out is no faith at all, which is captured well in James, one of the most Jewish epistles in the NT. Alms, prayer, and fasting are key aspects of Jewish piety and in other religious traditions as well (France 2007, 232). These three do not constitute a definitive list but are rather representative of how Jesus' disciples should practice acts of righteousness (Keener 1999, 207).

Another aspect that emerges in ch 6 is the highly relational nature of "your Father in heaven" who sees and rewards his faithful ones (vv 1*b*, 4*b*, 6*b*, 18*b*) and knows their physical needs, even before they ask (vv 8, 26, 30). This is an important perspective to bear in mind when interpreting 5:48 and the passages leading up to it, as Jesus is not legislating outward perfection but, in light of ch 6, is calling his followers to an intimate relationship with their heavenly Father who sees and knows them and will provide for them when they, for instance, always give to the one who wishes to borrow (5:42).

Interrupting Jesus' three-part teaching on true and false piety is the Lord's Prayer (6:9-13), which most fully expresses God's desire to be in relationship with his people as they pray for his kingdom to come and ask him for physical and spiritual sustenance. Keener notes that the prayer "is thoroughly Jewish in its content, form and language" (1999, 215). It appears to be specifically modeled after a synagogue prayer known as the Kaddish (Keener 1999, 215; France 2007, 243).

Although many English translations note that there is a doxological ending to the Lord's Prayer, it is left out of this commentary because it is not recorded in the earliest manuscripts. It is quite likely a later addition because many Christians adopted Jewish prayers, like the Lord's Prayer, which typically conclude with a doxology (Keener 1999, 225).

IN THE TEXT

■ **1** In Jesus' stinging rebuke of the ostentatious piety of the scribes and Pharisees in Matt 23, Jesus explicitly states that "everything they do is done for people to see" (23:5*a*). In contrast, his followers are not **to practice** their **righteousness in front of others to be seen by them**. The scribes and Pharisees receive exactly what they desire—they are seen by others (6:2, 5, 16). However, if the disciples follow suit, they will **have no reward from** their **Father in heaven**. This is a reward for the future, particularly in light of 5:12 (France 2007, 235; Nolland 2005, 274), in which suffering persecution for the gospel will also be rewarded.

■ **2-4** Jesus first addresses how the disciples should **give to the needy** (v 2*a*). They are not to **announce it with trumpets, as the hypocrites do in the synagogues and on the streets, to be honored by others** (v 2*b*). There is no surviving evidence that the religious leaders blew a trumpet to draw attention to themselves, prompting some scholars to conclude that Jesus has chosen imagery to make an exaggerated point (Nolland 2005, 274; France 2007, 236). Regardless, the issue is self-aggrandizing behavior to receive **honor** or be extolled in the eyes of others. In contrast, honor or glory is for God, according to 5:16 (Nolland 2005, 275).

The disciples should give alms in secret such that the **left hand** does not **know what** the **right hand is doing** (6:3) with the result that they will be rewarded by their **Father, who sees what is done in secret** (v 4*b*). The religious leaders' desire to be seen by all reflect hearts of impurity and selfishness. Jesus himself puts it this way: "On the outside you appear to people as righteous but on the inside you are full of hypocrisy and wickedness" (23:28).

While it may be challenging to give in such secrecy, the point of the metaphor about the right and left hand remains: none of it should be done with even a hint of self-acclamation (Nolland 2005, 276). Matthew even shifts from the plural pronoun **you** in 6:2 to the singular form for **you** in v 3, as well as in vv 6 and 17, which heightens the emphasis on discreet giving (France 2007, 237).

■ **5-8** Jesus first addresses *where* the disciples should pray in vv 5-7 and *how* they should pray in vv 8-13. The hypocrites perform this act of piety so that they can **be seen by others** (v 5*b*) compared with being extolled by others in v 2. The point is the same: a self-centered desire for recognition. Jesus says that **they love to pray standing in the synagogues and on the street corners** (v 5*b*). Both are places that, just as in v 2, afford a perfect opportunity **to be seen by others**.

The posture of standing to pray is widely practiced in Judaism (1 Sam 1:26; Neh 8:5-6) as well as observing specific prayer hours, of which there are at least three in 2TJ (see Dan 6:10; *1 En.* 51:4; Acts 3:1; McGowan 2014, 183-

89). At these times, the hypocrites are out on the streets (Matt 6:5). Nolland translates **street corners** as "'public squares' to bring out the sense of a broad open place . . . providing a suitable contrast with the (narrow) streets of v. 2" (2005, 277). Those who become the center of attention, either in the synagogue or on the street, **have received their reward in full** (v 5*b*).

Jesus calls his disciples to **go into your room, close the door and pray to your Father, who is unseen** (v 6*a*). The **room** is likely the inner room of a home, possibly a storeroom (BDAG 2000, 988), eliminating the prospect of the disciple being seen by anyone. This piety is to be as invisible as God himself, who is likewise **unseen**. As with the reward for covertly giving alms, the one who prays in secret will also be rewarded by the **Father, who sees what is done in secret** (v 6*b*).

In vv 7-8, Jesus turns to how the disciples should pray, providing a segue for the Lord's Prayer (vv 9-13). Unlike the **pagans** who **keep on babbling** (v 7) to their gods in order to secure their attention through **many words**, Jesus reiterates the immanence of the disciples' heavenly **Father, who sees what is done in secret** (v 6*b*) and **knows what you need before you ask him** (v 8*b*). This movement is echoed in Isa 65:24: "Before they call I will answer; while they are still speaking I will hear." Jesus strikes at the motivation of the heart: it is not necessary to use many words to get God's attention and then inform him of human need.

Matthew's use of *battologeō*, "babbling," and *polulogia*, "many words," essentially describes "an approach to prayer which values quantity (and perhaps volume?) rather than quality" (France 2007, 240). Pagans were known for long, babbling prayers to secure the attention of their deities, and some Jewish texts also warn against verbose prayers (see Eccl 5:2 and Sir 7:14). For Jesus, the issue is "the attitude of faith which underlies and inspires . . . the prayer" (France 2007, 241).

■ **9-15** Now that Jesus has taught his disciples where they should pray (vv 5-6) and how not to pray, like the pagans (vv 6-7), he declares **this, then, is how you should pray** (v 9*a*). Implied in this statement is a level of fluidity as Jesus is not commanding his hearers to pray these exact words but is rather teaching them what true prayer necessarily entails (Nolland 2005, 285; Davies and Allison 1988, 599).

Structurally, the Lord's Prayer has two parts:

1. Three supplications in the third-person singular imperative directed to the Father: **hallowed be your name** (v 9*b*); **your kingdom come** (v 10*a*); **your will be done, on earth as it is in heaven** (v 10*b*). These first three "are in effect a doxology, an act of worship, associating the praying community with God's purpose in the world" (France 2007, 243).
2. Three supplications in which the disciples bring their own needs before God: **give us today our daily bread** (v 11); **and forgive us our**

debts, as we also have forgiven our debtors (v 12); **and lead us not into temptation, but deliver us from the evil one** (v 13).

Jesus' instruction to address God with the paternal designation **our Father** reflects his own intimate communion with God, into which he invites the disciples. In Matt 11, Jesus addresses God as "Father" as the one who gives revelation to "little children" (v 25). Then, in v 27, he explains the intimacy he shares with his Father: "No one knows the Son except the Father, and no one knows the Father except the Son and those to whom the Son chooses to reveal him." Jesus repeatedly refers to God as Father in the sermon (e.g., 5:16, 45; 6:1, 4, 6, 8, etc.), and now he invites his disciples into a familial relationship with their heavenly Father who will provide for even their most basic of needs.

The supplication **hallowed be your name** is a call for the name of God to be honored and recognized by all. In Isa 29:23, the sanctification of God's name is associated with the manifestation of his rule. Similarly, in Ezek 36, God will sanctify his name by delivering his people from exile: "I will show the holiness of my great name [by delivering Israel], which has been profaned among the nations, the name you have profaned among them" (v 23*a*). The name of God was profaned by the nations and Israel and so he sent them into exile (v 22), but now that he will act to deliver them and cleanse them from all impurity, his name will once again be sanctified (v 24).

This association in Ezekiel is a relevant background for the audience of Jesus who sees exile as continuing in their own day. This prayer, coupled with Jesus' earlier kingdom proclamation (→ Matt 4:15-17), signals that restoration has dawned: it is time to pray for the hallowing of God's name, and hence Israel's restoration, which leads into, then, a supplication for God's reign to be realized: **your kingdom come** (v 10*a*).

The third supplication, **your will be done, on earth as it is in heaven,** encapsulates the preceding two as God's will is to have his name hallowed and his kingdom come. According to Keener, "The hallowing of God's name, the consummation of his reign, and the doing of his will are all variant versions of the same end-time promise: everything will be set right someday" (1999, 220).

In the second half, the supplicant asks for specific requests, which naturally flow out of that which is implicitly affirmed in the first part: the sanctification of God's name, the manifestation of his rule and the realization of his will, all of which function for the good of his people. The first petition for **daily bread** (v 11) reflects utter dependence upon God for the most basic of needs (Ps 104:14-15, 27-28). The unusual Greek term *epiousios*, translated **daily**, can mean "daily rations," "essential for survival," or "bread for tomorrow" (Keener 1999, 221). Others have suggested an eschatological significance: the bread of the great messianic banquet (Hagner 1993, 149-50). Since Jesus mentions **today** as well, it is likely sufficient bread for today, a "daily ration" and, based on context, refers to literal bread (see Matt 6:25-26). This recalls the daily bread, or manna, that the Israelites received from God in the wilderness and is a testimony of his faithfulness to his people, which is assumed in the Lord's Prayer.

Next, Jesus invites them to ask God to forgive their **debts** as they do likewise for others who owe them (v 12). Since they do not owe money to God, **debts** likely involves sin (see Nolland 1999, 223). The parable in 18:23-35, which is about forgiving debts, is elicited by a question about how many times one should forgive offenses (vv 21-22). France argues that "debt is a metaphor for offenses which need to be forgiven" (2007, 249-50).

The point of 6:12 is peace with God and one another. The necessity of seeking reconciliation, in this case forgiving offenses, when we seek the very same thing from God, is an important theme in Matthew (5:23-25; 6:14-15; 18:23-35; see also Sir 28:1-8). The priority of forgiving others is captured in the tenses of "forgive" in Matt 6:12: **forgive** [present tense] **us our debts, as we also have forgiven** [perfect tense] **our debtors**. The disciples should not seek forgiveness from God until they have forgiven others (→ vv 14-15 below).

Jesus concludes with a petition for protection from **the evil one** (v 13*b*). The **temptation** or "testing" in which **the evil one** seeks the stumbling of his victims recalls the experience of Jesus in 4:1-11 (→ 4:1). While some want to define what this testing might include, such as a great eschatological test of God's people (see Keener 1999, 223 n. 182), it is best to leave it open-ended as Jesus himself does. That Matthew has in mind **evil one** versus "evil" is supported by the literary context of the sermon. Certainly the evil one is at work, oppressing many with sickness and paralysis as Matthew records just before the sermon (4:24).

Keener argues that the petition **lead us not into temptation** (6:13) does not mean "deliver one from experiencing it" (1999, 225). That is, we should pray to avoid it, but that may not always be the case. This is a petition and not a promise! Although we are never promised not to be led into temptation or a period of testing, Jesus emphatically asserts that we should always pray for deliverance from the evil one. Testing in other parts of Scripture serves a redemptive value (see Gen 22:1 and Deut 8:2; France 2007, 251).

■ **16-18** Now that Jesus has described how the disciples should pray, he turns to how they should fast. Again, they should not be like the **hypocrites** who use acts of piety to draw attention to themselves: **do not look somber as the hypocrites do, for they disfigure their faces to show others they are fasting** (Matt 6:16*a*). This false piety is extreme: looking outwardly sad and downcast with an unrecognizable countenance solely to attract attention. This drama reflects the meaning of *hupokritēs* as a description for the masks that actors would don during a performance (Keener 1999, 206, 226). According to rabbinic literature, Jewish "fasts not only included abstention from food but other forms of self-abasement like not shaving, washing one's clothes, [and] anointing" (Keener 1999, 228). The hypocrites like to play up the physical effects that come with fasting.

In biblical tradition, Israel fasted in response to a situation, which required supplication (2 Sam 12:16-23), repentance (1 Kgs 21:27), or both (Neh 1:4-11; Dan 9:3-19). In Nehemiah and Daniel, fasting accompanied prayers of petition for deliverance from exile as well as confession of national sin. This movement is also reflected in Zech 8 in which fasts are turned to feasts when the Lord returns to Zion, marking the end of exile (Wright 1992, 235). Jesus affirms fasting after he is gone, which may well reflect a continuation of exile (Matt 9:14-15) but restoration from exile has begun (→ 4:12-17). *Already* restoration is occurring in the ministry of Jesus, but it is *not yet* complete.

As with almsgiving and praying in such a way as to be seen by others, the ones who highlight the physical toll of fasting **have received their reward in full** (6:16*b*). Jesus wants his disciples to conceal its effects by putting **oil on** their **head** and **washing** their **face** (v 17), so that **only . . . your Father, who is unseen** will see this act of piety**; and your Father, who sees what is done in secret, will reward you** (v 18). Oil not only moisturizes skin, according to Greek literature, but also cleanses it in an attempt to mitigate the physical appearances that come with a fast (see Keener 1999, 227). Followers of Jesus will use oil for this purpose in contrast to those who fast for their own self-aggrandizement.

Zechariah questions the motivation behind the fasts of exilic Israel, asking, "Was it really for me that you fasted?" (Zech 7:5*b*). Similarly, the prophet Isaiah castigates Israel for fasting while not addressing the social injustices of the nation (Isa 58:7-8). It appears that Israel's fasts, just like the contemporaries of Jesus, were for reasons other than turning their hearts toward God and living lives that meet the spiritual and physical needs of others.

FROM THE TEXT

Jesus gives his disciples a depiction of true religious devotion that is not based on performance but a pure heart that only God sees. Although we may find the command, "Be perfect, therefore, as your heavenly Father is perfect" (5:48) daunting and unattainable, 6:1-18 reveals that the heavenly Father desires relationship with his people. He is a Father who sees in secret the devotion of his people. God rejects self-aggrandizing religion, but, nonetheless, still expects acts of righteousness whether it be feeding the hungry or caring for the orphans and widows around us (see Isa 58:7-8). Relationship with the heavenly Father as described in Matthew describes an inward purity that results in transformed acts of devotion in our world that reflect his loving character. This is what it means to be the holy people of God.

In the midst of Jesus' teaching on what the Father expects of his children is the Lord's Prayer. This presents a necessary counterpoint to the expectations God has for his people, since it is concerned with his children turning to God to meet their needs. Before we ask anything, we are to recognize our place as ones under the kingship of God who desires to make his saving purposes known. In the second half, Jesus teaches the disciples to bring specific requests to the Father, such as physical sustenance, forgiveness for sins, and protection from the evil one. All of these things are the ways in which the holiness of God is manifest or "hallowed" on earth. We, as the holy people of God, are to be to others what our heavenly Father has been to us: people who restore and renew.

4. True Treasure (6:19-34)

BEHIND THE TEXT

In the first half of Matt 6, Jesus teaches the ways that his disciples are to relate to their heavenly Father. In the second half, vv 19-34, Jesus speaks of the ways that they are to relate to the world. There are four sections of teaching, each of which thematically relate to each other. In vv 19-21, Jesus warns his disciples not to stockpile treasures on earth, but rather treasures in heaven. He then addresses the eye (vv 22-23); a healthy eye is necessary for spiritual health and well-being. Then, in v 24, he warns the disciples in stronger terms about storing up treasures on earth and why they need healthy eyes. Finally, in vv 25-34, Jesus offers encouragement and consolation to those with healthy eyes who refuse to serve money over God (v 24*b*) or store up treasures on earth over those in heaven (vv 19-20).

France insightfully notes that when the disciples pray for "bread" in v 11 of the Lord's Prayer, they are "set free from material anxiety and can instead concentrate on the kingdom and righteousness of God (6:33) which are the prayer's primary focus" (2007, 257). Although the NIV breaks up vv 24-34 into two paragraphs, it is important to see it as one literary unit. Jesus asks a series of rhetorical questions in the first part (vv 25*b*-30) and then reaffirms what he has implied through those questions in vv 31-34: God will indeed look after his people if he cares for even "the birds of the air" (v 26*a*) and "the flowers of the field" (v 28*b*).

IN THE TEXT

■ **19-21** Jesus begins with a command that flows naturally out of his teaching on true piety and the promise of heavenly reward. Because of the Father's provision, the disciples are **not to store up . . . treasures on earth, where moths and vermin destroy, and where thieves break in and steal** (v 19). Unlike the modern Western world, ancients would store their equity, valuable goods or currency, in the home versus in a bank (France 2007, 258). These things are subject to decay and theft. The reference to moths consuming could imply textiles and various costly fabrics (Nolland 2005, 298).

More to the point, material goods are finite and of limited value, something that wisdom writers recognized (Prov 23:4-5; Eccl 5:13-17). Jesus is not prohibiting material wealth per se as Matthew's verb "to treasure" "refers to accumulation, not simple possession" (Davies and Allison 1988, 630). Jesus does promise that God will provide his people with "all these things" (v 33*b*).

In contrast, Jesus exhorts his disciples to **store up for yourselves treasures in heaven, where moths and vermin do not destroy, and where thieves do not break in and steal** (v 20). Unlike the materialism of v 19, **treasures in heaven** are not subject to destruction or theft. A variety of Jewish texts attest to the incorruptibility of heavenly treasures, which are of ultimate value.

As with "reward," Jesus does not define the **treasures**, but given that they are **in heaven**, they are associated with the Father and are eternal. Despite the attempts of some scholars to define them (e.g., Davies and Allison 1988, 632), we need to satisfy ourselves with not knowing and having faith that they will far exceed the things offered by this world. This requires trust for which Jesus advocates in v 25. Later, Jesus challenges a man who has faithfully obeyed the Law but the affections of his heart still fixate on material possessions he cannot give up for the sake of "treasure in heaven" (19:21).

It all comes back to the heart, an idea captured in 6:21: **For where your treasure is, there your heart will be also**. What one prizes in the present reveals the heart's focus. In vv 19-21, there is an echo of ancient Israel whose hearts became set on the idols and images of the pagan nations as they distrusted the Lord and his faithfulness. In Deut 8, Moses warns the Israelites, once in the land, not to forget the Lord who has given them all of their possessions (v 11), otherwise, their "heart[s] will become proud" (v 14). The subsequent
6:22-23 disobedience of Israel in the land revealed that their hearts no longer treasured the Lord and his commands (see Deut 30:17-18). Exile was the consequence.

Jesus himself refused to succumb to a similar temptation to trust in the idols of power and authority (→ Matt 4:8-9). Rather, he chose to worship the unseen God and "serve him only" (4:10). A heart that loves God, to which Moses calls the Israelites (Deut 6:5), "produces activity that will stockpile treasures in heaven and not on the earth" (Nolland 2005, 299).

■ **22-23** To properly understand what Jesus means when he says **the eye is the lamp of the body** (v 22*a*) we must consider the function of the eye in ancient thought. Basically, ancients believed that the "eye was quite literally a source of light, and the thought in vv. 22-23 is clarified and unified" by this assumption (Nolland 2005, 300). This is why the eye is a **lamp of the body**.

Jesus continues, **If your eyes are healthy, your whole body will be full of light** (v 22*b*). As a lamp, the eyes guide the individual and if functioning properly, they will absorb that light into the body. However, Davies and Allison argue that since the eye is a source of light, it is not a conduit to absorb from its surroundings (1988, 638). Based on their dubious analysis of the way the conditional clause functions in v 22*b*, they argue that "a good eye is evidence of inner light" (1988, 638). However, a plain reading illustrates that a good eye leads to a body full of light, a reading that a majority of scholars support.

The Greek word translated **healthy** (*haplous*) "pertains to being motivated by singleness of purpose . . . single without guile, sincere, straightforward" (BDAG 2000, 104). This recalls Jesus' exhortation on single-minded devotion on storing up treasures in heaven (v 20), which reveals a pure heart (v 21) and anticipates v 24 in which he affirms that is it impossible to love two masters, both God and money. If our eyes are focused on treasures in heaven, this will lead to a body full of light.

France suggests that the way Jesus crafts this imagery in v 22 implies that light is crucial for the "proper functioning of the body (person) and that this light is in some way dependent on the condition of the eye" (2007, 261). When we consider that many references to light in the OT are associated with God (e.g., Ps 104:2; Dan 2:22; Hab 3:3-4), Matthew's logic becomes clearer: as we seek that which is of God, our eyes are a lamp, having single-minded devotion to God and, as a result, we become full of him and his light and in that way can let our "light shine before others" (5:16*a*).

However, if the **eyes are unhealthy**, the **whole body will be full of darkness** (6:23). There is a chiastic pattern at work in which vv 20 and 22, the inner elements, express storing up treasures in heaven and having healthy eyes, whereas the outer elements express storing up treasure on earth (v 19) and having eyes that are unhealthy (v 23*b*). At the very center of the chiastic structure is v 21, which centers on the heart, in keeping with two other moments in the sermon (5:8, 28). Below is a diagram of the chiastic structure:

A: storing "treasures on earth" (6:19)
  B: storing "treasures in heaven" (v 20)
    C: "where your treasure is, there your heart will be also" (v 21)
  B': **healthy** eyes lead to a body **full of light** (v 22*b*)
A': **unhealthy** eyes lead to a body **full of darkness** (v 23*a*)

A pure heart is commensurate with eyes that are unwavering, functioning as a light, reflecting the things of heaven, and, consequently, the body is full of light. Meanwhile, an impure heart is commensurate with eyes that are **unhealthy** (*ponēros*), meaning "diseased" (Nolland 2005, 301). Since the eye is ill, it cannot function as a lamp and shed light in the interior of one's being. Therefore, the **whole body** is **full of darkness** (v 23*a*).

In context, a diseased eye is one that fixates on earthly treasures (v 19) and is enslaved to money (v 24). The lamp that is the eye, in this case, is not illuminating the interior of one's being, the heart. Jesus concludes that if **the light within you is darkness, how great is that darkness!** (v 23*b*). If the light to be internalized cannot enter because of diseased eyes fixated on things not of God, the light becomes darkness and darkness is all that is left.

■ **24** Just as in vv 19-21, in vv 22-23, Jesus is presenting his disciples with two different ways of relating to the world and, by implication, to God himself. In v 24, Jesus makes explicit what has been implicit all along: **No one can serve two masters**. This is the language of slavery, of which Matthew's audience would be well aware. Jesus explains two different types of slave-master relationships: **Either you will hate the one and love the other, or you will be devoted to the one and despise the other. You cannot serve both God and money** (v 24).

According to Nolland, this reflects a situation where two masters share a slave and the master who treats his slave well receives his or her affections (2005, 303-4). However, "when God is one of the masters . . . any consideration of dual service becomes totally impossible" (Nolland 2005, 304). Jesus calls his followers to a radical, unwavering obedience to "treasures in heaven" that reveal a pure heart (vv 20-21) and single-minded devotion enabling a spiritual interior saturated with light.

It is not possible to stockpile "treasures on earth" (v 19) and have diseased eyes that prohibit the light from entering (v 23) and think that one can serve God at the same time. This call to unwavering devotion to God as opposed to that which pagans pursue, once again, recalls Israel who was prohibited from serving the Lord and idols of pagan nations at the same time (Exod 34:10-16; Deut 4:23-24).

The last word of this section, in v 24*b*, is "money" (*mamōnas*) referring to "'resources,' 'money,' 'property,' 'possessions'" (Davies and Allison 1988, 643). It recalls the first injunction not to be storing up "treasures on earth" in v 19. This correspondence is no coincidence: the lure of wealth is real and giving into its lure comes at a high cost when it displaces trust in the heavenly Father. The disciples must "tear the mind away from worldly enticements and fix all attention on the Father in heaven" (Davies and Allison 1988, 643).

6:25-34

■ **25-34** Since Jesus prohibits the disciples from seeking what the world desires and the attendant enslavement to it, "money" and stockpiling "treasures on earth," Jesus consoles them: **Therefore I tell you, do not worry about your life** (v 25*a*). He defines what would entail worrying about one's life: **what you will eat or drink; or about your body, what you will wear**. Eating and drinking are fundamental to sustain life. Jesus is calling them to trust their heavenly Father for not only the most basic things but also the most crucial.

Trusting God for food recalls Satan's testing of Jesus to turn stones into bread since he was hungry after forty days of fasting (4:3-4). However, Jesus modeled what trust in the heavenly Father looks like and now calls his disciples to the same. Nolland notes that food and clothing are paired in Jewish texts (e.g., Deut 10:18; Tob 1:17) and are portrayed as essential to life. It is these that give life to the body (2005, 308-9). Put another way, "Food maintains the 'life' (continued existence), and clothes protect the body" (France 2007, 267).

In the first rhetorical question, Jesus asks, **Is not life more than food, and the body more than clothes?** (v 25*b*). There is a movement from the greater to the lesser, which is often a hallmark of rabbinic teaching (Davies and Allison 1988, 648): from life and the body, without which one simply does not exist, to food and clothes, which require a living being. In context, Jesus is calling his disciples not to be anxious about the lesser things because this stress will suffocate the greater, life and body (Nolland 2005, 309-10).

Jesus uses **the birds of the air** (v 26*a*) as an illustration of the ways in which God looks after them with food: **they do not sow or reap or store away in barns, and yet your heavenly Father feeds them**. The use of nature to make a theological point is well attested in Jewish literature. Jesus then follows up with two rhetorical questions that make his point well: **Are you not much more valuable than they? Can any one of you by worrying add a single hour to your life?** (vv 26*b*-27). Since these birds do not do the work of the farmer—sowing, reaping, and storing—how much more will God look after the disciples, who can do such things?

In the second question, the word for **hour** in Greek means "forearm" and "cubit" (BDAG 2000, 812), a unit of measure, while the word for **life** can mean the "period of one's life" or "bodily stature" (BDAG 2000, 435-36). Taking **life** as not the latter but life stage, a meaning not attested in Greek usage, Nolland argues the statement implies: "You cannot by worrying gain the seniority to which you aspire" (2005, 311). In his opinion, Jesus prohibits worrying about achieving a social stature to secure employment to meet financial needs.

The NIV's **add a single hour** is a more natural reading of the Greek text that reflects usage of the underlying Greek terms elsewhere. Further, food and clothing provide sustenance and protection; they do not guarantee upward mobility. The main point is that anxiety regarding these things accomplishes nothing and leaves little room to trust the heavenly Father who provides.

Jesus then raises the concern that his followers would have about clothing in v 28*a* and uses **the flowers of the field** as an example of something for which God provides: **They do not labor or spin** (v 28*b*). The latter term is used elsewhere to denote the fabrication of textiles (e.g., Exod 35:25-26 LXX). Solomon was not dressed as finely as one of the flowers (Matt 6:29; see 1 Kgs 10:1-25) and that if **God clothes the grass of the field**, which is subject to destruction in a short period of time (see Isa 40:6-8), **will he not much more clothe you—you of little faith?** (Matt 6:30).

None of these flowers work for their beauty, unlike what is required for the production of clothing—laboring and spinning (v 28*b*). "God gives them existence and life, and God provides for them. If He does that for the lower forms of life, He will do no less" for his people (Manson 1957, 112).

Matthew will repeat the accusation, **you of little faith** (*holigopistos*) later (8:26; 14:31; 16:8). In each passage, the disciples struggle to trust Jesus in a difficult situation. Its usage here demonstrates that much faith and trust is required due to the radical obedience to which Jesus call them. However, "In the present context the reader is encouraged to overcome 'little faith' by reflecting upon the lessons drawn from nature in 6:26-30 and by hearing afresh Jesus' promises in 6:32-3" (Davies and Allison 1988, 656).

Recalling his admonition not to worry in v 25, Jesus once again calls his disciples to the same in v 31: **So do not worry, saying, "What shall we eat?" or "What shall we drink?" or "What shall we wear?"** Echoing the injunctions of vv 22-24, Jesus states that the **pagans** pursue **all these things, and your heavenly Father knows that you need them** (v 32). The pagans' vain pursuit of material things is not unlike the vain babbling of their prayers, all of which reflects a distrust in the gods they worship (v 7). Pagans need to continually curry favor with the gods for blessing and well-being in the present (Ehrman 2004, 27).

The disciples are to pursue **his kingdom and his righteousness** (v 33*a*), which is the reign of God and his faithfulness that defines this reign. Then, as the disciples live in submission to God, **all these things will be given to you as well** (v 33). The referents of **these things** are the basic necessities that Jesus assures his followers God knows they need (vv 31-33).

Despite the possessive pronoun **his** indicating that it is God's righteousness, Nolland contends that the disciples' righteousness is in view, "the righteousness that God requires of us" (2005, 315). However, the disciples can pray for the kingdom to come in the Lord's Prayer because God is faithful, a well-attested OT understanding of "righteousness" (*dikaiosunē*) (→ Matt 3:13-15 sidebar, "Righteousness"). Further, the text is clear: seek **<u>his</u> righteousness**, that is, God's own moral integrity. God invites us to seek his faithfulness/righteousness so that we will realize his reign and depend upon him to meet our needs. This is the context from which we pray, "Give us today our daily bread" (see 6:11).

In light of God's faithful reign, Jesus concludes, **Do not worry about tomorrow, for tomorrow will worry about itself** (v 34*a*). They are to concentrate on today, for **each day has enough trouble of its own** (v 34*b*). It's important to see v 34*b* in connection with the Lord's Prayer where Jesus calls the disciples to be concerned only with the present: they are to ask for daily bread today trusting God for his provision in the present.

FROM THE TEXT

The key theme in 6:19-34 is unwavering trust in our heavenly Father to provide for our needs. Many of those who live in the modern, industrialized first world and enjoy the benefits of the free market economy may find the idea of trusting God for food and clothing quite foreign. Because of the geopolitical and economic imbalances of global life today, much of earth's population knows what it is to be without basic necessities.

However, Jesus' injunction at the end of v 24, "you cannot serve both God and money," is a statement applicable to poor and rich alike, transcending both time and geography, because it centers on the heart. A life lived for the purpose of stockpiling wealth on earth at the expense of God and others results in an enslavement, oftentimes accompanied by anxiety and worry, making unwavering trust in God impossible.

For Wesley, serving money involves

> loving the world; desiring it for its own sake; the placing our joy in the things thereof, and setting our hearts upon them; the seeking (what indeed it is impossible we should find) our happiness therein; the resting with the whole weight of our souls, upon the staff of this broken reed, although daily experience shows it cannot support, but will only "enter into our hand and pierce it." ("Sermon on the Mount: Discourse 9" in Wesley 1978, 5:382)

5. Relationship with Others and God (7:1-12)

BEHIND THE TEXT

Matthew 7 contains a series of shorter discourses, each of which concerns relationships: within the community (vv 1-5), with those outside (v 6), and with the heavenly Father (vv 7-11). The section ends with a concluding exhortation that, if followed, will ensure harmonious relationships with everyone (v 12).

a. Relationship with Others (7:1-6)

IN THE TEXT

■ **1-2** Jesus begins with a command: **Do not judge, or you too will be judged** (v 1). He follows with a rationale: **In the same way you judge others, you will be judged, and with the measure you use, it will be measured to you** (v 2). The second statement about measuring, which applied to the measuring of goods in ancient commerce (see McEleney 1994, 492), refers to the degree or severity of judgment that a disciple applies to another. This, then, dictates the level of judgment that the disciple receives in return.

The agent of the passive verbs (e.g., **you too <u>will be judged</u>**) is God. God, as righteous and just, is the one who will ensure that the disciple is judged or measured accordingly (see Matt 16:27; Rom 2:6). In light of Matt 7:3-5, this opening command and its explanation function as a warning against overly harsh critique and criticism. God will not let that go unpunished. Reciprocity is evident earlier in 6:14-15, where Jesus teaches that the disciples are only forgiven when they have forgiven others.

God as Judge

According to Gen 18:25, God is judge of the whole world—a concept actually connected to his role as Creator. God first judges when he pronounced his creation "very good" (Gen 1:31), and the heavens continually declare him faithful, making him a righteous judge (Ps 50:6). As the ultimate source of all good things

(Matt 7:11; Jas 1:17), God is the only one perfectly suited to render justice or to determine what is "good" and what is not. Through this work, God will right the wrongs of this current fallen world (Rom 2:1-11; Jas 4:12).

The God who creates in the beginning is the same God who judges at the end of the ages—"the Alpha and the Omega" (Rev 21:6). Matthew often refers to the final judgment at "the end of the age" when God will judge rightly and deal with evil (Matt 13:39-40, 49-50). Because God is a righteous Creator, we can entrust the final judgment to him (13:24-30, 43) relieving his people of the need to harshly criticize others (7:1-2).

■ **3-5** While one could interpret vv 1-2 as an injunction prohibiting anyone from judging another, vv 3-5 make it clear that this is not the case. Jesus requires the disciple to **first take the plank out of** their **own eye** and then that disciple **will see clearly to remove the speck from** the eye of another (v 5). There is no prohibition against judging others. Jesus is concerned with how the disciple administers a critique and, later in the Gospel, details how a disciple is to confront another (18:15-17).

The **speck of sawdust** (*karfos*) denotes a "small piece of straw, chaff, or wood" (BDAG 2000, 511) while the **plank** (*dokos*) refers to a load-bearing beam (BDAG 2000, 256). This absurd illustration is memorable, serving as a warning against hypocritical behavior in the church. Jesus even repeats it twice (7:3-4). Rather, the **hypocrite**, with the "plank-sized" sin, needs to **first take the plank of out of your own eye, and then you will see clearly to remove the speck from** another's **eye** (v 5). Unlike the scribes and Pharisees who intentionally deceive (see ch 23), the prospective hypocrite whom Jesus addresses is completely unaware of a serious personal issue but yet highlights an insignificant issue in the life of another.

■ **6** This short parable is difficult to interpret because Jesus provides no referent for **dogs** and **what is sacred** as well as for **pearls** and **pigs**. One possibility is that Jesus is referring to the Gentiles. In the first half of Matthew, there is an emphasis on the Jewish mission: Jesus saves "his people from their sins" (1:21), and when he sends the disciples out to minister they are not to "go among the Gentiles" (10:5*b*). Jesus himself refers to Gentiles as "dogs" in 15:26, a term of derision elsewhere in Jewish tradition (e.g., Deut 23:18 LXX [19 HB]). In the parable, **what is sacred** or holy (*to hagios*: "holy thing") is to be kept away from **dogs**, reflecting the Levitical system of separation (e.g., Lev 11). Likewise, **pearls**, something of great value and a simile for the kingdom of God (see Matt 13:45-46), should not be given to **pigs**, unclean animals (Lev 11:7-8).

There are a few references where dog and pig occur together as profane animals (e.g., *1 En.* 89:42; 2 Pet 2:22). In light of this, as well as Jesus' use of "dog" later in the Gospel and the Jewish focus of the disciples' mission in the first half of Matthew, these likely refer to Gentiles. However, this parable equally applies to anyone. Just as disciples must be discerning about their own character before judging another, they must also discern the character of those outside who may simply **trample them under their feet** (Matt 7:6*b*). This reflects a level of hostility toward the disciples (see 10:14, 16-18), or, worse yet, those outside as **dogs** may **turn and tear** the disciple **to pieces** (France 2007, 277). This is reflected in Prov 23:9: "Do not speak to fools, for they will scorn your prudent words."

FROM THE TEXT

In Matt 7:1-5, Jesus is calling his followers to be aware of their own shortcomings before they take it upon themselves to help others with their faults. Humility and authenticity are to characterize Christian community (Phil 2:3-4), so much so that Jesus warns his followers that the excessiveness with which they judge another, without first having their own house in order, God will accordingly judge them. It is a call for discerning one's own life first and foremost.

This continues in Matt 7:6, but this time defining the disciples' interactions with those outside the faith community. The disciples must be mindful of those to whom they minister, as these can squander the message or even harm the disciples. Although Jesus teaches that hostility will come, v 6 could be a call to mitigate those encounters, if possible, by deciding not to preach the gospel if it is not wanted.

b. Relationship with God (7:7-11)

IN THE TEXT

■ **7-8** The warning that characterizes vv 1-6 changes to one of invitation in vv 7-11. The divine passives of vv 1-2, which express the giving of God's judgment, now in vv 7-8 express the generosity of God's benevolence. Jesus exhorts the disciples in v 7: **Ask and it will be given to you; seek and you will find; knock and the door will be opened to you.** Jesus follows this with a rationale in v 8, which is essentially a restatement of v 7 but broadens the invitation to **everyone**. While most agree that the meaning of **ask**, **seek**, and **knock** do not refer to specific requests (France 2007, 280; Keener 1999, 245), Nolland relates each of these to different aspects of the Sermon on the Mount; for example, **ask** recalls the Lord's Prayer (1999, 325). It's more likely that each line in v 7, and then again in v 8, reflects synonymous parallelism of Hebrew poetry as opposed to each referring to an aspect of the sermon.

Some suggest that Jesus is not emphasizing persistence but is merely calling his followers to ask God for their needs (France 2007, 280; Davies and Allison 1988, 679). These verbs, however, can express a progressive aspect: keep asking, keep seeking, and keep knocking (v 7). This aligns with the Lord's Prayer in which the disciples are to pray each day, persistently: "Give us today our daily bread" (6:11). Followers of Jesus are to turn to their heavenly Father daily for all of their needs, letting "tomorrow . . . worry about itself" (6:34).

Jesus is not calling the disciples to be like spoiled children whining and complaining to their heavenly Father about their selfish needs. The illustration in 7:9-11 guards against this: these are children who ask for necessities of life: **bread** (v 9) and **fish** (v 10). These things are basic items in a Palestinian diet, which corresponds with the promises Jesus made earlier (6:25-34; Keener 1999, 246).

■ **9-11** Jesus now describes the nature of the God who will inspire the disciples to ask, seek, and knock. God is a **Father in heaven** who gives **good gifts to those who ask him!** (v 11*b*). Good earthly fathers will provide for their children when they ask, a point communicated through parallel rhetorical questions: **Which of you, if your son asks for bread, will give him a stone? Or if he asks for a fish, will give him a snake?** (vv 9-10).

Although scholars, ancient and modern, have proposed various connections between **bread/stone** and **fish/snake** (Keener 1999, 246 n. 229), the imagery highlights a contrast: earthly fathers sustain the lives of their children with **good gifts** (v 11). They do not provide things that serve no purpose (i.e., a **stone**) or could harm them (i.e., a **snake**). The phrase, **though you are evil,** likely refers to the moral fallibility of earthly fathers, as opposed to wicked or morally corrupt parents. Davies and Allison put it this way: "Notwithstanding that they continually whirl about in the abyss of sin, even human beings can show compassion and give unselfishly" (1988, 683).

Despite fallibility, earthly fathers can still meet the needs of their children, and so **how much more will your Father in heaven** look after those who turn to him (v 11)? The invitation to ask in vv 7-8, coupled with the affirmation of the goodness of the one to whom they ask in vv 9-11, reiterates *how* the disciples are to pray, as evident in the Lord's Prayer (6:9-13).

c. A Concluding Exhortation (7:12)

■ **12** This concludes not only the implications of Jesus' teaching on relationships with others (vv 1-6) and God (vv 7-11) but also the core teaching of the sermon. What Jesus' followers are to do to others is to be shaped by the preceding ethical content in the Sermon on the Mount thus far (Nolland 2005, 330). God is a heavenly Father who gives "good gifts" to those who ask (v 11). The disciples, **so in everything,** must treat others as they would want to be treated (v 12).

Some argue that **do to others what you would have them do to you** originated with Jesus in contrast with the rabbinic version: "What is hateful to you, do not do to your neighbor" (*b. Šabb.* 31a). It is unlikely that this negative version was interpreted as license to do less for the other. Both versions communicate the same idea: genuine concern for the other (Nolland 2005, 329).

As in vv 7-8, Jesus follows his command with a reason: **for this sums up the Law and the Prophets** (v 12). This recalls 5:17*b*, in which Jesus came "to fulfill" the Law and the Prophets, which is evident in hearts filled with love for one another. Love like this reflects the holy love of the heavenly Father (→ Matt 5:17 and 5:48). Jesus confirms this later when he states that loving others, as well as God, are the precepts upon which hang "all the Law and the Prophets" (22:40).

FROM THE TEXT

This text has been the object of much abuse by a prosperity gospel that teaches that God will give you anything (e.g., luxurious homes and vehicles), if you only ask! According to Michael Taylor, "In some traditions wealth has been regarded as a sign of divine blessing, often with the implication that the poor are to blame for their poverty" (2003, ix).

Jesus' sermon teaches the disciples that God will provide for our *basic* needs, "what you will eat or drink" or "what you will wear" (6:25). The disciples are to pray for "daily bread" (6:11). For the majority of people in the world today, these still remain serious needs, but the affluence of the West blinds the beneficiaries of such wealth to the simplicity of Jesus' teaching. This truth should embolden all Christians to do to others what we would have them do to us: give when we see need! In this, we reflect the love of our heavenly Father.

6. Warnings and Responses (7:13-29)

BEHIND THE TEXT

Jesus offers a series of exhortations and warnings that act as "an existential response to what has been heard and warn[s] of the consequences of failing to respond" (France 2007, 285). Jesus begins with a call to "enter through the narrow gate" that leads to a narrow road, implying that few will accept the challenges of the sermon (vv 13-14). He then warns his followers about threats from without, "false prophets" who are known by their fruit or lack thereof (vv 15-20).

Next, Jesus refers to those of his own who believe that their charismatic manifestations would earn them entrance into eternal life (vv 21-23). Finally, Jesus likens the one who obeys his words with the wise builder who constructs his house on the rock versus the foolish builder who builds on the sand, the latter of which ends in disaster (vv 24-27).

Matthew concludes the sermon with a transition statement (vv 28-29). Each of the oral discourses in Matthew, the first of which is the Sermon on the Mount, ends with a formula quotation to mark the conclusion of oral discourse and the resumption of the narrative (see v 28; 11:1; 13:53; 19:1; 26:1).

a. The Narrow Gate (7:13-14)

IN THE TEXT

■ **13-14** Jesus calls his audience to **enter through the narrow gate** (v 13*a*). However, **only a few find it** because **small is the gate and narrow the road that leads to life** (v 14). Many enter the **wide** gate and the accompanying **broad . . . road that leads to** eternal **destruction** (v 13). These metaphors imply the difficult challenges contained in the sermon and that few can handle them. Further, what one chooses now has implications for the future. Entering **through the narrow gate** now will ensure **life** in the future. Jesus refers to eternal life at a number of points throughout Matthew (18:8-9; 19:16-17, 29; 25:46), which is also "the exact opposite of the ultimate ruin referred to in the preceding verse [v. 13]" (Hagner 1993, 179).

In some OT texts, two roads or ways are used as a metaphor to describe two different lifestyles, each of which have very different consequences. This same metaphor is also found in a variety of Greek and Roman literature as well (Keener 1999, 250). The Psalmist writes: "For the LORD watches over *the way* of the righteous, but *the way* of the wicked leads to destruction" (1:6; see Jer 21:8). Jesus' words are also reminiscent of Moses at points in Deuteronomy, where the Israelites can choose blessing by obedience to the Law or curse by disobedience (11:26-29; 30:15-18). Jesus presents his disciples with two alternatives and exhorts them to choose the one that leads to life.

It is not surprising that this is a less popular journey, but not to choose it comes at great cost—**destruction**. In Matt 25:31-46, those who did not give in the way Jesus commands in 5:42 or apply the golden rule in 7:12, and yet consider themselves "righteous" or faithful (25:37-39), will face "eternal punishment" (25:41, 46). Although the narrow road is not easy (see 5:11-12; 10:16-23), it comes with great reward—eternal **life**.

b. False Prophets (7:15-20)

■ **15-20** Jesus warns the disciples about **false prophets** (v 15*a*) who are difficult to detect because **they come . . . in sheep's clothing** (v 15*b*). On the inside, **they are ferocious wolves**. The OT and other ancient literature attests to the fact that wolves prey upon lambs (see Keener 1999, 253), and the people of God in the OT are referred to as **sheep** (see Ezek 34).

Jesus reveals the motivation of these **false prophets**: as **wolves** they wish to ravage the Christian community who are the **sheep**. Davies and Allison list possibilities for the identities of these **false prophets**, which include Pharisees, Zealots, Essenes, Gnostics, and Jewish Christians (1988, 701). It is more likely that they refer to any group who are possibly charismatic (Matt 7:22), whose lives "show no evidence of the good fruit of righteousness" (Hagner 1993, 182) and, as a result, leave a wake of division and strife.

Jesus alerts his followers to false prophets and messianic pretenders elsewhere (7:22; 24:5, 10, 24) and warns them about inauthentic fellow believers (24:12, 48-51) (Keener 1999, 251). Preservation of the community is a major theme in Matthew, which suggests that both internal and external threats were very real (→ Introduction, under Matthew's Community).

As we have seen elsewhere, lifestyle in the kingdom is of utmost importance (e.g., 5:16). The key to discerning a false prophet is **by their fruit** (v 16*a*). This harkens back to John the Baptist's chastisement of the Pharisees and Sadducees who had all the appearance of religious devotion but not a lifestyle that cohered with a repentant heart (→ Matt 3:7-10).

To make the point that false prophets are in fact incapable of bearing fruit, Jesus asks yet another rhetorical question: **Do people pick grapes from thornbushes, or figs from thistles?** (7:16*b*). He then develops the agriculture metaphor, which functions as a response to his previous question: **every good tree bears good fruit** and **a bad tree bears bad fruit** (v 17). In v 18 he states the same point negatively. It is difficult to keep one's true nature hidden, as Jesus himself recognizes in Matt 12:34*b*: "For the mouth speaks what the heart is full of." Similarly, "Many ancients recognized that, despite all pretense, an evil person's nature was bound to emerge" (Keener 1999, 253, citing Prov 27:22; 1 Tim 5:24-25).

Consequently, echoing the words of John the Baptist, **Every tree that does not bear good fruit is cut down and thrown into the fire** (Matt 7:19; 3:10). This is a warning to would-be false prophets who intend to lead the disciples astray and, for Matthew, fracture the community to whom he writes. Jesus concludes with a restatement of 7:16*b*: **Thus, by their fruit you will recognize them** (v 20). This section demonstrates the importance of righteous ethical behavior, which Jesus has just articulated in the sermon, for life in the kingdom of God.

c. Entrance into the Kingdom (7:21-23)

■ **21-23** This saying appears to depict an eschatological scene of judgment. Those who felt that they did the will of God will ask Jesus **on that day** to admit them into the kingdom of heaven (v 22*a*). The temporal phrase, **on that day**, denotes "the day of the Lord" when he judges evil (Amos 8:9; Joel 2:1-2). Jesus will respond that **only the one who does the will of my Father who is in heaven** will enter (v 21*b*). Jesus continues, **Many will say to me on that day, "Lord, Lord, did we not prophesy in your name and in your name drive out demons and in your name perform many miracles?"** (v 22).

The phrase, **in your name**, is repeated three times. It is likely an invocation of the power of Jesus to perform a miraculous deed, similar to the way in which the apostles performed signs and wonders in Acts (e.g., 3:6, 16; Hagner 1993, 187). Despite the charismatic activities of these people and their plea marked by **Lord, Lord**, Jesus still refuses them: **I never knew you. Away from me, you evildoers!** (Matt 7:23).

Addressing Jesus as **Lord** in this context does not indicate an affirmation of his divinity but, at the very least, "implies a serious level of engagement with him, as illustrated in chap. 8 to follow" (Nolland 2005, 339). The first part of Jesus' response in 7:23, **I never knew you**, is a statement of rejection directed at fraudulent disciples who were not obedient to the will of the Father (see v 21*b*). Jesus is certainly not opposed to charismatic activity, as he will later commission his disciples "to drive out impure spirits and to heal every disease and sickness" (10:1*b*). However, something more is needed and that is "good fruit" (7:19), which follows from doing the will of God.

This is not the case for the "false prophets," who may be in view here. They seek to destroy the community despite the performance of signs and wonders. At the judgment, Jesus reveals their true identity: **evildoers** (*tēn anomian*: "the lawless ones"). Jesus may allude to Ps 6:8 [v 9 HB, LXX]: "Away from me, all of you who do evil." The evil or "lawless" in this psalm and elsewhere are those who have no regard for the Lord, his law, or his people (see Pss 89:22 [23 HB]; 94:20; Rom 6:19). Jesus uses similar language to dismiss those who claim to be righteous but were not due to their oversight of "one of the least of these" (Matt 25:40) and are likewise denied entry into the kingdom (25:41).

d. House upon the Rock (7:24-27)

7:24-27 ■ **24-27** Now that Jesus has warned his disciples about the difficulty of his teaching (7:13-14), threats to the stability of the community both from without (vv 15-20) and within (vv 21-23), he exhorts his disciples to put into practice the content of the sermon: **Everyone who hears these words of mine and puts them into practice is like a wise man who built his house on the rock** (v 24). Doing the will of the Father, although articulated in a variety of ways, is a major theme in the last three sections of teaching in ch 7. Beginning at v 15, Matthew uses the Greek word *poieō* several times: bear (*poieō*) fruit (vv 17, 18, 19), do (*poieō*) God's will (v 21), and practice (*poieō*) Jesus' words (vv 24, 26).

To practice what Jesus has taught is to build one's spiritual life on a firm foundation, just as the **wise man who built his house on the rock** (v 24*b*). When **the rain came down, the streams rose, and the winds blew and beat against that house; yet it did not fall, because it had its foundation on the rock** (v 25). However, the one who hears the words of Jesus and chooses **not** to **put them into practice is like a foolish man who built his house on the sand** (v 26). This house **fell with a great crash** when the storm came (v 27).

France indicates that "the parable itself is simple and self-explanatory in a country where heavy rain can send flash floods surging down the normally dry wadis with devastating effect" (2007, 296). The two contrasting behaviors, one characterized by the obedience of the **wise man** and the other by the disobedience or even apathy of the **foolish man** is reminiscent of the wisdom tradition in which the wise are contrasted with the foolish (Prov 10:1, 8; Eccl 10:2; Nolland 2005, 343).

It is Jesus' teaching, **these words of mine**, and not that of his heavenly Father's, that is the **rock** (*petra* [Matt 7:24]). God is often described as a rock who is sure and faithful (Deut 32:4, 18; Ps 18:2, 31 [3, 32 HB]) and in whom Israel can trust. This image has now transferred to God's Messiah in whom the Law and the Prophets are fulfilled, something that no rabbi would claim to do. **These words** refer to the entire sermon, which reveals a new covenant established by the Messiah. In this covenant, the Law is written upon the heart arising out of "a completely new relationship between God and his people" (Brower 2005, 122; → Matt 5:17).

e. *Conclusion (7:28-29)*

■ **28-29** Matthew concludes the sermon by recounting the amazement of the crowds **at his teaching, because he taught as one who had authority, and not as their teachers of the law** (vv 28*b*-29). These are the same crowds that gathered around Jesus at the beginning of the sermon and are now convinced of his authority (5:1). Matthew 7:29 reproduces the exact wording of Mark 1:22. Mark does not record anything Jesus teaches in the synagogue but only what Jesus does: he exorcises an unclean spirit (vv 21-26). Following this, the crowds express that this is "a new teaching—and with authority!" (v 27). Matthew, on the other hand, places this statement after the sermon to highlight the authoritative words of Jesus.

In Matt 8—9, Jesus will demonstrate that he has authority, not only through his teaching but also through his deeds (8:9; 9:6, 8; 21:23). The *deeds* of Jesus follow hard on the heels of this *teaching*, both of which point to the reign of God inaugurated by the Messiah (→ the summary statements in 4:23 and 9:35) and reveal God's ecclesiological and eschatological saving purposes for his people (→ 5:17-20).

FROM THE TEXT

These warnings and exhortations reflect a major theme in Matthew's Gospel, which James puts well: "Faith by itself, if it does not have works, is dead" (2:17 NKJV). A key tenet of Protestant theology is salvation by grace through faith (Eph 2:8) and, at first glance, it appears that Matthew advocates salvation by works. However, it is important to keep the rest of Matthew's theology in focus: Jesus is Immanuel, "God with us" (Matt 1:23), who establishes a new covenant between us and God whereby we can bear good fruit (7:17*a*) and do "the will of [the] Father" (v 21*b*). All of this is possible because of the sacrificial work of Jesus who died "for the forgiveness of sins" (26:28) and promises to be with us for eternity (28:20*b*).

C. Mighty Deeds of the Messiah (8:1—9:34)

This second narrative panel in Matt 8—9 offers a series of vignettes from the healing ministry of Jesus, which is summarized in 4:23-25. Throughout these two chapters, the popularity of Jesus continues to grow. Crowds follow him (8:1), often bringing those who need healing (8:16; 9:2, 32). Others follow Jesus because they themselves are in need (9:20, 27) or petition on behalf of a loved one (8:5-6). These moments demonstrate that Jesus as Messiah both teaches and heals with authority. These are the words and deeds of the Messiah that manifest the reign of God. In the ministry of Jesus, exile is coming to an end because the light of this reign has dawned (4:12-17).

1. Three Miracles of Jesus (8:1-17)

BEHIND THE TEXT

The first two accounts record the healing of people who were ritually unclean and therefore from whom most Jews would distance themselves: a leper (vv 1-4) and a Gentile (vv 5-13). Jesus performs the unthinkable and touches the leper. He then heals the Gentile's servant with a word from a distance. After these healings, he cures the fever of Peter's mother-in-law (vv 14-15). Crowds of needy persons continue to come (v 16). Matthew summarizes Jesus' activity as the fulfillment of the role of the Servant of Yahweh from Isaiah (v 17).

8:1-2 *a. Cleansing of a Leper (8:1-4)*

IN THE TEXT

■ **1-2** After his sermon, Jesus comes **down from the mountainside** with **large crowds** (v 1). These **crowds** (5:1-2) recognize his authoritative teaching and want to follow him. Hagner suggests that "the majority followed Jesus more out of curiosity than belief" (1993, 198). Matthew, however, shows that the crowds recognize that his authority is unique (7:28-29): And behold [untranslated in the NIV] **a man with leprosy came and knelt before him** asking that Jesus **make** him **clean** (8:2).

The Law is clear: those with leprosy are unclean and they must remain outside of community until they are declared clean by the priest. They then offer the requisite sacrifices (Lev 13—14). Thus, this man is likely in a rural area and has heard about Jesus' healing power (Matt 4:23-25). Some texts imply that leprosy was considered incurable by natural means (Exod 4:4-6; Num 12:9-15; 2 Kgs 5:1-27). This man's state is hopeless, but he recognizes Jesus' healing power: **Lord, if you are willing, you can make me clean** (Matt 8:2*b*).

The leper does not appeal to God for healing but to Jesus, who responds, "I am willing" (v 3*b*). Matthew's audience would know that only God can heal (see 2 Kgs 5:10-11 for Naaman's healing). Matthew does not spell out the implications of Jesus' miracle. Rather, "the reader is left to ponder the Christological implications" (France 2007, 308). Readers already know Jesus as Immanuel (Matt 1:23), God with us in salvation (→ Matt 1). Further, this leper addresses Jesus as **Lord** (*kurios*), the Greek name for Yahweh/Lord in the LXX. With this background and with Jesus' miraculous deed, the term may function as a verbal clue pointing to Matthew's high Christology (see 7:21; 8:8; 12:8). Of course, "lord" is also a form of address used by an inferior to a superior (Keener 1999, 267), which may be the usage at the historical level.

■ **3-4 Jesus reached out his hand and touched** him (v 3*a*). The impurity of leprosy is contracted through touch (e.g., Lev 13:46; Num 5:1-4). But rather than being contaminated, Jesus purifies the leper. With Jesus, purity is now a contagion. Recalling the declarations of the priests, Jesus declares, **Be clean!** (Matt 8:3*c*; see Lev 13:6, 13, 17, etc.) and **immediately he was cleansed of his leprosy** (Matt 8:3*d*). Unlike the priests who would only make this announcement after a leprous sore was healed by natural means, and the supplicant offered up the required sacrifices, Jesus merely touches this man and speaks an authoritative word.

Jesus then prohibits him from telling anyone about this (v 4*a*). Rather, he commands him to **go, show yourself to the priest and offer the gift Moses commanded, as a testimony to them** (v 4*b*). In Mark's account, the first thing this man does is exactly the opposite: he spreads the news (Mark 1:45)! As with other instances in Matthew, the understanding and obedience of those who relate to Jesus is more evident (e.g., compare Matt 14:33 with Mark 6:52), and so the man's obedience is implied, unlikely though it might be on historical terms.

The command to appear before the priest enables the leper to return to the community, having been declared clean (Hagner 1993, 200; France 2007, 308). Hagner argues that it has little to do with Jesus complying with the Law as articulated in Lev 13—14 (1993, 200). Jesus has come to fulfill the Law and the Prophets (Matt 5:17), but not the laws of ritual purity as Jesus clearly breaches those. Rather, his healing touch purifies this man, and purity is the goal of the Law (→ 5:48). Jesus enables this man to experience the beatitude that "the pure in heart . . . will see God" (5:8). This man's healing will be **a testimony to them**, the priests as well as others (8:4*b*), demonstrating that Jesus not only heals and purifies but also restores this man to the community, which fulfillment of the Law facilitates.

b. Healing of the Centurion's Servant (8:5-13)

■ **5-6** This is the first reference to a Galilean location since 4:13. Upon returning, **a centurion came to him, asking for help** (v 5). Jesus will minister to another impure person, this time a Gentile (see Acts 10:28). Because of Capernaum's location, being near the border of the tetrarchy of Philip and on a trade route, Roman soldiers would be stationed there (Hagner 1993, 203).

This **centurion** is in charge of one hundred foot soldiers (or eighty, according to Keener 1999, 264). Several centurions play a role in the NT (Mark 15:39; Luke 7:5; Acts 27:1). Another one, along with a contingent of soldiers, will declare Jesus as "the Son of God" (Matt 27:54).

The centurion also addresses Jesus as **Lord** (see 8:2): **"Lord," he said, "my servant lies at home paralyzed, suffering terribly"** (v 6). The Greek word for **servant** (*pais*) can also mean "son" but only in John 4:51 does the word clearly mean this. Matthew uses the word to mean "servant" elsewhere (Matt 12:18; 14:18), likely referring to "a house slave" (Davies and Allison 1991, 21; France 2007, 312; contra Hagner 1993, 204 who advocates for "son"). This **servant** is likely the centurion's only family, as they were prohibited from having regular families during their years of service (Keener 1999, 266). The servant's paralysis and pain might be due to "what we could call polio or a stroke . . . ; in either case there would be no prospect of a medical cure" (France 2007, 312). Another opportunity has arisen for the Messiah to demonstrate his authority.

■ **7-10, 13 Shall I come and heal him?** (8:7) is not an offer actually to enter the house of a Gentile, which was strongly discouraged in 2TJ. Rather, Jesus' response questions the presumption of the centurion that Jesus, a faithful Jew, would do such a thing. Thus, the centurion responds that he is unworthy: **Lord, I do not deserve to have you come under my roof** (v 8*a*). The centurion recognizes that Jesus can heal: **But just say the word, and my servant will be healed** (v 8*b*). He then compares Jesus to himself: **For I myself am a man under authority, with soldiers under me** (v 9*a*) to whom he gives orders, and they obey (v 9*b*).

This story and the one about the Canaanite woman (15:22-28) constitute a type-scene in which two or more stories with similar patterns communicate specific themes. They have similar elements: a Gentile asks Jesus to heal a loved one who suffers greatly (8:6 // 15:22); Jesus' initial response is unfavorable (8:7 // 15:23-24, 26); the supplicants make a case (8:8-9 // 15:25, 27); upon hearing this, Jesus acknowledges their great faith and performs the healing (8:10-13 // 15:28). Both stories reaffirm that Jesus has indeed come first for Israel, the chosen people (1:21; 10:6) because he does not immediately respond like he does with Jews (8:3, 15; 9:6, 22, 25, 29). However, in Matthew, faith is foundational for healing (see 9:28-29 and 13:58). Both the centurion and the woman demonstrate such faith, and Jesus affirms it (8:10; 15:28). He declares that the centurion's faith exceeds that of any Jew: **Truly I tell you, I have not found anyone in Israel with such great faith** (v 10*b*).

■ **11-12** There are eschatological consequences for Israel's lack of faith and presumption of election based on ethnicity. At the great eschatological banquet, **many will come from the east and the west** and will join the patriarchs **in the kingdom of heaven** (v 11). The idea of a messianic banquet is derived from Isa 25:6 and "Jewish tradition soon made it a blessing specifically for Israel" (France 2007, 317).

In contrast, Jesus predicts that **many**, that is, Gentiles, will come from lands outside of Israel to join the patriarchs. Davies and Allison contend that the **many** are "unprivileged Jews" (1991, 28) in light of Ps 107 and Isa 25—27. But this in unconvincing. Jesus is contrasting this Gentile's "great" faith with the faith of ethnic Israel (France 2007, 317-18). Jews who do not bear fruit worthy of repentance and believe that Jesus is God's Messiah, **will be thrown outside, into the darkness, where there will be weeping and gnashing of teeth** (Matt 8:12).

In Greek, the phrase "the sons [note the NIV's accurate translation, **subjects**] of the kingdom" is one Jesus will use again in 13:38 to describe those who will receive salvation. Jesus, as faithful Israel (→ 4:1-11), is now, as the Lord's Messiah, redefining the conditions for entrance into this new nation requiring faith in him, which overrides any ethnic superiority. Those who exhibit this faith are the true **subjects of the kingdom** (v 12*a*), such as the centurion (v 13).

The imagery in v 12*b* is Matthew's way of depicting eschatological judgment (13:42, 50; 22:13; 24:51; 25:30; Hagner 1993, 206) at the core of which is separation from the presence of God, being cast **outside. Darkness** is often a feature of such separation in Jewish tradition (e.g., Wis 17:21; Tob 14:10; *1 En.* 63:6). The **gnashing of teeth** may refer to anger (Job 16:9 LXX; Ps 34:16 [17 HB]; Davies and Allison 1991, 31) in response to this unexpected exclusion, or it could indicate simple mourning (Keener 1999, 269).

Jesus reapplies this language to faithless Israelites when it usually applies to godless Gentiles (France 2007, 316). However, not every Israelite will experience this judgment! "Perhaps 8:11f. should be understood as a prophetic threat, a word which speaks of damnation not as certainty but as a prospect demanding repentance" (Davies and Allison 1991, 31).

c. Healing of Peter's Mother-in-Law (8:14-15)

■ **14-15** Jesus' healing of **Peter's mother-in-law** who is **lying in bed with a fever** (v 14) is yet another account of his power to heal. Fever in the ancient world was considered a disease in itself rather than a symptom (Hagner 1993, 209). Peter's mother-in-law is able to serve them after she is healed, which "may make emphatic the model for discipleship: after Jesus transforms a person, the person serves him" (Keener 1999, 271).

After Jesus **touched her hand**, immediately **the fever left her** and she is restored to full health: **she got up and began to wait on him** (v 15). Matthew amended Mark's "wait on them" (1:31) to **him**. Jesus, and his ability to heal, takes center stage in these miracle accounts with little mention of the disciples.

d. Summary Statement (8:16-17)

■ **16** According to the parallel account in Mark, Jesus visited Peter's home on the Sabbath after having exorcised "an impure spirit" in the synagogue (1:21-31). France argues that Matthew does not indicate the day (2007, 321), but Matt 8:16*a*, **when evening came, many who were demon-possessed were brought to him**, may imply that Jesus visited Peter's home on the Sabbath.

Jesus healed the centurion's servant with a spoken word (v 13); now **he drove out the spirits with a word and healed all the sick**. This mode of deliverance is different from other exorcists of Jesus' day who would employ "elaborate incantations and techniques" (France 2007, 312; see also Keener 1999, 272). This verse also notes the continued popularity of Jesus' healing and deliverance ministry, recalling the earlier summary about Jesus' ministry drawing "large crowds" from every direction. The light of God's reign is dawning for those who are healed, signaling the beginning of the end of the exile that they and their ancestors have endured for generations (→ 4:23-25).

■ **17** The last use of a formula quotation indicating fulfillment of an OT prophecy was in 4:14. Here Matthew uses it to validate Jesus' healing ministry. In Isaiah's fourth servant song (Isa 52:13—53:12), the servant, considered to be the nation or a remnant thereof, will remove the covenant curses of exile, which include physical illness (Deut 28:59-61; Watts 2015, 90). In Isaiah, the servant effects his restoration through his own suffering, rejection, and death (vv 5, 8, 10-12).

Matthew's Use of Isa 53:4 in Matt 8:17

His citation reflects dependence on the MT rather than the LXX, which is evident in the following.

Matt 8:17	MT Isa 53:4*a*	LXX Isa 53:4*a* [NETS]
"He took up [*lambanō*] our infirmities ['sickness' (*astheneia*)] and bore [*bastazō*] our diseases [*nosos*]"	"Surely he took up [*nāśā'*] our pain ['sickness' (*ḥoliy*)] and bore [*sābal*] our suffering [*mak'ōb*]"	"This one bears [*pherō*] our sins [*hamartia*] and suffers pain [*odunaō*] for us"

Matthew's use of "he took up" (*lambanō*) reflects the MT's "he took up" (*nāśā'*) versus the LXX's "This one bears [*pherō*]." Further, the MT reads "sickness" (*ḥoliy*), and Matthew uses *astheneia* ("sickness, disease") instead of *hamartia* ("sins"), which is in the LXX. In the second line, Matthew's use of "bore" [*bastazō*] reflects the MT's "bore" [*sābal*], but his use of *nosos*, "diseases," is not reflected in the MT or LXX. However, Matthew uses this term in his summaries of Jesus' healings (4:23; 9:35; 10:1), which calls attention to the relationship of this citation to Jesus' healing ministry.

Some scholars link this citation, which describes the restorational work of the servant, to other instances of Isaiah in Matthew that point to the Suffering Servant (i.e., Isa 53:10-12 in Matt 20:28; and Isa 53:12 in Matt 26:28). The difficulty is that Jesus does not suffer in Matt 8—9, but his vocation as the servant will ultimately involve suffering on behalf of others (26:28; Isa 53:10-12; see Carson 1984, 205-7). Davies and Allison contend that this citation coheres with the context of Matt 8—9, and less with the passion, because Jesus "identifies himself with humanity in its suffering," just as the servant does (1991, 38).

In contrast, Rikk Watts argues that it has nothing to do with the passion or the humility of Jesus. Rather, it reveals that he heals comprehensively as God's divine Son (2015, 92; note Jesus heals "all the sick" in 8:16). Watts disagrees that Jesus does this work as the Messiah or even soon to be suffering servant-Messiah:

> Matthew does not make his first explicit identification of Jesus' Davidic identity and his healings (9:27-31) until well after he has firmly established Jesus' healing . . . via two earlier summary statements (4.23-24 and here, 8.16), neither of which have explicit messianic associations. (2015, 85)

Watts' sharp division between the divine and messianic identities of Jesus is overdrawn as they pertain to his healing ministry. First, Jesus as Messiah inaugurates God's reign for the sick and the marginalized (→ 4:12-17, 23-25). Second, his messiahship is the unifying factor for both healings and his suffering, both of which restore the fortunes of God's people. The fact that Matthew makes this point explicit after 8:17, in 9:27-28, and then again in 12:18-21 does not undercut this. Rather, it confirms what is already implicit.

Jesus' messianic vocation as the servant-Son of Yahweh involves healing and exorcism, bringing restoration to those who suffer the curses of exilic life (→ 12:18-21, in which Matthew quotes Isa 42:1-4, a portion of the first servant song). At the same time, his vocation as the servant-Son will ultimately involve suffering on behalf of others (Matt 26:28; Isa 53:10-12), which he does as King/Messiah of the Jews (Matt 27:37). Matthew's use of Isaiah in 8:17 signals no separation between Jesus' messianic death on the cross for the forgiveness of sins with his Galilean ministry of physical healing and deliverance. The last story (9:1-8) in the next triad of miracle accounts (8:23—9:8) highlights the authority of Jesus, as Son of Man, both to heal and forgive. 8:17

Some holiness preachers and theologians in the nineteenth and twentieth centuries have grounded the healing ministry of Jesus in the atonement. Van De Walle examines a number of individuals in the holiness movement who locate the physical healings of Jesus in the atonement (see Van De Walle 2009, 112-46). They claim that since sickness originally entered creation through the sin of Adam and Eve and that the atonement covers this sin, healing can occur now. In this way, Jesus really does take up our sickness and bear our diseases (v 17). But to press this to imply that healing must always occur because of the finished word of Christ is a step too far.

FROM THE TEXT

The first two stories demonstrate that the work of Messiah Jesus is comprehensive. For the leper, he not only heals but also purifies so that he can rejoin his Jewish community. The healing of the centurion's servant not only results in physical restoration but also demonstrates that the Messiah's work extends to non-Jews. Matthew's quotation of Isaiah in 8:17 shows that Jesus does this work as Yahweh's servant because God's heart is concerned with the total restoration of an individual physically, religiously, and socially. Once Peter's mother-in-law is healed, she begins to wait upon Jesus, which is what she would naturally do when a guest is in her home. The heart of our heavenly Father is revealed in the ministry of Jesus: God desires to heal and restore the whole person! May we be aware of the ways God would use us to extend the ministry of Jesus as described in these verses.

2. The Cost of Discipleship (8:18-22)

BEHIND THE TEXT

As France notes, here are "two case studies . . . of men who wish to join Jesus when he separates himself from the 'crowd'" (2007, 324). After witnessing Jesus exorcise "with a word" and heal "all the sick" (v 16*b*), some wish to follow him: first, a teacher of the Law (v 19) and then a disciple (v 21). These two discipleship accounts (vv 19-22) are between Jesus' orders to the disciples to cross over to the other side (v 18) and their obedience (v 23). This bracketing contrasts the obedience of those who left all to follow him (4:18-22) with those who may not be ready for discipleship (8:20) or to abandon familial responsibilities (v 21).

IN THE TEXT

■ **18-19** After having **the crowd around him** since the beginning of his Sermon on the Mount (5:1), Jesus **orders** his disciples **to cross to the other side of the lake** to have time with them alone (8:18; see 14:13; contra Nolland 2005, 364). Jesus has only called four so far (4:18-22) but others have followed and from this group he will identify twelve (10:1-4). A **teacher of the law** comes to Jesus and says, **Teacher, I will follow you wherever you go** (8:19*b*). Matthew does not often portray the scribes or **teachers of the law** in a positive light (5:20; 7:29; 9:3; 12:38).

Outsiders, like this scribe, address Jesus as **Teacher** in Matthew (12:38; 19:16; 22:16). Still, he is resolved to follow him wherever he goes. France suggests that this disciple only has in mind the journey across the lake, but the adverb **wherever** makes such a limitation unlikely (2007, 326). Davies and Allison suggest that this individual is not desiring to follow Jesus at all and is turned away for it (1991, 41). This is also unlikely.

■ **20** We do not know if Jesus grants this man his request. Rather, he emphasizes the cost of discipleship (see also 8:22). Unlike the animals that have a home, **foxes have dens and birds have nests**, Jesus as **the Son of Man has no place to lay his head**. This reflects Jesus' itinerant ministry, not the lack of a permanent dwelling (see 4:13). Even that night, Jesus is not sleeping in a home but in a boat (8:24). He will not have a home in the Gentile territory of the Gadarenes in which he ministers the next day (vv 28-34); rather, the inhabitants "plead with him to leave their region" (v 34*b*). His disciples will soon share in this as well (10:14, 16-20, 21-22, 34-36; Nolland 2005, 366). Following Jesus and fishing for people (4:19) involves dislocation and unexpected events. However, Jesus does return home to Capernaum in 9:1 (see 13:53-58).

Son of Man

Jesus uses the phrase **the Son of Man** thirty times in Matthew, just over twice as many compared with Mark. In each case, it is a title that only Jesus uses to refer to himself. Scholars used to agree, on the basis of a number of biblical and extrabiblical texts, that the return of the Son of Man to judge and to save was a widely held expectation among the Jews, which Jesus himself fulfilled (Matt 24:37-39; Mark 8:38). However, Geza Vermes began to examine the use of the phrase in Aramaic sources as a circumlocution for "I." This is also evident, at times, when comparing Gospel parallel texts (e.g., "Son of Man" [Matt 16:13] versus "I" [Mark 8:27]) (Vermes 1973, 160-91). Others, however, argue that it means "man" or "a man" (Lindars 1983, 19-24; Casey 1976, 147-54).

The most fruitful studies have been those that examine the OT meaning of the term and how it relates to Jesus' use of it. Morna Hooker argued that in Mark, for example, Jesus' appropriation of the term is modeled on the "one like a son of man" in Dan 7: "the authority, necessity for suffering, and confidence in final vindication, which are all expressed in the Marcan sayings, can all be traced to Dan. 7" (Hooker 1967, 192). Daniel 7 is also at play in Matthew: Jesus will speak of the earthly authority of the Son of Man (e.g., 9:6), his suffering (e.g., 16:12), and his future glory (e.g., 24:30). According to France, "Like his parables, the title 'the Son of Man' came with an air of enigma, challenging the hearer to think new thoughts rather than to slot Jesus into a ready-made pigeonhole" (2007, 327). In short, the definition of Son of Man in the Gospel is filled with content by the life and ministry of Jesus, the Son of Man.

Jesus' first use of the term **the Son of Man** here points to his lowly and humble status, like the Servant of Yahweh (see v 17), who is at the whim of his circumstances and the unpredictable nature of his ministry. Similarly, in Dan 7, the "one like a son of man" is a symbol for the holy ones who suffer under the tyrannical Seleucid Empire of Antiochus IV Epiphanes (Dan 7:14, 27). Just as Son of Man in Daniel refers to the nation of Israel, Jesus may also use the term to prepare his followers for the challenges of discipleship. Jesus redefines what it means to be Israel, which, for the time being, involves dislocation and discomfort. The Son of Man knows what it means to share "with his disciples in all the insecurity of their human condition" (France 2007, 328) as well as the difficulties that come with the proclamation of the gospel.

■ **21-22** Now **another disciple** comes **to him** desiring to follow Jesus (v 21*a*). However, he asks Jesus: **Lord, first let me go and bury my Father** (v 21*b*). This is a legitimate request: Elijah granted Elisha a similar request (1 Kgs 19:19-21). Whatever the precise circumstances, his request is rooted in the Mosaic commandment to "honor your father and your mother" (Exod 20:12; see also Lev 21:1-3; Nolland 2005, 367). One later rabbinic text highlights the duty when a relative dies: that person is freed "from all the commandments stated in the Torah" (*b. Ber.* 31a). If this text reflects earlier practice, Jesus' response in Matt 8:22 would be offensive to Jewish sensibilities: **Follow me, and let the dead bury their own dead** (v 22).

Just as James and John immediately stopped mending their nets and left their living father on his own (4:21-22), disciples must also be prepared to leave the dead as well for the call of Jesus (3:10). The idea of the dead burying the dead is, on the surface, nonsense if referring to the physically dead carrying out such an activity. In defense of Jesus, some claim he was talking about the "spiritually dead," those who have rejected Jesus (Davies and Allison 1991, 56). But it is in the nonsense of the idea that meaning is found. Jesus is saying to this man what you are concerned with will fix itself; rather, you need to deal with what is before you, the call of the kingdom. In this case, "even the most basic of family ties must not be allowed to stand in its way" (France 2007, 330; see 4:22; 10:37; 12:46-50; 19:29).

FROM THE TEXT

Discipleship has a cost, and this is the first moment where Jesus explicitly teaches about what following him entails. We do not know if these prospective disciples ended up following him, but Matthew's audience knows that the call of God may result in both physical dislocation (i.e., having no place to lay one's head) and social discomfort (i.e., not fulfilling expected social customs). Although Wesley does not use the term "discipleship," he recognizes that the call of Christ has supremacy in the lives of believers and that it should be rooted in the love we have for our Master. For the disciple, "All the commandments of God he accordingly keeps, and that with all his might. For his obedience is in proportion to his love, the source from whence it flows" ("The Character of a Methodist" in Wesley 1978, 8:344).

3. Three More Miracles of Jesus (8:23—9:8)

BEHIND THE TEXT

The first two of these miracle stories occur on the journey Jesus takes to the other side of the Sea of Galilee. He first calms the stormy sea (8:23-27), and on the other side, two unclean, demonized individuals confront him (vv 28-34). Upon returning to Capernaum, Jesus both forgives the sins and heals the paralysis of a man brought to him (9:1-8). The area of the Gadarenes, where Jesus encounters the two demonized men, is Gentile territory in the Decapolis, not under Herodian control. The exact location is uncertain ("Gerasenes" in Mark

5:1 // Luke 8:26; "Gadarenes" in Matt 8:28), although Davies and Allison plausibly argue for Gergesa because of its proximity to water and a steep cliff (1991, 79). The presence of pigs guarantees that this is Gentile territory.

These three stories center on further revelation of Jesus' identity, signalled by the question of the disciples in the first account: "What kind of man is this? Even the winds and the waves obey him!" (8:27*b*). Whereas once "the crowds" pondered Jesus' authority (7:28), it is now Jesus' disciples. In the second account, Jesus' authority over the demonic extends to unclean, Gentile territory (8:28-34). In 9:1-8, Jesus demonstrates not only power to heal but also the authority to forgive sins.

a. Calming the Storm (8:23-27)

IN THE TEXT

■ **23-25** In v 23, the disciples follow Jesus' order in v 18 to go to the other side: **Then he got into the boat and his disciples followed him**. Having heard Jesus' challenge to the two prospective followers (vv 18-22), the disciples know the cost of following him wherever he goes. While traveling across the lake **a furious storm came up . . . , so that the waves swept over the boat** (v 24*a*). This lake is known for the rapid development of high winds and waves due to surrounding mountains and its location in the Jordan valley (France 2007, 336; Keener 1999, 278).

In the midst of this storm, **Jesus was sleeping** (v 24*b*). The disciples wake him and ask that he **save** them because they are **going to drown** (v 25). This may echo Jonah who was awakened in a storm but, unlike Jesus, appeals to God for deliverance (Jonah 1:4-6, 14; Nolland 2005, 371, lists additional links but some apply more to Mark's version than Matthew's).

The disciples also address Jesus as **Lord!** (v 25). While this term may simply refer to a person of superior status, given Matthew's usage thus far, and its echo of the Greek name for Yahweh in the LXX, it contributes significantly to Matthew's Christology. The disciples are in need, like the leper (v 2) and the centurion (v 6), all of whom address Jesus as **Lord**. The disciples' request now that Jesus **save** (*sōzō*) them is fitting since it is often used when seeking deliverance from a hostile situation (Keener 1999, 280 n. 53).

■ **26-27** Jesus chastises them for their **little faith** (*oligopistos*), asking them, **Why are you so afraid?** (v 26*a*). Jesus used this same word in 6:30 to describe those who fail to trust in their heavenly Father for basic needs; how much more will he now, through Jesus, deliver them from this mortal danger (France 2007, 336)? Fear and distrust are at the root of the lack of faith in both cases. Jesus then performs the miracle: he **rebuked the winds and the waves** and the seas were then **calm** (v 26*b*). This control over the natural world falls under the domain of God himself, which is highlighted in the Psalms (e.g., 89:9 [10 HB] and 106:9) as well as in Job (38:8-11).

While the disciples witness Jesus performing miracles for others, now they are learning for themselves the identity of Jesus and ask, **What kind of man is this?** (v 27*a*). In the next scene, the demons recognize the identity of Jesus immediately (v 29*a*). For the disciples, Jesus' identity gradually unfolds while Matthew's audience has insider information, beginning in the birth narrative. They know, as do we, that Jesus is Immanuel, God with his people, exercising Yahweh's authority as his Messiah, over the chaotic and life-threatening seas. Later, on another stormy sea journey, the disciples recognize this: "Truly you are the Son of God" (14:33).

Matthew's use of **men** in 8:27 as opposed to **disciples** in v 23 may imply a contrast between the mortal status of the disciples and the one in their midst who reigns over the natural order and is more than a mere man (Gundry 1982, 156-57). It is unlikely to be another character group whom Matthew wishes to distinguish from the disciples, as Nolland argues (2007, 327). The power of Yahweh is with Jesus to perform a miraculous feat, but it will take some time before the disciples comprehend his identity.

b. Exorcising a Legion of Demons (8:28-34)

■ **28-29** As soon as Jesus arrives **at the other side** in the Gentile territory **of the Gadarenes, two demon-possessed men** who lived among **the tombs met him** (v 28*a*). These two were controlled by demons and became so violent that no one else **could pass that way** (v 28*b*). In some Jewish texts, **tombs** are associ-
8:28-29 ated with demons and magic (*Jub.* 22:17; *T. Sol.* 8:9; *b. Ber.* 18b; Keener 1999, 281). This, and Matthew's observation about violence, implies that "these demons are inordinately powerful—hence the narrative's opening suspense and Christological impact" (Keener 1999, 281). From the perspective of ritual purity, these men are unclean, having lived among the tombs. This is the first moment Jesus enters Gentile territory to extend the reign of God over the marginalized, something he will do again (Matt 15:21-28).

In Mark 5:1-20, there is only one man; Matthew has two. Davies and Allison list a variety of proposals to explain this movement (1991, 80), but none convinces them or France who cites Davies' and Allison's list as well (2007, 339). Matthew elsewhere doubles characters who are individuals in Mark (see Matt 9:27-31 and 20:30-34 // Mark 10:46-52). Perhaps Matthew is following an OT injunction that legitimate testimony is based on "two or three witnesses" (Num 35:30; Deut 17:6; 19:15), but this has difficulties of its own (France 2007, 340; Keener 1999, 282). Jesus elsewhere heals individuals as well (see Matt 8:14-15). As France notes, "The reason for Matthew's 'seeing double' remains a matter of speculation" (2007, 340).

The men themselves do not address Jesus, but only the demons (see Mark 5:9, 12) that harass them. They perceive him as a threat to their existence asking, **What do you want with us, Son of God? . . . Have you come here to torture us before the appointed time?** (Matt 8:29). Some argue that the

Greco-Roman concept of a "divine man" (*theios anēr*) is a helpful category for Jesus' ability to heal as the Son of God. Such an individual is a human with divine attributes, one of which is the ability to perform miracles. Preference for this background, however, is fraught with difficulties (Keener 2011, 51-53).

A Jewish background is more fruitful but indecisive. **Son of God** in Jewish tradition refers to angels, Israel, or Messiah. Matthew's presentation of Jesus as Messiah, Son of God (Matt 1:1; 16:16) as well as a new embodiment of the nation that is also God's son (Matt 2:15; 3:17) goes beyond either the Jewish or the Gentile background.

The demons know that their **appointed time** (v 29*b*) is short. In *1 En.* 55:4, the Messiah will reign over demonic forces while a messianic priest in *T. Levi* 18:12 will oversee the binding of Beliar, an opponent of God in a variety of Jewish 2T texts. Here, Jesus as Messiah, Son of God, delivers those oppressed by the ultimate enemy in the present time, as opposed to the future; indeed, "the Kingdom of God has come upon" these men (12:28), which means judgment for the demons now (Keener 1999, 286).

■ **30-31** Matthew indicates that there was **a large herd of pigs . . . feeding** not far away (8:30). This is clearly Gentile territory: pigs are unclean (Lev 11:7; Deut 14:8) and no faithful Jew would farm or consume them. Demons need to have a host (see Matt 12:43-45) and so they beg Jesus to send them into the nearby swine (8:31). This is a fitting home for these demons that initially inhabit men who live among tombs, which are also considered unclean (see the literature cited in Keener 1999, 281), and now wish to inhabit unclean animals.

■ **32-34** Jesus grants their request: **Go!** (v 32*a*). This simple command contrasts Jesus with magicians who would use various techniques (e.g., incantations) to exorcize (France 2007, 338). As soon as the demons **went into the pigs, . . . the whole herd rushed down the steep bank into the lake and died in the water** (v 32*b*). From a Jewish perspective, this would be welcomed, but more importantly, the demons are clearly gone from the men. It is likely that the swine **died** but not the demons (v 32*b*). Given that the sea is a place of chaos and hostility (see v 26), Jesus sent the demons to their rightful home.

The swineherds, who **went into the town and reported all this** (v 33), would have been outraged. As a result, **the whole town went out to meet Jesus** but, unlike the crowds thus far in Matthew, they urge **him to leave their region** (v 34). He will also soon be resisted by his own people (9:34; 12:24; 13:57-58; France 2007, 343).

c. Healing a Paralytic (9:1-8)

■ **1-2** Jesus crosses back over the lake and returns to Capernaum, where his ministry began (4:13-17) and he healed the centurion's servant (8:5). In Mark, Jesus is likely in his own home (2:1), but Matthew omits several details (see Mark 2:4*a*). Rather, **some men** merely bring to Jesus **a paralyzed man, lying on a mat** (Matt 9:2*b*). Unusually, Jesus does not act immediately; all those who have come to him thus far have been healed immediately (see 8:1-5, 6-13, 16). Instead, Jesus declares, **Your sins are forgiven** (9:2*b*). It was due to **their faith** (v 2*b*) that he makes this declaration, which likely refers to the **men** who carried him as well as the man himself (Hagner 1993, 232); again, faith is foundational for Jesus to heal and now to forgive.

Matthew reveals a new dimension of Jesus' authority: he can do that which only God can do—forgive sins (see Exod 34:6-7; Isa 43:25; 44:22). Jesus might be dealing with the root of the man's paralysis. Several OT texts draw a connection between sickness and sin (Lev 26:14-16; Isa 33:24; Jer 16:3-4). In Ps 32, the supplicant confesses that his body is decaying because of unconfessed sin (vv 3-4) and after his confession, he is physically restored (vv 5-7). Jesus' salvation, as in the psalm, encompasses the entire person (→ Matt 8:17) and when sin and sickness "are intertwined, God wishes to deal with both (Jas 5:14-16)" (Keener 1999, 289).

Forgiveness of sins was usually associated with the eschaton and "was built up on the OT promises of forgiveness linked to the assurance of restoration beyond the period of the Exile" (Nolland 2005, 381). The punishment for Israel's sin was exile and now that Jesus, Yahweh's Messiah, comes and offers forgiveness, the end of the exile has begun (see Jer 34:31-34; Ezek 36:24-26, 33; Wright 1996, 268-74).

■ **3** The scribes, the custodians of the Torah and halakhah associated with it, take issue: **This fellow is blaspheming!** Blasphemy includes a variety of offensive words or actions against God or his people, such as insulting his name (Lev 24:11), disbelieving his power (2 Kgs 19:4; Ps 74:18), or persecuting his people (Isa 52:5; Ezek 35:12). Jesus is guilty of blasphemy here because his claim to forgive sins, as a man, is reserved for Yahweh. He is arrogating divine prerogatives to himself.

■ **4-7** Jesus has divine insight into the thoughts of these scribes (see 12:25*a*; 22:18), because he questions their unstated comments recorded in Matt 9:3: **Why do you entertain evil thoughts in your hearts?** (v 4*b*). France claims that Jesus' "seeing their thoughts" (**knowing their thoughts** [v 4*a*]) results from his perceptive reading of their body language (2007, 347), but Matthew states that he "perceived" their thoughts.

Thus far, Jesus has not used the term **evil** (*ponēros*) to describe the character of his opponents. When the Pharisees accuse Jesus of exorcising by "Beelzebul, the prince of demons" (12:24), he labels them as "evil," for it is out of their hearts that they speak such things (12:34). In Jerusalem, he will accuse the Pharisees and Herodians of hypocrisy because of their "evil intent" when questioning him (22:15-18). In our passage, Jesus asks them why they **entertain** [*enthumeomai*] **evil thoughts**. They consider the prospect that Jesus is a blasphemer.

Jesus then asks his questioners if it is easier to pronounce that **sins are forgiven** or to give the command **get up and walk** (9:5). Claiming to forgive sins is easy to say, but healing paralysis is a different matter. So Jesus proves that he has forgiven sins by healing the paralytic: **But I want you to know that the Son of Man has authority on earth to forgive sins** and so Jesus tells the man, **Get up, take your mat and go home** (v 6), which he promptly does (v 7). The phrase **Son of Man**, along with the term **authority**, alludes to Dan 7 in which the heavenly "one like a son of man" is endowed with "authority, glory and sovereign power" (vv 13-14). Now, Jesus as the Son of Man, on earth, manifests his authority to execute a prerogative of Yahweh. Jesus is "Immanuel," God with us!

The Gospel authors develop the scene in Daniel and apply it to Jesus. Jesus as Son of Man is no longer passive like the Danielic figure, but actively exercises his authority on earth and will again in the future (16:27-28). In Jewish texts, which pre-date Matthew, the Son of Man is a heavenly figure who is likewise active, judging and punishing those who have oppressed God's people (e.g., *1 En.* 48:4-10 and *4 Ezra* 13:1-13*a*).

For Matthew, the Son of Man exercises Yahweh's authority on earth to forgive sins, and through this, Matthew reveals another aspect of Jesus' identity. Authority is a key piece of Matthew's presentation of Jesus (Hagner 1993, 233): he teaches with authority (7:29); heals with authority (8:9); and now he forgives sins with authority (9:6). Soon he will commission his disciples to minister with authority (10:1, 7-8).

■ **8** The **crowd** returns in this narrative after their absence from the Gadarene
exorcism (8:28). They are **filled with awe [*fobeō*] and . . . praised God, who** 9:8
had given such authority to man. Unlike John's Gospel, Matthew does not explicitly equate Jesus with God (Hagner 1993, 234); however, the **crowd** recognizes that Jesus' unusual authority can only be from God himself. Their **awe** is not "fear" (*phobeō*) as some suggest (France 2007, 343; Nolland 2005, 383) but wonderment or amazement at Jesus' authority and so praise God. This same "crowd," however, will eventually join those opposed to him (see 27:20).

Matthew states that such **authority** was given to **man** when it is "the Son of Man" who performs these miraculous deeds (see v 6). Hagner suggests that this "may reflect an ecclesiastical concern of his about the ability of Christ's representatives to forgive sins in the sense of declaring God's forgiveness or non-forgiveness in 18:18" (1993, 234). The disciples are able to heal and exorcise because of this authority as well (10:1-2), things heretofore only Jesus has performed, but this always seems to be a derived authority in connection with Jesus and his mission. This movement is reflected in Acts, in which the early Christians perform the same deeds of Jesus, and God receives praise as a result (Acts 3:8-9).

FROM THE TEXT

Some interpreters have applied allegory to the account of Jesus calming the wind and the seas. But this puts the interpreter at the center and overlays the text with an interpretation likely foreign to Matthew. For example, the world represents the storm and the boat is the church being tossed around by a hostile and unbelieving world; however, Jesus will bring the church through the storm to her heavenly home (see Peter Chrysologus, *Sermons* 50.2). Similarly, a more recent scholar suggests that this text is "a kerygmatic paradigm of the danger and glory of discipleship" (Bornkamm 1963, 52-57, cited in France 2007, 335). No doubt these are interesting homiletical lessons.

Matthew, however, wants the focus to fall particularly on Jesus and his identity. These three miracle accounts begin to answer the question posed by the disciples after Jesus rebukes the wind and the waves: "What kind of man is this?" Jesus is "Immanuel . . . God with us" (Matt 1:23): the one who exercises Yahweh's authority over the hostile forces of nature and the destructive effects of demonic influence; the one who exercises Yahweh's unique role of forgiving sins. As with the first three miracle accounts in 9:1-15, divine power is at work in Jesus for the sake of people. Whether it results in deliverance from mortal danger, release from demonic oppression, or forgiveness of sins, Jesus, as the Servant of Yahweh, is solely concentrated on the other. May we as Christ followers reflect that same love toward the other in our day-to-day lives.

4. Critiques of Jesus and His Followers (9:9-17)

BEHIND THE TEXT

9:9 In these two stories, Jesus teaches on the nature of his ministry through critiques from the Pharisees (v 11) and the disciples of John (v 14). These two episodes mark the beginning of opposition and resistance, which becomes more pronounced as the Gospel progresses. France comments that the narratives "together . . . provide a startling perspective on the new values of the kingdom of heaven which will increasingly put Jesus and his movement on a collision course with traditional Jewish piety" (2007, 351). The religious leaders' disapproval of Jesus culminates in 12:14, in which the Pharisees begin to plot about "how they might kill Jesus."

a. Calling of Matthew and a Critique of Jesus (9:9-13)

IN THE TEXT

■ **9** Jesus now calls a fifth disciple, a tax collector named **Matthew**. Jesus **saw** him while **sitting at the tax collector's booth**. He was likely a customs official because he was stationed at a booth and collected tariffs on goods crossing the border between Antipas' and Philip's territories (Keener 1999, 293; Gundry 1982, 166). Jews loathed tax collectors because they worked for Rome. They levied rates as high as thirty or forty percent (Keener 1999, 292). Jesus seems unconcerned about the public perception in calling such a person. Keener notes that "whereas Jesus warned a scribe who was a would-be follower about the cost

(8:19-20), he openly invited a despised tax gatherer to join his circle (cf. 18:17)" (1999, 292). Jesus gives a brief command, **Follow me** and, as with the first four disciples (see 4:18-20), **Matthew got up and followed him** (9:9*b*).

■ **10-11** Jesus then has **dinner at Matthew's house** along with **many tax collectors and sinners** as well as **his disciples** (v 10). Matthew's use of the Greek word for "reclining" (*anakeimai*), which is untranslated in the NIV, describes a seating arrangement for a banquet or celebratory meal (Nolland 2005, 385).

The addition of **sinners** widens the group to include those who have no regard for Torah obedience (Tob 4:17; *Pss. Sol.* 2:34; 13:1; Keener 1999, 295). Reference to **tax collectors and sinners** appears frequently in the Gospels (Matt 11:19; Luke 15:1; 18:9-14). France asserts that combining sinners with tax collectors highlights the disdain the general populace had for the latter (2007, 351). Further, Jesus breached Pharisaic purity rules by eating with them (Borg 1984, 78-95, cited in Keener 1999, 296). Tax collectors and sinners defile, and for Jesus to eat with them is highly inappropriate (Nolland 2005, 387). What is more, Jesus sharing a meal with these individuals communicates that they are his equals and that, in his eyes, they have value and worth.

From the Pharisees' perspective, holiness could not be preserved in such a context, but, as we have seen in 8:1-4, Jesus is redefining holiness. Already, he has touched a leper which did not contaminate Jesus but, rather, healed and purified the leper (8:1-4). This story and the one here expresses that "for Jesus, holiness is contagious, outgoing, embracing, and joyous. It transforms and brings reconciliation" (Brower 2005, 129).

This holiness does not center on exclusion and separation but centers on mercy and love. There are injunctions against associating with sinners, but this is so that one is not influenced by them (Pss 1:1; 119:63; Prov 13:20; Keener 1999, 297). This is not the case here. In the presence of Jesus, tax collectors and sinners are welcome, as well as other marginalized individuals (see Matt 8:16, 26-34). In contrast, the Pharisees, with their concern for maintaining ritual purity, ask Jesus' disciples, **Why does your teacher eat with tax collectors and sinners?** (9:11*b*).

■ **12-13** When Jesus hears this question, he responds that **the sick** and **not the healthy . . . need a doctor** (v 12). Then, in rabbinic fashion (the Pharisees describe him as **teacher** in v 11*b*), he commands them, **But go and learn** the meaning of Hos 6:6, **I desire mercy, not sacrifice** (Matt 9:13*a*). To make such a statement to the Pharisees would be highly insulting as he insinuates that they may have not even read it (Keener 1999, 298)! In the LXX, the prophet calls Israel to show mercy in human relationships. Here Jesus invites the Pharisees to have mercy on the outcast. Instead, they are behaving just like their rebellious ancestors whose "mercy is like a morning cloud and like morning dew when it goes away" (Hos 6:4*b* NETS). Jesus will cite Hos 6:6 again when the Pharisees challenge him for permitting the disciples to pluck heads of grain on the Sabbath (Matt 12:7).

Jesus then explains how the quotation relates to his ministry when he says, **For I have not come to call the righteous, but sinners** (9:13*b*). These are the sick, the sinners, the tax collectors, in other words, the ones whom God desires to save (e.g., Deut 30:3) and on whom he shows mercy (e.g., Isa 40:1-3; Hos 2:19 [21 HB]). Jesus is doing just this when he calls one of them to follow him and eats with his compatriots.

Later in the chapter, other outcasts—two blind men—recognize Jesus as the "Son of David" and plead that he have mercy on them and heal them, which he does (Matt 9:27-31). Jesus indeed fulfills Isa 53:4 by taking up "infirmities" and bearing "diseases" of those in need (NRSV). If he has come for the sick (Matt 8:16) and sinners (1:21) alike, then it is natural to suppose that he will be with them. The Pharisees, however, with their emphasis on religious exclusivity, have no room for mercy; they shun the tax collector and sinner because they would defile the Pharisees' purity and so, in an ironic way, they become the real sinners (see 26:45).

b. Critique of the Disciples and Teaching on Fasting (9:14-17)

■ **14** John's disciples ask him, **How is it that we and the Pharisees fast often, but your disciples do not fast?** Pharisaic fasts, and presumably those of John's disciples as well, were routine (Luke 18:12; Matt 11:18). The feast at Matthew's home triggers the question (France 2007, 356). Jesus had instructed his disciples to fast in secret and so if they were it would be unbeknownst to these other groups (Keener 1999, 300).

Wright comments that the practices of the Pharisees, as well as other Jewish groups, would be well known in each community, and, more importantly, the unique praxis of each group demonstrates their understanding of holiness (1996, 276; see also Brower 2005, 29-37). Fasting and mourning are associated with the exile, Israel's greatest disaster, which resulted in separation from the presence of God and his blessing (Zech 8:19; Wright 1992, 234-35).

Jesus has come announcing and demonstrating that God is King and the end of the exile is at hand (→ Matt 4:17), which results in a different behavior for him and his followers, demonstrating a kind of holiness different from that of the Pharisees or John's disciples (see 9:14). Now is the time to feast, and with the most unlikely of people, "tax collectors and sinners" (vv 10-13).

■ **15-17** Jesus offers two responses to John's disciples, both of which highlight that indeed "the kingdom of heaven has come near" (4:17*b*). God is now reigning in a new way through his Messiah, Jesus, which has implications for practices and structures of Jewish piety (see 6:1-18).

In his first response, Jesus uses the metaphor of a **bridegroom** (9:15). Jewish weddings are times of celebration and joy "with which any signs of sorrow seemed conspicuously incongruent" (Keener 1999, 300). While he, as the bridegroom, is present with **the guests**, they do not **mourn**. However, **the**

time will come when the bridegroom will be taken from them at which point the guests **will fast** (v 15).

For the first time in Matthew, Jesus makes a veiled reference to his crucifixion. The Greek verb translated **will be taken** (*apairō*) likely points to the arrest and eventual crucifixion of Jesus (Matt 26:3-5, 14-16, 45-50, 55; 27:27-37). France suggests that it is "a violent and unwelcome removal, with a possible echo of Isa 53:8," but there is nothing in this text or other occurrences of the verb to support this (2007, 356; BDAG 2000, 96). In the meantime, it is not a time for mourning but for rejoicing with his followers; there will be times for fasting when he is gone (6:16-18).

In his second response, Jesus uses two metaphors about a **garment** (9:16) and **wineskins** (v 17). Sewing **a patch of unshrunk cloth on an old garment** will make **the tear worse**. As the patch dries out, the fabric will shrink and rip the original garment worse than what it was. Similarly, **new wine**, which is not yet fully fermented, cannot be poured into **old wineskins**. As wine ferments, gases are released and pressure builds, bursting **the skins . . . ; the wine will run out and the wineskins will be ruined**. Well-used **wineskins** cannot be strained any further without bursting (Hurtado 1983, 31-32). Rather, **new wine** belongs in **new wineskins** so that **both are preserved**.

These metaphors speak of something new being imposed on something old, with destructive consequences. In context, they imply incompatibility between Jesus and a religious system that cannot and will not accommodate the new reign of God now revealed in him. Already, the scribes have accused Jesus of blasphemy (v 3), and the Pharisees questioned his disregard of ritual purity by eating "with sinners and tax collectors" (v 11). Finally, after Jesus performs another series of miracles, they will accuse him of operating by "the prince of demons" (v 34).

Nolland contends that the imagery of v 16 "has a potential for use with a continued valuing of the old coat (after all, the focus is on the fate of the coat, not that of the piece of cloth used for patching)" (2005, 391). It is clear, however, that the system or context represented by the coat and old wineskin is incompatible with what is new, and when the two mix, destruction results. Nolland is overexegeting this passage when he concludes that "the new does not need to be constrained by the old, and that only in this way can that which is of value from the old be preserved" (2005, 392). There is no indication in the context of vv 16-17 that Matthew's Jesus affirms the religious system represented by the scribes and Pharisees; Matt 23 should remove any doubts about this!

It is worth pointing out, however, that Matthew is not envisioning a new religion in favor of an old one. He is critiquing a Pharisaic way of being Israel or a religious system that provides little room for mercy for the marginalized. Jesus demonstrates that the holiness of Israel's God welcomes both the sick and the sinner.

FROM THE TEXT

One of the damaging legacies of modern holiness movements is an emphasis on legalism, a religion constituted by "external performance targets" (Brower 2005, 130). Far too often, we have been guilty of a Pharisaic version of holiness in which we believe that God or his people will be contaminated by that which is unclean and so protection of purity was achieved by shunning places or activities that would be considered "worldly." However, moral rectitude begins with hearts filled with the love of God through the indwelling presence of the Spirit and has little to do with one's chosen associates.

The Pharisees believed that Jesus would be contaminated by the sinners and tax collectors, just as they believed he would be contaminated by the lepers, the demon possessed, the blind, and the lame—all groups the Pharisees deemed unclean. However, it is for these ones that Jesus has come, and it is to these ones that the holiness of God extends through his Son, demonstrating unconditional love, mercy, and acceptance to the completely undeserving. The heart of the holy God is expressed in redeeming mission. What are the ways God would have his church unconditionally love and be with those who some would deem "unclean" and "defiling" today?

5. Four More Miracles of Jesus (9:18-34)

BEHIND THE TEXT

9:18-19

Matthew concludes this narrative panel with a third group of miracle stories. The first two are intercalated with one another where the account of Jesus raising the synagogue leader's daughter (9:18-19, 23-26) surrounds the account of the hemorrhaging woman (vv 20-22). In these stories, Jesus again breaches purity rules and, instead of being contaminated, heals those considered unclean by his touch. Again, the holiness of Jesus works outward and is not defiled by that which is unclean. This is the case when he shares table fellowship with ritually impure sinners and tax collectors. In the last two accounts, Jesus heals two blind men (vv 27-31) and delivers a mute demonized man (vv 32-34). Indeed, the exile is coming to an end as the holy and purifying power of the heavenly Father is at work through his anointed Son for the restoration of the outcast.

a. Raising of a Daughter and the Healing of a Hemorrhaging Woman (9:18-26)

IN THE TEXT

■ **18-19** Jesus has not even finished his teaching about the wineskins in v 17 and "behold" **a synagogue leader came and knelt before him** (v 18*a*). The Greek text reads only **leader** (*archōn*) while the NIV's **synagogue leader** is likely influenced by Mark 5:22 and Luke 8:41, where he is explicitly identified as such. He indicates that his **daughter has just died. But come and put your hand on her, and she will live** (Matt 9:18*b*).

France argues that it is unlikely that the temporal link, "while he was saying this," implies that Matthew wants his audience to see a connection between these healings and the teaching about the wineskins (2007, 362). However, these intercalated stories are mutually interpretive. Jesus embodies the new wine that cannot be contained by the old system, whose adherents would never make contact with a dead body (Num 19:11-12) or a bleeding woman (Lev 15:33) because both are ritually impure.

The synagogue leader demonstrates a bold faith by believing that Jesus can bring his deceased daughter back to life, especially when there is no evidence thus far that Jesus has done this (France 2007, 262). Elijah and Elisha did raise the dead in the OT (1 Kgs 17:17-24; 2 Kgs 4:32-37). This synagogue leader believes that Jesus can do this miracle as well. Jesus and his disciples promptly **got up and went with him** (Matt 9:19). Matthew's mention of **the disciples** here is important because Jesus will soon commission them to do the same (10:7-8).

■ **20-22** While Jesus and the disciples are traveling to the synagogue leader's house, an unclean woman, due to a chronic menstrual flow, **came up behind him and touched the edge of his cloak** (9:20). She also exhibits strong faith when she says to herself, **If I only touch his cloak, I will be healed** (v 21). The plan to **touch his cloak** is especially offensive since whatever she touched would become unclean (Keener 1999, 303).

Keener argues that "Matthew clarifies her touch of Jesus' cloak; she touched his 'fringe' [*kraspedon*]" (1999, 303). In Num 15:38-39, *kraspedon* refers to the tassels on the corners of garments to call Israel to covenantal obedience. Matthew uses this term merely to refer to the edge of his cloak.

Matthew omits the detail in Mark of Jesus perceiving "that power had gone out from him" and questioning the disciples who touched him (Mark 5:30). Matthew simply states that **Jesus turned and saw her** and encourages her: **Take heart, daughter . . . your faith has healed you** (Matt 9:22*ab*). Again, for Matthew, the emphasis falls on the person of Jesus and what he can accomplish.

Matthew does not indicate how Jesus knew this woman touched him or of her subsequent healing. However, Jesus has already exercised supernatural insight (see v 4); he appeals to the same insight here (Davies and Allison 1991, 131). Thus, "just as the Father knows his children's requests before they ask him (6:8), so too, apparently, does Jesus know what believers need before they ask" (Davies and Allison 1991, 130).

The woman was healed **at that moment** (9:22*c*). The Greek word for "healed" here is *sōzō*, which is usually translated "to save." This woman's disorder created social barriers in addition to its physical effects, so she is healed or saved on several levels (Keener 1999, 304). Further, Jesus' healing of this woman highlights her dignity and value, as well as that of the young girl in vv 23-26. In many ancient cultures, including Jewish culture, women were subjected to various forms of oppression. The harsh nature of OT ritual purity laws for women is well documented in recent studies (Davies 2003, 2-3; Harrington 2012, 70-78). However, in the ministry of Jesus, "societal oppression of women for religious or social reasons is not part of the way the new people of God are called to display their holiness before the world" (Brower 2012, 160).

■ **23-26** Jesus enters **the synagogue leader's house** and sees **the noisy crowd** (v 23) mourning the death of this child. Hired mourners and flutists were customary funeral attendants (Keener 1999, 304; Nolland 2005, 397). He commands them to leave because **The girl is not dead but asleep** (v 24*b*). This crowd does not recognize Jesus' authority since **they laughed at him** (v 24*c*).

According to some estimates, "In poorer parts of the Empire perhaps half of the live births did not survive past their mid-teens" (see Keener 1999, 304, for the literature cited). Curiously, Jesus has the crowd removed and then he simply takes her **by the hand, and she got up** (v 25), much like he did with Peter's mother-in-law (8:15; Nolland 2005, 398).

In the OT, "the hand of the Lord" often occurs in singular form and so Matthew might be echoing those moments to highlight the divine power at work in Jesus (Exod 9:3; 14:31; Josh 4:24, etc.; Davies and Allison 1991, 126). Jesus only heals by touch in these episodes, which reinforces what happened when he healed the leper: not just by words but also by touch is the Holy God now at work through his Messiah healing and saving the marginalized and the outcast. As a result, **news of this spread through all that region** (Matt 9:26), just as it had at the beginning (4:24-25).

b. Healing of Two Blind Men (9:27-31)

■ **27** As Jesus leaves the area of the synagogue leader's house, **two blind men** follow **him, calling out, "Have mercy on us, Son of David!"** This recalls the two demoniacs in 8:28 who come out to meet Jesus, but these blind men do not see him as a threat (contrast 8:29), rather as a merciful healer (for Matthew's tendency to double characters, → 8:28).

Son of David

The phrase "Son of David" occurs ten times in Matthew, far more than any other Gospel; the Gospel authors are the only ones who use it. In Matthew's opening sentence, he identifies Jesus as "the Messiah the son of David" (1:1). In the OT and 2TJ literature, the Son of David is the Messiah who will fulfill the promises made to David of an everlasting royal dynasty, at the head of which is a king from David's seed (2 Sam 7:10-16). Many of the prophets, speaking about restoration after the Babylonian exile, speak of the Davidic king as one who will reign with justice (Jer 23:5) and rule over a restored Israel (Ezek 37:21-22) with a rebuilt temple (Zech 6:12-13).

In the *Psalms of Solomon*, a text that dates from the mid-first century BCE, the Son of David will inaugurate his reign through violence. He will "destroy the unrighteous rulers . . . purge Jerusalem from gentiles . . . [and] drive out the sinners from the inheritance" (17:22-23). In later Jewish literature, like the *Psalms of Solomon*, the Son of David's "rule takes on eschatological and universal dimensions not found in the prophets [e.g., 1QM 11:1-18; 4QFlor 1:11-14]" (Bauer 1992, 767).

In four instances, Matthew associates the Son of David with mercy: those in need call him "Son of David," asking that he have mercy on them (Matt 9:27; 15:22; 20:30, 31). Many Jews, including Jesus' own disciples, believed that the messiah would reign through military might as depicted in the *Psalms of Solomon*, but in the Gospels Jesus exercises his messianic vocation through suffering and death (see 16:16-22). Those who need healing appeal to his mercy for their deliverance, not to his ability to overthrow the Romans, the enemy of Israel for Jews in the 2TP.

Jesus embodies the message of the Sermon on the Mount by showing mercy to those who need it (5:7; Nolland 2005, 400). The Messiah, Son of David, is one who heals the blind and restores the speech of the mute (12:22-23; 21:14-15). This is the merciful work of the Messiah as Jesus himself will affirm in 11:5.

Some suggest that the connection between Jesus healing as David's son stems from Jewish tradition in which Solomon is portrayed as a healer (Davies and Allison 1991, 136). But Matthew does not connect Jesus with Solomon in 9:28-31
this manner. Rather, Jesus as Messiah is one who reigns over sin, impurity, and disease, which is evident in Matt 8—9. It is these things as well as demonic influence that constitute the ultimate adversaries of Israel and are the covenant curses of exile (see Deut 28:59-61). The healings, purifications, and deliverances performed by the Messiah, the Son of David, inaugurate a once and for all return from exile (Wright 1996, 191-96).

■ **28-31** Jesus then enters the house, likely his own in Capernaum, and asks the blind men if they believe that he is able to heal them, to which they affirmatively respond, **Yes, Lord** (Matt 9:28). This question, again, highlights the necessity of faith in order for Jesus to heal, evident at a number of points (see 8:10; 9:2, 22; 15:28). After Jesus touches **their eyes**, he affirms their faith: **According to your faith let it be done to you** (9:29).

For Jews, blindness was associated with impurity. In Lev 21:20, a man with blindness was prohibited from becoming a priest, and, at Qumran, the blind were prohibited from Yahweh's temple for as long as they lived, lest the city itself become defiled (11Q20 12:6). When Jesus later enters the temple as Yahweh's Messiah, he heals the blind and the lame (Matt 21:14). The healing power of Jesus not only heals but also purifies. In this passage, Jesus performs the healing in secret. But in the context of Matthew's whole narrative, Jesus as

Messiah cleanses the impure through healing, making them holy and whole, just like their heavenly Father (5:48).

Isaiah 35:5-6 is the background of both this story and the following one (Matt 9:32-34). Isaiah 35 describes the work of Yahweh when he delivers Israel from Babylonian captivity. He will establish a highway called "the Way of Holiness" (v 8*a*) and "the unclean will not journey on it" (v 8*b*). On this highway, the "eyes of the blind will be opened and the ears of the deaf unstopped . . . and the mute tongue [will] shout for joy" (vv 5-6*a*). Jesus fulfills Isaiah's promise of establishing his holiness now in the present, as opposed to an undefined time in the future, in the lives of what the establishment have written off as unclean.

France notes that healing in his home provides a private setting making "it possible for Jesus to attempt to keep their healing a secret" (2007, 366), and he commands the men to secrecy in v 30. The word Matthew uses for **warned them sternly** (*embrimaomai*) only occurs here in Matthew (see Mark 1:43) and might stem from their understanding of Jesus' identity: he is the Messiah, Son of David. Jesus, however, wishes to conceal this truth for now.

MATTHEW

When they receive their sight, Jesus orders them to tell no one about this (Matt 9:30), but they disobeyed and **spread the news about him all over that region** (v 31). It is not surprising that the crowds reappear in v 33 as the word continues to spread, which has been the case from the beginning (4:24; 9:26).

c. Exorcising a Demon (9:32-34)

9:32-33

■ **32-33** As Jesus is leaving the house, a demonized man who **could not talk was brought to** him (v 32). This man is likely deaf as well since **could not talk** (*kōphos*) is also used in Matthew to describe deafness (11:5). The physical and psychological effects of demonic influence are varied in the Gospels (12:22; 17:15; Mark 5:5). Sometimes when Jesus delivers an individual from a demon, it results in a physical healing; in this case, **the man who had been mute spoke** (Matt 9:33*a*). Enabling the blind to see and the mute to speak is indeed the work of the Messiah who not only heals (11:5) but also purifies these individuals who are defiled by their ailments, particularly in light of Isa 35.

In response, the **crowd was amazed** and they recognize that Jesus' ability to heal is like no other: **Nothing like this has ever been seen in Israel** (Matt 9:33*b*). Their amazement matches the response of the disciples when Jesus "rebuked the wind and the waves" (8:26-27; Nolland 2005, 403) as well as other moments when Jesus heals (9:8, 26, 31; France 2007, 368).

This response of amazement is strategically placed by Matthew because it concludes his anthology of miracles and, consequently, highlights the unique authority of Jesus to do such things. He places a similar statement at the conclusion of the Sermon on the Mount about Jesus' unique authority to teach, not like "the teachers of the law" (7:28-29). The reference to **Israel** in 9:33 is a subtle affirmation that indeed Jesus has come to rescue "his people from their sins" (1:21) and whatever other ailments would hinder them from being a holy and purified people of God.

■ **34** The Pharisees witness Jesus exorcising the demon and conclude that **it is by the prince of demons that he drives out demons**. Earlier they question Jesus' choice to "eat with tax collectors and sinners" (9:11). But this goes much further. They now accuse him of operating according to the power of Satan; their hostility grows as the narrative progresses (14:5; 21:46; 26:3-5; 27:20; Nolland 2005, 404). Matthew's audience knows that this is false since Satan himself unsuccessfully tested and tempted Jesus in 4:1-11. Jesus later explains the absurdity of such an idea (12:24-29). He does not respond to the Pharisees, possibly because they address the crowds and not him (Davies and Allison 1991, 139).

This moment also anticipates opposition to the Messiah's followers who will perform the very same mighty deeds of Jesus, about which he warns them in the following chapter (Davies and Allison 1991, 138).

FROM THE TEXT

These four accounts reiterate Matthew's message in these two chapters. The healing and purifying power of Jesus Messiah completely restores the outcast and marginalized. Whether it is the isolated leper, the despised tax collector, or the oppressed woman, Jesus expresses the unconditional love of the Father through his purifying touch of the leper, table fellowship with the tax collector, and restoration of the woman. Another consistent theme is the necessity of faith to receive that which Jesus offers (8:10, 13; 9:2, 22, 28-29).

In our own faith communities, it is important that we continually remember that the exalted Jesus, through his Spirit, still heals and purifies today, in some cases leading to full emotional and physical healing of individuals. However, some Christians, feeling the need to explain why there are those who do not get healed, resort to hurtful excuses, for example, that the supplicant does not have sufficient faith. When praying for the sick, it is our responsibility to do just that—pray for the sick—and leave the healing up to God in his time and in his way.

D. Messiah Jesus Commissions His Disciples (9:35—10:42)

In this section, the disciples transition from merely observing Jesus' inauguration of the kingdom to participating in it. Jesus called four disciples at the beginning of Matthew to "fish for people" (4:19*b*). Now this call extends to twelve disciples (10:2-4). This is Matthew's second discourse section. In it, Jesus commissions the disciples to proclaim and enact God's reign, as Jesus himself has done, and warns them about the hostile reception that they will receive. Jesus himself has already experienced resistance from the religious leaders (9:3, 11, 14, 34), and the disciples should expect nothing less.

I. A Plentiful Harvest, but Few Workers (9:35-38)

BEHIND THE TEXT

Although the disciples may not yet fully understand Jesus' identity (see 8:27), the demons in the region of the Gadarenes know that he is the Son of God. For Matthew, the Son of God is the Messiah who exercises power over demonic forces and heals the sick (→ 8:28-29, for comment on "Son of God"). The disciples heard the exchange between their master and the demons, but their level of understanding is unclear. Now they learn that despite the power and authority of the Messiah, there is too much work for him alone. The disciples will inaugurate God's reign in both word and deed just like the Messiah who leads them.

IN THE TEXT

■ **35** This verse summarizes Jesus' ministry. He travels **through all the towns and villages** of Galilee, **teaching in their synagogues, proclaiming the good news of the kingdom and healing every disease and sickness**. Matthew uses essentially the same statement to describe the beginning of Jesus' ministry (4:23). His audience has a clear idea of what the proclamation of the gospel includes because of the Sermon on the Mount in Matt 5—7 and what the healing ministry of Jesus entails because of the collection narratives in Matt 8—9. These five chapters contain the words and deeds of the Messiah. Matthew has replaced Galilee in 4:23 with **all the towns and villages**, which is the same terminology Jesus will use to describe the itinerate ministry of his disciples in 10:11. This subtle change foreshadows their transient ministry (Nolland 2005, 406 n. 2).

■ **36 Compassion** motivates Jesus to proclaim the gospel. The Greek word for **compassion** (*splangchnizomai*) connotes deep pity or sympathy (BDAG 2000, 938). Whenever Matthew uses this term, it is always followed by action (14:14: healing; 15:32: feeding; 18:27: forgiving debt; 20:34: healing blindness). It's a word "which describes the Jesus of the gospel stories in a nutshell" (France 2007, 373).

Jesus observes that the crowds, which continue to grow, are **harassed and helpless, like sheep without a shepherd** (v 36*b*). The sheep/shepherd metaphor appears in the OT particularly when Israel's leadership is in question (1 Kgs 22:17; Ezek 34:4-6; Zech 13:7) or when Israel needs a leader (Num 27:17-18). In Matt 2:6, Matthew quotes a combination of Mic 5:2 [1 HB] and 2 Sam 5:2 to make the point that the Messiah is Israel's shepherd, which was David's role as king (Ps 78:71-72). Jesus is Israel's shepherd who shepherds the ever-increasing crowds.

Without a shepherd, sheep are vulnerable to a variety of predators and other dangers. This renders the sheep **harassed** [*skullō*] **and helpless** (*riptō*). According to Matt 8—9, the crowds are **harassed**, or made "weary" (BDAG 2000, 933), by demonic oppression, chronic illness, and socioreligious alienation. The Greek word for **helpless** refers to something that is laid down or put aside (BDAG 2000, 906), a fitting adjective for those who are harassed in such ways. These metaphorical sheep are in dire need of a leader who can heal and restore.

This is also an implicit critique of the leaders of Israel who value religious devotion over acts of mercy and compassion, like the leaders of Ezekiel's day who have "not strengthened the weak or healed the sick or bound up the injured . . . [but] have ruled them harshly and brutally" (Ezek 34:4). In contrast, Jesus has not come for "the healthy . . . but the sick" (Matt 9:12*b*), not for "the righteous, but sinners" (v 13*b*). In doing so, he fulfills the desire of Yahweh (see 9:13*a*).

■ **37-38** For Jesus, the need is too much: **The harvest is plentiful but the workers are few** (v 37). The almost continual presence of the crowds when he teaches and heals means that the harvest is ready (5:1; 7:28; 8:1, 18; 9:8, 33, 36; Nolland 2005, 408). Consequently, Jesus exhorts his disciples to **ask the Lord of the harvest** to meet this great need and, therefore, **to send out workers into his harvest field**. Jesus does not ask them to pray for more shepherds, but for "workers" (vv 37-38). "The disciples . . . will carry on Jesus' mission to these sheep" (Keener 1999, 309). In the OT, "harvest" refers to God's judgment (e.g., Isa 17:4-6; Jer 51:33; Hos 6:11). In Matt 13:24-30, it refers to both salvation and judgment and here to the healing and restoring work that the disciples are about to commence.

The Lord (*kurios*) is God himself to whom Jesus encourages the disciples to pray. This request is a specific example of the Father's will for which Jesus taught the disciples to pray in 6:10*b*. God, however, does not send the workers but rather Jesus does (10:1, 5). That Jesus assumes this role, as opposed to God, is another demonstration of Matthew's high Christology. Although God is the one who sends Jesus (10:40), Jesus is his Messiah who forms a new Israel and commissions her to engage in God's saving purposes for his people (see 10:5).

The eschatological gathering or harvesting of God's people (see Deut 30:1-5; Isa 27:12-13; Ezek 34:11-16) begins now. The end of the exile has dawned and the workers will rescue the lost sheep of Israel. In Ezek 34, Yahweh himself concludes Israel's exile by performing the tasks that his rebellious and negligent shepherds should have done: he will "bring back the strays," "bind up the injured," and strengthen "the weak" (34:16). For Matthew, God is now in the midst of his people in Jesus, Immanuel, who inaugurates the long-awaited return from exile (Hays 2014, 38-39).

FROM THE TEXT

Compassion motivates Jesus to restore the "harassed and helpless" (Matt 9:36*b*), which reflects the nature of God (Exod 34:6; Lam 3:22). It is a virtue that results in concrete acts of healing and liberation to the marginalized throughout Scripture. In Matthew, the needs are many and Jesus requires the assistance of his followers. In our world today, there are far too many harassed by the circumstances of life that often render them helpless and cast aside. The compassion and mercy of God himself, fully revealed in his Son, enables us not only to see the need around us but also to respond to it in tangible ways.

2. Jesus Commissions Twelve Disciples (10:1-15)

BEHIND THE TEXT

After asking the disciples to "ask the Lord of the harvest . . . to send out workers into his harvest field" (v 38), Jesus calls "his twelve disciples" and empowers them with the same authority that he has demonstrated "to drive out impure spirits and to heal every disease and sickness" (10:1; see also 9:35*b*; 4:23*b*). Matthew's connection between the call for workers and Jesus' subsequent commissioning of the disciples indicates that this harvest is about manifesting God's reign for the benefit of the sick and demon possessed. Jesus forms a new Israel that will be a blessing (Gen 12:3; Isa 49:6).

Jesus' calling of twelve disciples (Matt 10:1-4) recalls the formation of Israel as twelve tribes (Gen 49:28; Josh 13—21). Through Jesus' baptism (3:16-17) and his testing by Satan (4:1-11), Matthew reveals that Jesus embodies a new and faithful version of Israel. Wright comments that "Israel had not had twelve visible tribes since the Assyrian invasion in 734 BC, and for Jesus to give twelve followers a place of prominence [especially in light of the above texts in Matthew] . . . he was thinking in terms of the eschatological restoration of Israel" (Wright 1996, 300).

IN THE TEXT

■ **1** After **Jesus called his twelve**, he **gave them authority to drive out impure spirits and to heal every disease and sickness**. This verse provides a theological framework for what follows. Later, Jesus commands the disciples to "*go* . . . to the lost sheep of Israel" and as they do, they are to proclaim God's reign and "heal the sick, raise the dead, cleanse those who have leprosy, drive out demons" (vv 6, 8*a*). Without v 1, Matthew's audience would have little understanding of how simple Galileans could perform such mighty and miraculous deeds.

■ **2-4** Matthew refers to **the twelve** as **apostles**. Although this term becomes a formal designation in early Christian literature designating leaders in the church (Rom 16:7; Gal 1:17), it is still a relevant term on a literary level because of its etymology: "one who is sent" (*apostolos*). Jesus calls these **twelve**

apostles in order to "send" (*apostellō*) them on mission to manifest God's reign wherever they go (v 5). Keener contends that there is a prophetic background to this commissioning: "When Jesus 'sends' disciples . . . the disciples stand in the tradition of the prophets [who are also sent by God] (21:34, 36; 23:37), John (11:10), and Jesus himself (15:24; 21:37)" (1999, 314-15).

The first four names—**Simon (who is called Peter) . . . Andrew; James son of Zebedee, and his brother John** (v 2*b*)—are those whom Jesus called at the beginning of his ministry (4:18-22). That Peter's name appears first both here and in 4:18 highlights "his prominence throughout the story as leader of the group, which will be strongly underlined in 16:17-19" (France 2007, 378). Jesus calls Matthew at his tax booth later in his Galilean ministry (9:9). Other than **Matthew the tax collector** and **Judas Iscariot, who betrayed him** (10:3-4; Matthew [9:9]; Judas [26:23-25; 27:3-5]), Matthew makes no mention of the other apostles, implying that his emphasis is not on specific individuals who constitute the group but the numerical significance of twelve (France 2007, 378).

■ **5-6** The statement in 10:5*a* that **these twelve Jesus sent out with the following instructions** introduces his teaching in this second discourse, which will conclude in v 42. Matthew's Jewish emphasis is clearly evident in v 5*b*, a passage unique to Matthew, where Jesus prohibits the disciples from going **among the Gentiles or** entering **any town of Samaritans**. According to Hagner, "The Samaritans were despised as racially intermixed and disloyal to the law, and the Gentiles were viewed as outright pagans" (1993, 270). In the birth narrative, Jesus "will save *his* people from their sins" (1:21*b*) and fulfills the Law and the Prophets (5:17) as God's Messiah. In 8:7, Jesus appears unwilling to heal a servant of a Gentile centurion. His call in 10:6 to **go rather to the lost sheep of Israel** who are "harassed and helpless, like sheep without a shepherd" (9:36*b*; Keener 1999, 315) should not come as a surprise. As the chosen people of God (Gen 12:1-3; Exod 19:1-6), ethnic Israel is the primary focus of the ministry of Jesus at this point, not merely a specific segment of the nation, as some argue (e.g., Nolland 2005, 416-17).

However, Israel is chosen for a redemptive purpose, to be a blessing (Gen 12:1-3; Isa 49:6), a theme that will also come into focus as the Gospel progresses, culminating in Matt 28:19. The exclusivity of the command is more symbolic and does not disparage the Gentiles, who already have played a key role in Matthew's story (e.g., the Gentile women in his genealogy and the magi who worship the Messiah-King).

Further, this prohibition does not represent the pre-Easter Jesus movement and then after the cross it automatically extends to the Gentiles, as Davies and Allison suggest (1991, 168). Instead, Matthew reflects a covenant theology in which God sends Jesus and, by implication, his emissaries first to the ones whom Yahweh originally chose, who will eventually bless the Gentiles to whom Jesus ministers a couple of times (8:5-13; 15:21-28). The very same movement, of beginning with the Jews first and then ministering to the Gentiles, is evident in Luke-Acts (e.g., Acts 1:8) and Paul's ministry (e.g., Rom 1:16).

■ **7-8** **As** they **go**, they are to proclaim the same message that Jesus himself proclaimed beginning in 4:17: **The kingdom of heaven has come near**. They demonstrate this reign through their actions when they **heal the sick, raise the dead, cleanse those who have leprosy, drive out demons** (v 8*a*), which Jesus demonstrated in Matt 8—9. Hagner drives a wedge between proclamation and healing when he suggests that "the commission in its literal terms [e.g., heal the sick] applied fully only to the apostolic age" (Hagner 1993, 272). However, there is nothing in the text to warrant this assessment.

At the end of the Gospel, Jesus calls his followers not only to baptize those to whom they minister but also to teach "them to obey *everything* I have commanded" (28:20). This would include not only the proclamation of the gospel but also performance of the mighty deeds that manifest its saving power. "Discipleship means learning from Jesus and acting upon what one has learned" (Davies and Allison 1991, 446).

The disciples are not to profit financially when they perform these deeds, because they have received this authority at no cost: **Freely you have received; freely give** (v 8*b*). The word for **freely** (*dōrean*) refers to "a gift, without payment" (BDAG 2000, 266). Likewise, Paul never prevailed upon his churches to meet his personal financial needs (2 Cor 11:7), which is "in contrast with the common practice of itinerate philosophers and teachers who expected not just board and lodging but fees as well" (France 2007, 3984). The rabbis also speak of teaching the Torah freely because it is received freely (*b. Bek.* 29a; Hagner 1993, 272). In Acts, Simon the sorcerer attempted to purchase divine empowerment, for which he was strongly condemned (Acts 8:18-23). Both the reception of power as well as its effects are a free gift.

■ **9-10** At the same time, the disciples must have their basic needs met, and since they are performing kingdom work, **the worker is worth his keep** (Matt 10:10*b*). The word for **keep** (*trofē*) refers to food elsewhere in Matthew (3:4; 6:25). They must trust their heavenly Father for food, or, more broadly, basic needs (see 6:25-34). He prohibits them from taking **any gold or silver or copper** or a **bag for the journey or extra shirt or sandals or a staff** (10:9-10*a*). To set out on such a journey without these provisions would be unusual (Hagner 1993, 272). For example, the staff was used to ward off wild animals, and an extra shirt is necessary when the original becomes soiled. Some suggest that this distinguished the disciples from Cynics, itinerate philosophers who would have had **sandals and a staff** as well as a **bag** (Keener 1999, 317-18; Park 1995, 106-13).

Cynics

Cynicism is an ancient Greek philosophy dating from the fourth century BCE. It protests comfort and materialism and stresses living in harmony with nature and pursuing a life of virtue. One of its early founders lived in a large glass jar in Athens, embodying the rejection of wealth. During the time of Jesus, some Cynics became itinerate preachers who expounded their beliefs on the streets of Greco-Roman cities and often expected remuneration for their services. Many of them were recognized by their beards, staffs, and knapsacks (Fiore 2000, 243).

Some scholars have argued that Jesus was a Cynic because of his itinerant lifestyle and his rejection of power and money (e.g., Downing 1992). However, there are significant differences, not the least of which is that there is no evidence of Cynic preachers in the Levant in the first century (Evans 2012, 219).

Nolland argues that the adjective **extra** only applies to **shirt** and so Jesus prohibits **sandals or a staff** (2005, 418; see Mark 6:9 where Jesus allows sandals). However, in all three Synoptic Gospels, these injunctions imply that "travelling in an impoverished state . . . will make visible a trust in God, and God alone, for [their] needs" (Nolland 2005, 417).

■ **11-13** For lodging, the disciples are to **search there for some worthy person and stay at their house until you leave** (v 11*b*). The Essenes, a religiously strict sect of the 2TP, stayed with other Essenes when they traveled (Josephus, *J.W.* 2.124-27), but there is likely no connection between them and Jesus' followers.

Essenes

The Essenes are one of the three Jewish sects that Josephus describes in his writings (Josephus, *Ant.* 13.171). Forming in the second-century BCE, they strictly adhered to the purity laws found in Leviticus in order to maintain holiness. Membership was limited to Jewish males; they shared their goods with one another and welcomed fellow traveling Essenes into their homes. Eventually some formed a separatist sect outside of Jerusalem in the Judean wilderness. They believed that God would one day vindicate them as a restored and purified holy temple by destroying both Romans and unclean Jews. The writings known as the Dead Sea Scrolls, discovered in 1947, preserve their interpretation of a number of OT texts and rules of the sect. There are a number of unique parallels between the beliefs of this community and those of the early Christians, for example, the congregation as the temple.

The **worthy person** is one who is receptive to and supportive of the disciples' ministry (Nolland 2005, 419). Some might already have known of Jesus and his disciples and so would open their homes (France 2007, 386). The command to **stay at their house until you leave** likely means that the disciples are not to engage in activities that are not related to the work of ministry: when their work is done in that **town or village**, it is time to go (Nolland 2005, 419). When they come into **the home**, they are to **give it** their **greeting** (v 12). Ancient Jewish greetings include a blessing of peace (Keener 1999, 320; 1 Chr 12:18; 1QS 2:9; *4 Bar.* 7:35).

This leads to the next statement: **If the home is deserving, let your peace rest on it** (Matt 10:13*a*). The **home** that is **deserving** houses the **worthy per-**

son mentioned in v 11, who receives the disciples and their message. In these homes, the disciples will find fellowship. However, if that **home** is not deserving, then the disciples should not dispense peace and instead sever fellowship, which Jesus describes in v 14.

■ **14-15** When there are those who **will not welcome** the disciples **or listen to** their **words**, they are to **leave that home or town and shake the dust off** their **feet** (v 14). Jesus himself will be rejected by the inhabitants of Chorazin, Bethsaida, and Capernaum (11:20-21; 13:53-58). Just as he pronounces judgment on these towns later in Matthew, the disciples are to sever fellowship with those who reject the gospel.

They symbolically enact this by **shaking the dust off** their **feet**, as Paul and Barnabas do much later in Pisidian Antioch (Acts 13:51). Some postulate that this is drawn from Jews allegedly wiping dust from their feet when they return to Palestine from Gentile territory (see Keener 1999, 320 n. 22). There is no evidence to support this.

In Matt 10:15, Jesus concludes with a grave warning for those who reject the gospel. Their fate will be worse than the **judgment** experienced by **Sodom and Gomorrah** (v 15; Gen 19:24-28). Throughout the Scriptures, "the prophets have employed Sodom as the epitome of evil, a city that merited judgment (Is 13:19; Jer 50:40; Zeph 2:9) and regularly applied the image to Israel (Deut 32:32; Is 1:10)" (Keener 1999, 320-21). This background highlights the severity of rejecting God's chosen Messiah and reinforces a repeated theme in Matthew that judgment awaits those who resist the gospel (e.g., 23:33-36; 24:36-41, 45-51).

FROM THE TEXT

The empowering and commissioning of the disciples in Matt 10:1-16 is foundational for the Great Commission that concludes the Gospel (28:18-20). Jesus endows the disciples with authority to carry on his inauguration of the reign of God not only through their preaching but also through the performance of mighty deeds. Without these workers, the people will remain "harassed and helpless" (9:36*b*), beaten down by the injustices and oppression that can characterize life in a fallen world. The world today needs laborers who will bring the good news with more than words. Matthew's Gospel does not know of a compassion that does not result in liberation for the poor and the oppressed and healing for the sick. One of the hallmarks of John Wesley's ministry as well as those who followed after him was the proclamation of a gospel that enacts the message of rescue and deliverance to all regardless of age, race, or social class.

3. Warnings about Persecution (10:16-23)

BEHIND THE TEXT

Matthew 10 begins with Jesus endowing the disciples with authority to exorcise and heal (v 1). In v 13*b*, however, he introduces the prospect of rejection and what the disciples should do if that occurs (v 14). In this section, vv 16-23, he explains what form rejection may take, from being "handed over to local councils [or] flogged in the synagogues" (v 17) to being "brought before governors and kings" (v 18). The disciples should not worry about what to say to their adversaries, since "the Spirit of [their] Father" will speak through them (v 20). Matthew's audience would be aware of both Jewish and Gentile persecution. Jesus continues with a series of "messianic woes" which include familial strife (v 21) and everyone hating the disciples because of him (v 22). Finally, the disciples will still be fleeing from one town to the next when "the Son of Man comes" (v 23). These warnings would also be applicable to Matthew's audience, who themselves are experiencing Jewish and Gentile hostilities as they carry out the Great Commission (28:18-20).

IN THE TEXT

■ **16** This proverbial saying functions as warning to the disciples before they embark on their mission. As "apostles" (*apostellos*) (10:2), Jesus is **sending** (*apostellō*) the disciples **out** (v 16*a*; see also v 5). However, they go **like sheep among wolves** (v 16*a*). Jesus and the disciples are vulnerable, like sheep, and those who reject the gospel will use violence, like **wolves**, to stop its spread. Jesus has already used a similar metaphor, albeit with different meaning, in 7:15 (Nolland 2005, 422-23).

Therefore, they need to **be as shrewd as snakes and as innocent as doves** (10:16*b*). Being like sheep does not mean that the disciples are intellectually naive about the prospect of persecution but, rather, they are to be as **shrewd** [*fronimos*; in Gen 3:1 the serpent is *fronimos*] **as snakes** in order to minimize it. The term *fronimos* is the same one used in the LXX of Gen 3:1 to describe the cunning behavior of the serpent who tempted the man and the woman.

In contrast, the disciples are to be wise in avoiding needless harm. Since the snake/serpent is a hostile creature in biblical thought, "Jesus here offsets that more obvious connotation of snakes by a balancing animal image, the harmlessness of doves . . . they need the cunning of snakes without the venom" (France 2007, 391). But the focus is not "harmlessness" but "innocence" (*akeraios*, meaning "unmixed," "pure," or "innocent") (BDAG 2000, 35). Disciple behavior must be completely above reproach (Nolland 2005, 423), an exhortation particularly pertinent to a period when the church is established and becomes the object of the world's hostility (France 2007, 390). Jesus was both innocent and shrewd with his own persecutors to prolong his ministry (e.g., 21:23-27); therefore, it is quite reasonable that his followers did likewise.

■ **17-20** In 10:17-18, Jesus describes two contexts in which the "wolves" will persecute his followers. First, the disciples should be **on . . . guard** because they **will be handed over** [*paradidōmi*] **to the local councils** [*sunedrion*] **and be flogged in the synagogues** (v 17). There is no evidence that the disciples experienced these things during the earthly ministry of Jesus, but they did after (see Acts 5). Jesus himself will be "handed over" (*paradidōmi*) to the Jewish authorities (26:2).

The **local councils** or "sanhedrins" oversee respective synagogue communities. They can execute punitive action against the guilty, which includes flogging (Nolland 2005, 423). Davies and Allison postulate that Matthew's audience was aware of Jewish Christians who defamed the Jewish leadership and so were flogged as a result, which Paul experienced (2 Cor 11:23-24; 1991, 183).

Second, in Gentile lands, the disciples **will be brought before governors and kings as witnesses to them and to the Gentiles** (Matt 10:18*b*). The Greek term for **governor** (*hēgemōn*) "describes various types of Roman provincial administrators" (Keener 1999, 323). Matthew's use of the plural, **governors**, along with the reference to **kings**, points to a period beyond the ministry of Jesus (Keener 1999, 323).

Gentile persecution is **on my** [Jesus'] **account**, which will provide an opportunity for the disciples to make known this gospel message to the Gentile world **as witnesses** (Nolland 2005, 424). This could be seen as a threat to the stability of the Roman Empire (see Acts 16:21). But the fact remains: "Persecution and official opposition will . . . contribute to the spreading of the gospel rather than stifling it" (France 2007, 392).

In Matt 10:19*a*, Jesus is explicit that persecution is not a possibility but a certainty: **but when they arrest you**. While this seems like a foreign idea to Western Christians, for many Christians in other parts of the world, as well as
10:21-23 for the early Christians, persecution is a given. Keener remarks:

> So much was persecution a guarantee for a true disciple (2 Tim 3:12) that the leaders of the apostolic church would probably have questioned the authenticity of the witness of those not experiencing any (cf., e.g., 5:11-12; Acts 5:41; 14:22; Gal 5:11; 1 Thess 3:3; Rev 1:9). (1999, 321 n. 27)

Jesus has already instructed the disciples about the blessing and reward that comes from persecution (see 5:10-12).

The disciples should **not worry about what to say or how to say it** when handed over to the authorities, because **the Spirit of your Father** will be **speaking through you** (10:19-20). Just as the disciples are to trust God for material sustenance when in need (6:25-34), so, too, when they are in need of spiritual guidance (France 2007, 392-93). Nolland contends that this is likely a testimony about "a reality that is tangibly present in and with the speaking" (2005, 425). However, the text seems clear that this is divine illumination through the Spirit: **it will not be you speaking, but the Spirit . . . speaking through you** (10:20).

■ **21-23** Scholars refer to the distress and violence depicted in these verses as "messianic woes," a period of rebellion and strife preceding the Lord's judgment (Hagner 1993, 278). The familial strife in which **brother** betrays **brother, father** betrays even **his child**, and **children . . . rebel against their parents** (10:21) is an echo of Mic 7:6, where an increase in social and familial turmoil becomes a harbinger of God's judgment (Mic 7:2-7; Nolland 2005, 425). Going beyond the echo of Mic 7:6, Jesus describes rebellious children who **have** their parents **put to death**, which likely refers to state-sanctioned martyrdom, such as James underwent in Acts 12:1-4 (France 2007, 394).

Those who are devoted to Jesus, proclaiming his word and performing mighty deeds, **will be hated by everyone because of me** (Matt 10:22*a*). This may echo the LXX version of Mic 7:6: "the enemies of a man are the men in his house" (NETS). The prospect of hostility from family members highlights the cost of following Jesus, especially in a culture "in which the opinion of family members was paramount" (Keener 1999, 324).

However, deliverance will come for the faithful because **the one who stands firm to the end will be saved** (*sōzō*; v 22*b*). **Saved** has to do with rescuing an individual from a hostile situation and fits the present context. Until that time, Jesus teaches that when the disciples **are persecuted in one place, flee to another** (v 23*a*). They are to avoid prolonged hostility if possible by obeying Jesus' earlier exhortation to "be as shrewd as snakes and as innocent as doves" (v 16*b*), which involves knowing when to escape. Further, "They should not waste time throwing the pearls of their message of the kingdom of God before the unresponsive pigs and dogs of the towns which refuse them (7:6)" (France 2007, 395).

Finally, the disciples **will not finish going through the towns of Israel before the Son of Man comes** (10:23*b*). In other words, as Nolland argues, "Jewish Christians will not have used up all the towns in Palestine as places of temporary refuge . . . before they are relieved of their problem by the coming of the Son of Man" (2005, 427). This might also refer to a premature end to the disciples' evangelistic activity (Hagner 1993, 278), but the context favors the former since Jesus has just spoken about fleeing from one town to the next in v 23*a* and being hated by all in v 22*a*.

Many contend that this is a prediction of Jesus' second coming or the Parousia, in which he will come to deliver his faithful followers (e.g., Nolland 2005, 427; Davies and Allison 1991, 190). According to these scholars, Jesus expounds on his return as the Son of Man in Matt 24. There, however, Jesus teaches that the gospel will be proclaimed "in the whole world" before the end comes (24:14), which challenges this view. Some suggest it refers to the destruction of the temple, which would have occurred at least ten years earlier for Matthew's audience.

Other options include the death and/or resurrection of Jesus, Pentecost, or the Gentile mission (Hagner 1993, 279). Hagner makes a convincing case for the Son of Man's coming as referring to the temple's destruction because it marks the transition from the Jewish mission to the Gentile one (1993, 280), now that Israel's most sacred institution has been judged by God for her rebellion against his anointed. This coheres with the cessation of the disciples' missionary activity in Jewish towns when the Son of Man comes. France tracks along similar lines but stops short of identifying the Son of Man's coming with the temple's destruction (2007, 398).

The terminology, **Son of Man** (*ho huios tou anthrōpou*) and **comes** (*erchomai*) in 10:23*b*, echoes the celestial scene of Dan 7 in which Daniel, in a vision, sees the "one like a son of man [*hō huios anthrōpou*], coming [*erchomai*] with the clouds of heaven" (v 13*a*). His coming into the presence of God marks his vindication over the beastly, oppressive empires that have ravaged God's people over which "he was given authority, glory and sovereign power" (v 14*a*; for a detailed discussion on the meaning of the "coming" Son of Man, see Snow 2016).

At this point, because there is little context to support any of these proposals, the basic meaning that Jesus will not let his followers suffer interminably for the proclamation of the gospel and will deal with those who have persecuted his people (see Matt 10:26) is sufficient. Whatever the historical event might be that points to the coming of the Son of Man in v 23, it represents Jesus' everlasting dominion and sovereignty.

4. Encouragement in the Midst of Persecution (10:24-33)

BEHIND THE TEXT

These verses mark a reprieve from the warnings of arrest, persecution, and strife that accompany the proclamation of the gospel. Jesus first describes the relationship between himself and his disciples. While they are not above him, they are to be like him (vv 24-25*a*). However, since the context of this
10:24-25 teaching focuses on suffering on account of Jesus (e.g., v 18), it implies that the disciples will share in his suffering; this is how they will "be like" him.

Jesus then consoles them because those who reject them will receive their comeuppance and these ones cannot destroy the soul (vv 26-28). Further, the disciples are under the constant care of their heavenly Father who has even numbered the hairs of their heads (vv 29-31), and they will be rewarded for their faithfulness in the midst of opposition (vv 32-33).

IN THE TEXT

■ **24-25** In v 24, Jesus employs two parallel statements to describe his relationship with the disciples. The idea that **the student is not above the teacher** needs little explanation; the Twelve are those who learn from Jesus their teacher as other students learn from their rabbi. The word for **student** is *mathētēs*, a term that Matthew uses elsewhere to refer to the "disciples" (9:14; 10:1; 11:1; 28:16), and the word for **teacher** is *didaskalos*, typically used by the adversaries of Jesus when addressing him (e.g., 8:19; 9:11; 12:38). Here Jesus uses these to describe the disciple/rabbi relationship.

The second statement in 10:24*b* that likens the disciples to servants is a bit surprising. The Greek word for **servant** (*doulos*) actually denotes a slave; slaves have no rights and "are duty-bound only to their owners or masters, or those to whom total allegiance is pledged" (BDAG 2000, 260). The word for **master** is *kyrios*. In 6:24, God is the "master" or *kyrios* and now it is Jesus (→ 8:2, 6, 25, 27).

France is correct that *kyrios*, which the NIV translates as **master**, "need carry no more than polite deference, but which for Matthew probably has stronger connotations, as Jesus' own comments on the title in 7:21 indicate" (2007, 401). The disciples as "slaves" and their teacher as "lord" distinguishes their relationship from the ones of other students and their rabbis; Jesus is more than just a teacher or rabbi, and the disciples are ones who obediently serve him.

The goal of a disciple/rabbi relationship is that **students** are **to be like their teachers, and servants like their masters** (v 25). Disciples not only obey the teaching of their rabbi but also conform their lifestyle to his. For Jesus' disciples, this means rejection and persecution (9:34), which will intensify as the Gospel progresses (France 2007, 401; see 10:17-23).

Jesus concludes with a cryptic statement expressing the solidarity between him and his disciples: **If the head of the house has been called Beelzebul, how much more the members of his household!** (v 25*b*). **The members** of a Greco-Roman household embraced the ideas and practices of **the head of the house** (see Balch 1988, 28). These **members** are "not so much the owner's family as the wider group of household slaves and clients who came under his patronage and control" (France 2007, 402). This would, however, likely include the family members as **members of his household**, just as in the OT quotation in vv 35-36 below, in which the members of a man's household are his actual family (Davies and Allison 1991; see also Balch 1988, 25-36). So, **if the head of the house has been called Beelzebul**, a strong term of derision (→ 12:24), the **members of his household** are likewise objects of this derision.

In Greek, the verb for **has been called** is in the active voice and the verse should be translated "if they have called the head of the house Beelzebul." The Pharisees are the only ones who use the designation and direct it at Jesus in 12:24 and, before this, they refer to him as "the prince of demons" in 9:34 (Davies and Allison 1991, 195). Jesus is telling the disciples that the ones who persecute him will also be the ones who oppose them (10:17-18; Davies and Allison 1991, 197).

■ **26-27** Jesus now consoles his disciples: **So do not be afraid of them** (v 26). The antecedent of **them** are the "wolves" (v 16*a*), likely referring to the Pharisees, among whom Jesus sends his disciples and who will be guilty of delivering them "over to the local councils" and flogging them "in the synagogues" (v 17). The disciples are not to fear them because a time will come when they will be called to account: **For there is nothing concealed that will not be disclosed, or hidden that will not be made known** (v 26*b*). France and Hagner assume that this future revealing only refers to the gospel message (2007, 402-

3; 1993, 285), but the preceding context, which centers on the persecution of the disciples, implies judgment for adversaries.

Although *2 Baruch* postdates Matthew, the language of *2 Bar.* 83:3 is similar to Matt 10:26*b* and refers to eschatological judgment (see also *4 Ezra* 64:64-66): "He [the Most High] will certainly investigate the secret thoughts and everything which is lying in the inner chambers of all their members which are in sin. And he will make them manifest in the presence of everyone with blame." Davies and Allison suggest that "the thought of [this] apocalyptic revelation brings comfort" (1991, 203 n. 8).

The disciples are to live in anticipation of that day by revealing now the gospel message: **what I tell you in the dark, speak in the daylight** and **what is whispered in your ear, proclaim from the roofs** (Matt 10:27). France comments that "the disciples' duty is not merely the negative one of avoiding fear [as in v 26], but the positive one of bold proclamation in the face of opposition" (France 2007, 402). They will have opportunity to make known the gospel message when they are "brought before governors and kings as witnesses to them and to the Gentiles" (v 18).

■ **28-31** In v 28, Jesus provides another reason why the disciples should not fear their adversaries: they can only **kill the body** [*sōma*] **but cannot kill the soul** (*psuchē*) (v 28*a*). Rather, they should fear God, **the One who can destroy both soul and body in hell** (v 28*b*; for the significance of "hell," → Matt 5:21-26, "Hell" sidebar). An eschatological dimension is evident since physical martyrdom only affects life in this age and not eternal life in which the soul continues to exist. In Hebrew thinking, the soul and body are not separate entities. At creation, when God breathes into the human, the human becomes a "living being" (*psuchēn zōsan*).

In the 2T and NT periods, likely under Hellenistic influence, humanity is considered a dualistic being composed of body and soul, although some argue that this view is reflected in Hebrew thinking (e.g., Gundry 1976, 117-34). In both Testaments, "'Soul and body' provide a comprehensive designation for all that makes up a person" (Nolland 2005, 437). Jesus teaches the disciples that the power of their adversaries, which can only destroy the physical body, does not compare to God's power, which can also destroy the soul, for which there is no resurrection or resuscitation (see also Matt 5:29-30, in which the "whole body [can] be thrown into hell"). This is known as annihilationism, a view held by a number of evangelical scholars (Ellis 1997, 199-219; Stott 1989, 312-29).

Jesus then consoles the disciples using an analogy from nature (see "the birds of the air" and "the flowers of the field" in 6:26, 28). In 10:29, **two sparrows** are only worth **a penny**, but **yet not one of them will fall to the ground outside your Father's care**. The Greek word for **sparrows** (*strouthion*) refers to any type of small bird, and two of them are worth very little—an *assarion*, translated **penny,** which is worth about a sixteenth of a denarius. A denarius is a day's wage for a laborer (20:2; Nolland 2005, 437). If something so insignificant as small birds remain under God's care, how much more will he care for the disciples?

Some claim that the phrase **outside your Father's care** refers to God's presence, but Davies and Allison note that the Greek word for **outside** (*aneu*) usually means "'without the knowledge and consent of' (BDAG 2000, 78) when used of persons" (1991, 208). Applied to Matthew, all of God's creation falls under his knowledge. Jesus illustrates this in 10:30 that **even the very hairs of** [their heads] **are all numbered**. The inability to number a head of hair is a proverbial idea (Pss 40:12 [13 HB]; 69:4 [5 HB]), and for Jesus only God can do this (France 2007, 404).

The phrase "not a hair of his head will fall to the ground" occurs a few times in the OT to denote the protection extended to certain individuals for their faithfulness (see 1 Sam 14:45 and 2 Sam 14:11; France 2007, 404). However, Jesus does not promise protection but tribulation (Davies and Allison 1991, 209). He is emphasizing the greatness of God's knowledge, which transcends human ability and in this the disciples should find comfort. Recalling Matt 10:29, Jesus concludes: **So don't be afraid; you are worth more than many sparrows** (v 31).

■ **32-33** Although untranslated in the NIV, Matthew begins v 32 with an inferential conjunction, "therefore." These verses not only logically follow the consoling words in vv 26-31 but also the warnings in vv 17-23. The disciples can rest assured that just as their heavenly Father knows their current plight 10:32-33
of trial and tribulation in the present for faithfulness to the gospel or, as Jesus puts it in v 32, for acknowledging Jesus **before others**, he will one day **acknowledge** that one **before my Father in heaven**. However, the one who does not **acknowledge** Jesus now, but **disowns** him **before others**, he **will disown before** his **Father in heaven** (v 33).

The referent of **others** before whom the disciples confess include their adversaries, "the local councils," "synagogues," and "governors and kings" (vv 17-18) (Davies and Allison 1991, 215). This is the same day of reckoning when the harmful deeds of the adversaries of Jesus' disciples will be made known as well (v 26). France notes, "The issue is not merely obedience to Jesus' teaching, but the explicit 'acknowledgment' of him as Lord before a hostile world" (2007, 405).

For Jesus' followers, this will either be a day of vindication for those who have unashamedly proclaimed the gospel or judgment for those who have capitulated to their enemies. This scene is reminiscent of the vindication of the "holy people of the Most High" in Dan 7:13-14, 27 when the Ancient of Days rules in their favor for their faithfulness in the midst of persecution.

The scene in Matthew is **before** [*emprosthen*] **my Father in heaven**, which recalls the "one like a son of man" who "was led into his presence" or brought "before" Yahweh. The "little horn," who symbolizes the oppressive Seleucid king Antiochus IV Epiphanes, is also judged by Yahweh and destroyed for oppressing the faithful (Dan 7:8-11). However, there are no terminological correspondences with Dan 7, but there is a thematic correspondence between the two scenes (→ Introduction). Jesus depicts a great cosmic scene of judgment, reminiscent of the one in Dan 7.

Eschatological judgment is a major theme in Matthew. Jesus is the cosmic Judge who permits into heaven only those who do "the will of my Father who is in heaven" (Matt 7:21*b*) and "will reward each person according to what they have done" (16:27). Jesus assumes prerogatives of Yahweh and, in fact, "is thus not just a revealer but the focus of God's eschatological saving action and the criterion of judgment" (Davies and Allison 1991, 215).

Jesus as the one who acknowledges his followers **before** his **Father in heaven** becomes "the criterion of judgment" and ensures vindication for those who suffered "because of" (10:22*a*) him while on earth. According to Nolland, this scene is not judicial and discounts Matthew's use of *emprosthen* as implying such a context since "the same word is used of Peter's denial in a nonjudicial context in Mt. 26:70" (2005, 439 n. 110). However, Matthew uses it generically to describe the audience in front of whom Peter denies Jesus.

5. Consequences of Faithful Discipleship (10:34-39)

BEHIND THE TEXT

10:34-39

The first section, vv 34-39, describes the difficulties of faithfulness to Jesus while the second one, vv 40-42, indicates the blessing that comes from welcoming the disciples of Jesus. Jesus begins by stating that he is the reason for the tribulation that the disciples will experience. He has not "come to bring peace to the earth, . . . but a sword" (v 34*b*). The imagery of the sword describes the effect of the gospel message—rebellion on the part of those who refuse to accept it. As France notes, "God's kingship is one which always has and always will lead to violent response from those who are threatened by it (11:12)" (2007, 407).

Jesus describes this conflict in graphic language in 10:35-36, depicting unbridled familial strife perpetrated by those who do not accept the gospel. Jesus then warns his own followers of the high cost of following him, which may mean forsaking family ties for the gospel (v 37). In vv 38-39, he calls all of his followers to a cruciform life where, paradoxically, those who lose their lives will find it and those who seek to save it will lose it. Verses 37-39 "draw out the implications of 10:34-36: one must not love father or mother more than Jesus" (Davies and Allison 1991, 217). However, in vv 40-42, Jesus describes the reward that comes to those who care for and accept the beleaguered disciples.

IN THE TEXT

■ **34-36** Given all of the previous warnings Jesus gives the disciples (vv 17-28), the statement that **I did not come to bring peace, but a sword** is not surprising (v 34). However, the Messiah's reign is associated with peace in the OT (Isa 9:6-7 [5-6 HB]; 11:6-9). In the Sermon on the Mount, Jesus himself refers to "peacemakers" as "blessed . . . , for they will be called children of God" (5:9), but he also reserves a beatitude for those who are insulted, persecuted, and falsely accused (vv 11-12), indicating that his reign of peace will be accompanied by conflict. As many agree, the sword to which Jesus refers is not literal but is "a metaphor for conflict and suffering" (France 2007, 408; see also Davies and Allison 1991, 218), and Jesus is ultimately responsible for this strife as he emphatically claims: **I did not come to bring peace, but a sword**.

Jesus quotes Mic 7:6 in Matt 10:35-36, a text that is likely in the background of v 21. He returns to the theme of familial division to reinforce that the **sword** he brings will disrupt even family ties: **For I have come to turn "a man against his father, a daughter against her mother, a daughter-in-law against her mother-in-law"** (v 35). The net result: **a man's enemies will be the members of his own household** (v 36).

Micah 7:6 is part of a catalog of wickedness and rebellion that overtook Israel just before the Assyrian invasion of 722 BCE (7:12). Jesus appeals to this text to highlight the level of animosity and hatred that characterize those who reject the gospel. As Blomberg puts it, "Jesus is speaking of what he came to do and simply lapses into biblical language because of the parallels in the two situations" (2007, 37).

Family Values in Palestinian Judaism

For modern Christians, the apparent diminishment of family values because of the gospel may be difficult to accept (Matt 10:21-22, 34-37; see also 12:46-50). In biblical times, family included relatives beyond immediate family members. This is unlike the modern definition of family constituted by father, mother, and children. In Scripture, priority of the family and the care of its members is consistent in which "family-centeredness should be understood in a directly literal sense: the family *is* the *center*, not only of the social interaction of its members, but of the system of meaning out of which such cultures arose" (e.g., Exod 20:12; Deut 21:18-21; Prov 30:17; Matt 15:1-9; McVann 1998, 75-76). Self-identity and meaning are not founded upon self-differentiation from family, as in modern, Western cultures, but rather through the traditions established and perpetuated by the family (McVann 1998, 77; Malina 2001, 139-40). For Jesus to claim that the gospel undermines such an established and valued institution would be scandalous to many Jews.

■ **37-39** In Matt 10:37, Jesus explains the implications of the sword, which severs family ties. He requires exclusive allegiance, which may mean disregarding the wishes of **father or mother** if those are at cross-purposes with the gospel (v 37*a*). The same applies for **son or daughter** who may seek to influence negatively a disciple of Jesus (v 37*b*). To heed the wishes of family over the call of the gospel renders one **not worthy of** Jesus. Nolland comments that "the ties that bind are relativized in favour of a newly found, more fundamental tie" (2005, 441). Jesus himself rejected his own family in favor of a new one: "For whoever does the will of my Father in heaven is my brother and sister and mother" (12:50). This is a costly allegiance in light of the central role that the family had in Greco-Roman as well as Jewish society.

In 10:38, Jesus broadens his call to exclusive allegiance with an exhortation to live lives of selflessness for the sake of the gospel: **Whoever does not take up their cross and follow me is not worthy of me**. This is a call to live cruciform lives, to embody the self-giving life of Jesus himself who will bear both a metaphorical and literal cross, costing him his life in obedience to his Father's will (26:39). France argues that Jesus is primarily referring to their literal deaths in 10:39 (2007, 411), but the context is allegiance in this life at great cost. Will the disciple avoid persecution, suffering, and familial strife or enter into these things for the sake of Jesus? The road of discipleship, even if it ends with a literal cross, is about denying oneself of anything that hinders obedience to Jesus.

The picture of taking up a cross derives from the Roman background in which criminals were compelled to bear their own cross, likely the crossbeam, before being crucified on it (Nolland 2005, 441); in Matthew, Jesus is too weak to carry his own cross from the beating he received by Pilate's soldiers (27:27-32). Crucifixion not only was a gruesome form of capital punishment but also was associated with shame and disgrace. Neyrey notes that crucifixion was reserved for the lowest segment of society, such as "criminals and slaves, who utterly lacked any honor ascribed them by birth or virtuous deeds" (1998, 139).

Just as those disciples who fail to love Jesus more than their family, those who refuse to bear their cross are also **not worthy of** him (10:37). In v 39*a*, Jesus explains the consequence for refusing allegiance to him: **Whoever finds their life will lose it**. Those who refuse to live life under God's reign and would rather control their own destiny will surely lose it. Life (*psuchē*) does not refer to soul as in 10:28 but "'life,' perhaps even 'self'" (Davies and Allison 1991, 224).

There is reward for those who surrender their lives to God in the present: they **will find it** (v 39*b*). At the same time, to obey Christ in the present, to bear one's cross now, means eternal life in the future (see vv 32-33). All of these passages have an eschatological dimension. Jesus has inaugurated the kingdom of God, but it is not yet here in its fullness (→ 3:2). In this kingdom, the call of the cross for the disciples is to be realized now in the midst of a hostile world, but the reward for a cruciform life is yet to come, in which they will receive eternal life and recognition before their heavenly Father.

FROM THE TEXT

One of the key beliefs of the Wesleyan-holiness tradition is the need to consecrate or dedicate one's life to God and his purposes. Jesus concludes his warnings about persecution and strife, which will characterize the life of his faithful disciples, in 10:37-39 with a call to unconditional, selfless obedience to him, which is the basis for a Wesleyan understanding of consecration. This involves crucifying selfish desires in favor of fulfilling the desires of Christ and his expectations for life in the kingdom (see Gal 2:20).

Opposition to the gospel will come from a variety of sources: religious authorities, political leaders, and even the closest members of one's own family. Given the ability of synagogue-based Sanhedrins to isolate the disciples of Jesus from their religious communities, political leaders to pronounce the death penalty, or the family to disown one of their own, Jesus calls his disciples to trust in their heavenly Father who even knows about the well-being of almost worthless birds and numbers the hairs of the disciples' heads.

This is radical teaching, especially for contemporary evangelicals in the Western world for whom nuclear Christian families are a prized treasure. For some, they are even the measure of faithful discipleship! This conception of the family would be completely foreign to Jesus. Devotion to him and his call outweighs everything, even the family. In Matt 10:25, Jesus assures his disciples that this is a journey of which he is well aware and is one that he will experience himself, but, like him, they, too, must trust in their heavenly Father.

6. Reward for Support of the Gospel (10:40-42)

BEHIND THE TEXT

The addressees change from Jesus' disciples to those who would show them hospitality for even their most basic needs. This recalls Jesus' earlier instruction that the disciples are to greet the inhabitants of the home that receives them, and let their peace remain there if that home is deserving (10:12-13). Now the emphasis falls upon the compensation that those who show hospitality will receive (Davies and Allison 1991, 225). Carrying on with the eschatological tone evident at various points, Jesus promises that a heavenly award awaits those who accept his disciples. Later, he expands on this and describes an eschatological scene of judgment that is reserved for those who did not welcome his followers and the rewarding of those who did (25:31-46).

IN THE TEXT

■ **40-42** Jesus' opening line that **anyone who welcomes you welcomes me, and . . . the one who sent me** (10:40) underscores the solidary that the disciples have with Jesus. This theme is dominant in ch 10, and a clear statement of it comes naturally at the conclusion of this chapter. The disciples not only share in the authority of Jesus (v 1) but are also to become like him in his suffering (v 25).

Matthew 1:23 is also in the background in which Jesus is introduced as "Immanuel—God with us." Jesus is the one sent by God and now Jesus sends his disciples. To welcome the disciples is to welcome God! According to Jeremias, "God himself enters houses with Jesus' messengers. What a statement!" (1971, 239, cited in France 2007, 413 n. 7). This is what it means for Immanuel to dwell with his people.

Matthew 10:41 has a proverbial ring and makes the point that the one who welcomes the disciples as prophets and righteous ones in all of the right ways will be rewarded accordingly. At the same time, the disciples, like prophets, are both sent and Jesus sees the disciples continuing in the tradition of the prophets (5:12; 23:34; Nolland 2005, 444). The focus, however, is on the reward due those who welcome them.

Most commentators see an implicit identification of the disciples as prophets and righteous ones, which is evident in their interpretation of the **prophet's reward**, for example, the prospect of hearing the prophet speak (Davies and Allison 1991, 227) or receiving a blessing from him (1 Kgs 17:8-24; 2 Kgs 4:8-37; France 2007, 414).

But, like other moments in Matt 10, this is eschatological and the **prophet's reward** is likely in the age to come, just as it would be for the prophet of old who suffered much in the current age out of faithfulness to God. The referent of **righteous person** is less determinant than **prophet**, but whomever Jesus has in mind, this person is likewise faithful to God's will and will be rewarded accordingly. In the OT, the "righteous" are the ones faithful to God in contrast with the "wicked" (e.g., Ps 1:5-6) (France 2007, 414).

Jesus concludes that there is no form of help for his followers that is insignificant, as **anyone** who **gives even a cup of cold water to one of these little ones who is my disciple . . . will certainly not lose their reward** (Matt 10:42). Nolland argues that the reward is in contrast to the **prophet's** and **righteous person's reward** since **a cup of cold water** pales in comparison to the work of, for example, a prophet (2005, 445). However, Matthew makes no distinction among various **rewards**, which is supported by the parable of the talents in 20:1-16.

France indicates that the reference **little ones** recurs often in Matthew and is likely Matthew's manner of referring to his community (see 18:1-14; 25:31-46). Not unlike children, Matthew's church goes "out to represent Jesus in a hostile society[,] [has] no status and may easily be pushed aside" (France 2007, 415). However, there must be some difference between the **little ones** and those whom Jesus exhorts to care for them. This last section of teaching, beginning in v 32, is for the wider community of Matthew, that is, those who are not itinerate preachers (Davies and Allison 1991, 231). Those who welcome these **little ones**, even in the most insignificant ways, will receive a reward.

FROM THE TEXT

By concluding the discourse with this exhortation, Matthew underscores the need for a genuine and supportive community for those on the front lines of ministry. The hostilities that accompany a faithful proclamation of the gospel take a toll on the disciple, and Jesus recognizes that others can offer support and sustenance, all of which continue the work of the kingdom. Paul himself was grateful for the tangible support that the church in Philippi offered him (Phil 4:14-19).

At the same time, modern disciples of Jesus who are not in professional ministry still suffer hostilities because of faithfulness to Jesus and the gospel. These hostilities can take many forms from professional disadvantagement to fearing for one's personal safety. In this way, the church should be a place where anyone can identify as a "little one" and so receive the support and encouragement he or she needs.

E. The Messiah and John the Baptist (11:1-30)

BEHIND THE TEXT

Chapter 11 plays a pivotal role in the Galilean ministry section of Matthew's Gospel (4:12—18:35). Two components constitute this ministry: the Sermon on the Mount (5—7) and the performance of mighty deeds (8—9). In ch 10, Jesus commissions the disciples to preach the gospel and perform the same mighty deeds as he did. John then sends his disciples to see if Jesus is the Messiah (11:2-3). For the rest of ch 11, Jesus responds to this question. He is the Messiah to come, just as John was the one whom God sent to prepare his way (vv 4-15); however, neither one was universally accepted (vv 16-24).

Matthew illustrates this by pointing to the Galilean towns that did not repent, failing to become as "little children" (vv 20-25). Instead, they chose to be "wise and learned" in their own eyes (vv 25-26). In chs 12—18, Matthew will recount further hostility in which Jesus is rejected by the religious establishment as well as instances in which the "weary and burdened" turn to him for rest (vv 27-30) and ultimately salvation.

1. Resumption of Jesus' Ministry in Galilee (11:1)

IN THE TEXT

■ **1** This verse concludes Jesus' second discourse in Matthew. The phrase, **after Jesus had finished instructing his twelve disciples**, is similar to the one at the conclusion of the Sermon on the Mount (7:28*a*). In each case, Jesus transitions from teaching to itinerate ministry. In 11:1, he will move **on from there to teach and preach in the towns of Galilee**, thus summarizing Jesus' Galilean ministry once again (4:23; 9:35).

2. John's Inquiry about the Messiah (11:2-6)

BEHIND THE TEXT

John was imprisoned just as Jesus began his ministry in Galilee (4:12). John himself does not appear again in Matthew's narrative as an active character. After he prepares the Lord's way (3:3*b*), he recedes into the narrative background. John is now imprisoned and so must send his disciples to inquire about Jesus (see 14:1-12; 17:11-13). Matthew's strategic placement of this inquiry and Jesus' response to it provides an important interpretive lens for understanding Matt 4—10: "Jesus is the Coming One of John's preaching, the Messiah of prophecy who, through his proclamation to the poor and his miraculous and compassionate deeds, bring to fulfillment the messianic oracles uttered so long ago by Isaiah the prophet" (Davies and Allison 1991, 242).

IN THE TEXT

■ **2-3** Having **heard about the deeds of the Messiah**, John sends **his disciples** (v 2) to see if Jesus is **the one who is to come** (v 3*a*). This question follows the mighty deeds of Jesus in chs 8—9 and then, in ch 10, his commissioning of the disciples to go and do likewise but not without persecution and possibly death. While in prison, John has heard of this activity. **The deeds** of Jesus, however, seem at odds with the ministry of judgment originally prophesied by John that he would "baptize . . . with the Holy Spirit and fire" and "clear his threshing floor, . . . burning up the chaff with unquenchable fire" (3:11-12), all of which has yet to occur.

■ **4-5** In response, Jesus tells them to return **and report to John what you hear and see** (v 4), or as Matthew puts it, they are to recount "the deeds of the Messiah" (v 2). What they **hear** includes the teaching in Matt 5—7, as well as moments of teaching in Matt 8—9 (e.g., 8:10-12, 18-22). John has only heard about these things and certainly the miracles because he inquires about "the deeds of the Messiah."

Matthew uses this story to signal the character of the Messiah's mission. Absent is the judgment motif about which John prophesied in 3:11-12. The fundamental orientation of the kingdom of God and the messianic deeds that manifest it ministers grace and healing to the "harassed and helpless" (9:36*b*). Judgment is for those who refuse to accept the Messiah and oppress the marginalized (see ch 23).

Luz rightly indicates that the OT and 2TJ literature does not depict a messiah who performs miracles (2001, 132 n. 20), which might indicate why John has to ask if Jesus is "the one who is to come" (10:2). Matthew makes this connection on two occasions (12:22-23; 20:30-34), which demonstrates the type of messianic reign Jesus describes in 11:4-5.

This unexpected connection likely prompts John's question about Jesus' identity (11:3). Some have pointed to 4Q521 where a messiah will perform the very same things mentioned in 10:5 (see, e.g., France 2007, 424 n. 20), but this text does not actually specify that the messiah performs these things. Rather, the Lord himself will do them in a future messianic period (Nolland 2005, 450; Novakovic 2007, 225-29).

This coheres well with Matthew's presentation of Jesus as Immanuel, God with us. Through the Messiah, Immanuel is at work, performing miraculous deeds: **The blind receive sight, the lame walk, those who have leprosy are cleansed, the deaf hear, the dead are raised, and the good news is proclaimed to the poor** (v 5).

In ch 10, Jesus empowers the disciples to perform these things in order to expand his work as the Messiah who is inaugurating God's reign over blindness (9:28-31), paralysis (8:5-13; 9:1-8), leprosy (8:1-4), deafness (9:32-33: the Gk. word behind "could not talk" [*kōphos*] also means "deaf"), and death itself (9:18-19, 23-26). This work demonstrates Jesus' proclamation of **the good news**: under God's reign, sickness and death are overcome (→ 4:23).

Matthew adds **to the poor** at the end of the list, which parallels Luke's "blessed are you who are poor" (6:20) but not Matthew's "blessed are the poor in spirit" (5:3). Possibly Matthew is alluding to the LXX of Isa 61:1, in which Isaiah is anointed "to bring good news to the poor . . . and recovery of sight to the blind" (NETS).

The list of deeds has additional allusions to Isaiah: "Then will the eyes of the blind be opened and the ears of the deaf unstopped. Then will the lame leap like a deer, and the mute tongue shout for joy" (Isa 35:5-6*a*). Other texts from Isaiah that prophesy Israel's deliverance are in the background as well: Isa 26:19; 29:18; 42:7 (Davies and Allison 1991, 242). Since Isa 35 is a promise of deliverance from exile, Matthew's audience is reminded once again that the grand purposes of God are coming to fruition in Jesus, who brings the exile to a long-awaited end.

■ **6** Jesus concludes his response with an implicit warning: **Blessed is anyone who does not stumble on account of me**. To stumble in Matthew is to veer off the path of salvation either through one's own attitudes or those of another (→ Matt 5:28). Those who believe that Jesus is the Messiah on the basis of what he says and does will be blessed. Jesus, however, states this in a negative form that implies a warning. Those who **stumble on account of me** are those who refuse to believe what they have witnessed in his Galilean ministry.

France claims that "the attitude which led to his [John's] question is not conducive to spiritual insight" (2007, 425), or according to Davies and Allison, the inquiry reflects a "waning faith" (1991, 239) and so Jesus directs this beatitude at John. These conclusions are difficult to substantiate. What John has heard about does not line up with what he prophesied Jesus would do. Jesus leads with welcome for sinners, not judgment and condemnation. Further, there is little support for a wonder-working messiah in 2TJ. His question about the messianic identity of Jesus stems from an incomplete understanding, not from lack of faith. Jesus praises him as one of the greats of biblical history (11:11), a surprising assessment if John was losing his faith.

3. Jesus' Description of John's Ministry (11:7-15)

BEHIND THE TEXT

After describing the nature of his ministry to John, Jesus now explains John to the crowd. It is not clear if the crowds have been aware of John's imprisonment, but some may have heard John personally and been baptized by him (v 7*b*). John is not swayed by expectations (v 7*b*) and confronted those in authority when the need arose (14:3-5).

Dressed like Elijah, John was a prophet and even more, since he himself is the object of the fulfillment of OT prophecy (11:9-10). His ministry marks a transition from the era of "all the Prophets and the Law" (v 13*a*) to their fulfillment in Jesus. However, not everyone accepts this, including the governor Herod Antipas who has imprisoned him. Others may be questioning how this one, now jailed and awaiting death, is a key person in the changing of the ages preparing the way of the Messiah. Jesus recognizes that this is a difficult truth to accept, but it must be believed (vv 14-15). In the passages following v 15, Jesus illustrates the importance of having ears that can hear because not everyone welcomed their ministry (vv 16-24).

IN THE TEXT

■ **7-8** It is curious why Jesus would not include **John's disciples** in his teaching **about John** and how John relates to himself since they, including John himself, have little idea about the messiahship of Jesus (v 7*a*). Further, the ministry of John has little purpose outside of Jesus. In vv 7*b*-9*b*, Jesus asks **the crowd** a series of questions about the identity of John, which he then answers in vv 9*c*-10.

He first asks, **What did you go out into the wilderness to see? A reed swayed by the wind?** (v 7*bc*). Jesus assumes the crowd knows John and likely some would have been baptized by him, although Galilee is not among the named places from which people came (see 3:5).

The imagery of **a reed swayed by the wind** is a metaphor for one easily swayed by opinions or events (France 2007, 426; Hagner 1993, 304). John preached an unambiguous message, so this is an ironic question (see 3:7-12). Another ironic question follows: did they go out to see **a man dressed in fine clothes** (11:8*b*), some powerful figure? Clearly not: **Those who wear fine clothes are in kings' palaces** (v 8*c*). John wore "camel's hair, and . . . had a leather belt" and ate "locusts and wild honey" (3:4).

■ **9-10** John lived, dressed, and preached like a prophet, and so Jesus tells the crowd that this is who they went **out to see** (v 9*a*). But, John was **more than a prophet** (v 9*c*). In v 10, Jesus quotes Mal 3:1 (see Matt 3:3): **I will send my messenger ahead of you, who will prepare your way before you** (v 10*b*). The **messenger** is John, **the one about whom it is written** (v 10*a*), and, as in Mal 3:1, the Lord is the one who sends **my messenger**. John was **more than a prophet** since he himself is now the object of OT prophecy.

The phrase **ahead of you** (*pro prosōpou sou* [v 10*b*]) is found in the LXX of Exod 23:20 (NETS), in which the Lord promises to send "my angel in front of you" (*pro prosōpou sou*). In Exodus, the "messenger" is the Lord's angel who guides Israel in the wilderness and, later, is the same term used to refer to the prophets (2 Chr 36:15; Isa 44:26; Hag 1:13; Davies and Allison 1991, 249). John is a prophetic messenger sent ahead of Jesus.

Matthew's second line of the quotation (Matt 11:10*c*) reflects the Hebrew text of Mal 3:1, but he adds **your** to indicate that the **way** being prepared is for someone other than the Lord, which in context is Jesus. Finally, the phrase "before me" in Mal 3:1 is replaced with **before you**, for which Jesus is also the antecedent.

While it is clear that this quote reaffirms John as the eschatological forerunner of the coming of Jesus (see France 2007, 428, and Davies and Allison 1991, 250), the contexts of Mal 3:1 and Exod 23:20 both center on the Lord's judgment. In Malachi, the coming of his messenger presages the coming of the Lord himself, who "suddenly . . . will come to his temple" (Mal 3:1*b*); "But who can endure the day of his coming?" (v 2*a*). Earlier, Malachi chastises the priests for corruption (see 2:1-17) and so now the Lord comes in judgment. Likewise, Israel must heed the angel of Exod 23:20 in the wilderness and "not rebel against him; he will not forgive your rebellion, since my Name is in him" (v 21*b*).

This intertextual background forms an unstated correspondence beginning in Matt 11:15 where Jesus describes the misperceptions of people regarding both John and himself. This then leads to his denunciation of the rebellious towns of Chorazin, Bethsaida, and Capernaum, who refuse to recognize his work as Messiah. The threat of judgment, which has been prophesied by John (3:12) and is found in the contexts of these OT texts, is increasing.

■ **11-12** In 11:11-14, John is a transitional figure who is the greatest of all those who precede the coming of Christ (Hagner 1993, 305-6). Despite his appearance and the desolate location of his ministry, Jesus affirms that **among those born of women there has not risen anyone greater than John the Baptist** (v 11*a*). John's greatness is founded upon his call to be the Lord's messenger. His current incarceration is evidence of his obedience to this call (see 14:3-4).

Jesus then says that **whoever is least in the kingdom of heaven is greater than he** (11:11*b*). His point is not to disparage John but to highlight the inferior era of which John is a part in contrast with the era now inaugurated by Jesus. Davies and Allison claim that the preceding comments about John in vv 9-11*a* now become "a foil for the surpassing greatness of the kingdom" (1991, 251). His work is one of preparation for Jesus and his followers, and so these ones are **greater than he** (v 11*b*).

Life in the kingdom is accompanied by violence and hostility, as Jesus repeatedly warns his disciples in Matt 10. **From the days of John the Baptist,** who was arrested at the beginning of Jesus' ministry, **until now, the kingdom of heaven has been subjected to violence, and violent people have been raiding it** (v 12).

Before considering violence and the kingdom, scholars debate if John is indeed part of **the kingdom of heaven**. Verse 12 seems clear that John is a member of the kingdom (Davies and Allison 1991, 253-54), despite his work of preparation for the one who comes after him. But France claims that John is situated solely in the old era (2007, 429). In favor of the former, the work of John and Jesus is very much connected, which is the point of 11:7-15. Further, Jesus distinguishes between "all the Prophets and the Law" that perform their revelatory work "until John" (v 13), and John himself is included with the violence associated with the kingdom in v 12 (Hagner 1993, 307). Hagner is correct: "As a transition figure, John can be considered either as part of the old (e.g., v 11; cf. Luke 16:16) or as part of the new (vv 12, 13)" (1993, 308).

The two lines about the kingdom are in synthetic parallelism in which the second one, **violent people have been raiding it**, explains how it has been **subjected to violence** (Davies and Allison 1991, 256). While there are many different ideas on what Jesus means, he likely refers to the "messianic woes" or a period of suffering in the inaugurated kingdom that precedes the full deliverance of his followers (Davies and Allison 1991, 256; others also see this referring to suffering associated with the kingdom: Hagner 1993, 307; France 2007, 430).

Jesus inaugurates this period with his own coming and, as Matt 10 reveals, opposition takes many forms (see vv 17-23, 34-39). Matthew's audience may interpret the line **violent people have been raiding it** as referring to zealots who wish to co-opt the early Christian movement for their insurrection against Rome (France 2007, 430). This much we do know: "The kingdom of heaven has been and remains subject to violent opposition" (France 2007, 430).

■ **13-15** John is the culmination of the prophetic work of **all the Prophets and the Law** that **prophesied until John** (11:13). Scholars note the reverse order here of **the Prophets** and then **the Law** compared with the usual "the Law [and] the Prophets" (e.g., Matt 5:17). Possibly Matthew wishes "to underline the prophetic side of the Scriptures" (Davies and Allison 1991, 257) since the context focuses on John as the fulfillment of prophecy about Elijah.

John is one who prepares the way for the "one who is more powerful than" he (3:11) and this one, Jesus, comes to "fulfill" the Law and the Prophets (5:17). This does not mean the Law and the Prophets are now irrelevant but that which they promised, or required in the case of the Law, is now fulfilled (→ 5:17). Matthew reveals throughout his Gospel what aspects of the Law and the Prophets are fulfilled, and these overshadow all others, such as the double love command in 22:37-40. With the coming of John, **the Prophets and the Law** have served their purpose and cease to be the main components of divine revelation.

Through John's dress, the wilderness setting, and his announcement of a greater one for whom he prepares the way, Jesus affirms that John **is Elijah who was to come** (v 14*b*). This reinforces the point of v 13: the Prophets and the Law have their function until John whose coming "conjures up the final passage in the prophetic corpus [i.e., Mal 4:5-6]" (Davies and Allison 1991, 258). Indeed, "there has not risen anyone greater than John the Baptist" (v 11*a*).

Jesus recognizes, however, that not all embrace the message of John, and so his listeners have a choice: **if you are willing to accept it** (v 14*a*). John's incarceration did not further the nationalistic hopes of Israel's restoration that some may have linked with him. There is evidence of the expectation of Elijah's return in the later 2TP (France 2007, 431; see Sir 48:10 and Matt 16:14). However, John has not failed, despite the expectations of others.

Jesus concludes by warning his disciples and the crowds: **Whoever has ears, let them hear** (11:15; 13:9, 43). This saying is found in NT contexts where hearing is not sufficient but rather obedience to or agreement with the preceding teaching. Faith and acceptance are required to comprehend what God has done through John and is now doing through Jesus (see 13:11-17).

FROM THE TEXT

In the kingdom of God, things are not always as they seem. John's question about Jesus' messianic identity is evidence of this. He prophesied that Jesus would come in judgment (3:12), but instead he ministers healing and restoration to the marginalized (11:5). While Jesus will judge those who oppose him, his inauguration of God's reign is characterized by mercy and salvation, all of which points to the fundamental nature of his Father whom the Son reveals (v 27). As followers of Jesus, our love and care for the marginalized will also tell the world about the type of God we serve.

4. A Hostile Reception for Jesus and John (11:16-24)

BEHIND THE TEXT

Jesus begins with an assessment of how his ministry and that of John's have been received (vv 16-19). In vv 2-6, he is a Messiah who performs miracles and preaches "good news . . . to the poor" (v 5). John, on the other hand, is a transitional figure who has prepared the Messiah's way, fulfilling OT prophecy (vv 7-15). However, "this generation" (v 16*a*) expected something much different from what it received and, like children who do not get their way, it levels harsh and irrational accusations against those who have disappointed it.

Because of John's deprivation and austerity, folks assert that he has a demon. The opposite of this is Jesus who allegedly eats and drinks in excess and so people claim that he is extravagant, even unconcerned with the type of company he keeps. Jesus' teaching about "this generation," which is characterized by a failure to accept both John and Jesus, becomes a fitting segue for a rebuke of three Galilean towns who fail to recognize his messiahship and repent (vv 20-24).

IN THE TEXT

■ **16-17** The question, **To what can I compare this generation?**, builds on the uncertainty in vv 14-15: only some are "willing to accept" that John is the promised Elijah (v 14), and then in v 15 Jesus exhorts his listeners to believe that this is the case, despite his imprisonment: "Whoever has ears, let them hear."

In Matthew, those who do not accept John and Jesus align themselves with **this generation**. Later, Jesus includes religious leaders in this who seek signs because of disbelief and will be judged accordingly (12:39, 41, 42; 16:4; see also 23:36). He also castigates the disciples for their inability to exorcise a demon, which aligns them with an "unbelieving and perverse generation" (17:17). References to "this generation" echo Deuteronomy in which the Israelites are called "a warped and cooked generation" for their rebellion against Moses (Deut 32:5; Davies and Allison 1991, 260).

11:16-19 Jesus likens **this generation** to **children sitting in the marketplaces and calling out to others: "We played the pipe for you, and you did not dance; we sang a dirge, and you did not mourn"** (vv 16-17). Since **children** shout this saying **in the marketplaces . . . to others**, it appears that the setting is a children's game. Dancing to the pipe occurs at weddings and singing a dirge happens at funerals (France 2007, 433). Because men typically dance at the former and women mourn at the latter (see Keener 1999, 341, who cites Jeremias and Hooke 1972, 161), it could be that the pipe players are women (or girls) criticizing the men for not participating and the singers are the men (or boys) who do the same with women who refuse to mourn (Davies and Allison 1991, 261). As a child's game, there are those who wish to play the game and those who do not. Jesus applies this to the adults of "this generation" rebuking them for their childish ways because John and Jesus have failed to perform expected tasks identified in vv 18-19.

■ **18-19** Childish sentiment is evident in its response to John's asceticism of **neither eating nor drinking** with the accusation, **He has a demon** (v 18). Meanwhile, Jesus as **the Son of Man** does the opposite, **eating and drinking**, and is then criticized: **Here is a glutton and a drunkard, a friend of tax collectors and sinners** (v 19*ab*; for Jesus as **the Son of Man**, → 8:20). The antecedent of **they**, the ones who make the false accusations, are the current "generation" of 11:16-17 who have uninformed and childish expectations of John and Jesus.

"This generation" played the pipes for John but he refused to dance. Few have understood his prophetic ministry and ascetic lifestyle (3:4). The accusation that John is influenced by **a demon** may stem from his physical appearance due to self-deprivation of food and drink (see Mark 5:5) and the wilderness where he ministers (see Matt 4:1).

As for Jesus, they "sang a dirge" and he did not "mourn" (11:17) but rather celebrates by eating and drinking (see 9:10). Coupling "the pipe" of the saying in v 17 with Jesus who "came eating and drinking" connotes celebration and joy, quite the opposite of mourning (v 19*a*). The Pharisees question the disciples about Jesus who is eating "with tax collectors and sinners" (9:11*b*) at Matthew's house. Further, unlike John's disciples who fast, Jesus and his disciples celebrate until "the bridegroom [is] taken from them" (9:15*b*). Neither John nor Jesus measure up to the misguided expectations of "this generation."

According to France, most interpret Jesus as the one playing the pipes and John singing the dirge. The generation, then, fails to celebrate and mourn (2007, 434). Part of the difficulty in interpretation stems from the lack of precision in Jesus' use of the comparative "it is like" (11:16*b* NRSV), leading Nolland to conclude that "the point of comparison in the likeness is not necessarily between this generation and the children calling out" (Nolland 2005, 461; see also France 2007, 433).

But the antecedent of **they** in vv 18-19 and that of "we" in v 17 can only be members of "this generation." Or, put another way, "those who speak . . . their complaint in v 17 (the children) are like those who speak . . . their complaint in vv 18 and 19" (Davies and Allison 1991, 262), all of whom are the spokespersons of "this generation."

Jesus concludes with a cryptic statement that defends the unwelcomed behavior of John and Jesus: **But wisdom is proved right by her deeds** (v 19*b*). Matthew will develop the connection between wisdom and Jesus in vv 25-30; in 12:1-8, he is the personification of Wisdom when he redefines Sabbath law. Some have argued that this saying identifies Jesus with wisdom (Hagner 1993, 311; see Dunn 1996, 196-98), but that is making too much of such a short statement.

Matthew indicates that the wise behaviors of John and Jesus will be vindicated. In Jewish wisdom tradition, living wisely leads to blessing and vindication, or as Hagner puts it, "to find Wisdom is to find life (cf. Prov 8:32-36; Sir 24:1-22)" (1993, 311). God will completely vindicate or demonstrate the wisdom in the work of John and Jesus in the future when the kingdom of God is fully realized, but even now "the deeds of the Messiah," as listed in Matt 11:5, bring life to those who accept them (Nolland 2005, 464; Davies and Allison 1991, 265).

■ **20-22** Jesus begins to **denounce** or reproach **the towns in which most of his miracles had been performed, because they did not repent** (v 20). These small Jewish **towns** on the Sea of Galilee do not compare with the major Gentile cities of Sepphoris and Tiberias (France 2007, 437). The **miracles** or "mighty deeds" (*dunameis*) are "the deeds of the Messiah" (v 2) listed in v 5 (see examples in chs 8—9).

These express that the kingdom of heaven is drawing near and Israel's exile is coming to an end. The Lord and his anointed reign over that which oppress the people of God: blindness, leprosy, deafness, and death itself (11:5). Since Jesus performed **most of his miracles** in these **towns** and many still refused to repent, the intensity of Jesus' rebuke is harsh. Resistance toward Jesus now extends beyond the religious leaders.

The expression **woe to you** (v 21) is a declaration of judgment for those who refuse to obey God or recognize his sovereignty (see Jer 13:27; Mic 2:1; Zeph 2:5). Nolland suggests the phrase addresses those "whose situation is miserable," but Jesus does not portray the inhabitants of these towns as victims (2005, 467). Later, he directs the same denunciation at his religious opponents and Judas (Matt 23:13-32; 26:24).

Using hyperbole, Jesus asserts that if the same **miracles . . . were performed in Tyre and Sidon, they would have repented long ago in sackcloth and ashes** (11:21). This is particularly insulting since Tyre and Sidon are Gentile cities and were regularly condemned by the prophets for rebelliousness against God and hostility toward Israel (Isa 23:1-17; Ezek 26—28), and now Jesus states that their inhabitants are more open to the gospel than the Jews. **Sackcloth and ashes** is a fixed phrase in the 2TP associated with ritual mourning
11:23-24 (Esth 4:3; Dan 9:3).

Finally, since Chorazin and Bethsaida did not repent, **it will be more bearable for Tyre and Sidon on the day of judgment** (Matt 11:22). According to France, "The comparison of fates on the day of judgment is a repeated motif (cf. 10:15; 12:41-42) which is designed to emphasize the guilt of the Jews who failed to respond to Jesus rather than to pronounce on the destiny of the Gentile people as such" (2007, 438).

■ **23-24** Jesus singles out his hometown, **Capernaum**, where he began to preach the good news, and, thus far, its inhabitants have been open to him (8:5-17; 9:1-34; France 2007, 439). But the religious establishment is not as welcoming (9:3, 11, 34). Matthew associates Jesus' settling here with the fulfillment of prophecy. The land of darkness and death, the effects of the Lord's judgment, is now the object of his light and life (→ 4:12-17).

The taunt in 11:23*a* echoes the same one that Isaiah directs toward the king of Babylon (Isa 14:13-15): **And you, Capernaum, will you be lifted to the heavens? No, you will go down to Hades**. Jesus condemns Capernaum for its arrogance and consequent rejection, expressing that its final fate is **Hades**, death, and destruction (v 23*a*). Matthew's reference to "the wise and learned" in v 25, for whom the Father has not "revealed" these things, creates an unstated correspondence with the pride and self-importance of the Babylonian king who attempted to become "like the Most High" (Isa 14:14*b*), leading to his downfall.

Hades

This term occurs twice in Matthew (11:23 and 16:18) and only appears four times in the Gospels. The Greek word *hadēs* translates the Hebrew *sheol*, which denotes the abode of the dead (e.g., Isa 14:11; Job 17:13-16). It is contrasted with heaven (e.g., Isa 14:11-15) and is depicted as "a place of 'darkness' (Job 17:13), 'dust' (Job 17:16), and the place where the worm feasts (Job 17:14; 24:19-20; Is 14:11)" (Lunde 1992, 309). Jesus' reference to "Hades" as the destiny of Capernaum probably alludes to Isa 14:13-15. In 2T literature, there is hope of a return from *hadēs* (Wis 16:13; Sir 48:5; Lunde 1992, 310), but Jesus leaves little hope for this, which reflects the OT outlook.

Compared with Matt 11:21-22, Jesus makes an even more dramatic contrast claiming that if the miracles he performed had been done in Sodom, **it would have remained to this day** (v 23*c*). This highlights thoroughgoing resistance toward him, to which Matthew will refer later (13:53-58).

Consequently, **it will be more bearable for Sodom on the day of judgment than for you** (11:24). The prophets use **Sodom** both to illustrate the wickedness of Israel (Jer 23:14; Isa 3:9) and its consequent demise and to describe the judgment that the Lord will bring upon the nation (Jer 49:18; Lam 4:6). Jesus, as a prophet, now aligns Capernaum with the rebelliousness of historic Israel.

FROM THE TEXT

The proverbial saying in Matt 11:19*b*, "But wisdom is proved right by her deeds," which immediately precedes Jesus' denunciation of three Galilean towns, is a hinge connecting vv 16-19 and vv 20-24. "This generation" has not welcomed or understood these deeds as well as the ministry of John because they were expecting something much different. The "wisdom," or the ways in which Jesus and John have conducted themselves in accordance with God's will, although not pleasing to "this generation," will be vindicated or proven true.

This vindication includes not only the restoration that the deeds of the Messiah provide in the present but also, in light of the material following v 19, the judgment of those who refuse to acknowledge his messiahship (vv 20-24). The latter is the beginning of what will become a major theme in Matthew: judgment for those who rebel against the Messiah. The three Galilean towns' rejection of Jesus put them on par with godless cities that "not only . . . currently existed [Tyre and Sidon] but also . . . [with] any that ever existed [Sodom]" (Chrysostom, *Hom. Matt.* 37.4).

At some future point, the Lord will execute the judgment that Jesus speaks over these cities, which begins now with the withholding of revelation (v 25). One long-held tenet of the Christian faith is the reality of a final judgment and, despite how uncomfortable this is for some modern Christians, it cannot be avoided and to ignore it would nullify a large portion of Jesus' teaching in Matthew (e.g., Matt 23—24).

5. Concealment and Revelation of the Kingdom (11:25-30)

BEHIND THE TEXT

The temporal marker "at that time" connects the prayer of Jesus (vv 25-27) with his condemnation of Chorazin, Bethsaida, and Capernaum (vv 20-24). Verses 25-26 mark a transition from the condemnation of the "wise and learned," whom readers are to associate with the Galilean towns, to the "little children" who are first and foremost the disciples who willingly accept the gospel message and take upon themselves Jesus' yoke (vv 28-30). Revelation of "these things" comes to the "little children" from God through his Son who has the divine prerogative of determining the ones to whom he reveals the Father (v 27).

Although it appears that this revelation is limited and predetermined, it is open to "all you who are weary and burdened" (v 28). By reflecting the dependence of a child on a parent, the crowds who turn to Jesus due to the burdens they bear and the weariness that comes as a result will receive "rest for [their] souls" (v 29*b*). The yoke that Jesus exhorts his audience to bear is wisdom in the form of a new Torah, which Matthew illustrates in 12:1-14, that will liberate them from burdensome Pharisaic stipulations (23:3-4). In learning from Jesus, their new yoke will become "easy" and their new burden will be "light" (11:30).

IN THE TEXT

■ **25-26** In Matthew, the heavenly **Father** is one who knows his people (6:4, 6, 8, 18, 32) and to whom the disciples pray (6:9-13; 23:9; 26:53). In light of this, Jesus refers to his **Father** as **Lord of heaven and earth** (11:25), expressing that he is the Creator and sustainer of the world (Gen 14:22; Pss 115:15; 121:2) and, as such, is sovereign. Jesus praises God for this sovereignty and the accompanying ability to **have hidden these things from the wise** [*sofos*] **and learned** (*sunetos*) (Matt 11:25).

This prayer implicitly continues the condemnation of the Galilean towns in vv 20-24. In the OT, the Lord confounds those who are disobedient and refuse to acknowledge him (Isa 6:9-10; Dan 3:16). In Isa 29:14*b*, both "the wisdom of the wise [*sofos*] will perish, the intelligence of the intelligent [*sunetos*] will vanish" because of empty worship (v 13) and moral corruption (v 15).

According to Davies and Allison, "One is to think of the worldly wise, [persons] of secular sophistication who, though sagacious in their own eyes and crafty in their own devices, are yet far from true wisdom" (1991, 275). The leaders of Israel in Isaiah's day were guilty of arrogance and rebellion and so are the adversaries of Jesus in these towns.

The **things** the Father has hidden are difficult to determine. In context, intellectual apprehension of "the deeds of the Messiah" and the one who prepared his way are the most likely candidates (11:2-16). Jesus refers to those deeds as "miracles" (v 20), which failed to produce a response of repentance (vv 21-24) in three Galilean towns. The inhabitants' inability to apprehend the saving activity of God is the consequence of refusing to acknowledge the Messiah's deeds.

Instead, God has **revealed them to little children** (v 25). In the LXX, the word for **little children** (*nēpios*) is sometimes used to describe "the righteous" (Pss 18:7 [8 HB]; 114:6; 118:30). Later in Matthew, Jesus calls his disciples to "become like little children" (Matt 18:3) and states that "the lowly position of this child is the greatest in the kingdom of heaven" (v 4). For Matthew, **the little children** who received this revelation are humble, righteous, and repentant, unlike the arrogant and unrepentant to which Jesus refers in vv 21-24.

Concealing and revealing knowledge places v 25 in an eschatological context: "It was widely anticipated that the End would bring unprecedented knowledge and wisdom for the elect" (Davies and Allison 1991, 277). A number of OT and 2T texts reflect this: Jer 31:34; Hab 2:14; 1QpHab 7:1-14. The difference in Matthew and in other NT writings is that the Father has chosen to make **these things** known now through his Son. This is an invitation in the present for all of those who acknowledge need of the Father and believe in the work of his Son. This, as Jesus says, is what the **Father** was **pleased to do** (Matt 11:26).

■ **27** This verse attests to Matthew's high Christology in which Jesus is now 11:27
the locus of God's power and revelation. According to v 25, the "Father" has "revealed [these things] to little children," but the means of this revelation is Jesus: **All things have been committed to me by my Father** (v 27*a*). Some argue, appealing to Jewish wisdom tradition (e.g., Sir 51) that **all things** refer to wisdom (Matt 11:25-26; Luz 2001, 166; Hagner 1993, 320; Davies and Allison 1991, 279). While this is certainly true, one would expect the word "revealed" in place of "committed." The phrase "all things" encompasses not only the wisdom but also the deeds of the Messiah.

The investiture of the Son echoes the "one like a son of man" in Dan 7 who "was given [*didōmi*] authority, glory and sovereign power (v 14*a*). In Matt 9:6, the Son of Man has the authority to exercise his Father's prerogative of forgiving sins (→ 9:6). At the end of the Gospel, in 28:18, Jesus declares that "all authority in heaven and on earth has been given [*didōmi*] to me" (for a similar use of *didōmi/paradidōmi*, see Luke 4:6). For Matthew, God has endowed his Son Jesus not just with wisdom but also with authority and power to manifest his saving presence on earth.

Matthew 11:27 explains Jesus' exclusive reception of **all things . . . No one knows the Son except the Father, and no one knows the Father except the Son**. There are two different lenses through which one can interpret this mutual knowledge: (1) the alignment of Israel's will with that of the Lord's in the OT; or (2) a mystical union in which the Father and the Son know one another through more than the alignment of respective wills (see John 10:14-15; Luz 2001, 167-68). Option two interprets the knowledge that **the Son** and **the Father** share in a mysterious, suprarational relationship. Luz claims that this view seems at home in the 2T period with a movement toward a "mystical transformation of Old Testament faith" (Luz 2001, 168; see Wis 7:26-28). There is little evidence in Matthew as well as 2T literature for this.

Option 1 coheres with Matthew's presentation of Jesus, as true Israel, who is completely obedient to his heavenly Father and **knows** his will (→ 3:15—4:11). The Greek word for **know** in v 27*b* (*epiginōskō*) recalls the Hebrew *yada,* which expresses a close and intimate relationship between two parties, such as the Lord and the nation (Hos 13:4-5). This passage, then, is "a roundabout way of describing a reciprocal relationship . . . characteristic of Semitic languages" (Davies and Allison 1991, 281). Jesus' relationship with his heavenly Father is paradigmatic of the one that the Lord desired to have with his people (e.g., Deut 7:6-9; Hos 13:4-6; Amos 3:1-2), but this was never fully realized because of her disobedience.

The Son has the exclusive prerogative of revealing the Father **to whom** he **chooses** (Matt 11:27*b*). Jesus is the sole beneficiary of his Father's wisdom and power, and he now has the mandate to choose the ones to whom he will reveal salvation. This is not predestination wherein some are chosen to receive salvation and others not. He has chosen to keep the light of revelation from the wise
11:28-30 due to their failure to repent. Those who posture themselves as dependent children will receive wisdom and benefit from Jesus' saving work (vv 28-30).

■ **28-30** Jesus, the locus of God's revelation, welcomes everyone who responds to him: **Come to me, all you who are weary and burdened** (v 28*a*). For those who welcome the Son and recognize their need, the Son will reveal the Father (v 27). The **weary and burdened** recalls the "harassed and helpless" in 9:36*b*. Jesus calls **all** to find rest in him, not just his disciples (Nolland 2005, 476, contra Stanton 1982, 7).

Weary (*kopiaō,* fatigue from physical or spiritual exertion [BDAG 2000, 558]) and **burdened** (*fortizō,* the weight of a heavy load [BDAG 2000, 1064]) depict animals or humans attached to a yoke. Animals pull heavy loads, and humans—who put a yoke across their shoulders to distribute the weight (France 2007, 449)—bear a heavy load. The contrast with **my yoke** (vv 29*a*, 30*a*) is the wooden beam put across the shoulders of an individual.

Yoke also symbolizes various types of oppression (Gen 27:40; Exod 6:6-7; 1 Kgs 12:4-14; Isa 58:6, 9). For Matthew, the yoke borne by Jesus' audience is Pharisaic halakhah, which is burdensome and oppressive (Matt 23:4; Luz 2001, 172). It may also allude to economic and social burdens (France 2007, 448; Nolland 2005, 476). It could refer to any of these, but the narrative context, particularly 12:1-14, favors onerous obedience to the Law.

Halakhah

The halakhah of the Pharisees makes the Mosaic law applicable to a variety of circumstances. This is rooted in their desire to reflect God's purity in everything they do. Halakhah is derived from the Hebrew verb "to walk," a derivation that captures the comprehensive nature of this interpretation. All of Israel, including the Pharisees, are to "walk" in complete obedience to the Law in all things. While this interpretation was in oral form during the time of Jesus, it became codified in the Mishnah in the second century CE.

The Pharisees challenged Jesus when he breached their teaching, for example, when he heals on the Sabbath (Matt 12:1-8; see *m. Šabb.* 14:3-4). Their well-meaning desire to be holy in this way eclipsed the holy character of God as one who is merciful and gracious; God desires to heal! When this happens, the Pharisees' legal expectations become a "yoke" that is oppressive and wearisome in contrast with the one offered by Jesus (see also Matt 23:3-4).

Many scholars think the terminology of this passage parallels Sir 51:23-27 (France 2007, 447; Luz 2001, 171). The sage invites the "uneducated" to "draw near to me" (v 23 NRSV) and to "put your neck under her yoke, and let your souls receive instruction" (v 26 NRSV). The sage has "labored but little and found for myself much serenity" (v 27 NRSV). Matthew's Jesus reconfigures this imagery such that he becomes divine wisdom, something that the sage has merely received. For Jesus, "Wisdom's yoke is now his yoke, and it is he who offers rest to those who toil" (France 2007, 447). 11:28-30

T. W. Manson argues that the text of Sir 51, when it speaks of wisdom, is really referring to the Law, an identification that is reflected in a number of later Jewish texts (1938, 478, cited in Suggs 1970, 103 n. 7; Wis 6:4, 9; 9:9; Bar 3:9, 37—4:1; *T. Levi* 13:1-9). "Hence Jesus, in both [Matt] 11:27 and 29, and in contrast to Moses, is the perfect embodiment of God's purpose and demand and the functional equivalent of Torah. Law-giver and law are one" (Davies and Allison 1991, 290). This reading is strengthened when we consider Jesus' rewriting of Sabbath law in 12:1-14.

The promise of **rest** recalls the rest that accompanies possession of the promised land, where there is freedom from hostility. Israel will experience this if she is faithful to the Law (Josh 1:13; 2 Sam 7:11; 1 Kgs 5:4 [18 HB]; 8:56; Isa 63:14; Jer 31:2). Sadly, she is unfaithful, and rest is absent. While Jesus says nothing about the restoration of the land, rest from enemies and oppression fits in light of the compassion Jesus has on the "harassed and helpless" (Matt 9:36*b*). This is the end of Israel's exile in which she is delivered from the effects of the nation's disobedience and the lost sheep of Israel are found. The call to **learn from me** is to learn the wisdom Jesus offers, which brings much-needed rest.

Unlike the arrogant and proud opponents who refuse to learn from Jesus, or those Pharisees who "do not practice what they preach," but instead "tie up heavy, cumbersome loads and put them on other people's shoulders" (23:3-4), Jesus calls his followers to **learn from me, for I am gentle and humble in heart** (11:29). **Gentle and humble** parallels Jesus' earlier teaching about meekness in the Sermon on the Mount (5:5). All of these virtues are at the core of Jesus' identity. This does not mean that he lacks authority over hostility (e.g., 8:28-34; 23:13-26). At the same time, he is the servant of the Lord who "will not quarrel or cry out" (12:19*a*), as Matthew's Passion Narrative demonstrates (Luz 2001, 174), and "a bruised reed he will not break" (v 20*a*).

Obedience to this call results in **rest for your souls** (v 29*c*). **Souls**, in this context, represents the self as opposed to that "soul" that continues after death (→ 10:28). The line **you will find rest for your souls** alludes to Jer 6:16 where Israel can avoid her impending exile if she will turn from wickedness and behave uprightly, living in obedience to the Law. Now Jesus has been proclaiming an end to exile through teaching about the kingdom and his deeds, which mark its inauguration. The burdened and weary only need to turn to him and take his yoke upon them to receive this long-awaited rest, specifically, from demonic oppression, sickness, and onerous obedience to the Law.

In Matt 11:30, Jesus explains that **my yoke is easy and my burden is light**. This contrasts sharply with the onerous and burdensome Pharisaic halakhah. As ch 10 makes clear, following Jesus is not easy, so taking on his yoke does not mean that life is easy with no burdens to bear. However, when read in light of Jesus' ongoing conflict with the Pharisees, we see that his halakhah makes faithfulness to the Lord not onerous but rather liberating as the following passages (12:1-8 and vv 9-14) demonstrate.

FROM THE TEXT

Over their history, some holiness movements have been guilty of generating strict moral codes. Although their purpose was promoting holy living, the result was at times destructive, leading to the exclusion of those who did not line up with human expectations. When the gospel is reduced to a series of prohibitions, the life and freedom it gives fades into the background.

The "weary and burdened" in the time of Jesus bore the yoke of Pharisaic legislation, which was oppressive and onerous; some of the expectations of holiness denominations as they pertained to dress and behavior were equally burdensome. In Matt 11:28-30, Jesus offers a gospel of rest, liberty, and freedom. May we as a church preach and live that same gospel so that those burdened and wearied by the expectations of others or, more generally, by the cares of this world will know the light and easy load of obedience to Jesus Christ.

F. Resistance to the Messiah's Ministry (12:1-50)

BEHIND THE TEXT

Resistance to Jesus continues in Matt 12. The Pharisees challenge him in a variety of ways (see vv 2, 10, 24, 38). In ch 11, "this generation" (vv 16-19) is unsatisfied with the ministries of John and Jesus and then, in vv 20-24, the inhabitants of three Galilean towns will be judged for their failure to repent. A series of vignettes in ch 12 provides readers with specific examples of the resistance Jesus encounters.

The ending of ch 11 provides the theological framework for the first two conflict accounts (12:1-8 and 9-14). Jesus is the Son on whom true wisdom rests, which he offers to wearied and burdened souls (11:28-30). In the next two narratives, Jesus' type of wisdom reorients the Law toward the exercise of mercy and compassion. However, this comes at a cost. After Jesus heals a man with a withered hand on the Sabbath, the Pharisees plot to destroy him (12:14).

After Matthew's longest quote of an OT text showing that Jesus is an Isaianic servant-Messiah (vv 18-21), the Pharisees engage in slanderous speech. They contend that he exorcises by the power Beelzebul, to which Jesus responds that this is impossible and that those who make such an accusation can never be forgiven (vv 24-37). Also, the Pharisees and their scribes wish to see a sign. Jesus has demonstrated his messianic authority in their presence (see 9:32-34 and 12:22-24). The request stems from wicked and adulterous hearts. Jesus' fictive family are those who do the will of his Father and have forsaken all to follow him. In short, "Chapters 11-12 have revealed a wide variety of reactions to Jesus among his Galilean contemporaries, and the parables of ch. 13 will explain how such a divided response has come about" (France 2007, 495).

1. Challenged by the Pharisees (12:1-14)

BEHIND THE TEXT

In these conflict stories, Jesus is challenged by the Pharisees for what they consider an abrogation of Sabbath law. However, as true wisdom, Jesus teaches his disciples, through his words and actions, what Yahweh intended for Sabbath. Meeting human need takes precedence over Sabbath observance, fulfilling Yahweh's desire for mercy over religious devotion (see v 7).

Sabbath

Yahweh commands Israel to keep the Sabbath holy for two reasons:

1. God himself sanctified it by resting from his work after creating the heavens and the earth (Exod 20:8-11; Gen 2:2-3).

2. It is to remind Israel that God redeemed her from slavery in Egypt (Deut 5:15*a*).

Sabbath is a time to worship Yahweh and reflect on his faithfulness to the nation both as Creator and Redeemer. That Sabbath is a day of rest for the good of Israel is reflected in 2TJ literature: God "created this day for a blessing and sanctification and glory" (*Jub.* 2:32).

Because Sabbath is a holy day, there are a series of laws that safeguard it. By the second century CE, the Mishnah refers to thirty-nine prohibited forms of Sabbath work (*m. Šabb.* 7:2), which includes legislation related to agriculture and construction, for example. Much of this is oral tradition in the time of Jesus. There are also consequences for breaching Sabbath law, one of which is death (Exod 31:12-17; Num 15:32-36). This penalty is the basis for the Pharisees' plot to destroy Jesus after he heals a man's withered hand (Matt 12:13).

a. Challenged in a Grain Field (12:1-8)

IN THE TEXT

■ **1-2** **At that time** links this narrative and the following one (vv 9-14) with Jesus' teaching in 11:25-30. These stories illustrate that bearing the yoke of Jesus results in rest for weary souls in contrast with the oppressive yoke of Pharisaic halakhah. The first is set in the Galilean **grainfields on the Sabbath** (12:1*a*) through which Jesus and his disciples are walking. However, it is not
12:1-2 until the Pharisees see **his disciples . . . pick some heads of grain and eat them** that they say to Jesus, **Look! Your disciples are doing what is unlawful on the Sabbath** (vv 1*b*-2). His disciples are breaching Sabbath halakhah by plucking heads of grain. Since Jesus, as a rabbi, is responsible for his students, they address him directly and question him about **his disciples** (v 2; see Daube 1972-73, 4-5). Jesus, in turn, responds (vv 3-8).

In order to safeguard the holiness of the Sabbath, the Pharisees developed a complex set of rules governing behavior so that Sabbath became more of a burden than a rest. The rabbinic text *m. Šabb.* 7:2 records "thirty-nine categories of activity which were to be classified as 'work' for this purpose, some of which are very specific . . . , others so broad as to need further specification" (France 2007, 455).

The specific offense is difficult to determine. Was it the distance traveled, that is, beyond a "Sabbath day's journey" of two thousand cubits? Or, was the disciples' plucking 'work' and so they contravene the fifth commandment (Exod 20:9-11; 34:21)? The latter seems most likely (see Matt 12:1*b*-2).

Nolland suggests that Deut 23:25 [26 HB], which allows a needy Israelite to enter a neighbor's field, not to harvest but to pluck the heads of grain with one's hand, can account for the disciples' actions (2005, 482). Since it is permissible to prepare food for immediate consummation on the Sabbath (*Jub.* 50:8-10, 12; *m. Šabb.* 7:2), a sympathetic application of Deut 23:25 [26

HB] may justify the disciples' work (Nolland 2005, 482). If the Pharisees do have this text in mind, they do not agree with Jesus' application of it. It is difficult to know, however, if Jesus is even appealing to it. He alludes to other biblical texts in Matt 12:3-8.

■ **3-6** Jesus responds with an abbreviated and revised account of 1 Sam 21:1-6 [2-7 HB]. Have the Pharisees **read what David did when he and his companions were hungry?** (Matt 12:3). Later, Jesus asks the temple leaders (21:16) and Sadducees (22:31-32) if they have **read**. This question implies that they cannot claim ignorance. They fail to see how the ministry of Jesus coheres with Israel's Scriptures.

Jesus' reference to 1 Sam 21:1-6 [2-7 HB] highlights the human need of an authoritative figure and his compatriots and that this, as Matt 12:4 implies, takes precedence over legal concerns. A variety of proposals consider how the story of David addresses the accusation of the Pharisees (see Nolland 2005, 483). The most evident connection is that just as David can breach OT law by virtue of his royal authority, so can Jesus due to his authority as Messiah.

Jesus modifies 1 Sam 21:1-6 [2-7 HB] in at least four ways. The text of 1 Samuel does not record David eating the bread, nor do his companions enter the sanctuary at Nob (for the rest, see Snow 2016, 84-85). In Matthew, Jesus says that David **entered the house of God, and he and his companions ate the consecrated bread—which was not lawful for them to do, but only for the priests** (Matt 12:4). "By means of these modifications, . . . Jesus highlights that David and his followers execute a task reserved only for the priests" (Snow 2016, 85).

On the Sabbath, the priests replaced the bread of the presence in the tabernacle. Only the priests could consume the bread from the preceding week (Lev 24:5-9). This necessarily involved preparing food on the Sabbath. However, Yahweh permitted the priests to perform this in the tabernacle and later in the temple, which Jesus recognizes in Matt 12:5: **The priests on Sabbath duty in the temple desecrate the Sabbath and yet are innocent**. Sacred places seem to be exempt from some laws, which, for Jesus, means that "the non-work requirement of the Sabbath is not absolute" (Nolland 2005, 484). Put another way, Chilton and Neusner comment that "what was not to be done outside of the Temple, in secular space, was required to be done in holy space, in the Temple itself" (1995, 142; Milgrom 2001, 3:2099).

Jesus highlights David and his companions executing priestly prerogatives in "the house of God" (v 4) and, then, in v 6, Jesus announces, **I tell you that something greater than the temple is here**. There is a connection between the "unlawful" priestly activity of David and his followers in the sanctuary and the "unlawful" action of Jesus' disciples in a Galilean grainfield on the Sabbath. The disciples perform the guiltless work of the priests who prepare the bread of the presence on the Sabbath.

In v 6, Jesus implies that he himself transcends the holiness of the temple: **I tell you that something greater than the temple is here**. Jesus is not merely holding David up as a precedent for breaching Sabbath law for the sake of human need on the basis of royal authority, or demonstrating when a Sabbath rule does not apply. Matthew has already established that as the Son of Man, and elsewhere, Jesus has the authority to do that which Yahweh can, for example, forgive sins and calm stormy seas.

Here, Jesus clearly expresses that the holy institution that represents the holy presence of Yahweh is now inferior to the presence of Jesus himself who **is here**. Consequently, in the presence of Jesus, the laws that once applied only to the priests in the temple now apply to all of those associated with him, such as the disciples who can guiltlessly pluck heads of grain to meet human need.

From vv 3-6, Matthew's logic once again reflects his high Christology: if the temple is a space where Sabbath laws do not apply, or stated another way, "temple service takes precedence over sabbath observance" (Davies and Allison 1991, 314), how much more is that the case for those who follow Jesus, the "something" greater than the temple?

While some have suggested that the referent of **something greater** is "mercy" in light of v 7 (see, e.g., Keener 1999, 356), it seems more relevant to view **something greater** as referring specifically to the authority of Jesus (Davies and Allison 1991, 314; France 2007, 461). For Matthew, Jesus' authority places him functionally on par with Yahweh himself (see 9:6, 8; 21:23, 24; and, especially, 28:18) and **something greater** than the temple, given that it symbolizes Yahweh's presence, could only be Jesus and his authority.

Matthew also uses the same terminology in 12:41-42 where the referent of "something greater" again refers to the authority of Jesus, which the Pharisees reject (France 2007, 460-61). Yahweh's presence is no longer mediated through priests and the temple but is fully present in the person of Jesus; he is "Immanuel, . . . 'God with us'" (1:23)!

France, referring to Y. E. Yang, indicates "that if the guiltlessness of the priests derived from their being 'in the temple,' [then] that of the disciples derives from their being with Jesus, the one who is 'greater than the temple'" (France 2007, 462 n. 41; Yang 1997, 182-83). By defending their guiltlessness, Jesus is not rejecting Sabbath law but, as 12:7-8 reveal, is restoring its divinely intended purpose.

■ **7-8** Jesus' implicit admonishment of the Pharisees in v 3, "have you not read," is intensified when he accuses them of not knowing the meaning of Yahweh's words: **I desire mercy, not sacrifice**, citing Hos 6:6. The prophet highlights the wickedness of Judah, a nation that has "broken the covenant" and is "unfaithful to me [Yahweh]" (Hos 6:7). Even the priests are murderous and wicked (v 9). When Jesus quotes Hos 6:6 here and in Matt 9:13, he implies that the Pharisees' strict obedience to ancestral traditions eclipses mercy. In 9:13, they ask why Jesus is eating with "tax collectors and sinners" and now accuse his disciples of "doing what is unlawful on the Sabbath" when they satisfy human need (12:2).

In both stories, Jesus responds with **mercy**. For Matthew, **sacrifices** refers to Pharisaic observance that is inhibiting acts of mercy. If the Pharisees had understood how their obedience to the Law prohibits showing mercy, then they **would not have condemned the innocent** (v 7*b*), that is, the disciples. In vv 9-14, the Pharisees do not show mercy toward a man with a withered hand.

In the final verse, Jesus brings his response to a climax. Jesus can restore the true intention of Sabbath law *because*, or **for**, he is **the Son of Man** who **is Lord of the Sabbath** (v 8). Matthew's use of **Son of Man** is a development of the Danielic figure who now exercises divine prerogatives (→ 9:6). The same is true here.

The phrase **Lord of the Sabbath** recalls pentateuchal texts that "contain the phrase 'a sabbath of/to Yahweh' expressing that the sabbath day belongs to Yahweh and is under his dominion" (Snow 2016, 87). The authority of Jesus, the "something greater," enables him to exercise Yahweh's reign over Sabbath. He restores it to a day of blessing in which the disciples can eat without condemnation and receive mercy when it otherwise would not have been granted. Thus, Jesus' "yoke is easy and [his] burden is light" (11:30).

Further, Jesus fulfills the *purpose* of Sabbath just as he fulfilled the Law in 5:21-47. Here he rejects onerous scribal traditions that subvert the purpose of Torah-Sabbath laws (see also France 2007, 456). Matthew may have intentionally omitted Mark 2:27 lest it diminish his emphasis on Jesus' authority (Davies and Allison 1991, 315; France 2007, 462-63).

b. Challenged in a Synagogue (12:9-14)

IN THE TEXT

■ **9-10** Jesus then moves on to **their synagogue**, likely the "Pharisees' synagogue," to demonstrate that he will exercise his authority even in their territory. France suggests that **their** "begins to hint at the growing rift between Jesus and the synagogue establishment" (France 2007, 463). In 12:10, Matthew sets up a tense scene. Present is **a man with a shriveled hand** and, in Matthew, Jesus always heals those who are sick (4:23-34; 9:35). The Pharisees, meanwhile, are **looking for a reason to bring charges against Jesus** and so they ask him: **Is it lawful to heal on the Sabbath?** (v 10*b*).

The question **Is it lawful?** recalls the Pharisees' previous statement about the **unlawful** activity of the disciples. Although there is no prohibition against healing on the Sabbath in the Mosaic law, the rabbinic sources confine it to specific occasions when healing or saving life is permitted, such as the prospect of imminent death (*m. Yoma* 8:6). A man with a withered hand hardly falls into this category!

■ **11-12** Jesus responds with a question of his own. Reminiscent of OT casuistic laws, he asks them about **a sheep** that **falls into a pit on the Sabbath**. He implies that they would surely rescue it: **will you not take hold of it and lift it out?** (v 11). The OT advocates care for livestock (Deut 22:4; Prov 12:10), but some Mishnaic texts prohibit helping an animal in distress on Sabbath (*b. Šabb.* 128b; *m. Besah* 3:4).

However, the question in Matt 12:11*b* assumes that most people would aid an animal, especially Galilean farmers (Luz 2001, 188). Then Jesus employs a rabbinic form of argument that moves from the lesser to the greater: **How much more valuable is a person than a sheep!** (v 12*a*). He concludes that it is **lawful to do good on the Sabbath** (v 12*b*); similarly, the disciples can work to eat on the Sabbath to satisfy hunger.

■ **13-14** Jesus then turns to the man with the lame hand and tells him to **stretch out your hand** and when he does **it was completely restored, just as sound as the other** (v 13). But the Pharisees **went out and plotted how they might kill Jesus** (v 14). For them, Jesus is a lawbreaker; consequently, the rift between him and the religious establishment continues to widen (see 9:34).

At the same time, the Pharisees' plotting to kill Jesus *on the Sabbath* reveals a profound irony. For Jesus, human need takes precedence over Sabbath law, mercy over sacrifice. As the preceding story demonstrates, he is "Lord of the Sabbath" and as such restores this day to its original purpose of restoration and blessing while the Pharisees seek to murder him.

FROM THE TEXT

The Pharisees as a whole were likely sincere people who were trying to live lives of holiness, including keeping the Sabbath holy. But their rule-based approach to holy living became legalistic and petty. At various points, Matthew highlights the deleterious effects that this approach had on them and those who do not measure up to their standards (e.g., Matt 23:13-36).

In the ministry of Jesus, mercy and love triumphs over pedantic halakic Sabbath legislation, which can prohibit doing good and loving one's neighbor (7:12; 22:39-40). Wesley comments that Jesus

> brought it back to its original standard, to its just and natural extent. Accordingly both his words and his actions showed that we may do works of necessity and mercy on this day; that we may do whatever cannot be done on another day, or not without manifest inconvenience, such as giving ourselves decent and proper recreation; as feeding and watering of cattle—for this is a work of necessity; that we may relieve our sick or hungry neighbour—for this is a work of mercy. ("On the Sabbath," Wesley 1987b, 4:75-76)

Contemporary Sabbath observance needs to have at its center love and mercy, unhindered by legalistic dos and don'ts. Sabbath is a set apart time for the worship and praise of our creator God and for the enjoyment of fellowship with others along with the created order in which we live. Holiness traditions need to guard against making it a day of dreary legalistic practice.

2. The Ministry of the Servant-Messiah (12:15-21)

BEHIND THE TEXT

Isaiah 42:1-4, quoted in Matt 12:18-21, is the longest OT quotation in Matthew. It encapsulates much of Jesus' ministry even if it is difficult to make specific connections. Matthew has already alluded to Isa 42:1 in Matt 3:17 (→). In 8:17, he quotes from Isa 53:4 (→ Matt 8:17). Here, Jesus is the servant-Son/Messiah who brings justice to the poor and oppressed, resulting in hope for the nations. The form of Matthew's quotation adheres to the MT with some influence from the LXX (for details, see Nolland 2005, 492-95).

IN THE TEXT

■ **15-17** Somehow Jesus becomes **aware of this**, the plot to kill him, and he **withdrew from that place** (v 15*a*). This does not stop **a large crowd** from following him or stop Jesus from continuing his healing activity on the Sabbath day, since **he healed all who were ill** (v 15*b*). Jesus healing "all" is uniquely Matthean (4:23; 9:35). He will "withdraw" again after hearing about the death of John (see 14:1-13). Jesus removing himself from potentially hostile situations will end when he arrives in Jerusalem (e.g., 22:15-40).

Jesus warns the crowd **not to tell others about him** (12:16), a command we see again after Peter's confession (see 16:16-20). While Matthew's Jesus does not silence the demons who confess his identity as in Mark, the "messianic secret" may still be important (see 8:4; 9:30). In 12:15-16, Jesus demonstrates his messianic authority to heal the sick, already shown in Matt 8—9 (→ 8:1—9:34 C. Mighty Deeds of the Messiah), and affirmed by Jesus in 11:2-6. For now, he does not want them to make known the source of this power. However, immediately following the quote, Jesus heals a blind and mute man before "all the people" and gives no command for secrecy (12:22-23). If Matthew does intend to preserve Mark's messianic secret, then it is a diminished version (Neyrey 1982, 468).

Matthew indicates that **this was to fulfill what was spoken through the prophet Isaiah** (v 17), which leads to the quotation of Isa 42:1-4. But how does Jesus' command to secrecy fulfill this prophecy? Commentators recognize the incongruity of this quote with its context (Nolland 2005, 492; Luz 2001, 193). Probably "Matthew inserts the quotation, because at this point in his gospel he wants to use the Bible to remind his readers of the entirety of the story of Christ" (Luz 2001, 192).

Jesus is the Servant of Yahweh who speaks and acts with authority, reorienting the Sabbath as its Lord (11:25—12:14) and healing the sick (11:2-6;

12:15-16). As the servant, Jesus will not endorse violent or militaristic aspirations (→ 16:21-23). France suggests that this peaceful and gentle depiction shows Matthew's audience that conflict comes to Jesus; he himself does not go looking for it (2007, 469). This contrasts with the depiction of the Messiah in *Pss. Sol.* 17:21-30 who establishes Yahweh's reign through violence.

■ **18-21** The language of Matt 12:18*a*, **Here is my servant whom I have chosen, the one I love, in whom I delight**, recalls Jesus' baptism (see 3:17). The Greek term for "servant" (*pais*) usually means "child" in nonbiblical Greek (Luz 2001, 193; see Wis 2:13-18 for an exception) and, according to Luz, Matthew intends this familial designation. But most argue that *pais* means "servant" since this is the usual meaning in the LXX (Nolland 2005, 492; France 2007, 471 n. 21), including its use in Matt 8:6 (→). Jesus is not only the servant-Messiah but also in light of his baptism the servant-Son of Yahweh (see Ps 2:2, 7; 4Q174).

Matthew 12:18*b*, **I will put my Spirit on him**, also recalls the baptism narrative in which the Spirit descends upon Jesus (see 3:16*b*). He is the Spirit-filled servant-Son/Messiah who will **proclaim justice to the nations** (12:18*b*). In Isa 42:6-8, this proclamation involves being "a light for the Gentiles" (v 6*b*) and being empowered "to open eyes that are blind, to free captives from prison and to release from the dungeon those who sit in darkness" (v 7). This coheres with Matthew's summary of the divinely empowered messianic ministry of Jesus in Matt 11:2-6, which begins with Israel but will eventually include **the nations** or Gentiles (8:5-12; 15:21-28; 28:16-20).

Luz argues that "justice" (*krisis*) means judgment since it does elsewhere in Matthew (10:15; 11:22, 24; 12:36; 2001, 194). But this does not fit the context either here or in Isaiah. Jesus has just been healing and delivering the oppressed, which marks a reversal of injustice (e.g., 12:15; see also 23:23 where Matthew uses *krisis* as justice). In Isaiah, the servant brings healing and restoration to exiled Israel and the nations, which demonstrates Yahweh's righting of wrongs (see Goldingay 2005, 474, cited in Blomberg 2007, 42; Hagner 1993, 338). Of course, Jesus does judge his adversaries in 12:22-50 and in Matt 11 (Neyrey 1982, 464-65). These moments of judgment will culminate in final eschatological judgment (e.g., 13:37-43; 25:31-46), when he sets the world to right once and for all, which is an act of justice.

The one who brings **justice to the nations** (12:18*b*) will do so without violence and aggression: **He will not quarrel or cry out; no one will hear his voice in the streets** (v 19). This is a general comment, which aligns with Jesus' acceptance of suffering at the hands of his enemies (see 26:50-54, 67-68; 27:27-31). In the meantime, he does not draw attention to himself, as shown in his command of silence given to those whom he heals in 12:16 (France 2007, 469) and his withdrawal from the synagogue when he learns of the Pharisees' plot to kill him (vv 14-15).

But Jesus does not shy away from conflict when he labels the Pharisees a "brood of vipers" in 12:34 or as members of a "wicked and adulterous generation" in v 39. Matthew's Jesus is not a "flat" character but a round one who responds in different ways depending on the situation.

According to v 20, the servant will not harm others, no matter how useless they may be in the eyes of others. **A bruised reed** is not worth anything as it is no longer useful for measuring, but, yet, Jesus **will not break** it (v 20*a*), and although **a smoldering wick** needs to be extinguished, Jesus **will not snuff** it **out** (v 20*a*). In both cases, "What is normally thought to be beyond valuing is preserved from its expected fate" (Nolland 2005, 494). For Jesus, this involves sitting at table with "sinners and tax collectors," fulfilling God's desire for "mercy, not sacrifice" (9:13*b*; see Hos 6:6). It also involves defending his disciples to the Pharisees (see Matt 12:1-8, see esp. v 7).

He will carry on with this ministry of compassion and mercy **till he has brought justice through to victory** (v 20*b*). To do so means that Jesus has successfully fulfilled his ministry "as the one who establishes God's will and righteousness in the world" (Davies and Allison 1991, 327). The full manifestation of God's righteousness, something for which Jesus' followers seek (5:6), will mark the restoration of the marginalized, oppressed, and downtrodden.

Because of his work, **in his name the nations will put their hope** (12:21). In Matthew, ministry to the nations begins with the chosen nation, Israel (e.g., 1:21; 10:5-6), but the reign of God will extend beyond her (8:5-12; 15:21-28; 28:16-20). This finds its basis in the covenantal promises to Abraham (Gen 12:1-3), which is reiterated in the prophets (e.g., Isa 49:6). Jesus, as one who represents the nation of Israel, is the one who will fulfill the Abrahamic promises that she will become a blessing to the nations. Matthew hints at this both in his genealogy with the mention of Gentile women and then in his birth narrative with the appearance of Gentile astrologers.

FROM THE TEXT

Matthew uses OT quotations to confirm the identity of Jesus and the purpose of his ministry. Based on Isa 42:1-4, Jesus is the servant-Son/Messiah who brings justice to the sick and marginalized and exorcises by the power of the Spirit with whom he is indwelt (Matt 12:18, 28). He will not engage in violent, revolutionary activity to advance his mission (v 19), but he cares for the weak and the oppressed and will do so until justice wins the day (v 20). Because of these things, "in his name the nations will put their hope" (v 21).

Today, it is crucial that the church, like Jesus, ministers from a place of theological and biblical reflection, which informs theological practice. Everything that Jesus does is ultimately rooted in the missional love of God for his people and the nations, as revealed in the Scriptures. This is a mandate to which the church needs to give serious intellectual and practical attention.

3. Further Challenges by the Pharisees (12:22-45)

BEHIND THE TEXT

The exorcism of a demon from a blind and mute man "so that he could both talk and see" (v 22) elicits polarized responses. The crowds are amazed and question if this might be "the Son of David?" (v 23). Their awareness of Jesus' identity is growing. In 9:33, they had merely observed in response to another exorcism that "nothing like this has ever been seen in Israel." The Pharisees, on the other hand, reject the very foundation of Jesus' ministry, accusing him of using the power of Beelzebul (12:24). This is more specific than their designation "the prince of demons" in 9:34. The lines of rejection are becoming increasingly clear and, by the end of ch 12, the lines of allegiance will be clear as well when Jesus identifies his true followers (vv 46-50).

IN THE TEXT

a. Exorcisms by Beelzebul (12:22-37)

■ **22-23** Beginning the next scene with **then**, Matthew associates the quotation from Isa 42 with the healing of **a demon-possessed man who was blind and mute** (Matt 12:22*a*). Unlike the last healing in vv 15-16, after which he commanded silence, here he heals before **all the people** (v 23*a*) whereupon they ponder whether he is the Messiah: **Could this be the Son of David?** (v 23*b*; → Matt 9:27, "Son of David" sidebar). As servant-Messiah, Son of David, Jesus continues to bring justice to Israel both healing this man's eyes and restoring his speech. He manifests Yahweh's rule by the mighty deeds he performs (see also 9:27; 11:2-6; 15:22; 21:14-15).

■ **24 The Pharisees** respond very differently from the crowd by unambiguously declaring that Jesus operates according to the power of **Beelzebul, the prince of demons** (v 24*b*).

Beelzebul

"Beelzebub" is based on the Latin and Syriac versions of the NT (France 2007, 478 n. 21). However, **Beelzebul** is attested in a variety of early mss., although some lack the first "l." It is not clear how this name became associated with Satan in the Gospel tradition, but it is associated with pagan deities in the OT, such as the Canaanite god Baal, a deity whom the Israelites chose to serve, at times, over Yahweh. Baal combined with the Hebrew ending, *zebûl*, together means "Baal (lord) of the height" or "of the house" (France 2007, 478; Davies and Allison 1991, 195). Alternatively, later NT mss. that read "Beelzebub" may recall the god of Ekron, *baal zebûb* (2 Kgs 1:2-6).

The most plausible background is the "Lord of the height," denoting his heavenly authority (Twelftree 1992, 164). This is paralleled in one Jewish text where *Beelzeboul* is depicted as a ruler of demons (*T. Sol.* 3:6). For Matthew, the name is interchangeable with Satan, who is the ultimate adversary of Jesus (see Matt 12:26-27; Mark 3:22-23).

Matthew 12:22-24 forms a "type-scene" with 9:32-34 in which Matthew adds additional elements to this exorcism narrative that serve his thematic purposes. In 9:32-34, Jesus delivers a demon-possessed man who is not only mute but both blind and mute. The crowds are amazed, claiming that "nothing like this has ever been seen in Israel" (v 33*b*); now they searchingly ask if Jesus could be **the Son of David** (Matt 12:23*b*), a question posed in a manner that expects an affirmative response.

Even Matthew's choice of verb for **astonished** is more dramatic and intense than "amazed" in 9:33*b* (France 2007, 447).

The Pharisees respond that **it is only by Beelzebul, the prince of demons, that this fellow drives out demons** (v 34). In Greek, Matthew's placement of **this fellow** (*houtos*) suggests a scornful response (Davies and Allison 1991, 335). Further, the Pharisees name this demonic prince Beelzebul, marking an explicit rejection of his authority. Unlike the crowds who ponder the messianic authority of Jesus, the Pharisees have made up their minds: "We have therefore moved beyond 'academic' debate on the validity of Jesus' teaching and practice [e.g. 12:1-8, 9-13] to the realm of personal abuse and character assassination" (France 2007, 475). Comparing 9:32-34 with this account demonstrates that the crowds are growing in their awareness of Jesus' identity while the Pharisees acknowledge his power but attribute it to the demonic realm.

■ **25-28** Jesus responds because he **knew their thoughts** (*enthumēsis*; v 25*a*; see 9:4 for the same discernment). He will deal with not only their accusation but also "the motivation which gave rise to it," which is evident in vv 30-32 (France 2007, 479). Jesus responds by expressing the absurdity of their accusation (see 9:3-8). 12:25-28

He begins with common ground: if a **kingdom**, **city**, or **household**, is **divided against itself will be ruined/will not stand** (v 25*b*). Jesus then applies this to the Pharisees' accusation: **If Satan drives out Satan, he is divided against himself. How then can his kingdom stand?** (v 26). The application to the kingdom of Satan, which is one kingdom, anticipates a negative response to his question: it will not stand! For early Christians and other Jews of the 2T period, a sinister, evil kingdom exists: "Satan, like God, has a kingdom, a well-ordered and organized host of powers and influences that heed the beck and call of their dark Lord" (Davies and Allison 1991, 336; see, e.g., 2 Cor 11:14-15; Rev 12:7-9; 4Q268 10 ii.1-13). In Matthew, this kingdom is opposed to that of the kingdom of God that Jesus inaugurates, but he has authority over it (4:1-11; 8:28-34; 9:32-33; 12:22; 13:37-39; 15:21-28).

In 12:27, Jesus asks the Pharisees to consider another implication of their accusation (see v 24). If it is true that Jesus **drive[s] out demons by Beelzebul**, then **by whom do your people drive them out?** (v 27). Are the exorcism activities of **your people** [lit. "your sons"], those associated with the Pharisees, illegitimate as well? Other Jewish groups exorcised demons (Mark 9:38; Tob 8:1-3; 1 Sam 16:14-23), so Jesus' ministry is not unique. If they were to make such a false accusation against their own people, just as they are doing to Jesus, then **they will be your judges** (Matt 12:27*b*).

Jesus concludes by revealing the true source of his authority: **But if it is by the Spirit of God that I drive out demons, then the kingdom of God has come upon you**. This statement reinforces Matthew's quotation of Isa 42:1-4 above, where Jesus is depicted as the Spirit-filled servant-Messiah of Yahweh (Matt 12:18). In Luke 11:20, Jesus exorcises "by the finger of God" (see Exod 8:19), but Matthew's choice of **Spirit of God** (Matt 12:28) coheres with his theology of immanence: Jesus is Immanuel, God with us! Through the Spirit, the holy God is with his people in the person of Jesus, and the Spirit is the means by which he establishes God's reign in the lives of his followers.

France argues that Matthew's departure from his usual phrase ("kingdom of heaven") to **kingdom of God** is due to "the context [which] requires a more 'personal' reference to God himself than the more oblique language of his heavenly authority" (2007, 480). In the presence of the Spirit-filled Jesus, Satan's kingdom will not stand (v 26; Davies and Allison attribute the difference to style only: "kingdom of God" parallels "Spirit of God" and is the opposite of "his [Satan's] kingdom" [1991, 339]).

The conjunction **but**, at the beginning of v 28, could imply that the exorcisms of Jesus are unlike those associated with the Pharisees. The difference is rooted in identity: it is *Jesus* who casts out demons and, by virtue of his Spirit-filled messianic authority, does so in far less dramatic ways than other Jewish and Hellenistic exorcists, which included chants and incantations (for common features of Hellenistic exorcisms, see Meier 1996, 8-9; and Jewish exorcisms, see Davies and Allison 1991, 338 n. 25).

■ **29** This short parable describes the level of assault that Jesus is launching against the kingdom of Satan. There is no way that he is in league with him, and so Jesus describes in another manner his power over him (Nolland 2005, 501). In light of v 28, he is not just casting out demons "by the Spirit of God" but is attacking Satan, **the strong man** (v 29). This parable recalls Isa 49:24-25 LXX in which exiled Israel are the "spoils" in the possession of "a mighty one" (v 24 NETS). Yahweh will take that "mighty one captive, [and] he will take spoils" (v 25*a* NETS). In Isaiah, the "mighty one/strong one" refers to the nations who oppress exiled Israel. If Matthew has this text in mind, he applies it to Jesus' work of delivering oppressed and exiled Israel from bondage to her ultimate enemy, Satan.

The language of "binding" or "tying up" is paralleled in other Jewish literature to refer to the binding of the devil (*1 En.* 10:4-5; *Jub.* 48:15, 18; *T. Levi* 18:12) and demons (*1 En.* 54:3-5; *Jub.* 10:7; Luz 2001, 205 n. 70). The Greek word for **possessions** (*skeuos*) has a range of meaning, which can include the human body (BDAG 2000, 928). Jesus, exorcising "by the Spirit of God," frees those who are Satan's **possessions** because, in some unseen spiritual manner, he **ties up the strong man** (Nolland 2005, 502). Others have interpreted the **house** as humans (for a history of interpretation, see Luz 2001, 205 n. 72) and so an overemphasis on one-to-one correspondence in Matt 12:29 is misguided; rather, the parable's value is found as a description of the power of Jesus who overcomes **the strong man**.

■ **30-32** Now that Jesus has established that he is not in league with Satan, he turns his attention to the Pharisees, beginning with a general warning: **Whoever is not with me is against me, and whoever does not gather with me scatters** (v 30). The Pharisees are certainly not with Jesus and do not gather with him either. Thus far in Matthew, particularly in ch 12, the Pharisees completely reject Jesus and wish to have him destroyed (v 14). They are not "with him" as are his disciples (vv 3-4). For others, however, this is a summons to declare one's allegiance: no one can sit on the fence.

The gathering to which Jesus refers echoes moments in Ezekiel, for example, in which Yahweh "gathers" exiled Israel (e.g., Ezek 34). Matthew does not explicitly indicate that the Pharisees "scatter," but since they do not "gather," they essentially scatter God's people, something for which the pagan nations are guilty (Zech 1:19-21). Jesus inaugurates a return from exile that is evident at various points in Matthew and Matt 12:30 contributes to it (→ 3:1-3; 4:23-25; 9:2).

In 12:31, Jesus homes in on the Pharisees, whose accusation does not fall into the category of **every kind of sin and slander** that **can be forgiven**, but, rather, is **blasphemy against the Spirit** and **will not be forgiven**. The NIV translates the first occurrence of **blasphemy** (*blasphēmia*) as **slander**, which is a common meaning both in the LXX and pagan Greek literature (see Twelftree 1992, 75). 12:30-32

In 9:3, the scribes accuse Jesus of "blasphemy" for arrogating to himself the status of God. Here Jesus exorcises "by the Spirit of God" (v 28) and, as prophesied by Isaiah, is the one on whom Yahweh places his "Spirit" (v 18). So the Pharisees are guilty of a slanderous form of blasphemy when they accuse him of being empowered by Satan. Such blasphemy **against the Holy Spirit will not be forgiven, either in this age or in the age to come** (v 32*b*; for a survey of the history of interpretation of the unpardonable sin, Lammé 2012, 20-27).

What distinguishes this type of unforgivable blasphemy from **a word against the Son of Man** (v 32*a*)? Nolland interprets "the Son of Man" as a generic reference to humanity and so forgiveness for sins against others is possible (2005, 504), while blasphemy against the Spirit demonstrates an opposition to the forgiveness and healing Jesus has come to give and so forgiveness is naturally not possible.

France rightly understands "the Son of Man" to refer to Jesus himself and that which is spoken against him is forgivable since one may be ignorant of his true identity, whereas the Pharisees, who have witnessed Jesus' ministry, have emphatically rejected him and aligned him with the demonic realm (2007, 484).

Although the crowds are growing in their recognition of Jesus, the Pharisees have decided in 9:35 on what basis Jesus operates, and now they reject him completely, explicitly attributing his power to Beelzebul in 12:24; forgiveness is impossible with such a disposition because they have, in effect, rejected the whole pattern of God's redemptive story culminating in the words and deeds of the Messiah. In contrast, the crowds searchingly ask if Jesus is the Son of David (v 23*b*) and so the prospect of salvation for them is much more hopeful.

■ **33-37** Jesus now condemns the Pharisees for their harsh accusation and expresses why it is impossible for them to be forgiven. He begins with a generally accepted syllogism as he did in vv 25-26: **Make a tree good and its fruit will be good, or make a tree bad and its fruit will be bad, for a tree is recognized by its fruit** (v 33). The imperative **make** reflects the proverbial nature of this saying as opposed to a literal command (France 2007, 485).

Bearing good fruit is a distinct theme in Matthew. John warned the Pharisees and Sadducees to "produce fruit in keeping with repentance" (3:8) and warned them that trees that do "not produce good fruit" will be destroyed (v 10). Jesus taught the same idea in 7:17-18. The tree failing to produce "good fruit is cut down and thrown into the fire" (v 18*b*). Although Jesus does not describe what happens to bad trees in 12:33, the judgment language of 3:10 and 7:18 lurks and emerges in 12:36-37 and 39-42.

The Pharisees have rejected John's warnings and made accusations about Jesus that reflect inner corruption (9:34; 12:24): they are bad trees bearing bad fruit through their words, having already begun to plot Jesus' death (v 14), in addition to their slanderous accusation. Jesus labels them a **brood of vipers** (v 34; → 3:7) and rhetorically asks them, **How can you who are evil say anything good?** (12:34*a*; see 3:7; 23:33). They cannot, **for the mouth speaks what the heart is full of** (12:34*b*; Nolland 2005, 507). Jesus justifiably condemns his adversaries as **evil** for their slanderous rejection of him (v 35). Ironically, they themselves have become like Satan/Beelzebul, who is also opposed to the reign of God in Jesus (4:1-11). Matthew uses the same word for **evil** (*ponēros*) to describe the Pharisees here as he does for "the evil one" in 13:19, 39 (France 2007, 485). The lines of conflict between Jesus and the Pharisees are clearly drawn!

In 12:35, Jesus applies the imagery of v 33 to humanity in general and explains how words reflect the state of the heart: **A good man brings good things out of the good stored up in him, and an evil man brings evil things out of the evil stored up in him**. Since Jesus addresses the Pharisees directly in v 34, in between vv 33 and 35, the evil that they speak against Jesus comes from **the evil stored up in** them (v 35*b*) and they are the bad tree that can only produce bad fruit (v 33).

In vv 36-37, Jesus concludes his indictment with a warning: **the day of judgment** is coming when **everyone will have to give account . . . for every empty word they have spoken** (v 36).

Judgment

In the OT, Yahweh's judgment reveals his moral integrity to put what is wrong with the world to right: curse/punishment for the wicked and blessing/deliverance for the faithful. Israel is often the object of Yahweh's punishment for her rebellion (Jer 7:9-15) as well as the nations who oppress her (Isa 13). Reflecting the OT, Matthew refers to a future judgment as well, but it begins now with Jesus, who condemns those who reject him, namely, his religious opponents (12:32; 23:13-36; see also 11:22-24). At some future point, Jesus will exercise judicial prerogatives, fulfilling his words of warning and condemnation during his earthly ministry (7:22; 16:27; 24:30-31; 25:31-33). In the OT, Yahweh's judgment also results in the vindication/reward of the righteous (e.g., Hos 2:18-23 [20-25 HB]; Ezek 36:24-36), which is true when Jesus judges as well (see Matt 16:27; 24:31).

The word **empty** (*argos*) does not describe meaningless words but rather ones that do not reflect the truth (France 2007, 486, and the literature cited), which indicts the Pharisees for their malicious accusation against Jesus (12:36). In contrast, Hagner argues that Jesus

> sharpens the call to righteousness by noting the danger not only of obviously bad words [as in 5:22*b*] but even of seemingly neutral words that
> may, however, imply, presuppose, or in some indirect way aid what is 12:38
> bad even by being themselves merely ineffectual and empty. (1993, 350)

In either case, **empty** words are ones that lead to nothing good, of which the utterance of the Pharisees is an example.

This section is a warning to watch one's words, as they reveal the state of the heart and have implications for the future, specifically, at the judgment: **words** that are spoken will either acquit or condemn (v 37). Both terms imply a judicial setting of eschatological judgment. The state of the heart (vv 33, 35) and the attendant words that one speaks in the present have eternal consequences.

b. Demand for a Sign (12:38-45)

■ **38** Matthew indicates that **some of the Pharisees and teachers of the law** now challenge Jesus: **Teacher, we want to see a sign from you** (v 38). Nolland suggests that these **teachers of the law** are "scribes of Pharisaic persuasion. He [Matthew] sees the legally learned as appropriate spokespersons for the request being made" (2005, 509-10). If this is so, one would expect to see them in v 3 where there is a question about a legal concern.

Matthew continues to portray the Pharisees as unrelenting in their desire to challenge Jesus. This now includes a specific group from among their ranks. In v 3, they question Jesus about the unlawful activity of his disciples;

in v 10, they search for grounds to accuse him; in v 14, they plot his death, and in v 24, they accuse him of exorcising by the power of Beelzebul. Even their use of **Teacher** to address Jesus aligns with other moments in Matthew where "outsiders" use this term to address him (→ 8:19). For each accusation, Jesus defends his actions, to which they have no response. The request in 12:38 may be legitimately asking Jesus to prove his authority (so Davies and Allison 1991, 354), but its use here implies hostility. They want to see a demonstration of power on their terms.

■ **39-42** Jesus responds that **a wicked and adulterous generation asks for a sign!** (v 39). This coheres with his earlier question in which he calls the Pharisees a "brood of vipers" (v 34). Again in 16:4 Jesus responds to "the Pharisees and Sadducees" who ask for "a sign from heaven" (16:1). That marks the end of dialogue between Jesus and the Galilean religious leaders.

The Pharisees' request for a sign when "Jesus has already worked more than enough miracles to persuade an open mind (cf. 11.2-4)" (Davies and Allison 1991, 353) represents a rebellious attitude similar to the unfaithfulness of historic Israel. He has already condemned "this generation" in 11:16-19 in which it, like the scribes and Pharisees, has misguided expectations of both John and Jesus (→ 11:16-19).

The Pharisees will receive a sign **but none will be given it except the sign of the prophet Jonah** (v 39*b*). The explanations for this are many. Matthew includes **prophet**, which emphasizes the prophetic role of Jonah and may, by implication, point to a similar status for Jesus as well who warns of judgment in this section. The explanatory conjunction **for** at the beginning of v 40 indicates that the referent of this sign is found in vv 40-41. However, the association of Jonah who **was three days and three nights in the belly of a huge fish** with the **Son of Man** who **will be three days and three nights in the heart of the earth** is not immediately clear, aside from the fact that Jesus was not dead for this long.

Jonah is the intertextual framework for Matt 12:40-41 through reference to Jonah 2:1*b* LXX: "Jonah was in the belly of the fish three days and three nights." There are a few options for the purpose of this quotation:

1. the length of Jesus' internment of three days (Nolland 2005, 511).
2. the resurrection that follows is "God's one great sign to Israel" (Davies and Allison 1991, 355).
3. France, in arguing for a connection between "resurrection and proclamation" (2007, 492), asserts that while Jonah proclaimed the word of God after his deliverance from death, Jesus does so before it.

Resurrection and the length time in the whale/tomb are certainly in view, but the meaning of the sign is found in the work of Jonah and Jesus *after* **three days and three nights** (Matt 12:40). After his resurrection, Jesus becomes the vindicated Son of Man and as such will judge those who have rejected his messianic authority (Matt 24:30, 36-44). During his earthly ministry, Jesus warns his listeners about judgment at the hands of the Son of Man, just like **the prophet Jo-**

nah warns the Ninevites about impending judgment after three days and three nights in the belly of the whale. It is **the Son of Man**, however, who will bring that judgment to fulfillment at some point after his resurrection.

In 12:41, Jesus rebukes the Pharisees for their lack of repentance (see John's earlier call in 3:7-10). To claim that **the men of Nineveh will stand up at the judgment with this generation**, who then **condemn it**, would be scandalous to the Pharisees. With their emphasis on ritual purity and personal holiness, how could repentant pagans condemn them?

Luz argues that in Jewish texts, the righteous participate in the final judgment, not Gentiles (2001, 219-20; Dan 7:22 LXX; Wis 3:8; *Jub.* 24:29). But these Gentiles **repented at the preaching of Jonah** (Matt 12:41*b*); the Pharisees did not repent. If the Ninevites repented at Jonah's preaching, how much more should the Pharisees repent **now** that **something greater than Jonah is here**? The Pharisees' rejection of Jesus is profound.

Similarly, another well-known pagan, **the Queen of the South** will also **rise at the judgment with this generation and condemn it** (v 42*a*). She traveled **from the ends of the earth to listen to Solomon's wisdom, and now something greater than Solomon is here** (v 42*b*; see 1 Kgs 10:1-10). The implication for the Pharisees is the same: they have witnessed the preaching, teaching, and miracles of Jesus only to respond with consistent challenge and rebuke. The logic of the rebuke in Matt 12:40-41 is the same in 11:20-24 (Hagner 1993, 354-55). Jesus highlights the responsiveness of Gentiles to God versus Jews, which is a recurrent theme in Matthew (2:1-2; 8:10-11; 21:43; 28:19; Hagner 1993, 355). 12:43-45

Jesus is the **something greater than Jonah** and **Solomon**. He is greater than a well-known prophet and greater than one of Israel's greatest kings. His wisdom transcends Solomon's, for he himself is true wisdom and one who reorients Torah, such as Sabbath law, so it can be a source of blessing and life (→ 11:28—12:8 and France 2007, 493). He, as the **something greater**, is the very presence of God himself (→ 12:6).

■ **43-45** According to Luz, allegorical interpretation of this passage has reflected anti-Semitism (2001, 222). There is also a tendency, prima facie, to interpret vv 43-45 as a parable with no relationship to the practice of exorcism (e.g., France 2007, 494, and Nolland 2005, 514). But this story probably has intrinsic meaning like the parable of the sower in 13:3-9. The key to understanding the parable is found in 12:45*b*: **That is how it will be with this wicked generation**. Those who fail to recognize Jesus and fail to repent remain in a perilous position. The judgment that will befall them will be worse than their current situation.

The exorcised spirit travels **through arid places seeking rest and does not find it** (v 43*b*). But demons do not like to be without hosts (see 8:28-34). Hence, after finding no rest, the **impure spirit** (12:43*a*) decides to **return** to its host (v 44*a*). "The demon finds no rest in isolation because it is its nature to torment others. Evil always seeks to enlarge itself" (Davies and Allison 1991, 361).

Upon arriving, it finds **the house unoccupied, swept clean and put in order** (v 44*b*). In spite, it **goes and takes with it seven other spirits more wicked than itself, and they go in and live there** with the result that **the final condition of that person is worse than the first** (v 45). Possibly such a clean habitation requires more demonic power to return it to its unclean state (France 2007, 494).

Matthew's narrative placement of this parable implies that the clean-swept house is the Pharisees who have ritual purity and outward acts of righteousness in order (see Matt 23). But such religious devotion does not make them immune to evil (see 12:34-35, 38-39). They resist Yahweh's anointed by accusing him of operating by Beelzebul.

Judgment is coming (vv 39-42), directed against "a wicked and adulterous generation" (v 39*a*) and against those whose words deserve condemnation (v 37*b*). This is one instance of the judicial work of the servant-Messiah that describes in v 18*b* above (Neyrey 1982, 464-65). Reading vv 43-45 in this context suggests that this judgment will unleash a far greater form of calamity than the Pharisees and scribes are currently manifesting. Indeed, **the final condition of that person** [interpreted as Jesus' opponents] **is worse than the first**. This is the fate, most notably expressed in the temple's destruction (→ 16:27-28), that awaits **this wicked generation**.

FROM THE TEXT

12:22-45 The slanderous accusation by the Pharisees that Jesus exorcises by the power of Beelzebul and their desire, along with the scribes, to see a sign elicits lengthy responses from him, which seal their fate. In one of those responses, Jesus implies that the Pharisees are guilty of the so-called unforgivable sin, since they attribute the work of the Holy Spirit to that of Beelzebul.

There have been a variety of interpretations in the history of the church about what constitutes "blasphemy against the Spirit" (v 31)/speaking "against the Holy Spirit" (v 32), some of which have caused an enormous amount of anxiety for some Christians who have continually wondered if they are guilty of this sin. Because of the many ways that this text has been abused, Luz would only preach from it in order to argue "*against* the text in the service of an examination of its consequences" (2001, 210).

This underscores the fact that modern teachers and preachers must handle it with great care, not least because they are in positions of authority. This is especially the case for those in congregations who have "a sensitive conscience or for children who might be catching parts of a sermon intended for adults" (Brower 2012, 118). There is no specific sin that believers can commit that will disqualify them from receiving grace and mercy. There is no cap on God's grace and love for his people; Matthew makes it clear that Jesus has come for the sinner (e.g., 9:13*b*) and to forgive sin (1:21; 26:28).

The narrative context is important. The Pharisees have rejected the messiahship of Jesus, which he has amply demonstrated to them. But they refuse to acknowledge it and, instead, accuse him of working in league with Satan (9:32-34; 12:22-24). Such a stance eliminates the prospect of forgiveness, but this does not limit the love of God. Rather, the Pharisees have chosen to resist the Messiah, and God, as a gracious heavenly Father, respects that.

This is not a specific "sin" committed by the Pharisees but a posture of rebellion against God's saving purposes revealed in Jesus Messiah. Even the three major interpretations of "blasphemy against the Holy Spirit" in the Western church do not reflect an inadvertent or unintended committal of this sin. These interpretations include a denial of the divinity of Jesus (Athanasius), apostasy from the Christian faith, or rejection of the Catholic church (Augustine; see Luz 2001, 207-8).

The challenge for contemporary Christians is not to prematurely make judgments about God's work when it occurs in surprising ways and in unlikely places, "lest we be found opposing the work of the Spirit" (Brower 2012, 118) This is partly what leads to the Pharisees' rejection of Jesus: his demonstrations of mercy and grace for the marginalized and outcast were regrettably just too foreign for them.

4. True Followers (12:46-50)

BEHIND THE TEXT

Both Matt 11 and 12 end on an encouraging note. In 11:25-30, Jesus welcomes the weary and burdened to take upon themselves his yoke of wisdom, which leads to liberation. In this passage (12:46-50), Jesus affirms his closest followers by asserting that they are now his true family because they, like him, do the will of his heavenly Father (note that Jesus never refers to God as "our" heavenly Father, only "my" or "your" Father; see France 2007, 496 n. 5). Much of the material leading up to these passages in chs 11 and 12 records challenges to and rejection of Jesus' messiahship. Matthew likely places these stories here to keep in view that, despite persecution and hardship, the gospel is still an invitation and those willing to accept it are welcome (4:17).

Jesus' teaching that those who do the will of his Father replace his biological family would shock his original hearers as well as Matthew's audience (→ Matt 10:34-36 sidebar, "Family Values in Palestinian Judaism"). However, doing the will of the Father as revealed in Jesus is of paramount importance in God's kingdom and takes precedence over biological ties, no matter how important they may be. Replacing his mother with his disciples would unsettle an ancient audience as well since the mother and eldest son have a unique relationship in Palestinian culture (Malina and Rohrbaugh 2003, 73).

IN THE TEXT

■ **46-47** Not since the birth narrative has Matthew mentioned Jesus' **mother**. Now she and his **brothers** make an appearance and wish **to speak to him** (v

46*b*). However, they are **outside** and Jesus is **still talking to the crowd** (v 46*a*). Matthew has not indicated where Jesus has been teaching the crowds and conversing with the Pharisees other than that he "withdrew" from the synagogue in 12:15. **Outside** likely stems from Mark's placement of Jesus in a crowded house to which his family comes attempting "to take charge of him" (Mark 3:20-21). In Matthew, like Mark, Jesus learns that his family is standing **outside, wanting to speak to him** (Matt 12:46; see Mark 3:32). Further, in both texts, Jesus does not address them and merely refers to them for illustrative purposes (Mark 3:31-35).

■ **48-50** Jesus only **replied to** the individual who alerted him to the presence of his family with a question and does not go outside to see them: **Who is my mother, and who are my brothers?** (v 48). **Pointing to his disciples**, these are his true family: **Here are my mother and my brothers** (v 49). By repeating both **mother** and **brothers** to describe the makeup of Jesus' true family in v 49, who are actually the very ones outside wanting to see him, he dramatically breaks with Palestinian familial social convention.

Jesus continues, **For whoever does the will of my Father in heaven is my brother and sister and mother** (v 50). In previous instruction to the disciples, Jesus states this same idea in much harsher terms (→ 10:35-37). Although he does have biological sisters (see 13:56), Matthew's reference to **sisters** in 12:50 reflects his concern for the meaningful role of women in God's saving purposes, which he introduced in the genealogy. It may also indicate the presence of women disciples in his ministry (France 2007, 498; see 27:55-56). Nolland suggests that the plural **brothers** in v 49 encompasses sisters as well, although this is difficult to substantiate (2005, 517). More likely, Jesus is only referring to his **brothers** since his sisters are simply not there and would be at home, according to social convention (Luz 2001, 225).

Discipleship characterized by doing the will of **my Father** recalls earlier moments in which Jesus teaches the disciples to pray for the Father's will (6:10), calls them to "seek first his kingdom and his righteousness [understood as faithfulness]" (6:33), and exhorts them that "only the one who does the will of my Father who is in heaven" (7:21) will gain entrance into the kingdom. Intimacy with God through which comes awareness of his will is the righteousness that exceeds that of the scribes and Pharisees (5:20; France 2007, 498).

Members of this new, redefined family, some of whom have left biological members behind (4:18-22), "will receive a hundred times as much and will inherit eternal life" (19:29; France 2007, 496). These are those who "have entered into a new relationship with God as . . . their 'heavenly Father'" (France 2007, 496). This group of Jesus' followers are distinguished from the crowds, and so this passage provides a bridge to his parables, which reveal "the knowledge of the secrets of the kingdom of heaven" exclusively for his disciples (e.g., 13:10-11).

FROM THE TEXT

For Jesus and his followers, family is not constituted by biological and traditional ties but rather by devotion to the heavenly Father. This marks a significant departure from the cultural customs expressed in both the OT and in first-century Palestinian culture. The gospel can bring division as the preceding exchange between Jesus and the Pharisees makes clear (see also 10:34-37).

The teaching in 12:49-50 becomes foundational for early Christian conceptions of the community of faith since, like the disciples and Jesus himself (as depicted heretofore in Matthew), early Christians also severed ties with their biological families in addition to other social entities and were subsequently adopted into the family of God. "The practical effect of the early Christian movement was to replace family-centeredness with a church membership-centeredness, and to create the church as the new family, or the community of the new age (e.g., Acts 2:42-46)" (McVann 1998, 78; for further examples, see 2 Cor 6:18; Gal 6:10; Eph 2:19; 1 Tim 5:1). In the Western, modern world, some Christians have emphasized the sanctity of the nuclear family to the exclusion of one's true family, the church, but this is where our real brothers, sisters, and mother dwell, all under the care of our heavenly Father.

G. Parables about the Kingdom of Heaven (13:1-53)

BEHIND THE TEXT

Division is a dominant theme in Matt 13. This chapter, a series of parables plus interpretation, explains why the disciples constitute the true family of Jesus, the ones who do "the will of my Father in heaven" (12:50), while "this generation" and the religious leaders in particular reject him (11:17-20; 12:2, 10, 14, 24, 38-39). As long as the crowds fail to repent, they, too, are aligned with "this generation" and will not comprehend the reign of God in Jesus (12:23). Until they do turn to him, Jesus speaks to them in confounding parables (13:10-11, 13-15, 34). Jesus' interpretation of the parable of the sower declares that the disciples have privileged knowledge and not the crowds (vv 11-15).

France summarizes the movement of this chapter well:

> The parables provide a variety of models for understanding this conundrum [why Israel resists Yahweh's Messiah], by highlighting sometimes the varied nature of the hearers (vv. 3-9), sometimes the unexpected nature of the message (vv. 31-33, 44-45), and sometimes the division which is an empirical reality of human society in relation to God (vv. 24-30, 47-50). (2007, 499)

Jesus intentionally teaches the disciples instead of merely speaking to them *and* the crowds. Nolland indicates that this "is fundamental to the dynamic of the materials" (2005, 522). Kingsbury labels the chapter a major "turning point" because Jesus now begins to reject his religious adversaries and focus on those who embody the new Israel, his disciples (1969, 130; → 3:16-17 and BEHIND THE TEXT for 10:1-15).

There is little agreement on the organization of the parables, which suggests that we need to interpret each one in turn and appreciate its specific nuances (for various proposals see France 2007, 500; Davies and Allison 1991, 371; Luz 2001, 230).

I. Setting: Teaching by the Lake (13:1-3*a*)

IN THE TEXT

■ **1-3*a*** The opening line, **that same day Jesus went out of the house and sat by the lake** (v 1), connects Jesus' teaching about his true family, those who do "the will of my Father in heaven" (12:50), with the following parables. Understanding the parables is reserved for his disciples and not for the crowds who have now gathered en masse (see 13:11, 36). Jesus sitting, as opposed to standing, expresses his authority as a teacher (France 2007, 502; see also 5:1; 24:3).

"Many crowds," translated as **large crowds**, have come to Jesus (v 2). His popularity grows quickly, as Matthew indicates elsewhere (4:24; 9:26, 31, etc.). As a result, he **got into a boat and sat in it, while all the people stood on the shore** (v 2). France suggests that the disciples are also in the boat where they can ask him privately about the parables (v 10; France 2007, 501). However, Matthew's description that "the disciples *came to him*" (v 10*a*) challenges this idea. He introduces the content of his third major discourse in v 3*a*: **Then he told them many things in parables** (the first two discourses are Matt 5—7 and 10).

Parables

Scholarship on the meaning and function of the parables is voluminous, characterized by many debates and a variety of methods of study. For an excellent discussion on parables, see Snodgrass 2008. The term "parable" (*parabolē*) is a variegated literary form from a simple proverb (Luke 4:23) to a multilayered story (Matt 22:1-14; see France 2007, 502), and its OT counterpart, *mashal*, likewise has several forms.

There is some agreement on the following classification of the parables: *similitude*—an extended simile; *example story*—a narrative where the behaviors of an individual are to be emulated or rejected; *parable*—an extended metaphor in which aspects of a story communicate specific truths; and *allegory*—a story containing a number of metaphors (Snodgrass 1992, 593). In each of these forms, parables do not communicate meaning at a surface level; rather, intentional understanding and perception is required to learn from them (France 2007, 502). Classifications of the parables should never replace the importance of analyzing their literary contexts and their contribution to themes of the Gospel when determining meaning; it is easy to lose sight of the forest for the trees in parable analysis.

2. Parable of the Sower (13:3*b*-9)

BEHIND THE TEXT

This first parable is more aptly titled the parable of the soils since the emphasis is on the four types of terrain upon which the seeds fall; this emphasis continues in its interpretation (13:18-23). In each scene, the result of seeding increases, but it is only in the fourth that plants produce a crop (v 8). In the first, the seed does not even germinate (v 4). Jesus will reveal to the disciples the meaning of this parable in vv 18-23 after highlighting their privileged position as those who receive "the knowledge of the secrets of the kingdom of heaven" (v 11), in contrast with those who don't understand (vv 13-15).

IN THE TEXT

■ **3*b*-4** The imagery of **a farmer** going **out to sow his seed** (v 3*b*), probably wheat or barley, would be familiar with Jesus' rural Galilean audience. Appeal to the imagination is prompted by the untranslated **"Look!"** in the Greek text, which appears first in v 3*b* (Nolland 2005, 525). The farmer as a wasteful scatterer of seed on unfertile terrain is not the point. Rather, "The typical sower in first-century Palestine was a subsistence farmer with a limited plot of land at his disposal" (Nolland 2005, 525), and since seeds are light and easily blown by the wind, some may end up on poor soil.

So **as he was scattering the seed, some fell along the path** (v 4*a*). The hardened ground of a path, free of vegetation, provides an unobstructed view for **the birds** who **came and ate it up** (v 4*b*). Some have suggested, because the seed has fallen "beside the path" as opposed to on it, that the field has not yet been plowed and so the birds eat the seed beforehand, but the text is not clear at this point (Davies and Allison 1991, 382; France 2007, 504 n. 6). The main point is that this terrain makes the seed vulnerable.

■ **5-6** The next area is the **rocky places** on which **some** of the seed falls, **where it did not have much soil** (v 5). In v 6, readers learn its fate once it germinates: **But when the sun came up, the plants were scorched, and they withered because they had no root**. The Greek for **rocky places** (*petrōdēs*) describes a "rocky area with little topsoil" (BDAG 2000, 810), which is commonplace in the geography of Galilee (France 2007, 504). The plant roots cannot penetrate the soil to where there is moisture, so they quickly dry up. They start well, but quickly wither under the sun.

■ **7 Other seed fell among the thorns, which grew up and choked the plants**. These plants have grown for some time before they are overtaken by **the thorns**, which "would appear to mark an advance over the fate of the first two groups of seed" (Davies and Allison 1991, 384). The thornbushes have depleted the soil of moisture and nutrients necessary for plant growth (France 2007, 505).

■ **8-9** Finally, the **other seed fell on good soil, where it produced a crop—a hundred, sixty, or thirty times what was sown** (v 8). Matthew reverses Mark's order of thirty, sixty, and a hundred. Nolland suggests that the ordering from highest to lowest creates a chiasmus "between the three statements of fruitfulness and the three kinds of failure" where more growth is evident with each successive terrain (2005, 528).

The **good soil**, because of the crop it produces, stands in stark contrast with the other terrains upon which seeds have fallen. Luz dismisses a contrast for a number of reasons; for example, he claims that "the descending series of the figures in v 8 . . . would ruin the point of the contrast between the present time of failures and the 'abundant' yield that nevertheless results" (2001, 242). Given that no seed has provided *any* crop in the preceding three scenarios, the descending figures of crop yield in v 8 hardly undermine a contrast!

It is unclear if these crop yields refer to the number of grains found in each plant or the number stalks produced by each seed. According to France, even the highest yield in the list, **a hundred**, is not "miraculous" by ancient standards (2007, 505; Davies and Allison 1991, 385). This argument is dependent upon references to agricultural yields in ancient texts (Brower 2012, 122-23). Although the **good soil** functions the way it should, producing a proportional amount of crop, "most farmers would consider a hundredfold yield extraordinarily fortunate" (Brower 2012, 122).

The exhortation in v 9, **Whoever has ears, let them hear**, is a call to understanding that comes about by spiritual engagement with the parable. This understanding is only possible with open and receptive hearts (v 23), which will produce a bountiful crop. Jesus directs this invitation at the crowds and disciples alike.

3. Reason for the Parables (13:10-17)

BEHIND THE TEXT

This section is a response to the disciples' question as to why Jesus speaks to the crowds in parables (v 10*b*). He begins by highlighting their privileged status. Because they do "the will of [his] Father" (12:50), "knowledge of the secrets of the kingdom of heaven" (13:11) is given to them. Indeed, they will receive more knowledge, while what knowledge the crowds have "will be taken from them" (v 12).

Then Jesus cites Isa 6:9 twice, in Matt 13:13, 14, and Isa 6:10 in Matt 13:15, which is at the heart of his explanation: the crowds' doubt and disbelief render them incapable of hearing and seeing, illustrated by three of the four soils (vv 4-7). According to France,

> In answer to the disciples' question these verses [vv 11-17] explain why Jesus teaches in parables, but that explanation is itself based on the content of the parable: the failure of some of the soil to receive the seed

is a comment on the human condition which Isaiah's prophecy sets out. (2007, 507)

Isaiah 6 follows a series of prophecies condemning Judah for her rebellion (e.g., 5:7-30). The judicial blinding that comes upon Israel in 6:9-10 is a result of her persistent disobedience and rebellion. There are moments in which Isaiah calls Israel to repentance as well (see Isa 1:16-20), just as Jesus holds out hope that the Israel of his day will turn to him (see Matt 13:9).

Jesus quotes the LXX version of Isa 6:9-10 in Matt 13:14-15 almost verbatim. Because he utters the fulfillment formula quotation himself (v 14*a*), whereas Matthew does so elsewhere, some argue that vv 14-15 "are a (very early) post-Matthean interpolation" (Davies and Allison 1991, 394). There are equally convincing reasons that these verses are original with Matthew (see France 2007, 513; Nolland 2005, 535). The utterance of this citation formula may be different because "it lacked the degree of Christological focus that is a uniting feature of the [other] citations he has marked in this way" (Nolland 2005, 535).

In vv 16-17, Jesus blesses the disciples because of their ability to hear and see, unlike those depicted in vv 13-15; the content of what the disciples now understand is something that only the faithful ones of ages past longed to see and hear. This does not mean, however, that the opportunity for repentance has closed for the ones who cannot comprehend the parables. This incomprehension is a reflection of their state before Jesus, which will become their fate if they do not repent (Brower 2012, 129).

IN THE TEXT

■ **10-12** The scene shifts from Jesus teaching the "large crowds" (v 2) to **the disciples** coming **to him** and asking, **Why do you speak to the people in parables?** (v 10). The meaning of parables is not self-evident. They require affective and intellectual openness, a response of both heart and head (see also vv 18-23). In Luke, the disciples ask more generally about Jesus' teaching **in parables**. Here they ask the meaning of the preceding parable (see Luke 8:9).

Jesus responds, **Because the knowledge of the secrets of the kingdom of heaven has been given to you, but not to them** (Matt 13:11). The separation between the disciples and the crowds is clear. Jesus' true family are "his disciples" (12:49*a*). Reception of **secrets** about the reign of God, **the kingdom of heaven**, distinguishes insiders and outsiders (see 11:25). The interpretation of the parable in 13:18-23 is the continuation of revelation with more to come (e.g., 11:2-6; 12:46-50; 16:16-17; 17:1-9; 26:20-29), all of which focuses on "the *presence* of the kingdom in Jesus and his ministry" (Davies and Allison 1991, 389).

Revelation of knowledge for the faithful is found in Dan 2, in which Daniel receives revelation from God about the kingdom of Nebuchadnezzar, about which the wise know nothing (Dan 2:18-19, 27-30, 47; France 2007,

511). Further, a variety of Jewish texts speak of "mysteries" that God reveals to certain groups (Davies and Allison 1991, 389: Num 12:8; 1QS 9:17; *4 Ezra* 12:36-37).

Matthew 13:12 continues to distinguish between those who receive "the secrets" and those who do not: **Whoever has will be given more, and they will have an abundance. Whoever does not have, even what they have will be taken from them** (see also 25:29). This proverb, describing economic inequities, also applies to the spiritual world where "both gain and loss are compounded" (France 2007, 512). This highlights the importance of spiritual apprehension of the parables and that there are consequences for not having "ears" that can "hear" (13:9).

What knowledge the disciples have, God will add to it **and they will have an abundance** (v 12*a*). Nolland contends that the punitive second part of the proverb in v 12*b* plays out in Matthew's narrative because "Jesus no longer addresses them [the crowds] with directness about matters concerning the kingdom of heaven" (2005, 534). While this may be true, Jesus still has compassion and heals them (14:13-14; 15:30-32), teaches them (15:10; 23:1), and invites some even to follow him (20:29-31). Matthew's placement of 13:12 does not indicate that the door of invitation has been closed (→ vv 45-46).

■ **13-15** Paralleling Mark and Luke, Matthew reverses Isaiah's order of "listening/hearing" and "looking/seeing" (Isa 6:9): **Though seeing, they do not see; though hearing, they do not hear or understand** (Matt 13:13*b*). This is another reason why Jesus speaks **to them in parables** (v 13*a*). The NIV leaves out the conjunction "because" (*hoti*) at the beginning of the quote. According to Davies and Allison, this conjunction "makes the parables a *response* to unbelief: they are uttered *because* people see and do not see, because they hear and do no hear" (1991, 392; Luz 2001, 246).

Matthew uses **understand** several times here and elsewhere (vv 14, 15, 19, 23, 51; see also 15:10; 16:12; 17:13). Understanding is predicated upon the faith necessary to receive "knowledge of the secrets of the kingdom of heaven" (v 11). This is true for the disciples. The Pharisees' disbelief in the messiahship of Jesus (9:34; 12:1-14) has resulted in wrongly attributing his mighty deeds to the power of Beelzebul (v 24).

Jesus prefaces his quotation with the comment, **In them is fulfilled the prophecy of Isaiah** (13:14*a*). Matthew explicitly links the obduracy of those outside of the disciple group with the fulfillment of Scripture. This text appears elsewhere in the NT to describe "unbelief, and on more than one occasion it was employed to justify missionaries turning from an obdurate Israel to the Gentiles" (Davies and Allison 1991, 393; Acts 28:26-27; Rom 11:8).

Matthew adopts the LXX's use of the future tense for "hearing" and "seeing," which softens the imperatives in the MT: "Be ever hearing, but never understanding; be ever seeing, but never perceiving" (Isa 6:9). Likewise, in Isa 6:10, the LXX has changed the imperative in the MT from "make the heart" to a statement of fact: "for this people's heart has grown fat." France notes that "even in the LXX form the text is a devastating indictment of the people's condition, but at least it places the responsibility on them rather than on God and his prophet" (2007, 514; see also Davies and Allison 1991, 392).

The problem is that Israel's **heart has become calloused; they hardly hear with their ears, and they have closed their eyes** (Matt 13:15*a*; Isa 6:10*a*). This imagery parallels that of ears that no longer hear and eyes that cannot see, all pointing to a profound spiritual insensitivity and blindness. If they would but **see with their eyes, hear with their ears, understand with their hearts and turn, and I would heal them** (Matt 13:15*b*; Isa 6:10*b*).

Matthew concludes that this is the current state of Israel outside of Jesus' faithful followers. God has not caused this to come upon his people; they have rebelled, just as ancient Israel in Isaiah's day, but if they do turn and repent, God will restore them (see also Luz 2001, 247), a theme that appears elsewhere in Matthew (4:17; 7:7; 11:28) and is the reason why Jesus has come (1:21).

Although France puts the emphasis on human responsibility in his interpretation, he still maintains a divine election of "to some and not to others" for the ability to hear and see (2007, 515). But 13:12 describes the *consequence* of rebellion, not its cause, and, on the other hand, the blessing of obedience.

■ **16-17** Unlike the crowds and Pharisees who fail to see and hear, Jesus says to his disciples: **But blessed are your eyes because they see, and your ears because they hear** (v 16). As in vv 11-12, he draws a clear line between his followers who understand and to whom mysteries are revealed and those who do not because of their unbelief. This beatitude recalls the ones in the Sermon on the Mount with the major difference that the disciples are blessed *now* whereas their blessing is a future reward (5:4-9).

With an explanatory **for** (*gar*), Jesus elaborates that **truly I tell you, many prophets and righteous people longed to see what you see but did not see it, and to hear what you hear but did not hear it** (v 17). The NT refers to the OT period as one of anticipation at seeing the fulfillment of God's promises (see John 8:56; Heb 11:13-16; 1 Pet 1:10-12). Matthew's reference to **righteous people** (Matt 13:17*a*) replaces Luke's "kings" (Luke 10:24), which coheres with two other references to righteous people in 1:19 and 23:29. All are "significant people of faith from the past" (Nolland 2005, 537 n. 51). Now the disciples get to personally witness and participate in this fulfillment!

The *Psalms of Solomon*, a first-century BCE Jewish text, reads: "Blessed are those born in those days, to see the good things of the Lord" (18:6*a*). The context is the purifying work of the Messiah who will restore Jerusalem and establish a holy people. In Matthew, the disciples are **blessed** for they **see** the promised work of the Messiah in their day who likewise forms holy followers (Matt 13:16; see 5:48). The disciples also **hear** (13:17*b*), an uncommon way of perceiving the fulfillment of God's promises (Davies and Allison 1991, 396). This is Jesus' usage: "the deeds of the Messiah" are "heard" and they signal the end of Israel's exile and the dawn of a new era in God's saving activity (11:2-6 [→]).

The use of both "see" and "hear" in 13:16 may derive from Isa 6:9-10, contrasting others who cannot see or hear. Luz comments that "the disciples *are* not understanding people, but they *become* such through Jesus' instruction" (2001, 247). But while the disciples still have more to learn, they have come to Jesus (Matt 11:28) and are the ones who do the Father's will (12:50). Therefore, they receive the revelatory activity of the Son (11:29; 13:11-12, 16-17).

4. Interpretation of the Parable of the Sower (13:18-23)

IN THE TEXT

■ **18** Given the privileged position of his disciples who now see and hear what the prophets longed to know (v 17), Jesus exhorts them: **Listen then to what the parable of the sower means** (v 18). This exhortation follows naturally from the beatitude in v 16 and is quite different from Mark, where Jesus questions the disciples' ability to understand (Mark 4:13).

■ **19** First, Jesus explains the meaning of the seed that was sown "along the path," which the birds subsequently ate (Matt 13:4). This refers to **anyone** who **hears the message about the kingdom and does not understand it** (v 19*a*), the fate of those who are "ever hearing but never understanding" (v 14*a*; see v 13*b*). This recalls moments in chs 11—12 where Jesus did preach the message, but it was met with disbelief and rejection, resulting in incomprehension.

The failure to **understand . . . the message about the kingdom** is why Jesus teaches in parables (see 13:13). But for the disciples, understanding is "that extra dimension which will take [them] beyond merely hearing what Jesus says to grasping its true meaning" (France 2007, 520; see 13:23, 51; 15:10; 16:12; 17:13).

Although the seed is sown in the **heart** in which someone **hears the message** but **does not understand it, the evil one comes and snatches away what was sown in their heart** (v 19*b*). These hearts are like the hard path where the word could take no root (v 4*b*) and, with the agency of **the evil one**, no crop is produced, just like the birds who eat up the exposed seed on the path (v 4*b*).

Later Jewish literature describes the devil or demons as birds (*Jub.* 11:11; *Apoc. Ab.* 13; *Sanh.* 107a; Davies and Allison 1991, 400). **The evil one** is another term for Satan and the devil (→ Matt 4:1-2 sidebar, "The Devil") and is the one who seeks to lead the faithful into temptation and see their downfall (see 5:9-14). His work here is no different.

■ **20-21** The second type of terrain is the **rocky ground** (see 13:5). This terrain **refers to someone who hears the word and at once receives it with joy** (v 20), an understandable response, especially if one is healed and decides to follow Jesus. However, an overzealousness that does not count the cost of discipleship will share the same fate as the seed (see vv 5*b*-6).

Jesus warns his disciples about persecution "on my account" from Gentile and Jewish leaders (10:18; 24:9-10) and about the dissolution of families (10:21-22, 34-39; see also 5:10-12). If these followers are not prepared for these challenges, **they have no root**, and they, like the seed, **last only a short time**. The **trouble or persecution** that **comes because of the word** has the same effect as the scorching sun on plants: **they quickly fall away** (13:21; see v 6*b*). The term **fall away** (*skandalizō*) is a favorite of Matthew to describe various ways that one falls off the path of salvation (see 5:29): the harsh realities of persecution and trouble resulting from the gospel cause some to fall away.

■ **22** The seed sown among the thorns develops much further than the seed that ends up on "rocky ground" (vv 5-6). This seed **refers to someone who hears the word, but the worries of this life and the deceitfulness of wealth choke the word, making it unfruitful** (v 22). Jesus recognizes the barriers to discipleship in the Sermon on the Mount: "Do not worry about your life, what you will eat or drink; or about your body, what you will wear" (6:25; see also 6:28*a*, 31, 34). There is no need for his disciples to worry about **this life** since their heavenly Father will meet these physical needs (6:32).

On the other end of the spectrum is a preoccupation with deceitful, excessive wealth. The security and comfort it brings is false, a theme well-attested in the wisdom tradition (e.g., Prov 11:28; 23:4-5) (France 2007, 521). Jesus warns his disciples about this in the sermon as well and prohibits its accumulation (Matt 6:19) because no one can serve two masters, "both God and money" (v 24*b*; → 6:19 and 6:24). Jesus calls his followers to a radical, trusting obedience in the goodness of their heavenly Father so that they should not worry about insufficient wealth or be deceived by its excesses.

■ **23** The seed that lands **on good soil refers to someone who hears the word and understands it** (v 23*a*). The ability to hear and understand, as opposed to hearing and *not* understanding in v 19, results in a fruitful **crop, yielding a hundred, sixty or thirty times what was sown** (v 23*b*). This comprehension is contingent upon hearts that believe. They are fertile soil in which the seed takes deep root and is, therefore, not snatched away by "the evil one," or fails to grow into fruitful plants because of the difficulties of this life.

In the OT, a plant or tree firmly rooted represents faithfulness to God in times of difficulty (Jer 17:8 and Ps 1:3; Luz 2001, 249). Luz contends that Matthew is concerned with understanding as "first of all a matter of the head," although he recognizes that bearing fruit involves action and obedience (2001, 250). However, these are insufficient in themselves: it is only when the word makes its home in the heart that the disciple can withstand challenges and live out the ethical demands of the kingdom despite the personal cost (see also 6:21, 24; 22:37-38).

A deeply rooted faith is the seed that **produces a crop**. The Greek verb behind this phrase (*karpoforeō*) contains the word for "fruit" (*karpos*) denoting outward actions that indicate a repentant heart (France 2007, 522; see 3:8, 10;

7:16-20; 12:33; 21:43). The one who hears and understands naturally lives out the values of the kingdom (Luz 2001, 250; see 7:23-27).

Although Jesus does not identify the sower in the interpretation, the one who plants in the OT is God himself, or his appointed emissaries (e.g., Ps 80:7-11 [8-12 HB]; Jer 1:10), and Jesus later indicates that the sower of "the good seed is the Son of Man" (Matt 13:37). Like God in the OT, Jesus supplies his disciples with the seed needed to yield the required fruit for reflecting his reign on earth.

FROM THE TEXT

This first parable explains why Jesus is not unequivocally accepted by all. Some still refuse to repent and believe in the gospel even after witnessing the Messiah's deeds. However, Jesus does not speak in parables to prevent his listeners from being healed as a form of punishment. Rather, he does so because they are already spiritually obtuse due to their own disbelief.

The ability to hear the parables and comprehend is contingent upon one's choice to believe. The choice to accept or reject his gracious invitation is open to all and so, the seed-word sown in various terrains/hearts produces various results, but none of this is predetermined by God. Jerome and Chrysostom, for instance, both place responsibility on Jesus' hearers for their rebellion (see ACCS 2001, 1a:271-72). "Hence, if Jesus' ministry has not brought about what one might have anticipated, the fault lies neither with him nor with God but with human sin and hardened hearts" (Davies and Allison 1991, 375).

5. Three More Parables about the Kingdom of Heaven (13:24-33)

BEHIND THE TEXT

Jesus' private teaching to his disciples has now concluded. Since he is speaking in parables, he resumes his address to the crowds (vv 3, 10, 34). The next three are parables of "the kingdom of heaven" (vv 24-30, 31-32, 33) describing "different aspects of the new reality which has come into being through Jesus' ministry" (France 2007, 524). The parable of the sower has the same purpose.

a. The Parable of the Wheat and the Weeds (13:24-30)

IN THE TEXT

■ **24-26** This parable is thematically and terminologically related to the fourth scene in the preceding parable (vv 8, 23), although the imagery has shifted from "good soil" to **a man who sowed good seed in his field** (v 24). The "fruitful" scenario in v 23 rendered by "good soil" is still maintained here with the major difference that this man's adversary comes and **sowed weeds among the wheat, and went away** (v 25*b*), while he and his servants were asleep (v 25*a*).

As a result, **when the wheat sprouted and formed heads, then the weeds also appeared** (v 26). The type of weed sown is darnel and is poisonous because of a fungus that accompanies it (Luz 2001, 254; Nolland 2005, 545). Since it grows with the wheat, even having physical similarities with it, darnel can "render the crop commercially useless as well as potentially harmful" (France 2007, 526).

■ **27-30 The owner's servants** are surprised that there are now weeds growing among the wheat: **Sir, didn't you sow good seed in your field? Where then did the weeds come from?** (v 27). Luz comments that they should not be shocked since the appearance of weeds are unavoidable in farming (2001, 254), but it is likely the magnitude of the infestation that is unusual (see Nolland 2005, 546 n. 74).

The NIV's **Sir** is *kurios* in Greek, which for Matthew is likely more than a form of address from an inferior to a superior, since, in his interpretation, Jesus identifies the owner as "the Son of Man" in v 37 (Davies and Allison 1991, 413; → 3:3; 7:21, 22; 12:8). The man responds that **an enemy did this** (13:28*a*), and the servants ask him if they should remove the weeds (v 28*b*). Roman law prohibited sabotaging someone else's crops (see Kerr 1997, 108-9).

In an effort to preserve the crop produced by the good seed, the man wants them to wait lest they **uproot the wheat with** the weeds (v 29*b*). The term **uproot** (*ekrizoō*) is used in the LXX to describe the removal of evil (Wis 4:4; Zeph 2:4), which anticipates Jesus' interpretation of the parable in Matt 13:37-43 (Davies and Allison 1991, 414).

Rather, **Let both grow together until the harvest** (v 30*a*). Then "the man" will command the ones harvesting to **first collect the weeds and tie them in bundles to be burned; then gather the wheat and bring it into my barn** (v 30*b*). The separation comes at harvest. Pulling the weeds out now would also destroy the wheat since roots would be intertwined. The gathering of the wheat into the barn and the burning of the weeds recalls John's depiction of final judgment (→ 3:12).

b. The Parable of the Mustard Seed (13:31-32)

IN THE TEXT

■ **31-32** Jesus describes **the kingdom of heaven** as **like a mustard seed, which a man took and planted in his field** (v 31*b*). Although this seed **is the smallest of all seeds**, when it becomes a fully-grown plant, **it is the largest of garden plants and becomes a tree, so that the birds come and perch in its branches** (v 32). This parable contains hyperbole: a mustard seed is not the smallest seed and birds nesting in the branches of this two-meter-tall garden plant is unlikely, even if birds consume mustard seeds.

This exaggerated picture points to the miraculous nature of the kingdom, which should not be underestimated. Some argue that the growth of the mustard seed and the influence of the leaven, in the next parable, emphasize the working of God through natural processes (e.g., Nolland 2005, 554), but the images in both parables suggest something more.

Although the NIV has **perch** (*kataskēnoō*), the Greek verb means "to nest" in the sense of a dwelling (BDAG 2000, 527; Nolland 2005, 551 n. 89). The image of birds nesting in trees is found in OT texts describing the greatness of earthly kingdoms (Dan 4:10-12 [7-9 HB]; Ezek 17:22-24; 31:5-6). The birds do not represent the inclusion of the Gentiles (contra Luz 2001, 262). Rather, the parable depicts two contrasting realities about the kingdom of heaven: despite its insignificant beginning, it will become a miraculously glorious realm.

Admittedly, it has a humble beginning with the itinerate mission of Jesus and the Twelve, but a time will come when it will be visible to all, just as the mustard seed grows into a "tree" (e.g., Matt 24:30-31). Present failure to recognize Jesus' messianic authority masks the greater reality yet to be made known.

c. The Parable of the Leaven (13:33)

■ **33** This parable also offers contrasts that focus on the growth of the kingdom: **The kingdom of heaven is like yeast that a woman took and mixed into about sixty pounds of flour until it worked all through the dough**. Although
13:33 there is nothing miraculous in yeast, or, most likely, a small amount of fermented dough (Nolland 2005, 553), leavening such a large quantity of dough is unusual since that amount could feed around a hundred people (Jeremias and Hooke 1972, 147). The kingdom will not only dramatically/miraculously grow into a large tree but will also affect everything around it. Usually the effect of leaven is considered negative (e.g., Lev 2:11; Matt 16:6; 1 Cor 5:6), but here it is used in a positive way.

But what is **yeast** here? The NIV's **mixed into** can also mean to "hide" (BDAG 2000, 274) and forms a verbal thread with other cognate forms of this word in 11:25 and 13:35, 44. The messianic authority of Jesus has been "hidden [*kruptō*] . . . from the wise and learned" (11:25) and instead "knowledge of the secrets of the kingdom of heaven" have been given to his disciples, "but not to them [the crowds]" (13:11).

The parables contain "things hidden [*kruptō*] since the creation of the world" (v 35; see also v 44). The hidden truths of the kingdom contained in the parables (13:35) and in the mighty deeds of Jesus (11:20), like the hidden yeast, are those things that concern, among other things, its mysterious and miraculous growth. For example, the inhabitants of three Galilean towns in 11:20-24 failed to recognize that the deeds of the Messiah should lead to repentance and, hence, the growth of the kingdom. But these things will not remain hidden forever (France 2007, 527).

FROM THE TEXT

The last two parables, which Jesus does not interpret, have been subject to different allegorical interpretations (Luz 2001, 258). Both Augustine and Luther contended that they describe the miraculous growth of the church, which starts with humble beginnings and will end with worldwide domination. Luther puts it this way,

> The church is the Kingdom of God, because all other secular kingdoms fight against her, (she) who is alone, and weak, and despised, and nothing, but they do not conquer her. Instead, in the end she conquers all kingdoms and converts them to herself. (Luther, *Kritische Gesamtausgabe*, 38.563, cited in Luz 2001, 258-59)

The hope of the church conquering other nations is too triumphalist, at least as an institution. A more redeeming approach might focus on the positive role that the church as the people of God can have in society without the attendant desire to control political and social spheres and, instead, seek to restore and deliver the lost wherever they may be found.

6. Further Reason for the Parables (13:34-35)

IN THE TEXT

■ **34** Matthew reminds his readers of the modus operandi of Jesus, who **spoke all these things to the crowd in parables** (v 34*a*) and says nothing **to them without using a parable** (v 34*b*). Jesus has already given the reason for parables in vv 13-15. However, not all his teaching is in **parables** despite the emphatic assertion in v 34 (e.g., chs 5—7); Matthew's point is not to make fine distinctions about the way Jesus teaches but that his "public teaching, even when not cast in a form we would recognize as *parabolē*, remains elusive, challenging, and unsettling, leaving his audience in a dilemma as to what response they should make" (France 2007, 530). For some characters, their response is very clear and determined (see 21:45-46). 13:34-35

■ **35** Jesus' teaching again appeals to Scripture, Ps 78:2, but Matthew, not Jesus, cites the OT. He does not indicate which **prophet**, perhaps because the quotation is not from the prophets (Nolland 2005, 556). The speaker of the psalm is Asaph, who is considered a prophet (1 Chr 25:2; France 2007, 530; Davies and Allison 1991, 425).

Matthew quotes verbatim the LXX version of Ps 78:2*a*: **I will open my mouth in parables**. The second half, **I will utter things hidden since the creation of the world**, reflects a creative rendering of the MT (Nolland 2005, 556; Davies and Allison 1991, 426). This quote shares two terminological correspondences with Matt 13: "parable" and "hidden," a connection that requires further reflection.

In the psalm, the "prophet" calls the nation to make known "hidden things, things from of old" (Ps 78:2*b*) to "the next generation" of Israel. These things are "the praiseworthy deeds of the LORD, his power and the wonders he has done" (78:4*b*) as well as his law (v 5). If the next generation of Israel knows the deeds and law of God, they will not rebel as their ancestors did in the wilderness (vv 8-22).

Here Matthew evokes not only the content but its context. So Jesus' parables contain truth about the kingdom that when comprehended lead to deliverance and salvation, just like the hidden things in the psalm (see 13:33). For the crowds, however, these things remain "hidden" (*kruptō*; Nolland 2005, 556), but Jesus is **utter**[ing] **things hidden** as he reveals the kingdom mysteries in parables for those with eyes to see and ears to hear, which is precisely the message of Jesus' last parable.

France claims that the context of the psalm is irrelevant (2007, 530). However, if Jesus recapitulates the history of the nation is his person and ministry, this psalm is quite apropos seen in the light of the hostilities Jesus has encountered thus far from the Israel of his day (see 23:29-32). Thus, that which is hidden must be made known for the sake of the nation and this occurs now through parable teaching.

7. Explanation of the Parable of the Weeds and Wheat (13:36-43)

13:36-39

IN THE TEXT

■ **36** Jesus again teaches in private (see 13:18-23). With only his disciples in **the house** (v 36*a*), they ask him, **Explain to us the parable of the weeds in the field** (v 36*b*). Jesus' explanation focuses on the symbolic significance of **the weeds** and that of the one who sowed them.

■ **37-39** Jesus interprets the parable of the weeds by means of allegory (vv 24-30) and then in vv 40-43, he explains the action of the harvesters by allegory (v 30*b*). The catalogue of allegorical equivalences in vv 37-39 provide the interpretative framework for the eschatological judgment scene in the following verses (vv 40-43; France 2007, 532).

Jesus identifies himself as **the one who sowed the good seed**, a task he performs as **the Son of Man** (v 37; → Matt 8:20, "Son of Man" sidebar). This title functions as an expression of Jesus' coming authority as judge in 13:41, when he will put an end to evil (Nolland 2005, 559; see also 24:30-31). As both the sower and judge, "the Son of Man has in his hand not only the sowing but also the harvest and thus the entire history of the world" (Luz 2001, 268).

In v 38*a*, **the field is the world, and the good seed stands for the people of the kingdom**. Some interpreters have narrowed the meaning of **the world** to the church, which has determined applications (→ FROM THE TEXT below). Matthew's Jesus, however, has in mind the world at large, or "the sum total of everything here and now" (BDAG 2000, 561) in which both the faithful and faithless live. The identification of **good seed** with the **people** [lit. "sons"] **of the kingdom** recalls the seed in vv 8 and 23 that landed on "good soil" and its subsequent successful germination and growth; this soil/seed and the resultant growth are those who both hear and understand the word.

The NIV's **people of the kingdom**, as opposed to the familial term "sons," is less precise and so should probably be translated as "sons and daughters." This expresses an intimate connection with the kingdom, over whom God reigns (see v 43), similar to the children of Matthew's "heavenly Father" who can ask him for anything (7:9-11). "Sons of the kingdom" also appears in 8:12 (lit.), but in a very different manner to describe those who *assume* membership in God's family on the basis of Jewish ethnicity (→ 8:11-12).

Nolland suggests that the phrase "provides a bridge between the historical people of God (as the natural heirs of the kingdom [in 8:12] . . .) and the actualisation of kingdom membership that is taking place with the coming of Jesus" (2005, 559). "Sons of the kingdom" is in contrast with **the weeds** [who] **are the people** [lit. "sons"] **of the evil one** (v 38*b*). The one behind the sowing of these sons is **the devil** (v 39*a*) and is the enemy of the man who sowed "good seed" (vv 24-25).

Nolland argues that Matthew intends "evil," not the evil one, but this disrupts the correspondence with the sower's enemy and the parallelism with the evil one in v 19, who actively steals the word sown in the heart (France 2007, 535; see 6:13). The work of the evil one in both texts expresses "the power of the devil in the world and the responsibility he bears for human failing" (Davies and Allison 1991, 429).

The final movement of the parable talks about the harvest (13:30), which Jesus interprets as **the end of the age,** [where] **the harvesters are angels** (v 39*b*). The term "age" is used in apocalyptic texts to denote various eras over which God has control (e.g., *4 Ezra* 7:113; *1 En.* 16:1; *T. Levi* 10:2), and so the conclusion of this **age** will be marked by his judicial dominion, which Jesus describes in Matt 13:40-42.

■ **40-42** Final judgment awaits **everything that causes sin** [*skandalon*] **and all who do evil** (v 41*b*). Their fate is that of the weeds that are **pulled up and burned in the fire** (v 40*a*). Jesus' reference to *skandalon* and **all who do evil** (*anomia*) could allude to Ps 141:9*b* [140:9*b* LXX] (Davies and Allison 1991, 430). The psalm is a prayer for deliverance "from obstacles [*skandalon*] of those who practice lawlessness [*anomia*]."

For the work of judgment, **the Son of Man** is aided by **his angels** who **will weed out** [lit. "gather" or "collect"] **of his kingdom everything that causes sin and all who do evil** (Matt 13:41). Yahweh "gathers" exiled Israel to bring them back into the land (Deut 30:4; Zech 2:10 [11 HB]; see Matt 24:30-31); however, here the Son of Man, once again executing a divine prerogative, gathers for judgment (*1 En.* 54:6; 63:1; see Sim 1999, 693-718).

This work of the Son of Man for the sake of **his kingdom** (Matt 13:41*b*) underscores his royal authority, which Jesus Messiah already exercises during his earthy ministry. The connection between the Son of Man and the kingdom, which Matthew highlights more than the other Gospels (see 16:28; 19:28; 25:31-34; France 2007, 536), creates a continuity between the kingdom Jesus inaugurates in the present and the one he will consummate in the future. This hope is rooted in Dan 7:13-14 where the "one like a son of man" receives God's kingdom.

At this judgment, everything associated with evil will be cast **into the blazing furnace, where there will be weeping and gnashing of teeth** (Matt 13:42). Hell is not described as a furnace in the NT, but burning might recall the burning garbage heaps in the valley of Hinnom (18:9; 23:33; → 5:21-26, "Hell" sidebar). Most likely, however, Dan 3:6 LXX forms the background of Matt 13:42*b*: "They will throw him into the furnace of fire" (NRSV). Matthew's Jesus reverses the imagery from association with suffering out of faithfulness to God in Daniel to punishment because of sin. Fire is associated with judgment in both Testaments and elsewhere, which coheres with **the blazing furnace**.

Finally, Jesus identifies this inferno as a place of **weeping and gnashing of teeth**, which is a uniquely Matthean phrase describing the suffering and tribulation for those who refuse to acknowledge Jesus and the demands of his kingdom (see 8:12; 13:50; 22:13; 24:51; 25:30).

13:43 ■ **43** After the elimination of sin and evil, **then the righteous will shine like the sun in the kingdom of their Father** (13:43*a*). This language of vindication is inspired by Dan 12:3. It has two links with Matt 13:43*a*: "And those who are intelligent will *shine* like the splendor of the firmament, and some of the many *righteous*, like the stars forever and anon" (Dan 12:3*a* NETS [Theod.], emphasis added). Shining also appears elsewhere to describe the eternal state of the righteous after suffering (Wis 3:7; *1 En.* 39:7). The language of Matt 13:43 appears again in 17:2 at the transfiguration, which may imply that Jesus' followers, after suffering out of faithfulness, will share in the eschatological glory of Jesus himself (Davies and Allison 1991, 431; Nolland 2005, 561).

The allusion to Daniel is more relevant. Daniel 11 describes a period of tribulation and distress due to the hellenizing campaign of Antiochus IV Epiphanes, but his end will come (Dan 11:45). Daniel 12:1-3 then depicts the final judgment of those who followed him and the vindication of those who did not. This background parallels the time before the Son of Man's judgment of the devil, who is still at work attempting to derail one's faith, as Jesus himself says in the parable of the sower (Matt 13:19). Davies and Allison indicate that "both parables make it plain that while the victory of God's kingdom is sure, *the way from here to there is hampered by unbelief and its effects*. In other words, both address the same problem of evil" (1991, 408) whether it is disbelief or the work of the enemy.

Many commentators reject reflection upon the period between the sowing of the weeds and their removal, since Jesus mentions nothing about it in his explanation. However, Matthew evokes the context of texts he cites: the allusion to Dan 12:3*a* in Matt 13:43*a* invites such reflection. Further, Jesus devotes a substantial amount of teaching on the cost of discipleship elsewhere (10:16-23, 26-31, 34-39; 16:24-27; 24:9-14).

Luz argues that at the Parousia "the kingdom of the Son of Man is changed into the Kingdom of the Father" paralleling Paul's teaching about Christ handing over the kingdom to God (2001, 270; 1 Cor 15:24). But Matthew's high Christology would suggest otherwise: the Son of Man's kingdom is that of the Father's! Jesus inaugurates the kingdom of heaven, which denotes the reign of God, in his earthy ministry (Matt 4:17) and often executes divine prerogatives as he does so (8:25-26; 9:6). He will one day come as judge, also in the place of God, to consummate that reign (13:43; 24:30-31).

Jesus concludes this interpretation with an exhortation he has already used in 11:15 and 13:9 to encourage spiritual and intellectual engagement with this teaching: **Whoever has ears, let them hear** (v 43*b*). These words are encouragement for the disciples to continue to be children of their heavenly Father despite their present circumstances, because they will be rewarded and evil will be judged (v 38*a*).

FROM THE TEXT

Cyprian, Origen, Augustine, and Luther contended that this text is a divine acknowledgment of the persistence of sin in the church, whether it takes the form of heretical teaching or sinful behavior, and it will not be eradicated until the return of Christ. This reading assumes that "the field" (v 38) is not "the world" but rather the church. Luz cites Zinzendorf, an eighteenth-century German reformer, who "admonishes the 'brothers and sisters' to take care that 'the field of Jesus Christ bear as few weeds as possible,' but an 'institution . . . without spots and wrinkles' (Eph 5:27!) is not possible" (Zinzendorf 2:944, cited in Luz 2001, 272). 13:36-43

More recently, others have advocated for tolerance of behaviors and beliefs that diverge from the church's accepted teaching since Jesus/the owner demands coexistence of the wheat and the weeds (Luz 2001, 273), but this is clearly in tension with Matt 18:15-17.

Although their coexistence is a major component of the parable, the weeds are children of the devil who face judgment and removal from the kingdom. They symbolize hostile forces from without, not from within, and can make the life of the disciple very challenging in the present. This is supported by Matthew's use of Dan 12:3 in Matt 13:43 where the vindication of God's people follows suffering at the hands of external adversaries. This implicit warning about the difficulties of life in the kingdom of heaven is reflected in Jesus' concluding exhortation, "Whoever has ears, let them hear" (v 43*b*).

8. Three Final Parables about the Kingdom of Heaven (13:44-50)

BEHIND THE TEXT

While Matthew gives no indication of a public audience, he has already established that Jesus teaches the crowds in parables because of their obduracy (see vv 11-15, 34) and readers should not assume anything different here (France 2007, 534). The first two parables highlight both the hiddenness of the kingdom and its great value while the final one parallels the message of judgment and separation in the parable of the wheat and weeds, especially vv 40-42. Each of these parables is unique to Matthew.

a. The Parable of the Hidden Treasure (13:44)

IN THE TEXT

■ **44** This parable and the next one describe **the kingdom of heaven** as something hidden, which aligns with earlier teaching on "the knowledge of the secrets of the kingdom of heaven" (v 11) given only to the disciples (see also vv 33, 35). But these parables imply that the kingdom can be found. Jesus
13:44 likens the kingdom to **treasure hidden in a field**, which is discovered by an unsuspecting **man**. Hiding coins and other precious metals in the ground was a common practice in the ancient world before the security of banks and safety deposit boxes (see Davies and Allison 1991, 436 n. 7, and Luz 2001, 276-77, for ancient literature that refers to this practice).

The man is likely a laborer for a landowner (France 2007, 540-41). Not wanting others to find the treasure, **he hid it again, and then in his joy went and sold all he had and bought that field**. This apparently deceptive behavior should not distract contemporary readers from Jesus' point that the kingdom is of great value and "is worth any cost to seize this unique and unrepeatable opportunity" (France 2007, 540).

J. D. M. Derrett, after discussing Jewish legislation, concludes that this would be an acceptable action (1970, 6-13; for criticisms of Derrett, see Luz 2001, 277 n. 20). Davies and Allison remark that there is just too much missing from the parable to fairly evaluate this man's behavior (1991, 436). The **joy** of possessing the treasure is the characteristic of the kingdom (see Rom 14:17*b*). Finding the reign of God and living under it is worth relinquishing all ties and possessions that are required of prospective disciples (see 8:21-22; 16:24-26; 19:21).

b. The Parable of the Fine Pearl (13:45-46)

IN THE TEXT

■ **45-46** The second parable compares seeking **the kingdom of heaven** to a **merchant looking for fine pearls** (v 45). Merchants buy and sell wholesale pearls and travel extensively to do so (see BDAG 2000, 325), which implies that the kingdom is not only for the disciples (see vv 11-17 and 12:46-50), but also for any who seek it (see 6:33). Davies and Allison contend that, like the treasure in the field, this pearl is not available for all (1991, 439), but the imagery of the seeking merchant undermines this.

Pearls were far more valuable in the ancient world than today (Davies and Allison 1991, 439; Nolland 2005, 566; see also 1 Tim 2:9; Rev 17:4). The merchant eventually finds **one of great value** and sells **everything he had** so that he can purchase it, paralleling the response of the man in the preceding parable. The disciples themselves embody this abandonment (4:18-22; see also 19:27), since it is the most valuable "treasure/pearl" on earth and, despite its veiled presence, requires a sacrificial response on the part of those who desire it.

c. The Parable of the Dragnet (13:47-50)

IN THE TEXT

■ **47-48** Jesus now likens **the kingdom of heaven** to **a net that was let down into the lake and caught all kinds of fish** (v 47). Dragnets are quite large with one end
open having floats on the top and weights on the bottom to collect a variety of marine creatures (BDAG 2000, 910). Once back on shore, **the fisherman . . . collected the good fish in baskets, but threw the bad away** (v 48). The identification of the kingdom with the net that collects both **good** (*kalos*) and **bad** (*sapros*) fish parallels the parable of the weeds (vv 25-26). A time of separation comes (vv 29-30). The bad fish are those considered unsellable because they are diseased or ritually unclean (see Lev 11:9-12; France 2007, 543).

■ **49-50** As with the parable of the wheat and the weeds, Jesus interprets this one eschatologically, using it to describe the final judgment: **This is how it will be at the end of the age** (v 49*a*). The fishers are **the angels** who **will come and separate the wicked from the righteous** (v 49*b*), "the bad" and "the good" fish respectively. **The wicked** (*ponēros*) are those who reject the Messiah and persist in a lifestyle of sin and lawlessness (see v 41*b*) and are "the people [lit. 'sons'] of the evil one" (*ponēros*, v 38*b*). It is **from the righteous** that Jesus will **separate the wicked** (v 49*b*).

France comments that "until the final judgement there can be no separate existence for the true people of God: the wicked will be in the middle of them, like the wolves among the sheep in 7:15" (2007, 543; see also 25:32 for eschatological separation). Jesus repeats the imagery depicting the fiery fate that awaits **the wicked** (vv 49-50), which he used earlier in v 42 (→).

FROM THE TEXT

Like the parable of the wheat and the weeds, these parables have been interpreted as referring to the church (Luz 2001, 282). Both depict the church coexisting with evil members until the final judgment. Gregory the Great, a sixth-century pope, argues just this point (see ACCS 2001, 1a:288). However, Jesus describes not the church but "the kingdom of heaven" as a dragnet, which is an acknowledgment that life under God's reign includes those who refuse to accept it. This is not limited to the church. Recent interpretations introduce a missional component in which the time before the separation provides an opportunity for repentance. Matthew's Jesus is concerned, however, with eschatological judgment and the fate that awaits those who fail to accept the kingdom.

9. Concluding Parable and Transition (13:51-53)

IN THE TEXT

■ **51-52** Jesus now questions his disciples, which assumes a private setting (vv 46-50; see vv 10, 34, 36): **Have you understood all these things?** (v 51*b*). **These things** refers to preceding parable teaching. The disciples' **Yes** affirms that they have the requisite faith for understanding, unlike the crowds (→ vv 13-15). "The knowledge of the secrets of the kingdom of heaven" (v 11) has been given to them.

Jesus then teaches a final parable about **every teacher of the law who has become a disciple in the kingdom of heaven** (v 52*a*). He begins with **therefore**, which is not inferential but additive building upon v 51 and so may be translated, "And in this way, it will happen that every scribe" (Luz 2001, 286; for the same use of this conjunction, see 18:23; Davies and Allison [1991, 445] suggest "so then" or "well"). France argues that **therefore** is purely inferential but does not explain how this parable functions as a conclusion to the preceding ones (2007, 544).

Jesus appears to link the importance of kingdom understanding with the teachers of the Law, professional Scripture scholars, who become disciples. Thus far, however, they have been his adversaries (9:3; 12:38). For those who repent and become disciples, this **is like the owner of a house who brings out of his storeroom new treasures as well as old** (13:52*b*).

This simile reflects the Jewish-centric presentation of Jesus in Matthew. The learning of the scribes who know the Law and its application (**the old treasures**) coheres with the kingdom of heaven inaugurated by a Messiah who has not come to abolish the Law but to fulfill it (5:17; **the new treasures**) Luz (2001, 287) identifies the "old" as the Scriptures and the "new" with the gospel.

Continuity with the Scriptures of Israel and the Mosaic law is an important theme in Matthew, and these scribes "have the special task of combining the 'new' with the 'old'" (Luz 2001, 288). What is **new** occurs first because Jesus' inauguration of the kingdom of heaven and his fulfillment of OT prophecy gives meaning to what has come before, the **old**.

Most commentators argue that **every teacher of the law** refers to the disciples themselves, a term that Jesus later uses to denote those whom he sends out to the "teachers of the law and Pharisees" (23:34; see France 2007, 546; Davies and Allison 1991, 444-45; Nolland 2005, 571). Another translation for **become a disciple** (*mathēteuō*) is simply "discipled," in the sense of having been instructed by Jesus (Davies and Allison 1991, 446), which aligns with the preceding verse in which he questions his disciples if they have "understood" his parable teaching. "In this way," then, they are teachers of the Law who have been instructed in the kingdom of heaven and are able to bring out new and old treasures.

Based on the imagery of one who **brings out of his storeroom**, Nolland comments that "this scribe is a discipling disciple: the treasure he has gained is a treasure he passes out to others" (2001, 571). This is the teaching ministry by which the disciples teach others "to obey everything I have commanded you" (28:20*a*). The "teacher of the law" in 13:52 can refer both to trained scribes who become disciples and to the disciples themselves who instruct others with "new treasures as well as old."

Perhaps **every teacher of the law** interpreted as a professional scribe is
a veiled self-reference to the author himself (e.g., Goulder 1974, 375; Davies
and Allison 1991, 446). This option is difficult to substantiate, not least be- 13:53
cause of the anonymous authorship of Matthew and that Matthew would not
have considered himself a scribe.

■ **53** Matthew draws Jesus' teaching to a close with a transitional statement, which is similar to the way he concludes all five of his major teaching discourses (8:1; 11:1; 13:53; 19:1; 26:1). In a few of these cases, like this one, Matthew indicates that Jesus has finished teaching and that he is now moving on to a new location, which here is a return to his hometown, Nazareth (v 54).

H. Resistance to Jesus and John (13:54—14:12)

BEHIND THE TEXT

Matthew's remaining narrative sections (13:53—17:27; 19:1—23:39; 26:1—28:20) do not exhibit the same cohesive structure as 8:1—9:34 and 11:1—12:50. They largely follow Mark's order, but Matthew tailors these stories to the needs of his audience. Through the rejection Jesus encounters in his hometown of Nazareth (13:54-58), Matthew's audience sees that the familial separation introduced in 12:46-50 extends to religious alienation (13:57). This rejection is becoming personal, and the disciples will soon align themselves with these adversaries as they spurn the idea that he must suffer (16:22) and desert him at his arrest (26:56*b*).

The beheading of John the Baptist for his prophetic work (14:1-12) introduces yet another dimension of hostility that, although focused squarely on John, anticipates the rejection of Jesus in Jerusalem (21:45-46; 26:3-5, 65-68). Jesus relates John's suffering to his own in 17:9-13. Matthew's placement of John's martyrdom and Jesus' rejection after parables that explain why there are divided responses to Jesus, reveals that rejection is rooted in the inability to understand and "leads not to indifference but to hostility. Those who do not grasp the secrets of the kingdom of heaven necessarily find Jesus [and John] offensive" (Davies and Allison 1991, 453).

I. Resistance in Nazareth (13:54-58)

IN THE TEXT

■ **54*a*** Upon Jesus' arrival in Nazareth, **his hometown** [*patris*], **he began teaching the people in their synagogue** (→ 2:22-23). Nolland argues that **his hometown** is Capernaum (2005, 574; see 4:13), but *patris* connotes the locale of one's upbringing and ancestry (BDAG 2000, 788). The phrase **their synagogue** functions as a "verbal thread" beginning in 4:23, which Matthew uses in a summary statement (see also 9:35). In 12:9, "their synagogue" refers to the synagogue in Capernaum where the Pharisees begin to plot Jesus' death (12:14). The recurrence of this phrase may signal a rupture between Jesus (and his followers) and this institution. Jesus does not teach in a synagogue again after 13:54-58, but we should not conclude that he has forsaken his people (Davies and Allison 1991, 455). He will still minister to them (14:34-36; 15:1-20, 29-31).

■ **54*b*-56** The first rhetorical question from the crowd indicates that Jesus did more than teach: **Where did this man get this wisdom and these miraculous powers?** (13:54*b*). France claims that Jesus performed no miracles here, with the crowds asking their question based on hearsay (2007, 549). But v 58 indicates that he did perform miracles there, just not many. Earlier Jesus taught that true wisdom is in him (→ 11:28-30) and demonstrated his messianic authority through mighty deeds (see 9:27-31; 12:13, 15, 22-23).

In response, the synagogue crowd was **amazed** (13:54*a*; see 7:28; 22:33). Davies and Allison suggest that this verb has a negative connotation (1991, 455), but it is more likely a natural response to the wisdom and power of Jesus that exceeds the crowd's expectations of the rabbi (see Luke 4:16-27 and Dunn 2006a, 216-22). The synagogue crowd initially recognizes his power and wisdom. But their subsequent questions seek to reduce him to the level of the mundane and ordinary: **Isn't this the carpenter's son? Isn't his mother's name Mary, and aren't his brothers James, Joseph, Simon and Judas? Aren't all his sisters with us?** (Matt 13:55-56*a*).

The Greek word for **carpenter** (*tektōn*) refers to a variety of construction skills, including woodworking and masonry (BDAG 2000, 995). The lack of reference to Joseph could imply that he is deceased (France 2007, 549). Most likely Jesus carried on the family business (Mark 6:3). The names of Jesus' brothers would be well-known to Matthew's audience (Acts 1:14; 12:17; 1 Cor 9:5; Jude 1:1; see France 2007, 549-50, for a hypothesis about the presence of Jesus' sisters). In light of Matt 12:46 where his family is outside wanting to question Jesus, they now become the basis of the synagogue's rejection of him.

In 13:56, the crowd restates their initial question about **where** Jesus acquired **all these things** (see v 54*b*). Their knowledge of Jesus' family, "a family of modest means in a carpenter's household" (Nolland 2005, 576), is incommensurate with Jesus' extraordinary wisdom and power. References to Jesus' family here do not necessarily mean that they are now decidedly against him, as Luz suggests (2001, 303), but Matthew does not mention them again.

■ **57-58** Not surprisingly, **they took offense** [*skandalizō*] **at him** (v 57). Matthew uses *skandalizō* to describe those thrown off the path of salvation by suffering or evil from within or without (see 5:28-30 and 13:21). For those who reject him, Jesus is the source of stumbling (→ 10:34-36). They will not be blessed: "Blessed is anyone who does not stumble [*skandalizō*] on account of me" (11:6, 20-24). MATTHEW

Jesus' proverbial response, **A prophet is not without honor except in his own town and in his own home** (13:57*b*), is not from Scripture (but see Jer 1:1; 11:21-23). The idea that those who become great are rejected by their own is well attested in Greek literature (Davies and Allison 1991, 460). Jesus anticipates the story of John's martyrdom for his prophetic work. Jesus' fate as the one who comes after John (Matt 3:11) is likewise ominous. 13:57—14:2

Matthew reports that Jesus **did not do many miracles there because of their lack of faith** (13:58). Mark states that Jesus "could not do" many miracles there (Mark 6:5). For Matthew, "inability [in Mark] has become refusal; Jesus is indisputably in charge" (Davies and Allison 1991, 460). The connection between faith and healing, which appears so often in the Gospels, remains unchanged (see Matt 8:28-29). The disbelief of this crowd aligns them with the faithlessness of "this generation" (17:17; France 2007, 550).

2. Resistance from Herod Antipas (14:1-12)

IN THE TEXT

■ **1-2** Herod Antipas learns of Jesus' ministry about the same time as the Nazareth synagogue crowd: **<u>At that time</u> Herod the tetrarch heard the reports about Jesus** (v 1).

Herod Antipas

Herod Antipas is the son of Herod the Great and Malthace, a Samaritan and the latter's fourth wife (Josephus, *J.W.* 1.562). Herod Antipas' rule as **tetrarch** is below that of a king (Josephus, *Ant.* 17.318; BDAG 2000, 1000). Matthew calls Antipas "king" in v 9, likely reflecting common parlance. His father appointed him ruler of Galilee and Perea before his death in 4 BCE, and Antipas reigned until 39 CE. Antipas likely lived in Tiberias, his capital city, but the location of John's martyrdom was Machaerus in Perea, on the eastern side of the Dead Sea, where Herod the Great built a palace (Josephus, *Ant.* 18.119; Hoehner 1992, 324; idem, 1980). John's death occurred sometime between him sending his followers to inquire about Jesus in 11:2 and Herod's appraisal in 14:1-2.

John was beheaded because he condemned Herod's marriage to his brother Philip's wife, Herodias, who was the granddaughter of Herod the Great and daughter of Herod's son Aristobulus, the half-brother of Antipas. Herod Antipas fell in love with Herodias while visiting his brother in Rome. The name "Herod Philip" evident in modern scholarship is likely not his actual name, reflecting Mark who calls him Philip and Josephus who refers to him as Herod (e.g., Josephus, *Ant.* 18.116). Herod Antipas divorced his current wife, King Aretas' daughter, so he could marry Herodias, which provoked a military conflict (see Josephus, *Ant.* 18.109-14).

Upon hearing the reports about Jesus, Herod says to his royal attendants,
14:3-5 **This is John the Baptist; he has risen from the dead! That is why miraculous powers are at work in him** (v 2). Matthew's placement of these words on Herod's lips (unlike Mark's account) highlights the political threat of John. In Matthew, Herod wants to kill him (v 5*a*); in Mark, he protects John from Herodias, his wife (Mark 6:19*b*-20).

The rumor of John's resurrection surfaces again in Caesarea Philippi (Matt 16:14). There is no connection between resurrection and possession of miraculous powers per se in ancient sources (Nolland 2005, 580). But Herod's assumption that a resurrected John would possess **miraculous powers** parallels the testimony about Jesus by the crowd (Davies and Allison 1991, 467), serving to underscore the solidary between John and Jesus. There is, however, no account of John performing miracles.

■ **3-5** In 14:3-12, Matthew provides a flashback to explain Herod's paranoia about John (v 2). John challenged Herod about taking his brother's wife as his own, **saying to him: "It is not lawful for you to have her"** (v 4). In Greek, the imperfective tense form of **saying** connotes a routine protest on the part of John about the illicit union, possibly to the masses, until his arrest. Except for the case of Levirate marriage (see Deut 25:5-10), an Israelite is prohibited from taking his brother's wife in marriage, as this would be considered incest (Lev 18:16; 20:21; Hoehner 1992, 323).

Herod **wanted to kill John** but didn't since **he was afraid of the people, because they considered John a prophet** (v 5). John's martyrdom casts a dark shadow over Jesus, who is likewise rejected as a prophet (see 17:9-13). Persecution of the prophets, well known in Jewish tradition (see, e.g., Jer 26 and Lam 2:20), is a theme Matthew regularly invokes (Matt 5:12; 17:12; 21:33-41; 22:3-6; 23:29-36). The prophetic solidary that John and Jesus share leads to their deaths. It also constrains their opponents who must deal with John and Jesus without antagonizing the crowds since they are both considered prophets (14:5; 21:46).

■ **6-12 On Herod's birthday the daughter of Herodias danced for the guests** (14:6). Josephus indicates that her daughter's name is Salome (*Ant.* 18.136). Herodian parties were known for their debauchery (Keener 1999, 399-401). Salome's dance must have been so seductive that Herod swore **to give her whatever she asked** (v 7).

On the advice of Herodias, Salome makes a gruesome request: **Give me here on a platter the head of John the Baptist** (v 8). To preserve his honor among his guests, Herod orders the beheading but he **was distressed** (vv 9-10; see Mark 6:20). Although Herod was distressed, Matthew explicitly indicates that Herod wants to kill John (Matt 14:5*a*), which reflects Matthew's disdain for the Herods in his narrative.

Matthew states that **his head was brought in on a platter and given to the girl, who carried it to her mother** (v 11). John has died an unjust death, the result of a precipitous offer. **John's disciples** retrieve **his body and buried it**, and **then they went and told Jesus** (v 12). Joseph of Arimathea does the same thing after Jesus' crucifixion (27:57-60). At hearing this news, Jesus withdraws from the crowd for a time (14:13*a*).

FROM THE TEXT

The life of a prophet is dangerous. John was arrested for his prophetic work just before Jesus began his ministry (4:12-13), but the events are narrated together to make the point that the fate of John awaits Jesus as well. Jesus is maligned by the synagogue in Nazareth because they refuse to believe his words and accept his deeds. Herod Antipas is fearful that John's hearers will rebel against him because John rebukes him for his immoral behavior. The synagogue crowd and Herod Antipas are united in their rejection of God's emissaries.

John and Jesus have a similar relationship with institutions. Jesus taught earlier that new wine will burst old skins and a new patch cannot be sown on an old garment (→ 9:16-17). The prophetic voice brings the word and activity of God in new and unexpected ways, but religious and political structures often cannot accommodate it (Johnson 2011, 49-51). John calls Israel to repentance, and Jesus continues this call so that she can be free from bondage to sin and sickness.

John's challenge to "King" Herod leads to his death. In the case of Jesus, the Sanhedrin, the Jewish ruling body that has close political ties to the Romans, view his ministry as a threat for which he pays the ultimate price. In Acts, his followers carry on with his prophetic work, calling all to repentance, offering forgiveness to the sinner (Acts 2:38-39), and healing the sick (3:1-10). They, too, pay a heavy price for this (4:3, 27-30; 5:33, 40), but Jesus warned his followers early on about the cost of following him (Matt 10:16-23).

I. Mighty Deeds of the Messiah Continued (14:13-36)

BEHIND THE TEXT

The tone of the narrative changes dramatically in the following three miracle stories: Jesus gifts the multitudes with an unexpected supper (14:13-21), walks on water (vv 22-33), and heals all those who even touch the edge of his garment (vv 34-36). These high moments, however, are short-lived. Jesus is promptly challenged by the "Pharisees and scribes . . . from Jerusalem" about his disciples who eat with unclean hands (15:1-2 NRSV). In the meantime, Matthew reaffirms through these stories that Jesus is Immanuel, God with us.

1. Feeding of the Five Thousand (14:13-21)

IN THE TEXT

■ **13-14** Upon hearing the news of John's execution, Jesus **withdrew by boat privately to a solitary place** (v 13*a*). Herod now knows of him (France 2007, 560), so, as he did when John was first arrested, he departs (see 4:12). He also withdraws after hostile encounters with the Pharisees (12:15; 15:21). It is not clear to which locale Jesus has retreated, but likely outside of Antipas' domain, northeast of the Sea of Galilee (France 2007, 561).

When the crowds hear of his whereabouts, they **followed him on foot from the towns** (v 13*b*). Jesus remains popular in Galilee (see 4:23-25; 8:1, 16; 12:15; 14:34-36; 15:29-31). Despite his need for solitude, **when Jesus landed and saw a large crowd, he had compassion on them and healed their sick** (v 14), echoing the compassion he had for the crowds in 9:36. Jesus' compassion leads to restorative action (→ 9:36). It is through the disciples, in addition to himself, that Jesus exercises compassion. Here he provides another opportunity for them to act with compassion (see 14:16).

■ **15-21** Their first response is to ask Jesus to send the crowds back **to the villages** so they can **buy themselves some food** (v 15). But Jesus tells them, **They do not need to go away. You give them something to eat** (v 16). To the disciples, this was "a hollow joke" (France 2007, 562). It may echo Elisha's command to his servant, "Give it to the people to eat," referring to twenty loaves of bread with which he expects to miraculously feed one hundred men. His servant likewise responds with incredulity (2 Kgs 4:43-45; Davies and Allison 1991, 488).

In Matt 10:8, Jesus exhorts the disciples to perform miracles and here he may expect them to do it again. However, they did not understand what he was asking: **We have here only five loaves of bread and two fish** (14:17); basically, they have nothing at all faced with the prospect of feeding five thousand men excluding women and children.

Jesus asks for the bread and the fish and requests that **the people . . . sit** [*anaklinō*] **down on the grass** (v 19*a*). The verb *anaklinō* describes a posture of reclining at a banquet (e.g., Luke 7:36; 12:37; BDAG 2000, 65), which anticipates the Last Supper at which Jesus "reclines" (*anakeimai*) with his disciples (26:20). Davies and Allison comment that "after directing the crowd to sit down, Jesus, acting like the host at a regular Jewish meal, . . . distributes the food to his disciples who in turn distribute it to the crowd" (1991, 490). He multiplies the food by **taking the five loaves and the two fish and looking up to heaven, he gave thanks and broke the loaves** (14:19*b*).

Jesus looks to his heavenly Father for the provision of food, reflected in the Sermon on the Mount (6:25-34) and in the supplication: "Give us today our daily bread" (6:11). He models ways of relating to the Father that he expects of his followers. The verb **gave thanks** (*eulogeō*) can also mean "to bless." Since most Jewish prayers "bless God" for his provision, instead of offering thanksgiving, Jesus is praising God when he looks up to heaven before he breaks the bread and gives it to **the disciples** (14:19*c*; Luz 2001, 314 n. 56; France 2007, 562; in *m. Ber.* 6, the supplicant blesses God for a variety of provisions).

The verbs "take," "bless," "broke," and "give" all occur in the Synoptic accounts of the miraculous feeding as well as the Last Supper narratives (France 2007, 558). Davies and Allison list nine terminological parallels between 14:13-21 and 26:20-29, some of which are not in Mark, which implies that Matthew makes an even more conspicuous link between the two scenes (1991, 481; see also Nolland 2005, 592). "The feeding of the crowd is therefore presented as a 'foretaste' of the central act of worship of the emergent Christian community" (France 2007, 558) and, consequently, anticipates the creation of a large table, beyond the twelve disciples at the Last Supper (26:20-29), that includes Gentile and Jew alike. In 8:11 (→), Jesus has already predicted such an eschatological feast. This is another proleptic moment signaling that the gospel is for all nations (28:19).

Some claim a Mosaic background for the feeding of the five thousand, in which Moses oversees the miraculous provision of manna for the Israelites, also in the wilderness (Exod 16). Allison argues that manna in Exodus, the Last Supper, and the messianic banquet are thematically connected in Jewish tradition (Allison 1993, 238-42). However, connections with the Last Supper and the eventual messianic banquet seem more relevant to Matthew. Further, Jesus is not in a wilderness area, but in a solitary place (Nolland 2005, 589).

The disciples gave the multiplied bread and fish **to the people** (Matt 14:19*c*) and **they all ate and were satisfied** (v 20). To be **satisfied** (*chortazō*) is to be completely full of food, not lacking anything (BDAG 2000, 1087), recalling the satisfaction that awaits those who hunger now (5:6); for Nolland, a connection between 5:6 and 14:20 is "no more than a coincidence of language" (2005, 594), but the many verbal threads in Matthew suggest otherwise.

There were **twelve basketfuls** [*kofinos*] **of broken pieces . . . left over** (v 20*b*). The type of basket used here, *kofinos*, is quite large and is specifically used by Jews, which may suggest a completely Jewish crowd. In the next feeding account, this type of basket is not mentioned (see 15:37), corresponding to Jesus ministering in Gentile territory (France 2007, 563, 603). Since the baskets are large, there are copious amounts of bread and fish left, echoing miracles by Elijah and Elisha (1 Kgs 17:16; 2 Kgs 4:6-7, 44; Davies and Allison 1991, 491).

Matthew records the number of those present, highlighting the magnitude of the miracle Jesus performs: **The number of those who ate was about five thousand men, besides women and children** (v 21). The Greek text actually reads "without women and children," and so could be understood as only five thousand men present, but there are other instances in Greek literature where the preposition is understood as "besides" or "in addition to" (see BDAG
14:22-24 2000, 1095; France 2007, 564-65).

2. Jesus Walking on the Water (14:22-33)

IN THE TEXT

■ **22-24 Immediately Jesus made the disciples get into the boat and go on ahead of him to the other side** (v 22*a*). While they are doing so, he sends the crowd on their way (v 22*b*). Matthew's **immediately** is likely influenced by Mark (see Mark 6:45). Jesus still has not been alone since his departure to "a solitary place" (Matt 14:13), which prematurely ended (vv 13*b*-14*a*); he urgently desires **to pray** to his heavenly Father, which he does **on a mountainside by himself** (v 23*a*).

Solitary prayer is another exhortation from the Sermon on the Mount that Jesus himself practices (6:5-6; see 14:19; Davies and Allison 1991, 502). Davies and Allison contend that the mountaintop setting contributes to a Moses typology (see 5:1-2) and is resumed later (see 17:1-8; 1991, 502). Moses was also on Sinai alone (Exod 24:2), but it is unclear how this relates to Jesus walking on the water (Matt 14:25) and, especially, the confession that he is the Son of God (v 33).

In v 23*b*, **later that night** Jesus was **alone**, which means that the disciples have been out on the lake for some time. This sets up v 24: **the boat was al-**

ready a considerable distance from the land, buffeted by the waves because the wind was against it. The Greek for **buffeted** means to "torment" or "harass" (BDAG 2000, 168) and is used to describe the effect of sickness in 8:6. Nolland comments that this verb's use in 14:24 "may suggest that human suffering is not far from sight; readers are invited to think in terms of their own experiences of being buffeted by life" (2005, 600).

■ **25-27** Jesus comes to the disciples **shortly before dawn** (lit. "at the fourth watch of the night," between 3 a.m. and 6 a.m.) **walking on the lake** (v 25). In the OT, God can walk on the sea: he "walks on the sea as on dry ground" (Job 9:8 NETS); "In the sea was your way, and your paths in many waters, and your footprints will not be known" (Ps 77:19 [20 HB; 76:20 NETS]; see also Hab 3:15). The disciples are naturally **terrified** at this sight perhaps due to limited visibility in the twilight: **"It's a ghost," they said, and cried out in fear** (Matt 14:26).

Fear is often a response to an epiphany (see Gen 15:1; Exod 20:20; Luke 1:12; Rev 1:17). However, the disciples cry out because they think it is **a ghost** or an apparition (BDAG 2000, 1049), such as an evil spirit who dwells in the water (Nolland 2005, 601) or "a disembodied spirit . . . where a physical body would sink" (France 2007, 569; see also Nolland 2005, 601). Jesus **immediately** reassures them: **Take courage! It is I** [*egō eimi*]. **Don't be afraid** (Matt 14:27).

The response, **It is I**, can also be rendered "I am," which is Yahweh's self-identification in Exod 3:14 and elsewhere, which may be another, albeit veiled, contribution to the divine authority of Jesus and his power over the sea/water (Davies and Allison 1991, 506; Luz 2001, 320; France [2007, 569 n. 14] demurs but the context favors this identification).

■ **28-33** The account of Peter attempting to walk on the water is unique to Matthew. Initially it demonstrates strong faith by Peter who **got down out of the boat, <u>walked on the water</u> and came toward Jesus** (v 29*b*). Compared to Mark, Matthew downplays the disciples' weak faith and lack of understanding, so this unique vignette fits. Even Peter's request to come to Jesus (**if it's you**), when a second earlier they thought the figure was a ghost, represents a degree of faith. In response, Peter steps out of the boat.

This recalls the empowering of the disciples to exorcise demons and heal the sick in 10:1, just as Jesus does (9:35). This Messiah shares his authority, which is reflected in Jesus' request to his disciples that they feed the crowd (14:16). France thinks this is "a cautionary tale" (2007, 568) against presumption, but Jesus chides Peter for "little faith" and "doubt" (v 31*b*), not because he stepped out of the boat.

Once Peter **saw the wind**, fear overtook him and he began **to sink** (v 30*a*). He **cried out, "Lord, save me!"** (v 30*b*). This cry parallels that of the disciples in 8:25 ("Lord, save us!") and occurs in Ps 69:1-3 [2-4 HB] as a plea of deliverance from threatening waters. The echoes of Yahweh's dominion and salvation here makes **Lord** (*kyrios*) as a title likely (→ Matt 8:2, 25). Jesus **immediately** saves him: **Jesus reached out his hand and caught him** (14:31*a*);

this echoes Ps 18:16*b* [17*b* HB]: "he [Yahweh] drew me out of deep waters" (see also Ps 144:5-8).

Jesus chastises Peter: **"You of little faith," he said, "why did you doubt?"** (Matt 14:31*b*). (For the meaning of **little faith** in Matthew → 6:30, and, for some of the disciples who "doubt" → 28:17*b*.) According to Davies and Allison, "Jesus is there to save *despite* inadequate faith" (1991, 509), but Matthew's point is that Immanuel, God with us, saves *because of* human weakness.

Unlike 8:26*b*, in which Jesus rebukes "the wind and the waves," the winds calm as soon as he steps into the boat (14:32). This still expresses his authority, paralleling Yahweh's rule over hostile waters (Job 26:11-12; Pss 65:7 [8 HB]; 89:9-10 [10-11 HB]). The disciples then **worshiped him, saying, "Truly you are the Son of God"** (Matt 14:33).

If there were any lingering doubts about Matthew's high Christology, this dispels it. Jesus is introduced as God's Son at his baptism. While that context may be limited to his status as Yahweh's anointed King (→ 3:17), no such limitations apply here. That Jesus can walk on the water and that his presence in the boat calms the rough waves reaffirms Matthew's high Christology: this is not only the Messiah/Son of God but also the Lord/*kurios* delivering his people by being present with them. Once again, Jesus' identity as Immanuel, God with us is confirmed.

The disciples' recognition of his sonship represents an increase in understanding that grows (→ 16:16; Davies and Allison 1991, 510). Luz rightly
14:34-36 points out that the confession by Peter in 16:16 is "the resumption and intensification of this confession [in v 33] by all of the disciples" (2001, 319).

3. Further Healings (14:34-36)

■ **34-36** The disciples and Jesus sail to **Gennesaret** (v 34), likely located on the northwest coast of the Sea of Galilee (Davies and Allison 1991, 511). This reference comes from Mark, who notes geographical locations more than Matthew (see Mark 6:45 compared to Matt 14:22). Matthew mentions Galilean villages at specific points: the beginning of Jesus' ministry (4:13-14: Capernaum); lack of repentance (11:20-24: Chorazin, Bethsaida, Capernaum); lack of faith (13:54-58: Nazareth).

In Gennesaret, the response is completely different: as soon as **the men** recognized Jesus, they **sent word to all the surrounding country** and **people brought all their sick to him** (v 35). Those bringing the sick **begged him to let the sick just touch the edge of his cloak** (v 36*a*; see also 9:20-21 and note Acts 19:12, in which "handkerchiefs and aprons" become conduits of healing). Everyone who did was healed (Matt 14:36*b*).

This summary statement reminds Matthew's audience that the Messiah/Son of God continues to inaugurate God's reign and the end of exile through physical healing (→ 4:13-17, 23-25). In 15:1-2, the Pharisees challenge Jesus about his disciples eating with unclean hands, which makes sense if they had just been ministering in the unclean marketplaces as recorded in Mark 6:56, the parallel text to Matt 14:36. It is unclear why Matthew has left this out.

FROM THE TEXT

A unifying feature of the first two narratives is Jesus' power to perform deeds associated with Yahweh. Furthermore, he invites the disciples to do the same. When Jesus miraculously feeds the multitudes, he first praises his heavenly Father who makes all provision possible, but Jesus himself provides the food. In some ways, this parallels his exhortation to the disciples in 9:38. They are to "ask the *Lord* of the harvest . . . to send out workers," a prayer that Jesus subsequently answers himself. This is another instance of the subtle but perceptible eliding of Jesus with Yahweh. Next, his walking on the water and rescue of Peter recalls the divine activity of God in the OT from his dominion over and salvation from threatening waters to his self-identification of "I am."

In both accounts, the disciples could participate: Jesus asks them to feed the multitudes and then permits Peter to walk on the water. By performing these deeds and inviting the disciples to do likewise, Jesus is a Messiah who shares the divine power of Yahweh and consequently forms a new Israel that can bring healing and restoration to the world. This is the inaugurated reign of Israel's God. In what ways should the church today continue this inauguration so that others will know that Immanuel is present in her midst?

J. Jesus Challenged about Ritual Purity (15:1-20)

BEHIND THE TEXT

This story brings the momentum generated by the last three miracle accounts (14:13-36) to a brief halt. After this, Matthew continues with more accounts of Jesus' miracles without hostile interference (15:21-39). Matthew abbreviates many of Mark's, but the contours of this one remain. Some of the differences are significant. He excludes Mark's description of the Pharisees' ritual purity practices (Mark 7:3-4), assuming his audience would already know this information. Jesus quotes Isa 29:13 after his question about breaking a commandment for the sake of tradition (Matt 15:3-9), which is more logical than Mark's order (France 2007, 578).

The reference to God uprooting what he has not planted (15:13-14), from Matthew's own source material, condemns the scribes and Pharisees. The challenge by the Pharisees and scribes and the response by Jesus (vv 3-11) results in a "breach between Jesus and the scribal establishment [that] is irreparable" (France 2007, 575). His redefinition of impurity (v 11) offends them (v 12), but the Pharisees have already made up their minds about Jesus in any case (see 9:34; 12:24).

IN THE TEXT

■ **1-2** News from Galilee of this controversial Jesus has reached the **Pharisees and teachers of the law . . . from Jerusalem** (15:1). This is just the beginning of hostility from Jerusalem. On three occasions Jesus predicts that he will suffer at the hands of the Jerusalem elite (16:21; 17:22; 20:18-19).

These leaders accuse the disciples of breaking **the tradition of the elders** by failing to **wash their hands before they eat!** (v 2). The Galilean Pharisees have already questioned Jesus about their lack of Sabbath observance (12:2), which breaches Pharisaic halakhah as is the case in 15:2. Jesus himself is also guilty since he is breaching purity boundaries by ministering to the unclean: a leper (8:3-4), a Roman centurion (8:5-13), two Gentile demoniacs (8:28-34), sinners and tax collectors (9:10-13), and a menstruating woman (9:20-22).

The maintenance of ritual purity was a fundamental tenet of scribal Pharisaism (→ "Ritual Purity" sidebar below), and this **tradition of the elders** becomes codified in the Mishnah in the third century CE. This oral tradition is not found in the Law itself. **The elders** refers to well-known scribes who developed the halakhah, which protected observant Jews from Torah-breaking.

Ritual Purity

The call for Israel to be holy is rooted in the holiness of God, who expects his people to "be holy" as he "is holy" (Lev 11:44; 20:26). The holiness of the people of Israel, as well as their places and things, such as the temple, requires the maintenance of a holiness derived from God himself (Brower 2005, 24). The question on the minds of 2TP Jews is how to maintain a state of purity and holiness, given that a variety of sources of impurity contaminate.

Ritual impurity or being in a state thereof results from touching dead bodies (Num 19:11), consuming certain foods (Lev 11), or emitting a bodily discharge (Lev 12:2). Another source of impurity is immoral activity (Lev 18), also known as moral impurity, which is not separate from ritual impurity in the Torah (Wenham 1979, 20-21). These can also defile the holiness of God's people, which Jesus himself teaches (Matt 15:11; Mark 7:21-23).

The Pharisees' requirement of handwashing reflects the custom of the temple priests who did so before they executed their priestly duties (Exod 30:17-21; 40:30-32; Lev 22:4-7). Borg notes that "members of a Pharisaic fellowship . . . were committed to . . . eating *every* meal in that degree of purity observed by the officiating priests in the temple" (1984, 80-81). Unlike the priests who performed ritual washing exclusively in the temple, the Pharisees, as a lay movement, practiced purity laws, such as this one, in the public sphere.

Handwashing stems from their concern to maintain ritual purity by *separation*. This is evident when they chastise Jesus earlier in Matthew for eating with "tax collectors and sinners" (Matt 9:11). The Pharisees desire that the whole nation embrace their way of being Israel. As Brower notes, "If God's people were called to be a kingdom of *priests*, then the purity rules for Temple service should be expanded to include the whole of Israel and the whole land" (2005, 30).

■ **3-6** Jesus does not immediately address the specific accusations. Rather, he confronts a more fundamental issue about **your tradition** (v 3), the Pharisaic halakhah, of which ritual handwashing would be included. Jesus argues that, far from enabling obedience to **the command of God** (v 3) it is fostering disobedience. He cites the fifth commandment, **Honor your father and mother** (v 4*a*; Exod 20:12), and a supporting text: **Anyone who curses their father or mother is to be put to death** (Matt 15:4*b*; Exod 21:17).

The Pharisees, however, are guilty of breaching this commandment by uttering a vow from scribal tradition: **But you say that if anyone declares that what might have been used to help their father or mother is "devoted to God," they are not to "honor their father or mother" with it** (Matt 15:5-6*a*; see *m. Ned.* 8:7 for similar vows). That which is **devoted to God** is *qorban*, although Matthew has not included this term from Mark 7:11; such devoted items are "something consecrated as a gift for God and closed to ordinary human use" (BDAG 2000, 559).

Basically, what is dedicated through the vow immediately becomes inaccessible to anyone else and belongs exclusively to the temple treasury (France 2007, 580; Davies and Allison 1991, 523). It seems to have been used as a "work-around" to avoid the obligations to a parent, a kind of first-century tax avoidance scheme! According to rabbinic sources, it was not always invoked with the purest of intentions (see *m. Ned.* 5:6, in which the *qorban* vow is used as retaliation against another person).

Jesus argues that in uttering this vow, they **nullify the word of God for the sake of your tradition** (v 6*b*). The abuse of *qorban* as a means to avoid fulfilling the fifth commandment renders the Pharisees guilty; they have breached an actual command of God. Elderly people in much of the world, then and now, were completely dependent upon their children and the latter were required to care for their parents (see Sir 3:12-16; Prov 28:24; 1 Tim 5:4). The *qorban* vow is about "service to God . . . [and] can never be isolated from service to fellow human beings" (Davies and Allison 1991, 525).

■ **7-9** Jesus then calls them **hypocrites** for their double standard (see Matt 23:13, 15, etc.) and claims that **Isaiah was right when he prophesied about you** (15:7). His quotation of Isa 29:13 reflects the LXX: **These people honor me with their lips, but their hearts are far from me. They worship me in vain; their teachings are merely human rules** (Matt 15:8-9). The leaders of Israel relied on their own wisdom and kept their plans hidden from Yahweh but still had the appearance of devotion (Isa 13:14-15). Now Jesus condemns the scribes and Pharisees for the same kind of false religion, although outwardly they appear extremely pious.

The Pharisees and scribes' interpretation of *qorban* law is hypocritical. Their observance of it and other like things because of their "tradition" prevents true Torah observance. "God has been effectively excluded from his own worship—and that is also the effect of the displacement of the commandment of God by scribal tradition" (France 2007, 582). This form of religion degenerates into preoccupation with ritual purity (vv 11, 17-19 [esp. vv 17-19]). Purity is at risk of becoming wholly external, a matter of performance. But this misses the point; it's about purity of heart (→ 5:20).

■ **10-14** This exchange is not private, and Jesus now turns his attention from the Pharisees and scribes to **the crowd**, exhorting them to **Listen and understand** (15:10*b*). To "listen/hear" and "understand" is to apprehend the "secrets of the kingdom of heaven" (13:11; see also 13:23, 51), but this is contingent upon faith. Jesus then utters a short "parable" (15:15) that, like the parables in ch 13, requires the ability to hear and understand: **What goes into someone's mouth does not defile** [*koinoō*] **them, but what comes out of their mouth** (v 11). To **defile** is to render ritually impure (see 4 Macc 7:6). A cognate noun, *koinos*, refers to things used in the cult as common and "therefore defiled in relation to the need for cultic purity" (Nolland 2005, 620; see 1 Macc 1:47, 62).

This is an offensive statement since it appears to undermine the very basis of the Mosaic purity laws. Matthew's use of **mouth**, not found in Mark, "makes the application to food and speech [the Pharisaic use of vows] more direct" (Nolland 2005, 619). Jesus' statement in Matt 15:11 does not invalidate the ritual purity system of the OT, but relativizes it in favor of "the more important matters of the law" (23:23), just as Hosea does not unequivocally reject the temple's cult in favor of acts of mercy (Hos 6:6). Davies and Allison refer to this as "relative negation in which all the emphasis lies on the second limb of the saying" (1991, 529; see also 2 Chr 30:18-20).

The disciples point out to Jesus, in private, that **the Pharisees were offended** [*skandalizō*] **when they heard this** (Matt 15:12), referring to Jesus' direct teaching about "what defiles" (v 11*b*). The Nazareth synagogue crowd also took offense (*skandalizō*) at Jesus' teaching and mighty deeds (see 13:56*b*-57). He becomes a source of destruction rather than salvation, which Jesus illustrates with the following: **Every plant that my heavenly Father has not planted will be pulled up by the roots** (15:13). But, in the meantime, they must be left where they are (v 14*a*).

In the OT, Israel is planted by God (Isa 5:7; 60:21; 61:3; *Pss. Sol.* 14:3-4) and, in keeping with the parable of the wheat and weeds, what should not have been planted will be removed (13:24-30, 37-43). "That the Pharisees are not a planting of God, as Jesus' word directly indicates, is a slap in the face of their sense of election" (Luz 2001, 333). Neither ethnicity nor obedience to a scribal tradition masquerading as authentic piety immunizes against judgment

(→ 8:10-12). John has already warned their Galilean counterparts about the prospect of judgment (see 3:7-10).

The future uprooting of the religious leaders places this controversy on an eschatological level. The Pharisees and scribes will be judged because of their hypocrisy. These **blind guides** and their followers **will fall into a pit** (15:14), a metaphor for failure and destruction (Ps 7:15 [16 HB]; Prov 26:27; Davies and Allison 1991, 53). Their misguided teaching will be exposed (see Gamaliel's logic in Acts 5:34-39). Their condemnation anticipates Jesus' warning against the teaching of the Pharisees in Matt 16:5-12 (Nolland 2005, 623).

■ **15-20** Peter says to Jesus, **Explain the parable to us** (15:15) referring to the aphorism in v 11. In Matthew, Jesus tones down his rebuke of the disciples for this request (see Mark 7:18) but he still asks, **Are you** [plural] **still so dull?** (Matt 15:16). Peter, from this point on, speaks on behalf of the disciples (e.g., 16:16, 22; 18:21), confirmed by Jesus' response with the plural **you**. They should have understood given their privileged status, but, alas, they have not, and there is more incomprehension to come (16:8-9).

Jesus' explanation reflects his desire that they comprehend his teaching (Luz 2001, 333); therefore, he gives a short description of the human digestive system and the waste it produces (15:17). Neither the food nor unwashed hands are a source of impurity. Rather, **the things that come out of a person's mouth come from the heart, and these defile them** (v 18).

One of the first things to come **out of the heart** are **evil thoughts** (*dialogismos*, v 19*a*). The word *dialogismos* denotes "evil machinations" (BDAG 2000, 232) as opposed to a momentary thought. The heart, as the seat of our affections, emotions, and will, is capable of either great good or great evil first in thought and then in word and/or deed. For Matthew's Jesus, **evil thoughts** manifest as **murder, adultery, sexual immorality, theft, false testimony, and slander** (v 19). Immoral thoughts and actions are what truly defile in the sight of God.

A number of 2T texts associate virtues/righteousness with purity and vices with impurity (1QS 5:13-14; Josephus, *Ant.* 18.117; *Jub.* 20:5; Ezra 9:11; Ps 119:9; Rom 1:24). France notes that **sexual immorality** following as it does **adultery** and the same for **slander** with **false testimony** cautions "the reader against sheltering behind a too limited definition of 'adultery' and 'false testimony,' in much the same way that 5:21-28 took us behind specific acts of murder and adultery to a wider area of culpability" (2007, 586).

The Pharisees' practice of a highly respected ritual purity does not remedy hearts that are filled with **evil thoughts**, which they have repeatedly manifested (see Matt 9:35; 12:14, 22). Consequently, they align them with an "evil . . . generation" (16:4 NRSV). In 12:34, Jesus labels the Pharisees as "evil" because they are incapable of saying "anything good . . . for the mouth speaks what the heart is full of." Their overemphasis on ritual purity creates a piety that overlooks the heart and, hence, prohibits them from becoming the holy nation and priestly kingdom that they desire, in much the same way that other scribal traditions lead them to breach the Mosaic law.

Jesus concludes that the vices above (in addition to others) **are what defile a person** (15:20*a*). His last line, **but eating with unwashed hands does not defile** (v 20*b*), is both a logical conclusion of what he has just taught in vv 11 and 17-19 and a response to the Pharisees' critique of the disciples in v 2.

FROM THE TEXT

To be holy, as God is holy, means having hearts that are pure and righteous, a connection Jesus captures when he says, "Blessed are the pure in heart, for they will see God" (5:8). Having hearts that love God and others fulfills the Law and results in a purified and holy people (see 5:21-48). In contrast, the Pharisees' fixation with external practices to maintain ritual purity, while rooted in a desire to be a holy people, cannot deal with inner attitudes of the heart. "This stress on the heart, on interior life of religion, on intention and attitude, is indeed found throughout Matthew and is a chief characteristic of the whole of his Gospel" (Davies and Allison 1991, 539). Wesley contended that outward acts of piety must be linked with purity of intention. If not, believers will "place all religion in attending the prayers of the church, in receiving the Lord's Supper, in hearing sermons, and reading books of piety; neglecting meantime the end of all these, the love of God and their neighbor" ("Upon our Lord's Sermon on the Mount" in Wesley 1984, 1:593). Purified hearts that love God and neighbor fully should characterize the life of any disciple.

15:21-39

K. The Ministry of the Messiah outside of Israel (15:21-39)

BEHIND THE TEXT

Jesus now retreats to Gentile territory to manifest God's reign. Matthew's first reference to Gentiles is the magi (2:1-2), and Jesus first enters Gentile lands in the region of the Gadarenes (8:28-34). After he healed the servant of a Roman centurion (8:5-10), he predicted that Gentiles would join faithful Jews at the messianic banquet (8:11-12). Matthew's Jesus has come to save Israel from their sins (1:21), but he is also the Messiah who forms a new Israel. This new Israel will include others who will participate in Israel's vocation of being a blessing to the nations (Gen 12:1-3; Isa 49:6). He will commission his followers to do the same (Matt 28:19-20).

Jesus now heals a Gentile's daughter (15:22-28) and then both heals and feeds a multitude of Gentiles (vv 29-39). France comments that "the whole of the second half of ch. 15 thus puts into practice the message of its first half, the relaxation of the Jewish 'purity' culture which had hitherto kept Jew and Gentile apart" (2007, 591). In Jesus, the two become one purified people of God.

I. Healing of the Canaanite Woman's Daughter (15:21-28)

IN THE TEXT

■ **21-24** Jesus now withdraws "from that place," possibly the area around Gennesaret (see 14:34), the last locality that Matthew mentions. This is the third time that he withdraws after confrontation (12:15) or the prospect of it (14:13). He retreats to **the region of Tyre and Sidon** (15:21). Davies and Allison argue that Jesus has not left Jewish territory since the woman **from that vicinity came to him** (v 22*a*), and there were Jewish settlements further to the west allowing Jesus to withdraw from Galilee but remain in Israel (1991, 546; but see Luz 2001, 338-39). However, Matthew links the phrase **from that vicinity** with **the region of Tyre and Sidon**, coastal cities on the Mediterranean. Mark, on which Matthew is relying, locates Jesus in Gentile territory for this scene and the following feeding miracle (Mark 7:24-37).

The prophets often rebuke **Tyre and Sidon** for hostility toward Israel (→ Matt 11:21). Matthew refers to the woman who comes to Jesus as **Canaanite** (15:22*a*) and from the area of Tyre and Sidon (BDAG 2000, 1077). In Matthew, these cities function symbolically "to evoke scriptural images of the original inhabitants of Palestine as objects of scorn and enemies of Israel" (Nolland 2005, 632). Despite this, she **came to him, crying out, "Lord, Son of David, have mercy on me!"** (v 22*a*). Clearly, Jesus' fame has spread to other Gentile territories (4:25: Decapolis).

Her use of two christological titles, **Lord, Son of David**, reveals a profound understanding of Jesus' identity that transcends that of the disciples (14:33*b*), others that Jesus has healed (9:27*b*), and those that have witnessed this work (12:23). "Her confession of faith is a recognition of the saving intervention of the God of Israel through his messiah" (Nolland 2005, 632). Her request for help, coming from a Canaanite, in Gentile lands, also indicates that the gospel extends beyond Israel's borders.

Matthew has implied at numerous points that Jesus exercises divine prerogatives, such as forgiving sin (9:1-12) and calming the seas (8:23-29; see also 3:3). In Matthew, **Lord** often connotes a high Christology in which Jesus becomes part of the divine identity (7:21, 22; 8:2, 6, 21, 25; 9:28; 12:8; 14:28, 30; see Bauckham 1998a, 25-42). Further, her plea to **have mercy** echoes many psalms, in which the supplicant seeks Yahweh's mercy (6:2; 9:13; 25:6).

This woman pleads for **mercy** because her **daughter is demon-possessed and suffering terribly** (15:22*b*). In response, **Jesus did not answer a word** (v 23*a*)! He has never done this with those who request healing. He even responded to the Roman centurion, another Gentile, but did not offer to heal his servant immediately (8:7). His disciples are no better as they **urged him, "Send her away, for she keeps crying out after us"** (15:23*b*).

Jesus answers her, **I was sent only to the lost sheep of Israel** (v 24), which is in keeping with the message of the angel to Joseph that Jesus "will save his people from their sins" (1:21*b*) and his instruction to the disciples that they minister only "to the lost sheep of Israel" (10:6). The **lost sheep** refers to the nation of Israel who are without a shepherd and are, consequently, "harassed and helpless" (→ 9:36). France claims that Jesus makes this reply to the disciples and that the woman overhears it (2007, 593) but this is speculative.

■ **25-28** The woman is persistent and **knelt before him**, petitioning, **Lord, help me!** (v 25; see 8:2; 9:18). Her continued supplication again echoes language from the Psalms (69:6 [LXX; 7 HB] and 78:9) and continues to bolster Matthew's high Christology. Even this does not change his mind, because Jesus responds that **it is not right to take the children's bread and toss it to the dogs** (*kunarion*) (Matt 15:26).

The **children** refer to Israel (see Exod 4:22; Deut 14:1; Isa 1:2; Hos 11:1). "Dog" is a Jewish term of derision for Gentiles (→ Matt 7:6). Some commentators, such as Nolland, suggest that the woman refers to a domesticated dog versus a wild one, based on the Greek word Jesus uses (*kunarion*; 2005, 634), which creates a fitting contrast with **the children** of a household (Luz 2001, 340).

This woman astutely responds that **even the dogs eat the crumbs that fall from their master's table** (v 27), a common occurrence in the ancient world. Davies and Allison comment that "the woman dutifully recognizes both the priority of Israel and Jesus' obligation in that regard" (1991, 554). She also recognizes, however implicitly, the vocation of Israel to be a blessing to the nations (Gen 12:1-3; Isa 49:6). Both her persistence and wisdom prompt Jesus to acknowledge her **great faith** and, consequently, **her daughter was healed at that moment** (Matt 15:28).

This woman's **great faith** stands out against the "little faith" of the disciples (8:26; 16:8) and Peter (14:31). She knows that the saving power of Israel's God is at work in the Messiah, an insight that the religious leaders fail to believe and the disciples are starting to realize. While Jesus preserves the election of Israel in 15:24, 26 in keeping with his own vocation to save the lost sheep, faith in the Messiah demolishes the barriers of election and ethnicity that characterize Judaism in the 2T period.

Faith broadens the blessing of God to the nations and recovers what the purpose of God was all along. In context, the **bread** thrown to this woman in the healing of her daughter becomes a bridge between the bread Jesus miraculously multiplied for the Jews in 14:13-20 and the bread he will multiply again for the Gentiles in 15:32-39 (Nolland 2005, 634).

2. Feeding of the Four Thousand (15:29-39)

IN THE TEXT

■ **29-31** Jesus leaves the region of Tyre and Sidon, **went along the Sea of Galilee** and **then he went up on a mountainside and sat down** (v 29). Mountains are located on the eastern shores of the Sea of Galilee in the Decapolis. Matthew links the Sea of Galilee with the Gentiles receiving the gospel (4:13-16), and now his readers see this fulfilled (Gundry 1982, 318). After the feeding miracle (15:32-38), Jesus returns via boat to Magadan (v 39) in Jewish territory; the Pharisees and Sadducees requesting a sign confirms this (16:1). The exact location of Magadan and Mark's Dalmanutha are unknown but are likely near the Sea of Galilee (Davies and Allison 1991, 574).

After witnessing the sick healed, the Gentile crowds give praise to **the God of Israel** (15:31; but see Cousland 1999, 14-23, and France 2007, 597 n. 6). While Matthew does not explicitly indicate that Jesus is in Gentile lands, and he only ministers to Gentile individuals, Matthew's narrative placement of vv 29-39 following the healing of a Gentile suggests that this episode signals that Jesus brings blessing to the Gentiles. The way that Matthew summarizes healings that occurred in Jewish territory (14:34-36) may also point to the same work of the Messiah now in non-Jewish lands (15:30-31; France 2007, 597; see also Gundry 1982, 317-19). This view supports the theological coherence of Matt 15.

The last time Jesus went up a mountain was in 5:1-2. Now **great crowds** come **bringing the lame, the blind, the crippled, the mute and many others, and laid them at his feet; and he healed them** (15:30). The crowds have already come to Jesus from the Decapolis for healing (see 4:23) and now he comes to them. Matthew repeats this list in 15:31 to highlight the success of Jesus' healing ministry: **the mute speaking, the crippled made well, the lame walking and the blind seeing** (v 31*a*). The crowds are **amazed** at witnessing this and **praised the God of Israel** (v 31*b*).

The reign of God inaugurated by the Messiah in the land of Israel is equally available to those outside of the nation. With the exception of healing the **crippled**, Jesus performs each of these miracles in Israel (mute: 9:32-33; lame: 21:41; blind: 9:27-30; Davies and Allison 1991, 568). These are "the deeds of the Messiah" (11:2), whose mission is first to the lost sheep but also to the nations.

Just as in 11:5, 15:31 echoes Isa 35:5-6*a* [LXX]: "Then the eyes of the blind [*tuphlos*] shall be opened, and the ears of the deaf [*kōphos*] shall hear; then the lame [*chōlos*] shall leap like a deer, and the tongue of stammerers shall be clear" (NETS). This passage shares three terminological correspondences with Matt 15:31: "blind" (*tuphlos*), "deaf"/"mute" (*kōphos*), and "lame" (*chōlos*), which may point to an allusion. Isaiah 35 culminates with the redeemed exiles coming to Zion (v 10). If Matthew is alluding to this passage, it supports Zion themes discussed below and "the reader is reminded that in Jesus' healings the time for the fulfilment of the Isaianic promises has dawned" (Nolland 2005, 639). Exile is ending.

Davies and Allison argue that healing on a mountain evokes Zion theology from the OT in which *Jews* come to the presence of God to be healed. They assert that "in Jewish expectation, Zion is the eschatological gathering site of scattered Israel, a place of healing, and the place of the messianic feast" (1991, 566; see also Donaldson 1985, 128-31).

Other "Zion" texts depict the Gentiles coming as well. Davies and Allison cite Mic 4:6-7 as evidence for Zion as a place of healing, but it is healing for Israel *and* the nations (see Mic 4:1-5; see also Isa 60:1-3 for the gathering of Israel and Gentiles to Zion). The scene in Matt 15:29-31 foreshadows the last mountain on which Jesus commissions his followers to make disciples of "all nations" and asserts that his presence will be "with [them] always" (28:16-20), the latter of which evokes Zion texts as well where the redeemed are in the presence of God.

■ **32-33** The two feeding stories (14:13-21; 15:32-39) form a type-scene in Matthew in which both not only share common themes and terms but also exhibit differences that are thematically important. Unlike the first feeding account in which the crowd had only been with Jesus for a day (14:15), this Gentile crowd has been with him for **three days and have** [had] **nothing to eat**
15:32-39 (15:32*a*). Jesus does not want to dismiss them on an empty stomach or **they may collapse on the way** (v 32*b*). He does not ask the disciples to feed them as he does in 14:16, but they gather that Jesus wishes to provide food, and then they question where they would find **bread in this remote place to feed such a crowd** (v 33*b*). Surprisingly, they do not ask Jesus to perform a feeding miracle as he did a short time earlier. It is less surprising that Jesus rebukes them later for misunderstanding his teaching and being concerned about having no bread (16:8-11; France 2007, 602).

■ **34-39** Jesus asks the disciples, **How many loaves do you have?** (15:34*a*) and they respond, **Seven . . . and a few small fish** (v 34*b*). The use of a diminutive in Greek for **small fish** underscores the deficient amount of food for such a large crowd and sets up the thoroughly miraculous nature of the feeding. After seating the crowd (→ 14:19), Jesus **took the seven loaves and the fish, and when he had given thanks** [*eucharisteō*]**, he broke them and gave them to the disciples, and they in turn to the people** (15:36).

Matthew's use of **given thanks** versus "blessed" (*eulogeō*; 14:19) "gives the text a perfect parallel in the Eucharistic tradition preserved in Luke 22:19 and 1 Cor. 11:24" (Davies and Allison 1991, 573). This still reaffirms a connection with the Last Supper in which Jesus and his disciples will recline around a table, which anticipates a greater feast to come for both redeemed Jew and Gentile (→ 8:10-12; 14:15-21; 26:20-29).

The disciples collect **seven basketfuls of broken pieces** of leftover bread and fish (15:37*b*). Matthew's use of a different word for "baskets" (*spuris*), contrasted with *kophinos* in 14:20, may support a non-Jewish setting (→ 14:20). Jesus fed **four thousand men, besides women and children** (15:38). Allegorical interpretations for the meaning of the **seven** baskets and **four thousand** fed (see Luz 2001, 346) are unconvincing. France wonders if the four thousand Gentiles being fed here and the five thousand Jews in the first story preserves Matthew's emphasis on the priority of the latter (2007, 600). Jesus sends the crowd on its way and he sails back to Jewish territory in **the vicinity of Magadan** (v 39).

FROM THE TEXT

Jesus' healing of a Canaanite woman's daughter in Gentile territory (15:21-29) aptly follows the ritual purity controversy in which the Pharisees defend their traditional notions of what defiles (vv 1-20). Jesus, however, incisively labels them as hypocrites because genuine contamination comes from evil hearts, which they have exhibited, for which their adherence to scribal teaching on ritual purity offers no solution.

Assuming that Jesus continues his ministry in Gentile territory with the feeding of the four thousand, he models for his disciples how the boundaries erected by the Pharisees of avoiding anything unclean come down under his reign as Messiah. Building on the healing of the Canaanite woman's daughter, Jesus heals all of the Gentiles brought to him and then gifts that same crowd with a bountiful provision so that all are full.

What does it mean for holiness people to question the legitimacy of boundaries that we have erected so that we do not become defiled? What are the essentials upon which we must all agree (e.g., beliefs and practices) that distinguish us as set-apart people and what are nonessentials? Having established this, what are the ways in which we as Christ's faithful followers can creatively minister to those whom other Christians may consider "unclean"? These questions need to be asked again and again lest we miss the forest for the trees!

L. Request for a Sign (16:1-4)

BEHIND THE TEXT

In this narrative and the one following it, Jesus' warning against the teaching of the Pharisees and Sadducees (16:5-12) marks the conclusion of his Galilean ministry and the beginning of his journey to Jerusalem. The Pharisees have repeatedly challenged Jesus (9:11, 34; 12:2, 24, 28; 15:1-2) and even plotted his death (12:14). These two narratives, then, function as "a kind of final indictment of the Pharisees (and Sadducees) in the first main part of the Gospel" (Hagner 1995, 457).

IN THE TEXT

■ **1** Jesus returns to Jewish territory, Magadan (15:39), and **the Pharisees and Sadducees** test (*peirazō*) him **by asking him to show them a sign from heaven.** These same leaders were warned by John to "produce fruit in keeping with repentance" (3:8). These groups have different beliefs but they unite "against what is perceived to be potentially threatening to the status and welfare of each group" (Hagner 1995, 455). They did not heed John's words and now test Jesus just as the devil did (4:1-11). Matthew's use of *peirazō* aligns them with the supramundane opposition to Jesus. Peter will do the same in the following narrative (16:23). They test him in order to find "something that could be used against him" (Hagner 1995, 455). The Pharisees will do this again in 19:3 and 22:18.

The Pharisees and scribes have already requested a sign, but Jesus refused (see 12:38-39). They want **a sign from heaven**, that is, a sign from God himself (see 6:9; Hagner 1993, 455), or, perhaps a cosmic sign (Luz 2001, 348). But the Pharisees, according to Matthew, would not have accepted it even if God had provided one. In fact, they fail to see that Jesus is himself the sign from heaven. Their hostility is unrelenting here and elsewhere (see 12:3, 10, 14, 24). The Sadducees will later challenge Jesus on their own (22:23-32).

■ **2-4** Jesus responds with a proverb about interpreting the weather, **the appearance of the sky** (v 3*b*). When the sun sets and **the sky is red**, the clouds from stormy weather have moved off to the east, and so **it will be fair weather** (v 2). Early the next day, if **the sky is red and overcast**, a front is moving in from the west, and **today, it will be stormy** (v 3*a*). Then Jesus says, **You know how to interpret the appearance of the sky, but you cannot interpret the signs of the times** (v 3*b*). He implies that they have been given many **signs** but miss them, especially what God is doing now through his Messiah (see 8:1—9:34; 11:2-6). The temple leaders will respond to Jesus with similar incomprehension (21:23).

Jesus labels the Pharisees and Sadducees **a wicked and adulterous generation** for seeking **a sign** (16:4; see 12:39). This language aligns them with Israel's rebellion by failing to trust in Yahweh's saving plans. It will receive no sign, **except the sign of Jonah**. Although Matthew leaves out "prophet," in contrast with 12:39, the import remains: Jesus is a prophet like Jonah who announces judgment on the unrepentant and rebellious (→ 11:21-23). Jesus quickly withdraws after this confrontation (16:4*b*; see 4:12; 12:15; 14:13). He will no longer speak to the Galilean leaders.

M. Warning about the Pharisees and Sadducees (16:5-12)

IN THE TEXT

■ **5-6** Jesus and the disciples **went across the lake**, probably to Bethsaida, from where they would go to Caesarea Philippi, the setting for the next scene (16:13-28). For this journey, **the disciples forgot to take bread** (v 5), a detail that explains the disciples' misguided response to Jesus in v 7.

Since they are together, Jesus teaches them: **Be careful . . . Be on your guard against the yeast of the Pharisees and Sadducees** (v 6). Leaven has a positive metaphorical sense in 13:33, but it can also denote a corrupting influence (Hagner 1995, 459). The imagery comes from the Passover ritual (France 2007, 609 n. 9; Exod 12:15, 19); for Paul, it signals an infectious moral corruption (1 Cor 5:6-8). In the rabbinic tradition, leaven represents evil inclinations.

The warning about the Pharisees and Sadducees follows their confrontation with Jesus, so they are aligned with "a wicked and adulterous generation" (Matt 16:4). The connotations of leaven, coupled with Matthew's negative portrayal of these leaders, leaves little doubt that their teaching is evil and at odds with the Messiah's ministry.

■ **7-12** The disciples take Jesus' warning literally: **It is because we didn't bring any bread** (v 7). Jesus hears this and chastises them for it, but not quite as harshly as in Mark (see Mark 8:17-21): **You of little faith, why are you talking among yourselves about having no bread?** (v 8*b*). **Little faith** (*oligopistos*) has characterized the disciples earlier when they doubted Jesus' ability to rescue them from the stormy sea (8:26) and then Peter when he began to sink after having taken a few steps on the water (14:31). In 6:30, it refers to those who doubt God's provision to meet physical need, whichs seem to capture its subsequent uses in Matthew.

Jesus then asks, **Do you still not understand?** (v 9*a*), a question that has "the effect of sharpening the rebuke" (Hagner 1995, 459). Earlier, Jesus declared that "understanding" has been given to the disciples and withheld from others (13:11, 16-17). France's assessment is correct: "Perception and dullness will continue to jostle in Matthew's portrayal of the disciples as they wrestle with the demanding new values of the kingdom of heaven" (2007, 608). At the end "they understood" (v 12*a*; Davies and Allison 1991, 588), but more incomprehension lies ahead (e.g., 16:23).

Jesus then asks if the disciples **remember** (*mnēmoneuō*; 16:9*a*) the miraculous provision in the two feeding stories (vv 9*b*-10). The verb *mnēmoneuō* connotes more than just recalling a memory but "being mindful, paying heed [such that the disciples] . . . should engage its implications for the present" (Davies and Allison 1991, 591; see also BDAG 2000, 655). If Jesus needs bread, the disciples should know that he will not need yeast belonging to the Pharisees and Sadducees as an ingredient.

He then asks, **How is it you don't understand that I was not talking to you about bread?** (v 11*a*). Forming an inclusio, Jesus exhorts the disciples, yet again, to watch out for **the yeast of the Pharisees and Sadducees** (vv 11*b*, 6). Mark ends the account at this point, but Matthew explains that the disciples understood that Jesus was not speaking about literal yeast but, rather, **the teaching of the Pharisees and Sadducees** (v 12*b*).

Pharisaic and Sadducean beliefs have crucial differences (→ Matt 3:7-10 sidebar, "Pharisees and Sadducees"), so the teaching to which Jesus refers is their unified opposition to himself. They see his words and deeds as a threat. Hagner suggests their teaching is centered on a shared messianic nationalist agenda (1995, 46), but this is unlikely for the Sadducees, who are not looking for current renewal through God's Messiah.

FROM THE TEXT

Both the disciples and the religious leaders fail to understand Jesus' identity. While the disciples eventually understand, they initially fail to trust him. This failure is on a much larger scale with the Pharisees and Sadducees. They desire to overthrow him. Both accounts are a reminder that no matter the knowledge one acquires, "in the realm of the knowledge of God [it is still possible] to exist in . . . darkness" (Hagner 1995, 456). The issue both for the disciples and Jesus' opponents is their inability to trust in him. It is not surprising that Jesus calls children "the greatest in the kingdom of heaven" (18:4) for their ability to trust wholeheartedly in him.

IV. JOURNEY TO JERUSALEM: MATTHEW 16:13—20:34

With Jesus and the disciples in Caesarea Philippi, Matthew focuses on the revelation of Jesus' identity as the servant-Messiah and the disciples' inability to grasp this vocation. Mark goes to greater lengths to highlight their incomprehension (see Mark 10:35). Jesus is about to meet his demise in Jerusalem, where "they will confront the hostile power of the religious authorities of Israel" (France 2007, 628). Jesus must prepare his disciples. His fate demands faithful followers who value the kingdom over their own lives. Matthew's fourth discourse considers the inner life of the nascent Jewish Christian community (Matt 18), but the impending suffering of Jesus and the attendant cost of following him dominates the teaching (17:9-13, 22-23; 18:1-5; 19:1-2, 16-30; 20:17-19).

A. Jesus Is the Messiah (16:13-23)

BEHIND THE TEXT

This section begins with a dialogue between Jesus and his disciples and then between Jesus and Peter. Peter declares that Jesus is "the Messiah, the Son of the living God" (16:16). Jesus in turn responds with a beatitude and a description of Peter's role in the building of "my church" (vv 17-19). After warning the disciples to tell no one about his messiahship (v 20), Jesus predicts his suffering in Jerusalem (v 21), to which Peter strongly objects (v 22). This elicits a sharp rebuke from Jesus (v 23) who then talks about the cost of following him, for which there is future reward (vv 24-28). Despite the acrimony between Jesus and Peter, this section serves "to record the establishment of a new community, one which will acknowledge Jesus' true identity and thereby become the focus of God's activity in salvation-history" (Davies and Allison 1991, 603).

IN THE TEXT

■ **13** After crossing the Sea of Galilee, Jesus and his disciples journey northward **to the region of Caesarea Philippi**. This region is the most northern part of the historic land of Israel, once belonging to the tribe of Dan. Caesarea Philippi is outside of the land of Israel and is a well-known locale for the worship of pagan deities, especially the Greek god Pan. It is here that Herod the Great also built a temple in honor of Caesar Augustus. Peter's confession in v 16 that Jesus is the Messiah, the Son of the "living God," challenges the lifeless idols of this pagan land and its imperial cult (Brower 2012, 227).

When **Jesus** arrives in **Caesarea Philippi, he asked his disciples, "Who do people say that the Son of Man is?"** (v 13; → Matt 8:20 sidebar, "Son of Man"). Jesus refers to himself as **the Son of Man** several times (see 9:6; 10:23; 11:19; 12:8, 32, 40; 13:37, 41), but there is little indication that this is a widely recognized title. France suggests that "Matthew's decision to use 'the Son of Man' here perhaps reflects his awareness of the open-ended and puzzling nature of this designation as used by Jesus during his ministry" (2007, 615).

■ **14-16** The responses demonstrate that "the Son of Man" was not a title but functioned as a prophetic category: **Some say John the Baptist; others say Elijah; and still others, Jeremiah or one of the prophets** (v 14). **Elijah** was expected to return in the future (Mal 4:5-6 [3:23-24 HB]; Sir 48:10) but, for Matthew, he has come in **John the Baptist** (→ Matt 3:4). Possibly, the mighty deeds Jesus performed evoke **Elijah** for some.

Jesus experienced a similar rejection to **John** (see 13:57*b* and 14:1-12); he links his ministry with John's (11:16-19; 21:23-27). Reference to **Jeremiah**, not found in Mark or Luke, may derive from the message of judgment Jesus directs toward the temple (Menken 1984, 23). Menken suggests that the reference to

Jeremiah intentionally reflects Matthew's emphasis on this prophet, who "is the prophet of the rejection and the passion of the Messiah" (1984, 23). All the proposals by the crowd find some basis in Jesus' ministry.

Jesus then asks the disciples: **But what about you? . . . Who do you say that I am?** (Matt 16:15). **Simon Peter** responds, **You are the Messiah, the Son of the living God** (v 16). For once, the disciples are correct. Peter, as spokesperson, believes that Jesus is the Messiah in light of what they have witnessed (→ 11:2-6 for the connection between messiahship and mighty deeds).

The title **the Son of the living God**, along with the lengthy response by Jesus, are unique to Matthew (see Mark 8:29*b*). This highlights the familial relationship that Jesus as Messiah has with God (see Matt 3:17; 11:27; 17:5*b*). "Son of God" was a designation for Israel's kings, which coheres with Matthew's messiahship emphasis (see 26:63*b*). In 2 Sam 7:14, Israel's Davidic king is God's son, and in Ps 2:7, God addresses the Messiah as his son. The DSS also make this connection, likely due to these texts (4Q174; France 2007, 618). Two demoniacs address Jesus as "Son of God" (Matt 8:29), and the disciples make the pronouncement when he calms the stormy sea (vv 26-27).

This declaration, occurring in the middle of Matthew, confirms for his audience that Jesus is his anointed king with whom he shares a unique relationship (see 3:17). The adjective **living** reflects the Jewish polemic against pagan worship of lifeless gods (see Wis 14:8-31; 2 Macc 7:33; 15:4; 3 Macc 6:28).

■ **17-20 Jesus replied, "Blessed are you Simon son of Jonah, for this was not revealed to you by flesh and blood, but by my Father in heaven"** (v 17). **Son** 16:17-20
of Jonah may refer to Peter's father John (see John 1:42). **Jonah** likely results from its Semitic version (*Iōannēs*), from which either Jonah or John can be rendered in Greek (France 2007, 620). But Davies and Allison think **son of Jonah** is intentional because Peter's declaration results from divine prophetic inspiration (1991, 622; see also Gundry 1982, 332), or it may recall the prophetic/preaching ministry of Jonah himself (Keener 1999, 426; → Matt 12:39-41).

Peter receives the *makarism* or "beatitude" because he is the recipient of divine revelation, similar to Jesus himself (11:25-27; see 13:16-17; France 2007, 619). Jesus addresses only Peter ("you" in 16:17-19 is singular). France attributes Matthew's emphasis on Peter to his foundational role in the formation of the church as recorded in Acts (2007, 613). In light of Matt 13:16, Luz notes that "it is important to observe once again here that in 16:16-17 not only Peter but all the disciples were called blessed by Jesus" (2001, 362).

Human reasoning, **flesh and blood** (v 17), is in contrast to divine revelation (see 1 Cor 15:50; Eph 6:12). Peter's declaration is from Jesus' **Father in heaven** (Matt 16:17*b*). The heavenly Father reveals truth to his children, confirming the attentiveness of God that Jesus depicts in 6:4, 6, 8, 18, 32.

In 16:18, Jesus connects the name of **Peter** (*Petros*), "rock" (*Kēphâ*) in Aramaic, with his identity as **this rock** (*petra*) [upon which] **I will build my church, and the gates of Hades will not overcome it**. There is no surviving evidence that *Petros* was a proper name in ancient times (France 2007, 621), which renders its use here poignant. Early in Acts, Peter is the leading figure of the early church and becomes "the initiator of the new direction which made the community of Jesus followers distinct from its Jewish heritage (Acts 10-11)—'*my ekklēsia*'" (France 2007, 613).

The **church** that Jesus establishes in his ministry does not refer to the later institution that distinguishes itself from Judaism but, rather, is the formation of a new Jewish community that is founded on the shed blood of Jesus and, as such, is the locus of God's saving activity through his Messiah (→ 26:20-29). In the LXX, the Greek terms for "church" (*ekklēsia*) and "synagogue" (*synagōgē*) are translated from "the Hebrew *qahal*, denoting the 'assembly or congregation' of Israel" (Schrage 1979, 7:802; see also Davies and Allison 1991, 629). This new congregation of Israel is in continuity with the OT people of God through which God's saving promises are now revealed.

The use of **rock** imagery to describe the foundation on which Jesus builds his **church** recalls Jewish texts where stones or rocks refer to sacred places or the architecture of the Jerusalem temple (Gen 28:22; Isa 28:16; Zech 4:7-10; 1QS 8:4-8; 4Q164). This imagery also describes the dwelling of God's people (1 Cor 3:10-11; Eph 2:20; 1 Pet 2:4-8). The Twelve and those that join them become the new dwelling of God, a new holy temple in the world, and in this community the exalted Christ dwells (Matt 1:23; 18:20; 28:20).

As for this community, Jesus continues, **the gates of Hades will not over-**
16:17-20 **come it** (16:18*b*). Hades is the dwelling place of the dead, much like Sheol. In a number of texts, the gates of Hades/Sheol denote the place of mortal danger or death (e.g., Isa 38:10; Wis 16:13; *Pss. Sol.* 16:2). France indicates that "the 'gates' thus represent the imprisoning power of death: death will not be able to imprison and hold the living church of God" (2007, 624), just like Jesus himself overcame death "on the third day" (→ Matt 16:21, below) and promises life for his disciples (→ v 25, below).

Others suggest that **the gates** represent the realm of demons whose assault on the church will not be victorious (Davies and Allison 1991, 632-34). In 2T literature, the underworld is the habitation of evil spirits (*1 En.* 22:1-14; 51:1; 103:5-8; *Jub.* 5:10; 22:22; Josephus, *J.W.* 3.374-75; 1QH 6:22-29). **Hades** is an active force in light of similar grammatical structures in the LXX (Davies and Allison 1991, 633). It is likely that the **gates of Hades** refers to both realms: death and the demonic.

Jesus gives to Peter **the keys of the kingdom of heaven** (Matt 16:19*a*), which represent an authority exclusive to him. Davies and Allison argue that the **keys** relate to the gates mentioned in v 18: "In other words, both vv 18-19 have to do with doors or gates" (1991, 632) and, hence, the delegated authority to open and close them (see Isa 22:22*b*: "what he opens no one can shut, and what he shuts, no one can open." Keener holds that the authority given to Peter and the disciples enables them to welcome people into the kingdom (1990,

430). Peter and the church open a door to the kingdom of heaven for those outside. In contrast, the scribes and Pharisees lock people out (Matt 23:13).

Jesus continues, **Whatever you bind on earth will be bound in heaven, and whatever you loose on earth will be loosed in heaven** (v 19*b*). Joel Marcus argues that binding and loosing is the release of the power of the kingdom to combat the demonic realm expressed in "the gates of Hades" (1988, 443-55). Jesus gives his disciples authority over that which plagues helpless and harassed Israel, such as demonic influence and sickness (10:1-8). The keys represent the authority to exclude hostile forces from the community. Or, they "unlock the gates of heaven . . . [which] will swing open, and the kingly power of God . . . will break forth from heaven to enter the arena against the demons" (Marcus 1988, 455).

France argues that the object of binding and loosing are "things, issues, which are being tied or untied, not people as such" (2007, 626). This is supported by the rabbinic literature (e.g., *b. Sabb.* 31a-b), along with 18:18, and coheres with the context since Jesus has just warned against the false teaching of the Pharisees and Sadducees (Davies and Allison 1991, 639), the ones who "shut the door of the kingdom in people's faces" (23:13) due to the onerous demands of the oral law (23:4). Luz comments that "Peter's task is to open the kingdom of heaven for people, and to do it by means of his binding interpretation of the law" (2001, 365), which is now fulfilled by loving God and neighbor (→ 22:37-40).

France prefers a future perfect passive translation of "bind/loose" that is rendered "will have been bound/loosed," since this portrays Peter as "not the initiator of new decisions for the church, but the faithful steward of God's prior decisions . . . [and so] the saying becomes a promise not of divine *endorsement*, but of divine *guidance*" (2007, 627).

The more difficult reading, as printed in the NIV, is likely correct: Peter and the disciples (in 18:18) are initiating activity that heaven then endorses. Matthew is clear that God is the one who reveals and leads his people (e.g., 18:18-20), but the language of binding and loosing beginning with the church highlights the important role that his people play in the enactment of his saving purposes whether it be manifesting his reign over sickness and death or preserving orthodox teaching.

Jesus orders the **disciples not to tell anyone that he was the Messiah** (16:20), lest his ministry be cut short by the religious leaders before he gets to Jerusalem, where other messianic pretenders have risen and fallen (see Wright 1992, 170-81).

■ **21-23** In v 22 Peter refuses to accept that Jesus must suffer and die at the hands of the temple leadership (v 21). But this is his messianic vocation, unlike violent messianic pretenders, and the militant messiah of the *Psalms of Solomon* (see 17:23-27). In contrast, Jesus **must go to Jerusalem and suffer many things at the hands of** the temple leaders, **the elders, the chief priests and the**

teachers of the law (16:21*a*). These temple leaders orchestrate the crucifixion of Jesus (26:3-4, 57).

A messiah who suffers has no precedent in the OT or other 2T Jewish literature, and Jesus will continually remind the disciples about this plight (17:22-23; 20:18-19). He **must . . . suffer many things**. The implication of **must** is that this is the will of his Father (see 26:23-24, 31, 54, 56): "The Son of Man will go *just as it is written* about him" (26:24).

But there is no explicit scriptural language that states this. Rather, this redemptive suffering evokes other images from Jewish tradition. First, he is the Suffering Servant from Isa 53 whose "life [is] an offering for sin" (v 10) and who bears the "iniquities" of Israel (v 11), which is a role Jesus introduces in Matt 12:15-21.

Second, his death "for many" (20:28) echoes the Maccabean martyrs who suffer for the sins of the nation (2 Macc 7:18). In 4 Maccabees, a later text, the suffering of the martyrs atones for the nation (4 Macc 6:28-29). Third, the righteous sufferer depicted in Pss 22 and 69 also informs the suffering of Jesus. The righteous sufferer endures trial and hardship out of obedience to God and is later vindicated by him, which parallels the resurrection of Jesus. This background becomes explicit in Matt 20:28 when Jesus indicates that "the Son of Man" will "give his life as a ransom for many," and when he explains the redemptive purpose of his shed blood in 26:28.

The death of Jesus is not the end of the story, however, because **on the**
16:21-23 **third day** he will **be raised to life** (16:21*b*). At his resurrection, and specifically, when the disciples are reunited with him in Galilee, the holy community established by his resurrection is inaugurated (see 26:31-32). The passive **be raised** implies God's vindication of the Messiah.

France diminishes any echo of Hos 6:2 in the phrase **on the third day** (2007, 633; likewise Nolland 2005, 687), despite the terms shared by Matthew and the LXX. Still, the resurrection marks the inauguration of a new community (see Matt 26:31-32); Hosea promised the restoration of God's people "on the third day" (Hos 6:2*b*). The reuniting of the disciples with Jesus after his resurrection marks the formation of a new holy community centered around the resurrected Messiah (→ Matt 26:31-32).

Peter protests the servant-Messiah vocation of Jesus: **This shall never happen to you!** (16:22*b*), which he delivers as a stern **rebuke** (v 22*a*; see 8:26 and 17:18 for other uses of "rebuke"). Luz bases Peter's rebuke not so much on the prospect of Jesus' suffering but that Peter himself and the disciples will share the same fate (2001, 382). They do desire glory (20:21), but it is doubtful that they even understand that Jesus needs to suffer, let alone themselves. In response, Jesus rebukes Peter: **Get behind me, Satan!** (16:23*a*), just as he rebukes Satan himself in 4:10.

Peter is echoing the temptation of Satan to fulfill the will of the Father without the cross. Peter, who was just blessed for his divinely received confession in 16:16, now relies on his own wisdom. The kingdom of this world has no place for redemptive suffering and death. Opposition between the powers of this age and Jesus is dominant in the Gospels. Satan tempted Jesus at the beginning with the offer of power and authority that did not include suffering. Peter's rebuke of Jesus reflects the same idea, which earns him the label **Satan**. This rebuke contrasts sharply with the divine origin of Peter's confession in v 16.

Peter is now **a stumbling block** (v 23*b*). If Jesus were to heed Peter, he will deviate from the mission of God. Peter has **merely human concerns** and does **not have in mind the concerns of God** (v 23*b*; → 13:41). The "'rock' on which the church is to be built proves instead to be a stumbling block" (France 2007, 635). What a change from Peter's declaration in 16:16!

FROM THE TEXT

There is a rich, and complicated, tradition of interpretation reflected in Orthodox, Catholic, and Protestant sources on the meaning and relevance of 16:18-19 (see Luz 2001, 373-75). Verse 18, in which Jesus identifies Peter as "this rock [on which] I will build my church," is the basis for apostolic succession in both Orthodox and Catholic traditions. In the latter, papal authority, as embodied in the pope, is accorded the same authority as Peter himself, which he received directly from Jesus. According to Vatican II, "'God's word . . . was entrusted to the apostles by Christ the Lord and the Holy Spirit' and handed down by them 'to the successors . . . in its full purity'" (cited in Luz 2001, 370). Luz observes that later Catholic sources in the post-Constantine era prioritized the role of v 18 in order to legitimate the papacy.

Such is not the case in the few centuries after Christ. Origen, for example, refers to Peter as a model disciple but attributes no unique authority to him. In some texts of the fourth and fifth centuries, "The idea of an almost mystically understood identity of the Roman bishop with Peter is often more important than the idea of succession" (Luz 2001, 371).

However, it was not long before the Catholic church espoused a papacy where Peter's unique status lived on through succeeding popes. A number of historical factors, such as the rise of certain heresies and the emerging dominance of the Roman church, necessitated this. When the pope made decrees, he did so not on his own authority but rather from Peter's whose authority the pope exercised. This meant that the pope, in light of v 19, has the ability to forgive sins and excommunicate. Such decrees are considered to be "God's word."

The Protestant Reformers, along with some Orthodox thinkers, argued that the rock is Peter's confession that Jesus is God's Son or that the rock is his faith (Luz 2001, 373). Peter then becomes a model of faith in Christ, which is reflected in his confession. His subsequent denial of Christ's suffering reveals his human weakness and thereby becomes one with whom subsequent Christians identify: discipleship is characterized by victory and difficulty. The church of Jesus Christ started with a less than perfect group of disciples, to whom Christ remained faithful despite their moments of faithlessness and disbelief. A church founded upon disciples like these should be a source of hope and encouragement for Christians today.

Further, while Peter is a central figure in this passage and in the subsequent early Christian period, the imagery of Peter as "this rock" on which "I will build my church" ultimately points to the formation of a holy community founded upon the sacrificial work of Jesus on the cross (see 20:28; 26:20-29) and "the gates of Hades will not overcome it" (16:18*b*). Although Peter receives the keys in v 19*a* and what he binds/looses on earth is bound/loosed in heaven (v 19*b*), the community "binds/looses" under the guiding presence of the exalted Christ (18:18-20).

In the time of Matthew's audience, likely in the 80s CE, Peter is now martyred, and the church carries on the work once the responsibility of the apostles. The Christian church has a great responsibility to be faithful stewards of both the teaching of the gospel of Jesus Christ and its embodiment in the world, demonstrating grace and mercy wherever and whenever God's people come together. She should never become an avenue for the divine sanctioning of politically motivated actions or ideals in our world, as has occurred in church history, rooted in misinterpretation of 16:18-19.

B. The Cost of Following the Messiah (16:24-28)

16:24-26

BEHIND THE TEXT

Jesus' teaching on discipleship in 16:24-26, coupled with the description of his fate (v 21), sets the tone for the journey to Jerusalem. "The shadow of the cross thus falls across this whole southward journey, as Jesus tries to get his disciples to understand the paradoxical and unwelcome nature of his mission" (France 2007, 628).

However, Jesus will be raised again, just as those who lose their life for him "will find it" (v 25*b*). Further, reward will come when the Son of Man appears (v 27) and manifests "his kingdom" before the deaths of some of his followers (v 28). The prospect of future reward for various trials and tribulations, including martyrdom, should encourage the disciples in the present.

IN THE TEXT

■ **24-26** Jesus **then** explains the implications of his servant-Messiah vocation: **Whoever wants to be my disciple must deny themselves and take up their cross and follow me** (v 24). The present tense of **follow** (*akoloutheō*) indicates that discipleship is a daily choice and should reflect "determination to stick to the chosen path" (Davies and Allison 1991, 671). He is calling them to live cruciform lives defined by the great sacrifice that he will make in Jerusalem.

Jesus may be preparing his followers for martyrdom in vv 24-25 (France 2007, 636). But he is primarily dealing with the heart and its affections (see 10:38). Jesus' followers must make a daily choice to keep Jesus and his commands a priority. Hagner comments, "To deny oneself—indeed to die to oneself—this is what it means to 'follow' Jesus" (1995, 483).

Jesus explains why they should choose a life of self-denial: **For whoever wants to save their life will lose it, but whoever loses their life for me will find it** (16:25). The disciples are faced with two choices, each with different consequences. Those who seek personal security and comfort will surely **lose it** (see 19:21-22). Genuine followers of Jesus accept a life of sacrifice, and the original disciples learn this lesson after Jesus' resurrection. In his greatest moment of need, they desert him (26:56*b*), and his most vocal disciple, Peter, denies him three times (26:58, 69-75).

In contrast, those prepared to take up their cross and lose **their life** (*psuchē*) will find true life. The loss of **life** to which Jesus refers is life defined by selfish desire. However, the one who relinquishes this kind of life will receive new life both now and in the future; a life with God through his Spirit that focuses on "one's true being, and thus life that transcends death" (Hagner 1995, 484; → 10:39).

Jesus explains, by two rhetorical questions, the futility of desiring to save one's life. He first asks, **What good will it be for someone to gain the whole world, yet forfeit their soul?** (16:26*a*). Satan tempted Jesus with "all the kingdoms of the world and their splendor" (4:8) only if Jesus would worship 16:27-28
him in return (4:9). Giving into temptations such as this results in a forfeiture of the **soul** (16:26*b*) since the kingdom of this world has values and ideals at odds with the kingdom of heaven. See Jesus' earlier warning to his followers: "You cannot serve both God and money" (6:24*b*).

In the second question, he underscores the gravity of the decision: **Or what can anyone give in exchange for their soul?** (16:26*b*). The center of life with God both now and in the future can never be substituted by material things, no matter how alluring. Davies and Allison suggest that the second question is inspired by Ps 49:7-9 [8-10 HB], which speaks about the inability of humanity to effect their own redemption (1991, 674).

■ **27-28** In Matt 16:27, Jesus provides an eschatological rationale for obedience to him in the present: **For the Son of Man is going to come in his Father's glory with his angels, and then he will reward each person according to what they have done**. The statement evokes Dan 7:13-14 where "the one like a son of man" comes to the Ancient of Days to receive "authority, glory and sovereign power" (see Matt 10:23). Jesus has already exercised this "authority on earth to forgive sins" (9:6), and one day he will exercise authority to reward the faithfulness of his followers.

The line, **then he will reward each person according to what they have done** (16:27), shares language with Ps 62:12 [13 HB] and Prov 24:12 (see also

Sir 35:22 and *T. Job* 17:3). These texts reflect "a stereotyped phrase or expression" (Davies and Allison 1991, 676). Again, Jesus performs tasks specifically associated with Yahweh by rewarding the faithful (see Matt 9:6; 10:23; 13:41). The phrase **going** [*mellō*] **to come** can indicate imminence (16:27; see the use of "going" in 17:22; Hagner 1995, 485). This fits with Jesus' pronouncement that some will not experience **death before they see the Son of Man coming in his kingdom** (16:28).

Like Yahweh, the Son of Man is aided by **angels** (v 27) in his work (see Zech 14:5) and is associated with heavenly **glory** (see Exod 15:11; Isa 6:1-3). The description is reminiscent of celestial scenes in which Yahweh is portrayed as a judge in the presence of heavenly beings. The most relevant is Dan 7:10, in which the Ancient of Days judges beastly empires in his celestial abode surrounded by heavenly creatures (see also 1 Kgs 22:19-20; Ps 82:1; Isa 6). This background suggests a judicial context for the Son of Man's coming with the authority, like Yahweh, to reward his faithful for **what they have done**.

This reward by the Son of Man is unique to Matthew (see Matt 5:16; 6:1; 11:19). At the conclusion of the Sermon on the Mount, Jesus commends the one who "hears these words of mine and puts them into practice" (7:24) and, later, as eschatological judge, he offers a reward for the one who cared for "the least of these brothers and sisters of mine" (25:40) and punishment for those who did not. For Matthew, the gospel that is not embodied or lived out is no gospel at all and, in the present context, this involves giving one's life for Mes-
16:27-28 siah Jesus no matter the personal cost.

Jesus continues to speak about the future in 16:28, but the timing of this event, **the Son of Man coming in his kingdom** (v 28*b*) will occur in the lifetime of his disciples: **some who are standing here will not taste death** (v 28*a*). Jesus prefaces this prediction with a solemn opening: **Truly I tell you**, which emphasizes the gravity of what he is about to say.

But to which historical event is Jesus referring? Suggestions include Pentecost, the destruction of the Jerusalem temple, the transfiguration, Jesus' resurrection, and the Parousia, or second coming (Davies and Allison 1991, 677-79). The transfiguration is an unlikely candidate since Matthew indicates that this occurs "after six days" (17:1*a*). This temporal marker is too specific to cohere with the far less determinant phrase **will not taste death**.

Many commentators favor the Parousia (e.g., Davies and Allison 1991, 678-79; Gundry 1982, 341-42), supported by moments where it seems that the Son of Man's coming does depict this event (19:28; 25:31). Arguing against this, France claims that many of Jesus' predictions about his coming will be fulfilled in the lifetime of either his disciples or others to whom he speaks (2007, 637; 10:23; 16:28; 24:30, 34; 26:64). However, France is reticent to posit a historical event (2007, 641). It may be that some of these references (e.g., 10:23; 16:27-28; 24:30-34) are fulfilled in the lifetime of the disciples and function as temporal judgments in anticipation of his final eschatological appearing before all (19:28; 25:31).

The destruction of the temple seems the most likely option because it at least marks the *beginning* of vindication (→ 10:23) and occurs in the lifetime of **some** of those listening to Jesus. God's judgment on the institution that symbolizes hostility toward Jesus and his followers (→ 24:1-31) is their "reward" for what they have done. This is supported by the judicial scene in 16:27 and is foreshadowed by Jesus' symbolic halt of the sale of sacrificial animals in the Court of Gentiles. Here he declares that the temple has become "a den of robbers" (→ 21:13*b*). It is no longer fulfilling God's saving purposes and, moreover, in Matthew, it is a symbol of hostility toward Jesus Messiah whose leaders despise him (21:15). Through this event, Jesus comes as a judge **in his kingdom** anticipating "the renewal of all things, when the Son of Man sits on his glorious throne" (19:28*a*; see also *1 En.* 62:5).

FROM THE TEXT

Jesus teaches that discipleship has a great cost and that "he does not do something for those who do nothing" (Davies and Allison 1991, 681). In *The Cost of Discipleship*, Bonhoeffer coined the phrase "cheap grace" and defines it as "grace without price; grace without cost!" (1959, 45). To ignore this teaching of Jesus would constitute the clearest instance of "cheap grace." Death to self, a favored phrase of holiness preachers, begins with a full surrender of our own aspirations to the will of God as revealed in Christ Jesus. This involves a rejection of the values and ways of living of this world.

Single-minded devotion to Christ requires relinquishing those things that invite us to find peace and security outside of intimate relationship with him. While this is not an easy road and the cost is great, the reward is even greater since our hearts will, to use Paul's language, come "alive to God" (Rom 6:11). For Wesley, this type of devotion should characterize the life of every believer (Oden 2012, 244).

PART TWO: MATTHEW 17:1—28:20

Arseny Ermakov

C. The Transfiguration (17:1-13)

1. On the Mount of Transfiguration (17:1-8)

BEHIND THE TEXT

The transfiguration story is intrinsically linked with the previous chapter; it continues with the theme of the revelation of the true identity of Jesus. Peter's declaration of Jesus' messiahship and divine sonship (16:13-20) is paralleled and supported by God's confirmation: "This is my Son, whom I love" (17:5). Witnessing the divine glory in Jesus by Peter, James, and John (17:2) is seen by some as a fulfillment of the promise in 16:28 (France 2007, 644).

The placement of the transfiguration event in the narrative marks its importance. The voice from heaven at the baptism reveals Jesus' identity (3:13-17), right before his public ministry in Galilee. Now we hear the voice of God again as Jesus is on his way to Jerusalem, before the drama of the Messiah's suffering and death unfolds. The divine confirmation of Jesus' identity at these points serves as a guarantee that what happens next is in accordance with God's will. Jesus' practice of healing, cleansing, exorcism, and forgiveness of sins are grounded in the power of God, not of Beelzebul (12:22-32). Sufferings and the death of the Messiah are not an incomprehensible deviation from the plan (16:21-23) but the divinely ordained path for the Son of Man (17:22-23).

The transfiguration story is rich in OT allusions, predominantly taken from the Exodus story. Exodus 24 and 34 provide most of the parallels: six days (Matt 17:1↔Exod 24:16), three companions (Matt 17:2↔Exod 24:1), a high mountain (Matt 17:1↔Exod 24:12), a shiny face (Matt 17:2↔Exod 34:29), tents/huts (Matt 17:4↔Lev 23:27, 34) a cloud (Matt 17:5↔Exod 24:16), the voice of God from the cloud (Matt 17:5↔Exod 24:16), and the fearful reaction of the people (Matt 17:6 ↔ Exod 34:30). Other allusions could be detected as well: Gen 22, Ps 2, and Dan 10:5-9.

These striking parallels with Exodus lead some scholars to conclude that Matthew portrays Jesus as the new Moses (Allison 1993, 243-47). However, the allusions are ambiguous since they do not fit the Exodus pattern precisely. None of them provides the key for unlocking the meaning of the story. Moreover, there are no exact parallels to this event in biblical or other ancient traditions (Keener 2009, 437).

Matthew is not just describing Jesus in terms of Moses. But by weaving together images from Exodus and other traditions into the story and portraying the manifestation of the divine presence in similar terms to the Sinai theophany, Matthew actually redefines Jesus' identity. He is not just a prophet like Moses, he is greater than Moses.

The transfiguration story is bracketed by sayings about the last days (Matt 16:27-28 and 17:11-13). Jewish eschatological expectations create a context for the event. The appearance of Elijah and Moses on the mount (17:3)
17:1 is not accidental. Old Testament traditions envisage the coming of Elijah and a prophet like Moses in the last days (Keener 2009, 438). In this context, the transfiguration recasts and reinterprets the vision of the future in light of Jesus the Messiah, the Son of God, as well as providing a *proleptic* look into the days to come. The moment of Jesus' glorified appearance is a foretaste of the future coming of the Son of Man "in his Father's glory" (16:27).

IN THE TEXT

■ **1** Matthew introduces the episode with a brief time reference: **after six days**. On the one hand, it ties together the two episodes of the gradual revelation of Jesus' identity (16:13-27 and 17:1-8). On the other, it indicates a short time period between the prophetic pronouncement "some who are standing here will . . . see the Son of Man coming in his kingdom" (16:28). This is an anticipatory but not final fulfillment (Nolland 2005, 699).

The disciples' experience at the transfiguration is the second focal point. Jesus took with him three close disciples: **Peter, James and** his brother **John**. In spite of their lower status in relation to Moses, Elijah, and Jesus, the three play an important role. Every scene contains a reference to their experience of the event (France 2007, 643): Jesus **took** them (17:1), **led them up**, was "transfigured before them" (v 2); the heavenly figures appeared to them (v 3); they offered to build dwellings (v 4); the "cloud overshadowed them" (v 5

NRSV); God addressed them: "Listen to him!"; they were "overcome by fear" (v 6 NRSV); "Jesus came and touched them" and comforted them (v 7); "they looked up" (v 8); it was their vision (v 9).

Jesus purposefully takes this chosen group to witness the revelation of his divine identity. They as a group are on a journey of discovery of who Jesus truly is. Thus the transfiguration event is about this communal experience of divine presence and revelation.

The **high mountain** is not named by Matthew. This silence opens the issue to speculations. The Galilean landscape provides a range of possibilities, with Mount Hermon and Mount Tabor as the most likely (Davies and Allison 1991, 646). In the narrative context, the mountain serves as an allusion to the Sinai theophany and provides a natural setting for the experience of divine revelation since mountains have often been associated with closeness to God (Boyer 2017, 1-9).

■ **2** Jesus **was transfigured** [*metemorphōthē*] **before them**. Matthew uses a rare Greek word to describe what has happened to Jesus (see Rom 12 and 2 Cor 3:18). In our story, transfiguration is a change of Jesus' appearance: **his face shone like the sun, and his clothes became as white as the light**. Matthew's unique description of Jesus' shining face (see Mark 9:3 and Luke 9:29) alludes to Moses' experience of divine presence at Sinai (Exod 34:29).

The imagery of light and white garments is often associated with otherworldly human, angelic, and even divine appearance (see Isa 6:1-3; Rev 1:12-16; 4:4). The language here reflects the disciples' experience of the heavenly world breaking into the human realm. Matthew recasts those images to demonstrate, though briefly, Jesus' place among heavenly beings and—even more—his divine identity through the medium of the Voice from heaven.

Jesus' glorified appearance was revealed before the cloud of the divine presence came down (Matt 17:5; see Exod 34). Luz also notes that Christ's transformation points to the future hope of bodily resurrection of Jesus and his followers (2001, 399); the theme appears later in the post-transfiguration discourse (Matt 17:9).

■ **3** The significance of the appearance of Moses and Elijah has been debated. The traditional view that they represent the Law and the Prophets doesn't gain much support from modern interpreters. The prevailing opinion leans toward their role in Jewish eschatological schemes: the expectation of Elijah (Mal 4:4-5 [3:22-23 HB]) and a prophet like Moses (Deut 18:15-19) to come back again in the last days. So, the appearance of Moses and Elisha might signal "the coming of the messianic age" (France 2007, 648). Whatever was expected from the great prophets of the past was redefined and fulfilled with a greater magnitude in the mission of Jesus and John the Baptist. However, both interpretations of the heavenly figures point in the same direction—the Scripture and eschatological expectations find their fulfillment in the figure of Jesus the Messiah.

Neither Matthew nor Mark reveal the content of the conversation between Jesus and the heavenly visitors. Luke, on the other hand, suggests that they were talking about future suffering, resurrection, and ascension (Luke 9:31). Whatever happens to the Messiah in Jerusalem is validated by the key prophetic figures of Israel.

■ **4** Peter's suggestion to **put up three shelters** could be taken in different ways: as a gesture of Middle Eastern hospitality, as a reference to the Jewish festival of booths (Lev 23:39-44) or even as an attempt to mark a theophany by building sacred shrines (Hagner 1995, 493). Matthew is less critical of the disciples' idea; he omits Mark's remark: "He did not know what to say" (Mark 9:6). Perhaps, the disciples were hoping that the holy figures would stay and play their part in the unfolding drama of the last days; this might explain their further discussion about Elijah's eschatological role (17:10).

■ **5** The appearance of **a bright cloud** (or a cloud full of light [*phōteinē*]) signals God's presence. The Scripture itself and later Jewish traditions associate this kind of cloud with the visible manifestation of divine glory or Shekinah (Exod 24:15-16; Isa 4:5; Ezek 1:4; 2 Macc 2:8). Here Matthew clearly parallels the disciples' experience on the Mount of Transfiguration to the one of Moses at Sinai (Exod 24:15-18).

The story culminates with God speaking from the cloud: **This is my Son, whom I love; with him I am well pleased. Listen to him!** This statement brings the key aspects of Jesus' identity together by alluding to the messianic interpretation of the following texts: Ps 2:7, divine sonship; Isa 42:1, suffering servant; and Deut 18:15, prophet like Moses. God confirms Jesus' identity to the close disciples (see Matt 3:16-17) before they witness the final act of the messianic tragedy and triumph unfold in Jerusalem.

The divine command **listen to him** could be interpreted at two levels. At the level of the immediate context, it's a reference to Jesus' prediction of Messiah's death and resurrection, which is hard for the followers to accept (16:21-23; 17:22-23). The disciples have to understand the events in Jerusalem as the divine plan of redemption and reject the human way of thinking about the future of the Messiah (16:23). At the level of the overall Gospel narrative, the command could refer to listening to the authoritative teaching of Jesus in general. Matthew is particularly interested in Jesus' teaching and exposition of the Torah and even structures his Gospel around the five key discourses. There is also opposition to his teaching and practice from the teachers of the Law. At the transfiguration, God confirms the extraordinary authority of the Messiah to reinterpret, amend, suspend, draw attention to the neglected commandments, and even act contrary to the Mosaic law (Jackson 2008, 14-31). Jesus is the bearer of truth and the proclaimer of the will of God; obedience to his words is expected.

■ **6-8** The disciples' reaction to the divine presence is very similar to other scriptural encounters: **they fell facedown to the ground, terrified**. Fear mixed with worship often marks human response to theophany (Gen 28:16-17; Exod 20:18-20; Ezek 1:28; Rev 1:17). But the parallels between Daniel's experience and Matthew's account are particularly striking (Luz 2001, 398). In two different vision accounts, Daniel receives a "vision" (Dan 8:16; 10:7), hears the voice of a heavenly figure (Dan 8:16; 10:9) and "fell prostrate" in terror (Dan 8:17; 10:9). Then the angel touches Daniel (Dan 8:18; 10:10, 18), sets him on his feet, and comforts him (Dan 10:18).

This final episode of the transfiguration narrative adds an intimate stroke to the portrait of the glorified Messiah. Jesus appears to be a compassionate and caring Lord (see Matt 8:23-27) who comforts his terrified followers: **Don't be afraid**. He uses this phrase again in the postresurrection encounter with the women (28:5, 10); this creates another parallel between the transfiguration and resurrection stories.

The story finishes as it started with Jesus and the three disciples on the mountain. The heavenly figures disappear and the disciples **saw no one except Jesus** (17:8). The final comment reveals the real focus of the story; it is about Jesus and his divine identity.

FROM THE TEXT

The transfiguration story is rich in meaning and symbolism. Matthew alludes to OT texts in order to describe this extraordinary event and communicate the sense of otherworldly presence. All aspects—transfiguration, the appearance of the heavenly figures, and theophany—serve the same purpose of revealing Jesus' identity. The brief moment of glorified appearance points to the Easter glory of bodily resurrection, to the enthronement and exaltation of the Son of God (Luz 2001, 396-97), and even to the second coming of the Son of Man (Nolland 2005, 701).

It also unmistakably reveals—according to the traditional interpretation—the divine identity of the Messiah. The conversation with the heavenly visitors both marks out the continuity between the work of Jesus, Moses, and Elijah in the history of Israel's redemption and redefines Jesus' role in the ushering in the kingdom of heaven. He is evidently bigger than the second Moses or the prophet of the last days. At the event's culmination, the divine voice confirms the divine sonship, Messiah's destiny, and the authority of Jesus' words.

The mystery of transfiguration takes place for the disciples' sake. They as a community participate in the journey of discovery of Jesus' true identity. But there is more to it. The Eastern Christian tradition treats this communal participation in Jesus' transformation as a promise of the future resurrection and transfiguration of the bodies of Jesus' followers, "changing them into a better condition" (Luz 2001, 401).

The holiness overtones of the transfiguration story are often missed by modern commentators. In the symbolic world of ancient Judaism, the presence of God and heavenly figures (including angels) indicate the supreme level of purity and holiness: nobody and nothing that does not meet such requirements can be found in their presence (Ermakov 2014a, 171-72). In this framework, the Matthean account of Jesus' transfiguration could be seen as a disclosure of his supreme heavenly holiness. What is more intriguing is that God's holy presence descends on the disciples (17:5). This could imply their holy status as the followers of Christ and the leaders of the new holy people of God. But this status is part and parcel with the mission of God as they have to leave the mountaintop and return to the valley where the harsh realities of serving suffering humanity await (see 17:14-20).

2. The Coming of Elijah (17:9-13)

BEHIND THE TEXT

This episode introduces a change in scenery; the mountaintop has been replaced by descent from the mountain. Matthew uses this episode to clarify some aspects of transfiguration and provide the final explanation to the questions surrounding the figure of Elijah (see 11:1-19). This passage places the mountaintop event into the context of Jewish eschatological expectations: how does the appearance of Elijah fit into the scheme of future events? Matthew also brackets the transfiguration story with the future vision of Jesus' death and resurrection (16:21-28↔17:9-13).

17:9

IN THE TEXT

■ **9** On the way down, Jesus commands the disciples not to tell anyone of the vision. Among other Gospels, only Matthew uses the Greek word *horama* (vision) to describe the transfiguration event. This word has been used in Acts (9:10; 10:3; 11:5; 16:9) and Daniel (7:1-2; 8:26; 12:4, 9) in reference to divine revelations in the form of a vision. This raises some questions about the nature of the event: was Jesus transfigured physically? Or did the disciples receive a vision of the glorified Christ? Hagner suggests that in this particular context *horama* does not necessarily refer to "a supernatural vision" but simply to things that they have seen (1995, 498). In any case, the transfiguration story depicts the disciples who peeked behind the curtain of earthly reality and saw who Jesus truly is.

This passage also continues the Matthean motif of secrecy (see 8:4; 9:30; 16:20). At this point, the disciples have to be silent since this vision might only add to the confusion about Jesus' identity, mission, and future (see 16:13-23). Things will make more sense after the resurrection of the Son of Man: the appearance of the risen Lord will dispel the disciples' bewilderment. In this context, Matthew sees transfiguration as foreshadowing Jesus' resurrection when his exalted identity will be revealed to everybody (Hagner 1995, 498).

■ 10 The sight of Elijah on the Mount of Transfiguration puzzled the disciples since the teachers of the Law have taught **that Elijah must come first**. This belief is based on Mal 4:5-6 [3:23-24 HB] where YHWH sends the prophet to reconcile the people of God before the day of the Lord. However, the notion of Elijah as the Messiah's forerunner has been debated in NT scholarship (Harrington 1991, 157-62). Allison is confident that the traces of this belief could be found in different Jewish traditions (1984, 256-58). The question about Elijah not only reveals Jewish eschatological expectations but also indirectly aims at figuring out Jesus' identity. If Elijah has not come yet, who then is Jesus? (see Matt 16:14).

■ 11-13 Jesus affirms this rabbinic eschatological view with a remark that Elijah **will restore** [*apokathistēmi*] **all things** (17:11). The text itself does not elaborate on what restoration of **all things** entails. Davies and Allison provide a list of Elijah's deeds expected by different Jewish traditions: reconciliation of families and neighbors; preach repentance; ingathering of God's people and purification of a remnant; explanation of unclear texts from the Torah; restoration of bottles of manna, sprinkling water, and anointing oil; and resurrection of the dead (1991, 715).

Jesus clarifies the matter: **Elijah has already come** (v 12*a*). But the restoration of people of Israel and the preparation of the way of the Lord has been met with violence: **they . . . have done to him everything they wished**. This is a clear reference to the beheading of John (14:1-12). This rejection and killing of the prophet of the last days has also been echoed in 23:37. Matthew removes any doubt: **he was talking to them about John the Baptist** (17:13). The same connection was made earlier (11:14). But this time, the disciples have been made aware that the fate of the forerunner foreshadows the fate of the Messiah himself: **The Son of Man is going to suffer at their hands** (17:12*b*). The motif of rejection of God's messengers by Jewish authorities is picking up momentum (see 16:21; 17:22-23).

FROM THE TEXT

This passage clarifies the issue of Elijah's return and his role in the coming of the kingdom of heaven. Matthew removes ambiguity from Jesus' answer in Mark 9:9-13. Elijah of the last days, prophesied in Mal 4:5 [3:23 HB], is John the Baptist whose ministry is seen as restoration of all things. The eschatological events anticipated by Jewish religious teachers have been fulfilled in the relationship between John the Baptist and Jesus of Nazareth. John is the one who restores the people of God and prepares the way for the Messiah.

However, Jesus' take on the question of Elijah not only affirms those eschatological views but also reinterprets and redefines them. The forerunner of the Messiah foreshadows his fate by dying from the hands of Jewish authorities. The continuity in ministry and proclamation between John the Baptist and Jesus the Messiah stretches further as both of them experience rejection, suffering, and death.

D. Liberation of a Boy with a Demon (17:14-21)

BEHIND THE TEXT

The beginning of the passage continues with allusions to Exodus that flow from the transfiguration story. In Exod 32:15-20, Moses was met with peoples' apostasy after coming down from Mount Sinai; Jesus faces an "unbelieving and perverse generation" and finds "little faith" in his disciples (Matt 17:17, 20). This seems to be the key to the problem the disciples faced. Jesus has given them authority over demons (10:1), but they were unsuccessful in casting it out this time. The root of the failure is found within the followers themselves: "You have so little faith" (*oligopistian humon*). Thus this exorcism story is different from others; it has a clear focus on the issue of faith (*pistis*). Moreover, the story raises questions about interconnections between physical affliction and demon possession.

Matthew narrates the story with minimal details and removes some ambiguities found in Mark's version (see Mark 9:14-22; Luke 9:37-45); about two-thirds of the Markan story has been omitted (see Mark 9:20-27). The passage has two parts: exorcism encounter (Matt 17:14-18) and a short saying about faith (vv 19-20).

The absence of v 21 from the NIV and NRSV has to be noted. Scholars see the sentence "but this kind does not come out except by prayer and fasting" as an interpolation or a later addition to the early text. Bruce Metzger has suggested that this addition reflects the early church's emphasis on "the necessity of fasting" (1975, 101). Some manuscripts insert just "by prayer," others add "by prayer and fasting" (see Codices Ephraemi Rescriptus, Washingtonianus, Regius, Bezae, etc.). The verse itself is missing from some of the important textual witnesses (Codex Sinaiticus, Codex Vaticanus, Codex Coridethianus, etc.). Different versions of the Matthean text share these readings with Markan textual traditions (Mullins 2007, 398). The editors of modern critical editions of the NT felt that the removal of v 21 would better reflect the early text of the Gospel and provide the earliest recoverable reading.

IN THE TEXT

■ **14-16** Matthew reports that when the three disciples and Jesus came down from the mountain, they were met by the crowd and a man pleading for his son. They have quickly learned that the rest of disciples have attempted to heal the boy and failed. The narrator uses the language of worship (Hagner 1995, 503) in the description of the encounter between Jesus and the father:

approached (*prosēlthen*), **knelt before** (*gonupetōn*), **Lord** (*Kyrie*), **have mercy** (*eleēson*) (vv 14-15*a*). He appeals to Jesus for help and healing since his son **has seizures** [*selēniazetai*] **and is suffering greatly** (v 15*b*).

The NRSV describes the affliction in modern terms: "he is an epileptic." Here we need to exercise caution in making a modern diagnosis for phenomena in the past. The NIV provides more careful translation and avoids the anachronistic reading for *selēniazomai*—an affliction ancients described as people who "fall down in moonlight" (*selene*, "the moon"). France's suggestion "subject to fits" is most appropriate in this context: this "demon possession resulted in fits" (2007, 659-60). At this point in the story, readers have no idea that those fits are caused by a demon. But the interconnection between spiritual and physical become evident later.

■ **17-18** The phrase **unbelieving and perverse generation** (v 17) echoes Deut 32:5, 20 and fits very well into the wider Matthean motif of faithlessness (see Matt 11:16; 12:39-45; 16:4) that finds it culmination in 23:34-36, where peoples' unbelief leads them into rejection of the divine messengers and results in punishment and destruction. Jesus publicly expresses his frustration at peoples' disbelief: **How long shall I stay with you? How long shall I put up with you?** It is hard to avoid the impression that the failed disciples are included into that category. Both the unbelieving crowd and the disciples' "little faith" (v 20) concern Jesus.

Jesus rebuked the demon, and it came out of the boy, and he was healed at that moment (v 18). The object of Jesus' rebuke is unclear. The pronoun *autō* could be translated as "him" or "it." So, it could refer to the boy or the demon. The NIV opts for **the demon**, the NEB prefers "the boy," and other translations use "him." Now readers discover that the boy is demon possessed. At the rebuke the demon leaves the boy and he is healed; here exorcism results in healing. In spite of peoples' unbelief, Jesus has demonstrated his strength and authority over the powers of evil. He restores health and liberates from demonic oppression.

■ **19-20 Then the disciples came to Jesus in private** (v 19)—away from the crowd and public attention the disciples wanted to inquire about their shameful failure in casting out a demon. Mark 6:6-13 and Luke 9:1-6; 10:1-17 report that the disciples were successful exorcists prior to this incident. However, in Matthew's Gospel the disciples had no previous experience. They are surprised at this outcome since they received authority to do these things (Matt 10:1). What is lacking? Are there special techniques or more powerful words? Jesus is blunt: **Because you have so little faith** (*oligopistian* [17:20*a*]). Authority given is not enough; faith is also necessary (France 2007, 662). However, "a weak faith . . . produces the same effect as no faith" (Hagner 1995, 505).

Truly I tell you emphasizes the importance of the saying that follows (v 20*b*). Jesus illustrates the power of faith or reliance on God through contrast between a small seed and a mountain. A person with the smallest amount of faith could do great things; **nothing will be impossible** (v 20*c*). This passage does not lend itself to promote the modern "can-do" attitude and "belief in oneself to do anything." It is firmly anchored in the mission of Jesus of proclamation of the gospel by word and deed, restoration of the people of God. It calls to have faith as relying on God, the source of every power.

FROM THE TEXT

The story illustrates the disciples' failed attempt to participate in the mission of God. They as Jesus' co-workers have received authority to confront the powers that oppress and harm the people of God. But they failed to exercise this authority because of little faith. The episode turns into a lesson about the importance of faith on the journey of discipleship. It also demonstrates Jesus' authority over demonic powers in the context of peoples' unbelief.

Although the incident with the boy evidently connects "fits" and demon possession, healing and exorcism, we as modern readers should resist the urge to link illness with individual sin or brain disorders with demonic activities. As Brower notes, "Such assumptions in the past led to tragic consequences" and mistreatment of afflicted children and adults (2012, 252-53). In the context of pastoral care, one has to take into account multiple aspects of human condition including psychological, physical, and mental well-being. Moreover, the context of other healing stories in the Gospel of Matthew prevents us from generalization and seeing all expressions of "fits" or "epilepsy" as a result of activity of evil spirits.

In the Gospel, diseases are rarely connected with demonic possession or sin; they are part of the general human condition and living in the fallen world. The point of the healing and exorcism stories is to illustrate the work of restoration of the people of God through Jesus the Messiah, the Son of God; and this particular event exemplifies a holistic act of salvation: restoration of both body and soul.

The issue of relationship between faith and healing is a contentious one. However, some Christians take a judgmental tone and appropriate Jesus' voice from this story (and other passages) to shame those who for one reason or another haven't received healing or those who are suffering from a chronic or terminal illness. They quickly make their own diagnosis of others—"lack of faith."

This passage does not give any license for heaping up guilt, manipulating feelings, or pronouncing verdict over the faith of others—unless one wants to usurp God's place. If anything, the passage might actually speak into the inability of some church leaders to lead and to serve—exemplified by the apostles who had "little faith."

E. Teaching on the Way: Community (17:22—20:34)

1. The Second Passion Prediction (17:22-23)

BEHIND THE TEXT

This second prediction of Jesus' death and resurrection has parallel texts in Mark 9:30-32 and Luke 9:44-45. Matthew differs in one aspect—the reaction of the Twelve. He omits the motif of misunderstanding and hiddenness; the disciples are fully aware of the meaning of the prediction.

The saying seems to appear randomly wedged between two unrelated stories. However, this position could be connected to other episodes (Matt 17:14-20 and vv 24-27). Future events in the Messiah's life could further shake even the little faith of the Twelve, so Jesus warns them again. The temple plays a crucial role in the Passion Narrative and culminates in the connection made between the death and resurrection of Jesus and the destruction of the temple in 26:60. The temple tax incident also hints on complete reliance on God—practical expression of the disciples' faith.

Most scholars count this prediction as the second announcement of Jesus' suffering and death (Hagner 1995, 506). However, Jesus hints to his future in 17:9, 12 as well. The passage has a straightforward structure: (1) betrayal into the hands of men, (2) death, (3) resurrection, and (4) reaction of the disciples.

IN THE TEXT

■ **22 When they came together in Galilee**—it is not clear who had gathered: only the Twelve or other followers as well. Matthew 17:24—18:25 describes the last moments of Jesus' teaching and actions in Galilee; afterward the group will be traveling to Jerusalem (19:1-2). Perhaps Jesus gathers the group for a pilgrimage to Jerusalem (Davies and Allison 1991, 733). If this is correct, then the text implies a wider audience for the proclamation of the fate of the Messiah (as opposed to a private setting in 16:21).

The prediction about **the Son of Man** is built around three key verbs: "to be betrayed" (*paradidosthai*; NRSV); "they will kill" (*apoktenousin* [v 23]); "he will be raised" (*egerthēsetai*). The first verb (*paradidomi*) is in the passive voice (be given, handed over, or betrayed). The absence of a concrete subject creates ambiguity. Is it a reference to Judas who betrays Jesus? Or is it a reference to God who gives his own Son? This verb will play an important role in the Passion Narrative (chs 26—27).

Into the hands of men (17:22) is an inescapable reference to Jewish authorities. The whole sentence echoes Dan 7:25 and Isa 53. In the first passage the son of man and the saints are given to the enemy of God and in the second, the servant of YHWH has been subjected to suffering.

■ **23** The second verb, *apoktenousin* (**they will kill him**), has been used by Matthew in reference to persecution and killing of the prophets (see Matt 10:28; 23:34; 24:9). Jesus and his disciples will share the fate of the foregoing messengers of God. Although there is continuity in suffering, Jesus will turn a new page—**he will be raised to life** (*egerthēsetai*). The third verb, *egeirō* (to raise up, to arouse from sleep), is also set in passive voice. But here the subject is clear: this is the work of God. This is a *divine passive*, which implies divine action. What happens to Jesus in this prediction is not a series of unfortunate events but is driven by divine intervention. Both verbs, *giving up* and *raising up*, may be divine passives.

The disciples were filled with grief or became very sorrowful (*elupēthēsan sphodra*; see 26:22 and 26:38). The first prediction was met with refusal (16:22-23), and now with acceptance and sorrow. It is a fitting response to the proclamation of the Messiah's suffering (Hagner 1995, 508).

FROM THE TEXT

The Gospel narrative gears up toward its culminative events that start
to unfold from 26:1. The predictions anticipate further developments in the
story and prepare the disciples and readers for the final showdown. Jesus repeats these words several times and tries to convey something important about
17:23 messiahship: the Son of Man has to go through death and resurrection before
he appears triumphant over his enemies. The path of the Messiah through suffering to vindication is also the one that his disciples will follow (16:24-28).
The predictions also convey the sense of divine purpose and action.

2. On the Temple Tax (17:24-27)

BEHIND THE TEXT

At the center of this unique story is the issue of paying the tax in support of the Jerusalem temple. Every free Jewish male over twenty years of age was obligated to pay the half-shekel tax every year (including Israelites living in Diaspora). The commandment from Exod 30:11-16 served as a foundation for this practice. However, this in itself did not require an obligatory annual temple tax. This gave rise to disagreements between the main groups within 2TJ.

The Qumran sectarians taught that the temple tax must be paid only once in a lifetime (4Q159 fr. 1 ii 6-12). The Sadducees rejected the practice on the basis that it should be done voluntarily (*m. Šek.* 1:4-5; Luz 2005, 414-15). The Pharisees, by contrast, emphasized the compulsory nature of this religious tax (*m. Šek.* 1:3; 2:4). The tax was established in the first century BCE and existed till the destruction of the Jerusalem temple in 70 CE. Later, the Romans established in its place the tax called *fiscus Iudaicus* to pay toward the temple of Jupiter Capitolinus that was built on the site of the devastated Jerusalem temple (Sanders 1992, 156).

Jesus' teaching is about the nature of this payment toward the temple; the teaching about paying the civil taxes to Roman authorities comes later in the narrative (22:12-22).

IN THE TEXT

■ **24-25*a*** Jesus and the disciples returned to Capernaum. Jesus lived there and it served as the base for their Galilean ministry (4:12-13; 9:1). It may have been seen as an official residence for taxation purposes (Hagner 1995, 511). In the first episode of the story, Peter meets temple tax collectors who inquire whether or not Jesus (and perhaps his followers) pays this two-drachma contribution (roughly equivalent to a half-shekel). Peter's reply is clear: **Yes, he does** (17:25*a*).

■ **25*b*-26** In the second episode, Jesus used Peter's encounter with the tax collectors as a teaching opportunity to explain why they pay the tax. This is interesting since the relationship between Jesus and the temple is ambiguous (see 21:12-22; 26:57-68). Jesus bases his answer on a parallel drawn from the existing taxation system in which, it seems, the members of the royal family were exempt from **duty and taxes** (17:25*d*). It's not clear who Jesus compares to the **children** of the king—his followers or the Jewish people in general? Jesus stresses the voluntary nature of the contribution. Perhaps he believed that the temple should not be supported by obligatory taxation (Bauckham 1988, 74).

■ **27** Jesus and his followers pay the tax not out of obligation **but so that** they **may not cause offense** (*skandalizō*). Jesus often confronts wicked leadership or challenges Pharisaic beliefs and practices. But this is a secondary issue. Jesus abstains from exercising his rightful freedom so as not to make a stumbling block to proclamation of the gospel. Scholars have long noted similarities between this passage and practices of the Apostle Paul's ministry (Davies and Allison 1991, 748; see 1 Cor 8:12-13; 10:31-33; 2 Cor 9:16-15 for clear examples).

There is no description of the miracle through which Peter finds the money in the mouth of a fish. Some suggest that Jesus meant for Peter to fish, sell the fish, and pay the tax out of that (Jeremias 1971, 87). But that suggestion misses the point of the story; if one is willing to sacrifice freedom for the sake of the gospel, then God will provide: **a four-drachma coin** is exactly what's needed to pay the tax for two (Mounce 1991, 172).

FROM THE TEXT

In spite of the fact that the followers of Jesus were not obliged to support the temple and its worship through the tax, they are willing to pay in order not to offend the Jewish authorities and, perhaps, the wider Jewish public. The story could be reflective of the problems of early Jewish Christian community still worshiping in the Jerusalem temple and a part of the wider Jewish community.

The specifics of the story are largely irrelevant for contemporary Christians, although forms of church taxes are paid in some European countries. However, it lays a foundation for a more general application. One should be prepared to sacrifice rightful freedom out of a concern for others and the proclamation of the gospel (Hagner 1995, 513). Jesus often challenges Pharisaic practices and clearly offends them (see ch 23), but here he chooses to avoid unnecessary resentment. Should we be more prepared to compromise where fundamental beliefs are not at stake? It should also motivate some Christians to fulfill their social obligations without rancor (Keener 2009, 444).

3. The Discourse on the Church (18:1—19:12)

a. Who Is the Greatest? (18:1-4)

BEHIND THE TEXT

This passage introduces the fourth set of Jesus' teachings, widely known as the Discourse on the Church (18:1-35). Jesus addresses challenges in dealing with sin in the community of boundless grace and forgiveness. Teaching on the communal life of the church (*ekklesia*) starts with leadership and true greatness.

18:1 An image of "a little child" (*paidion*) takes central stage in 18:1-14. The perception of children and childhood in the ancient world was different from ours. The Greek word *pais/paidion* ("a little child") can also mean "a slave" (Luz 2001, 428). Thus, children had a low social status, particularly in the Greco-Roman world. The head of the household had absolute authority over his children, could sell them into slavery or put them to death. Children had no property rights until they reached maturity or when they were legally declared adults by their father (Treggiari 2003, 137-38).

The abandonment and even killing of unwanted infants—on the grounds of disability, illegitimate paternity, economic hardship, or bad omens—was widely practiced in the ancient world as well (Harris 1994,1-15; Evans-Grubbs 2013, 83). Adding to that a high rate of infant and child mortality completes the picture of "the weakest and most vulnerable" members of ancient societies (Malina and Rohrbaugh 2003, 336). In the world of 2TJ, the picture was a little bit different: children were seen as the gift and blessing from God, and parents had responsibility to raise them in obedience to the Torah (see Deut 6:7; 11:19).

IN THE TEXT

■ **1** By formulating the question in general terms, **Who . . . is the greatest** [*meizōn*] **in the kingdom of heaven?**, the disciples were actually trying to disguise their own quest for status, power, and authority. It's particularly telling since

Jesus has already provided an answer in 5:19: "Whoever practices and teaches these commands will be called great [*megas*] in the kingdom of heaven."

The issue was sparked by the previous events. The Twelve were given authority to preach and perform acts of power (10:1-10). However, after Peter's confession Jesus acknowledges Peter's leading role (16:18-19), talks about his own impending death (v 21), takes Peter, James, and John on the Mount of Transfiguration (17:1), witnesses the failure of the rest of the disciples to cure a boy (v 16), and makes Peter pay the temple tax on their behalf (vv 24-26). So, who is the greatest? Peter? The "transfiguration trio"? All of them wanted to know the answer: those who felt excluded from the privileged relationship with Jesus and those who presumed their newly gained importance.

The disciples' question also reflects cultural values; the key ones were the pursuit for honor and avoidance of disgrace. Honor (or affirmation of a person's worth) came from status or could be achieved by behaving in accordance with a group's values and expectations (deSilva 2004, 125). The question betrays this cultural drive for status among peers.

■ **2-3** Illustrating his answer, Jesus calls a little child to stand in their midst. The physical presence of a little person (versus a great person) embodying "social insignificance" and "indifference to greatness" (Hagner 1995, 517) challenges the disciples' cultural assumptions about leadership. This prophetic act signals the rearrangement of the social order and accepted values that come with the in-breaking of the kingdom. Those on the fringes of society are at the center of divine concern.

Then comes the warning to the Twelve: **Unless you change** [*straphēte*] **and become like little children, you will never enter the kingdom of heaven** (18:3). They have to change (repent, turn around) their mindset toward leadership and status in order to be a part of God's work in these last days. They cannot be driven by the human agenda of greatness and at the same time participate in the life and mission of the new holy people of God. Matthew emphasizes that it is important not only to receive the kingdom like a child (10:15) but to be like a child (Nolland 2005, 731), recognizing one's insignificance, vulnerability, and, perhaps, powerlessness.

■ **4** The phrase **whoever takes the lowly position** means to give up one's social status, to accept undeserving and inappropriate treatment, and to give honor to others (Malina and Rohrbaugh 2003, 92). For the Twelve it implies more than a mental exercise. It comes close to humiliation: "Accept the low social status which is symbolised by the child" (France 2007, 679). They must put aside their culturally fuelled concern for self-value, power, authority, and honor and reorient themselves to the low and vulnerable status of a child and a servant.

So then, who is the greatest? The one who renounces the pursuit of honor, humbles oneself, and is prepared to be treated like a child: "those who humble themselves will be exalted" (23:12). True greatness and honor in the kingdom of heaven comes through humility and renunciation of one's importance. In spite of Jesus' stern warning, this radical reorientation is hard to accept. The Twelve continue to struggle with the notion of such humiliation, and the issue surfaces again in 20:26-28 and 23:11-12.

FROM THE TEXT

The passage raises an array of questions in relation to power and authority within the community of faith. Jesus subverts fundamental cultural assumptions by questioning notions of honor and shame, social positioning ("great ones" vs. "little ones," "upgrade" vs. "downgrade"), greatness, humility, and servanthood. He calls for renunciation of the obsession with self-importance and taking self-denial seriously (Nolland 2005, 732). The new leaders of the holy people of God are to reflect the values of the kingdom and challenge widely accepted cultural patterns. Jesus emphasizes the seriousness by issuing a troubling warning: "Unless you change . . . you will never enter the kingdom of heaven" (18:3).

In modern Western culture, the child in the middle might not appear to be a strong prophetic action but it sends an unsettling message for modern Christian readers nonetheless. First, Jesus teaches us to challenge unspoken assumptions about leadership within the church that often unconsciously appropriates practices and values from the wider culture: the world of business or tribal cultures or different ideologies.

Second, the message of embracing the position of powerlessness and vulnerability should trouble our "middle class" communities of faith who wholeheartedly embrace the corporate ideas about success, prosperity, and management. This ancient notion of humility uncompromisingly clashes with the modern obsession with reputation, claims to rights, appeals to entitlements, and clinging to privilege.

Third, the passage calls to abandon this (often unconscious) quest for raising one's social position at the church's expense by getting into leadership within the communities of faith.

Fourth, all of these culturally driven concerns should be put aside and focus should be placed on serving each other in humility regardless any social, ethnic, gender, or cultural boundaries.

b. Causing to Stumble (18:5-9)

BEHIND THE TEXT

In vv 4-6, Jesus makes a shift in the language from "this child" (*paidion touto*) to "these little ones" (*tōn mikron toutōn*). He gradually transitions from a particular child who represents a low-status person, to "one such child" who represents Christ himself, to "little ones" who represent a group of people "who believe in me" (18:6). Now Jesus uses the image of a little child as a metaphor for those who belong to the community of Christ. Jesus' followers are like little children (children of the heavenly Father [see 23:9]) and the Twelve should take proper care of them. The leaders of the holy people of God are called not only to embrace the status of servants but also to give people of low status the same respect as they would to Jesus himself, and serve them as they would serve Christ. Moreover, they must not to give any reason for believers to lose their faith.

IN THE TEXT

■ **5 Whoever welcomes one such child in my name welcomes me**. The Twelve should demonstrate their humility by welcoming **one such child**. Welcoming is an act of hospitality and inclusion. The leaders of the holy people of God should extend their care and protection to the most vulnerable in society. But there is more. By welcoming children, they extend hospitality to Jesus who associates himself with the lowest of the low.

■ **6 If anyone causes one of these little ones . . . to stumble**. Hospitality and welcoming are juxtaposed to **causes . . . to stumble**. The phrase suggests a range of possibilities. First, it could describe a failure in welcoming "little ones" on the bases of their low social status. Leaders and members of the community are warned against despising them and not showing a serving attitude.

Second, it could be an action that leads others to sin or to take an offense (see vv 8-9, 15, 21). This could have referred to sexual abuse, particularly in the context of vv 8-9. The seriousness of that offense is underscored by the vivid language of punishment by drowning by attaching the heavy communal millstone that was usually operated by a donkey (Keener 2009, 449). Thus the language **causes . . . to stumble** could refer to any action that prevents "little ones" from following Jesus.

■ **7** Jesus understands the human condition well; it is almost impossible in the fallen world (*kosmos*) to avoid things that lead people to stumble: **such things must come**. But this is no excuse for irresponsible acts toward others and putting stumbling blocks on their path of following Christ. Jesus proclaims "woe" twice, to the world in general and to individuals within it: woe to the world because it not only contains "stumbling blocks" but also is affected by them (France 2007, 682), and to particular persons **through whom they come**.

Later Jesus pronounces similar "woes" upon the Pharisees (23:13-32) or Judas Iscariot (26:24) that point to the kind of stumbling blocks that Matthew has in mind. Life is full of opportunities to stumble, and the members of the community should be aware of that. But one cannot just blame the world, society, and the way things are. Further in the text, the idea of self-imposed limitation creates the sense of responsibility for one's own sins that affect others (Hagner 1995, 522).

■ **8-9** Jesus gives examples of things that might cause a person to stumble and sin: **your hand or your foot** (v 8). He uses vivid and shocking language to draw attention to the seriousness of the issue. The passage is *not* a call to practice self-mutilation, despite amputation as a part of punishment for certain sins in the OT (see Exod 21:23-25; Lev 24:20; Deut 19:21; 25:11-12). The language is metaphorical.

There are a few options in navigating this discourse. First, the references to hands, feet, and eyes could be understood as euphemisms for sexual activity. Matthew has already used similar language in Matt 5:28-30 where the right eye and the right hand may refer to stimulation of sexual desires. Moreover, the OT often uses the word "feet/legs" (*raglayim*) in reference to male/female genitals (see Deut 28:57; Ruth 3:4; Isa 7:20); the same could be said about the word "hand"(*yd*) (see Isa 57:8; Song 5:4). If that is the case, then the vivid and strong condemning language of the passage could be interpreted as a dire warning against sexual misconduct or even against the sexual abuse of children within the community (Collins 2007, 450-52). "Scandalizing the little ones" would definitely deserve drowning "in the depths of the sea" (Matt 18:6) or throwing **into eternal fire** (v 8).

Second, "hands" and "feet" could also be understood as the means of carrying out sinful intentions in general (Davies and Allison 1991, 765-67). The Scripture often refers to hands in contexts of different sins and to feet as "the means of transport to the place where sins are committed" (Marcus 2009b, 691). Perhaps this could imply that the principles rising out of dealing with sexual sins could also be applied to other areas of human behavior.

18:8-9 Third, the passage could be seen as a communal parable that illustrates excommunication of a member of the body of Christ who causes offense in order to protect the whole community; cutting off a limb or gouging an eye out is metaphorical language that refers to the removal of a person from the community (Harrington 1991, 265).

If something causes one to stumble, it should be dealt with without hesitation and restraint. Radical action is taken to forestall grave consequences. The danger of stumbling blocks is further emphasized by the language of judgment. The Twelve should take Jesus' warning about them seriously: instead of receiving life eternal some could be thrown into the Gehenna of fire (*tēn geennan tou puros* or **the fire of hell** [v 9]).

Gehenna

Gehenna (*geennah*) is a Greek rendering of the Aramaic name for the Valley of Hinnom (*gehinnom*; see Isa 31:9; 66:24; Jer 7:32). In the time of the kingdom of Judah, the place was associated with human sacrifices to Molek (2 Kgs 16:3; 21:6) and later referred to as the place of divine judgment (Jer 7:32; 19:6). In 2TJ, Gehenna refers to the fiery abyss of the final judgment and destruction (Jeremias in *TDNT*, 657-58). It is better to deal with the root of the problem now than to be punished in the world to come.

FROM THE TEXT

The Twelve as the leaders of the new holy people of God should serve others, "these little ones," with a spirit of respect and hospitality. They also must avoid or remove anything that causes others to stumble on the path of following Jesus. It is hard to miss the communal context of this passage. Whatever a leader of the church does affects not only that individual but the whole community of faith.

Some might appeal to this text to justify the practice of self-mutilation or self-harm. Eusebius reports of an incident of self-castration allegedly performed by young Origen—an early Christian theologian (third century CE)—who interpreted another Matthean text (19:12) "in too literal and extreme a sense" (*HE* 6.8). While Eusebius attributes such an action to an "immature and youthful mind," there could be different reasons at play. Under no circumstances is self-mutilation an appropriate reading of this passage. Although people might appeal to the Bible, pastorally, it is important to get to the root of the problem that could often be found in anxiety, depression, inner struggle, sexual insecurities, or negative body-image.

To navigate the issue in terms of biblical interpretation, one might first challenge assumptions behind a dualistic understanding of the human person (body versus spirit) and the negative view of the created material world. Second, an appeal to the holistic anthropology in the wider biblical context and particularly to the positive treatment of the human body (see, e.g., Gen 18:10-14
1:27-31; Ps 139:13-14; 1 Cor 6:19) could be helpful. Third, to counter any literalistic interpretation, one has to pay attention to the context of the passage and recognize the metaphorical nature of this, and other, texts. The rhetorical strategy of vivid and shocking language has been employed to draw hearers' attention to the gravity of the issue and the urgency of dealing with the root of the problem.

c. The Parable of the Lost Sheep (18:10-14)

BEHIND THE TEXT

Matthew puts the parable of the lost sheep (18:12-13) in a context that is different from Luke's (Luke 15:4-7). Framed by vv 10 and 14, the parable receives a distinct focus. While in Luke, Jesus addresses the Pharisees and emphasizes the joy of finding and welcoming sinners (Luke 15:1-2), Matthew is concerned with finding "these little ones," that is, the members of the Christian community that have gone astray (18:14). This difference reflects Luke's *missional* focus and Matthew's *pastoral* concerns. The NIV and other modern translations omit v 11 as it does not appear in key ancient manuscripts (see Codices Sinaiticus and Vaticanus). It reflects a later addition influenced by Luke 19:10.

Guardian Angels

Early and medieval interpreters saw this passage as a proof text for the existence of guardian angels (see Acts 12:15; Heb 1:14), while some later commentators saw it as reflecting special divine care for "the little ones." Belief in guardian angels could be traced in 2TJ and later rabbinic traditions (Lutz 2001, 441-42). According to their views, these angels occupy the lowest position in the angelic hierarchy (*T. Adam* 4) and do not normally see God (*Midr. Qoh.* 49b). They also play a role in the final judgment by recording or reporting on the deeds of people (*3 Bar.* 12-13; *2 En.* 19:4). On the other hand, the Matthean text suggests that these angels belong to the highest order of the angels of the presence who see God's glory. They have often been associated with the seven archangels (Tob 12:15; *Jub.* 1:27; *1 En.* 9:1; 1QSb 4:25; 1QH 6:13) who played a variety of roles (priestly, judicial, revelatory, intermediary, etc.) and resided in the heavenly court/temple (EDEJ 2010, 329-30).

IN THE TEXT

■ **10-11 Do not despise one of these little ones**. Again, Jesus warns the apostles not to disregard or treat with contempt (*kataphronein*) the members of the congregation. They might appear unimportant, occupying the lowest niches of ancient society or playing an insignificant role in the community of faith, but they are very precious in the eyes of God. The "little ones" have been represented by the angels of the presence that **always see the face of my Father**—the highest in angelic hierarchy (see Ps 8:5 [6 HB]). Thus the leaders of the people of God must defy widespread cultural attitudes of disdain toward people of lower social standing. As the followers of Jesus they should act counterculturally.

■ **12-13** Jesus illustrates the appropriate attitude toward the "little ones" by the parable of the lost sheep. The central character demonstrates extraordinary concern for just one lost sheep: **If a man owns a hundred sheep, and one of them wanders away** (v 12). The parallels are hard to miss. The OT often uses the image of shepherd and flock in relation to YHWH and Israel (see Isa 40:11; Ezek 34:31; Mic 7:14). This shepherd represents God the Father who lovingly cares for each of Jesus' followers. The parable not only illustrates a theological point but also calls hearers to action. The Twelve ought to imitate God the Good Shepherd and show the same attitude toward the "little ones" who might have wandered away or stumbled (Davies and Allison 1991, 767).

■ **14** A change in the language occurs: "my Father" (v 10) turns into **your Father** [*tou patros hymōn*] **in heaven** here. This variation not only states that God is the Father of all (Jesus, the Twelve, and the "little ones") but also implies that the disciples should take him as a role model (see 5:42-48). As Jesus the Son of God embodies the love of God, so the disciples emulate the divine passion for the lost and marginalized. God is **not willing that any of these little**

ones should perish. *Apolētai*, or "perish," is a strong word to describe the fate of those who stumble and wander away. Leaders must do everything possible to seek and restore those precious little ones who stumbled: "The mission to rescue little ones who have been led astray is motivated by the concerns of God and angels gathered before him" (Nolland 2005, 743).

FROM THE TEXT

This parable concludes the section on leaders, their role and attitudes toward others in the community of faith (Matt 18:1-14). The passage reveals Jesus' vision for genuine Christian leadership: humility, kindness toward children, refraining from offending others, serious self-control, and deep concern for fellow believers that enhances communal living, serves the common good, and flourishes in faith (Davies and Allison 1991, 777). "Matthew's audience should be ready to lament leaders . . . who are more concerned with their own reputation and position than with the needs of the people" (Keener 2009, 450). The story calls the disciples to imitate God's love not just by welcoming into the community but by doing their utmost if someone stumbles or wanders off.

d. Dealing with Sin in the Church (18:15-20)

BEHIND THE TEXT

Second Temple Judaism provides examples of communal practices of reproof and reconciliation, rooted in the Levitical command: "Rebuke your neighbor frankly so you will not share in their guilt" (Lev 19:17). Leviticus 19 calls the people of Israel to imitate God's holiness in every aspect of their life, and part of that experience includes reproving sinful behavior. However, Leviticus couples the command to rebuke with the command to love one's neighbor (v 18). The holy people of God are called to admonish one another in love.

The Qumran community developed its own practices of reproof based on this command: "They shall rebuke one another in truth, humility, and charity" (1QS 5:24-25). The *Rule of the Community* describes a three-stage process of dealing with sinful behavior through an annual review of the members of the congregation. They were encouraged to solve issues between themselves, then in the presence of a witness and then to bring it "before the Congregation" (1QS 5:23—6:1). There are similarities and differences between the Qumran and Matthean practices of reproof. They are both rooted in Lev 19 (see Kister 2010, 212-29; van de Sandt 2005, 178-92).

Jesus also outlines three stages in dealing with sin within the community of followers: (1) privately between two individuals (18:15), (2) in the presence of two or three witnesses (v 16), and (3) before the whole church (v 17). The process is aimed at reconciliation and restoration of the broken relationship.

Verse 15 contains a textual variant that might affect interpretation of the passage: some manuscripts contain "against you" (see, e.g., Codices Alexandrinus [sixth century CE], Regius [eight century CE], and Washingtonianus [fourth century CE]); others lack that phrase, see Codices Sinaiticus [fourth century CE] and Vaticanus [fourth century CE]). The NIV editors suggest that the phrase is a later addition taken from Luke 19:10. The absence of the phrase would suggest a general context of dealing with any sinful behavior; its presence would envisage a specific situation of broken relationships between two individuals.

IN THE TEXT

■ **15-18 If your brother or sister sins** (Matt 18:15). The passage does not clarify what sins are in view; it appears to be a broad category that might include a range of transgressions against members of the community (see chs 5—6). Jesus outlines the steps toward reconciliation based on Scripture. Leviticus 19:17 informs the first step: **point out their fault, just between the two of you**. The second step has Deut 19:15 in mind: **every matter may be established by the testimony of two or three witnesses** (Matt 18:16). These practices were originally for criminal offenses, but Jesus appropriates them for the new holy people of God (Harrington 1991, 269). These steps should be taken on the basis of the offender's response: **if they will not listen**. Unwillingness to repent will then lead to community involvement. Now the whole church will attempt to resolve the matter.

Treat them as you would a pagan or a tax collector is ambiguous (v 18). In a Jewish Christian community these people could have been seen as unclean or immoral; thus the language suggests exclusion. But Matthew depicts them in a positive light: tax collectors (see 9:9-13; 11:19) and Gentiles (see 8:5-13; 15:21-28) accept the good news. If that is the case, then the phrase could imply treatment with love and not expulsion. The former interpretation is more likely.

The authority originally given to Peter (16:19) is now extended to the wider community of disciples: **whatever you bind on earth will be bound in heaven** (18:18). In the context of communal discipline, it refers to the power of exclusion or restoration into the *ekklesia* through offering forgiveness of sins. Whatever decision has been made, it has the imprint of divine authority (Harrington 1991, 269).

■ **19-20** Jesus elaborates further on the way communal decisions ought to be made: agreeing (*sumphōveō*) and praying play an important part. The heavenly Father will hear prayers of the faithful because they gather in the name of Jesus the Son of God to do justice and make peace.

But there is more: **For where two or three gather in my name, there am I with them** (v 20). The phrase is set in the context of church discipline and, perhaps, refers to the presence of witnesses (see v 16). As the community gathers to deal with offenses and exercise given authority **about anything** (or "any case"; v 19), Jesus is present in the decisions made. Moreover, the passage strongly connects the steps of reconciliation and the use of power with prayer and the experience of the divine presence. Thus worship plays an important role in the process of communal restoration. This saying also indicates a departure from rabbinic traditions where the presence of God was experienced through reading Torah (*m. ʾAbot* 3:2-3, 6); it is now through gathering and evoking Jesus' name (Davies and Allison 1991, 789-90).

FROM THE TEXT

Jesus does not shy away from the realities of communal living: discord and sinful behavior happen. He outlines a pathway of dealing with sin within the church. One striking feature is the communal nature of the process; though one person might have sinned, the whole *ekklesia* is affected and involved at the final stage of reconciliation. The holy people of God were given the authority to practice reproof, love, forgiveness, and discipline if necessary. Within this community of forgiveness and restoration, the acts of reconciliation are inseparable from prayer, worship, communal harmony, agreement, and the experience of the divine presence.

The text raises the issue of divine and communal authority that might unsettle modern readers. Jesus does not discuss the abuse of that spiritual authority and the misuse of that mandate "to bind and loose." However, if the appeal to heaven is to justify decisions that do not promote harmony and agreement, or do not reflect love in reproof, or do not reflect a spirit of forgiveness and prayerfulness in worship—genuine questions must be raised about the appropriateness of the decision.

e. The Parable of the Unforgiving Servant (18:21-35)

BEHIND THE TEXT

The parable is set in the context of dealing with sin among Jesus' followers. After outlining the steps for reconciliation, Jesus now turns to a proper reaction of a person who is offended by somebody's sinful behavior. Thus Matthew underlines the main principle behind practices of discipline and reconciliation within the church. The disciples' authority to "bind and loose" should be rooted in the kindness of God who offers limitless forgiveness. The community and its individual members should practice mercy since God has offered grace to everybody.

IN THE TEXT

■ **21-22** Now Peter inquires of Jesus how many times to forgive a member of the community who sins (*hamartēsei*) against him. By asking for a number, Peter may mirror rabbinic logic. The Babylonian Talmud recalls a tradition attributed to rabbi Jose ben Judah who taught that "if a man commits a transgression, the first, second and third time he is forgiven, the fourth time he is not forgiven" (*b. Yoma* 86b). Jesus raises Peter's **seven times** to **seventy-seven**. The Greek numbers (*hebdomēkontakis hepta*) could be interpreted in two ways: **seventy-seven** or seventy times seven.

But to count numbers is to miss the point. These numbers allude to Gen 4:24, "If Cain is avenged seven times, then Lamech seventy-seven times." Jesus subverts numbers of vengeance turning it into "a model of unlimited forgiveness" (Mounce 1991, 177). Instead of vengeance, the followers of Christ should practice unbounded forgiveness. Perhaps this provides a practical example of how the believers could surpass righteousness "of the Pharisees and the teachers of the law" (5:20).

■ **23-27** Jesus illustrates both the necessity and limitlessness of forgiveness by telling a parable about a Gentile king and his unmerciful servant. This story, unique to Matthew, contains three main scenes: the king forgives an enormous debt (18:23-27); the servant does not forgive a small debt (vv 28-30); the king punishes the unmerciful servant (vv 31-34). In the first episode, the king wished to settle his accounts and calls his *douloi* (slaves, servants). "Servants" could be interpreted as a reference to financial officials (Snodgrass 2008, 68) or provincial satraps (Keener 2009, 458) who were responsible for gathering taxes/revenue for the royal treasury.

One of those servants was brought to the palace; he owed the ruler **ten**
18:23-30 **thousand** talents (v 24). This enormous amount of money roughly equals the annual revenue of a wealthy Roman province (Mounce 1991, 177; see Strabo XVII 1.13) or to six million day wages for a laborer (Turner 2008, 450). Since the servant could not repay such a large sum, the king gives orders to sell all (*panta*) that the official has including **his wife and his children**. Jewish tradition prohibits the sale of wives and children into slavery (Jeremias and Hooke 1972, 211). The sale makes no financial sense—such a debt is unimaginable for a servant. This is punishment (Harrington 1991, 270). Hearing the harshness of the king's ruling, **the servant fell on his knees** and begged for another solution. The plea to **pay back everything** (*panta*) is unrealistic, but the lord/master (*kyrios*)—moved by compassion—cancels the debt and lets him go.

■ **28-30** The experience of extraordinary royal forgiveness teaches the functionary nothing. As soon as he is released, **he found one of his fellow servants who owed him a hundred silver coins** ("denarii" [NRSV]; v 28) and demanded repayment of the debt.

This second episode contrasts the king and the unmerciful servant. First, the official owed the king six million denarii and now asks for repayment of a hundred. Second, the servant treats his fellow servant in an aggressive and disrespectful manner. Third, the plea of the debtor is reasonable; it is feasible to pay that kind of money (about hundred days' wages) if a creditor shows patience. Fourth, the servant shows no pity toward his fellow servant. Fifth, he imprisons the man "until he [could] pay back all he owed" (v 34). The servant's behavior is in stark contrast to the king's benevolence. He was unable to show mercy to others, though he had experienced it himself.

■ **31-34** The final episode brings secondary characters to the scene: **When the other servants saw what had happened, they were outraged** (*elupēthēsan sphodra*; v 31; see 17:23; 19:22; 26:22). The injustice and blatant hypocrisy of the unmerciful servant drives them to tell the ruler what has happened. The enraged king calls him "a wicked slave" and reminds him of the generosity he has experienced. There is the crux of the story: **Shouldn't you have had mercy** [*eleēsai*] **on your fellow servant just as I had on you?** (18:33). Injustice, hypocrisy, the failure to exercise mercy and forgiveness results in severe punishment: the master turns him over to the torturers (*tois basanistais*).

■ **35** The moral of the parable echoes the Sermon on the Mount: "But if you do not forgive others their sins, your Father will not forgive your sins" (6:15). Jesus sternly warns his audience that those who are unwilling to forgive should not expect forgiveness. Those who have experienced the forgiveness of God should demonstrate the spirit of mercy to others within the community of faith. Failure to do so might involve punishment from God. However, forgiveness should be offered from the heart (see 5:8, 28; 6:21). The message here is simple: if one wants mercy from God, one must be merciful to others (Harrington 1991, 272).

FROM THE TEXT

Jesus' call to practice limitless forgiveness is rooted in the character of God and the Christian experience of divine mercy. The parable clearly alludes to it using familiar language: the lord *having compassion* toward his servant *forgives* the debt (see 6:12) and *releases* him. Having experienced forgiveness from God, one should extend mercy to others. This is a fitting end for the discourse on the church.

The whole chapter has covered key practical aspects of living and leading within the community of faith. Recognizing the reality of brokenness within the world and the church, Jesus calls the Twelve to a different vision of leadership based on humility, care, inclusion, servanthood, self-denial, and—most of all—forgiveness. He also warns them about the effects of sin on a leader and other members of the congregation and provides the steps for reconciliation. The pathway leads through repentance and willingness to forgive that is rooted in divine grace. Finishing the discourse with the call to limitless forgiveness, Jesus provides a vision for the holy people of God: "The community cannot tolerate sin without confrontation and reproof, but must always love and forgive without limits" (Snodgrass 2008, 74).

Forgiveness is not the same as ignoring the sin or ignoring the victim of sin. This is a counter-lesson that the church has recently needed to learn. Forgiving sins never validates the cover-up tactics from church leadership that has been recently revealed in child sexual abuse cases. Establishing transparent systems of power, responsibility, and, above all, accountability must be set up to prevent all kinds of abuse within the community of faith. If, despite these systems, abuse occurs, forgiveness never means circumventing the due process of legal responsibility.

f. About a Man Divorcing His Wife (19:1-12)

BEHIND THE TEXT

Matthew uses his traditional formula "when Jesus had finished saying these things" to indicate the end of a teaching section (see 7:28; 11:1; 13:53; 26:1). The summary in 19:1-2 bridges to the next part of the story. Jesus and his followers left Galilee, the home province, the place of active ministry and proclamation, and went to the province of Judea. The ultimate destination is Jerusalem (see 16:21). Matthew marks the milestones: leaving Galilee (19:1), progress on the way (19:15), on the way to Jerusalem (20:17), leaving Jericho (20:29), and approaching Jerusalem (21:1).

This section (chs 19—20) describes events on the way to the heart of Judea. Matthew's account of the journey itself is sparse; the focus is teaching "on the way" (20:17). The blessing of little children (19:13-15) and the healing of two blind men (20:29-34) are the only episodes describing action. All of these teaching episodes—in one way or another—address disciples and their concerns, even those that start as an inquiry from an outsider (Pharisees [19:3] or a rich young man [v 16]). Some teaching has parallels with previous sayings of Jesus. Others serve as an extended explanation: about divorce (5:31-32 with 19:1-9), about welcoming children (18:1-5 with 19:13-15), about riches (6:19-24 with 19:16-26).

IN THE TEXT

■ **1-2** This Matthean bridge focuses on two points. First, location changes: from Galilee to Judea. Matthew's remark about **the other side of the Jordan** (19:1) suggests that Jesus took a route through Perea and around Samaria. Matthew, however, may not be precise here: the borders of Judea did not cross "the other side of the Jordan." Second, Matthew notes that **large crowds followed** [*ēkolouthēsan*; see 4:20-22; 8:23] **him** (19:2), but this time Jesus is not teaching but healing (see 5:1-2). His journey through Judea is very different from his travels in Galilee. It is not filled with actions of power and proclamation of the kingdom. Judea and Jerusalem in particular are more associated with suffering and conflict with the religious and civic authorities than active and successful ministry.

■ **3-6** Jesus' first encounter on the way is with the Pharisees. This fits into ongoing conflict with religious leaders as they **came to** him to **test him** (19:3).

This time they raise the issue of divorce: **Is it lawful for a man to divorce his wife for any and every reason?**

Rabbinic Views on Divorce

The Mishnaic tractate *Gittin* discusses the questions related to divorce and provides insights into that particular conversation. The school of Shammai permitted divorce only on the grounds of the wife's unchastity, which was generally understood as *any form of sexual immorality* or marital unfaithfulness (Keener 2009, 463). For the school of Hillel, on the other hand, "any matter of indecency" meant *any reason* that a husband finds indecent, "even if she spoiled his dish" (*m. Git.* 9:10C). Rabbi Aqiba goes even further: a man could divorce "if he found someone else prettier than she" (*m. Git.* 9:10E). The question in the text is carefully formulated and reflects this Pharisaic halakic debate over the interpretation of the ambiguous phrase "any matter of indecency" (see Deut 24:1).

The Pharisees intend to drag Jesus into a technical discussion: "What are the legitimate grounds *for a man* to divorce his wife according to Deut 24:1-4?" This specific question is an aspect of the wider issue of family and divorce that sees marriage as a contract that could be broken by a husband (Harrington 1991, 273).

Jesus begins his response with a lesson in reading and interpreting the
Scripture: **Haven't you read**? (Matt 19:4). Instead of engaging in proof texting
and discussing the technicalities of language, Jesus sets divorce into the wider 19:3-6
context of the story of God in the Torah. For him, the divine intention at creation of male and female should lie at the foundation of the practical theology
of marriage. Here Jesus is not only drawing the appropriate framework for
interpreting Deut 24:1-4 but also providing the theological basis for his radical
statement on marriage in Matt 5:31-32.

Jesus fuses two texts from Gen 1:27 and 2:24 together to make his argument. He uses the traditional rabbinic method of exegesis called *gezerah shavah*, that is, "interpretation of one text in the light of another text to which it is related by a shared word or phrase" (Instone-Brewer 2002, 137). The argument is simple: God has created male and female and united them in marriage, **so they are no longer two, but one flesh** (Matt 19:6).

These texts were traditionally used against polygamy, but Jesus takes an unexpected turn: **therefore what God has joined together, let no one separate**. Since God has created male and female with a purpose of uniting them in a monogamous marriage; this union—ideally—should not be broken (Instone-Brewer 2002, 138). Divorce, the separation of husband and wife, is against the divine purpose of lifelong marriage. If that is so, then how should we interpret Moses' statement about divorce? Does the husband have any legitimate reasons for divorce?

■ **7-9** Such a radical vision of marriage as an unbreakable, lifelong union puzzles the Pharisees. **"Why then," they asked, "did Moses command that a man give his wife a certificate of divorce and send her away?"** (v 7). Does Jesus reveal a contradiction between Genesis and the Deuteronomistic law? Here we need to note a change in language. Jesus uses the word "to permit" (*epitrepo*) instead of the Pharisaic "to command" (*entellomai*). For him, Moses' instructions regarding divorce should be seen as a concession, not a command (Harrington 1991, 273): **Moses permitted you to divorce your wives because your hearts were hard. But it was not this way from the beginning** (v 8).

For Jesus, Moses allowed divorce, in spite of God's original intentions for marriage, because of male hardness of heart; that is, their rebellious nature or weakness and failure. David Instone-Brewer suggests that "hardness of heart" should be understood as stubbornness to repent. If this is correct, then according to Jesus the divorce law could be applied if a guilty party stubbornly refuses to repent and to give up adulterous behavior. On the other hand, if a spouse repents, the innocent partner could forgive and not divorce (2002, 144). This fits well with Matthew's emphasis on limitless forgiveness (18:15-35). Divorce is permitted but not compulsory; it's not a command. For Jesus, Moses permits divorce because of human failure to forgive or to repent.

Anyone who divorces his wife, except for sexual immorality [*porneia*], **and marries another woman commits adultery** [*moichatai*]. Jesus does not discard Moses' authority but interprets this law on the basis of divine intentions: what God has united must not be divided. In this light "any case" could be only when "one flesh" has been compromised by infidelity. Here Jesus provides a very restrictive reading of Deut 24:1-4. He sees divorces on any grounds other than infidelity as invalid, perhaps siding with the "conservative" school of Shammai. However, divorce becomes an acceptable option if reconciliation is impossible.

In Jesus' interpretive framework of the Torah based on divine intentions at creation, a male partner who divorces on any grounds apart from adultery is still seen as married. Jesus' approach to marriage as a lifelong union makes male-initiated divorce virtually impossible. Thus he reiterates the seriousness and importance of marital union and indirectly protects women, who were more vulnerable in ancient marriage, from possible abusive practices of "easy divorce and remarriage."

■ **10-12** The issue of divorce unexpectedly rolls into the discussion about single living as the disciples react to the impossibility of divorce: **it is better not to marry** (*gamēsai*; Matt 19:10) then. According to traditional customs, divorce makes remarriage possible. But it is not so according to Jesus. Not surprisingly, the impossibility of divorce and remarriage has been perceived by the Twelve as a harsh commandment (Luz 2005, 500).

The disciples' reaction reveals that **not everyone can accept this word** (v 11). Robert Gundry interprets "this word" or "this teaching" in reference to the prohibition for Jesus' male followers, who could not remarry after divorce except on the grounds of infidelity (1982, 381-82). Voluntary abstention from marriage is not something that they are looking forward to, and it was not perceived as something normal within ancient Judaism anyway. Later rabbinic tradition recalls Rabbi Eleazar's interpretation of Gen 5:2 (the parallel passage to Gen 1:27): "Any man who has no wife is no proper man" (*b. Yebam.* 63A).

Jesus goes even further and turns to an uncomfortable image: **for there are eunuchs** (*eunouchoi*; v 12). There are three kinds of eunuchs, those males: (1) born with damaged reproductive organs; (2) **made . . . by others**, referring to castration as a punishment, torture, or cruelty to prisoners of war, to male harem servants, or to priests of certain pagan religious traditions; (3) and those who voluntarily committed to "unmarried life or to sexual ascetism" (Luz 2005, 502).

It appears that Jesus uses this unusual analogy to describe those within the church "who had to divorce their wives because of adultery and who are not free to remarry and to produce children with a new wife" (Luz 2005, 500). This comparison might have been perceived as offensive. Eunuchs would be seen not just as single persons but as not even proper males, experiencing exclusion and shame. The rabbinic tractate *Tosefta Megillah* 2.7 marks them and other males with damaged genitalia as the least holy among all other categories of Jewish males (see Lev 21:20-21; Deut 23:1).

But Jesus redefines this "offensive" imagery into something honorable: **eunuchs for the sake of the kingdom of heaven** (Matt 19:12). They have been
restored and welcomed into the new people of God (e.g., Acts 8:26-40) in fulfillment of Isa 56:3-7. Those who do not remarry out of obedience to Jesus' command demonstrate honorable dedication to the kingdom of heaven. It is another aspect of radical self-denial: marriage and having children is not compulsory. There is nothing dishonorable in staying single.

The one who can accept this should accept it. Jesus repeats twice that this choice is not appropriate for everybody; not everyone can accept this. The phrase could be interpreted as the call to divorced men, the followers of Jesus, to dedicate themselves to the cause of the kingdom of God. Becoming "a eunuch" is an act of radical self-denial that not only brings reputational losses in the ancient world but also sacrifices vital relationships and sexuality for divine purposes. Later in the chapter, Jesus returns to a similar issue related to sacrificing family ties for the sake of the kingdom (see 19:27-30).

FROM THE TEXT

The passage starts off as a technical rabbinic debate over marriage law (Deut 24:1): What are the lawful grounds for a male to file for divorce? Jesus interprets this law in the wider context of Scripture: the ideal at creation of humans is to become and remain "one flesh" in marriage. Thus this Deuteronomistic law doesn't allow any divorce apart from the grounds of "indecency," restrictively understood as marital infidelity.

Jesus recognizes that in the fallen world even what God put together could be broken through human unfaithfulness. In that case, divorce is possible but not unavoidable, since to divorce is not a commandment but a permission. It could be seen as a last resort if a spouse remains unrepentant. This virtual impossibility of male-initiated divorce could be seen as protective of women as a more vulnerable party in ancient Jewish marriage.

Apart from the interpretive limits of the passage, this is clearly a male-oriented text: the conversation about a male-initiated divorce turns into the issue of male adultery by remarriage (continuing the conversation about male adultery and lustful gaze from 5:27-30). The example of eunuchs further illustrates the point about male sexuality that could be offered as sacrifice.

The circumstances of women in regard to marriage and divorce are not even on Matthew's radar. Mark, on the other hand, includes women into the discussion in the parallel passage (see Mark 10:1-12). What would be valid female grounds for divorce? In this scenario, the wife is represented as a guilty party; what should happen when a male is a guilty party? Matthew doesn't say. Does Jesus have the issue of violence in the family in mind? Hardly, but that cannot be ignored in discussions of the breakdown of the covenantal relationship of marriage.

What would be Jesus' take on other reasons for divorce in Exod 21:10-11? Or Paul's permission to separate in the case of abandonment (1 Cor 7:10-16)? This passage has strict limitations in addressing the overall issue of divorce. However, Jesus does challenge some ancient Jewish male perceptions related to marriage: marriage, ideally, should stay unbroken; being single or celibate is a possibility as a response to the will of God. Surprisingly, neither marriage nor divorce are compulsory (Instone-Brewer 2003, 65-69).

Jesus responds to the issue of marriage and divorce in the very particular social realities of the ancient world: arranged marriages, contractual relationships, extended families, social and financial implications, patriarchal society, and so forth. Some of those social realities remain the same but others are significantly different. To navigate a pastoral response in the realities of a modern Western nuclear family might be very challenging. It is just as challenging to read this passage into circumstances of the non-Western world.

Recognition of the applicable limits of this passage in a different time and place should drive us to look more closely at Jesus' overall approach to the issue: one that is grounded in the wider context of Scripture and the purposes of God for human flourishing revealed in Christ. This would allow us to steer away from a legalistic debate over marriage and divorce toward a creative dialogue and practice that is guided by the spirit of forgiveness and love that are very close to the Matthean Jesus.

Unfortunately, this text and the similar ones have been used to create shame and guilt, even to exclude people from the church who for one reason or another could not stay married. In some instances they are treated as second-class church members. This is far away from Jesus' intentions in this passage. Serious questions need to be addressed. What, for instance, would be an appropriate response in the realities of modern pastoral ministry to remarried couples with children or couples who bypassed the official institution of marriage? These are far from easy questions to answer and require solid theological and biblical foundations with deep love and pastoral sensitivity. For help in navigating through some of the issues raised by this text, see Alex R. G. Deasley (2000) and David Instone-Brewer (2002).

F. The Little Children and Jesus (19:13-15)

BEHIND THE TEXT

The blessing of the little children continues Matthew's theme of family relationships and the kingdom. It follows the extended discussion on marriage, divorce, and "celibacy" addressing some controversial issues within Judaism at the time.

Malina and Rohrbaugh note that our modern romanticized perception of childhood is different from the realities of the ancient world. Disease, malnutrition, violence, abuse, hard work, and other factors contributed to a high rate of child mortality. Sixty percent were dead by the age of sixteen and over seventy percent would have lost one or both parents before reaching adolescence (2003, 336). Without any support system (apart from that of the wider family) children and orphans took their place alongside vulnerable members of society (→ 18:1-4).

God has a special concern for their well-being and fair treatment (see Deut 10:17-19; 14:28-29; Ps 82:3). They often relied on divine protection and provision. In this context, parents' motivation to bring their children to Jesus is understandable. When the fate of their children was often outside of their control, bringing children to be blessed by "a holy man" comes out of deep parental concern for children's protection and future well-being (France 2007, 727).

IN THE TEXT

■ **13** The little children **were brought** (*prosēnechthēsan*) to Jesus. This verb is often used by Matthew to describe bringing sick people to Jesus for healing (see 4:24; 8:16; 9:2, 32; 14:35; 17:16). Here, parents brought their children for Jesus **to place his hands on them and pray for them**. This could be interpreted in two ways. First, children were brought for healing, perhaps, because they were sick and dying (Malina and Rohrbaugh 2002, 336). Jesus has already healed some people by touching and laying on of hands (see 8:3; 9:18).

Second, it could be for blessing of the children (see Gen 48:14-15). The rabbinic tractate *Masekhet Soperim* recalls a tradition of bringing thirteen-year-old boys to be blessed by the elders of Jerusalem on the evening of the Day of Atonement (*Sop.* 18:5). Mark understands this event exactly in this light: Jesus "placed his hands on them and blessed them" (Mark 10:16; see vv 13-16).

But the disciples rebuked them. The reason is not clear. Perhaps they thought that Jesus had more important things to do than to attend to children whose prospects of survival were unclear. Their low position in society could also have added to that negative attitude.

■ **14-15 Let the little children come to me, and do not hinder them** (v 14). Whatever the event might be—blessing, healing, or both—the message is clear. Jesus cares for the little ones. This symbolic laying on of hands is a practical demonstration of divine care, inclusion, and recognition of the child's value (see 18:2-5) **for the kingdom of heaven belongs to such as these**. Despite their low status in the society, they take special place in the kingdom. Children matter not only to their parents but also to God himself.

FROM THE TEXT

This brief episode concludes the section in the narrative where Jesus
challenges some widespread perceptions in regard to marriage and children.
For him, marriage is not obligatory. But once partners are married, his ideal is
lifelong relationship. As in 18:1-3, Jesus dignifies small children as participants
19:14-15 in the kingdom. This story celebrates children and their place in the heart of
God. It is not surprising then that the passage has been used to support the
church's practice of infant baptism and dedication.

G. Teaching on the Way: Discipleship (19:16—20:28)

1. The Rich Young Man (19:16-30)

BEHIND THE TEXT

This story has two parts: the encounter with the rich young man (19:16-22) and the following teaching on discipleship (vv 23-30). It is built around a set of questions from a young man, the disciples, and finally, Peter. The encounter circles around the same key issues: covenantal righteousness, wealth, possessions, self-denial, status, rewards, and following Jesus. Matthew uses the language of being saved (*sōthēnai*; v 25), inheriting eternal life (*zōēn aiōnion*; vv 16-17, 29), and entering the kingdom of God (*eiselthein eis tēn basileian tou theou*; v 24) as synonyms.

The dialogue begins and concludes with the issue of inheriting eternal life (vv 16, 29). The key question of entering the kingdom of God is set in the context of the covenantal faithfulness of Israel to God through following the commandments of the Law. But Jesus—without rejecting the importance of the Law—redefines that notion. In these last days, ultimate obedience to the divine will is reflected in self-denial and following the Messiah.

The argument is structured in the following way:

- *Jesus and the rich young man* (vv 16-22). Question: "What good thing must I do to have eternal life?" Answer: "Keep the commandments," give "your possessions . . . to the poor, and . . . follow me." Reaction: The young man is unable to do it because of many possessions.
- *Jesus and the disciples* (vv 23-26). Reaction: "It is hard for someone who is rich to enter the kingdom of heaven"; almost impossible. Question: "Who then can be saved?" Answer: Salvation is in the hands of God.
- *Jesus and Peter* (vv 27-30). Reaction: We gave up everything and followed you. Question: What's the reward? Answer: Receive eternal life and rewards when Jesus becomes the king.

Matthew contrasts the story with the previous blessing of the little children (vv 13-15). This young man is a stereotypical righteous person, an embodiment of the Deuteronomistic vision of blessing and prosperity for those who obey the commandments (Deut 28:1-14; see Ps 1). Moreover, he longs for rabbinic wisdom and spiritual guidance. Surely, people like that, faithful to the covenant, are worthy to enter the kingdom of heaven! But the kingdom belongs to the low-status little children; a rich, righteous, high-status man goes away empty-handed. Jesus engages ancient stereotypes of righteousness, reinterprets scriptures, redefines the boundaries of the people of God, and challenges followers to think deeply about true discipleship.

IN THE TEXT

■ **16-20** Matthew does not identify the main character at the beginning of the story; we learn that he was a young rich man only at the end (v 22). A stranger (**a man**) approached Jesus and asked: **Teacher, what good thing must I do to get eternal life?** (v 16). This passage has often been interpreted as an example of "salvation by works" in Judaism. Some also assume that the text refers to salvation of the soul and eternal life as commonly understood in the Christian tradition. However, in the context of 2TJ and the progression of the passage, the young man's question is: "What should I do to be part of God's coming rule/the kingdom of God?" The answer is straightforward: being in covenant relationship with the God of Israel demonstrated through following Torah.

Jesus begins answering his question with a strange remark about **good** (*agathon*; v 17) that appears at first glance to be out of place: **There is only One who is good**. But this provides a framework for understanding what follows: **If you want to enter life, keep the commandments**. The goodness of God is the foundation of the commandments that Jesus selectively cites. They are about being good toward others: **You shall not murder, you shall not commit adul-**

tery, you shall not steal, you shall not give false testimony, honor your father and mother (vv 18-19).

This list is summed up by the commandment to love one's neighbor. Because God is good, a believer has to do good to others and even more, love them. Imitation of divine goodness is reflective of covenantal relationship. The commandments of loving neighbor and taking care of the poor come from Lev 19:10-15, 18. In their original context, they stem from the call to the people of God to imitate God's holiness (vv 1-2).

The young man confirms that he has been following the commandments. But could there be something that has escaped him, something that could prevent him from entering the kingdom: **What do I still lack?** (Matt 19:20).

■ **21-22** At first, Jesus refers to obedience to the covenantal law as one of the aspects of being part of the kingdom. This does not deviate from commonplace understanding. But Jesus does not stop here and redefines that notion. **If you want to be perfect** (*teleios*), Jesus states, you have to make two more steps: **go, sell your possessions and give to the poor, and you will have treasure in heaven. Then come, follow me** (v 21).

Matthew has already used the word "perfect" to describe attitude toward others: Jesus called the crowd to be perfect in love as their heavenly Father embracing friends and foes (5:48). In this passage, "to be perfect" is also used in reference to others: selling everything and giving it to the needy. This commandment from Jesus may be a practical, but rather radical, interpretation of the Law with its concern for social justice and care for the well-being of the poor (see Lev 19:10, 15).

Giving all possessions to the poor will not only show the young man's love toward his neighbor but also take it to another level. It will also test his love toward the God of Israel whom the Shema calls to love with all one's strength, that is, with one's possessions (Deut 6:4). Perfection in goodness and love could be demonstrated through unreserved surrendering of all possessions. Moreover, this could be a vivid demonstration of the kingdom at work: "Renouncing possessions and giving to the poor reflects a great reversal of things that brings with it the coming kingdom of God" (Barton 1994, 214).

Giving up possessions is the first step on the new journey of following Jesus. This is the key to the whole conversation. In Matthew, Jesus the Messiah is ushering in the kingdom of heaven, and following him and his interpretation of the Torah is to set oneself in the salvific work of God. To complete the list of commandments, **to be perfect** the young man needs to respond to Jesus' call to **follow me** through the radical act of love and self-denial and join him on the mission of God (Matt 19:21).

The full answer to the initial question, "What good thing must I do?", arrives here as a raw challenge: leave everything you have and follow me. This is what other disciples have already done. But for the young man (*neaniskos*), this message is hard to accept, for **he had great wealth** (*ktēmata polla*; v 22).

The tragic irony is that he was unable to do that one good thing in order to enter life eternal. Wealth turns from being the sign of blessing from God for those who obey him (Deut 28:1-14) into a stumbling block for fulfillment of God's will. This is a perfect illustration of Matt 6:19-24: the man is torn between securing treasure in heaven and serving money. This story redefines wealth and also the notion of righteousness. Obedience to the Torah is coupled with radical self-denial and following the Messiah. This righteousness evidently "surpasses that of the Pharisees and the teachers of the law" (5:20) and leads to the kingdom of heaven.

■ **23-26** Jesus uses the encounter as an opportunity to teach the disciples. Attachment to wealth makes it extremely hard, even impossible, to respond to the call of radical self-denial and total commitment to following Jesus. The hyperbole of **a camel** and **the eye of a needle** illustrates the point: **it is easier for** the impossible to happen rather than **for someone who is rich to enter the kingdom of God** (v 23). This reply shocks the Twelve. If this righteous, blessed man—obedient to Torah, an embodiment of Ps 1 ideals—is not good enough, **Who then can be saved?** (v 25).

The final answer to the rich young man's question is that it is a gift from God. In the days of the Messiah, the kingdom of God is breaking into this world through the mission of Jesus. Those who thought it was based only in obedience to the Law turned out to be mistaken. In these last days, responding to the Messiah's call and embracing his mission by radical following (19:29) sets one on the path to the kingdom of God.

■ **27-30 We have left everything to follow you! What then will there be for us?** (v 27). Unlike the rich young man, the Twelve answered Jesus' call, gave up what they had, and followed (see 4:18-22; 9:9-13). What is the reward? In his answer, Jesus sets an eschatological perspective: **At the renewal** [*palingenesia*] **of all things** (19:28). Discourses on reward and punishment (see chs 23—25) are a feature of Matthew's Gospel (Barton 1994, 208-9). Here Jesus looks into the future restoration of the people of God and establishment of the divine rule to promise well-deserved rewards. When Jesus becomes the king, his close companions will be given significant roles: "His disciples will be revealed as the most important persons among the Jewish people" (Harrington 1991, 281). They will rise from humble fishermen to the princes of Israel: **You . . . will also sit on twelve thrones, judging the twelve tribes of Israel**. The Twelve will become the leaders of the new holy people of God. This dramatic reversal of roles demonstrates the nature of the kingdom of heaven: **last will be first** (19:30).

Other disciples will not go empty-handed. Their feats of faith are no less impressive: leaving their possessions behind, breaking family relations, and rejecting obligations toward close relatives **for my sake** (v 29). This radical renunciation of possessions and cutting off family ties adds to the Matthean picture of true discipleship (Barton 1994, 214). It fits together with self-control (5:21-30, 33-37), private piety (6:1-18), almsgiving (5:42), fasting (6:16-18), self-denial and cross-bearing (16:24-26), avoidance of putting stumbling blocks before others (18:5-9) and, perhaps, celibacy for some (19:11-12). Such self-denial and discipline mark out dedicated followers and the whole community of faith gathered around Jesus the Messiah. It is not surprising that this whole passage inspired monastic movements of the past and encourages modern readers to simple and sacrificial living.

Significant sacrifices and generous future rewards are the key elements of the passage. Every character in the story has been promised eschatological recompense: treasure in heaven for the young man (v 21); the twelve thrones for the apostles (v 29); and to all followers a hundred times as much of what they left behind. Radical renunciation and self-denial for the name of Jesus is not meaningless; it carries great rewards in the future and particularly **eternal life** (*zōēn aiōnion*).

FROM THE TEXT

In his answer to the young rich man's question, Jesus redefines the traditional notion of righteousness that secures one's place in the coming kingdom of God. It is not enough just to be bound to God by a covenant relationship and obedience. To bring things to perfection, one must demonstrate the radical love toward God reflected in giving up everything for the sake of God's mission and following his Messiah. These last days, as the kingdom of heaven is breaking in and turning things upside down, demand radical change in life and total dedication. But not all could respond to that call. There is a danger of being enticed by wealth, social standing, and other cares of human life.

Thus following Jesus requires self-denial and rejection of things that could cause stumbling. But the rewards are much greater. Hardships and rewards of discipleship are at the center of this passage. Being part of the divine rule, entering life eternal, though ultimately the gift of God, is predicated on following Jesus and his practical interpretation of the Torah that is firmly rooted in imitation of God's goodness, love, righteousness, and holiness.

Jesus' call to renounce possessions, marriage, and even family sounds challenging for both ancient and modern readers. Historically, Christians responded to this call in different ways: from communal living in the early church (Acts 2:42-47) to the monastic movements in late antiquity; from spiritual renewals and self-denial appeals in modern times to choosing to live simply.

The passage raises hard questions. The answers are neither easy nor predetermined. What does it mean to follow Christ in the realities of modern cultures across the world? Is it even possible today? What does self-denial look like in the life of "middle class" Christians? What things prevent us from undertaking this salvific journey? Questions continue.

Unfortunately, the self-denial language is often reduced to a banality of money given for charities or mission work. It also can't be shrunk to ministerial calling in the church or overseas missionary appointment. There is no "two-tier" system of discipleship; all are called to follow Christ in such a way that reflects the upside-down values of the kingdom of heaven and the character of God. The lenses of individualistic spirituality also have to be removed in order to find an answer to the question, What does it mean to follow Christ as a community of faith?

The text's radical message pushes readers to think counterculturally. It goes against rampant consumerism and encourages simple living. It rejects the pursuit of individualistic well-being and supports social consciousness and responsibility. It resists modern evangelical versions of "the prosperity gospel" and inspires generosity of spirit. No commentator can dictate an answer; no follower of Jesus can avoid the questions. This radical thrust of Jesus' call must be heard afresh in every time and place.

2. The Parable of the Workers in the Vineyard (20:1-16)

BEHIND THE TEXT

Matthew carefully creates the context for this parable. First, he brackets it by similar sayings with reversed word order:

- 19:30 "But many who are first will be last, and many who are last will be first."
- 20:16 "So the last will be first, and the first will be last."

Second, the whole section of 19:16—20:34 wrestles with the issues of
status, greed, power, and true discipleship. The parable itself is addressed to the Twelve in response to the issue of status and reward for those who left everything and followed Jesus (19:27-30): "you . . . will also sit on twelve thrones" (v 28). Later, the question about sitting on the right and left in the kingdom of heaven is met with "whoever wants to be first must be your slave" (20:27).

Third, the parable has also been bookmarked by Jesus' statement about his own death and humiliation (20:17-19). This illustrates what it means to become last. Fourth, this section culminates with the exemplary behavior of two blind beggars who demonstrate the humble attitude of the true followers of Jesus.

Such an intertwined and complex narrative structure creates an interpretive focus for the parable. The disciples are concerned with fair reward, status, and power; Jesus opposes that culturally driven pursuit for honor. In the kingdom this logic has been reversed. True discipleship cannot be based on a desire for rewards and status in the coming kingdom. Rather, sacrificial servanthood and a humble attitude mark out the true disciples of Christ.

This challenges some traditional interpretations. Many see it as an illustration of divine grace in salvation, an argument against salvation by work and merits, or a prophetic insight into acceptance of the Gentiles who will later join the mission of God. But none of these does justice to Matthew's deliberately crafted narrative.

Jesus builds this parable on the scriptural image of a vineyard representing the people of Israel and its owner—YHWH himself (Isa 5:1-7; Jer 12:10). But Jesus redefines that image. The hired workers represent his disciples—the leaders of the new holy people of God gathered around the Messiah—who participate in the mission of God by ushering in the kingdom and serving the community of faith. The time of harvest may refer to the time of spreading the good news of the kingdom (see 13:39); and receiving a day's pay might have eschatological overtones and refer to future judgment and reward (Harrington 1991, 284).

IN THE TEXT

■ **1-7** Matthew uses **the kingdom of heaven is like** as an introduction to the parables (v 1). Jesus illustrates the principles of the kingdom by comparing it to hiring seasonal workers at harvest: **a landowner who went out early in the morning to hire workers for his vineyard**. This was normal practice in rural Palestine: a vineyard owner comes to a marketplace (*agora*) where he can find day workers for picking grapes (vv 2, 4, 7).

Unlike normal practice (Hultgren 2000, 37), this landowner (*oikodespotēs*) hires workers in stages: early in the morning (around 6 a.m. [v 1]), at noon (v 5), throughout the day, and at dusk (v 6). The story gradually builds up the contrast between those hired in the morning and those hired closer to the evening. The expected differentiation in wages drives the plot forward. The owner has agreed to pay **a denarius for the day** with the first party (v 2), and **whatever is right** with the rest (v 4). A denarius was an average payment for the twelve-hour workday that lasted from sunrise to sunset (Snodgrass 2008, 370). All would assume proportionate pay according to hours of work. Those hired later would not expect to be paid for the whole day.

■ **8-12 When evening came** (v 8). The Torah requires payment of a hired worker on the evening of that day (Lev 19:13; Deut 24:14-15). The owner orders his manager to pay first those who were hired last and to pay the first last. When those who were paid first received a full day's wage for a partial day's work, expectations of those workers who worked all day were understandably high. If the master gives a whole day's pay to laborers who worked just a few hours, **they expected to receive more** (Matt 20:10).

But their hopes were dashed. They got the normal rate—**a denarius**. Their feeling of entitlement and expectations based on their understanding of fairness created a sense of injustice. And the workers **grumble** [*egongyzon*] **against the landowner** in spite of the fact that they have received their wages (v 11). From their perspective, the problem is, **You have made them equal** [*isous*] **to us** (v 12). The last hired who were paid first received an undeservedly high amount, and the first hired got paid the agreed amount. This reversal illustrates one of the main points of the parable: "The last will be first, and the first will be last" (v 16). The parable takes an eschatological tone: in the kingdom of heaven God might reward in a similar way.

■ **13-16** The landowner responds to one of the representatives of the group: **I am not being unfair** or unjust **to you, friend** (v 13; see 22:12; 26:50). He keeps his word and they received the agreed payment. The owner can do whatever he wants with his money. The problem is somewhere else: **Are you envious** [*ho ophthalmos sou ponēros*] **because I am generous?** (*agathos*; 20:15). This could be literally translated as "Is your eye evil because I am good?" Here the metaphor of "an evil eye" describes envy, similar to 6:23. The workers are jealous because the owner is generous to others. But this generosity shows "God's freedom to be gracious" (Luz 2001, 534) and illustrates further the divine ability to provide generous gifts and rewards (see 19:26-30).

At the end, Jesus formulates the moral of the parable: **The last will be first, and the first will be last** (20:16). This reverses his previous saying from 19:30. In the context of 19:16-29, "The first will be last, and the last will be first" meant that the least in the society—who left everything and followed Jesus—will become first in the kingdom when Jesus becomes the king.

But this parable teaches the disciples a different lesson. Those who think that they have a higher status or deserve more might find themselves being last. In the time of "great reversal" God might surprise the leaders of the people of God with his radical generosity. Though the Twelve will become "the judges . . . of Israel" (19:28 NEB), they have to remember that if they get their focus wrong in their mission of the kingdom, they might become the last. This is another paradox of the kingdom.

FROM THE TEXT

The story likens working in a vineyard during harvest to the outworking of the kingdom of heaven. The landowner hired the laborers to toil in the vineyard; God has invited the Twelve to participate in his mission and to serve his people. At its center is the remarkable generosity and goodness of the landowner and the jealousy of those who felt entitled to more for their hard work. Here Jesus challenges the disciples' concerns and attitudes toward rewards in the kingdom (see 19:27-30; 20:20-28). His followers should not claim any special status over others before God due to "hard conditions" or "long period of service" in the kingdom (Pregeant 2004, 150).

Jesus warns leaders about the risk of becoming last if they get their priorities wrong. At the eschatological reversal, the disciples might see others—whom they reckoned to be worthless and unimportant—being lifted up and rewarded by the act of justice and the overwhelming mercy of God. Ultimately, the parable is about the way God acts in judgment and reward that often defies human ideas about fairness. It illustrates God's justice, grace, and an often-incomprehensible sense of generosity.

If this is the way the kingdom operates, what should the followers expect? On the one hand, participation in God's mission is not "a fruitless endeavor." God will reward justly and generously. But those who think they should receive more because of their selfless contribution or position in the community might find themselves disappointed since God does not act according to human ideas about justice.

Nor should the desire for power, status, and rewards guide their ministry. The proper motivation is a serving spirit and reliance on God's generous mercy, not calculation of rewards. The followers are to emulate divine generosity and not envy others. Otherwise those who might think of themselves as the first in the kingdom of heaven might find themselves last (Snodgrass 2008, 375-77).

3. The Third Passion Prediction (20:17-19)

BEHIND THE TEXT

Jesus' third prediction (see 16:21; 17:22-23) had been made on the way to Jerusalem (20:17) and provides more details. It includes a reference to the role of the Gentiles. This unholy alliance between the Jewish religious leaders and the Gentile authorities will be responsible for the Messiah's humiliation, torture, and crucifixion. Instead of a place from which good news is proclaimed, the sacred city—the center of worship and pilgrimage—becomes the place of injustice, rejection, and suffering of God's Messiah (see 23:37-39).

IN THE TEXT

■ **17** Matthew reminds his readers that Jesus is **going up to Jerusalem**. Signposts on the journey are noted: Galilee (17:22), Judea (19:1), Jericho (20:29), the Mount of Olives (21:1), and now Jerusalem (21:10). The passage mentions Jerusalem twice. As they slowly approach Jerusalem, this interlude—in anticipation of unfolding events—creates suspense and expectation. But for the disciples, this prediction redefines and challenges their vision of the future. Jerusalem will become the place of suffering of the Messiah, and not of his political triumph as envisioned in popular Jewish eschatology.

As with the other predictions, this is a private conversation. He **took the Twelve aside** and alerted them, for the third time, about the importance of these events. This is the true path of the Messiah, the cup that he is about to drink (see 20:22-23). But they still only understand dimly. No reference is made to their response (compare 16:22; 17:23). Could this signal acceptance or disbelief?

■ **18-19** The previous predictions focused only on Jesus' fate. But here, **we are going up to Jerusalem**. They will play their role in the coming tragic events. The passion will touch their lives on both personal and communal levels: betrayal, abandonment, denial, sufferings, death, and resurrection. They share the journey as a community, though in different ways. Following the footsteps of Jesus often involves suffering and even death (see 16:24-26).

This prediction adds more detail. We already know that Jesus will be betrayed (17:22), the religious leaders will be involved (16:21), and he will be killed and raised to life on the third day (16:21; 17:23). Here Jesus elaborates on the role of the leaders: they will sentence him to death (20:18) and **hand him over to the Gentiles to be mocked and flogged and crucified**. In doing so, Matthew creates links to the Passion Narrative: **will be delivered** (*paradothēsetai*) ↔betrayal by Judas (26:14-16, 47-56); the religious leaders **will condemn him** (*katakrinousin*)↔the plot to kill and the Sanhedrin trial (26:3-5, 57-68); **will hand him over** [*paradōsousin*] **to the Gentiles to be mocked** [*empaixai*] **and flogged** [*mastigōsai*] **and crucified** (*staurōsai*)↔trial before Pilate; humiliation, torture, and crucifixion by Roman soldiers (27:11-26, 27-44); he **will be raised** (*egerthēsetai*) from the dead↔resurrection on the third day (28:1-8).

This short description reveals Matthew's view: Jesus is portrayed as a victim, an object of the actions of others. The blame for his sufferings and death is placed on the Jewish authorities (→ 27:24-26). Though Jesus appears to have no control over the circumstances, these events will reveal his deep sense of self-denial and surrender to the divine will; this attitude is in stark contrast to the disciples' longing for power (see 20:20-28).

FROM THE TEXT

The third prediction redefines the disciples' perception of what is about to take place. It comes after the disciples' fixation on sacrifices and rewards. Jesus' reminder about his own ultimate sacrifice exposes their selfish thinking (Keener 2009, 484). The narrative contrasts humiliation, sufferings, and crucifixion with the disciples' desire to sit on thrones in glory (see 19:28; 20:21). Any claim to rewards and glory requires following Jesus on the path of suffering and death (see 16:24-26). But this is no mere individual pursuit. Embracing the suffering of Christ for the sake of the good news is a communal journey that affects believers as a community.

20:20-28

4. A Mother's Request (20:20-28)

BEHIND THE TEXT

Matthew now returns to the familiar themes: reward, status, suffering, and servanthood (see vv 16, 18-19). Surely the disciples would already comprehend what true greatness is in the kingdom. But no. They fail to grasp not only the way of the Messiah but the nature of following, discipleship, and leadership in the kingdom.

The petition of the mother of James and John contrasts with those of the Canaanite woman and her daughter (15:21-28) and the plea of the blind beggars (20:29-34) who exemplify key aspects of following Jesus.

IN THE TEXT

■ **20-23** The mother of James and John (the sons of Zebedee) approaches Jesus with a request. The woman is portrayed as a humble petitioner: she kneels before Christ and only speaks after he asks her a question. Perhaps she recognizes Jesus' royal authority. Later in Matthew, she is one of the faithful female disciples who stayed at the cross (27:55-56). The parallel story in Mark 10:34-45 does not mention her at all. Perhaps Matthew places her here to protect the reputation of her sons so that her request is the "naïve concern of the loving mother" (France 2007, 756). More probably, their attempt to avoid embarrassment by sending their mother to ask for them—ironically—characterizes them negatively (Turner 2008, 486).

Her request was not simple: to grant that her sons would sit at Jesus' right and left hands in his kingdom. As the Messiah and his followers get nearer to Jerusalem, James and John seek places of honor and power in anticipation that Jesus will become the King of Israel. Perhaps, in their minds, the arrival in the holy city will trigger the events that will lead to reestablishment of the throne of David. They want to ascend into the positions of power as Jesus' close viziers and trusted advisers, perhaps even preempting Peter or one of the others. They act as if they have not heard Jesus' words about the fate of the Messiah (20:17-19). Ironically, at the crucifixion, "the mock-up enthronement," the right and the left beside Jesus were occupied by bandits while James and John were in hiding (27:38).

Jesus' reply is addressed to the brothers; this is a strong hint that James and John are behind this request. They have not comprehended the magnitude and implications of their request. So Jesus asks them a question: **Can you drink the cup I am going to drink?** (v 22). The Scripture uses the cup metaphor for God's judgment or to describe a person's fate, suffering, or even death (see Ps 11:6; Isa 51:17; Zech 12:2). In Gethsemane, Jesus uses this traditional language of "this cup" to refer to his own impending suffering and death (Matt 26:39). In other words, Jesus asked them if they are prepared to suffer for the sake of the kingdom.

The brothers confidently affirm that they can drink that cup. But this, too, turns into an irony: when the time comes, these close disciples fled and failed to **drink from** the **cup** as they boldly promised (20:23; 26:31-35, 56). However, they will drink their cup of suffering for the sake of the kingdom but later in their lives.

In spite of their confident response, Jesus cannot grant their wish: **These places belong to those for whom they have been prepared by my Father**. After Jesus' teaching in chs 19—20 they should have known that there are no privileges in the kingdom (Luz 2001, 543; see 19:26; 20:1-16). Rather, the way to sharing in the glory lies through suffering and self-denial. They have to follow the path of Christ: through suffering to vindication, from humiliation to glory.

But even then, only the heavenly Father will decide who is worthy to receive these rewards. This again underlines the inadequacy of the disciples' question and demonstrates the radical difference between visions of power in human and God's kingdoms.

■ **24-28** The other ten disciples are annoyed with James and John after hearing about their request. They are indignant, not because of moral superiority but because the Zebedee brothers got there first. Despite the fact that they all have been promised prominent positions in the future, to "sit on twelve thrones" (19:28), their jealousy (see 19:9-15) betrays their weak grasp of Jesus' teaching on leadership and servanthood (see ch 18).

Jesus turns this incident into another teaching opportunity. He gathers the Twelve and lays out two contrasting examples of leadership: the rulers of the Gentiles and the leaders of the new holy people of God. He opposes "lord it over" (*katakyrieuousin*; 20:25) and "exercise authority [*katexousiazousin*] over" the people to becoming a "servant" (*diakonos*; v 26) or even a "slave" (*doulos*; v 27) to others. Jesus challenges deeply engrained cultural assumptions about leadership. Their relentless drive for honor and power reflects culturally approved patterns: to rise from poor fishermen to nobility in the kingdom of God. They want to climb that pyramid of power that existed in the ancient world with oppressive rulers at the top and powerless and disenfranchised slaves at the bottom.

Jesus tips that pyramid on its head: **Not so with you** (v 20). Their model of leadership is not the rulers of the Gentiles. Their last lesson was from children (see 18:2-4); here it is from those at the bottom: servants and slaves. In the paradoxical nature of the kingdom of heaven as opposed to the kingdoms of the world, true greatness is found not in a position of power but in sacrificial service to others. The disciples are called to deny claims to status of honor and power and to humble themselves to positions of dishonor and powerlessness; genuine Christian leadership comes from a serving attitude.

To live out this new radical pattern of leadership, the Twelve need to follow Jesus' example. He embodies sacrificial self-denial for the sake of others: **The Son of Man did not come to be served, but to serve, and to give his life as a ransom for many** (20:28). The Son of Man did not come to rule but to exercise authority in service to others through feeding the hungry, healing the afflicted, releasing captives from the bondages of possession, embracing the excluded, proclaiming forgiveness of sins, and so forth.

Here the phrase **the Son of Man** gains another dimension; it is connected not only to images of heavenly glory (16:27-28; 24:36-44; 26:64) or future suffering (17:22; 26:45) but also to the mission of God—serving others. Brower, however, suggests that "the son of man" language—based on Dan 7:13—points to Jesus and as well as to his followers. The title, thus, hints at collective participation in redemptive suffering and the mission of God that brings salvation to all of humanity (2012, 284-87).

The culmination of the servanthood motif comes in the ultimate act of sacrifice—giving life as **a ransom for many** (*lytron anti pollōn*). The meaning of the phrase is not clear here and has no other scriptural parallels. The OT uses the word "ransom" in two ways (see Brower 2012, 286-87, for more detailed discussion). Literally, it means a monetary price for a slave's freedom (Exod 21:30) or buying back things dedicated to God (Lev 27; Num 3:40-51).

In a metaphorical sense, the word denotes deliverance and salvation of people from oppression, enemies, evil, and so forth (e.g., Ps 130:8; Jer 15:20-21; 31:11). Thus Jesus' death is an act of service that brings deliverance to others (France 2007, 761). The disciples—following the Son of Man example—have to be prepared not only to become servants of others but also to give their lives (see Matt 16:24-28).

Matthew has been echoing and interpreting the Suffering Servant song from Isa 53:10-12 (but see Lutz 2001, 546). In Isaiah, the righteous servant gives his life as a redemptive offering that ushers in restoration of the holy people of God—"make many righteous" (Isa 53:11 NRSV). Here, one person suffers and many, the people, benefit. It does not imply that "many" equals "all" nor that it has a vicarious death with an elected few in mind (France 2007, 763). This Isaianic background fits well into the Matthean vision of Jesus, who brings redemption (1:21) and makes the covenant (26:28) through giving up his life for the benefit of many; this is "the saving action by which God establishes his new people" (Hooker 1994, 56).

However, seeing a developed theology of atonement—and particularly of "limited atonement" or "substitutionary atonement"—in this or other Matthean passages would be anachronistic. Perhaps, the emphasis is not on the nature of death per se but on the radical character of servanthood that culminates in giving his own life for the salvific benefits of others (Lutz 2001, 546).

FROM THE TEXT

The disciples misunderstand the nature of leadership in the kingdom. They act out the cultural values and male virtues of their day by pursuing positions of honor and power. Jesus confronts them with a countercultural paradigm and subverts their notion of authority. The leaders of the new people of God are to practice servanthood instead of oppressive rule. To be first in the community of faith is to embrace the position of a slave. Jesus is the ultimate example in selfless and sacrificial service to others.

The message of servanthood and radical self-denial for the sake of Christ and others is challenging for modern readers if taken seriously. It's hard to embrace Jesus' teaching and example in all cultures that encourage self-promotion, worship fame, value winners, despise losers, and generally operate in honor/shame paradigms. This goes against the human inclination to dominate others, a symbol of our alienation from each other apart from Christ.

How do today's church leaders express Christlikeness in their ministry? What does it mean to follow his example and to confront cultural patterns wherever we live? How do we live out the upside-down, inside-out values of the kingdom in contemporary communities of faith? These questions do not go away and should continually be at the forefront of our community and personal self-examination under the Spirit.

There may be a few ways to think about them: in societies that praise go-getters and worship success, to live out servanthood; in societies that worship money, to practice sacrificial giving and reliance on God; in societies that value individualism, to create healthy communities of faith; in societies that encourages consumerism, to exercise modesty and taking care of others; in the societies obsessed by well-being, to open our eyes to suffering in this world and to share the pain of others.

As today's holy people of God, we are called to serve each other and live together as a serving community that values each other. We encourage each other, recognize each other's gifts, break cultural boundaries, and help each other to live out our individual and communal calling in this world. These patterns of countercultural living may capture some of the kingdom values of the Matthean Jesus.

H. Jesus Heals Two Blind Men in Jericho (20:29-34)

BEHIND THE TEXT

This is the last miracle in Christ's ministry. The story has a doublet in Matt 9:27-31. Both episodes have two blind men (9:27↔20:30), a petition to have mercy (9:27↔20:30), the proclamation of Jesus' identity as Son of David (9:27↔20:30-31) and healing by a touch (9:29↔20:34). But minor dissimilarities and different contexts suggest slightly different interpretations. Here the two healed men show interest in following (20:34) instead of spreading the news (see 9:31). The triple public confession of Jesus as Lord and Son of David (see the private encounter in 9:28) signals interest in messianic identity. The stories form a literary connection between ministries in Galilee and Judea (Patte 1986, 284).

IN THE TEXT

■ **29 As Jesus and his disciples were leaving Jericho**, they leave an important ancient crossroads. The routes from Judea, Perea (modern Jordan), and the Jordan valley meet here. The city and its oasis, mentioned by Josephus, Pliny, and Strabo, was known for its palm grove, fountains, Herod's palace, and perfume production. In addition, it was a stopping point for Jewish pilgrims on their way to Jerusalem. Jesus and his disciples find themselves in the midst of pilgrims who engulfed Jericho at Passover.

■ **30-31 Two blind men** [*duo tuphloi*] **were sitting by the roadside** (v 30), probably begging for alms from the pilgrim crowds (Hahn 2007, 243). Disability in the ancient world was perceived as great misfortune or even divine punishment. The shame associated with physical deformity often led to marginalization, to exclusion from communities, and to poverty.

Some holiness groups treated blind people as unclean since they could not avoid contacting impure things (4QMMT B 49-54). Visual impairment could lead to exclusion from temple worship (Ermakov 2014a, 178). The effect on communal and family relationships is less clear. One thing is evident: for whatever reason these blind men found themselves on the fringes of social and religious life.

To attract Jesus' attention, **They shouted, "Lord, Son of David, have mercy** [*eleēson*] **on us!"** The crowd of pilgrims who were following Jesus rebuked them and tried to silence them. Matthew does not give reasons for this strange reaction. Perhaps, assumptions about the greatness of the Messiah did not allow them to see people in need and caused them to treat those blind beggars as unworthy of Jesus' attention (Patte 1986, 285) or they did not want Jesus to be delayed on his journey (Turner 2008, 491) or such public acclamation of Jesus could be seen as dangerous and rebellious in the charged political and religious atmosphere surrounding Passover. Whatever the reason, the two men persisted and Jesus heard them. In contrast to the crowd's lack of compassion, Jesus does not ignore their plea. Here the royal Messiah embodies the kingdom's ideals of servanthood and is prepared to serve the least.

The identification of Jesus as Lord (*kyrios*) and Son of David (*huios Dauid*) is important. Matthew uses *kyrios* extensively in relation to Jesus; this address often comes from the disciples and people in need of healing. More generally, the term "lord" was used in a variety of contexts and could indicate a relationship between a master and servants/slaves, a teacher and a disciple, a king and his subjects, or God and his people (*DJG*, 484-93). By bringing these two titles together, Matthew narrows the meaning of *kyrios* here to an identification of Jesus as the royal Messiah, the Messiah of Davidic lineage. It also echoes the tradition of another son of David—Solomon—who was known in Jewish tradition not only for his wisdom but also for possessing healing and exorcistic powers (Harrington 1991, 291).

Messiah from the House of David in Second Temple Judaism

The eschatological expectations of a messiah coming from the royal house of David are known in 2TJ. *Four Ezra* 12:32 envisages the coming of the Messiah at the end of days "who will arise from the posterity of David." The *Psalms of Solomon* picture the Messiah as a Davidic king who will purify Jerusalem, restore

Jewish people, and reestablish the land of Israel (*Pss. Sol.* 17-18). Some Dead Sea Scrolls refer to the Messiah of Righteousness as "the branch of David" (4Q252; 4Q285). In Matthew Jesus as the Son of David (see 1:1-17) fulfills the messianic expectations for restoring (see 9:27; 12:23; 15:22; 21:15) the people of God (*DJG*, 768-69). In the debate with the Pharisees, Jesus takes this identification even further—the Messiah has divine identity (see 22:41-45).

These men confessed Jesus to be the Messiah of Israel with the power and authority to heal them. Ironically, the blind men perceived something that escaped the "seeing" disciples and the crowd. This affirmation comes in anticipation of his triumphal entrance to Jerusalem (21:1-10). Jesus, the Son of David, the coming King of Israel, will arrive to the holy city but will be rejected by his subjects. He will be the Suffering Messiah, the Son of Man.

■ **32-34** Jesus asked them a question similar to the one he asked the sons of Zebedee and their mother in the previous story (see 20:21): **What do you want me to do for you?** (v 32). The question reveals the true desires of human hearts. The closest apostles wished to sit on the thrones in the kingdom of heaven; the blind men—**our sight** (v 33) or "that our eyes might be opened" (*hina anoigōsin hoi ophthalmoi hēmōn*).

According to R. V. G. Tasker (1961, 196), the Codex Nitriensis Curetonianus (an early Syriac version of the four Gospels) adds a line to the blind men's reply: "that we may see you." This addition interprets their desire not just for mere healing but as a desire to follow Jesus. But even without this later addition, this simple request adds another ironic touch to the story. The desire to see and then follow is juxtaposed against the concern for power and status. Perhaps the apostles were blinded or their sight was blurred by desires for glory. But the blind men—secondary characters in the Gospel story—see the true nature of discipleship.

Jesus had compassion [*splanchnistheis*] **on them and touched their eyes** (v 34). The Messiah on his way to Jerusalem for the Matthean climax pauses to show mercy to two disabled beggars. Jesus, the example to the Twelve of true greatness in the kingdom (see 20:20-28), serves "the little ones" (18:10-14). With their sight restored, they could return back to their normal lives and reconnect with their community. These disabled, poor, unclean, and insignificant members of the society were restored to health and now can fulfill their religious and social duties.

By associating with and extending his grace to them, the Messiah also restores their dignity. The shame associated with disability in the ancient world has been removed. This brief healing encounter demonstrates a holistic picture of restoration and salvation that affects all areas of their lives. The Messiah of Israel restores his people.

Immediately they received their sight and followed him. Now that they can see, they have chosen not to go back to their old lives but to join Jesus on the way. Their response to the merciful act of the Lord is to follow him.

FROM THE TEXT

This is more than just another healing story demonstrating Jesus' power and authority. It also reveals, through contrast with the previous episode (20:20-28), aspects of authentic discipleship: the blind men clearly perceive Jesus' true identity, publicly confess it, receive complete restoration, and follow him. The irony is strong: this perceptiveness and response to Jesus is something with which the Twelve struggle. Charles Talbert also notes a pattern of discipleship that emerges from the story: from spiritual blindness to seeing who Jesus is and to following him (2010, 242).

The episode also illustrates holistic restoration. Once on the fringes of the society, they now find their new place at the epicenter of God's work. Treated with dignity, the blind men were not only brought to health but also restored back to religious and communal life. Even more, they find their place among the new people of God who have been gathering around Jesus the Messiah. The kingdom of heaven bridges the boundaries of social exclusion and draws the restored men within. Through the work of the Messiah the kingdom breaks in, turning things upside down and restoring people in different aspects of their lives.

The confession of Jesus as Lord and Son of David emphasizes the royal aspect of his identity. He is the true King of Israel from David's line, already set out as important in Matthew's birth narratives (chs 1—3). This affirmation anticipates his royal visit to the holy city. The portrayal of Jesus' identity continues throughout his time in Jerusalem and culminates at the crucifixion as the wooden plaque over his head states, "THIS IS JESUS, THE KING OF THE JEWS" (27:37).

V. JESUS IN JERUSALEM: MATTHEW 21:1—25:46

A. Jesus' Arrival in Jerusalem (21:1-11)

BEHIND THE TEXT

Jesus' arrival in Jerusalem marks an important turn in the story: his last days in the holy city. Here, at the heart of the Jewish nation, the Messiah of Israel will prophesy, heal, teach, and confront the corrupt religious and civil establishment. In a tragic twist, the holy city will also become the place of rejection, suffering, and death of the Son of God. The crowd's acclamation "Hosanna to the Son of David" at the triumphal entry (21:9) will change to "Crucify him!" at the trial (27:22). Matthew wraps the event of entry to Jerusalem in Scripture.

Passover and Yom Kippur were the most important festivals in the Jewish calendar. Pilgrims flocked to Jerusalem from everywhere. E. P. Sanders estimates that from three hundred to five hundred thousand people could have been in attendance (1992, 128). Josephus mentions that whole families would travel to celebrate Passover (*Ant.* 11.109), bring sacrifices, and share the festive meal with relatives and friends. It is not surprising, then, to hear about children in the temple (see 21:15-16). Jesus enters Jerusalem surrounded by this pilgrim crowd ascending to the Temple Mount.

IN THE TEXT

■ **1-7** The road from Jericho brought Jesus and his disciples to the Mount of Olives that overlooks the holy city from the east. This brief remark sets the geographical context and alludes to Zech 14:4. Zechariah envisioned that in the last days YHWH himself will come to Jerusalem and "his feet will stand on the Mount of Olives."

At the village of Bethphage (from Aramaic, "the house of unripe figs"), Jesus makes arrangements for his so-called triumphal entry. Matthew signals its importance by including this preparation. Similar arrangements will be made for the Last Supper (26:17-19). Jesus sends two disciples to find a young donkey with its mother, with instructions to untie and bring them to him. The story is enigmatic, and Matthew offers no explanation apart from the fulfillment of prophecy. However, the phrase that sounds like a password—**the Lord needs them** (21:3)—shows Jesus' identity and authority and creates a sense that whatever takes place is happening in accordance to God's will.

Matthew's account creates an impression that Jesus rides two donkeys: the disciples put cloaks on *them* and he sat on *them*. A few explanations have been proposed to deal with that puzzling description. First, Matthew's bad grammar creates ambiguity and the second "them" refers to cloaks not donkeys. Second, Matthew misinterpreted the Hebrew parallelism in Zech 9:9 where the repetition refers to the same donkey and not to two animals. Third, Matthew uses a rabbinic way of interpreting the prophecy "and flexes his grammar" to serve his theological purpose (Garland 2001, 214). Fourth, the remark about two donkeys might reflect a reality when a young and unridden colt is still accompanied by his mother to calm him down in overwhelming circumstances of a large crowd (Morris 1992, 522).

The reference to two animals is important for Matthew since he wants the readers to grasp fully the symbolism behind Jesus' ride to Jerusalem (Hagner 1993, 594). He quotes Zech 9:9 as the frame of reference for understanding the event. This is, then, a prophetic reenactment that makes an unequivocal statement about the identity of the rider and his messianic purposes. Jesus is not just a Galilean rabbi on pilgrimage; this is an event of far greater magnitude. Zechariah's prophecy has been fulfilled: Jesus, the humble and righteous king from David's line, comes to Israel's capital to restore his people. The scene recalls David's return to Jerusalem as a victorious but humble and peaceful king after defeating his son Absalom (2 Sam 19—20).

■ **8-11** An exceptionally large crowd (*ho pleistos okhlos*) joins the procession. People spread their clothes and tree branches on the road in a public act of celebration and honoring of the coming king (see 2 Kgs 9:13). Repeated shouts of **hosanna** (Matt 21:9)—which literally means "save us"—turn into acclamations of praise and glory. The phrases are taken from Ps 118:25-26. The psalm is a king's song of thanksgiving and used in a festal procession into the temple courts (from the gates to the altar). Starting off as an individual thanksgiving (vv 5-24), it turns into communal praise as the worshipers unite with their king in the acclamation of "the saving power of God" (Anderson 2000, 103).

In an unexpected twist, Jesus' humble presence turns an annual pilgrims' ascension to the Temple Mount into a royal procession. The royal psalm sounds again as the messianic King comes to fulfill divine promises of restoration and salvation. This is the culminating moment in the motif of confession of Jesus' identity: the large crowd of Jewish pilgrims recognizes Jesus as the Son of David and not only single individuals (a Canaanite woman [Matt 15:22]; blind men [9:27; 20:30]). Secrecy has gone (9:27-31; 16:20). Jesus arrives in Jerusalem as the Messiah, the Savior, and the true King of Israel.

This unexpected royal procession has **stirred** (*seiein*; 21:10) Jerusalem. A large crowd approaching the city and acclaiming Jesus as the Davidic messianic King triggers some anxiety. The inhabitants are alarmed and puzzled: who is this? Jesus is unknown in the city. Pilgrims from Galilee may be better informed. For them, he appears to be **the prophet from Nazareth of Galilee** (v 11). This seems to be a common perception among people (16:14), but at the end of the story it will be also revealed that he is the King of the Jews (27:11) and the Son of God (26:63-64; 27:54).

FROM THE TEXT

The entry into Jerusalem turns into the public revelation and acclamation of Jesus' messianic identity. This is pictured as a royal procession into the 21:12-17
temple courts. Jesus' visitation of the holy city fulfills the old prophecy and vividly demonstrates the paradoxical nature of Jesus' messiahship: the humble king arrives on a donkey to serve his people and bring redemption through his own death (20:25-28). How quickly things change. Starting with the notes of celebration and triumph, Jesus' time of visitation will turn into a bitter conflict (21:23—23:36), culminate in a lament over Jerusalem (23:37-39), and end on the cross (27:45-54).

As we celebrate the kingship of Christ on Palm Sunday or during the feast of Christ the King, the image of the humble King points to the radical and countercultural nature of the kingdom of heaven. Jesus the King reveals the example of servanthood, suffering, and self-giving that confronts human patterns of leadership and questions existing structures of power.

B. Jesus at the Temple Courts (21:12-17)

BEHIND THE TEXT

In Jesus' time, the Jerusalem temple complex was one of the wonders of the Roman world. Renovated by Herod the Great on a grand scale, it occupied a territory roughly equal to thirty-five football fields. This imposing structure was surrounded by high walls with distinct public spaces. First, visitors would enter the outer court or the Court of Gentiles with colonnade porticoes on its sides; the events of Jesus' visitation (driving away traders, healings, and children's praise) took place here (21:12-16).

Three inner courts were separated by a wall and were off limits to any Gentiles under the penalty of death. The first inner court, the Court of Women, was open to all ritually clean Jews. It was separated by a gate from the Court of Israel (where only men were allowed entrance) and the Court of Priests—the central place for worship and sacrifices.

The temple building itself was located at the center of that court. It contained the sanctuary—divided into the holy place and the holy of holies—and storage rooms for supplies and ritual vessels. Josephus reports that the temple facade was pure white and some of its elements adorned by gold (Chilton et al. 2000, 1168-69).

The Jerusalem temple served as the center of religious life for Israel and its holy place. Most Jews believed that the Holy God himself dwelled within its walls. The divine presence demanded a high level of ritual purity; entering the temple without water purification in the special bathhouse was forbidden. The inner court and the sanctuary was the epicenter of temple worship; here the priests would bring daily offerings and sacrifices to God and lift praises and prayers on behalf of the people of Israel.

The temple was the place of celebration of different festivals and hosted
21:12-13 annual pilgrimages. Its courtyards also were filled with vibrant spiritual and intellectual life: rabbis were writing their tractates and taught their students as well as carried their theological and even political debates (Chilton et al. 2000, 1168-69).

On his arrival at Jerusalem, Jesus goes straight to the temple and takes immediate action in a public demonstration of messianic authority. At first, it appears Jesus protests against misuse of God's house for trade instead of prayer. The holiness of the temple has been compromised by corrupt commercial activity and unfair trade practices. But the quotes from Isa 56:7 and Jer 7:11 highlight that trade on the sacred precincts is just a symptom of what is really going on in the sanctuary. Biblical scholars usually interpret this prophetic enactment of casting away the traders in two ways: as a cleansing of the temple (Lohmeyer 1961, 36) or as a demonstration of its destruction (Sanders 1985, 61-76; Telford 1980, 59). Placed in the wider context of the Gospel narrative with its predictions of the temple's demise (see 23:37—24:35), Jesus' dramatic action speaks into that turbulent future of the holy place.

IN THE TEXT

■ **12-13** Jesus' appearance in the temple recalls Mal 3:1: "Suddenly the Lord you are seeking will come to his temple." Jesus the Messiah found the sacred space defiled. He drove out buyers and sellers and overturned the tables and seats of moneychangers and dove merchants. This trade was temple business: selling animals for sacrifices and changing coins to the Tyrian coinage for offerings and temple tax. Jesus' action is in the Court of Gentiles (France 2007, 783).

Stopping these activities would lead to the collapse of temple worship (Gray 2008, 25-26). Matthew does not elaborate on Jesus' intentions, but it is unlikely that Jesus expresses any antitemple sentiments at this point. His reaction might have been triggered by bringing such business on the sanctuary's premises (Eppstein 1964, 54-57) or by violating the sanctity of the temple through moral pollution from "immorally acquired money" (Regev 2004, 399-401).

In his address to the people, Jesus brings two scriptural references that help to explain his outrage: they have turned the temple into **a den of robbers** (Matt 21:13). Matthew uses the term *lēstai* (robbers) in description of—what may appear to be—buyers and sellers. Sanders suggests that the term "swindler" would be more appropriate (1985, 66). But this is not convincing.

This scriptural quotation comes from Jer 7:11. In that chapter, Jeremiah denounces the unrepentant sins of the people of Judah: stealing, adultery, idolatry, shedding blood, oppression of the poor, orphans, and widows. Because of their wrongdoings the house of the Lord is profaned and going to be destroyed (Jer 7:1-14). The sanctuary ceased to be the holy place and the house of God; it has become the gathering place of sinners. "Robbers" in this Jeremiah passage is the metaphor for the rebellious people of God who profaned the sanctuary.

21:14-17

Jesus will denounce the sins of religious leaders (see Matt 23); the Gospel story shows them to be wicked and sinful in the way they dealt with the Son of God (see 26:45). Thus, this intertextual reference points more generally to the activities of a corrupt priesthood and not just of market relationships. For Jesus, the wickedness of the priesthood and the activities of the people in the sanctuary make the temple unfit for worship and keep it from serving its purpose. By their deeds they actually profaned the holy place and brought imminent destruction on it (see 23:37—24:2; Evans 1997, 419-28). The Second Temple has not become "a house of prayer for all nations" as was expected in Isa 56:7. The action, then, may have been a prophetic action of judgment. It could also have been "purification" of the sanctuary (Dunn 2004, 466).

■ **14-17** The Messiah now brings healing at the heart of the Jewish nation, not just Galilee (11:15; 15:30-33). Instead of the money-making bazaar, the Son of David turns the temple into the place of restoration: "The blind and the lame came to him" (21:14). The praise of children—**Hosanna to the Son of David** (v 15)—connects Jesus' identity, healing, and proclamation of salvation. Jesus of Nazareth is the Messiah who brings restoration to his people.

The acclamations he received on the way to Jerusalem (v 9) are now being proclaimed at the center of the Jewish universe. But the climax has an ironic twist. It is children who praise the true King of Israel; thus the scripture has been fulfilled again: **From the lips of children . . . you . . . have called forth praise** (v 16). This episode adds to the Matthean theme of children who have a special place in the kingdom (see 18:1-6). Small children perceived who Jesus truly is, but the priests and the teachers of the Law remained blinded. They **saw the wonderful things he did** and still failed to recognize the Messiah (21:14).

After these encounters, Jesus leaves the temple for the night and comes back the next day. This is the rhythm of his pilgrimage life: he spends days in Jerusalem and nights in Bethany (26:6). This was a normal practice of pilgrims to find accommodation in nearby villages or bring their own tents and camp outside of the city in a "greater Jerusalem" as it were (Sanders 1992, 129).

FROM THE TEXT

Jesus' action in the temple contains several interwoven motifs: restoration of the people and confronting the religious establishment; pronouncement of judgment and revelation of his identity; exercising messianic authority and rejection by the leaders. This prophetic enactment exposed the sins of the people of Israel and its priesthood and signals the temple's doom (see 24:1-28). The incident has also planted the seeds of the future conflict (21:23—23:39) that led to Jesus' death on the cross.

The temple motif continues to play an important role: the false accusa-
21:18-22 tions against Jesus are built around the temple's destruction (26:61-62) and the culmination comes with tearing of the temple curtain in two at Jesus' death (27:21). The fates of the Messiah and the temple are interconnected; rejection of the true King of Israel leads to demise of the most holy place. The proclamation of salvation and acts of healing on the sacred grounds point to the holistic nature of Jesus' ministry where physical well-being does not escape his attention. The Son of David has vividly shown what the temple of God is supposed to be: the place of worship and restoration, not the seat of corruption.

C. Jesus and a Fig Tree (21:18-22)

BEHIND THE TEXT

Jesus returns to Jerusalem the next day, having spent the night in Bethany. This time it is a private entry. On the way he encounters a fig tree and his prophetic action turns into a lesson for the disciples. This story has three main parts: Jesus' deed (vv 18-19), the disciples' question (v 20), and the final pronouncement (vv 21-22). Matthew used this pattern for storytelling (action, question, response) before in the confrontation stories: 9:10-13 and 12:1-8 (Davies and Allison 2004, 147).

IN THE TEXT

■ **18** Matthew gives an impression that Jesus was eager to return to Jerusalem first thing in the morning (*prōi*, **early**). He has even skipped his breakfast: **he was hungry** (Nolland 2005, 850). This sets the scene for what is about to happen and, perhaps, also echoes language from Mic 7:1 with its context of judgment.

■ **19** On his way to the city, Jesus spots a fig tree and finds **nothing on it except leaves**. Here Matthew omits Mark's comment: "because it was not the season for figs" (Mark 11:13). John Nolland notes that it was still possible to find unripe edible figs in this time of the year (April) in Palestine (2005, 852). So, perhaps, Jesus was hoping to find some of those early figs, but the fruitless tree had nothing to offer to satisfy his hunger.

In the OT, the image of a fruitless fig tree symbolically represented the people of Israel and her failures as well as the consequences of God's judgment (Jer 8:13; Mic 7:1). In this temple context (see Matt 21—25), the fruitless fig tree may represent the failure of the people of God and particularly its religious elite. They profaned the temple and rejected the Messiah. The cursing of the fig tree may be a prophetic pronouncement of judgment over them: **Immediately the tree withered**. The symbolism becomes even clearer later when Jesus denounces the religious leaders and foresees the destruction of Jerusalem in 23:33-39.

■ **20-22** The disciples were **amazed** at such rapid withering of the fig tree (v 20; see Mark 11:20): **How did the fig tree wither so quickly?** But they have misunderstood the action. They are more concerned with how Jesus has performed such an act of power rather than with the judgment on the fruitlessness of the people of God. The disciples' question turns the cursing of the tree from a prophetic symbolic act to the issue of faith and power. The symbol of the barrenness of Israel turns into a teaching moment about the vitality of faith.

Jesus responds by teaching on the importance of faith and prayer. The disciples will be able to perform similar prophetic actions and even do bigger acts of power (**also you can say to this mountain**) if they **have faith and do not doubt** (Matt 21:21). What seems impossible is possible if a believer is in a close relationship with God, trusts him completely, and understands one's place in the mission of God. These things are not done for their own sake or to show off the disciples' power and authority. They powerfully demonstrate the divine presence and action in the breaking in of the kingdom of God.

The parallel story in Mark clearly presents Jesus' action as a proclamation of doom over the religious leaders and the temple (Mark 11:12-14, 20-24). The reference to "this mountain" (probably Zion) that could be removed by prayer points to the destruction of the temple (Telford 1980, 115, 119). In Matthew the connection between **this mountain** and the temple is less evident.

The disciples cannot do **whatever**, everything (*panta hosa*) they want without realignment with the divine will and without a close relationship with the only source of their power. Anything is possible only if based on "prayer with faith" (NRSV), that is, the connection with God, trust, and reliance on him. This emphasis is important for Jesus, because the disciples had misunderstood this aspect of following Jesus and participating in the mission of God in the past (17:14-20). Like the people of God in the past, they might fail to be faithful and fruitful. That is why Jesus reiterates again and again the same truths about the importance of faith (6:5-6; 7:7-11; 18:19-20).

FROM THE TEXT

The cursing of the fig tree completes the sequence of three symbolical actions in ch 21: triumphal entering of Jerusalem (vv 1-11), driving out the traders from the temple (vv 12-13), and cursing the fig tree (vv 18-22). All of these signal Jesus' authority and judgment brought on Jerusalem and its temple (France 2007, 793). Matthew brings together the symbolic action of judgment and the issue of faith as a warning to Jesus' followers that they can only be fruitful and perform deeds of power if they are in close relationship with God and understand their place in God's mission. They can do the same things that Jesus has done, but not as self-sufficient miracle workers: "the miraculous power available to the disciples to fulfill their calling, that is, in the living of the Christian life in fruitful discipleship" (Hagner 1995, 607). They need to realize that prophetic
21:23-27 acts of power, faith, faithfulness, and prayer are interconnected on the grand canvas of the breaking in of the kingdom of heaven.

D. Jesus' Debates with Religious Leaders at the Temple (21:23—22:46)

1. Debate One: By Whose Authority? (21:23—22:14)

a. Jesus' Authority Questioned (21:23-27)

BEHIND THE TEXT

Jesus returns to the temple for the second time after spending a night in Bethany (21:17). This time, the temple grounds (perhaps in the Court of Gentiles) serve as a scene for his teaching and confrontation with Jerusalem religious and civil leaders (21:23—23:38). He has a series of debates with different groups of the Jewish religious and political establishment: the chief priests (*archiereis*), the elders of the people (*presbyteroi tou laou*), the scribes/teachers of the Law (*grammateis/nomikoi*), the Pharisees (*Pharisaioi*), the Herodians (*Hērōdianoi*), and the Sadducees (*Saddoukaioi*). Later, this stand-off escalates and leads to the plot first to arrest (21:46) and then to kill Jesus (26:1-5). But the common people seem to support Jesus (21:46). The Jerusalem leaders questioned Jesus' authority after what he did the day before: the triumphal entry and the prophetic action in the temple (see 21:1-17). Jesus responds with questions and parables that challenge their authority instead (21:28—22:14).

IN THE TEXT

■ **23 By what authority are you doing these things?** Jesus enters the temple and starts teaching, but Matthew is silent on its content. The chief priests and elders challenge his authority (*exousia*). They have witnessed his action of driving out the traders (21:12-13), healing the blind and the lame (v 14), and heard him teaching the pilgrim crowds (v 23). All of that occurred on temple premises. This raised a legitimate question for the high priests and temple authorities: Who authorized this Galilean?

Readers already know that Jesus has been teaching and acting with extraordinary authority in Galilee (see 7:29; 9:6). Moreover, the source of his authority had been already revealed by the divine voice from heaven: "This is my Son . . . Listen to him!" (17:5; see 3:17). Now Jesus acts with the same messianic authority in the temple and Jerusalem. But the final answer to the leaders' question will be given right at the end of the Gospel story: "All authority in heaven and on earth has been given to me" (28:18).

■ **24-25*a*** Jesus refuses to give them a direct answer. Instead, he employs a traditional rabbinic technique of a counterquestion: **John's baptism—where did it come from? Was it from heaven, or of human origin?** (v 25*a*). If they will explain the ministry of John the Baptist, he will reveal the source of his authority. Has John's ministry been authorized by heaven or by humans? Does it come from God or is it self-appointed? Which is it? The question assumes that John and Jesus share the same source of authority (see 3:1-17; 11:1-19; 17:10-13). Indeed, John the Baptist has already acknowledged that Jesus' authority exceeds his own (3:13-14).

■ **25*b*-27** The question changes the dynamic; the leaders are not on the offensive anymore. Now they need to defend. They have started reasoning (*deilogizonto*) because they have a dilemma. If they admit that John's ministry came from God, they could be accused of not believing him and thus disobeying God himself (see 3:7). For Jesus, John is God's prophet of the last days (11:7-15).

But the religious leaders rejected John's ministry, saying that he was possessed by a demon (11:18). They cannot state publicly that John's baptism was just a human endeavor. How would the crowd (*tov ochlon*) react, since, for them, John was a prophet? Religious beliefs acquire political and public security implications. Similar concerns over public order are considered when the authorities decide to arrest Jesus. The fear of the people—a refrain in Matthew (21:46; 26:5)—guided the religious leaders in dealing with Jesus. He too was popular and perceived by the masses as a prophet like the Baptist (16:14).

The authorities made a politically pragmatic decision not to deny John publicly. They disguised their real views on John by an evasive answer: **We**

don't know (*ouk oidamen*; 21:27). So Jesus refuses to reveal his authority. But readers know that the authority of both John the Baptist and Jesus the Messiah come from heaven.

FROM THE TEXT

Readers already know that Jesus has divine authority. But the religious leaders stubbornly refuse to accept Jesus' authority and the authenticity of his ministry. The leaders cannot or will not perceive, recognize, and admit that God is at work in the ministry of the Messiah and his forerunner. Matthew shows that the kingdom of heaven is breaking in and the authority of stubborn religious leaders is under threat; they have attacked Jesus in a bid to protect it. This passage illustrates again one of the tragic ironies of the Gospel: the religious leaders deny the will and work of the God of Israel in these last days. By his repeated reference to the fear of the people, Matthew also signals that the conflict is with the religious establishment who are leading the people in the wrong direction, and not with the people.

b. The Parable of the Two Sons (21:28-32)

BEHIND THE TEXT

This unique parable opens a set of three stories addressed to the Jewish civil and religious authorities (21:28—22:14). It starts by questioning Jesus'
21:28-29 authority. These parables show that it is the leaders who are in danger of losing their authority and status as they persist in rejecting the work of God in the ministry of Jesus the Messiah (21:32, 43; 22:14).

Jesus sets this parable in an everyday setting: a Jewish peasant family taking care of its vineyard. The story centers on the relationship between a father and his two sons (see Luke 15:11) and particularly the issue of obedience. Torah has required obedience to parents from children and has seen it as a part of honoring them (Deut 5:16; 21:18-21). Obedience of children to their parents also brings honor to the whole family and boosts their reputation within the wider community. Disobedience does the opposite.

IN THE TEXT

■ **28-29 What do you think?** (v 28). At the beginning of the parable Jesus invites the audience to make their own judgment and then to apply it to their situation in a hope that they might change their minds or be convinced of their misunderstanding. Jesus introduces the main characters: **a man who had two sons** (v 28). The father asks his first (*prōtō*) son, perhaps the eldest one, to **work today in the vineyard**. The son's initial response is outright rebellion: **I will not** (v 29). He is purposefully disobedient, challenges the father's authority, and brings shame on both of them. However, the son **changed his mind** (*metamelētheis* could also mean "regret" or "repent") later and did what the father had requested in the first place. Initial rebellion and reluctance turned into obedience and eventual fulfillment of the father's will.

■ **30** The second episode shows the opposite reaction. The other son politely acknowledges his father's authority, **I will, sir** (*kyrie* here could be also translated as "lord" or "master"), and agrees to go to the vineyard. However, **he did not go**. Initial compliance turns into disobedience. Both sons have said one thing and done another. Rebellious words turn into obedient action; respectful words become an act of rebellion (see 7:15-20 and 23:1-4).

■ **31-32** Jesus asks, **Which of the two did what his father wanted?** (v 31). The answer is obvious: the first son who fulfilled the will of the father (*to thelēma tou patros*). But Jesus' interpretation of the parable has an ironic twist. The chief priests and the elders of the people are actually represented by the second disobedient son. It is God's will for his people to enter the kingdom of heaven as it is breaking in through the work of Jesus the Messiah and John the Baptist. Those who appear to be rebellious and disobedient at first, exemplified by **the tax collectors and the prostitutes**, respond with repentance and faith and thus enter the kingdom of God.

These people, "the sinful outcasts of society" (Hagner 1995, 614), are actually represented as the first son who goes into the vineyard and fulfills the will of the father. The Jewish leaders—who claim to be obedient to the divine will by following Torah, leading righteous lives, performing cultic duties at the temple, and waiting for the kingdom of God—actually disobey God's will in these last days by rejecting John's call to repentance and thus tragically find themselves outside of the kingdom.

Like the second son who did not change his mind, the authorities and the temple hierarchy are persistent in their rejection even after they witnessed that other people responded with faith (21:32). They **did not repent** [*metemelēthēte*] **and believe** (*pisteusai*).

Matthew's unique reference to John's ministry, **the way of righteousness** (*hodō dikaiosynēs*), could be translated in two ways. The NIV renders it as **John came to you to show you the way of righteousness**. John called the religious leaders to prepare the way of the Lord by repentance, belief, and purification (see 3:1-10). Or, the phrase could be translated as "John came to you in the way of righteousness" (NRSV). This could refer to the way John conducted himself, that is, "lived a godly life" (France 2007, 806) or as an allusion to him as Jesus' forerunner who started "the process of accomplishment of salvation" (Hagner 1995, 614). Another possibility is to recapture "the way of righteousness" as the mission of God. Thus John reveals what God is about to do and Jesus confirms his participation—"to fulfill all righteousness"—at baptism (3:15).

FROM THE TEXT

The parable illustrates the people's response to the message of John the Baptist and closely ties it with the issue of submitting to the divine will. The God of Israel calls his people to the way of righteousness and expects loving obedience, but Israel's response is disobedience. The parable also points to the continuity between the ministries of John the Baptist and Jesus the Messiah; both of them play a part in ushering in the kingdom of heaven. What they do is God's will, fulfilling his will. Modern Christian readers might find the themes of obedience and fulfillment of the Father's will, following the way of righteousness and not just talking about it, useful for spiritual reflection.

c. The Parable of the Tenants (21:33-46)

BEHIND THE TEXT

This is the second parable of the three (21:28—22:14) addressed to the religious leaders. The parable has Isa 5:1-7 in its horizon: the vineyard representing the people of Israel and the owner, YHWH himself. Jesus refers to Ps 118:22-23 to highlight the meaning of the parable and interpret it in this light. Jesus recasts the story of Israel in the light of the coming of the Son of God (see 21:38-39).

Rejection of divine messengers and the death of the Messiah have grave implications for the future of the people of Israel as well as their leaders. Jesus does not shy away from the language of judgment and points to the future reconfiguration of the kingdom of God (see 21:43-44).

Apart from references to OT scriptures, Matthew alludes to future events: Jesus has been condemned to death after he has given a positive answer to the question from the high priest, "Tell us if you are . . . the Son of God" (26:63).

This story features conflict over a vineyard or farmland. The vineyard has been leased and tensions between tenants and the landlord arose. In the parable, the landlord was asking for his share of harvest as part of lease payment, but the tenants were more interested in "possession and use" of the land (Snodgrass 2008, 284).

IN THE TEXT

■ **33-39** Jesus emphasizes the role of the landowner who has established the vineyard: he has planted grapevines, secured the property by setting up the wall and erecting a watchtower, and dug a wine press. Hultgren describes a similar press found in Nazareth: "the winepress is a bed-sized level area cut into the limestone for squashing grapes" (2000, 371). He has created all conditions for successful operations of the vineyard, leased it to the tenants, and left home.

At harvesttime, the landowner sends his servants to collect the crop share as lease payment, but **the tenants seized his servants; they beat one, killed another, and stoned a third**. So the owner sends other servants, but they were treated similarly. Green suggested that the failure to collect his share of harvest gave the tenants a reason for claiming it as their own (*DJG*, 179-80). Finally the landlord sends his own son in an attempt to establish control over his property: "Sending of the son is an indication that legal action was being taken" (Snodgrass 2008, 294). So, the wicked tenants decide to kill the heir to the property and claim his inheritance.

■ **40-41** Jesus addresses his audience with a question about the future of the wicked vineyard renters: **When the owner of the vineyard comes, what will he do to those tenants?** (v 40). He invites the temple leaders to finish the story; now they can decide the fate of the characters and assign just punishment for their evildoings. But by doing so, the authorities inadvertently predict their own future, since the parable is ultimately about them (v 45). In their own judgment, the landlord must punish the wicked tenants and rent the vineyard to others who **will give him his share** (v 41).

■ **42-44** The leaders' comment was met with a quote from Ps 118:22-23: **The stone the builders rejected has become the cornerstone** (*eis kephalēn gōnias*; Matt 21:42). The great reversal—as illustrated by the psalm—is one of the key characteristics of the coming kingdom. In this context, the saying highlights a rejection-vindication motif that will be later utilized in the Passion Narrative (see chs 26—27). At the end of the Gospel, the rejected Messiah receives "all authority in heaven and on earth" (28:18).

The reference to a **cornerstone** could also be interpreted as an allusion to the establishment of the new temple (26:60). This quotation also hints at the future judgment for those who have rejected Jesus the Messiah and particularly at the religious leaders standing now in front of him. The language of "being broken" or **crushed** by the stone points to judgment (21:44). This motif also finds later development in Matthew's little apocalypse (chs 24—25) with the imagery of the exalted Son of Man who delivers judgment.

This parable joins all these dots together. God is like the landlord; the vineyard represents the people of God; the servants and their treatment (beaten, killed, and stoned) represent God's messengers and prophets (see 23:29-36); the owner's son who was cast out and killed represents Jesus the Messiah (though some scholars would see John the Baptist); and the wicked tenants stand for the current religious and civil leaders of Israel. The time of harvest and settling of the accounts has eschatological overtones and points to the time of judgment (Blomberg 2012, 331-32).

The identity of the new tenants is not clear and open to interpretation. Three main suggestions have been made. First, the kingdom has been taken away from Israel and given to the Gentiles (Mounce 1991, 201). Second, in the great reversal the kingdom will be taken from the religious and civil establishment and given to those who responded to Jesus' call—the children, the poor, the disfranchised, the sinners, and the outcasts. Third, the people of God will be regathered around the Messiah and given new leaders—the Twelve (see 19:28). The more likely is a combination of the last two options.

■ **45-46** At this point the meaning of the parable became evident to the religious authorities. The prophetic action in the temple and now the direct words of Jesus reveal their wickedness and bring the conflict into the open. From that moment, Matthew reports, they were looking for an opportunity to arrest him. This Matthean remark sets in motion Jesus' predictions about his own sufferings and death. Ironically, they reenact the parable's wicked tenants in real life. In a perversion of justice, they have first decided to apprehend him and then to look for any legal reasons; this will be particularly evident in the Passion Narrative and its trial scenes (see chs 26—27).

But even at this point in the story, they will shortly attempt to trap Jesus in his words in order to create a legal case against him (see 22:15-40). However, the leaders could not arrest Jesus just yet because **the people held that he was a prophet** (21:46). Again, they are not ready to act against the will of the pilgrim crowd out of concerns for public safety.

FROM THE TEXT

In this parable, Jesus retells Israel's story in the tradition of OT prophecy with a couple of new twists. As in the Hebrew Scriptures, it illustrates divine grace and patience toward his rebellious people but also introduces the character of the Son of God who follows the prophets. Rejection and murder of the Messiah have two implications: judgment over the current temple authorities and establishment of different leaders who "will produce [the] fruit" of the kingdom (21:43; Snodgrass 2008, 286). In spite of resistance from the religious authorities, God will accomplish his redemptive purposes for his people through a great reversal of powers and reestablishment of the new holy people of God.

d. The Parable of the Wedding Banquet (22:1-14)

BEHIND THE TEXT

The parable of the wedding banquet is the last in the set (21:28—22:14) related to the judgment over those who reject Jesus the Messiah. The parallel between the invited guests of the banquet and the civil and religious leaders in Jerusalem (21:23) to whom the story is addressed is clear. As the guests reject the invitation to the wedding banquet of the king's son and mistreat his servants, so the leaders of Israel reject the Son of God and persecute God's prophets and messengers. Jesus' point is clear: "Those who dishonor the Son shame and dishonor the Father who sent him" (Keener 2009, 518).

The story is built around the relationship between the king and his vassals. It was customary to have extravagant royal public weddings and to invite nobles and officials. The problem lies in the behavior of the invited guests. In response to the king's invitation, they have deliberately insulted him by providing absurd excuses and mistreating his messengers. Such conduct is a sign of disrespect, disloyalty, disobedience, even outright rebellion. The king's rage was justified: the king was "avenging his honor by executing those who insulted him by scorning his invitation to eat" (Keener 2009, 520).

The Matthean story has its parallel in Luke 14:16-24. Both parables are rooted in the idea of the messianic banquet and refer to Jesus' inclusion of sinners and outcasts into his table fellowship. Rejection of Jesus is seen as self-exclusion from the banquet of the kingdom, which results in divine judgment. But Matthew's version is also different: the context is a royal wedding; the king's servants were killed; the murderers are executed and their city destroyed. While Luke subverts Pharisaic views on the nature of the messianic banquet, Matthew uses the parable to illustrate the fate of the Jerusalem leadership. The story anticipates the discourse on the last days and destruction of Jerusalem (23:33-39; 24:1—25:46).

IN THE TEXT

■ **1-7** The first part of the parable is built around the king's invitation to come to the wedding banquet for his son and the guests' refusal to do so. The story implies that the guests had received their royal invitations well before the banquet and agreed to come in the first place; it would have been unthinkable to reject the invitation from the person of the highest social status. The 22:1-7
second call to come (22:3)—which is repeated twice in the story—is just to inform the guests that the dinner is ready (Keener 2009, 519). Social conventions make their response shocking, offensive, and insulting—**they refused to come** (v 3).

In spite of their disrespect, the king sends even more servants in a bid to convince the guests to come (v 4). This demonstrates the king's benevolence, patience, and goodwill. More details are given for the invitation as well as the reasons for refusal. The feast is ostentatious, with meat as its centrepiece: **oxen and fattened cattle**. The king's status demanded the best feast and the finest entertainment.

By contrast, the response is staggering; some guests behaved as if they never agreed to come and continued with their daily business (v 5). Another **seized** the king's **servants, mistreated them and killed them** (v 6). The reaction of the king to such defiance was predictable: he **was enraged** (v 7). The wedding celebration quickly turns into a bloodbath. The king's soldiers **destroyed those murderers and burned their city**.

The first part of the parable continues the theme of the rejection of Jesus and his message by the Jewish establishment. The parable alludes to the messianic banquet, to Jesus as the Son of God, to the prophets and particularly John the Baptist, who had been killed (14:1-12). The point is clear: the ungrateful and rebellious guests represent "the chief priests and the elders of the people" (21:23). As a result of their stubbornness, punishment will surely fall upon them (22:7), hinting at the destruction of Jerusalem by the Romans in 70 CE (France 2007, 825).

■ **8-10** Despite these shocking events, the wedding celebrations are not canceled. The story takes an unexpected turn. The king decides to invite people from **the street corners** (v 9). Anyone, good or bad, is welcome at the king's table to celebrate. In contrast to the invited guests, the people respond with enthusiasm and **the wedding hall was filled with guests** (v 10). This king's ridiculous gesture turns the logic of the story upside down. Those who were deemed unworthy to come in the first place celebrate at the king's table; those who were deemed worthy to come turn out to be underserving and are destroyed.

The parable contrasts different responses to the king's invitation. This is a main theme of the Gospel: the people on the fringes of religious and social life in Israel happily respond to Jesus' message (see 9:10) while authorities and religious teachers utterly reject it. Thus, the parable illustrates the inclusive nature of the kingdom. The invitation to join and celebrate is for all.

■ **11-14** Here Matthew departs from the other Gospels by adding another incident. At the banquet, the king noticed a man **who was not wearing wedding clothes** (*ouk endedymenon endyma gamou*). An invitee to a royal wedding would have been expected to come in clothes fit for the occasion. But this man decides not to change his garments. Attending public festivities and appearing before the king in ordinary working clothes was perceived as insulting (France 2007, 826-27).

Perhaps the change of clothes symbolizes repentance and change (see Rev 19:8; Isa 61:10; 64:6). This person did not change despite his acceptance of the invitation. Matthew's parable includes a warning both to religious leaders who found themselves outside the kingdom of God and to those who enjoy the fellowship of the Messiah. Continual participation in the kingdom requires transformation. Being thrown out of the banquet is a possibility (Matt 22:13). "God's kingdom is a kingdom in which love and justice and truth and mercy and holiness reign unhindered. They are the clothes you need to wear for the wedding" (Wright 2004, 2:85).

FROM THE TEXT

This parable plays on contrasting responses to the king's invitation to the celebration of his son's wedding. The unexpected turn of events exemplifies the paradoxical nature of the kingdom itself. Those who zealously waited for it to come have failed to respond to God's message and to recognize the breaking in of the kingdom in Jesus' ministry. Instead, the king invites the poor and lowly. Ironically, religious and social outcasts celebrate the kingdom and share at the table of the Messiah (see 9:10). Everyone is invited to be part of the kingdom.

The reality is that people will respond in different ways: rejection, ignorance, acceptance, indifference, desire to follow but refusal to change are all possible. Each response has consequences. In the story, the joyful notes of celebration, salvation, and grace have been mixed with the disturbing tones of judgment, punishment, and destruction. And both the opponents and the followers of Jesus have to listen to them attentively.

2. Debate Two: Paying Taxes to Caesar (22:15-22)

BEHIND THE TEXT

This passage opens a set of discussions with the religious leaders over theological and practical issues (22:15-45). Matthew reveals the intention behind these rabbinic debates: "The Pharisees . . . laid plans to trap him in his words" (v 15). On the one hand, they challenge Jesus' authority publicly. On the other, they were looking for a valid reason for arrest and prosecution. A case of blasphemy would be ideal, but political disloyalty would suit.

This episode introduces a new group among Jesus' opponents—the Herodians. Little is known about them. They may represent supporters of the Herod the Great's dynasty (73-4 BCE). In Jesus' time, the Herodians likely would have backed Herod Antipas, the Jewish tetrarch ("ruler of a quarter") of Galilee and approved of the vassal arrangement with the Romans. This group could have been perceived as collaborators by more conservative Jews.

The poll tax (*knēsos*) was the presenting issue. This was from men, wom- 22:15-17
en, and slaves from age twelve to sixty-five; the tax has to be paid in Roman currency (Harrington 1991, 310).

IN THE TEXT

■ **15-17** The Pharisees take indirect action to entrap Jesus. They sent their disciples who could be witnesses and accusers in the future trial. They start their conversation with flattery, pretending to ask an innocent practical question from an authoritative rabbi. But ironically, their insincere praise turns into a true confession: Jesus is the one who teaches **the way of God in accordance with the truth** (v 16). In the beginning of the conversation, Jesus seems caught between Pharisees and Herodians, the religious conservatives and the collaborationists. Would he be able to satisfy both groups by an answer to such a politically loaded question?

Is it right to pay the imperial tax to Caesar or not? (v 17). "No" would be interpreted as inciting rebellion against the occupying Romans (since 63 BCE) who taxed the populace. The Romans had already dealt with a tax revolt (ca. 6-9 CE). Josephus reports that the leader of the rebellion, Judas of Galilee, encouraged his followers not to pay taxes and defy the Roman authorities: "They were cowards if they would endure to pay a tax to the Romans" (*J.W.* 2.117). "Yes" would have been interpreted by some radical conservative Jews as an act of betrayal and collaboration with the Gentiles or even worse—as an act of idolatry.

■ **18-22** Jesus sees through their ruse and calls them **hypocrites** (*hypokritai*; v 18). He asks to see a coin used for paying the tax. A silver denarius with an emperor's image—perhaps of Tiberius or Augustus—is provided. The denarius of the emperor Tiberius (14 to 37 CE), also known as a "tribute penny," contained an inscription "Caesar Augustus Tiberius, son of the Divine Augustus."

The depiction of a head of the divine Caesar, a son of a god, was sacrilegious to observant Jews. In contrast, Jewish coins from the Maccabean period (second century BCE) until the first Jewish revolt (first century CE) have—with some rare exceptions—no images of humans or animals. This illustrates Jewish observance of the second command (Exod 20:4-6) forbidding graven images because the coins could have been used for idol worship (Stoops 2000, 222-25).

So give back to Caesar what is Caesar's, and to God what is God's. Jesus approves the payment of the tax: **give back** (*apodidōmi*) what belongs to the emperor. But he shifts the focus to the central point: the things that belong to God. What do we owe God? Not just the temple tax (see 17:24-27) or even giving up material possessions (see 19:16-30). Jesus evokes here and then spells it out later—love God "with all your heart and . . . soul and . . . mind" (22:37). It is about giving back or dedicating to God everything and even one's life. In the context of Matthew, it ultimately means self-denial and following Jesus the Messiah (see 16:24). After these words, the Pharisees and the Herodians could not argue with Jesus and **went away** (22:22). Their trap failed.

Not only does the saying have a rhetorical value or illustrate Jesus' whit and illusiveness, but as N. T. Wright suggests, its subversive nature should not escape a perceptive reader. The call to give God what he deserves is set against Caesar's claims to divinity spelled out on the coin and—in the context of 2TJ—could be interpreted as the call to worship YHWH alone.

If that is the case, the aphorism, in effect, refuses paganism, undermines any human claim to divine status, puts the Roman emperor in his place, and questions pagan authority over Israel (Wright 1996, 502-6). Jesus offers a different vision of the kingdom to both Jewish collaborationists and rebels. He calls to real nonviolent revolution through joining the Messiah and his kingdom movement that "would come about through Israel reflecting the generous love of YHWH into the whole world" (Wright 1996, 507).

FROM THE TEXT

This passage does not encourage its readers to divide their lives into separate spheres: secular and sacred, material and spiritual. Jesus recognizes that certain obligations to the wider society and government should be respected but, at the same time, there are greater obligations toward God (Mounce 1991, 208). Jesus makes his listeners think about what things are due to God (as opposed to Caesar) and set the priorities right.

However, this aphorism could serve as a warning to modern Christians not to subsume the divine realm within Caesar's and to resist the temptation to sanctify the state in any form, whether it be "the divine right of kings" or electing "a Christian president or prime minister." It warns of dangers in setting state or political ideologies in the place of God or confusing the redemptive story of God with nationalist narratives. The history of Christianity demonstrates how easy it is to turn "God with us" or "In God we trust" into a political slogan that justifies anything. The church should resist any such embrace of the state that undermines and hinders its prophetic voice and the mission of God in this world.

3. Debate Three: About Resurrection (22:23-33)

BEHIND THE TEXT

Jesus' actions and teaching in the temple (see ch 21) have challenged different factions of religious elite. They are uniting against "the common enemy." This time Jesus is approached by the Sadducees (→ Matt 3:7-10 sidebar, "Pharisees and Sadducees"). According to Josephus, this priestly group rejected Pharisaic traditions and practices (including belief in resurrection) and insisted on the primary authority of the Torah, the first five books of the Bible (*Ant.* 18.11-18). This time they ridicule Jesus over the issue of resurrection. Matthew describes another attempt to trap Jesus in his words and undermine his authority as a teacher and interpreter of the Scripture.

IN THE TEXT

■ **23-28** The foundation of their hypothetic scenario is the commandment from Deut 25:5-10 dealing with levirate (from the Latin word *lēvir*, "brother in-law") marriage: **If a man dies without having children, his brother must marry the widow and raise up offspring for him** (Matt 22:24). The main concern of that ordinance is the preservation of the bloodline and name of the deceased person.

Levirate Marriage

Levirate law describes a situation when a husband dies before producing a male heir and demands the husband's brother to marry the widow and produce a son. However, if the brother-in-law does not want to carry out this "legally binding duty," a ceremony of *khalitsah* must be performed in the presence of the town elders. The widow should inform the elders that her brother-in-law refuses to marry her. The elders then summon the man and if he persists in his decision, the widow removes his sandal, spits in his face and denounces him as a man who "refuses to carry on his brother's name in Israel" (Deut 25:7; see vv 7-10). After this, she could legally marry outside of her husband's family (*NIDB*, 3:644). The

OT contains a couple of examples of levirate law at work (see Gen 38:1-30; Ruth 3:9—4:10).

In the passage, the seven brothers die childless one after another, leaving the widow to the next brother in accordance with the Law. The intention behind this made-up story is to reduce the idea of resurrection to absurdity (Harrington 1991, 312): **Now then, at the resurrection** [*tē anastasei*]**, whose wife will she be of the seven, since all of them were married to her?** (Matt 22:28). For the Sadducees, the notion of the dead coming back to life and the commandment about levirate marriage don't make any sense if put against each other. In other words, the idea of resurrection is nonsensical and has no justification within the Torah.

■ **29-33** Jesus' response demonstrates two main mistakes made by the Sadducees: **You do not know the Scriptures or the power of God** (*tēn dynamin tou theou*; v 29). They have misunderstood both the nature of resurrection and the wider narrative context of the Torah. For Jesus, the resurrection from the dead is not ridiculous since it lies within the abilities of divine power (see Rom 4:17). Moreover, the life in the renewed world could only be comparable to angelic existence. There issues of marriage are of no concern: **People will neither marry nor be given in marriage** (Matt 22:30).

Jesus also finds the idea of resurrection in the Torah, the authoritative scripture for the Sadducees. In Exod 3:6, 15-16 God introduces himself to Moses as the God of the patriarchs who are supposedly dead. But in argumentation similar to the rabbinic interpretation of resurrection in the Torah (see *b. Sanh.* 90b; Keener 2009, 528-29; Davies and Allison 2004, 3:233) Jesus concludes that God has spoken as **the God . . . of the living** (Matt 22:32). This presupposes that God still enjoys a personal relationship with Abraham, Isaac, and Jacob. Though their bodies have perished, they are still alive with God. His scriptural argument for resurrection breaks the logic of the Sadducees' *reductio ad absurdum* argument based on one of the commandments of the Torah. Jesus gives yet another lesson in scriptural interpretation to the religious leaders of Jerusalem.

When the crowds heard this, they were astonished at his teaching (v 33). Matthew's comment on the crowd's astonishment points out the gap between the ordinary people and their leadership in relation to Jesus. The crowd sympathizes with Jesus and is amazed by his teaching. Attempts to undermine Jesus' authority have an opposite effect. His responses to their logical traps build support from the crowd. He is an authoritative teacher unlike those religious authorities.

FROM THE TEXT

Jesus' views on resurrection are in common with the Pharisees (see Acts 23:8) and others in ancient Jewish thought (see *1 En.* 51, 104; Isa 26:19; Dan

12:2). The truthfulness of his words will be proven later. God's power will be demonstrated at the moment of Jesus' death (Matt 27:52-53) and resurrection (28:1-15). This argument foreshadows those events and provides scriptural foundation for it. The God of the living will raise Jesus, the victim of the religious leaders, from the grave. The Sadducees will be proven wrong again. Moreover, Jesus as authoritative interpreter of Scripture provides an example for his disciples to follow.

4. Debate Four: The Greatest Commandments (22:34-40)

BEHIND THE TEXT

Matthew's formulation of the greatest commandment occurs in confrontation with the Pharisees. Mark frames the dialogue as an inquiry from a friendly teacher of the Law (Mark 12:28-34). Luke situates this encounter earlier and couples it with the parable of the Good Samaritan (Luke 10:25-37). Matthew modifies the first love commandment by omitting "with all of your strength" (see Deut 6:5) and including "with all your mind" (*holē tē dianoia sou*) taken from the LXX. Mark and Luke include both readings (see Mark 12:30; Luke 10:27).

This is the last attempt to undermine Jesus' authority (Matt 22:15-40);
a Pharisee challenges him on the issue of the greatest commandment. The
question is not unusual (see Hagner 1995, 646). In his reply, Jesus brings two 22:34-36
commandments together: Deut 6:4-5 and Lev 19:18 on the basis of the shared
verb "to love" (*agapō*).

IN THE TEXT

■ **34-36** The Pharisees would have applauded Jesus' answer to the Sadducees (Matt 22:23-33). But they wish to test him further. Scholars have noted that the phrase **got together** (*synēhthēsan epi to auto*; "gathered together" [NRSV]) is an allusion to Ps 2:2: "the rulers band together against [*synēhthēsan epi to auto*] the LORD and against his anointed." This suits the Matthean portrayal of the confrontation between Jesus the Messiah (or the Anointed One) and the religious elite of Jerusalem (Matt 21).

One of the Pharisees—a representative of the group—was **an expert in the law** (*nomikos*) of Moses (22:35). This is Matthew's only use of this title. This signals that the issue at hand is central to understanding and interpreting the Torah (France 2007, 844). He approached Jesus and asked, **Which is the greatest commandment** [*entolē megalē*] **in the Law?** (v 36). The question is not aimed at undermining the importance of other commandments but rather at finding out the foremost commandment, a summation of the Law or the basic principles on which the whole of the Law is based.

Rabbinic traditions provide examples of similar discussions. Rabbi Shimon Bar Kappara has asked: "What short text is there upon which all the essential principles of the Torah depend?" (*b. Ber.* 63a). Rabbi Hillel has taught a converted Gentile: "That which is hateful to you do not do to another; that is the entire Torah, and the rest is its interpretation. Go study" (*b. Šabb.* 31a). However, the Pharisee's question had a more sinister purpose: it was aimed at undermining Jesus' authority if he gets the answer wrong.

■ **37-40** In his response, Jesus refers to the Shema (Deut 6:4-5), the core statement of Israel's faith recited daily by pious Jews. Recasting Moses' words, Jesus calls Israelites to **love** [*agapēseis*] **. . . God with all your heart** [*kardia*] **and with all your soul** [*psyche*] **and with all your mind** (*dianoia*; Matt 22:37; note "strength" in Deut 6:5); in other words, with one's whole being. The repetition of the word **all** (*holē*) indicates complete dedication of one's whole life to the Holy God of Israel. Originally, this commandment was set in the context of covenant renewal in Deuteronomy, and exclusive love toward YHWH was the only proper response to what he has done for Israel. **This is the first and greatest commandment** (Matt 22:38). No Pharisee could argue with that.

Love your neighbor as yourself (v 39). Jesus adds to the first commandment **the second is like it**. One cannot love God without loving a neighbor. The second love commandment comes from Lev 19:18 and has a fellow Jew in mind. However, the original context of the commandment follows the call from the Holy God to imitate his holiness (vv 1-2). Leviticus 19 explains what it means to be the holy people of God, and it is inseparable from love toward both fellow Israelites and foreigners (vv 18, 34).

For Lev 19, to imitate God's holiness means to imitate God's love for others. Jesus also redefines the notion of a neighbor: it is not just about a fellow Jew, but any person whom one comes across (see Luke 10:29-37). But Jesus goes even further in imitation of divine love and calls his followers to embrace even enemies (Matt 5:43-48).

All the Law and the Prophets hang on [*krematai*] **these two commandments** (22:40). The double love commandment summarizes and expresses the heart of the Torah and the whole of Scripture (see 5:16-20). It is the key to understanding and practicing the whole of the covenantal law: "Matthew saw the love commandment as giving meaning and direction to the whole Torah" (Harrington 1991, 316). The Scripture should be interpreted and practiced in the context of loving relationship with God and others, within the covenantal community of faith.

Matthew mentions no reaction to Jesus' words from the Pharisees or the crowd. They ask no more questions. It may not be coincidental that the hostile religious leaders finish attacking Jesus after his words about love for neighbor. In their own interpretation and practice of the Law, they were missing that key element—love. The way they have been treating Jesus is clearly going against the spirit of the Torah. Moreover, their failure to recognize divine work in the ministry of Jesus the Messiah and active opposition to it might signal lack of love toward God as well.

FROM THE TEXT

This purely rabbinic discussion over interpretation of the Torah (coupled with the Sermon on the Mount) turns into the foundation of Christian ethics. Complete, selfless dedication to God and serving others out of love have inspired and motivated Jesus' followers throughout centuries to great feats of faith.

The double-love commandment is not distinctively Christian, however. Nor is it a new commandment given by Jesus (but see John 13:34). This comes from the heart of the Torah. But Jesus, with the authority as the Son of God (see Matt 17:5) and "a prophet like Moses," brings them together in a unique way. They are not only signposts that point in the right direction for moral actions in everyday living but also hermeneutical lenses for interpretation and application of the Scripture.

Throughout the Gospel, Jesus clashes with the Pharisees over their interpretation and practice of the Torah because it neglects the big picture, missing its heart and spirit. This is particularly evident in the confrontation over healing on the Sabbath (see 12:1-14) where loving a neighbor overcomes the Pharisaic views on acceptable activities on the holy day. Jesus not only shows love to people around him but also exemplifies the love for God. He demonstrates complete self-denial and dedication to the divine will even if it leads to death on the cross (see 26:36-44). Jesus not only teaches but also embodies this double-love commandment and inspires his followers to do the same.

The double-love commandment is at the heart of the Wesleyan understanding of perfection and holiness. In *A Plain Account of Christian Perfection*, John Wesley notes, "By perfection I mean the humble, gentle, patient love of God and our neighbour, ruling our tempers, words, and actions" (Wesley 1987, 11:466). For him, the restorative work of divine grace and the presence of the Holy Spirit in the life of a believer are reflected in constantly increasing love for God and neighbor. This "perfect love" and holiness is expressed in complete devotion to God, in selfless acts of love toward people and growing in maturity (Greathouse 1979, 15).

5. Debate Five: Whose Son Is the Christ? (22:41-46)

BEHIND THE TEXT

Up to this point, Jesus was questioned by different religious teachers with the intent to challenge and undermine his authority (21:23). However, they have failed "to trap him in his words" (22:15). Now it is Jesus' turn to put them on the spot. He poses a set of related questions about the Messiah's identity: "What do you think about the Messiah?" (v 42).

This encounter has a double purpose. It demonstrates inadequacy of the teachers of the Law; they are unable to answer, what appears to be, a simple question from Jesus. But it also adds another argument in support of Jesus' messianic identity that has been gradually revealed through the entire narrative. The conversation adds to Peter's divinely inspired confession in 16:16 ("You are the Messiah, the Son of the living God") and provides an example of Jesus' interpretation of Ps 110:1.

IN THE TEXT

■ **41-42** Jesus starts their conversation with a simple question about the Messiah's sonship: **Whose son is he?** (v 42). The Pharisees provide the correct answer: **The son of David**. Their response reflects widespread Second Temple beliefs, deeply rooted in the Davidic covenant (2 Sam 7:13) and prophetic scriptures (Isa 11:1-10; Jer 23:5; Ezek 34:23-24). It also reflects the hope for restoration when the Messiah would reestablish the kingdom to Israel free from Gentile oppression. However, their answer does not satisfy Jesus.

■ **43-46** Jesus takes the interrogation further and gives another lesson in biblical interpretation. The second set of questions is now related to a psalm of David inspired **by the Spirit** (Matt 22:43). Psalm 110 is an enthronement psalm that was used during coronation ceremonies (Harrington 1991, 318). Jesus provides a messianic interpretation of it and perceives David as a prophet who foresees the future enthronement of the Messiah akin to the vision from Dan 7:13-14.

The first line of the psalm speaks of "the LORD" (Heb. *YHWH*; Gk. *kyrios*) who addresses "my lord" (Heb. *ʾadonay*; Gk. *kyrios*), that is, a newly anointed king or the future Messiah. Jesus argues that King David refers to the future Messiah, his son or descendant, as his Lord. But since a son has lower status than the father, the Messiah must be more than just David's descendant. Jesus' play on the word "lord" suggests that the Messiah is also the Son of God. This is Matthew's vision of Jesus' identity; he is both the Son of David and the Son of God (Turner 2008, 541).

Matthew remarks at the end of the story that **no one dared to ask him any more questions** (Matt 22:46). It is not a sign of agreement with Jesus' teaching but recognition of the failure to trap Jesus publicly. But for Matthew, it is also a sign of the pinnacle of Jesus' teaching.

FROM THE TEXT

This encounter with the Pharisees adds another brushstroke to the Matthean portrait of Jesus. He is the Son of David, the Messiah, but even more astonishingly he is also the Lord and the Son of God. The Scripture itself supports that notion. Moreover, this story takes the readers back to the issue of

Jesus' authority in 21:23. The text answers that question indirectly and brings the debate with religious leaders to a fitting conclusion.

At this point, they have given up attempts to undermine his authority by public questioning. However, the issue of Jesus' identity and authority resurfaces later in the narrative when Jesus is again questioned by religious leaders at the trial (26:57-68 and 27:11-26; see Turner 2008, 542).

E. Discourses on Judgment (23:1—25:46)

1. Jesus Denounces the Scribes and the Pharisees (23:1-12)

BEHIND THE TEXT

The last of Matthew's extended discourses starts with ch 23 and finishes at 26:1 with a traditional formula: "When Jesus had finished saying all these things." This discourse speaks of judgment over religious leadership, Jerusalem, and culminates with the universal judgment over "all nations" at the coming of the Son of Man. It also promises salvation and vindication for those who persevere and live faithfully. Chapters 23 and 24—25 are thematically interconnected, but 24:3 marks a change in setting and audience: Jerusalem, the scribes and the Pharisees, then the Mount of Olives and the disciples.

Chapter 23 describes the confrontation between Jesus and the religious
elite. In chs 21—22, his authority has been challenged by priests, the elders of 23:1
the people, scribes, the Pharisees, and the Sadducees. But they failed. Instead they achieved the opposite result: the people were amazed at Jesus' responses (22:22, 33). At the end of this confrontation in ch 23, Jesus denounces his opponents.

This extended criticism and harsh condemnation is unique to Matthew. The polemic against the teachers of the law (or the scribes) and the Pharisees has been interpreted by some as an indicator of conflict between "the Jewish Christians and the more powerful early rabbinic movement" (Harrington 1991, 327). Others trace it back to Jesus' own outrage at his opponents' religious practices and attitudes (Mounce 1991, 213). Both reasons are plausible.

The chapter divides naturally into three parts, addressing different audiences: 23:1-12—the disciples and crowd; vv 13-36—the Pharisees and teachers of the Law; vv 37-39—Jerusalem. It also contains different literary forms (Hagner 1995, 654): an exhortation (vv 1-12), woes (vv 13-33), a prophecy (vv 34-36), and a lament (vv 37-39).

IN THE TEXT

■ **1** Previously the religious leaders were trying to undermine Jesus' authority by challenging him publicly. Now Jesus turns **to the crowds and to his disciples** to reveal the true state of their leadership: it is riven with hypocrisy.

Hypokrisin appears six times in this chapter (vv 13, 15, 23, 25, 27, 29) and also has been used to describe Jesus' opponents elsewhere (6:2-16; 7:5; 15:7; 22:18). The gap between their teaching and practice, their public appearance and inner motivations, casts a shadow on their leadership and compromises their authority as teachers of the people.

■ **2-4** Jesus recognizes their authority to teach and interpret the Law and maybe even judge (Keener 2009, 541) since they **sit in Moses' seat** (23:2). The latter phrase could also allude to the preacher's seat in the synagogue. This Mosaic authority requires people to **do everything they tell you** (v 3).

Scholars differ on how to read this statement. Jesus has been criticizing their practices throughout the Gospel; some of their teachings are not particularly good either (see vv 16-26). Does Jesus acknowledge their quest for holiness? Does he agree that some ethical teachings of the Pharisees are acceptable (Keener 2009, 541)? Does he mean that their concern for preservation of the Scriptures is praiseworthy (Talbert 2010, 257)? Or is this statement meant to be an irony? Are they really worthy to occupy the seat of Moses (France 2007, 859)? Whatever the meaning, the focus is not on the Pharisaic teaching per se but on their failure to live by it.

Perhaps, then, it is a call to follow their teaching but not their example (see Pregeant 2004, 167). But this is unlikely. Jesus compares their practical interpretation of the Torah (or halakhah) to **heavy, cumbersome loads** (v 4) that they put on the shoulders of others. They make rules that they cannot follow themselves or fulfill minimally. By not practicing **what they preach** (v 3) they undermine their own authority. Their teaching is set in contrast to Jesus' teaching: "My yoke is easy and my burden is light" (11:30).

■ **5-7** The hypocrisy comes out in two ways: they don't do what they teach and what they practice is based on wrong motives: **Everything they do is done for people to see** (23:5). Some of their religious practices do not reflect extreme piety but the pursuit of prestige, honor, respect, and recognition. Jesus questions the way they treat the outward marks of an observant Jew: **They make their phylacteries wide and the tassels on their garments long.**

Phylacteries and Tassels

The practice of wearing phylacteries (Heb. *tefillin*) or small leather boxes with selected Torah passages "was widely observed toward the end of the Second Temple Period" (Glatt-Gilad and Tigay 1996, 854). It is based on a literal interpretation of commandments from Exod 13:9-16 and Deut 6:8. They were normally worn by observant Jews on the forehead and left arm for times of prayer. They had been originally designed to be a constant reminder of covenantal obligations and the commandments of the Torah but later also served as amulets containing "protective powers" (Glatt-Gilad and Tigay 1996, 854).

Fringes or **tassels** were special cords on each corner of one's garment. The practice of wearing them is based on Num 15:37-41 and Deut 22:12. These blue and later white cords were designed as a reminder to obey the Torah's decrees. Today these tassels can be found on Jewish prayer shawls and linen vests (Saldarini 1996, 352). Matthew notes that Jesus wore them as well (Matt 9:20; 14:36).

"Widening" could refer to wearing these elements of garment outside of set prayer times or making them look bigger (Mounce 1991, 215). According to the Matthean Jesus, in the Pharisaic mind the length of a cord or the size of a leather box would announce to others the amount of zealousness about the Law or the size of one's piety—which is never big enough.

Jesus also turns to their deferential seating order in assemblies and synagogues. Sitting by rank was a normal cultural practice in the ancient world (Keener 2009, 543). **The place of honor** was normally on the platform facing the congregation (v 6). But the teachers of the Law particularly enjoyed it (see Luke 14). They also enjoyed the respect signaled by being called **Rabbi** (Heb. "my master," "my lord" or even "my great one"; Matt 23:7). This public honor pointed to their knowledge, skills, and authoritative judgment over the issues related to the law of Moses.

Here Jesus exposes their true intentions. Their zealousness for the Law had become a pursuit for titles, places in the hierarchy, and the visible marks of righteousness and authority. They are concerned with recognition and appearance in the eyes of others. Their practices and attitudes did not stem from inward piety but were driven by the wider culture of honor and shame.

■ **8-12 But you are not to be called "Rabbi"** (v 8). Self-promotion and the quest for honor cannot be a foundation for genuine faithful practices. Here the cultural values of the ancient Mediterranean world clash with the ones of the kingdom. The disciples can learn from the Pharisees what not to do. The followers of Jesus have to realize that all honor belongs only to God and his Messiah. There is only one Master and **Father** (v 9)—God himself. There is only one **Teacher** (v 8)—the Messiah (see 26:25, 49). They cannot claim titles that belong to the only Great One; the disciples are all brothers. There is no rank or preferential treatment. 23:8-12

This is a vital lesson. Disciples should not seek respect and honor with preferential treatment or special titles. Jesus' followers should demonstrate the opposite attitude: "the greatest among you will be your servant" (v 11; note the play on words here: **rabbi**—"my great one"). Respect and honor come from serving others, not by having titles or occupying the places of power. They are very slow to learn the lesson.

FROM THE TEXT

By revealing the hypocrisy of the teachers of the Law and the Pharisees, Jesus teaches his disciples the true values of the kingdom. There is no justification for those who claim Mosaic authority and relentlessly pursue honor, concern themselves with appearing righteous in public, climbing hierarchical ladders, expanding the gap between teaching and practice, and abusing authority within the community of faith. The leaders of the new holy people of God should embrace opposite attitudes and practices (Malina and Rohrbaugh 2003, 116).

Jesus continues with the same line of thought initially taken in the Sermon of the Mount: The kingdom requires righteousness greater than that of the Pharisees and teachers of the Law (5:20). The true righteousness and greatness should be revealed in humility and servanthood, not in outward appearance or honorific titles.

Jesus also demonstrates the subversive nature of the kingdom: humbling of the exalted and exaltation of the humble. Here we hear eschatological notes of reversal. Those who sit in the seat of Moses and abuse Mosaic authority now will face judgment later. And the Twelve will assume the seats of power: "When the Son of Man sits on his glorious throne, you who have followed me will also sit on twelve thrones, judging the twelve tribes of Israel" (19:28). The disciples then struggled to resist the anti-kingdom of God cultural norms (see 18:1-5; 20:20-28). Would Jesus have some similar stern words for contemporary disciples?

2. Seven Woes (23:13-36)

BEHIND THE TEXT

23:13-36 Now Jesus turns from the crowds and his disciples and directly addresses "the teachers of the law and Pharisees" (23:13). In a prophetic style, he denounces his opponents by proclaiming seven woes against them. These are woes of judgment, not lament (Luz 2005, 115), the opposite of the blessings of the Beatitudes in 5:3-12 (Harrington 1991, 326). The righteousness of the Pharisees does not lead to blessing but to judgment. Matthew groups the insults, indicating the seriousness of the conflict between Jesus and religious authorities (Malina and Rohrbaugh 2003, 115).

The passage is full of bitter irony. Jesus mocks their rigorous adherence to purity rules by comparing them to unclean animals (23:33) and unclean spaces (vv 27-28). Their single-mindedness about following the Law is in reality two-faced as they transgress the Law and misinterpret its intentions in their everyday living. Righteousness ironically turns into hypocrisy and performance targets.

The issue that underpins the conflict is differing vision of holiness and its outward manifestation (→ Matt 3:7-10 sidebar, "Pharisees and Sadducees"). Their obsession with ritual purity and table fellowship practices reflect a holiness paradigm rooted in the idea of separation (Borg 1984, 96; Neusner 1973, 79; *m. Soṭah* 9:15). Pharisaic associations (Heb. *havurah*) maintained holiness through purification rituals, following their interpretation of Torah, and separating themselves from different sources of ritual impurity, including the unclean and sinful people. As opposite to separation, Jesus understands holiness as transformative, inclusive, and contagious. It draws people—who were deemed unclean, sinful, and unworthy—into the kingdom (see 9:9-13; Ermakov 2014b, 89-110).

IN THE TEXT

■ **13-14 You shut the door of the kingdom of heaven** (v 13). This accusation may be interpreted in two ways. First, they thought that they would inherit the kingdom because of their faithful following of Torah. But in reality, they could not enter because their righteousness emphasized purity of the body and ignored purity of heart (23:25-26). This interpretation prevented people from entering the kingdom rather than helping (Luz 2005, 116-17).

In contrast, Peter is given "the keys of the kingdom of heaven" (16:19) for opening it. People could enter the kingdom through the ministry of Jesus and his disciples; but they face closed doors if they listen to the Pharisees. Second, the religious leaders are hindering the spread of the gospel by opposing and rejecting the Messiah and thus shutting themselves and others from the kingdom (Harrington 1991, 325).

■ **15** Jesus sarcastically comments that the Pharisees **travel over land and sea to win a single convert**. The word *prosēlytes* (a proselyte) may refer to a Gentile convert to Judaism. The extent of any Pharisaic mission has been debated, but there is evidence of such activity in the second and third century CE (Keener 1999, 548), possibly in response to the growth of the Jesus movement. Converts should participate in rituals of purification and circumcision. But the result was the opposite: proselytes were **twice as much a child of hell as you are**. This may refer to an overzealous neophyte who exemplifies extreme Pharisaic attitudes, teaching, and the way of life (see Phil 3:4-6; Luz 2005, 117-18).

■ **16-22** Jesus illustrates their misinterpretation by the teaching on oaths and tithing. Verses 16 and 24 form an inclusio by starting and concluding the section with the same phrase: **you blind guides**. This spiritual blindness does not allow them to see God at work in Jesus' ministry (9:34; 12:24). But it also refers to their misinterpretation of Scripture and erroneous teaching.

If anyone swears by the temple, it means nothing; but anyone who swears by the gold of the temple is bound by that oath (23:16). Oaths were often given to support one's words and promises. In a Jewish context, people avoided mentioning God in those oaths and replaced his name with reference to the temple, the most holy place (Luz 2005, 199-120). The Pharisees attempted to make a distinction between oaths that are binding and those that are not. Jesus showed the flawed logic behind their practices (Talbert 2010, 258-259). Jesus makes his argument on the basis of a priestly understanding of contagious holiness: common things are sanctified by contact with holy objects (Exod 29:27; Lev 6:27 [20 HB]).

The holy temple makes its treasures sacred, and the altar consecrates sacrifices; they are obviously more important. Thus, swearing by the temple or the altar does not make the oaths void. In reality every oath ultimately—regardless of how one phrases it—appeals to God: **And anyone who swears by heaven swears by God's throne and by the one who sits on it** (Matt 23:22). Placed in the context of Jesus' teaching on oaths in 5:33-37, the passage shows the absurdity of Pharisaic practice of oaths in general: "One should not swear . . . since an oath really does obligate God, [and therefore] every oath is a misuse of his name" (Luz 2005, 120-21).

■ **23-24** Jesus accuses the Pharisees of paying attention to an insignificant issue of tithing garden herbs and neglecting more important things in the Law. The Torah required tithing of only certain agricultural products: grain seeds, oil, wine, fruits of the field, and trees (Lev 27:30; Deut 14:22-23). But their tradition has extended those requirements to everything that had been cultivated, including herbs (Luz 2005, 123). Their detailed rules and regulations eclipsed the heart of the Torah: **justice** [*krisin*], **mercy** [*eleos*] **and faithfulness** (*pistin*; Matt 23:23).

The irony is that in their zealousness for the Law and appearing righteous, they had neglected the essentials: "To act justly and to love mercy and to walk humbly with your God" (Mic 6:8). So they **should have practiced the latter, without neglecting the former** (Matt 23:23). In their practical interpretation of the Torah, the Pharisees should get the priorities right. The hyperbole
23:23-28 of a gnat and a camel (v 24) illustrates that absurd oversight: they filter their wine in order not to swallow an unclean insect (Lev 11:41), yet swallow a camel—one of the biggest unclean animals (v 4).

■ **25-26 You clean the outside of the cup and dish** (Matt 23:25). The fifth woe is built around the purity of utensils. Some rabbinic schools insisted that if an outside of a cup is contaminated then the whole vessel is unclean; its contents should not be consumed and must be thrown away. Others made a distinction between inside and outside; if only the outside has been rendered unclean, there is no need to throw away its contents (see Maccoby 1999, 152-54).

Jesus' response radically redefines the problem. Purity of utensils is irrelevant because their plates and cups are filled with moral uncleanliness: **greed** [*arpagēs*] **and self-indulgence** (*akrasias*). *Arpagēs* could also be translated as violence, plunder, or robbery. Thus what they eat was taken from others, perhaps from the widows and the poor (France 2007, 875). As with the essentials of the Law (vv 23-24), they have missed the key aspects of purity rules: if the inner is clean, **then the outside also will be clean** (v 26; see Mark 7:1-23). They needed to deal with impurity that comes from within.

■ **27-28** The illustration with **whitewashed tombs** (Matt 23:27) perfectly captures Jesus' point about outward appearance and inward impurity. According to the Torah, human bones and graves are sources of ritual uncleanliness; contact with them will render a person unclean for seven days (Num 19:16).

The Mishnah mentions a practice of whitewashing tombs around festival times in order to mark these unclean places to prevent pilgrims from inadvertently touching them and getting defiled, which would prevent them from participation in religious celebrations (*m. Šeqal.* 1:1). "Whitewashing" could also refer to decorative plaster adorning tombs; a beautiful place contains unclean human remains (Lachs 1975, 385-88). In either case, the point is clear: the Pharisees may appear righteous by following purity rules but inside their hearts are filled with hypocrisy and wickedness. They are defiled from within.

■ **29-32** The religious leaders were **build[ing] tombs for the prophets and decorat[ing] the graves of the righteous** (Matt 23:29). Josephus mentions, for example, that Herod has built "a monument . . . of white stone" at the entrance to David's tomb (*Ant.* 16.7.1). But for Jesus, these public monuments marking holy spaces and honoring people of the past highlights the hypocrisy of the current leadership since the prophets were murdered by people in power.

The claim from the **teachers of the law and Pharisees** that they would not have taken part in murdering the prophets testifies further to their two-facedness. In reality, they are no different from their ancestors. Building the tombs for the victims of their predecessors is a sign of continuity and not of repentance and distancing (Harrington 1991, 326). By persecuting Jesus and his followers, the religious leaders closely follow the footsteps of their forbearers.

■ **33-36** At the end Jesus asks a rhetorical question: **How will you escape being condemned to hell?** (v 33). Unfortunately, they won't. What their fathers have done to the prophets in the past, they will do to the messengers of the kingdom in these last days: **Some of them you will kill and crucify; others you will flog in your synagogues and pursue from town to town** (v 34). They rebel against God by rejecting his Messiah and his messengers.

The relationship between YHWH and the prophets of old is mirrored in the relationship between Jesus and his followers: **I am sending you prophets and sages and teachers**. Jesus has divine authority to send his disciples to proclaim God's will in this world. There is continuity in the mission of the people of God. But, unfortunately, they will face the same opposition as the prophets and of Jesus himself: the path of rejection, persecution, and death.

From the blood of righteous Abel to the blood of Zechariah son of Berekiah (v 35). The identity of Zechariah son of Berekiah is not clear. Some link it to the Zechariah of 2 Chr 24:17-27 who was stoned in the temple courtyard. This may have been the last murder in the biblical story since 2 Chronicles was the last book of the Jewish canon. Others identify him as Zechariah son of Bareis mentioned by Josephus (*J.W.* 4.5.4). He was killed by the Zealots in the middle of the temple around 69 CE (Hagner 1995, 677).

In either case, this statement illustrates the idea that from the beginning (Gen 4:1-12) and throughout Jewish history, the religious leadership leaves a bloody trail of murdered righteous people. The language of judgment here, **upon you will come all the righteous blood**, resonates with prophetic language from the OT (see Jer 22:17; Lam 4:13), and the act of spilling of innocent blood is one of the sins condemned by the Torah (Deut 19:10).

Similar language is also found later in the Passion Narrative: **His** [Jesus'] **blood is on us and on our children** (27:25 [→]). **On this generation** (Matt 23:36) of wicked leaders will come the punishment for "the whole biblical history of disobedience and murder" (Hahn 2007, 277). This also has been linked with the destruction of Jerusalem and its temple in the next passage (see vv 37-39). But all of that language is just a prelude to the drama of judgment that unfolds in chs 24—25.

FROM THE TEXT

This text has been used in the past to justify anti-Semitic attitudes. But Jesus' critique of specific Pharisaic practices is neither an attack on Judaism in general nor even all Pharisees. And it certainly has no ethnic relevance today. Rather, this critique is from within. Jesus stands here in the great OT prophetic tradition and—like the oracles of old—denounces and pronounces doom on unfaithful and hypocritical religious leaders. One of the biggest problems is that they are resisting God's will in these last days and using their authority to prevent people of Israel from following the Messiah. Anti-Semitism in all of its forms is inexcusable for anyone, and especially for Christians. Sadly, it is an indelible stain on the story of the church.

The church in general and the Wesleyan-holiness movement in particular could learn from this critique of the Pharisees who turn a genuine concern for purity and holiness into hypocritical separation from others and reduce righteousness to a set of legalistic performance targets. Jesus reminds us to take a holistic approach to righteousness that embraces a whole person: internal and external. Instead of separation, the practice of holiness should be based on justice, mercy, and faithfulness.

3. The Fate of Jerusalem (23:37-39)

BEHIND THE TEXT

After proclaiming woes against teachers of the Law and the Pharisees, Jesus addresses personified Jerusalem. The change in audience signals a bigger problem: his proclamation has been rejected not only by the corrupted Jerusalem leadership but also by its inhabitants; the people "were not willing" to gather around God's Messiah (23:37).

The passage mirrors the previous language (vv 29-36) but changes its tone. Woes turn into a lament that comes out of Jesus' love for Jerusalem and its people. They have brought judgment on themselves by resisting and ultimately rejecting God's message and salvation. But this prophetic message deviates from doom and offers hope at the end. Donald Hagner interprets this change as an indication of Jesus' grace. Israelites and their leaders have not been prejudged, and Jesus expresses his desire to "receive them back into his fold." However, the reality is that they have rejected the invitation and put themselves out of the divine "saving purposes" (Hagner 1995, 679).

IN THE TEXT

■ **37** Jesus addresses the holy city: **you who kill the prophets and stone those sent to you**. Tragically, Jerusalem—the center of religious life of Israel—turns into the place of persecution and death for God's messengers (see vv 31, 34-35). The holy place that should have been full of justice and peace is full of murder (see Isa 1—4). As in Isaiah, rejection of God's messengers in the past and present (Jesus and his followers) and ultimately the divine will for Israel will result in punishment and destruction.

The simile **As a hen gathers her chicks under her wings** evokes psalms that describe the caring and protective God of Israel (Pss 17:8; 36:7 [8 HB]; 57:1 [2 HB]; 61:4 [5 HB]). But here Jesus reapplies the image of YHWH to himself. It creates a sense of divine authority as well as his love for Jerusalem and its people; it is in a vivid contrast to damnation of the religious leaders. Jesus laments the failure to respond to his call to gather around the Messiah and be restored as the people of God.

■ **38 Your house** [*oikos*] **is left to you desolate**. Here Jesus directly refers to the destruction of the Jerusalem temple. It will be unpacked further in the next chapter (see 21:14; 24:15). The language implies divine abandonment and judgment. Jesus again uses traditional prophetic imagery: the divine presence withdraws from the temple and the city because of the people's sins (see Ezek 8:6-12; 9:3-9).

■ **39 Blessed is he who comes in the name of the Lord**, from Ps 118:26, first appears in Matt 21:9. Here it refers to the future, perhaps to the coming of the Son of Man in 24:37-51. The ambiguity leaves the open question: Is this future restoration or future judgment that will come from the exalted King of Israel? The phrase might refer to confession or recognition of the rejected Messiah since they did not accept Jesus when he first arrived in Jerusalem (see ch 21). The salvation of Israel then is contingent on her repentance and acceptance of Jesus as her Messiah (Keener 2009, 558). Thus the text could be interpreted as an extension of divine grace.

This is the last public teaching of Jesus. The next time he faces the Jerusalem crowd they will be rejecting him before his crucifixion (see 27:15-23). But when he appears to them as the exalted Son of Man, there will be no alternative but to acknowledge who he really is (Hagner 1995, 681).

FROM THE TEXT

In his last address to the festive crowds in the temple, Jesus expresses his heartfelt lament over the city and its inhabitants. The passage hints at two perspectives on the coming judgment. It will be experienced by "this generation" and then later in some distant future "you will not see me again until you say . . ." This will be more pronounced in the following chapters as Jesus expounds on the imminent destruction of Jerusalem and the future coming of the Son of Man (chs 24—25) where acceptance of his rule brings salvation and rejection—punishment (Hagner 1995, 681).

4. The Fate of the Temple (24:1-35)

BEHIND THE TEXT

The whole section of Jesus' engagements with the Jerusalem temple and confrontation with Jewish religious leadership (chs 21—23) culminates in 24:1-2, the explicit prediction of the temple's destruction. The first visit to the temple turned into an enacted prophetic proclamation of its doom, and the blame is solely placed on the religious leadership that defiled the very place of the divine presence. In the following section, Jesus elaborates further on the fate of the temple and the establishment of the new messianic age when Jesus reigns as the exalted Lord (chs 24—25).

This section poses serious problems to the widespread interpretation of the text as a prediction of the end of the world and attendant calculations of "the signs of the times." The single but significant reference to "this generation" in 24:34 throws this line of argument into a tailspin. Alternatively, this discourse could be interpreted as a vivid prophetic description of the destruction of Jerusalem and its temple in 70 CE (see N. T. Wright, G. B. Caird, M. Borg, C. H. T. Fletcher-Louis). This position could provide a very convincing case, particularly in relation to the Gospel of Mark (Brower 2012, 324-43). However, Matthew's version needs to be read on its own terms. One key point is the frequent use of *parousia* in referring to "the *coming* of the Son of Man" (vv 3, 27, 37, 39).

R. T. France argues that one should interpret the apocalyptic discourse in chs 24—25 as Jesus' response to two different questions from 24:3. The first one is related to the destruction of Jerusalem: "When will this happen?" The answer to this question stretches from 24:4 to v 35 and is structured around certain events and time references ("then," "immediately," and "those days"). These should warn the disciples to flee the destruction: "let the reader understand" (24:15).

The second question is about "the sign of your coming." Jesus gives an answer to it in 24:36—25:46. Ironically, he provides "signs" for the impending destruction of the holy city but no warning sign is given prior to the coming of the Son of Man: "about that day or hour no one knows" (v 36; France 2007, 889-901). N. T. Wright interprets this question not as a reference to "the second coming" but the question about Jesus' enthronement as a king: "'When will you come in your kingdom? When will the ages turn?' What come next are details of the plan to become a king and 'the birth pangs of the age to come'" (1996, 346).

According to France, Matthew brings these two questions together to dispel confusion: some Christians might interpret tribulations surrounding the destruction of Jerusalem as the sign of the coming of the Son of Man. But it is a false connection: "The disciples are therefore specifically warned against associating the *parousia* with the events predicted in vv. 15-31" (France 2007, 901). Thus France attempts to take a *via media* that interprets chs 24—25 as referring both to the destruction of Jerusalem and the future coming of the Son of Man without a direct correlation between the two. This may be the best way to tackle Matthew's "Little Apocalypse."

This discourse uses traditional Jewish prophetic and apocalyptic language. The Danielic tradition leaves the most visible mark: destruction of Jerusalem and the temple (Dan 9), the rumors of war (11:44), the tribulation (12:1), the abomination of desolation (8:13), and the appearance of the son of man on clouds (7:13) form the backbone of the Matthean apocalyptic narrative (Keener 2009, 573).

Wright notes that the imagery used by Matthew is rooted in the classic prophetic critique from within Judaism (see Isa 1—5; Ezek 34). Vivid prophetic language is found in Matt 24:29 that describes the destruction of the Jerusalem temple as a cosmic catastrophe (see similar prophetic poetry in Isa 13:10, Ezek 32:7-8, and Joel 3:14 [4:14 HB]). Another influence from the prophetic tradition is seen in the language of judgment and vindication.

Following traditional prophetic logic, the Matthean Jesus has already alluded to the judgment of religious leaders of the people of Israel (Matt 8:11-12; 22:1-14). Here the story reaches a devastating climax: the profaned temple, corrupt religious leadership, rejection of the will of God and his Messiah results in judgment and destruction. Thus this section is not about some distant unknown future. Rather Matthew's Jesus uses "Jewish images that indicate bringing of the story of Israel to its appointed climax" (Wright 1996, 362).

Matthew's "Little Apocalypse" invites different—often opposing—perspectives. However, paying attention to its immediate narrative, literary, and historical contexts will help in navigating through the text. One of the most unhelpful and unfortunately popular ways of interpretation thought is to take it out of its context and use it for calculating the time of "the end of the world." Ironically, Matthew argues against such views: looking for the signs of Jesus' second coming is futile since "the Son of Man will come at an hour when you do not expect him" (24:44).

Any approach that focuses on decoding "the future events" misses key points of the apocalyptic discourse. Jesus not only prophesies—in very general terms—about calamities surrounding the destruction of Jerusalem and its inhabitants but also expresses pastoral concern for his followers. He tells what the disciples should do in times of such turmoil. One thing is certain: being prepared is not about looking for signs or calculating days. It is about remaining a faithful follower of Jesus the Messiah.

IN THE TEXT

■ **1-2** This prediction of the temple's destruction follows the oracle on the fate of "this generation" (23:36; see vv 35-36) and Jerusalem (vv 37-38). Its splendor impressed Jesus' followers, simple Galilean peasants: **his disciples came up to him to call his attention to its buildings** (24:1). The Jerusalem temple was known for its beauty and impressive appearance; "it was, perhaps, the biggest sanctuary in the Roman Empire" (see Sanders 1992, 50-76). Josephus' description is extravagant:

> It was the most admirable of all the works that we have seen or heard of, both for its curious structure and its magnitude, and also for the vast wealth bestowed upon it, as well as for the glorious reputation it had for its holiness. (*J.W.* 6.267)

But Jesus is not impressed; even this magnificent temple would not be spared: **Not one stone here will be left on another** (v 2). The judgment on wicked religious authorities, a faithless generation, and the holy city culminates in the destruction of the most sacred place.

■ **3** Jesus leaves the temple and stops on the Mount of Olives on his way to Bethany (26:6). He reveals the fate of Jerusalem from the mountain that overlooks the holy city and its impressive temple. This move from the temple to the Mount of Olives echoes Ezek 11:23 and Zech 14:4-5. In Ezekiel, the divine presence or glory leaves the city and stops on "the mountain east of it." In the second prophecy, on the day of the Lord, God himself will visit Jerusalem and "his feet will stand on the Mount of Olives." Both of these passages are set in the context of judgment over Jerusalem and the enemies of YHWH. Zechariah 14:2, 5 have also been echoed in Matt 24:7, 16, 40-41 mentioning earthquake, people fleeing, and half of the population killed.

The disciples approach Jesus privately and ask him two important questions: **When will this happen, and what will be the sign of your coming and of the end of the age?** While Mark is only interested in the destruction of the temple (Mark 13:4), Matthew adds the second question about the sign of the *parousia* or Jesus' coming in glory. Perhaps Matthew was trying to clarify misconception that "so cataclysmic an event as the destruction of the temple must usher in the end of the present world order" (France 2007, 895). If that's the case, then the first question is addressed in 24:4-35 and the second from 24:36 onward. Davies and Allison, on the other hand, see 24:4-35 as an introduction to 24:36—25:30 (2004, 331).

Parousia

Parousia is a Greek term used by early Christians to refer to the coming of Jesus in glory. It is often associated with the second coming of Christ that ushers in the final consummation of the kingdom of God through universal judgment. The language and imagery associated with the term comes from OT theophanies and apocalyptic visions such as Dan 7. The term itself was used in the Greco-Roman word to describe both the arrival and presence of a Roman emperor in a province. L. J. Kreitzer notes that in the NT the advent of Jesus Christ is seen as a multifaceted concept: "As an act of vindication, a time of visitation, a decisive moment of judgment, a time of deliverance and the climatic event of consummation" (1997, 856-58).

■ **4-8** Jesus describes the atmosphere before the destruction of the temple—a time of unrest and tribulation. The language is similar to apocalyptic traditions found in *4 Ezra* 9:3: "There shall appear in the world earthquakes, tumult of peoples, intrigues of nations, wavering of leaders, confusion of princes" (see *Sib. Or.* 2; *2 Bar.* 70).

One sign of upcoming devastation is the appearance of messianic claimants **in my name** (Matt 24:5). Those who claim **I am the Messiah** (or the Christ) will attract many. Jewish history prior to and beyond 70 CE proves the point. The appearance of Jewish rebels and messianic figures is noted in Acts (5:36-37; 21:38) and later in the writings of Josephus (*J.W.* 2.13.4; 2.17.8-10; *Ant.* 17.10.5; 18.85-87). A telling example has Rabbi Akiva who identified the leader of the second Jewish revolt (132-135 CE) Simeon bar Kochba or "the son of the star" (see Num 24:17) as a messiah (*y. Ta'an.* 68d).

Early Christians could have witnessed **wars and rumors of wars** (Matt 24:6). The Roman-Parthian War over Armenia (58-63 CE), Boudicca's Revolt in Britannia (60-61 CE), the suicide of the Emperor Nero and the following political calamity and brief civil war known as the Year of Four Emperors (69 CE), and, of course, the first Jewish revolt that led to the destruction of Jerusalem (66-73 CE).

Famines and earthquakes (Matt 24:7) were part of life in the ancient Mediterranean. The first century CE witnessed devastating earthquakes (see Tacitus, *Ann.* 2.47; Pliny the Elder, *Nat. Hist.* 2.86.200): Lydia (17 CE), Ephesus with widespread destruction in Asia Minor (23 CE), and the volcanic eruption at Pompeii (62 CE). (See earthquake history of the region in Ambraseys 2009, 62-814.) Matthew also mentions earthquakes at the time of Jesus' death (27:51) and resurrection (28:2); these could be interpreted as omens of judgment and impending destruction (→ 27:51-54). Josephus mentions "so great a famine was come upon us" (*Ant.* 3.320; 20.51-53), which has been dated around 44-46 CE. Acts 11:28 also mentions a great famine in Palestine and Syria under Claudius (France 2007, 904). This passage also reveals a pastoral concern for the disciples. In time of instability and uncertainty Jesus warns them to **watch out that no one deceives** [*planēsē*] **you** (Matt 24:4) and don't be **alarmed** (*mē throeisthe*; v 6). These are not signs of the imminent "coming" or "destruction." These are natural events in human history and part of ancient life. They should be taken as **the beginning of birth pains** (v 8) that usher in "the suffering of Jerusalem" (France 2007, 904). **End is still to come** (*oupō estin to telos*; v 6) refers to the future destruction of the temple (see v 14) and not the end of the world.

■ **9-14** Here the focus shifts to the followers of Jesus. They will be affected as well; the faithful ones **will be handed over** (v 9; see parallels with Jesus' sufferings in 17:22) to the civil authorities for trial. They should expect persecutions and even death. But this time, hostilities will come not only from the Jewish community (see 10:17-23) but also from **all nations** (*pantōv tōv ethnōn*), that is, the Gentiles.

The rejection, oppression, and injustice (i.e., **the increase of wickedness** [v 12]) will have a devastating effect on the community of the faithful: **the love** [*hē agape*] **of most will grow cold**. This will manifest itself in the degradation of relationships with God and fellow believers: many will stumble and lose their faith; others will follow the false prophets. Hate (see 10:22) and betrayal (see 10:21) will spread within the community. The language of stumbling, handing over, and betrayal is strikingly similar to ch 26, where Jesus is being betrayed, handed over, and denied by the disciples.

MATTHEW

Jesus calls his followers to **stand firm** and remain faithful to **the end** (*eis telos*; 24:13). Salvation will be granted to those who persevere. The meaning of *eis telos* is not clear. France (2007, 907) offers a few options: the end of the age (which presupposes eschatological salvation), the destruction of the temple (which presupposes physical security), or continue in faith "for as long

24:9-22 as it takes" or to death (with salvation as "the ultimate spiritual security"). Whatever "the end" is, the readers anticipate its arrival soon (Luz 2005, 195).

Wars and natural disasters do not signal the coming destruction of Jerusalem and the end of the old order. The proclamation of **the gospel of the kingdom** heralds the end of the temple and the beginning of a new age (v 14). The end will come when the gospel spreads around the known inhabited world (*holē tē oikoumenē*), which included the Mediterranean basin and north and east of it, or the Roman Empire. Acts records the spread of the gospel from Jerusalem to the center of the ancient world—Rome (Acts 1:8). This contrasts with the mission of the Twelve in Matt 10:5-6; the news that the gospel will spread beyond Israel anticipates the great universal commission in 28:19. The gospel of the kingdom will reach all nations despite hatred of the followers of Christ.

■ **15-22** Having set the general context, Jesus moves to the events leading to the destruction of the temple. The appearance of **the abomination that causes desolation** (v 15) in the temple signals its impending destruction as well as devastation falling upon Judaeans. Matthew tries to clarify the confusion his readers might have had concerning this abomination (see Mark 13:14). He uses the neuter participle (**standing** [*hestos*]) to indicate that this is not a reference to a person but an object or an incident and he identifies the exact place where the abomination appears—**the holy place**, that is, the Jerusalem temple.

The phrase "the abomination of desolation" (*to bdelygma tou erēmōseōs*) comes from Daniel (8:13; 9:27; 11:31; 12:11). It refers to the desecration of the temple in 167 BCE under King Antiochus IV Epiphanes who placed a pagan altar and offered sacrifices on the top of YHWH's altar (see 1 Macc 1:54-59, 62-64). Matthew's readers should expect a similar abominable act of profanation and pollution of the most holy place that ushers in its destruction.

"The Abomination of Desolation" in the History of Interpretation

Several events in the history of the Roman occupation of Judea that could have been perceived as sacrilegious (France 2007, 913): the erection of the Roman-style eagle over the temple's gate by Herod the Great (*J.W.* 1.648-55); bringing the Roman legions' insignia to the holy city by Pilate (26 CE) (*J.W.* 2.169-72); Emperor Caligula's attempt to erect a statue of himself in "the temple of God" (40/41 CE) (*J.W.* 2.184-203; *Ant.* 18.261-309); occupation of the temple by Zealots (Josephus calls them "bloody polluters" who made the sanctuary "a shop of tyranny") during the first Jewish revolt (67/68 CE) (*J.W.* 4.150-57); the presence of Roman army standards (with idolatrous symbols) in the temple during its destruction in 70 CE (see Luke 21:20). Traditional interpretation has also connected "the abomination of desolation" with presence of a figure of antichrist (Keener 2009, 573-75). Robert Snow has suggested (in relation to the parallel passage in Mark 13) that "the abomination of desolation" refers to the actions of corrupted priesthood that have profaned the temple (2016, 141-43).

The Danielic language hints at the kind of event to expect and is general enough to accommodate a variety of possibilities. Historical information concerning the events in Jerusalem during the Jewish revolt is too sketchy to pinpoint exact events that would fit the predictions.

The appearance of the abomination (see different translations for abomination: "Appalling Horror" [Robinson 1927, 198], "Devastating Pollution" [France 2007, 913], "Abominable Sign" [Tasker 1961, 229]) signals rapid escalation and **those who are in Judea** should immediately find refuge in **the mountains** (Matt 24:16). The text is filled with urgency: those at work (**in the field** [v 18]) or at leisure (**on the housetop** [v 17]) must leave everything behind and move quickly. Delay risks death. This rapid flight would be hard for **pregnant women and nursing mothers** (v 19). But it won't be easier for those who stayed behind. Josephus, describing the horrors of the besieged Jerusalem, tells of a rich woman, Mary, who stayed within the city and in the time of famine "she slew her son, and then roasted him, and ate the one half of him, and kept the other half by her concealed" (*J.W.* 6.201).

Timing of the flight is also important: not **in winter or on the Sabbath** (v 20). Cold nights, rain, muddy hills, flooded wadis, the swollen Jordan river poses danger to the refugees (Hagner 1995, 701; Harrington 1991, 337). The reference to the Sabbath may betray the concern for Sabbath observance within the early Jewish-Christian community. In any case, urgent departure will make this observance impossible (Hagner 1995, 702), practically difficult (France 2007, 915), or will be severely limited by it (Mounce 1991, 225). Eusebius, an early church historian, notes that Early Christians took seriously that warning. Christians in Jerusalem "commanded by a revelation" left the city before the siege (*HE* 3.5.3).

Flight to Pella

Early Christian writers Eusebius (*HE* 3.5.3) and Epiphanius of Salamis (*Panarion* 29.7.7-8; 30.2.7; *Weights and Measures* 15) recall a tradition of a miraculous escape of the believers from the holy city just before the siege took place. It was said that an angel of God (in other versions Christ himself) told the faithful to leave "the royal capital of the Jews" because it would be completely destroyed. Christian refugees from Jerusalem found their new home in Pella, in the region of Decapolis (modern northwestern Jordan). The historicity of the story has been debated in modern scholarship (Brandon 1957, 167-84; Gunther 1973, 81-94; Pritz 1981, 39-43; Koester 1989, 90-106; Bourgel 2010, 107-38).

The great distress or tribulation (*thlipsis megalē*) is the reason of the urgent flight. This traditional apocalyptic, hyperbolic language of judgment (Dan 12:1; Joel 2:2; Rev 16:18) describes the horrors of Jerusalem's destruction: **unequalled from the beginning of the world until now** (Matt 24:21).
24:23-28 It emphasizes the seriousness of destruction and sufferings. Josephus, who witnessed the events, describes the horrors of the six-month siege of Jerusalem 70 CE: starvation, cannibalism, robbery, terror, conflicts between Jewish fractions, and futile attempts to escape the city (*J.W.* 5-6). Josephus claims that this was the worst disaster since creation: "Accordingly, it appears to me that the misfortunes of all men, from the beginning of the world, if they be compared to these of the Jews are not so considerable as they were" (*J.W.* 1.11).

Matthew uses the divine passive to point to God's intervention: **those days will be shortened** (v 22). No one would have survived in Jerusalem if God had not been merciful. He does that because of **the elect** (*eklektous*; "chosen"). This term often refers to Israel, but here it has been redefined. The chosen ones are the new holy people of God gathered around Jesus Messiah (see 22:14; 24:24, 31). This recalls the OT theme of God's mercy because of the righteous remnant (see Isa 4).

■ **23-28** The time marker (**at that time** [Matt 24:23]) connects the appearance of pseudomessiahs and false prophets to the events leading up to the destruction of Jerusalem. Again, Jesus warns against deception by their words and miracles (see v 4; Exod 7:22; 8:7 [3 HB]). Josephus confirms this:

> A false prophet was the occasion of these people's destruction, who had made a public proclamation in the city that very day, that God commanded them to get upon the temple, and that there they should receive

miraculous signs of their deliverance. Now there was then a great number of false prophets suborned by the tyrants to impose on the people, who denounced this to them, that they should wait for deliverance from God; and this was in order to keep them from deserting. (*J.W.* 6.5.2)

The calamity of the first Jewish revolt, the siege of Jerusalem, and the destruction of the temple would give rise to all sorts of messianic claims. The hopes for a messianic intervention to save the holy city are groundless, including the hopes of some of the elect that the imminent destruction of Jerusalem would usher in the return of Jesus the Messiah. False claims abounded: **"'Look, here is the Messiah!' or, 'There he is!'"** (Matt 24:23).

This passage juxtaposes false messianic claims with the future coming of the true Messiah. "Unlike the messianic pretenders, with their offer of 'signs,' the Son of Man will give no warning sign of his *parousia*" (France 2007, 918). Like lightning, his coming will be sudden, unexpected, and visible for everybody. It will be obvious to everyone and "not matter of dubious claims and speculation." The disciples are warned against associating the coming of Christ with the destruction of the temple (France 2007, 901). In other words, Matthew mentions the coming of the Son of Man in order to "distinguish it from the events currently being considered" (France 2007, 918).

Jesus finishes this part with an enigmatic simile about a corpse and **the vultures** (or "eagles"; v 28; *hoi aetoi*). In the context of v 27, the parable seems to illustrate "the unmistakable character of the parousia" (Hagner 1995, 707). As the gathering of vultures indicates the presence of a **carcass** (v 28), so the coming of the Son of Man will be visible to everybody. In the context of v 29, the saying may illustrate the destruction of Jerusalem. Eagles gathering over a corpse could allude to symbols on the standards of the Roman army (Mounce 1991, 225).

■ **29-31** The culmination comes immediately after the time of distress (perhaps referring to the war and the siege). The destruction is expressed through traditional apocalyptic and prophetic language: **the moon will not give its light; the stars will fall from the sky** (v 29). These do not signal the destruction of the whole cosmos but—in poetic form—describe the magnitude of the catastrophe and severity of the divine judgment (see Isa 34:4; Amos 8:9; Hag 2:6, 21). The language of the shaken universe may indicate the overthrow of systems of power, oppressive foreign enemies such as Babylon (Isa 13:10) and Egypt (Ezek 32:7) or even corrupted Zion (Joel 2:10, 31 [3:4 HB]).

Crispin Fletcher-Louis points to OT and 2TJ traditions regarding the temple as a representation of the cosmos in miniature (2002, 156-62). Its threefold structure corresponded, represented, and encapsulated "heaven and earth in its totality": "the sanctuary (supremely the Holy of Holies), the inner and outer courts, are allowed to correspond to heaven, earth, and the sea respectively" (Fletcher-Louis 2002, 157). He also illustrates his point by the description of the temple veil (see Matt 27:51) found in Josephus (Fletcher-

Louis 2002, 164): "For the scarlet seemed emblematic of fire, the fine linen of the earth, the blue of the air, and the purple of the sea. . . . On this tapestry was portrayed a panorama of the heavens, the signs of Zodiac excepted" (*J.W.* 5.212-13). It is not surprising then that Jesus describes the destruction of the Jerusalem temple in apocalyptic terms as the collapse of the universe.

Then will appear the sign of the Son of Man in heaven (24:30*a*). This verse provides a challenge for interpreters as it appears to connect the coming of the Son of Man with the destruction of the temple. However, a more detailed look at the apocalyptic language of the text and its intertextual links could provide an alternative pathway. The nature of the sign (*semeion*) is unclear. Moreover, the Greek behind this phrase provides two possibilities: the sign will appear in heaven or the sign of "the Son of Man in heaven" will appear.

The history of interpretation provides four possible explanations: (1) appearance of a cross in the sky; (2) a military imagery of a flag or a standard coupled with "a trumpet call"; (3) the sign is the Son of Man himself (Luz, 2005, 201-2); the sign is the destruction of the temple and in-gathering of the people (France 2007, 926).

Whatever the sign might be, it will be evident to **all the peoples of the earth** (v 30*b*) and they will mourn. This alludes to Zech 12:10-14, which speaks of the inhabitants of Jerusalem and the land of Israel mourning over "the one they have pierced" (Zech 12:10). Later in the Passion Narrative, Matthew uses other passages from Zechariah to signal the rejection of the Messiah (Zech 11:4-14; 13:7-9 ↔ Matt 26:31; 27:9-10).

If this passage fits in Matthew's messianic interpretation of Zechariah, then, perhaps, it is better to translate *pasai hai phylae tēs gēs* as "the tribes of the land," referring to the people of Israel, not to other nations of the world. In other words, the people of God will mourn the destruction of Jerusalem and comprehend the consequences of their rejection of the Messiah. This interpretation fits well with the previous statement in 23:37-39 and later in 27:24-25.

The Son of Man coming on the clouds of heaven (24:30*b*) is the key to understanding the passage. The whole scene comes from Dan 7:13-14 where an enigmatic figure of one like a son of man "on the clouds of heaven" comes before God in the heavenly throne room; there he was given authority, glory, and power. It is an upward movement: from earth to heaven and not vice versa. The change in the language has to be noted as well; Matthew uses *erchomenos* (**coming**) here and not *parousia* (→ Matt 24:3 sidebar, "Parousia" above). The reference to Daniel's vision here suggests the coming of the Son of Man into the heavenly presence of God, not his return to earth. Jesus evokes this apocalyptic image of vindication and triumph of the Son of Man in contrast to the previous references to the suffering and humiliated Son of Man.

The imagery communicates the message that Jesus is the true Messiah, vindicated by God himself. Wright suggests that Jesus has been vindicated in three ways: resurrection and ascension, the destruction of the temple as the center of opposition to the Messiah, and fulfillment of his prophecy. The news about his victory will be spread by messengers **from one end of the heavens to the other** (Matt 24:31; Wright 2002, 122-23). France summarizes the meaning of this passage:

> The time of the temple's destruction will also be the time when it will become clear that the Son of Man, rejected by the leaders of his people, has been vindicated and enthroned at the right hand of God, and that it is he who is now to exercise the universal kingship which is his destiny. That is how Daniel's vision is to be fulfilled. (2007, 924)

Verse 31 continues with the royal imagery of the glorified Messiah. After his enthronement, Jesus sends his messengers or angels (this could refer to either heavenly beings or humans) to **gather his elect**. Using the language referring to scattered Israel (Deut 30:4; Zech 2:10 [14 HB]; Isa 27:13), Jesus redefines it to talk about his followers. This relation between Jesus' exaltation and the future mission is fully seen after his resurrection. Matthew 28:18-19: "All authority in heaven and on earth has been given to me. Therefore go and make disciples of all nations." The gathering of the people refers to reconstitution of the people of God as well as to the mission of spreading of the good news of Christ's reign.

Matthew 24:29-31 should be understood as part of the answer to the question about destruction of the temple. Again Jesus uses apocalyptic imagery. This is an act of judgment over faithless Israel. It is also the beginning of the new order: the rule of the vindicated and enthroned Son of Man who will ingather the new holy people of God. Jerusalem and its temple will cease to be the center of the *missio dei* (France 2007, 928).

■ **32-35** In the future days of uncertainty and turbulence, deceit and betrayal, the faithful ones must be alert and wise. A fig tree could teach them a lesson. A budding tree that produces new leaves is a sign of the coming summer. Since the disciples already can read the signs of nature in the change of seasons, they should also pay attention to the signs of the coming destruction and the change of the old and the new age: **so . . . you know that it is near** (v 32).

What is more surprising is that **all these things** (v 33) will take place before **this generation . . . will pass away** (vv 34-35*a*). Here we find the most problematic statement for any interpretation that sees vv 4-31 as a prediction of the second coming of Jesus. The history of interpretation has proposed a few solutions: (1) Jesus and the early church were mistaken; (2) redefine "this generation" into "human" or "Jewish race"; (3) see a multiple fulfillment of this prophecy throughout history; (4) reinterpret "happened" into "will have started to take place"; (5) blend the historical perspectives in prophetic language where immediate and distant events have been brought together; (6) fulfilled in the death and resurrection of Jesus (Mounce 1991, 227-28).

All the tensions could be easily resolved by a simple recognition that this statement is related to the destruction of the temple in 70 CE (see 23:36; Hagner 1995, 715). The followers of Jesus and other Jewish people (the generation that has rejected him; see 27:25) will witness the destruction of the temple and the vindication of Jesus (Wright 1996, 362).

My words will never pass away (24:35*b*). This statement echoes Isa 40:8 and 51:6 and redefines "the word of YHWH" into "my words." Jesus' words have divine authority (see Matt 28:18-20) and could serve as a reliable guide to the future events (Hagner 1995, 716). This phrase also alludes back to a previous statement in 5:18. In this context the passing away of **heaven and earth** (24:35*a*) could be read as a reference to the destruction of the temple (see vv 29-31). The future destruction of the temple will fulfill Jesus' prophecy.

FROM THE TEXT

Jesus' oracle about the fate of Jerusalem and its temple is rooted in the great prophetic tradition of Israel. It describes the destruction of the city that has rejected God's Messiah. Its form, language, and content indicate genuine prophetic insight rather than a text written after the destruction took place (Hagner 1995, 703). But the text not only is about divine judgment but also expects "the great time of renewal." These tragic events mark the new beginning expressed in apocalyptic language: vindication of Jesus, ingathering of the new people of God, and inauguration of the new age of the Messiah's rule (Wright 2004, 338). The text is not just interested in "discernment of times"; it is pastoral at heart. Jesus urges the believers to be prepared, to stay strong in their faith, and to trust that they will be delivered in the time of tribulation.

Popular "last days teachings" often appeal to this passage assuming that it talks about *our* times and *our* near future. They attempt to force the text—despite its resistance—into a variety of dispensational eschatological scenarios. This "reading into the text" of modern anxieties and concerns is only possible if the passage gets disembodied, that is, taken out of its immediate historical and literary context, removed from its original audience, and its traditioned prophetic and apocalyptic imagery disregarded. But taking into account all these hermeneutical aspects provides a balanced and responsible interpretation of this challenging and symbolically filled text.

5. The Coming of the Son of Man (24:36—25:46)

a. Necessity of Watchfulness (24:36-44)

BEHIND THE TEXT

The next section concerns the coming (*parousia*) of the Son of Man in response to the disciples' second question: What is the sign of your coming (*parousia*) (24:3)? The answer is surprising. False prophets and messiahs will give signs (v 24) but no sign of Jesus' return will be given; the only sign is the Son of

Man himself (see 12:39-40). The return will be unpredictable, unexpected, and catch many unaware. But the faithful ones have to be prepared for that.

IN THE TEXT

■ **36-41** **About that day or hour no one knows** (24:36). In contrast to the previous section outlining the sequence leading to the temple's destruction, this section opens with the statement that the day and the hour are unknown. Only God knows the time of the Son of Man's *parousia*. The only thing clear is that many will be unprepared. The Noah story illustrates the point (Gen 6—8): the people were occupied with everyday life and had no idea of the judgment that was about to come until it was too late to escape the flood. The arrival was sudden and swept them away.

At the coming of the Son of Man something similar will occur: **One will be taken and the other left** (v 40*b*). People working in the field (see v 18) or at home will be caught by surprise. The coming will not only divide people but also take some away in judgment (see 25:32). Importantly, in this context, "taking away" is not about "rapture" or "taking into safety"; it is the language of judgment and destruction. The people will be taken away as those who were taken away by the flood (see 24:39). The Son of Man will return on a day and an hour when he is least expected. But the disciples have been warned, they know *what* is coming but don't know *when* this will happen.

■ **42-44** This unexpected arrival has pastoral implications. Followers are to be watchful and ready: **Therefore keep watch, because you do not know on what day your Lord will come** (v 42). Jesus illustrates the importance of alertness with a series of parables (24:42—25:30). The first one draws on a familiar image (see 1 Thess 5:2; Jer 49:7-13; Joel 2:1-11; Obad 4-8) of a thief coming at night. The disciples must be vigilant unlike the owner of the house. They must **Keep watch** (*grēgoreite*; Matt 24:42) and **be ready** (*ginesthe hetoimoi*; v 44). Not knowing the exact time of his arrival is no excuse. What that means in practical terms is spelled out later in 25:34-44.

b. A Wise and a Foolish Slave (24:45-51)

BEHIND THE TEXT

The second parable uses the relationship between a slave and his master to make the point. Jesus juxtaposes "a wise slave" with "a wicked one." Old Testament wisdom tradition illustrates foolish and wise behavior (Wright 2002, 130). The same motif runs through other parables of the set as well (25:2, 21, 26). Its logic is clearly seen in these parables: to be prepared is to be wise; not to be prepared after the warning is foolhardy. The wisdom of the faithful will be rewarded; foolishness will have catastrophic consequences.

IN THE TEXT

■ **45-47** A rhetorical question sets the scene: **Who then is the faithful and wise servant?** (v 45). In the first episode, the master gives a small task to his slave—to feed others **at the proper time** while he is away—supposedly on a business trip. The wise slave faithfully carrying out the task will be rewarded when the master comes back. He will promote him to be a manager of the whole estate. We find the same pattern later in the parable of the talents (see 25:21, 23).

The meaning is clear. The return of the master (or "the lord" [*kyrios*]) in 24:46 alludes to v 42. **It will be good for that servant** (lit. "blessed [*makarios*] that servant") alludes to the Beatitudes (5:3-12) and the future reward (25:46). Hultgren suggests that the image of a slave put in charge of providing food for others refers to the leaders who teach the faithful (2000, 162, 164). This makes sense since the parable is included in the private conversation between Jesus and his disciples (24:3). However, the parable could be applied to other areas of ministry as well (Nolland 2005, 1000).

■ **48-51** The second episode suggests that the slave could behave in a wicked or foolish way. Instead of carrying out his task, he usurps the master's authority, ignores his responsibilities, and abuses others: **begins to beat his fellow servants** (v 48). Since "the master takes his time," he also embraces the life of debauchery with "every intention of having the house back in order by the time the master returns" (Nolland 2005, 999). But the unexpected arrival cuts the slave's plans short and catches him off guard. The extended absence is no excuse for this wicked behavior.

The unexpected arrival results in punishment of the wicked slave. Slaves were property and a slave's life and fate were in the master's hands. But this punishment is intolerably harsh: **he will cut him to pieces** (*dichotomeō*; v 51). "Cut into pieces" or "cut in two" is a known form of a gruesome punishment (Luz 2005, 224-25). Jesus evokes this shocking image to illustrate eschatological judgment. Those who are not ready will share **a place with hypocrites** (see ch 23) and the same fate. The language of the parable explicitly connects it to the wider context of *parousia*: "day" and "hour" (v 50), "weeping and gnashing of teeth" (v 51).

FROM THE TEXT

The parable illustrates what it means to be ready or unprepared for the unexpected coming of the Son of Man. Jesus juxtaposes the story of "the faithful and wise slave" with "the wicked one." The wise one does his job faithfully; the foolish one abuses his power and neglects his tasks. Readiness is illustrated by fulfilling a given task and sluggishness by abuse and ignorance. This reflects the biblical wisdom tradition: the way of the wise leads to blessing, and the way of the foolish leads to destruction (see 5:1-12). Thus the parable, in the light of the impending coming of the Lord, calls the listeners to choose between two ways: wise and foolish, faithful and wicked.

The parable could also be interpreted as a warning to the new leaders of the people of God since it is addressed to the disciples (24:3). Given the task of caring for "the servants in his household" (v 45), they must not be like the Jerusalem religious leadership who abuse their power within the community of faith. As wise servants in the household of God, they should fulfill their task in the spirit of servanthood (see 18:1-14).

c. The Parable of the Ten Bridesmaids (25:1-13)

BEHIND THE TEXT

This is the third parable illustrating the idea of the unexpected coming of the Son of Man and the importance of watchfulness/readiness. If the previous parable warned that the coming may happen sooner than expected (24:48, 50), this one suggests that it may happen later (25:5) than expected (Snodgrass 2008, 518). All three parables are in the context of uncertainty surrounding the coming of the Son of Man: regardless of the timing, the believers should be wise and ready.

This unique Matthean parable combines the wisdom tradition with ancient marriage customs. The contrasting behavior of wise and foolish females is reminiscent of Lady Wisdom and Mistress Folly from the book of Proverbs (Wright 2002, 133). The difference between wisdom and foolishness is set in the context of ancient marriage customs (see 9:15; 22:2).

Marital language was often used by the prophets in description of the relationship between God and his people (Isa 54:4-6; Ezek 16:7-34; Hos 2:19 [21 HB]). But here, the parable redefines that imagery to describe the visitation of the Messiah, the bridegroom, who is going to set things right. Thus the hints of the judgment appear even in the setting of a wedding celebration (see 25:10-12).

Nuptial Rituals

The lack of a reliable description of nuptial rituals from first-century Palestine provides us with a range of reconstructed scenarios (see Snodgrass 2008, 512). The most plausible one has been suggested by Joachim Jeremias. Wedding festivities normally start in the late evening with the guests gathered in the bride's parents' house. Entertainment and food are offered while they are waiting for the bridegroom. The husband-to-be accompanied by a party of friends arrives late (half an hour before midnight) to pick up the bride. After negotiating the dowry, the wedding party travels back to the bridegroom's home in a processional ceremony in "a sea of light." The matrimonial ceremonies, banquet, and fresh entertainment take place there (Jeremias 1966, 137).

IN THE TEXT

■ **1-5** The parable compares the kingdom of heaven to what happens to young women at a wedding. The parable first introduces the main characters: ten virgins (*parthenois*) and a bridegroom. The young women have been participating in wedding celebrations; they could have been bridesmaids, servants, or friends/neighbors (France 1989, 350). Their role is to escort the newlyweds to the wedding feast. Since the procession normally takes place at night, they **took their lamps** (v 1) or "a torch" or "a lantern." The torches were wrapped with a cloth soaked in oil. Five of them took jars of oil for their torches and the other five did not. The oil jars were used for dipping torches before lighting them or getting the fire going (Blomberg 2012, 239). The wise girls thought ahead and prepared for all eventualities; the foolish ones did not. "Being wise means to have oil for the torches and foolishness—not thinking about it until it is too late" (Wright 2002, 133).

It was getting late and **the bridegroom was a long time in coming** (v 5*a*). The story does not explain the delay. Some speculate that the procession was held up due to prolonged bargaining with the bride's relatives over the dowry or the presents (Jeremias and Hooke 1972, 173-74; Blomberg 2012, 240). But this is irrelevant to the story. A long time waiting could be tiring, and the young women **became drowsy and fell asleep** (v 5*b*).

25:1-10 ■ **6-10** Finally a messenger announces the arrival: **Here's the bridegroom! Come out to meet him!** (v 6). The girls **woke up and trimmed** [*kosmeō*] **their lamps** (v 7) or put them in order. This might mean tightening and trimming the cloth, dipping torches in oil again and lighting them in preparation for the procession (Hultgren 2000, 173). Being wise here is not staying awake all the time, but being prepared and thinking ahead.

The foolish maidens face a problem: without oil their torches started to go out. The wise refused to share their oil with them on pragmatic grounds: **there may not be enough** (v 9). Because of the folly of others, the whole procession could be ruined if all torches go out. So, their advice to the foolish girls is to go and buy oil for themselves. At midnight?! This might sound plausible since everybody "would be up and about for such celebration" in a small village (Mounce 1991, 233); the foolish girls had no other choice but to try finding oil to buy in the middle of the night.

While they were away, the groom arrived. The wise maidens met him with torches lit and the whole wedding procession sets off to his house for celebration. Verse 10 notes—almost in passing—that the door of the house was shut. This is unusual for a rural wedding when doors would remain open during celebration (Keener 2009, 589). This countercultural element makes the narrative take an unexpected turn. Foolishness and unpreparedness have serious consequences: they are too late for the wedding feast.

■ **11-12** The third scene starts at the same location—at the closed door. The foolish girls return and wish to join the celebration. It is not clear whether or not they obtained oil. It doesn't matter; they are late and the door is shut. In his reply to the maidens' plea to enter, the bridegroom pronounces the formula of rejection: **I don't know you** (v 12). This phrase had often been used by rabbis to forbid certain disciples to approach them (France 1989, 352). Thus "the failure of the foolish to prepare for the bridegroom's arrival led to their total exclusion from the marriage festivities" (Mounce 1991, 233).

■ **13** The call for watchfulness could not be directly deduced from this parable since both wise and foolish fell asleep. But it summarizes the whole section 24:36—25:12, where the idea of not knowing the day or the hour is a repeated refrain (France 1989, 352). Craig Blomberg, however, suggests that *grēgoreō* could mean not just "to stay awake" but also "to be prepared" (2012, 241-42). In any case, it is a call to be ready, be prepared for the coming of the Lord since **you do not know the day or the hour** (see 24:36; 24:44).

FROM THE TEXT

The parable has a long history of allegorical interpretation. The story itself invites that kind of approach by using potent imagery (virgins, oil, sleep, etc.). But put in its immediate context, it illustrates a simple point: one has to show wisdom and foresight in preparation for the coming of the Son of Man. Though the parable does not spell out what readiness looks like in practical terms, Snodgrass concludes: "Readiness is an attitude, a commitment, and a lifestyle. It means living in ways that comport with the character of the kingdom and being faithful at all times" (2008, 518). Later in the narrative, in the parable of the talents (25:14-30) and by the simile of sheep and goats (25:31-46), Jesus explains what it means to be alert.

d. The Parable of the Talents (25:14-30)

BEHIND THE TEXT

This parable has the same motifs as the story of the wicked slave (24:45-51): departure and return; reward and punishment; delegation of responsibilities and servants' performance. The phrase "it will be like" (25:14) connects it to the preceding theme of alertness and watchfulness (v 13). But here, the focus is practical implications: to be prepared means to use the given time for the opportunities presented.

Many interpreters read the parable in connection with the Parousia. But Wright thinks the parable is rooted in the tradition of returning of YHWH to Zion and originally illustrated judgment over Jerusalem. The time gap implied in the story is between Jesus' resurrection and the actual destruction of the temple. The wicked slave represents religious leaders or those who did not respond to the Messiah's proclamation. The only people vindicated are those who responded to the news of the kingdom proclaimed by Jesus. Thus the parable originally was aimed at the Jewish leaders and not the church. Wright also recognizes that Matthew reinterprets these original motifs by placing them into the eschatological context of early church expectations and wrapping them in the distinct Matthean language of judgment, that is, references to darkness, weeping, and gnashing of teeth (Wright 1996, 635-39).

IN THE TEXT

■ **14-18** Jesus illustrates what watchfulness and readiness mean by what servants or slaves (*douloi*) do with entrusted money. Before going on a journey, a master summons his slaves and puts them in charge of part of his assets. They were given money in accordance with their ability to manage. This is serious responsibility with vast sums at stake. A talent or a bag of gold is a monetary weight of approximately thirty to forty kg. Depending on the value of coins, it could amount to twenty years' worth of a worker's wages (Snodgrass 2008, 528). The natural question is, How should this opportunity be used? The servant who received five talents doubled the amount; so did the one who received two talents. The third servant has decided to bury his master's money for safekeeping: he **dug a hole in the ground and hid his master's money** (v 18).

■ **19-30 After a long time the master of those servants returned and settled accounts with them** (v 19). Those who invested money wisely and made a realistic amount of profit (Scott 1989, 226) were praised and rewarded: **I will**

put you in charge of many things (v 21). Being a **good and faithful servant** (vv 21, 23)—being in charge of the master's money—meant using the opportunity for profit.

The third slave, on the other hand, played it safe. According to rabbinic tradition, he demonstrates responsible and legitimate behavior in trying to keep the money safe by burying it. This absolves him from further responsibility (Scott 1989, 228). However, this is not what the master expected; at the very least, he could have **put** his master's **money on deposit with the bankers** (v 27). The Torah (see Deut 23:19-20 [20-21 HB]) forbids charging interest to other Israelites but allows this practice in dealing with the Gentiles. But the servant has not done even that and blames the master. Since he perceived the master to be a harsh and unjust man, he decided not to risk in order to avoid possible punishment.

The irony of the story is hard to miss. The master turns out to be generous in giving rewards to others (vv 21-23) and the servant is punished for failing to invest and doing nothing. He is called **a wicked** and **lazy servant** (v 26) because he has not used time and opportunity wisely. Verse 29 spells out a master's approach to management: **For whoever has will be given more**. But those not using opportunities will lose what little they have. The consequences are severe: **Throw that worthless servant outside, into the darkness, where there will be weeping and gnashing of teeth** (v 30).

Scholars suggest a few possibilities for "the wicked servant" character: (1) Israelites who refused Jesus' proclamation of the coming kingdom; (2) the Pharisees and religious leaders who did not put the Law (the one talent given by the master) to proper use (Kistemaker 1980, 144); (3) Jesus' followers who failed to utilize their gifts while waiting for the coming of the Lord.

FROM THE TEXT

The story is not about praising successful investors but about being wise in using given opportunities. The parable illustrates this point by opposing good (*agathe*) and faithful (*piste*) servants to a wicked (*ponerē*) and lazy (*oknerē*) one. It also uses dramatic language to describe the consequences of their decisions: the wise ones are invited to share the master's happiness and the foolish one is thrown into darkness. Not knowing "the day or the hour" (23:36) is no excuse for doing nothing; passive waiting for the coming of the Lord could turn into a disaster, not the moment of joy. The time must be used wisely to take risks and maximize opportunities on the mission of God, not to waste them (France 2007, 951). Examples of those opportunities are provided later in the narrative (see 25:34-46).

This parable concludes the set illustrating the importance of watchfulness and readiness in the light of the coming of the Son of Man. The first parable warns about the unexpected and unpredictable nature of the event; the second one considers a scenario when the master comes earlier than expected (24:48, 50); the third one looks at when a bridegroom comes later than expected (25:5); the final one addresses the issue of what is the right thing to do in the time of waiting. The parables call Jesus' followers to stay faithful (*pistos*), to be wise (*phronimos*), to remain watchful (*grēgoreite*), and to be prepared (*hetoimoi*). This set could be seen as "an exhortation for followers of Jesus to be faithful in their obedience until his return" (Snodgrass 2008, 534).

e. The Sheep and the Goats (25:31-46)

BEHIND THE TEXT

The final scene of judgment of the nations provides no clue about timing but vividly describes its significance. This is the final section of "the Little Apocalypse" related to the *parousia* of the Son of Man. The passage is filled with prophetic allusions: the son of man given power over all peoples (Dan 7:13-14), the vision of God sitting on the throne (Zech 14:5), gathering of the nations (Joel 3:1-12), and the judgment of sheep by the divine shepherd (Ezek 34:17-22). All of that imagery comes from scenes depicting the future divine judgment over Israel or the nations.

Matthew rereads these images through the lenses of Jesus the Messiah. The judgment texts refer to the God of Israel, but Matthew applies them to the vindicated and glorified Son of Man (see Zech 14:5). The identity of the Danielic son of man (Dan 7:13-14) has been revealed in Jesus.

The exalted and vindicated Messiah executes his universal power and authority (see Matt 28:18) by bringing justice to all nations. The Matthean apocalyptic discourse begins with judgment over Jerusalem, its leaders, and the people of Israel and finishes with the images of the future judgment over all the nations. Judgment is based on their response to the gospel and their treatment of "the least of these brothers and sisters of mine" (25:40). It's the vindicated and enthroned Son of Man, the King, who settles accounts with both Jews and Gentiles; he blesses the righteous and punishes the wicked.

The interpretation of the whole passage depends on identification of those who are being judged (all nations) and "the least of these brothers and sisters of mine." There are a few possibilities. First, a universal interpretation sees all people being judged because of the treatment of the poor and disadvantaged. Second, the classic interpretation equates all nations to all Christians, and their judgment is based on how they have treated other Christians (the little ones). Third, the passage envisages the judgment of the Gentiles because of their treatment of Christians (Luz 2005, 267-74). The latter is the current dominating opinion.

Matthew uses the language of "little ones" and "brothers" to describe members of the community of faith (see 5:19; 11:11; 18:3-6; 12:50; 28:10). Moreover, in 10:40-42 a reward is promised to those who welcome the apostles,
25:31-33 "one of these little ones who is my disciple." Thus the passage likely foresees the judgment on the nations who treated or mistreated Christians. However, this does not exclude believers who mistreat others. The acts of kindness and hospitality toward "the little ones" are expected from the believers as well (see 18:5). R. T. France summarizes the message of the text as "judgment on how people responded to Jesus' representatives and ultimately to him. Response to them is measure of their response to the gospel of the kingdom" (2007, 958).

IN THE TEXT

■ **31-33** The final section of the Matthean apocalyptic discourse begins with the image of the exalted Son of Man and **all the nations** (*panta ta ethne*; 25:32*a*) gathered before his throne. This scene evokes Joel 3:1-12 [4:1-12 HB] where God enters into judgment with all the nations because of how they treated Israel. However, this section redefines this notion. Now the Son of Man judges nations because of how they treat the new people of God gathered around Jesus the King. Luz suggests that the people of Israel are also included with other nations and "they will be judged by the same criterion as all other people" (2005, 281). Harrington, however, insists that this episode is concerned with the judgment over the Gentiles as Matthew mentions judgment over Israel in a different context (see Matt 19:28; 1991, 358-59). But the judgment is not along ethnic lines but in accordance to treatment of "the little ones."

As a shepherd separates the sheep from the goats (25:32*b*) is traditional language for God and Israel: the shepherd and the flock (see Ezek 34:17-22). The simile about dividing goats and sheep at the end of a grazing day illustrates the upcoming judgment. Putting sheep on the right and goats on the left marks the king's favor to one group and disapproval of the other (France 1989, 356). The exalted king will divide the righteous from the wicked.

■ **34-40** The first group is separated for the reward and blessing: **Come, you who are blessed by my Father; take your inheritance, the kingdom prepared for you since the creation of the world**. This overwhelming gift of the kingdom of heaven and eternal life (Matt 25:46) comes out of their response to the hardships of others (see Isa 58:7-8; Ezek 18:7, 16); the righteous have extended hospitality and acted kindly toward **the least of these brothers and sisters of mine** (Matt 25:40). This demonstrates profound solidarity between the king and his people. Individually, the son of man represents the people of God; corporately, the believers represent Jesus himself. Ultimately, the acts of charity toward gospel messengers show the response to Jesus the Messiah and his gospel of the kingdom (Keener 2009, 605).

■ **41-46** The second group failed miserably. While circumstances required hospitality and kindness, they neglected "the little ones" in need: "Their judgment rests not on acts of wickedness but on their failure to respond compassionately when faced with human despair" (Mounce 1991, 236). Though "the least of these" (*elachistos*) may appear insignificant in the eyes of the nations, they actually represent the true King and Judge of all (Luz 2005, 280). To mistreat them is to offend the Lord; it is also indicative of rejection of the King's messengers and ultimately the King himself.

Matthew uses very potent judgment language. It continues with imagery from the preceding parables: separation between wise and foolish, righteous and wicked, blessing and punishment. But he also intensifies it. The blessed ones (*hoi eulogēmenoi*) are opposed to the cursed ones (*hoi katēramenoi*). Coming into the presence of the King is juxtaposed with departing from him. Inheriting the kingdom is placed in contrast with being thrown in the eternal fire, and eternal punishment is contrasted with eternal life. Such rhetoric warns that failure to welcome the King's emissaries and their message has serious consequences. Moreover, in doing so they side with the cosmic powers that resist the rule of God and as a result they will share the fate of **the devil and his angels** in punishment (v 41).

The Matthean imagery of eternal fire (*to pyr to aiōnion*) and eternal punishment (*kolasin aiōnion*) could be interpreted as "punishment in the age to come rather than punishment that continues forever" (France 2007, 967). Moreover, contrasted to having eternal life (*zōēn aiōnion*) this language could imply destruction rather than endless torment.

FROM THE TEXT

In the final section of his answer to the disciples' question about the coming of the Son of Man, Jesus pictures justice to all. The Son of Man as the enthroned and exalted King has a universal authority to judge the nations. Thus the coming of the Son of Man is the time of reckoning for everyone; judgment that would affect both Jews and Gentiles. Judgment is based on "the response of the nations to *disciples* in need" (France 1989, 355). In the light of Jewish prophetic traditions, the passage ascribes divine authority to the Son of Man to judge all the nations and redefines the people of God as the followers of Jesus (Wright 2002, 142).

Though primarily concerned with the Gentiles, this passage might also serve as a warning to Matthew's Christian community. The faithful must not mistreat their brothers and sisters but take care of "the little ones" in the spirit of hospitality and servanthood. Being prepared is to serve and act kindly on the basis of the highest standard of love (Luz 2005, 283).

VI. THE PASSION NARRATIVE: MATTHEW 26:1—27:66

The story of the events leading up to Jesus' death and burial is traditionally called "the Passion Narrative." It covers the last moments with the Twelve, Judas' betrayal, the arrest in Gethsemane, Jewish and Roman trials, humiliation, agonizing death, and burial. Jesus and his disciples are at the center of this unfolding tragedy. Here Matthew brings all of the christological titles together, revealing Jesus' true identity: the suffering Son of Man, the Son of God, the Messiah, and the King of the Jews. The betrayal and abandonment by the Twelve contrast with the faithfulness of female followers. The sufferings and vindication of Jesus and the story of the failure and restoration of the disciples serve as examples for those early Christians who faced persecution and rejection from the wider Jewish community.

But the Passion Narrative is not just descriptive. Matthew, like the other Gospel writers, interpreted the events. The death of the Messiah on a cross required serious explanation, particularly for a Jewish audience for whom such punishment could be easily perceived as a curse from God (see Deut 21:22-23). Scripture plays the crucial role for Matthew here as in the birth narratives. He uses direct quotations (Matt 26:31↔Zech 13:7; Matt 27:9-10↔Jer 32:8 and Zech 11:12-13; Matt 27:46↔Ps 22:1 [2 HB]), allusions (Matt 26:67↔Isa 50:6 and 53:3-5; Matt 26:64↔Dan 7:13), and a typological reflection on the suffering servant from Isa 53 and the righteous sufferer from Ps 22 (Green, McKnight, and Marshall 1992, 602-3).

Matthew's scriptural references (Matt 26:31, 56; 27:9) and Jesus' foretelling of the future (26:1-2, 20-24, 31-34) drive the narrative: the suffering and death of the Messiah is the divine plan of redemption and not the punishment of a false prophet. The events of passion week are within the purposes of God: **My Father . . . may your will be done** (26:42). The vicarious and redemptive death of the Son of Man brings salvation to the people of God and inaugurates the new covenant (v 28).

But divine necessity does not exclude human responsibility (Brown 1994, 29). Complex realities of injustice, betrayal, cruelty, and cowardice are interconnected in a web of decisions and responsibilities taken by the religious leadership (26:3-5, 56-69; 27:20), Judas (26:14-16; 27:3-10), Peter (26:31-35, 69-75), the disciples (26:36-46, 56), Pilate (27:11-26), soldiers (27:27-37), and the crowd (26:55-56; 27:20-26). Matthew counters these by including accounts of faithfulness and support from minor characters in the story (26:6-13; 27:19, 32, 54-56, 57-61).

Matthew's Passion Narrative covers the last five days of the final week during the Feast of Unleavened Bread/Passover in Jerusalem:

Wednesday (26:1-16):

- The last prediction of Jesus' death (vv 1-2)
- Plot against Jesus (vv 3-5)
- Jesus anointed in Bethany (vv 6-13)
- Judas agrees to betray Jesus (vv 14-16)

Thursday (26:17-75):

- The Last Supper (vv 17-30)
- Prediction of Peter's denial of Jesus (vv 31-35)
- Gethsemane (vv 36-46)
- Jesus' arrest (vv 47-56)
- Jesus before the Sanhedrin (vv 57-68)
- Peter denies Jesus (vv 69-75)

Friday (27:1-61):

- Judas hangs himself (vv 1-10)
- Jesus before Pilate, the Roman governor (vv 11-26)
- Roman soldiers mock Jesus (vv 27-31)
- The crucifixion (vv 32-44)
- The death of Jesus (vv 45-56)
- Burial (vv 57-61)

Saturday (27:62-66):

- Securing of the tomb (vv 62-66)

Sunday (28:1-15):

- Women at the tomb (vv 1-7)
- Women meet the resurrected Christ (vv 8-10)
- The Roman guards' report (vv 11-15)

A. From Bethany to Arrest (26:1-56)

1. The Final Prediction of Jesus' Death (26:1-5)

BEHIND THE TEXT

Matthew's introduction creates a framework for understanding the events. He brings two motifs together: Jesus' prediction of his own death (26:1-2) and the leaders' plot to kill him (26:3-5). This is both divine necessity and an evil plot in a mysterious dialectical relationship between human and divine wills.

IN THE TEXT

■ **1-2** Matthew's traditional formula indicates the end of the final discourse: **when Jesus had finished saying all these things** (see 7:28; 11:1; 13:53; 19:1). **All** (*pantas*) suggests that this was the last public teaching in the Gospel (see chs 5—7; 10; 13; 18; 23—25). This is the fourth and final prediction, echoing the earlier ones (→ 16:21; 17:22; 20:18-19). However, it omits the resurrection and includes a time reference: **the Passover is two days away** (26:2). This works at two levels: first, as a narrative time that explains the sequence of events about to take place; second, as a symbolic framework for understanding the death of Jesus—a covenantal redemptive sacrifice akin to a Passover lamb (see 20:28).

■ **3-5** Jesus' prediction is on the way to its tragic fulfillment. A group of chief priests and community elders, perhaps representatives of the Sanhedrin, gathered to develop a plan for apprehending and killing Jesus. The group was led by **the high priest, whose name was Caiaphas** (26:3). Josephus notes that he was appointed by Valerius Gratus, Pilate's predecessor as procurator (*Ant.* 18.29). Caiaphas was high priest from 18 to 36 CE (France 1989, 361).

They plotted (*synebouleusanto*) to arrest Jesus secretly or by trickery (*dolō*); it highlights the injustice and corruption of the leaders. The secrecy reveals their fear of Jesus' popularity among the pilgrims and residents of Jerusalem. **Not during the festival** (*mē en tē heortē*; v 5) is better translated as "not in the time of festival crowd" (Hill 1972, 333). Later they arrest Jesus during the festival but away from the public, thus preventing a riot.

FROM THE TEXT

By placing Jesus' prediction of his death and the authorities' plot to kill him side by side, Matthew makes several points. First, the suffering and death of the Messiah is both divinely ordained and a result of human conspiracy. Second, the religious leaders are shown again to be deceitful and unrighteous. Third, Jesus is a victim.

Matthew does not reveal the motivation behind the plot to kill Jesus. James Dunn sees the main reason as the challenge Jesus posed to the temple and its priestly elite. Their resentment grew after his public action and teaching in the temple (chs 21—23) after the triumphal entry into Jerusalem (2006b, 67-70). E. P. Sanders suggests that Caiaphas, maintaining public security, wanted to put down this troublemaker out of fears that Jesus could incite a riot during Passover celebrations (1995, 269).

2. Preparation: Anointing (26:6-13)

BEHIND THE TEXT

Matthew's next story sets the mood and interpretive lenses for what follows and illustrates a proper reaction to Jesus' prediction of his own death (26:2). To this point, the Twelve have not comprehended the gravity of his prediction and given no response to it (see 16:22; 17:23).

IN THE TEXT

■ **6-7** Matthew sets the scene carefully. Jesus has returned from Jerusalem to Bethany (see 21:17), a village located approximately three km. east of the holy city. He, the disciples, and an unknown woman find themselves **in Bethany in the home of Simon the Leper** (26:6). Away from the public eye and the pilgrim crowds, the woman's actions will teach the Twelve a lesson.

Ironically, the woman remains anonymous but the house owner, who does not play any significant role, has been identified. Simon was nicknamed "the Leper" because of a skin disorder. He may even have been cleansed by Jesus himself; his identification could serve as indication of an eyewitness source or of a person known in the early Christian community (Bauckham 2006, 81-84). In a similar story, the Gospel of John identifies the woman as Mary, sister of Martha and Lazarus (John 12:2-3). But the Synoptic Gospels keep her identity and intentions hidden (see Mark 14:1-9; Luke 7:36-50 places the story in a different context).

Matthew focuses on her actions. She brought a small bottle **of very expensive perfume** (*alabastron murou barutimou*; Matt 26:7*a*), a mixture of different oils with a pleasant aroma. While Jesus was reclining at the table she **poured** out (*katekheen*; v 7*b*) the ointment **on his head**; perhaps all of it. Anointing heads with oils at festive meals was a known custom across the ancient Mediterranean world and sometimes seen as a luxury (Luz 2005, 336).

■ **8-9** The disciples see this as a profligate action: **"Why this waste?" they asked** indignantly (v 8). The Twelve get something right about Jesus' teaching on riches (see 11:5; 19:16-22), and it fits with the traditional almsgiving to the poor on the eve of Passover. But their moral outrage is displaced; they got their timing wrong. The remark could have been suitable on a different occasion, but these are exceptional circumstances.

■ **10-12 She has done a beautiful thing** [*kalon*] **to me** (26:10). The disciples clearly misunderstood the meaning and importance of the woman's action.

This was not a waste; it was a good deed, an act of kindness and charity. There would be opportunities to serve the poor in the future. This is not a dismissal of the needy but, this time, Jesus is at the center of this event: **you will not always have me** (v 11). It was not about money or enjoying luxury; she did something special: **she did it to prepare me for burial** (v 12).

The woman turns the tradition of anointing at festive celebrations into a prophetic act of preparation for Jesus' coming sufferings and death (see Mark 10:31). Perhaps she does what in normal circumstances the family members or close friends of a deceased should have done. Matthew doesn't mention that Jesus' body was anointed according to burial traditions (Matt 27:59), nor that women came on the resurrection day to apply oils to the dead body (28:1; see Mark 16:1; Luke 24:1). Her anointing served that purpose (→ Matt 27:59-60). In this story, the woman's action is the proper response to Jesus' prediction of his death: anointing, serving him, and supporting on the path. It contributes to the prophetic character of the story.

■ **13** Although **what she has done will also be told, in memory of her**, this act of giving and prophetic symbolism was met with misunderstanding. Her actions were inappropriate in the male space within this private house. But Jesus affirms this unknown woman, celebrates her insight, and commends her sacrificial giving. Her servanthood is an honorable deed worthy of remembrance in the community of faith. She has been vindicated.

FROM THE TEXT

The unknown woman's action affirms the redefinition of messiahship: the Anointed One is not a militant but a suffering Messiah, the notion that the Twelve have struggled to accept. The disciples are also oblivious, despite Jesus' predictions, to the gravity of the events that are about to unfold. Once again it is a secondary character in the Gospel story illustrates, once more, true discipleship reflected in servanthood, support, and perceptiveness.

The story challenges any perception that female followers are insignificant in the mission of God. Sadly, some people have also cited this text to justify the existence of poverty. But this text does no such thing. On the contrary, the woman's gift serves as a model of sacrificial love and reminds Jesus' followers to use their own resources in selfless giving for the sake of the kingdom of heaven, including service to the poor (Keener 2009, 620).

3. Judas Offers to Betray Jesus (26:14-16)

BEHIND THE TEXT

Matthew tellingly juxtaposes the anointing story with Judas' treacherous agreement to hand Jesus over to the religious authorities. The contrast is stark. The unnamed woman comes to Jesus; the disciple named Judas Iscariot goes to his high-ranking enemies. She gives away expensive oil for Jesus; he receives money for Jesus' life. Her act of kindness is the opposite to Judas' act of betrayal. As with the woman's story, the story of Judas will be known within Christian tradition but for all the wrong reasons.

The scene of betrayal is brief. Readers know nothing about Judas' motives; France suggests disillusionment with Jesus as a messianic figure (2007, 978). The authorities show no interest in Judas or his reasons. Nor does the passage reveal how Judas knew about their desire to arrest Jesus. No details of their plan are given. Judas doesn't ask for money but is happy with the sum offered.

Matthew alone mentions the thirty pieces of silver (*triakonta argyria*). The amount of "blood money" is quite modest: perhaps a month's wages or so. Although it was enough to buy a burial plot later, money wasn't the only reason for betrayal (Hagner 1995, 761).

IN THE TEXT

■ **14-15** Matthew has already identified **Judas Iscariot** (v 14) as the betrayer (10:4). **Iscariot** may come from the Hebrew *ish qeriyoth* and means "a man of Kerioth." Or, it may also derive from the Latin *sicarius* (meaning "a dagger man"), a term used for a Jewish religious militant group (Harrington 1991, 363).

Judas wants to receive a reward for Jesus' life: **What are you willing to**
26:14-16 **give me?** (26:15). This desire for money and greed are more explicit drivers in
John's Gospel (John 12:4-6).

Thirty pieces of silver is the price assigned for betrayal (Matt 26:15). It plays a double role in the narrative. It demonstrates the fulfillment of the OT prophecy (Jer 19:11; Zech 11:13). It also serves as literary bookends at the beginning and end of the Judas story (see Matt 27:9-10).

■ **16** From this point, **Judas watched for an opportunity** to enable the chief priests to execute their plot and arrest Jesus in the sly way as they wanted (26:4). His role is to identify Jesus when he is not surrounded by the crowd so that Jesus could be arrested without public knowledge. The opportunity arrives in the garden of Gethsemane (v 47).

FROM THE TEXT

Judas' payment is contrasted with the sacrificial giving in the previous story: the woman gives to Jesus; Judas gets a bribe for Jesus' life. In the end, this act of betrayal does not pay off. He wants a profit but loses everything, including his own life, and his money goes to another person (27:3-10). The woman, on the other hand, gives a jar of perfume and gains much more (Keener 2009, 620-21). This illustrates the upside-down nature of the kingdom of heaven: those who sacrifice gain; those who seek profit lose (16:25-26; 19:27-30).

4. The Last Supper (26:17-30)

BEHIND THE TEXT

Passover (Heb., *Pesah*; Gk., *Pasha*) is celebrated as one of the three great pilgrimage festivals (along with Weeks and Tabernacles; see Lev 23:15-44). The festival commemorates the miraculous salvation of the firstborn, liberation from slavery, and escape from Egypt (see Exod 12). By the time of Jesus, the festivals of Passover and Unleavened Bread had been merged together into one eight-day period (see Lev 23:4-8; Deut 16:1-8).

On 14th of Nisan (a spring month in the northern hemisphere), pilgrims went to the temple to be purified by sprinkling of water and to sacrifice a Passover lamb; then they would attend a festive family meal that was accompanied by prayers and hymns. On the next day, the 15th of Nisan, festivities would continue with seven days of celebration of the Feast of Unleavened Bread (Sanders 1992, 132-33).

The number of pilgrims has been estimated from 300,000 to 500,000 (Sanders 1992, 128). Such crowds could have created tensions and sparked confrontation between the pilgrims, who celebrated the festival of redemption and liberation by the God of Israel, and the occupying Roman forces who controlled the holy city of Jerusalem.

Passover Meal

According to Exod 12:8, the Passover meal consisted of a few dishes: roasted lamb, unleavened bread, bitter herbs, fruit puree, and wine. The order of the Passover meal (*Pesah Seder*) consisted of four main parts:

1. Preliminary course: a head of the family pronounces blessing over the feast day and the first cup of wine; eating of an appetizer that included some herbs and a puree made of figs, dates, raisins, apples, almonds, spices, and vinegar;
2. Passover liturgy: the story of Passover is recounted; the first part of the Passover song of praise is sung; the second cup of wine is taken;
3. Main meal: blessing of the unleavened bread; the main meal of lamb, bread, bitter herbs, fruit puree, and wine; blessing of the third cup of wine;
4. Conclusion: the second part of the Passover song of praise is sung, praise over the fourth cup. (Jeremias 1977, 85-86)

Passover commemorates release from Egyptian oppression, entrance into the covenant with God, and establishment of the holy people of God. Matthew clearly identifies the Last Supper as a Passover meal but focuses on key moments. This has created some problems for scholars who try to identify the event's timing, order, and features (see Marshall 1980, 62-75; Dunn 2003, 772-73). However, the overall Passover context is crucial for understanding the Passion Narrative and Jesus' mission. He purposefully chooses the Passover celebration (out of many other Jewish festivals) for the final showdown.

In this context, Jesus' message is loud and clear. Through the blood and suffering of the Messiah, the new Passover Lamb, the God of Israel rescues his people from oppressive powers, forgives sins, establishes the new covenant, and restores them so that they might fulfill their true vocation in this world—to be the holy people of God on the mission of God. This new, redefined Passover celebrates the fulfillment of the scriptural promises of the coming of YHWH, deliverance of God's people, and establishment of the kingdom brought about by the righteous servant for "the many" (Wright 2016, 192).

The Passover meal narrative contains three key scenes: preparation (26:17-19), prediction of betrayal (26:20-25), and institution of the Lord's Supper (26:26-30).

IN THE TEXT

■ **17-19** Preparation starts from the disciples' question about the place for the Passover celebration. They desire to serve their Master; Judas wants to receive something for himself (Davies and Allison 2004, 457). Jesus then sends the disciples to a certain man in Jerusalem, notifying him that they will celebrate Passover in his house on this day. This gives an impression that Jesus has prearranged the accommodation.

Matthew's addition, **My appointed time** [*kairos*] **is near** (v 18; see Mark 14:14; Luke 22:11), highlights the impending culmination of the story—betrayal, suffering, and death. Matthew connects this notion of the hour with Judas, who was looking for an opportune time (*eukairian*) to betray Jesus (Matt 26:16) and whose arrival with the armed mob (v 45) signals that the hour (*hōra*) is near. The preparation scene highlights the importance of the event (see 21:1-6) and identifies the Last Supper as a Passover meal.

Chronology of the Last Supper

All of the Gospels place the events of the Passion Narrative within the framework of Passover celebrations. However, there is a discrepancy between the Synoptics and the Gospel of John. Matthew, Mark, and Luke identify the Last Supper as a Passover meal (Matt 26:2, 17-19; Mark 14:1, 12, 14, 16; Luke 22:1, 7-8, 13, 15) that was celebrated on Thursday evening, the 14th of Nisan, and Jesus' crucifixion occurred on the next day, Friday the 15th of Nisan. John, on the other hand, suggests that Jesus' trial and crucifixion took place on "the day of Preparation of the Passover" (John 19:14, 31). This places the Last Supper outside of official Passover celebrations.

Many attempts have been made to reconcile the two accounts: (1) Jesus and the disciples had "a special private Passover"; (2) they have celebrated in accordance to the calendar followed by the Qumran sectaries; (3) Passover could have been celebrated over two consecutive days due to the large number of

Passover lambs to be slaughtered; (4) two calendars were used during 2TP: Galileans counted days from sunrise to sunrise while Judeans counted from sunset to sunset. Thus, in John, Jesus the Galilean has celebrated Passover while his opponents—who arrested and trialed him—have not (*DJG*, 120-21). Interestingly, John focuses on Jesus' death as that of the Passover lamb, so his timing of the Last Supper coheres with his theological perspective. A possibility also exists that one of the Gospel traditions may be wrong about the actual day.

■ **20-25** It is **while they were eating** (Matt 26:21*a*) that the betrayer (*ho paradidous*) or the one who will deliver (*paradidomi*) Jesus to his enemies is revealed. It starts with passing remarks about the time and the celebrants gathering around the table. As the new day arrived at evening and according to Passover tradition (Exod 12:8), Jesus reclines with the Twelve for the festive meal. He takes the position of authority.

Interestingly, Jesus does not sit or recline during his trial, humiliation, and crucifixion. His opponents, on the other hand, do. This reflects his temporary loss of power and authority (Davies and Allison 2004, 545). Jesus will regain that authority when his enemies will see him "sitting at the right hand of the Mighty One" (Matt 26:64).

Readers already know who the betrayer is. But now the disciples face that reality: **Truly I tell you, one of you will betray me** (v 21*b*). Someone from the close circle of apostles, who shares in this intimate meal and a common bowl of *haroset* (a sweet paste made for dipping bitter herbs), will be gravely disloyal to the Messiah. Matthew uses the same phrase, "greatly distressed" (*lypoumenoi sphodra*; v 22*a* NRSV), to describe their reaction to Jesus' words as they heard about Jesus' death in 17:23. Their response to Jesus' revelation is a negative question, **Surely you don't mean me, Lord?** (26:22*b*). Betrayal would be unthinkable, they imply. However, they will all abandon Jesus at the end (see 26:31, 56).

In response, Jesus explains that the betrayal is part of his path toward Golgotha. **The Son of Man will go** in accordance with the Scriptures (v 24). But which scripture? Matthew does not have a particular passage in mind but the whole of Scripture. The span of the story from the covenant with Abraham to the Isaianic promises of restoration; through the Psalms of the righteous sufferer to the visions of Dan 7—the whole story is a bigger divine picture of salvation and redemption where the Messiah plays the central role. God's redemptive purposes have been revealed beforehand, and the Son embodies the divine will and faithfulness.

Although Judas' act of giving Jesus over to his enemies has been foreseen, his responsibility remains. The appearance of **woe** (*ouai*; v 24*b*; see 23:13-32) highlights the consequences of faithlessness. Judas' apostasy and, later, his death is a culminating point of the faithlessness of God's people that highlights the faithfulness of the Son of God.

Matthew singles out Judas who asks the same question as the rest of the disciples. He addresses Jesus not as "Lord" but **Rabbi** ("teacher"; 26:25*a*); Judas will do that again at the time of the arrest (see v 49). This time Jesus responds in a very direct way, **You have said so** (*su eipas*; v 25*b*). The phrase could also be translated as "Yes, it is you" since it confirms that Judas is the betrayer. Jesus knows what is going to happen but also the identity of his betrayer.

Matthew negatively portrays Judas (though not as negatively as in John 12:4-8; 13:18-30), but the Greek word *paradidomi* (deliver, hand over) doesn't necessarily have negative connotations. It might simply highlight Judas' instrumental role in delivering Jesus to his adversaries. Judas plays a part, a tragic one, in the divine plan of redemption.

■ **26-30** Jesus celebrates Passover, a family festival, in the circle of his disciples, his new family (see 12:46-50). He assumes the role of paterfamilias in leading the meal and explaining its meaning since every element of the Passover meal is symbolic representation of the Exodus experiences of the people of God (see Exod 12). **While they were eating** (Matt 26:26*a*), Jesus interrupts the traditional flow of the Passover meal, takes unleavened bread and a cup of wine, and reinterprets them in the light of his vicarious death.

First, he takes a piece of bread and gives thanks or pronounces blessing. Matthew does not give the words of the prayer but perhaps the Jewish traditional formula was used: "Blessed are you, Lord our God, King of the Universe, who brings forth bread from the earth" (Davies and Allison 2004,
26:26-30 470). Then Jesus breaks the bread, symbolizing the Messiah's suffering and death: **Take and eat; this is my body** (*touto estin to sōma mou*; v 26*b*). In this context, the phrase could be rendered as "this is myself" giving some support to the idea of Christ's presence in the Eucharist (*NIB* 8:471). But more likely, this should be seen primarily as a prophetic representational act. Instead of the Passover lamb, Jesus takes the central place at the Last Supper, offering his flesh and blood for the redemption of the people of God.

Second, Jesus takes a cup of wine, gives thanks, and offers it to his disciples: **Drink from it, all of you** (v 27). Normally, Passover celebrants would drink from their own cups. But here Jesus invites all, including Judas, to share one cup. Sharing his cup may be an invitation to participate in the suffering and death of Christ (see 20:22-23; 26:39, 42).

This is my blood of the covenant (v 28*a*) evokes the covenant ceremony from Exod 24:1-8 when Moses sprinkled both the altar and the people with sacrificial blood, the blood of the covenant, to ratify the new relationship between God and the Israelites and consecrate them as the holy people of YHWH (Nicholson 1982, 83). But this is more than simply a reenactment of the Exodus event. He is more than a new Moses. This is Jesus' own blood, and his blood establishes and seals the renewed relationship with God and sanctifies the new holy people of God gathered around the Messiah (Hooker 1994, 56).

In Exodus, the covenant ratification ceremony was followed by a celebratory meal that was shared by Moses, Aaron, the priests, and the leaders of the people of Israel in the presence of God (see Exod 24:11). Now, the leaders of the new people of God—the Twelve—share the covenant meal in the presence of the Messiah, "God with us" (Matt 1:23).

This is the blood **which is poured out for many for the forgiveness of sins** (v 28*b*). The language here echoes the Isaianic song of the Suffering Servant who pours out his life and bears the sin of many (Isa 53:12). In doing so, Jesus takes on the full vocation of the people of God and the servant Messiah. The result of the atoning death of Jesus is forgiveness of sins offered to his people (Matt 1:21), redemption, salvation, and restoration of the relationship with the Holy God (Marshall 1980, 100). Jesus' command to **take**, **eat**, and **drink** (26:26, 27) is an invitation open to all to participate in and embrace the salvific effects of his death (Davies and Allison 2004, 470).

Identity of the Servant in Isaianic Servant Songs (Isa 42:1-4; 49:1-6; 50:4-9; 52:13—53:12)

Since the Servant of YHWH is only named in Isa 49:3, his identity sparked a variety of interpretations. Three distinctive approaches have emerged: collective, corporate personality, and individual. A collective interpretation identifies the Servant with the nation of Israel or with the righteous remnant of Israel (as in 49:3). Corporate personality interpretations suggest that the Servant of YHWH refers to both "the prophet himself as representative of the nation, and the nation whose proper mission is being fulfilled" (Whybray 1983, 72). Another suggestion has been that the Servant does not represent an individual royal figure but the whole Davidic dynasty.

Individual interpretations connect the Servant's identity with a single historical or ideal eschatological figure. The prophets Moses and Jeremiah were identified as possible candidates as well as some ancient rulers, such as Zerubbabel (the governor of Judah under Persian rule, 538-520 BCE), Nebuchadnezzar II (the king of the Neo-Babylonian Empire, 605-562 BCE), or Cyrus the Great (the king of Persia, 600-530 BCE) (*DOTP*, 705). The prophet Isaiah has also been identified with the Servant (Whybray 1983, 70-77). However, both Jewish and Christian traditional interpretations connect his identity with the future Messiah (*DOTP*, 704).

The renewed symbolism of the Passover meal takes the disciples further in time—to the arrival of the kingdom in its fullness. The Last Supper anticipates the eschatological banquet **when I drink it new with you in my Father's kingdom** (Matt 26:29). Jesus, the exalted Messiah, celebrates his triumph with his people gathered around the table. This hopeful imagery not only hints at Christ's resurrection but also assumes restoration of the broken relationship between Jesus and his disciples.

The Passover meal would traditionally finish with the singing of Pss 114 to 118. Here the celebrants did not depart from that custom: **When they had sung a hymn, they went out to the Mount of Olives** (Matt 26:30).

FROM THE TEXT

The scene of the Last Supper is a complex and symbolically rich event. The final dinner with the disciples is set in the context of Passover celebration, the festival of Israel's redemption. This Passover feast is steeped in the drama of betrayal and broken relationships. But it is transformed into the covenantal meal and the crucial means of grace that celebrates forgiveness of sins, the vicarious death, and the life-giving presence of Christ.

While it reminds us of Jesus' previous meals with the Twelve (9:9-13; 14:13-21; 15:29-39), the Last Supper also departs from them. Out of this meal emerges a new symbolic world that centered on Jesus' vicarious death and his eschatological triumph. It reimagines and recasts traditions of Israel in the light of the redemptive work of God in Christ. Now the Passover meal celebrates the new exodus—freeing from the bondage of sin—that culminates in the establishment of the (new) covenant with the new holy people of God. At the Messiah's table time converges: it commemorates the past (the salvific work of God in Exodus), explains the present (Jesus' sacrificial death and its benefits), and anticipates the future—the messianic banquet in the kingdom of heaven.

26:17-30 Matthew's story of the Last Supper could not be told without the complexity of relationships and the tragedy of human brokenness. The Evangelist juxtaposes the establishment of the covenant with betrayal. The disciples repeat the path of Israel from the past: establishment of the relationship with God, breaking of the covenant, followed by restoration.

Matthew shows the community of disciples facing a crisis: Judas is looking for an opportunity to betray Jesus and the Eleven will soon abandon him. In just such a time, Jesus invites them to participate in the benefits of his death: salvation and forgiveness of sins. He welcomes them to the messianic feast, shares with them the meal of redemption of the holy people of God, and draws them into a close covenantal relationship. Hospitality, forgiveness, and restoration are openly and freely offered to those who might not be worthy.

The first "Holy Communion" is given to the weak in faith in anticipation of reconciliation through the atoning death of Christ. This could serve as a prime example for prevenient grace, inclusion, the importance of the Eucharist for restoration of communal relationships, and of an open communion table.

The Lord's Supper plays a crucial role in the life of the church in many ways. Matthew's rendering of the story highlights the fact that the communion goes beyond just remembrance or mere symbolism. At the communion table, our brokenness is met with the promise of restoration, our sin with forgiveness, our alienation with welcome, our self-interest with selfless self-giving, our weakness with the divine resolve, and our failure to follow with Christ's faithfulness.

The practice of Holy Communion also goes beyond individualistic piety. It is always a communal meal that celebrates the relationship between God and his people that is grounded in Christ's sacrifice. By gathering around the Lord's Table and sharing broken body and poured-out blood, the community of faith participates in the redemptive work of God in this world, partakes in Christ's sufferings, rises with him to the new life in the Father's kingdom, proclaims the good news, inspires to embody and to live out God's grace. No wonder that John Wesley encouraged Christians to receive the Lord's Supper as often as one can (Wesley 1978, 3:428-39).

5. Prediction of Peter's Denial (26:31-35)

BEHIND THE TEXT

This conversation between Jesus and Peter is about future events. The disciples will abandon their master, be scattered and regathered in Galilee; Jesus will die and rise from the dead; and Peter will deny Christ three times. The leading apostle challenges Jesus twice and the conversation finishes with Peter's rebuttal. However, the truthfulness of Jesus' words will be proved by the unfolding events (Davies and Allison 2004, 482-83).

IN THE TEXT

■ **31-32** It is not clear where the exchange takes place: on the Mount of Olives (see 26:30) or on the way to it. But Jesus starts it with a troubling topic. Judas is not the only betrayer; the rest of the Twelve will also leave their Messiah, **fall away** [*skandalisthesthe*] **on account of me** (v 31). Similar language is found in 18:6-9, where Jesus warns the disciples not to put stumbling blocks on the path of "the little ones" who are following him. Here, the fate of their Messiah, suffering and death on the cross, will cause them to stumble and fall away. They will, temporarily, abandon him.

Matthew sees their betrayal as fulfillment of Zech 13:7, striking of the shepherd and scattering the sheep. In its original context, the prophet predicts divine punishment of Israel. But Matthew reinterprets it not as punishment but as divine necessity: striking of the Messiah and scattering of the disciples is followed by resurrection and regathering of the people of God.

In spite of this gloomy prediction, there is a brighter future; **I will go ahead of you into Galilee** (Matt 26:32). This points toward Jesus' resurrection, restoration of relationship with the Eleven, and regathering of the Messiah and his apostles. Despite their disloyalty and betrayal, forgiveness and restoration are offered. Jesus, the Good Shepherd, takes care of his flock (see 18:10-14). They will meet the resurrected Messiah on the mountain in Galilee and be empowered to continue on the mission of God (28:16).

■ **33-35** Peter continues to challenge Jesus and presents himself as the most loyal disciple. He confidently avows, **Even if I have to die with you, I will never disown you** (26:35). He is like a proud cock boasting and challenging his teacher (Davies and Allison 2004, 487). He has come to terms with Jesus' impending death (which he fiercely denied before; see 16:21-23) and is prepared to sacrifice his own life. Jesus' response is full of irony; Peter's loyalist zeal will turn in eager disowning, **you will disown me three times** (26:34). The disciples' bravado to die with and for Jesus will be proven false. When the time comes, Jesus dies surrounded by mockers and in the company of criminals (27:32-44) while the disciples are on the run fearing for their own lives (26:56).

FROM THE TEXT

This dialogue focuses on several themes: Jesus' foreknowledge, divine providence, human frailty and responsibility, and most importantly, grace and restoration. In a theme from the exile, the scattered people will be regathered around the resurrected Messiah. Despite their disloyalty, betrayal, and denial, Jesus will restore the relationship and entrust them with his mission (see 28:16-20). Jesus knows his flock and what people are capable of. Stumbling and failing on the way of discipleship is a possibility. But the promise of restoration encourages followers of Christ not to give up completely but to rise up and continue on the journey.

6. In Gethsemane (26:36-46)

BEHIND THE TEXT

The passage focuses on Jesus' words of prayer and instruction to the disciples. It is organized around Jesus' prayer and the disciples' failure to stay awake: Jesus prays alone and returns to his disciples three times (26:39-41, 42-43, 44-46). Three prayers and the acceptance of the divine will are in contrast with three denials by Peter in vv 69-75, where he falls into temptation and rejects Jesus (France 1989, 374).

IN THE TEXT

■ **36-38** Jesus takes his disciples to an olive orchard on the lower slopes of the Mount of Olives (Hagner 1995, 782) called **Gethsemane** (v 36), a Greek transliteration of the Aramaic *gat shemane* (meaning "olive press"). Jesus calls Peter and the sons of Zebedee (see 17:1-8) to support him in the time of prayer and inner struggle: **Stay here and keep watch with me** (26:38). Matthew notes Jesus' angst by echoing the psalms of the righteous sufferer (see Pss 42—43). They are the framework for understanding Jesus' agony. They capture the depth of human pain: Jesus truly embodies the righteous Suffering Servant.

The language of "being sorrowful to death" emphasizes the distress as he is approaching his final hours. Brower reflects that both the dread of death and the fear of abandonment by God "plumb the extremities of human suffering" (1978, 271). In this emotional state, Jesus seeks the support of his close companions and turns to God in prayer.

■ **39-44** Jesus prostrated himself before God in surrender and intense anguish. The address to the Father and recognition of the divine will echo the Lord's Prayer (6:9-13). Jesus asks, **May this cup be taken from me** (26:39), a symbolic reference to suffering and death (see 20:20-28) that also echoes the language of the cup with the blood of the covenant (26:27-29). The prayer moves then from the plea for deliverance from death to trust in the divine will. Jesus' genuine desire to escape suffering is met by his resolve to fulfill the Father's will through vicarious and redemptive death.

Jesus then returns to his disciples and finds them sleeping. **Watch and pray so that you will not fall into temptation** (*eis peirasmon*; v 41*a*); this is another echo of the Lord's Prayer, "lead us not into temptation" (*eis peirasmon*; 6:13). Jesus' call to watchfulness is not only about staying awake now but also about staying faithful and avoiding the temptation to abandon him in the times of trial (see 24:42-43; 25:13).

The spirit is willing, but the flesh is weak (26:41*b*) has often been interpreted as reflecting the dualism of human nature where soul is superior to flesh and spirit is the antithesis to material (Davies and Allison 2004, 499). However, this phrase, particularly in a Jewish context, could be a proverb referring to the inner human struggle and weakness in the face of death (*NIB* 8:476). The Matthean juxtaposition of "the willing spirit" of Jesus and Peter's weakness illustrates the point.

Three times Jesus leaves his disciples, prays alone, and returns to find them sleeping **because their eyes were heavy** (v 44). This physical tiredness and the lack of watchfulness foreshadows, despite Jesus' warning, their imminent falling into temptation and abandonment of the Messiah.

■ **45-46** After the time of prayer and inner wrestling, Jesus is prepared to face his destiny with unflinching resolve: **The hour has come, and the Son of Man is delivered into the hands of sinners** (v 45). The Scriptures and Jesus' predictions are about to be fulfilled (see 17:22-23; 20:17-19; 26:2). The arrival of the betrayer inaugurates the final stage. Jesus goes out to meet Judas and his own fate face-to-face. The language of sinners (*hamartōloi*) opposing Jesus highlights his status of an innocent and righteous sufferer and the corrupt nature of supposedly righteous and holy religious leaders.

FROM THE TEXT

Jesus is the exemplar for Christians facing suffering and persecution for Christ. Jesus is the obedient Son who fulfills the will of the Father and stays faithful despite temptation and fear. Disciples in the time of trial should stay awake by avoiding temptation and departing from the path of following Jesus. They see the importance of prayer and surrender to God's big purposes.

The episode also highlights Jesus' humanness. At the hour of distress, Jesus looks for the support in prayer and physical presence from his close group of followers. In the Gospel story, they are not only called "to be with" him and "to follow" him but also to "watch with" him in the time of temptation. This highlights the importance of prayer, support, and even physical presence with members of the community of faith who find themselves in times of distress or depression due to their commitment to the divine will or in other difficult circumstances.

7. Jesus' Arrest (26:47-56)

BEHIND THE TEXT

Jesus' arrest includes four scenes: Judas' kiss (vv 47-50), cutting of a slave's ear (vv 51-54), Jesus' address to the crowd (vv 55-56*a*), and a note about the disciples' desertion (v 56*b*). The episode brings narrative threads together: the authorities' plan to apprehend Jesus in secret (26:5), Judas' role in betrayal (26:14-16, 21-25), and Jesus' perdition of his fate (17:22). Structurally, the passage could be organized around three of Jesus' addresses: to Judas (26:50), to the disciple (v 52), and to the armed crowd (v 55). The fulfillment of Scriptures, a key motif in the Passion Narrative, is mentioned twice. This is coupled with the fulfillment of Jesus' own predictions about his disciples' betrayal.

IN THE TEXT

■ **47-50*a*** Judas arrives with a band of armed men, probably from the temple guard, sent by the Jewish religious and civic authorities. Judas, concealing his intentions, addresses Jesus, **Greetings, Rabbi!** and kisses him. He places himself outside of the followers' circle by using this title, normally used by outsiders in Matthew; the disciples would address Jesus as "Lord." He also turns a kiss—the sign of friendship, peace, and respect—into an instrument of betrayal. He singles Jesus out from the rest so that the armed men could detain him.

Jesus' address to Judas as **friend** (*hetaire*) could be interpreted in two ways: a close relationship between them and Jesus' friendliness toward his betrayer (Davies and Allison 2004, 509); or, a way of distancing Judas by addressing him in "a polite cool generic form" as if his name was unknown to Jesus (*NIB* 8:477). The statement **Do what you came for** (*eph ho parei*) invites a variety of interpretations: (1) as a question it would sound like "Why do you come?"; (2) as a statement with a command, "Do what you are here to do"; (3) and as a comment of disappointment with Judas, "For *this* you come!" (Hagner 1995, 789). After these words, the guards arrest Jesus.

■ **50*b*-54** One of the disciples, in an act of resistance and loyalty, decides to defend his Master by attacking one person from the crowd. (John identifies the disciple as Peter; see John 18:10). This is ironic. Their resolve to remain loyal and to die with Jesus (Matt 26:35) resulted just in cutting off a slave's ear; not a major achievement! Their bravery and zealousness soon desert them.

Jesus de-escalates the situation: **Put your sword back in its place** (v 52*a*). Violence only causes further violence: **for all who draw the sword will die by the sword** (v 52*b*). Jesus' way is to love one's enemies and not to retaliate (5:38-39, 43-48). If fighting were the answer, Matthew notes that Jesus could have called **twelve legions of angels** (26:53). The Messiah's role is not to wage a war but to save and restore his people (1:21). Jesus resigns his power ("emptied himself of all but love," in Charles Wesley's memorable phrase) to fulfill his purpose: give his life for others. He allows this arrest to happen. At this ominous hour, nonviolent surrender is the way for the Scriptures to be fulfilled.

■ **55-56** Jesus addresses the armed crowd. This arrest, away from the pilgrim crowds and the public space of the sacred precincts, is dishonorable and betrays their evil intentions. They treat the Messiah of Israel as if he were a bandit or a rebel (*lēstēs*). Still, their plan to arrest Jesus by stealth (26:4) has worked. And it has **all taken place that the writings of the prophets might be fulfilled** (v 56*a*). Jesus surrenders on his own terms.

After these words, **All the disciples deserted him and fled** (v 56*b*). The initial act of resistance from one of the disciples turns into an act of abandonment by all. The actions of the armed crowd and of the disciples fulfill Jesus' word and ancient prophecies (see vv 31-35).

FROM THE TEXT

Several thoughts emerge from this passage. First, following the divine will is costly. Believers could be tempted not to drink the cup of suffering and find an easier way or resist it with violence. Jesus shows the resolve to follow the Father's will no matter the cost.

Second, redemption comes through the act of self-giving love and not by brute force or invasion by twelve legions of angels. The mission of God is not furthered by violence but by living out selfless love, exemplified by Jesus. That path may lead to suffering and death. Ancient and modern martyrs have proven again and again that Christians are strong when they are most vulnerable and weak (Wright 2016, 374-77).

Third, the passage illustrates "the way of God's kingdom is to absorb evil rather than inflict it, and brings the spiral [of violence] finally to an end" (*NIB* 8:477). But this is not just about the divine work of restoration of peace and bringing redemption. This is embedded into the mission of Jesus' followers. Peacemaking and the refusal of violence become part and parcel of our costly embodiment of the Sermon on the Mount: "Blessed are the peacemakers, for they will be called children of God" (5:9).

Fourth, this story and the whole Passion Narrative resist the modern, culturally driven, evangelical fixation on well-being where suffering is seen as a hurdle to overcome. This text calls us to recognize again that "suffering and dying is the way by which the world is changed" (Wright 2016, 368). Jesus has won his victory and brought redemption to his people by suffering on the cross; the mission of God is "cross-shaped." Suffering is a part of the redeeming work of Christ that has been accomplished on the cross and embedded into his followers' mission (16:24-26). The holy people of God have to recognize the proper place of suffering in the cruciform mission of God that they carry out in this broken world. This is never easy or without the plea, "My Father, if it is possible, may this cup be taken from me" (26:39).

B. Trials: Jesus, Peter, and Judas (26:57—27:31)

1. Jesus before the Sanhedrin (26:57-68)

BEHIND THE TEXT

Sanhedrin

26:57-68 In Matthew, Sanhedrin (from Gk. *synedrion*, "sitting down with") refers to the supreme council of Jerusalem that had certain authority over local governance, responsibilities over public order in the city, and limited judicial power. But generally, the term referred to regional assemblies of local leaders with responsibilities for tax collection and civil order. These were not always permanently organized bodies; some of them were assembled by rulers only for certain tasks. In Jerusalem, the council has also served as a link between the Jewish community and Roman authorities and exercized its powers in collaboration with them. The Sanhedrin included chief priests, elders, and teachers of the Law and possibly "leading citizens" (see 26:57). Normally, the high priest would preside over the council; at this time, Joseph Caiaphas served in that role (*AB* 5:976-77).

The episode is the culmination point in the Matthean portrayal of Jesus' identity. Jesus publicly affirms that he is the Messiah, the Son of God and the exalted Son of Man (26:63-64).

The trial scene does not follow the procedures outlined in the later rabbinic tradition (*m. Sanh.* 4-7). The organizers were concerned with the minimal conditions that would give it the appearance of legitimacy (Hagner 1995, 797). Even so, the trial looks dubious: held at night, on the eve of the holy day, with minimal attendance of the council members and with no proper witnesses. Thus R. E. Brown suggests that it was more like a pretrial questioning before turning Jesus to the Romans for legal inquiry (1994, 363).

■ **57-58** After his arrest, Jesus was brought to Caiaphas' house for questioning. This was where the scheme for his arrest had been hatched (26:3). The other disciples ran away (v 56), but Peter followed Jesus into the courtyard, setting the scene for Peter's denial (vv 69-75). Peter is in the company of the guards; the fear of being apprehended leads to Peter's betrayal.

■ **59-61** The "trial" adds to the picture of corrupt religious leadership involving perversion of justice and transgression of the Torah. The purpose was to lay charges against Jesus, **so that they could put him to death** (v 59; see vv 3-5). Ironically, they were unprepared since they were still looking for **false evidence** and **false witnesses** (v 60), in clear violation of Torah (see Exod 20:16 ↔Deut 5:20). Their moral bankruptcy is reflected in the questionable legality of the whole affair.

The appearance of following the Law, however, is upheld (Deut 17:6): two witnesses are found who are prepared to testify against Jesus. They accuse him of the plan to destroy the temple and rebuild it in three days. Nowhere in the Gospel story has Jesus made that statement directly (→ comments on the fate of the temple in 21:12-17 and 24:1-35). Perhaps his prediction of the temple destruction in a private conversation with his disciples (24:2) was misrepresented by the false witnesses and has become one of the reasons to justify his crucifixion (see 27:40).

The other Gospels interpret this language of destruction and restoration of the temple as a metaphor for Jesus' death and resurrection (Mark 14:58; John 2:19-22). This will signify the relocation of holiness and the divine presence into the new dwelling place of God, the new covenant community of "those who respond to Jesus' call" (Brower 2007, 69).

■ **62-63*a*** Any threat to destroy the temple could be seen as an act of desecration. It could also be seen as an instigation to rebellion against both the Roman and temple authorities. Insurrection would be a capital offense. When Jesus is accused, Caiaphas challenges him to respond: **Are you not going to answer?** (Matt 26:62). Jesus refuses to defend himself, evoking the imagery from Isa 53:7. His accusers interpreted the silence as an acknowledgment of guilt. But Jesus' silence is telling: he "submits to the faulty reasoning of his accusers and opponents in order to accomplish the will of God and so fulfil the scriptures" (Hagner 1995, 799).

■ **63*b*-66** The second line of accusation concerns Jesus' identity. Caiaphas charges Jesus by an oath to answer truthfully: **Tell us if you are the Messiah, the Son of God** (Matt 26:63*b*). Here Jesus offers a direct self-affirmation of his identity. Ironically, the high priest confesses who Jesus is: **You have said so** (v 64*a*). This is the first of a series of ironic proclamations of Jesus' identity from his enemies (see 27:17, 22, 29, 37, 43, 54).

Jesus admits that he is the Son of God and the Messiah and adds another christological image—**the Son of Man . . . coming on the clouds of heaven** (v 64*b*). This picture evokes Dan 7:13 and Ps 110:1 (see Matt 24:29-31) and sends a message to those who plotted against Jesus: the Mighty One himself will vindicate Jesus and give him authority over the universe. Their attempt to destroy him is futile. Matthew brings all the key christological titles together to reveal Jesus' true identity: the Messiah, the Son of God and the suffering and vindicated exalted Son of Man.

The high priest explodes in hypocritical righteous anger, tears his garments, and accuses Jesus of blasphemy. Although Jesus was not guilty because he didn't pronounce the divine name (*m. Sanh.* 7:5), Caiaphas interprets his confession as an insult to God since Jesus claims things that belong to God alone (Hagner 1995, 801). The high priest's accusation and theatrical action prompt the members of the assembly to pronounce the verdict; they have found what they were looking for. Jesus deserves to die as a blasphemer (see Lev 24:16). However, since the Sanhedrin did not have authority to carry out the death penalty, the execution would depend on the Roman authorities.

■ **67-68** Public humiliation follows. Its purpose is to undermine Jesus' lofty
claims of messiahship. Since he can't prevent physical abuse and mockery,
can't prophesy or perform deeds of power, he is not who he claims to be.
Through a series of "status degradation rituals" (see Matt 27:20-23, 27-44) and
his shameful death on the cross, the authorities try to destroy Jesus' credibil-
26:67-68 ity and turn him from a respected prophet and rabbi into a despised criminal
(Malina and Rohrbaugh 2003, 413). Jesus silently endures their insults, mockery, abuse, demeaning guessing game, and exemplifies, in a dignifying manner, his own teaching from 5:38-42. The scene also evokes scriptures, particularly the song of the Suffering Servant (Isa 50:6; 53:3-5) and the psalms of the righteous sufferer (Pss 22; 69—71).

FROM THE TEXT

The text raises moral dilemmas. When Christians are faced with perversion of justice, corrupted governmental, corporate, or church systems, with abuse of power, and physical demeaning, what is their response? Would we appeal to Jesus' unique example, who surrenders his powers and privileges to bring redemption to others and assume a position of powerless victim? Or being inspired by his vision of the kingdom would we challenge oppressive systems by living out righteousness, mercy, peacemaking, and love? Should we just hope for eschatological vindication or actively look for justice here and now? Jesus' example of peaceful resistance, open challenge, and surrender might guide in these complex issues. However, one should always remember that identification with the crucified Lord and participation in the redemptive mission of God might lead to suffering and, possibly, even to death.

2. Peter Denies Jesus (26:69-75)

BEHIND THE TEXT

This passage, coupled with the story of Judas (27:1-10), concludes the motif of betrayal and abandonment by the Twelve and fulfills Jesus' prediction about Peter (26:33-35). It has been placed between episodes of Jesus' trials before the Sanhedrin (vv 57-68) and at the governor's palace (27:11-26). The story is built around three challenges about Peter's connection to Jesus and his responses: "I don't know the man" (v 74). Two servant girls accuse him of being "with Jesus" (vv 69, 71) and the bystanders, "you are one of them" (v 73). The leading apostle renounces not only his master but also his ties to the community of followers.

As the story progresses, his eagerness to distance himself from Jesus escalates: first, he simply denies (v 70); then he denies "with an oath" (v 72); and finally he denies with "curses" and swearing (v 74). Peter not only renounces any connections with Jesus but also physically moves away from him: from the courtyard to the gateway and outside.

Apart from intensification and progression, Matthew uses juxtaposition and irony. Peter's denial before servant girls is set against Jesus' confession and faithfulness at the trial before the leaders of the Jewish people. While Jesus meets his enemies face-to-face, Peter retreats. Peter's rejection is highlighted by his previous confession of Jesus' identity (16:16) and boasting and swearing of allegiance (26:33-35).

IN THE TEXT

■ **69-70** While the other disciples deserted Jesus and fled (26:56) Peter follows and finds himself in the courtyard of the high priest's house. Here he is challenged by a servant girl (*paidiskē*): **You also were with Jesus of Galilee** (v 69). This charge could put him in danger of being arrested and more. He tries to escape by denying any association with Jesus despite his promise in v 35.

The low social status of the slave girl further highlights Peter's cowardice. The girl says Jesus is "of Galilee" (see Luke 23:6). Later Peter is identified as a Galilean. These Galileans are noticeable in Jerusalem. Peter is out of place in the high priest's house, and it raises the girl's suspicion. Galilee, their home province and place of comparatively successful mission, contrasts with Jerusalem, the place of trial and suffering.

■ **71-72** Peter, wanting to avoid further questioning, tries to leave the courtyard. But another slave girl accuses him of being **with Jesus of Nazareth** (26:71; a further pointer to his Galilean identity). The rejection story in Nazareth (13:53-58) is in parallel to what is happening in the holy city. The second denouncement comes with an oath: **I don't know the man!** (26:72). This intensifies Peter's denial. He knows who Jesus is: he is the Messiah, the Son of the Living God (14:33; 16:16).

■ **73-74** Later, another challenge comes from bystanders. Here the threat of arrest becomes real. They have recognized his Galilean accent, which betrays his identity, **Surely you are one of them** (26:73). This time Peter does not spare his words: **He began to call down curses, and he swore to them** that he does not know Jesus (v 74).

The object of cursing is not clear. Two interpretive possibilities exist. First, he calls divine wrath on himself if his words are not true. Second, he could have cursed Jesus in an attempt to prove that he is not one of the disciples (Davies and Allison 2004, 547). This intensifies the break from Jesus and has been done in front of two or more male witnesses. Such a public renunciation of ties with a former patron or master would have severed relationship irreversibly (Malina and Rohrbaugh 2003, 318).

■ **75** The dramatic ending comes when **a rooster crowed**. Peter recalls the words of Jesus, who predicted this act of disloyalty (see 26:34). Peter goes outside of the chief priest's courtyard and **wept bitterly**. He denied Jesus in front of many witnesses but sheds his tears of remorse away from the public eye. Even when recognizing his failure, Peter does not want to be compromised.

FROM THE TEXT

The story of Peter's denial introduces readers to the sensitive issue of
26:73-75 apostasy. Jesus has warned his disciples about times of persecution and the importance of staying faithful (10:16-23). But the leading apostle fails to confess (10:32-33), pick up his cross, and follow Christ to the end (16:24-26). Instead he fiercely denies his relationship with Jesus and the community of his followers in order to save his own life. The Gospel does not shy away from talking about failure and reveals the drama of following Christ in its raw complexity. When the time of trial comes, even the strongest in the community of faith may stumble and fall into temptation.

But this story is not only about human frailty. In spite of betrayal and unfaithfulness, after Jesus' resurrection Peter finds restoration and is called back to participate with others in the mission of God (28:16-20). The strongest may stumble but Jesus' forgiving embrace remains open for all. The story reveals a pattern of Christian discipleship: human failure is met by divine grace.

3. Judas Hangs Himself (27:1-10)

BEHIND THE TEXT

Matthew sandwiches the story of Judas' death between the short description of Jesus being sent to Pilate (27:1-2) and the trial at the governor's palace (vv 11-14). He also juxtaposes the stories of Judas and Peter (26:69-75). Judas' premeditated apostasy ends up in suicide; Peter's failure to remain faithful ends in repentance and future restoration (28:16-20). The episode brings to conclusion Judas' story, reveals the fate of "blood money," and shows—once again—the moral bankruptcy of the religious establishment.

Matthew interprets the events in the light of the OT. By bringing together Jer 32:6-14 and Zech 11:13 and interpreting them in each other's light, he tells his readers something about the evil shepherds of Israel who plot, kill, and use other people for their sinful purposes and discard them when the time comes. Matthew sees the whole story as the fulfillment of Scripture. Throwing money into the temple and purchasing the potter's field follow prophetic insights. The Hebrew wordplay between *yosher* ("potter") and *'osher* ("treasury"), based on the passage from Zechariah, underlines the explanation of the event: the priests prevented the money to be returned to the treasury (Keener 2009, 657).

IN THE TEXT

■ **1-2** The Sanhedrin has gathered again for the second hearing. They have interrogated Jesus first (see 26:57-68) in order to prepare the legal charge. Now is the time to bring him before the Roman authorities for the proper trial. This event echoes earlier predictions: "and will hand him over to the Gentiles" (20:19).

Judas Iscariot in the History of Interpretation

From early stages in Christian history, the story of Judas Iscariot raised a variety of historical, theological, and ethical issues. For the majority of believers and church fathers, the figure of Judas was univocally associated with apostasy and treachery; he was remembered as a villain, Satan's tool, a betrayer, a hypocrite, a money-monger (see, e.g., Chrysostom 1859, "Homily on the Betrayal of Judas," PG 49:373-92), and a thief. As the most evil character among the Twelve, he embodied the vices of avarice and greed and—as some extra-canonical traditions suggested—was possessed by the devil from childhood (*[Arab.] Gos. Inf.* 35). Moreover, Judas' example fuelled anti-Semitic attitudes (*ABD* 3:1095).

However, there were other perspectives. Early Gnostic texts, such as the recently discovered "Gospel of Judas," represented him as the most trusted and perceiving disciple. Other Christian voices were heard as well. Origen, a theologian from Alexandria (third century CE), was one of the first who made a serious attempt to wrestle with the story of Judas and its theological implications. He challenged some of the widespread perceptions of Iscariot as a personification of evil who was incapable of salvation.

Origen questioned Judas' responsibility: If Satan has entered Judas, who did the betraying then? Can Judas be really responsible? Origen also wrestled with the issue of Judas' place within the divine plan of redemption: If God decided to sacrifice his Son and Jesus goes willingly to death, then "betrayal" does not go against the divine will. Rather, it becomes a vehicle for carrying out these redemptive purposes. These and other unresolvable questions led Origen to conclude that "there is a mystery in the betrayal of Judas against Jesus" (Laeuchli 1953, 262-63, 265-66).

In recent years, many challenges to the traditional portrayal of Judas have been made. Scholars (such as Karl Barth, William Klassen, Hans-Josef Klauck, Anthony Cane) reassessed and reinterpreted Gospel accounts and their language (particularly the use of *paradidomi*). They have looked into possible motifs behind Judas' decisions (disillusionment, an honest mistake, a result of inner struggle and contradictions). Alternative scenarios have been posited: Judas' providential role in salvation; Judas as personal agent of Jesus who organized his peaceful "handing over" to authorities to avoid riots and bloodshed, and so forth. His suicide was seen as an act of solidarity or a sign of crushed hopes for establishment of the kingdom of God (see Harvey 2016, 4-16; *ABD* 3:1096).

Whatever stance is taken on Judas—condemnation or exoneration—a Christian interpreter should keep in mind William Klassen's question: "Is it too much to suggest that whatever Judas did, he too was covered by the intercessory prayer of Jesus from the cross: 'Father, forgive them for they know not what they do'?" (in *ABD* 3:1096).

■ **3-5** When Judas heard that Jesus was condemned to death, **he was seized with remorse** (v 3). The Greek word for "feeling remorse" (*metamelētheis*) could be also translated as "to regret," "to repent," or "to change one's mind." This provides two possibilities for interpretation of the event. Traditionally, the episode is seen as "a crime and punishment story." Judas gets what he deserves according to the law of Moses: "Cursed is anyone who accepts a bribe to kill an innocent person" (Deut 27:25). His suicide is a dishonorable death of regret (Keener 2009, 659).

On the other hand, Judas' actions could reflect repentance: he has changed his mind about what he has done, realized his own guilt and the innocence of Jesus, returned the money, and confessed his sin. In this light, suicide could be seen as an attempt on Judas' part to expiate for his own offense (Davies and Allison 2004, 562-63).

Tragically, this is not the way to restore the broken relationship with his Teacher. Judas' death also foreshadows the corporate responsibility for injustice and spilling the innocent blood (see 27:25) and evokes a similar story from 2 Sam 17:23.

Judas' confession is met with indifference. The priests did not care about his remorse and confession. There is no regret on their part: **What is that to us?** (Matt 27:4). They offer no opportunity for forgiveness: **that is your responsibility**. In the act of desperation and defiance, Judas throws the blood money—originally taken from the temple treasury—back into the sanctuary (*ton naon*). This symbolic act, again, hints at the fact that the temple has become the place of corruption (→ 21:12-17) and its priests are the evil shepherds of Israel.

This episode highlights three main issues. First, it continues the theme of Christ's innocence. Judas has realized that he played a role in the perversion of justice and committed a sin by betraying an innocent man. Even the priests have acknowledged Jesus' innocence indirectly: they have treated the thirty silver coins as blood money—money paid for taking an innocent life. Here Judas stands together with Pilate and his wife (27:11-26), who also refused to believe that Jesus was persecuted by the religious authorities for a crime.

Second, the story, once more, demonstrates the priests' hypocrisy: they are ready to make evil plots, bribe, and accuse innocent people but find it unacceptable—for purity concerns—to receive "blood money" back into the temple treasury (Keener 2009, 660; see 23:25-36).

Third, the tragic end of Judas' life—one step short of reconciliation—illustrates the complexity of the relationship between human responsibility, consequences, and the divine will. The Gospel narrative also puts two deaths in parallel: Judas takes his own life in an attempt to atone of his sin; Jesus gives his own life to redeem others.

■ **6-10** The only problem that concerns the priests is what to do with **blood money** (v 6). The thirty silver coins are now tainted with spilling of innocent blood and became unclean. They can't be returned to the temple since it will compromise the holiness and purity of the holy courts. The irony is that the holy place has already been defiled by the actions of the corrupted priesthood (see 21:12-13). They took the money in the first place from the temple treasury for the unholy purpose of facilitating Judas' betrayal. The result of that act is the death of an innocent person, which is a heinous crime according to the Law (Deut 19:16-21; 27:25; see also Gen 4:11).

The priests decide to buy a plot of land and turn it into an unclean space—a cemetery assigned for Jews who lived abroad. For Matthew, this explains where the name for the place—the Field of Blood (Aram.: *Akeldama*; Matt 27:8)—came from. Matthew finds its explanation in Jeremiah and Zechariah. For Matthew, the suffering of the innocent Messiah was prefigured even in that small detail.

FROM THE TEXT

The story of Judas is one that disturbs a thoughtful Christian reader. It raises an array of questions. Could Judas have been restored? How was his apostasy different from other apostles? Was his role in the economy of salvation predetermined? Has God—like the Jerusalem priests—discarded Judas after he has done his part? Would humanity's redemption have been possible without his act of handing Jesus over? Has he committed an unforgivable sin?

Matthew leaves these questions unanswered and even refuses to speculate on Judas' "eternal destiny" (*NIB* 8:484). Moreover, Judas' act of self-destruction is ambiguous. The plain reporting that "he went away and hanged himself" (27:5) is opened to interpretation. On the one hand, Judas' suicide could be seen as a confirmation of divine judgment and "a shameful crime" in the light of certain Jewish traditions (*J.W.* 3.8.5; *m. Sanh.* 10:2). On the other,

Matthew might not have viewed it as a wrongful act in the circumstances. Perhaps it was a result of genuine remorse and an attempt to expiate for his wrongdoings by taking his life in a version of a noble death (4 Macc 17:11-24; *Gen. Rab.* 27:27; Oropeza 2011, 76-77; Droge and Tabor 1992, 133). Did he cross the lines between suicide and martyrdom? The answer lies in Judas' intentions that the Gospel writer does not reveal.

This Matthean ambivalence gives us an opportunity to pause in our haste to condemn. Like the rest of the Twelve, Judas left everything and responded to Christ's call to follow, was given authority and appointed as an apostle, and participated in the mission of God. He also betrayed Jesus and recognized his failure but could not find the way out of the maze of intentions, decisions, and consequences. Feeling trapped and alienated, he took his life.

By placing Peter's story just before this tragic episode, Matthew suggests that there is always an alternative. Self-alienation, a deep feeling of remorse, guilt, and disorientation do not have to lead to self-destruction. In these dark hours of abandonment and betrayal, Jesus never showed animosity to any of his followers, including Judas. Placing themselves in the shoes of Peter and Judas, the Gospel readers should grasp the liberating truth about following Christ: those who stumble always have an opportunity to find new orientation, forgiveness, and restoration in the embrace of "love divine, all loves excelling."

The church's handling of suicide over the centuries as "a heinous crime" and an unforgivable sin was colored by the story of Judas. It was often connected with devil possession or faithlessness and apostasy that placed persons who committed suicide outside of the faith community and the saving grace of God. Refusal of Christian burial for suicides sent a message that there is neither peace nor place for them in this life or the world to come. The church could and should have done better. The issue of suicide continues to be shrouded in shame in many Christian communities. Often this attitude fails to consider the complex psychological, physiological, and social issues surrounding suicide, keeping the faithful distant from the reality of suicide and its consequences.

Suicide and the church's response to it remains a complex issue. But what is clear is this: The tragic story of Judas in Matthew—though it warns about the perils of apostasy—gives no permission for adding post factum shame or ostracization on the victims of suicide or their families. The passage resists being turned into a proof text for condemning suicide victims. But it does give us room to have honest conversations about suicide and to invite Christ to shed his light into those dark places of human experience. The story also provides an opportunity to confront our own judgment of others and ourselves, and gives a space for grace to be extended, not only in prevention but also in care for those grieving the loss.

4. Jesus before Pilate (27:11-26)

BEHIND THE TEXT

The Greek text of the Gospel refers to Pilate as *hēgemonos* (usually translated as "a governor")—a ruler whose official Roman title was prefect (Lat. *praefectus*). It is only at the later stage in history Roman officials in Judea were appointed as procurators and governors. The prefect was installed by and answered directly to the Roman emperor. The Roman administration was in charge of the military command, exercised judicial authority, and managed the finances of the province (Smith 2010, 94). Pilate served as the procurator of Judea from 26 to 36 CE with the official residence located in Caesarea. His presence in Jerusalem during the Passover festival is most likely related to security concerns: to keep an eye on Jewish masses and to prevent any civil unrest.

IN THE TEXT

■ **11-18** After interjecting the story of Judas (27:3-10), Matthew returns to the trial of Jesus. In vv 1-2, the readers have already learned that the Jewish authorities decided to put Jesus to death and took him to the Roman governor for the final legal trial.

Pilate's question, **Are you the king of the Jews?** (v 11), immediately gives the case political overtones. Jesus' accusers decided to present the matter as a possible case for revolt against Rome and not as a blasphemy (see 26:65-66). This put the Roman governor into an impossible position. On the one hand, Pilate is clearly reluctant to pronounce a judgment over this Galilean peasant particularly because **he knew that it was out of self-interest that they had handed Jesus over to him** (v 18). On the other hand, he has to respond to such accusations in order to protect Roman power in Judea.

In Matthew, Pilate is torn between the concern for justice and political necessity. This is surprising; he was known for executing people without a proper trial (Sanders 1995, 274). Since the case was presented to him as a political issue, he decides to cooperate with the Jewish authorities and reacts swiftly: execution was carried out only a few hours later (Keener 2009, 667). The life of a Jewish peasant is not a big price to pay for civil peace in Jerusalem at the time of Passover.

Jesus affirms his identity as the Messiah and the King of the Jews and refuses to answer other false accusations. Pilate offers another opportunity to respond: **Don't you hear the testimony they are bringing against you?** (v 13). According to Roman law, a refusal to defend oneself in court is interpreted as recognition of one's guilt (Keener 2009, 668). However, Pilate is impressed with Jesus' refusal to defend himself. This could be interpreted as honorable behavior in the presence of Roman authority. But readers know that his refusal is a sign of surrender to God's will, of the resolve to suffer to the end, and a silent statement of his innocence.

Pilate's way to resolve the tension between justice and political necessity is to pass responsibility of the verdict on to others by offering a Passover amnesty: **Which one do you want me to release to you: Jesus Barabbas, or Jesus who is called the Messiah?** (v 17). Though elsewhere unattested in Judea, Romans did pardon criminals in respect to local customs and during certain festivals. Since Jesus was not sentenced at this point, Pilate thinks of *abolition*—releasing a suspect before the trial (Keener 2009, 669).

In Pilate's eyes, Jesus poses no danger to Rome. It is only the local religious leaders who are concerned with his popularity among the pilgrims. So, he offers the crowd to choose between Jesus called Barabbas (or "son of the father," from Aramaic) and Jesus called Christ (or the Messiah). Jerusalemites have to choose between **a well-known prisoner** (v 16) and "that innocent man" (v 19).

■ **19** Matthew unexpectedly pauses in telling his story: Pilate's wife sent him a message about her dream. This is an interesting interlude. Dreams were often perceived as messages from the divine realm. Here an elite Gentile woman—a Roman noble—receives divine revelation of Jesus' innocence while Jewish religious leaders remained blind (France 2007, 1055). Scholars note that she exemplifies a number of Jewish and later Christian sympathizers among Gentile elites (France 2007, 1054; Brown 1994, 805-7).

■ **20-26** Since Jesus was more popular with the people in Jerusalem, Pilate
 thought that they would prefer Jesus to Barabbas and his dilemma could be resolved. But it was not the case. The religious leaders persuade the masses to insist on Jesus' execution. Matthew shows that Pilate makes an attempt to change the crowd's mind but the only response he gets is, **Crucify him!** (v 22). The people share with their leaders the responsibility and guilt in spilling innocent blood and thus, according to the Law, "they ironically invite a curse against themselves" (Keener 2009, 671).

In the final scene of the trial, Pilate washes his hands in front of the angry mob and declares, **I am innocent of this man's blood** (v 24). For Matthew, Roman authorities are not to blame for Jesus' fate. The full responsibility lies with the crowd and its leaders. This is in a reverse parallel with the previous story (vv 3-4): Judas takes responsibility for innocent blood; Pilate denies his (Davies and Allison 2004, 564).

In response to Pilate's symbolic action, **all the people answered, "His blood is on us and on our children!"** (v 25). Matthew's intention is quite evident here (since no other Gospel mentions this episode)—to highlight the crowd's responsibility and portray some Jews in the negative light. This is likely reflective of tensions and conflict within the Jewish community in the second part of the first century CE. Hostilities between the Matthean *ecclesia* and synagogue—between Jewish followers and those who rejected Jesus as the Messiah of Israel—surface in this and other Matthean texts (Hagner 1995, 828).

Some scholars have attempted to reinterpret the passage to soften Matthean negativity. It has been proposed to see "covering in blood" as a reference to a restorative and salvific event (akin to the covenantal ceremony in Exod 24:1-8) rather than the language of curse and punishment (Cargal 1991; Sullivan 1992). However, the wider context of the text implies judgment overtones and, at the same time, it contains no anti-Semitic agenda.

For Matthew, this ominous phrase is connected with the destruction of Jerusalem and its temple in 70 CE (see Matt 23:37-39) and must not be treated as "a perpetual curse" on the people of Israel that somehow justifies their persecution. The pattern of the passage reflects the OT prophetic tradition: rejection of God's messenger and his proclamation results in judgment and punishment. The rejection of Jesus by "this unbelieving . . . generation" (17:17) brings destruction to the old order and signals the birth of the new people of God, who will be gathered around the resurrected Messiah (France 2007, 1058).

Pilate's attempt to avoid his responsibility did not prevent him from cruelty: **he had Jesus flogged, and handed him over to be crucified**. Death sentences were often accompanied by severe flogging (27:26). The Romans used scourges—leather whips knotted with pieces of iron or bone—on slaves and noncitizens. Jesus, probably, was tied to a pole and scourged (Brown 1994, 851). Ancient readers would be all too familiar with this punishment and horrific scenes, and Matthew omits the gruesome details.

This episode—intentionally or not—unmasks some of the Matthean attempts to absolve Pilate. Ultimately, the fate of Jesus was in the hands of the Roman governor who had the full authority to execute or pardon despite the wishes of his subjects. Pilate and the religious elite, who have turned the crowd against Jesus, share that responsibility for the suffering and death of the Messiah of Israel; and no amount of water can wash that off.

FROM THE TEXT

Matthew clearly emphasizes the guilt of Jewish leaders in Jesus' death rather than of the Roman authorities. Pilate reluctantly executes his judicial responsibilities. He sentences Jesus to death—knowing of his innocence—under pressure from the crowd instigated by the religious authorities. Pilate decides to meet the people's demands since there was nothing at stake for Rome in this case except civic peace. But this political flexibility is only situational; Pilate knew how to execute Roman might on other occasions by slaughtering unruly Jewish masses (*Ant.* 18.55-62; Keener 2009, 667).

For Matthew, the whole case is a perversion of justice: the innocent man suffers and the criminal has been released. The trial of the Son of God unmasks the ugly state of affairs: the political and religious establishments commit crimes in the name of security. They fear losing power and control over the Jewish people. Political expediency overcomes fairness. Corruption overcomes righteousness. Clinging to power overcomes the value of human life. Jesus faces injustice with silent dignity (see Isa 53:7): no pleading, no defense. He has accepted his fate in Gethsemane (see Matt 26:36-46), endures his trials, and trusts his heavenly Father; and the faithful God turns the appalling reality upside down. Through the pain and death of the righteous sufferer God transforms injustice into redemption, hardship into salvation, mockery into truth, and rejection into the new beginning.

There is a dark side to the use of this story. Regrettably, this passage has been used to validate persecution of Jews by appealing to the role the crowd played in Jesus' execution. Its interpretation also contributed to nurturing anti-Semitic sentiments within, and persecution by, the church for centuries that tragically culminated in the Holocaust. It is clear that the text cannot justify revenge in any form. It must never be interpreted in a manner that supports anti-Semitism in any shape or form. Those attitudes are against the Christian spirit of love and forgiveness reflected in the Sermon on the Mount (5:38-40, 43-48). Ultimately, Christ's blood is the source of forgiveness for all, Jews and Gentiles, not of curse and condemnation (Hagner 1995, 827).

5. Soldiers Mock Jesus (27:27-31)

BEHIND THE TEXT

This episode reveals an upside-down world. Mockery and humiliation of
27:27 a Galilean peasant and condemned criminal ironically turns into an enthronement ceremony for the true King of Israel who will rule from the cross. In this carnivalesque event—when things are opposite to what they appear to be—the Roman soldiers proclaim Jesus' true identity; he is the King of the Jews, the Messiah from the house of David. Moreover, this event for Matthew evokes the Suffering Servant motif from Isa 50:6: "I offered my back to those who beat me, . . . I did not hide my face from mocking and spitting."

Matthew shapes the passage in a parallel structure (Davies and Allison 2004, 597) with the repetition of key words and actions; at the center is the scene of the soldiers kneeling and hailing Jesus as the King:

Jesus taken to the Praetorium (v 27)
Jesus stripped and clothed (v 28)
A crown on the head, a reed in hand (v 29*a*)
Kneeling and mocking (v 29*b*)
A reed strikes Jesus' head (v 30)
Jesus stripped and clothed (v 31*a*)
Jesus led away to crucifixion (v 31*b*)

IN THE TEXT

■ **27** Matthew reports that the Romans have gathered a whole cohort (*speiran*) of soldiers (roughly five hundred men) with one purpose in mind—to humiliate Jesus. This unit represents the whole of the Jerusalem garrison stationed in the Antonia Fortress, the Roman governor's residence (*praetorium*) in Jerusalem. However, some have suggested that the place of mockery could have been Herod's palace instead (Smith 2010, 94).

■ **28-30** In the mockery scene, soldiers use the imitations of the symbols of royal authority. The emperor's purple robe is represented by the scarlet cloak of Roman soldiers. The crown made of thorns stands for the radiant crowns of Greek kings and Roman rulers. It was likely not designed as an instrument of torture but as an imitation of crowns shaped to represent the sun rays; thus spikes were sticking outward (France 1989, 394). The royal scepter is fashioned out of a reed. The whole pretend dress-up game then culminates in kneeling and paying homage to Jesus by shouting, **Hail, king of the Jews!** (v 29). This evokes the Roman greeting of the emperor—"Hail, Caesar!" (Harrington 1991, 395).

Mockery leads to physical abuse: they spat on him and hit him on the head with the reed. Matthew's description is more about humiliation than torture per se. Flogging has already occurred (see v 26). This event fulfills Jesus' own prediction in 20:19: "and will hand him over to the Gentiles to be mocked and flogged and crucified."

■ **31** After finishing their cruelty, the soldiers returned Jesus' clothes and led him to the place of crucifixion. France notes that Romans would normally parade condemned criminals to the place of execution without any clothes on. But because of Jewish sensibilities toward human nakedness, they decided to cover him (France 1989, 394).

FROM THE TEXT

The story operates on two levels. On the one hand, Jesus the Messiah is being humiliated by soldiers in a theatrical demonstration of the power of Rome. This is what awaits rebels and self-proclaimed rulers of the Jews: extreme dishonor, humiliation, and death. This episode is juxtaposed with mockery by Jewish people at the cross (27:38-44). The true king was rejected and humiliated by both Jews and Gentiles.

But this mock coronation turns into a confession of Jesus' true identity. In an ironic twist, Roman soldiers kneel and pay homage to the King of the Jews. This grotesque event is followed by Jesus' way to the cross—the throne of suffering and redemption for the people of God. Though proclaimed as the King in mockery, Jesus becomes the King of the whole cosmos when God himself gives him power and authority at the end of the Gospel story (28:18). He is the King of all: Jews and Gentiles.

Jesus takes abuse with the meekness and dignity of the true king. His endurance sets an example for his followers who would experience humiliation, torture, and even death from Jewish and Roman authorities.

C. Crucifixion and Burial (27:32-66)

1. Crucifixion (27:32-44)

BEHIND THE TEXT

The Romans inherited the practice of crucifixion from other Mediterranean cultures and it was perceived by imperial nobility as a barbaric, cruel, and disgusting torture. It was normally reserved for members of the lower classes, slaves, and non-Roman citizens. The term "crucifixion" refers to different ways of attaching people to a pole by impaling, hanging, nailing, or tying; sometimes just to a vertical stake or a pole with a horizontal beam (Brown 1994, 945-47). Apart from a slow and agonizing death, crucifixion was associated with public humiliation and shame.

Crucifixion also served as a propaganda displaying the might of the empire and fate of its enemies. Matthew gives no attention to the details of this torture. Instead he uses the typology of the righteous sufferer taken from Psalms and Isaiah where suffering and death of a righteous one were explained by his loyalty to YHWH and not as divine punishment. This creates a direct parallel with the death of Jesus, who fulfills God's will (26:36-44) and drinks the cup of suffering in full (20:22-23).

IN THE TEXT

27:32-38

■ **32-38** Jesus was publicly paraded to the place of execution. He was forced to carry the crossbeam (Lat., *patibulum*) and possibly a wooden plaque around his neck with the charge written on it (Lat., *titulus*). Since Jesus was unable to carry his own cross due to the earlier scourging (27:26), the soldiers picked a random man from the crowd and made him carry the cross. Matthew mentions his name: **Simon** from **Cyrene** (v 32). He may have been remembered as a witness of Jesus' sufferings and later as a member of the Christian community.

Jesus was taken to Golgotha (translated from Aramaic as **the place of the skull** [v 33])—the site for execution outside of the holy city walls. Before crucifixion, the soldiers offered him a **drink**—wine mixed with bile, a narcotic to dull the agony (v 34; France 2007, 1066). Jesus refuses. The episode echoes the righteous sufferer motif and Ps 69:21 [22 HB] in particular. Casting lots over Jesus' clothes evokes Ps 22:18 [19 HB]: "They divide my clothes among them and cast lots for my garment." Matthew provides no details, simply noting that they nailed the *titulus* to the cross over his head. His crime—being the King of the Jews. Ironically, the false accusation, mockery, and Roman warning to potential rebels turn into the proclamation of his true identity. Jesus, the Messiah, dies for his people and reigns from the cross.

The Greek word for "robbers" (*lēstēs*; NKJV) could mean "bandits" (NRSV), "thieves" (KJV), or could also describe **rebels** or insurgents (v 38*a*).

But Matthew does not elaborate on the identity of the "robbers" or their offenses. For him, the fact that Jesus dies in the company of criminals echoes Isa 53:12, "he was numbered with the transgressors." The two robbers, crucified **one on his right and one on his left** (v 38*b*), takes readers back to the story of the disciples' request (20:20-28) to "sit at your right and . . . at your left in your kingdom" (v 21). Irony again is used: the disciples have failed to remain faithful and share the cup of suffering at the end despite their confident "we can" (20:22). Jesus dies, not in the company of his closest followers, but with the robbers who mock him.

■ **39-44** Matthew identifies a few groups gathered at the cross: soldiers, passers-by, and Jewish authorities. All of them—including the crucified criminals—insult the suffering Christ. Jesus is powerless on the cross despite his supposed identity. If he is the one who will supposedly destroy the temple (see 24:1-2; 26:60-61), the Son of God and the King of Israel, then he should come down from the cross and save himself. If he can't save himself, let God do it now. Thus, for them, the death on the cross proves that Jesus is not the true Messiah of Israel. This is the final scene of their rejection. The language and logic of their insults is reminiscent of the Wisdom of Solomon:

> He . . . boasts that God is his father.
> Let us see if his words are true,
> and let us test what will happen at the end of his life;
> for if the righteous man is God's child, he will help him,
> and will deliver him from the hand of his adversaries. (Wis 2:16-18 NRSV)

Come down from the cross, if you are the Son of God! (Matt 27:40) echoes Satan's temptation in 4:3, 6. This is the last temptation of Christ: to end his suffering and humiliation and to put his enemies to shame. But Jesus, the Son of God, stays faithful to the will of his Father: **he trusts in God** (27:43). He dies for the sake of his people and God vindicates his Son on resurrection morning.

Matthew uses the language of Ps 22:7-8 [8-9 HB] to describe mocking: "hurled insults, shaking their heads" (Matt 27:39↔Ps 22:7 [8 HB]), "He trusts in God. Let God rescue him" (Matt 27:43↔Ps 22:8 [9 HB]). Thus Matthew subverts the logic of the insults. Scripture has foreseen that this would happen to the righteous sufferer; thus the claims about Jesus stay true. What the Jewish authorities say in mockery turns into confession of his true identity as the Messiah and the Son of God. At every stage of the passion story, Matthew brings up the Scripture to show that the Messiah's sufferings are not divine punishment or an evidence of his falsehood. Whatever happens to Jesus had been preordained by God himself.

FROM THE TEXT

The mock coronation in 27:27-31 is followed by crucifixion—the parody on enthronement. The King of the Jews has taken his throne—the cross on the outskirts of the holy city. His celebratory acclamations, insults; his royal festive drink, cheap wine mixed with gall; his trusted viziers, dying robbers; his people, scoffers. Instead of joy, pain; instead of honor, humiliation. But the light of the Scripture subverts this grotesque show, and the mockery turns into proclamation of the truth: the righteous sufferer of Ps 22 is Jesus the Messiah and the Son of God.

Although the episode is a picture of total rejection and abandonment, there is always a glimmer of hope. Throughout the Passion Narrative, secondary characters come to Jesus' aid by performing small gestures. Though the Twelve abandoned him, Jesus is not alone. People along the way share his sufferings. Simon's story of carrying Christ's cross is one of those. It is a potent image that echoes the words of Jesus in 16:24-25 and reminds believers about the place of carrying the cross in following their Master.

2. The Death of Jesus (27:45-56)

BEHIND THE TEXT

Matthew tells the story of Jesus' last moments in three key scenes: (1)
27:45-50 death culminating in the final cry (27:45-50); (2) cosmic portents that end
with the centurion's confession (27:51-54); and (3) witnesses at the cross
(27:55-56).

The Matthean account mostly follows Mark's story and has subtle differences from Luke. Matthew highlights the expectation that Elijah might come to "save" (*sōsōn*) the Messiah (v 49); Jesus cries twice before his death (vv 46, 50); and has a reference to resurrection of the saints (vv 52-53). Description of physical agony is absent. Again, he wraps the event in OT allusions. For him, whatever happens on and at the cross fulfills the Scriptures and, ultimately, the will of God.

IN THE TEXT

■ **45-50** In the beginning of the death scene, Matthew reports unnatural **darkness** (*skotos*) that **came over all the land** (v 45) and lasted from noon to 15:00 (3 pm) (v 46*a*). It suggests divine displeasure with what is happening to Jesus. But there is more to it. The description echoes Amos 8:9: "'In that day,' declares the Sovereign LORD, 'I will make the sun go down at noon and darken the earth in broad daylight.'" The apocalyptic imagery of darkness over the land signals the end of the old age and the beginning of the new one with the death, and later, with the resurrection of the Messiah.

After a few short hours on the cross, **Jesus cried out in a loud voice, *"Eli, Eli, lema sabachthani?"*** (Matt 27:46*b*). In a mixture of Hebrew and Aramaic words, he recites the first line of Ps 22:1, translated into Greek for his readers: **My God, my God, why have you forsaken me?** (Matt 27:46*c*). Traditionally, this outcry was interpreted as "a cry of dereliction" and a sign of God-forsakenness and abandonment as Jesus dies under the weight of the sins of humanity. However, Jesus' cry is set in the context of the righteous sufferer typology that has been widely used by Matthew in the Passion Narrative (see, e.g., Ps 22:18 [19 HB]↔Matt 27:35-36). In Ps 22, the outcry of the righteous sufferer in the beginning of this personal lament reveals the sense of abandonment in the midst of suffering. But the psalm does not dwell on this motif; it moves from desperation to hope, from suffering to salvation, and from humiliation to vindication. As it progresses, the question in the beginning receives its answer later (see Ps 22:23-24 [24-25 HB]): "he did not hide his face from me, but heard when I cried to him" (NRSV), and the individual lament turns into communal praise.

By evoking the opening line of the psalm, Matthew invites his readers to keep in mind the whole of the text. Indeed, Jesus' outcry is laden with strong emotions of suffering and death, and this humiliating and painful experience might appear to be a sign of abandonment and curse by God. But, as with the psalm, the Gospel narrative provides the answer to this (almost rhetorical) question later. God has not forsaken Jesus; he was vindicated at resurrection and given universal authority (see Matt 28).

The similar sound of the word "God" (*Eli*) and the name "Elijah" (*Elias*) confuses the bystanders. They wonder if Jesus calls for Elijah's help and whether the prophet will come to save Jesus and take him down from the cross. This reflects a belief that Elijah would come from heaven when people are in danger (France 2007, 1077; for more on Elijah, see 17:10-13). The cry of suffering moved one of the bystanders to offer Jesus a drink—a sponge with *oxos*—cheap sour wine or **wine vinegar** (27:48). This refreshing drink was normally used by soldiers and laborers. Offering this drink to Jesus could be interpreted as continuation of mockery or, perhaps, more appropriately, as an act of kindness to dull his pain (France 1989, 399). For Matthew, this is another reference to the Scripture: "They . . . gave me vinegar for my thirst" (Ps 69:21 [22 HB]).

Jesus had cried out again in a loud voice (Matt 27:50*a*). This second cry echoes Ps 22 (see Ps 22:2, 5, 24 [3, 5, 25 HB]). Though it is not clear what Jesus shouted this time (see John 19:30), for Matthew, the scriptural pattern has been fulfilled again. After three hours of humiliating torture on the cross, Jesus **gave up his spirit** (*aphēken to pneuma*; Matt 27:50*b*). This could be interpreted in two ways: Christ simply stopped breathing (Hagner 1993, 847) or voluntarily relinquished his life (France 2007, 1078). Jesus has already referred to his own death as giving life willingly in the ultimate act of servanthood (see 20:28). Other Gospels also prefer the latter interpretation: at the last moment, Jesus has given his spirit to the Father (Luke 23:46; John 19:30). This fits well into the Matthean portrait of Jesus as the suffering Son of Man and the obedient Son of God (see Matt 26:36-42).

■ **51-54** Cosmic events occur. First, the sun is darkened (27:45), and now the **earth** violently shakes and **rocks split** (v 51*b*). The created order is in turmoil as it responds to the death of Christ. Its universal significance is further emphasized by what has happened in the temple, the symbolic representation of the ancient cosmos in miniature. Matthew uses the same word (*schizō*) to describe splitting of the rocks and tearing the curtain **in two** (v 51*a*).

It is uncertain which curtain was torn: the inner curtain (separating the holy of holies) or the outer one (covering the entrance to the sanctuary). A variety of interpretations of this symbolic act have been offered: (1) there is no need for the temple anymore; (2) it is a sign of its impending destruction (→ 24:29-31); (3) this opens the holy of holies to give direct access to God; (4) it is a sign of the destruction of the world, the coming of the end times, and the beginning of the new era of God's reign. In any case, the death of Christ sends "a shockwave" through the whole of the universe; the omens signal its magnitude and vindicate the suffering Messiah (Talbert 2010, 308).

Amid the portents of doom and destruction, broken tombs release the saints back to life (27:52). This story is unique to Matthew (an allusion to Ezek 37:13-14) and is symbolic: Jesus' death brings life to the holy people of God. It immediately illustrates that his death was vicarious and redemptive—truly "for many" (Matt 20:28). For Matthew, Jesus' death and resurrection inaugurates the rising from the dead for the faithful ones; and this event in Jerusalem anticipates resurrection for all believers (1 Cor 15).

The way Jesus dies by yielding his spirit and the following omens reveal that he was not an ordinary Galilean peasant: **Surely he was the Son of God!** (Matt 27:54). In Matthew, the centurion—a Roman officer in charge of a unit (*centuria*) of around one hundred men—is the first Gentile to confess Jesus' identity without mockery (see vv 40, 43). The words echo God's voice from heaven (3:17; 17:5) and follow the Jewish disciples' profession (14:33). Now, both Jews and Gentiles confess Jesus' true identity—though sometimes without full comprehension—and join the divine affirmation. This highlights the universal and inclusive character of the gospel, points toward the future inclusion of the Gentiles into the people of God (see 28:19), and alludes to Ps 22:27-28 [28-29 HB]. This scene is juxtaposed to the rejection and mockery Jesus receives from Roman soldiers and Jewish authorities (Matt 27:27-31, 39-44). The Passion Narrative vividly portrays the drama of rejection and belief.

■ **55-56** Matthew finishes the scene with recalling the disciples who witnessed Messiah's death on the cross: **Many women were there . . . They had followed Jesus from Galilee** (v 55). Though standing at a distance from the cross, they are the faithful followers who stayed with their Master from the beginning of his ministry in Galilee to the very end. Out of many, Matthew identifies three: **Mary Magdalene, Mary the mother of James and Joseph** [this is Matthew's way to refer to the mother of Jesus—see 13:55]**, and the mother of Zebedee's sons** (27:56).

The two Marys not only witness Jesus' death and burial (v 61) but also are the first witnesses and proclaimers of his resurrection (28:1, 9). By mentioning the mother of John and James (the sons of Zebedee; see 10:2), Matthew points to a tragic irony that the mother of Jesus' closest companions followed him to the end and her sons failed. This adds another stroke to the portrayal of this family whose contours were highlighted in 20:20-28.

FROM THE TEXT

For Matthew, the death of the Messiah, the Son of God is an event that reverberated throughout the entire creation. Heaven, earth, and even the temple—the center of the ancient Jewish universe—delivered apocalyptic omens signaling the arrival of the new age. The resurrection of the saints also points to the coming rule of God. Jesus dies with solemn dignity and self-control. The question he asks in the anguish of death evokes the whole of Ps 22 with its motif of suffering and vindication.

Although the full answer does not come immediately in the narrative, the Roman centurion's confession paves the way for it: "Surely he was the Son of God" (Matt 27:54). The final episodes of the Gospel reveal that God did not forsake his Son, and neither did some of his faithful followers. Jesus will be vindicated by the Father later by the mighty act of resurrection (see ch 27).

The brutality of crucifixion plunges God Incarnate right into dark realities of the suffering world. The gospel leitmotif of Jesus' *suffering for his people* culminates here. But the pastoral implications of it go far beyond. Like any other human, Jesus faces death; like any other living soul, he suffers. This utter solidarity with human condition reveals a confronting yet comforting truth—God *suffers with us* and his groaning creation. In the midst of the crushing feeling of abandonment and despair, Jesus cries out together with us, broken humans, "Why have you forsaken me?" (v 46). And this unconditional presence of Immanuel reassures—God is with us (1:23). Now, the Christ exalted fully understands, helps, and intercedes for those who suffer (see Heb 2:18).

Here, on the cross, God transforms suffering and death into the vital means of divine grace. Death gives life; suffering brings restoration. The Matthean employment of the motif of the righteous sufferer highlights another truth that goes beyond notions of suffering as punishment or discipline; it has redemptive purposes. Suffering and even death is an intrinsic part of the *cruciform* mission of God. The disciples are called to cross-bearing and *suffering with Jesus,* for his sake (Matt 16:21-26). Thus Jesus on the cross is the exemplar for the faithful: living out radical self-denial and faithfulness to God to the very end (see 16:24-28; 20:20-28).

But it is also a reminder of the mutuality of love: he suffers with us as we suffer with him. Later, the Apostle Paul recognizes life and death in Christ—whether or not we want it—as a vital pattern of the Christian journey (Rom 6:6; 2 Cor 4:11; Gal 2:20); dying of oneself, arising in Christ, suffering persecution, running the race of faith and, as Jesus did, "for the joy set before him he endured the cross" (Heb 12:2). Only in that light of the resurrection is Paul able to say: "For to me, to live is Christ and to die is gain" (Phil 1:21).

3. The Burial of Jesus (27:57-61)

BEHIND THE TEXT

The stories of Jesus' burial and securing of the tomb not only set the stage for the resurrection narrative (28:1-20) but also provide answers to a set of important questions: What has happened with Jesus' body? Who has buried Jesus? Where was he laid? And who are the witnesses of his burial? Matthew also includes this story in his Gospel to counter stories circulated within Jewish communities at the time; one of the prevalent ones was that the disciples just stole Jesus' body from the tomb (→ 28:1-15).

Roman and Jewish burial practices for executed criminals were strikingly different. Romans preferred to leave the executed on their crosses to rot as punishment and a warning to others in a public display of imperial power. However, on rare occasions authorities could give a body to relatives or friends
27:57-60 on their request. Jewish law (Deut 21:21-23), on the other hand, demanded that the dead be buried—even criminals—before nightfall. Normally that would be in a common grave (Talbert 2010, 309).

IN THE TEXT

■ **57-58** Both Jewish tradition and Roman practices have been followed in the burial of Jesus. The phrase **as evening approached** (v 57) indicates that Jesus was buried on the same day before sunset. At the same time, Joseph from Arimathea approaches Pilate, the Roman governor, to ask for permission to bury Jesus, the executed criminal—so called "THE KING OF THE JEWS" (v 37). Surprisingly, Pilate orders the release of the body without any hesitation.

Matthew describes Joseph of Arimathea as **a rich man** (*anthrōpos plousios*; v 57) and **a disciple of Jesus** (*autos emathēteuthē tō Iēsou*). Mark 15:43 and Luke 23:50 identify Joseph as a member of the Sanhedrin. For Matthew, this description echoes Isaiah's song of the Suffering Servant: "He was assigned a grave . . . with the rich" (Isa 53:9). Jesus' body will be put in a place envisioned by the prophet.

■ **59-60** What Joseph does next is full of dignity and care: he **took the body, wrapped it in a clean linen cloth, and placed it in his own new tomb** (Matt 27:59-60). The cemetery was located outside the walls of the sacred city, and tombs were carved out of limestone rock found there. Normally, a corpse could have been washed, anointed with ointments applied, and tightly wrapped in a linen cloth or with cloth strips. Then it was carried in burial procession to the place of rest. At the burial site, family, friends, and neighbors could offer their laments and pay last respects. The body then was left in the tomb for a period of time to decompose. At some point, bones were collected and put in a special stone box (an ossuary), and then the tomb space was reused for other deceased family members. The entrance to the burial cave was sometimes closed with a big stone to prevent looting (*ABD* 1:785-94).

While not all traditions were followed, Jesus receives a proper and dignified burial in contrast to the degradation of mockery, torture, and shameful crucifixion. Instead of being tossed in a common grave for criminals, Jesus' burial brings a sense of vindication. Joseph receives Jesus' lifeless body in contrast to what Roman soldiers have done. Joseph covers the naked, broken body with **a clean linen cloth** (v 59) as opposed to the shame of being crucified naked. Joseph offers his own tomb that no one has used before, the place of rest, as opposed to the cross, the place of agony (see Hengel 1977). Joseph of Arimathea, the follower of Jesus, honors his Master with these small gestures and restores his dignity as Jesus used to restore dignity and honor to others.

■ **61** The same women who witnessed Jesus' death (v 56) **were sitting there opposite the tomb**. They have seen his burial and noted its location. This brief observation is a guarantee that on the resurrection morning they will find the right tomb (see 28:1).

FROM THE TEXT

The scene of Jesus' burial is brief and serves as a prelude to the culmination point of the Passion Narrative and the whole Gospel in general—the Christ's resurrection. The women, the tomb, the big stone, and the issue of Jesus' body will reappear later in the story (see 28:1-10). This account is also filled with tragic irony and true discipleship. The absence of the Eleven and the appearance of Joseph of Arimathea are telling. It is not the closest disciples who take care of the body of their Master and pay last respects but an unknown—to this point in the Gospel story—follower. The examples of true and faithful discipleship come from the secondary characters in the Gospel (the women and Joseph). This dignifying burial is a gesture of love and servanthood as well as a sign of honor and vindication.

4. Guard at the Tomb (27:62-66)

IN THE TEXT

■ **62-64** Even after Jesus' death, the religious leaders were anxious. They see the Roman governor on the next day: **the one after Preparation Day** (*meta tēn Paraskeuēn*; v 62). This is a Matthean way to refer to the holiest day of the week—the Sabbath. Their request to Pilate was simple: to **give the order for**

the tomb to be made secure until the third day (v 64). They have remembered that Jesus has promised that he will rise from the dead on the third day. But for them, this statement is part of the false teaching that Jesus, the deceiver (*ho planos*), was spreading around. They were concerned that his followers might steal the body and tell everyone that Jesus' promise has come true. And **this last deception will be worse than the first**—that he is the Messiah and the Son of God (v 63).

The whole scene again shows the hypocrisy and cynicism of the religious leadership (see ch 23). What has happened to Jesus is of their design. In the beginning of the Passion Narrative, "they schemed to arrest Jesus secretly and kill him" (26:4). Later they arrested him under a false pretense (v 55), looked for false evidence (v 59) and false witnesses (v 60), and generated false accusations at his trial (vv 65-66). Now at the end, their final accusation of Jesus being a deceiver reveals the sad irony—those who are supposed to serve the God of Israel are the true deceivers (Berg 2014, 188-92). This theme of hypocrisy and deception continues as the religious leaders try to cover up the truth of Jesus' resurrection (28:12-15).

■ **65-66** Pilate agrees to provide **a guard** (*koustōdian*; 27:65) and gives them permission to do whatever they deem necessary to secure the tomb. The scene is set for another irony in the making—even a Roman guard is useless when God himself decides to intervene (28:2-3). The chief priests and the Pharisees have decided that it would be enough to seal the stone and put the guard at the entrance of the tomb; this should definitely prevent the disciples from stealing the body.

FROM THE TEXT

Securing the tomb is the final episode of the Passion Narrative per se, setting the scene for Matthew's explanation of why Jesus' body could not have been stolen by the disciples (see 28:1-15). The religious leaders of Jerusalem continue to plot against Jesus and his followers even after his death. Apparently, they remembered Jesus' words about resurrection, but the disciples did not. Their actions served one purpose—to undermine and prevent the spreading of the good news of resurrection. Even with the help of the Roman state, the corrupted religious leadership could not thwart the divine plan of redemption. And, ironically, the secured tomb becomes another strong argument for Jesus' bodily resurrection.

VII. RESURRECTION: MATTHEW 28:1-20

A. The First Witnesses of the Resurrection (28:1-10)

BEHIND THE TEXT

The story of Jesus' resurrection follows the account of precautions taken by the religious leaders and Roman authorities to protect the tomb from interference. Ironically, nothing can prevent or stand in the way of God's action. Matthew does not describe Jesus' resurrection per se. It takes place hidden from human eyes and remains a mystery of divine work. But its announcement comes loud and clear to the faithful women: earthquake, angelic appearance, dramatic unrolling of the tomb stone, scared Roman soldiers, and the message to the Eleven. The whole event challenges and subverts the existing power structures: the power of Roman authorities has been undermined by angelic intervention; the faithful women, not the eleven apostles, are the first to hear the good news of Jesus rising from the dead.

The idea of resurrection was not shared by everyone in 2TJ. The Pharisees believed in the immortality of the soul and possibility of resurrection (see *Ant.* 18.14-15). The Sadducees rejected that belief and insisted that the soul dies with the body (see *Ant.* 18.16). The difference is seen in Acts 23:6-8. The Scriptures allude to it only in a few brief passages: Isa 26:19; Dan 12:2; 2 Macc 7:9, 14. Those who believed in resurrection saw it as a future event marking the coming of the kingdom of God in its fullness; the righteous ones will be restored to life eternal and the wicked ones—for punishment and destruction (Harrington 1991, 411).

IN THE TEXT

■ **1** Out of many female followers who watched Jesus' crucifixion (27:55), Mary Magdalene and the other Mary (perhaps, the mother of James and Joseph [vv 56, 61]) wanted **to look at the tomb** on the morning after the Sabbath (28:1). Mark and Luke have a slightly different account with women wishing to anoint Jesus' body (Mark 16:1; Luke 24:1). With Matthew's strong emphasis on the security of the tomb (Matt 27:64-66), these women wanted to know what the Romans had done to secure it and if there were any possibility to get access to it ("you are looking for Jesus" [28:5]), so that they could pray and mourn.

■ **2-4** The appearance of **an angel** was accompanied by a great **earthquake** (*seismos megas*; v 2). Matthew refers to earthquakes as one of the signs preceding the final consummation of the kingdom (24:7) and mentions an earth-

quake in relation to Jesus' death (27:51, 54). Here the earthquake is linked by the coming of **an angel of the Lord** (28:2). This event evokes apocalyptic imagery; the fulfillment is close. Earthquakes accompanying both Jesus' death and the announcement of his resurrection signal the magnitude of the events and their central place in the unfolding drama of the last days. They demonstrate that God is at work bringing his redemption through the unimaginable acts of the death and resurrection of the Messiah.

The women witnessed both the actions and the appearance of the angel, who **came down**, went **to the tomb, rolled back the stone and sat on it** (vv 2-3). The angel's action shows divine power at work. He has undone what the religious and military authorities did to secure the tomb. Human opposition to God's plans failed. God is in control and not wicked human leadership. Matthew compares the angel's appearance to lightning and snow. The parallels with Jesus' appearance at transfiguration (17:2) are clear. The heavenly being reflects divine glory. Significantly, the angel did not remove the stone to let Jesus out, but showed the women that he was not there (28:6).

The Roman guard is another unwilling witness of the angelic appearance. Matthew tells the story with irony. The soldiers fail to secure the tomb as they find themselves face-to-face with a powerful heavenly being. The angel removes the stone with the official seal, defying the authority of Rome. Instead of fighting, the Roman soldiers are paralyzed with fear and **became like**

dead men (v 4). The guardians exchange places with Jesus: they appear dead while he is alive (Hagner 1995, 869). For Matthew even the empire is powerless in the face of divine action. The episode is juxtaposed with the scene of mockery by the governor's soldiers (27:27-31). They exercised their power over Jesus by humiliating him but are now helpless and humbled. The tables have been overturned; the soldiers are being mocked as cowards.

The moment of resurrection makes things right: God himself has vindicated Jesus, soldiers are humiliated, the authorities are rendered powerless, and the faithful women are rewarded. The powerless ones have witnessed the wicked plans of the powerful falling apart when confronted by divine determination. The kingdom is at work.

■ **5-7** The angel addresses the women who were looking for the crucified one (*ton esraurōmenon*): **He is not here; he has** been raised**, just as he said** (28:6). The text utilizes a *divine passive* to imply that God himself has raised Jesus from the dead. This is the reason—and nothing else—for his absence in the tomb. All has been predicted by Jesus (16:21; 17:23; 20:19), unfurled in the Passion Narratives (26:17-25; 27:11-44), and culminating in the resurrection (28:5-9). Jesus' resurrection has become the bedrock of Christian faith, the center of its proclamation and the source of its future hope. It was fundamental for the apostolic preaching (see Acts 3:15; 4:10; 13:30) and foundational for faith, practice, and eschatology as outlined by Paul in 1 Cor 15.

The core of the angelic message is wrapped in five verbs translated as commands: **do not be afraid** (*mē phobeisthe*; Matt 28:5), **come** (*deute*; v 6), **see** (*idete*), **go** (*poreutheisai*; v 7), and **tell** (*eipate*). The appearances of heavenly beings usually instill fear in humans (see Luke 1:11-13, 28-30). Unlike the soldiers, the women don't have to be afraid; the angel brings good news to them. He comforts them in a very similar way to Jesus at the transfiguration (17:7) and later at the resurrection appearance (28:10). He then tells them to **come and see** the tomb; this is why they came after all (28:1, 6). The angel encourages them not to just believe his words but to check for themselves. Now they see for themselves **the place where he lay**. The tomb is empty. While the angelic witness and the absence of a body are evidence of Jesus' bodily resurrection, they are not sufficient.

After seeing the tomb, the women are instructed to **go quickly and tell** the eleven disciples the good news of Jesus' resurrection: **he has** been raised **from the dead** (v 7). The two Marys are the first witnesses and become messengers of the good news. They are to tell the disciples to go to Galilee to meet the risen Lord. This is another fulfillment of Jesus' predictions (see 26:32). Indeed, all of Jesus' predictions now make sense; what appeared to be cryptic, unclear, confusing, and even confronting to the disciples has now been resolved with Jesus' coming to life.

In Matthew, Galilee is the place of the disciples' calling, apostolic commission, and participation in God's mission. Now it is also becoming a place of restoration. The Passion Narrative tells the story of the disciples' denial, betrayal, and desertion: "All the disciples deserted him and fled" (26:56). Though not worthy, the Eleven have graciously been given an opportunity to see their Master again. The angelic message that the faithful women must give to the unfaithful and doubting disciples is that Jesus' resurrection brings restoration to their relationship with him.

■ **8-10** The women wasted no time: they **hurried away from the tomb** (28:8) and **ran** to proclaim (*apangeilai*) the news of the empty tomb (see Mark 16:8). Matthew also notes that their hearts were filled "with fear" (*meta phobou*; NRSV)—despite the angel's assurance—mixed with "great joy" (*charas megalēs*; NRSV). The women who witnessed the death and burial of Jesus (27:55-56, 61) were overjoyed that Jesus is alive but, at the same time, fearful of the powerful divine intervention and angelic presence and, perhaps, sensing the magnitude of the unfolding events.

The story culminates with the appearance of the risen Lord on the way to see the disciples. They were looking for him in a graveyard and now he casually meets them on the road. Jesus' first word is a simple everyday greeting: **Greetings!** (*chairete*; 28:9).

The women recognize him immediately (see Luke 24:13-35). Their reaction is astounding: falling at his feet in worship. In their culture the grasping of feet is an expression of submission and homage usually paid to a ruler or a king (Hagner 1995, 874). Matthew implies that the risen Jesus is the Messiah and the King of Israel (27:42). Moreover, taking hold of Jesus' feet implies the physicality of the encounter. It is not just a vision or a hallucination. However, the language of worship (*prosekunēsan*) is particularly striking. Juxtaposed with the response to the angelic appearance and reinforced by imagery in 28:18, it points to the divine identity of the Risen One (Bauckham 2008, 57). By this seemingly impulsive act of worship, the women recognize Jesus as the Messiah, the Lord, and the Son of God.

The parallels between Jesus' and the angel's words are clear: **Do not be afraid. Go and tell my brothers to go to Galilee; there they will see me** (v 10). The risen Christ comforts them and repeats the angel's command to go and **tell** (*apangeilate*) the good news of resurrection. Again, Galilee is confirmed as the place of the second resurrection appearance and the place of reconciliation. Despite the disciples' betrayal, as a sign of reconciliation, Jesus continues to call them **my brothers** (see 12:40-50; 25:40). This almost fleeting encounter sets the stage for the climactic meeting of Jesus and his disciples in Galilee (Hagner 1995, 874).

FROM THE TEXT

This story brings different threads together: the fulfillment of Jesus' predictions, the revelation of his identity, and the subversion of the power of Jewish and Roman leadership. Moreover, juxtaposed with the failure of the

Twelve, the story of the faithful female followers of Jesus finds its culmination here. The two Marys become the first witnesses and proclaimers of the resurrection. The women not only heard the angelic message and witnessed the empty tomb but were the first to see the risen Lord.

This encounter makes the case for Jesus' resurrection complete: the angel's message and the empty tomb by themselves are not solid enough grounds for believing in it. The personal postresurrection encounters (see 1 Cor 15:5-8) are essential. Matthew also adds another brushstroke to the portrait of the faithful women: despite their fear and confusion, they follow the commands from the angel and Jesus himself and deliver their message to the disciples.

B. The Final Cover-up (28:11-15)

BEHIND THE TEXT

The story forms an inclusio to the whole of the Passion Narrative: it starts with the chief priests and the elders of the people (*hoi archiereis kai presbuteroi tou laou*) plotting to kill Jesus (26:3-5) and finishes with them planning to cover up his resurrection (28:12). The corrupt Jewish leadership opposes Jesus and his mission to the end. Even the news of his resurrection could not change their hearts. This episode belongs to the unique Matthean material and finishes the story of securing the tomb (27:62-66).

The whole resurrection narrative addresses false accounts of what has
happened. Matthew's story negates some of them and reduces the number of 28:11-15
explanations of the event. For example, the women might have just found the wrong empty tomb. But Matthew mentions that they knew the exact location of the tomb (27:61) and reached it on the resurrection day (28:1). Or Jesus just appeared to be dead and walked away after regaining consciousness. For Matthew, it is impossible since the tomb was "cut out of the rock," "a big stone" was rolled to block "the entrance" (27:60), and the religious authorities have sealed it and placed a guard (v 66). Thus Matthew leaves only two possible explanations for the empty tomb: resurrection or a stolen body. The story of the women describes what really happened, and the final episode with the guards reveals the roots of the rumor that the body was stolen (Keener 2009, 698).

This episode explains why early Christians hear a different story of Jesus' resurrection from their Jewish opponents: there was no resurrection; the disciples just stole the body. Matthew reveals that the alternative narrative was made up by the authorities who bribed the key witnesses—the guards. The soldiers were happy to comply and spread this lie.

The story of the guards and the chief priests is juxtaposed with the women's reaction to the resurrection. Like the two Marys, the guards also proclaimed (*apangellō*) what they saw (28:11). But this did not persuade the religious authorities. The refusal to believe and the attempt to cover up illustrate the hardness of hearts and prove Jesus' point about "this unbelieving

. . . generation." The same evidence was interpreted differently by the wicked priesthood and the elders. The empty tomb by itself might have different explanations, but personal encounters with the risen Lord and the testimonies of the faithful support the Christian claim.

IN THE TEXT

■ **11** At the same time, some of the Roman guards (*koustōdias*) hurried back to Jerusalem (since the tomb was located outside of the city walls) to report/proclaim (*apangellō*) to the chief priests. Their account contained **everything that had happened**. Although the priests were aware of divine action that took place at the tomb; the empty grave and angelic appearance have not convinced them of Jesus' resurrection.

■ **12-15** The priests and elders gather for the last time (see 26:3) to devise another plan since the previous one failed (see 27:62-66). They resort to bribery and offered the soldiers **a large sum of money** (28:12). Earlier the priests gave Judas money for betraying Jesus (26:15) and now they give money to suppress the news of his resurrection. The reality of Jesus' resurrection undermines their position and authority and highlights again that they set themselves against God and his Messiah.

Ironically, the story invented by the authorities is based on the scenario they were trying to prevent by sealing the tomb in the first place (see 27:64). But it also is intended to undermine credibility, subvert the narrative, and negate Christian claims about resurrection. In their presentation, the empty tomb is not the work of God but the result of a capital offense—grave robbery—and lies (Keener 2009, 713). The religious authorities project on Jesus' followers their own deceit and corruption.

But this fake story—not just the subversion of truth—puts the Roman soldiers in a dangerous position. Sleeping on duty is a serious offense in the Roman army and could lead to a severe punishment and even a death penalty (Card 2013, 250). The allure of money and the promise of protection—if the news of Jesus' missing body reaches the governor—convince the soldiers to cooperate; and they **did as they were instructed** or taught (*didaskō*; 28:15). For Matthew, this instruction adds the final stroke to the portrait of the religious authorities: their teaching is a lie wrapped in corruption.

Matthew notes that the fabricated story **has been widely circulated** among Jewish people of his day. The proclamation of good news went in parallel with the spreading of this false recasting of the events. We find an echo of that even later in the writings of Justin Martyr (second century CE) where he engages in a polemic with a Jewish rabbi Trypho who claimed:

> A godless and lawless sect has been started by a deceiver, one Jesus of Galilee, whom we nailed to the cross, but whose body, after it was taken from the cross, was stolen at night from the tomb by his disciples,

who now try to deceive men by affirming that he has risen from the dead and ascended to heaven. (Justin 2003, 108:2)

FROM THE TEXT

Despite all, the tomb is empty not because of the disciples or human intervention; it is empty because of God's action. Matthew juxtaposes two reports about the empty tomb: one from the women and the other from the Roman guards. The former is the basis of Christian proclamation and the latter is the source of rumors circulating in the Jewish community at the time. One is coming out as an account of personal witness to angelic message and the empty tomb as well as the experience of Jesus' appearance. The other is a result of corruption and an outward lie.

C. The Great Commission (28:16-20)

BEHIND THE TEXT

The final scene of the Gospel brings together and resolves two key themes: Jesus' identity and discipleship. The drama of the suffering and rejected Messiah, the Son of Man, had been resolved in the appearance of Jesus, the vindicated Messiah, the Son of God, as the exalted risen Lord who had been given authority over the created universe. The story of the disciples also finds its culmination here. It started enthusiastically with calling and unconditional following (4:18-21; 9:9-13) followed by the appointment of the Twelve (10:1). But later it has spiraled down, riddled with misunderstanding (16:21-23), failure (17:14-23), and betrayal (26:56).

Here readers find the restoration of the broken relationship with Jesus, and even more—the rekindled sense of purpose. Renewed, they have received instructions to continue on the mission of God. Now it does not focus solely on Israel (10:5-6) but embraces all the nations (see 24:14; 26:13). Jesus and his disciples are back to Galilee, where it all started (see 3:12, 18). This change in location has an important symbolic meaning, signaling the restoration of the broken relationship and the future fruitful mission for the followers. This scene marks the end of the Gospel story and the beginning of the disciples' ministry. It's a new stage in the disciples' journey, not its end.

The appearance of Trinitarian language in the baptismal formula ("in the name of the Father and of the Son and of the Holy Spirit" [28:19]) has sparked scholarly debates. Many commentators doubt that the formula comes from Jesus himself and more likely reflects later Christian confessions and practices (see Keener 2009, 717; France 2007, 1116-17; Hagner 1995, 888). In either case, the Trinitarian language here makes sense in its wider narrative context. It not only brackets the story of Jesus' mission with the presence of the Trinity at his baptism (3:13-17) but also summarizes and recognizes the involvement of all persons of the Trinity into the mission throughout the Gospel (Hartman 1997, 151).

Although the Great Commission pericope is unique to Matthew, it has parallels. The episode resembles the commissioning of the Twelve in 10:1-4; both times the disciples are sent to the mission in the authority of Jesus. Similar scenes of calling and commissioning are found in Scripture: Deut 31:14-15, 23; 1 Chr 22:1-16; Josh 1:1-9; Jer 1:1-10 (Davies and Allison 1988, 679-80). Matthew 28:18 also echoes Dan 7:13-14 where the enigmatic figure of "one like a son of man" receives "authority, glory and sovereign power" from God himself. In Matthew, this Danielic vision coupled with the sending of the disciples to all nations indicates the universal character of the kingship of the risen Christ.

IN THE TEXT

■ **16-17 Then the eleven disciples went to Galilee** (v 16*a*). Matthew's story assumes that the women had arrived and passed the message to the eleven disciples (see Luke 24:9-13) who remained together in Jerusalem (see Matt 26:13). This is the only time they were called **the eleven**. As commanded, they have traveled back to Galilee, about a three-day journey via Samaria.

Matthew does not identify **the mountain where Jesus had told them to go** (28:16*b*). Some have suggested the mount of transfiguration (Luz 2005, 621-22). If the transfiguration was seen as anticipation of Easter glory (→ 17:1-8) then perhaps the appearance of the risen Christ in the same location could make sense. Now all of the disciples (not the chosen three) can experience the presence of heavenly glory and the final revelation of the true identity of Jesus. This then creates an inclusio to the story of the Messiah's suffering that culminates in vindication (chs 17—28). Though location is important, the focus of the passage is on the event that takes place—the appearance of the risen Lord. Hagner suggests that we need to interpret it foremost as a place of revelation (1995, 884).

The disciples' reaction to Jesus' appearance is similar to that of the women: **When they saw him, they worshiped him** (28:17*a*; see v 9). Worship here refers to the physical act of bowing or prostrating. The followers' struggle to grasp Jesus' identity has been resolved here in the act of worship. Jesus is more than a human being or a rabbi; he is indeed the Son of God, the vindicated Messiah, and even more—the risen Lord who has authority over the whole of the universe.

But some doubted (v 17*b*) is an intriguing remark. Matthew uses a set of verbs to describe the disciples' actions. They **went** (*eporeuthēsan*) to Galilee in obedience to Jesus' command, **saw** (*idontes*) the risen Christ, **worshiped** [*prosekynēsan*] **him**, and **doubted** (*edistasan*). Even to this final point, the disciples experienced a mix of faith and unbelief. The object and meaning of the verb *distazein* ("to doubt") here is not clear. It is used only in Matthew (14:31; 28:17).

Scholars provided a range of suggestions: they had doubts about whether Jesus would forgive them; they had doubts concerning his identity; they were not sure how to behave in the presence of Jesus; they were afraid to approach him (Hagner 1995, 885) or not sure about appropriate ways of worshiping him (France 2007, 1112). Perhaps "doubt" describes all of these things: some of the disciples were not sure what they were seeing and how to respond to it. Confusion, hesitation, disbelief, fear, hope, and awe engulfed the Eleven as they found themselves in the presence of the risen Jesus whom they abandoned just a few days before.

■ **18-20** The NIV renders the Greek phrase "spoke to them saying" as **and said** (v 18*a*). This does not fully express Matthew's emphasis. He comes to them and speaks in an act of reassurance and reconciliation (see 17:7). He does not rebuke them. Their failure has been left behind and it has been "swallowed up in the much greater reality of the mission to which they are now called" (France 2007, 1112). Jesus reestablishes broken relationship through inclusion into the mission of God. He calls them to do that for which they were commissioned (see 10:1).

All authority in heaven and on earth has been given to me (28:18*b*). Matthew uses the *divine passive* here. Though the giver is not identified, the text implies that the authority has been bestowed by God. Understood in Trinitarian terms, God the Father is behind the resurrection, vindication, exaltation, and enthronement of Jesus, the Son of God. The act of ultimate obedience to the will of the Father has made redemption possible.

The enigmatic comment in 11:27 makes perfect sense now: "All things have been committed to me by my Father. No one knows the Son except the Father, and no one knows the Father except the Son and those to whom the Son chooses to reveal him." The promises of the future rule of the Son of Man have been fulfilled (19:28; 24:30-31; 25:31-34; 26:64). Jesus of Nazareth, who had been humiliated and crucified, is vindicated now by God himself; here resurrection is connected with enthronement and assuming power. The resurrected Lord possesses the authority attributed to God alone.

The Gospel motif of messiahship or kingship culminates here with an unexpected twist. Jesus is not just a descendant of King David (1:1-17), the royal Messiah (21:1-11), and the King of the Jews (see 27:29, 37). The final speech of the story reveals the universal character of Jesus' kingship; he is the King over the whole of the cosmos. The divine will exercised on earth as in heaven will be through Jesus, the exalted Messiah. The phrase **authority in heaven and on earth** (28:18*b*) echoes the Lord's Prayer (5:10). This is also set in opposition to 4:8-9, where Satan appears to have authority on earth over "all the kingdoms" (v 8).

Therefore go and make disciples of all nations (28:19*a*). One can experience Jesus' authority and kingship in the world through the people of God. Jesus reigns through his obedient followers on the mission of God. They were given royal authority to announce the good news of Jesus' universal reign and bring others to faith and obedience (Wright 2004, 208).

Jesus as the exalted Lord of all envisages universal mission: the good news is extended to all the nations (*panta ta ethnē*). In this light, Jesus' ministry focused on "the lost sheep of Israel" (10:6; see vv 5-6) in the first part of the Gospel serves as preparation for the universal mission of God. The restored Israel gathered around Jesus the Messiah and represented by the apostles is given the authority to embark on the mission to the entire world and to embrace both Jews and Gentiles. This is the firm foundation for his disciples' inclusive life and ministry.

The mission of the disciples is not just about proclamation of the good news. It is about making dedicated and faithful followers (see 19:27-30). The grammatical structure of the sentence reveals the true purpose of the Great Commission. It is built around the main imperative verb to **make disciples** (*mathēteusate*; 28:19) with subordinate participles: **go**[ing] (*poreuthentes*), **baptizing** (*baptizontes*), and **teaching** (*didaskontes*). The Eleven are called to make disciples by reaching all corners of the earth, baptizing new believers, and teaching them to obey Jesus' commandments so that they can join the new holy people of God in the mission of God.

The appearance of **baptizing them in the name of the Father and of the Son and of the Holy Spirit** and the Trinitarian formula comes as a surprise. Up to this point, baptism was practiced only by John the Baptist (3:1-12) and not by Jesus or his followers. Perhaps the phrase reflects early Christian practices. However, it may not be an anachronism or later addition; it comes out of the narrative logic of the Gospel itself. First, it echoes Jesus' baptism with its Trinitarian shape (3:13-17). Second, the formula affirms all of the Trinity as the actors of the story of redemption. For Matthew, the mission of Jesus, the obedient Son of God (3:17; 17:5), is driven by the will of God the Father (11:27; 24:36; 26:63-64) and empowered by the presence of the Holy Spirit (3:11; 4:1-11; 12:28-32). New disciples will be baptized in the new name, the name of the Trinity that made salvation possible.

Baptizing **in the name of** has two possible connotations. In Greco-Roman context, the phrase was used in legal documents to identify an owner and carries the idea of possession and belonging. In a Jewish context, the phrase is used in the sense of "with reference to," to act on behalf of another. The disciples have been given authority to bring persons into this new relationship—"relating the one being baptized to the Trinity" (Ferguson 2009, 135-36). Thus the apostles are called to bring people from all nations into the new covenant relationship with God through the visible act of baptism. It signifies belonging to God, inclusion into the new people of God on the mission of God, and new life under divine rule. In this sense, baptism has an eschatological perspective: inclusion into the kingdom of God now, which stretches to the end of days (Hartman 1997, 153).

Disciples are not called to make followers in their name but to make others disciples to follow Jesus, the true Teacher (23:10). Baptizing is accompanied by **teaching them to obey everything I have commanded you** (28:20*a*). This may assume that baptism serves as an entry point to becoming a disciple (Ferguson 2009, 138). **To obey everything** refers to Jesus' teaching and perhaps particularly to the Sermon on the Mount (chs 5—7) with its focus on the greater righteousness (see also 11:28-30 and 23:1-32). The kingship of Jesus is experienced by the new people of God through living in accordance with his commandments. A person who belongs to God reorients one's life around the divine will. And that will is missional.

The mission, teaching, and life of the community of faith rest on the assurance that **I am with you always, to the very end of the age** (28:20*b*). Their mission is not short-termed; generations of disciples will experience his empowering presence till the end of the ages. Matthew brackets the narrative of his Gospel with the idea of continuous divine presence with his people echoing the motif of YHWH's presence with Israel during the Exodus (see Exod 13:17—19:25). The story of Jesus, the Messiah, starts with the proclamation that "God [is] with us" (Matt 1:23), pauses with the promise "there am I with them" in the middle (18:20), and finishes with the assurance **I am with you always** at the end (28:20). In response to their hesitation and unbelief, Jesus reassures them that he will be in their midst, though unseen, to empower, to console, and to guide them in the mission he has given them (France 2007, 1108). With the reference to the consummation of the age, the promise stands for generations of Christians, including Matthew's contemporaries (Hagner 1995, 889).

FROM THE TEXT

The last episode of the Gospel focuses on the risen and exalted Christ. The final resurrection appearance proclaims the triumph of God and his Son. On the mountain, the suffering Messiah has been revealed as the Lord of all. God the Father has vindicated and exalted Jesus who willingly went through humiliation and death on the cross. The universal kingship of Christ is the foundation for the mission of his people: to bring all the nations under the rule and obedience to Jesus, the Son of God.

The Great Commission is unapologetically christocentric. It is *Jesus* who sends the apostles to make disciples for him, to baptize them in name of *the Son* (and other members of the Trinity), and to teach to obey *his* commandments, with the promise that *he* will be present with them on their mission to the entire world.

The last episode also highlights the relationship between the Messiah and his people. This is a great example of divine grace and restoration. Jesus appears before the bunch of betrayers and failures and entrusts them with an important task—to be emissaries of the kingdom. The resurrection and continual presence of the exalted Christ will empower the confused, doubting, and weak disciples to bring the good news of his reign to all corners of the earth.

The story of the gospel does not finish with the resurrection of Jesus. It takes its readers into the future. The apostles and the whole church are sent on the mission of God that embraces all people—the mission that continues to the end of time.